PRESSIONISM SYMBOLISM

The Belgian Avant-Garde 1880–1900

Royal Academy of Arts, London
7 July – 2 October 1994

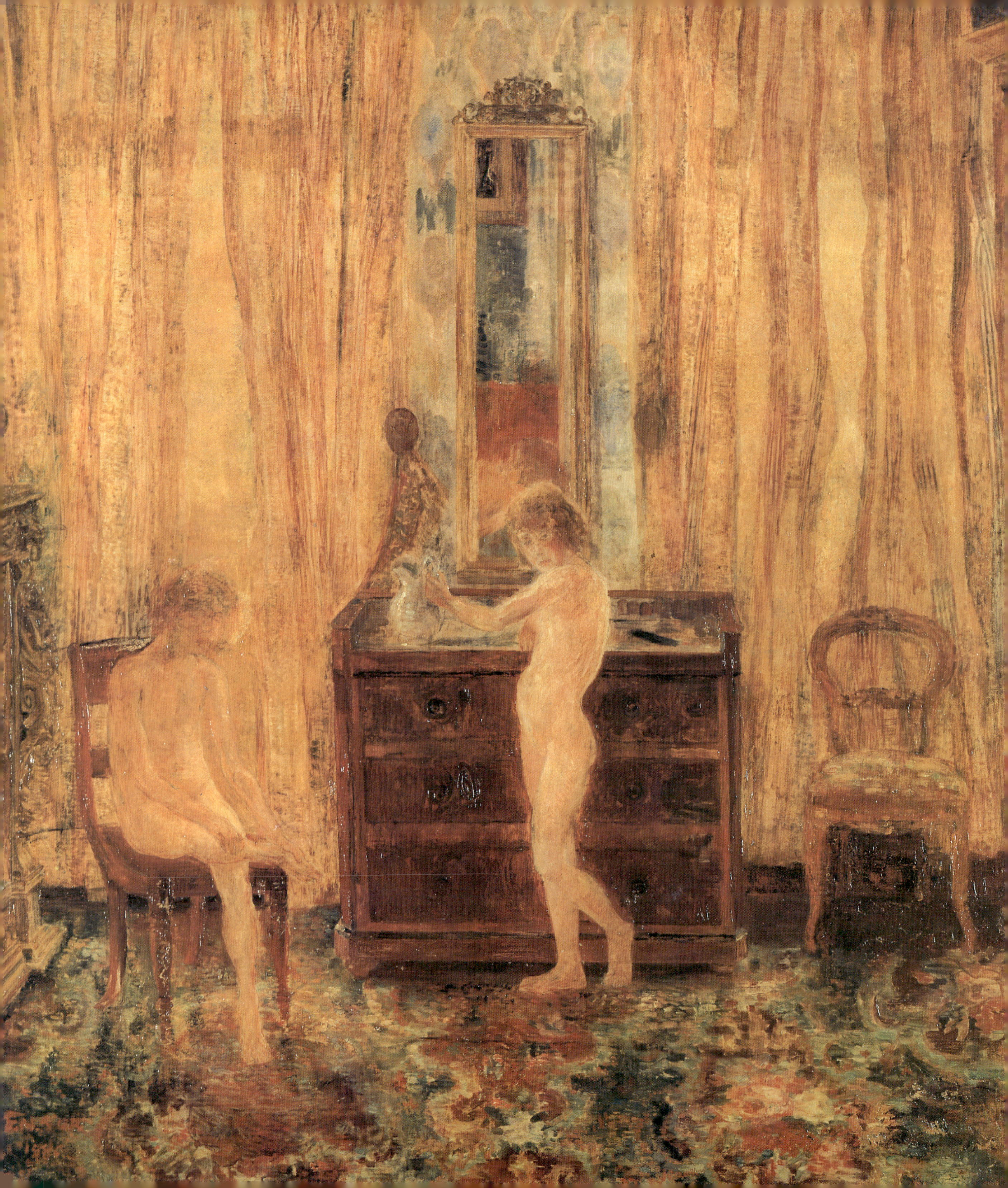

IMPRESSIONISM TO SYMBOLISM

The Belgian Avant-Garde 1880–1900

Edited by

MaryAnne Stevens with Robert Hoozee

with contributions by Jane Block, Jean F. Buyck,

Ronny Gobyn, Serge Goyens de Heusch and Robert Hoozee

ROYAL ACADEMY OF ARTS, LONDON

in association with LUDION PRESS, GHENT

This catalogue was first published on the occasion of the exhibition
IMPRESSIONISM TO SYMBOLISM: THE BELGIAN AVANT-GARDE 1880–1900,
Royal Academy of Arts, London, 7 July – 2 October 1994

The exhibition is sponsored by

GENERALE TRACTEBEL UM UNION MINIERE

The exhibition was organized by the Royal Academy of Arts, London.

The Royal Academy is grateful to Her Majesty's Government for its help in agreeing to indemnify the exhibition under the National Heritage Act 1980 and to the Museums and Galleries Commission for their help in arranging this indemnity.

Translated by Ted Alkins, Caroline Beamish, Margaret Curran, Beverly Jackson, Bob Symonds and Alistair Weir
Copy editor: Paul van Calster
Catalogue designed by Dooreman
Typeset by Ludion, Ghent, in Martin Majoor's Scala and Scala Sans
Lithography by De Schutter, Antwerp
Printed in Belgium by Die Keure, Bruges

ISBN 0-900946-45-8 (paperbound)
ISBN 0-900946-46-6 (clothbound)

Front cover: THÉO VAN RYSSELBERGHE, *Portrait of Octave Maus*, 1885 (detail), Musées royaux des Beaux-Arts de Belgique, Brussels [cat. 70]
Back cover: XAVIER MELLERY, *My Hallway, Light Effect*, c. 1889 (detail), Private Collection [cat. 43]
Frontispiece: JAMES ENSOR, *Children washing*, 1886 (detail), Private Collection [cat. 16]

Contents

Sponsor's Preface

1952 and 1994. Two significant dates. The first major event devoted to Belgian culture to be held in London since 1952.

Since then little of any significance has been done to make Belgium's rich and varied cultural heritage known to the British public, although many exhibitions of Belgian nineteenth- and twentieth-century art have been held during this period in other countries, such as France, Switzerland and even Japan. This may well explain the fact that Belgian artists do not seem to enjoy the reputation they deserve in Britain and that Belgium's cultural treasures of the last century are still pratically unknown here.

We were therefore particularly interested to learn of the Royal Academy's plans to organize an exhibition of late nineteenth-century Belgian painting and sculpture, and consequently we were only too pleased to offer it our support, especially in view of the fact that this exhibition reflects, in every respect, the aims of the patronage policy of Société Générale de Belgique's Group, and more particularly that of the other two partners directly involved with the exhibition, Tractebel and Union Minière.

For a considerable period of time now our three companies have played a leading role in the Belgian economy. The reputation of a country is largely determined by the creativity and dynamism of its population and the richness of its cultural life. We feel it is our responsibility to help preserve a cultural heritage of which we are justifiably proud and also to promote Belgian art abroad.

Although we have a long tradition as patrons of the arts, this exhibition is the first one with which we have been involved outside Belgium. London was not chosen purely by chance. We know the city well and value London's role as one of the world's most important financial centres. We also hope that this exhibition will demonstrate our interest in London as one of the world's leading cultural centres.

The exhibition 'Impressionism to Symbolism: the Belgian Avant-Garde 1880–1900' comprises seventy-one paintings and nine sculptures carefully selected to reflect the spirit of a particularly rich and creative period when Belgium found itself at the crossroads of several artistic trends. Individual reactions to the exhibits will no doubt vary, but we hope that this carefully prepared exhibition will stimulate interest in the art of this period.

We should like to express our appreciation to the many people responsible for organizing this remarkable exhibition. We offer our warmest thanks to the President of the Royal Academy of Arts, Sir Philip Dowson CBE, to the Librarian and Head of Education, MaryAnne Stevens who is curator of the exhibition and to all their colleagues, not only for their unrivalled knowledge of the arts but also for their patience and understanding in meeting our expectations.

We should also like to offer our thanks to the Belgian Ambassador in the United Kingdom, Baron Herman Dehennin, and to the Marquise de Cérenville, who first thought of the exhibition and drew our attention to the Royal Academy's plans.

It is with great pleasure that we have helped support this exhibition at the internationally renowned Royal Academy of Arts, thereby stimulating interest in Belgian art in one of the world's leading artistic and cultural centres, London.

VISCOUNT ÉTIENNE DAVIGNON

Chairman of the Board, Société Générale de Belgique
Chairman of the Board, Union Minière
Member of the Board, Tractebel

President's Foreword

The closing decades of the nineteenth century witnessed striking developments in Belgium, from rapid social, political and economic change to a burst of artistic activity which marked all aspects of that nation's culture: music and literature, architecture, applied arts, painting and sculpture. Fuelled by the need to assert its national identity, by proximity to European centres of the avant-garde, notably Paris and London, by its liberal press and publishing laws and by its passionate belief in the social role of the arts, Belgium fostered a cultural renaissance as vital, yet less rigid in its stylistic manifestations, as anywhere in Europe.

A myriad group of small exhibiting bodies, such as Les XX in Brussels or Als Ik Kan in Antwerp, numerous literary and artistic reviews and an articulate intellectual class supported a range of visual manifestations which reflected a particular combination of international innovations and native pictorial and literary concerns. Respect for the painterliness and naturalism of art of the Flemish Golden Age created dramatic, expressionistic images of Belgian landscapes and domestic interiors, while a search for truths that lay beyond the objects and experiences of everyday life informed a particular manifestation of Symbolist art – from the dream evocations of Khnopff to the hallucinatory masks and skeletons of Ensor. Alternatively, the concern to translate light into paint informed an exploration of both Impressionism and Neo-Impressionism, derived from France but endowed with a distinct tonality and an enduring concern to avoid the dissolution of form inherent in these programmes' pursuit of light. This exhibition takes a cross-section of such innovations, presenting works by Ensor, Khnopff and Rops, as well as by less well-known figures such as Mellery, Vogels, Van de Velde, Finch and Van Rysselberghe.

The exhibition has been selected by MaryAnne Stevens, Librarian and Director of Education at the Royal Academy, who has been expertly guided in this task by Robert Hoozee, Director of the Museum voor Schone Kunsten, Ghent. Its administration has been handled with great competence by Corinne Wellesley. Robert Hoozee has also been instrumental in securing the large team of scholars who have contributed to the catalogue, and has himself shared the task of editing the publication with MaryAnne Stevens and Paul van Calster. We have been enormously fortunate in having had the widespread and enthusiastic support of major museums and art galleries throughout Belgium. Not only have their staff made available to us important loans, but they have been more than generous in providing advice and information essential to the success of the enterprise. To their directors and curators we extend our deepest thanks, as we also do to all those private collectors who have so generously lent to the exhibition.

Finally, and most importantly, this exhibition could not have been presented at the Royal Academy without the positive support of our three Belgian sponsors, Société Générale de Belgique, Tractebel and Union Minière. Guided towards us by Madame la Marquise de Cérenville, they have guaranteed the realization of this project.

For many of our visitors, this exhibition will probably represent a voyage of discovery. We trust that it will bring enlightenment and enjoyment, as it defines a less well-known but vital part of the map of European cultural innovation at the end of the nineteenth century.

SIR PHILIP DOWSON CBE

President
Royal Academy of Arts

Executive Committee

Piers Rodgers (Chairman)
Secretary, Royal Academy of Arts

Allen Jones RA
Chairman, Exhibitions Committee of the Royal Academy of Arts

Norman Rosenthal
Exhibitions Secretary, Royal Academy of Arts

MaryAnne Stevens
Librarian and Director of Education, Royal Academy of Arts

Annette Bradshaw
Deputy Exhibitions Secretary, Royal Academy of Arts

Paul De Backer
Communications Manager, Union Minière

François Desclée de Maredsous
Secretary of the Board, Tractebel

Jean-Jacques Massart
Communications Director and Human Resources Director, Société Générale de Belgique

The Marquise de Cérenville

Sir Kenneth Corfield

Exhibition Coordinator
MaryAnne Stevens
Librarian and Director of Education, Royal Academy of Arts

Assistant Coordinators
Corinne Wellesley, Charlotte Stirling

Photographic Coordinator
Miranda Bennion

Acknowledgements

Serge le Bailly de Tilleghem
Mr Baneyds
Pierre Baudson
Melle Bessemans
Nadine Bigbie
Baronne Antoinette Bodson-Perier
Bernadette Bonnier
Jean F. Buyck
Colette Castermans
Suzanne de Cérenville
Colin Clark
Piet Coessens
Sir Kenneth Corfield
Joost De Geest
H.E. Baron Dehennin
Natalie Delvaulx
Patrick Derom
Michael Doran and
the Courtauld Institute Libraries
Eric Dossart
Françoise Dumont
Andrée Ferrant
Bruno Fornari
Catherine Gernay
Serge Goyens de Heusch
H.E. Mr John Gray
Eric Hennaut
Norbert Hostyn
Nicole d'Huart
Erwin Joos
Paul and Ellen Josefowitz
Samuel Josefowitz
Christian Klemm
Ellen Lee
Comte Henry de Limbourg Stirum
Liliane Lisens
Henk Mahieu
Jean-Jacques Massart
John Myerscough
Patrick O'Brien
Gisèle Ollinger-Zinque
Michael Palmer
Carl Peeters
Wendy Pollard
Joseph J. Rishel
Michelle Robinson
Liliane Sabatini
Laus Albrecht Schroder
Henry Strachie
Liliane Tackaert
Sabine Tavernier
H.E. Baron Vaes, KCMG
Jacques van Hee
Stefan van Raay
Van Rysselberghe Family
Emmanuel and Ines Vaxelaire

Lenders to the Exhibition

BELGIUM

ANTWERP
- C & R Antwerp
- Historical Museums, Plantin-Moretus Museum
- Koninklijk Museum voor Schone Kunsten

BRUGES
- Groeningemuseum

BRUSSELS
- Collection Crédit Communal de Belgique / Collectie Gemeentekrediet van België
- Collection de l'Etat Belge
- Galerie Patrick Derom
- Hôtel Charlier
- Musée Constantin Meunier
- Musée d'Ixelles
- Musées royaux des Beaux-Arts de Belgique / Koninklijke Musea voor Schone Kunsten van België

GHENT
- Museum voor Schone Kunsten

LIÈGE
- Collection particulière représentée par le bureau de recherches Leodico–98
- Musée d'Art moderne et d'Art contemporain
- Musée de l'Art Wallon

OSTEND
- Museum voor Schone Kunsten

TOURNAI
- Musée des Beaux-Arts

VERVIERS
- Musées Communaux

FINLAND

HELSINKI
- (Ateneum) The Finnish National Gallery

TURKU
- Art Museum

GERMANY

DARMSTADT
- Hessisches Landesmuseum

HAGEN
- Karl Ernst Osthaus-Museum

THE NETHERLANDS

THE HAGUE
- Gemeentemuseum

SWEDEN

- Private Collection Sweden–Norway

SWITZERLAND

BERNE
- Fondation Socindec

GENEVA
- Musée du Petit Palais

ZURICH
- Kunsthaus

U.S.A.

FORT WORTH, TEXAS
- Kimbell Art Museum

INDIANAPOLIS, INDIANA
- Museum of Art (The Holliday Collection)

NEW YORK
- The Hearn Family Trust

PROVIDENCE, RHODE ISLAND
- Museum of Art, Rhode Island School of Design

SPRINGFIELD, MASSACHUSETTS
- Museum of Fine Arts (The James Philip Gray Collection)

And all those lenders who wish to remain anonymous.

Editors' Note

ORIGINAL TITLES

Where available, the French or Dutch original titles given in Les XX, La Libre Ethétique or other pre-1920 exhibition catalogues have been included in the catalogue entries.
Purely descriptive titles (e.g. Self-portrait) and titles of comparative illustrations are given in English only.

DIMENSIONS

Dimensions are in centimetres, height before width.

AUTHORS OF CATALOGUE ENTRIES

APA	Anne Adriaens-Pannier
BF	Bruno Fornari
BV	Brita Velghe
DDC	Danielle Derrey-Capon
EL	Ellen Lee
FL	Frederik Leen
GOZ	Gisèle Ollinger-Zinque
HT	Herwig Todts
JB	Jane Block
LDJ	Leen de Jong
LS	Liliane Sabatini
ML	Marc Lambrechts
NH	Norbert Hostyn
PB	Pierre Baudson
RC	Roger Cardon
RH	Robert Hoozee
SC	Susan Canning

Introduction

Belgian Art 1880–1900

ROBERT HOOZEE

The only institution in the past two centuries of Belgian art to have aroused widespread international interest is the artists' society known as Les XX (Les Vingt, i.e. The Twenty).[1] This society, established in Brussels in 1883 and dissolved ten years later, helped channel an exceptionally creative phase in Belgian art, and its members included the most progressive and influential artists of the day; its chief aim was to provide them with a platform. At the same time, its annual exhibitions included the work of carefully selected guests who represented the best of European and American modern art. Extensive interest in Les XX has sprung in part from the group's own pronounced internationalism and in part from its ready assimilation into our orthodox view of the history of modern art (see Block).

Les XX has rightly been assigned a central role in this exhibition of Belgian art from c. 1880 to 1900. But the selection has the additional merit of a broader frame of reference. For to have focused exclusively on key figures such as Ensor (q.v.) and Khnopff (q.v.), or on Neo-Impressionism, would have been to give a skewed impression of the group, presenting it as wholeheartedly avant-garde in a twentieth-century sense. In fact many of its members, with Delvin (1853–1922), Vanaise (1854–1902) and Verheyden (q.v.) among them, had a more traditional bent. Furthermore, the group's later luminaries, such as Ensor and Khnopff, made their début at Les XX with works that can scarcely be called revolutionary. And among the foreign guests we find not only great modernists such as Seurat, Gauguin and Whistler, but also less innovative figures including the members of the Hague School (Hendrik Willem Mesdag, Josef Israëls and Anton Mauve).

Les XX remains an extremely important group to which we shall have to return several times in the following pages, but it is as well to recall that at every level the group was subtly intertwined with Belgium's varied artistic life. Les XX was not a sudden bright light come to illuminate an otherwise dull Belgian sky. Rather it was a vehicle that helped crystallize the available potential, and in that sense it pointed to the past as much as to the future.

The success of Les XX was undoubtedly related in part to the figure of its organizer, Octave Maus. But the artists themselves generated the essential dynamism of the group, with members regularly falling out of favour and resigning while others were welcomed in their place. When we run our eyes over the list of the twenty founding members, we gain an impression of the kind of artists that so respected each other in 1883 that they wanted to found a common society.[2] What this list reveals is not a group motivated by a destructive urge to jolt the world of art into a wave of innovation, but a balanced sample of the various shades of opinion that were present in Belgian art. It should also be noted that in its annual exhibitions, Les XX paid tribute several times to more venerable 'great masters' of Belgian nineteenth-century art; furthermore, its periodical, *L'Art moderne*, published lengthy articles on artists who had pioneered their own particular ideals.

THE 1860s AND 1870s: REALISM AND FRENCH INFLUENCE

From the mid-nineteenth century onwards, Belgian art began to respond wholeheartedly to the call for *modernité* that was resounding through Europe. The positivist aesthetics that favoured a personal and faithful rendering of the real world were formulated mainly in Paris, and although Realists in Brussels would not form their own group until 1868, Realism was incorporated into Belgian art at a fairly early stage.[3]

The fact that Belgium had a strong and liberal-minded middle class helps explain this swift response; from these ranks were drawn the artists' public and clientele. Another significant factor was the close relationship between Belgium and France. Belgium was often a host country to French émigrés whose radical ideas had made their homeland less than hospitable to them. Jacques-Louis David had been an illustrious exile after 1815. And after Napoleon III seized power in 1851, many fled from France to Belgium, including the writer Victor Hugo and the Socialist philosopher Pierre-Joseph Proudhon.

Gustave Courbet, the key Realist in the visual arts, had often visited Belgium. In 1846–1847, Courbet went on a study tour to the Netherlands and Belgium, and he occasionally returned in subsequent years to visit artist friends in Brussels, Antwerp and Ghent.[4] In 1851 he exhibited his *Stonebreakers* (destroyed) in the Brussels Salon. After this he regularly submitted work to the Belgian salons, and he energetically propagandized in Belgium (which he referred to as 'my country'[5]) on behalf of his own form of 'democratic realism'. In 1861 he addressed a conference in Antwerp, and in the 1868 Salon in Ghent he submitted some of his most anticlerical works.[6]

Other French artists may have been less present in person than Courbet in Belgian art circles, but their work was greatly in evidence. A study of the salon catalogues shows that from the mid-century onwards, French landscapes were regularly shown in Belgian salons. As a result, there was soon a large market for the new French art in Belgium. Jean-François Millet was especially popular; his major works, such as *The Angelus* (1859; Musée d'Orsay, Paris), were in Belgian collections for some time before finding new homes at the turn of the century, in other parts of Europe or in the United States.[7]

Given that Paris was a mere stone's throw away, it was understandable that the great city had a powerful magnetic appeal to Belgian artists, not only as a source of potential clients, but also because of the artistic debates that were so much part of the Parisian scene. The new landscape style that the Parisian artists evolved in the village of Barbizon around 1850 fired the enthusiasm of Belgian landscapists. From 1845 onwards Belgian painters were working in Barbizon, and soon comparable regional schools developed in Belgium itself, such as that of Tervuren near Brussels. By 1860, Romantic-Realist landscape had won widespread acceptance in Belgium. Portraiture and genre painting were developing their own modes of realism at the same time, and in these fields too it was French artists who led the way. Some Belgians, Joseph Stevens (1816–1892) and Félicien Rops (q.v.) spring to mind, spent extended periods in Paris, and others even made it their permanent home. The best known among the latter is Alfred Stevens (1823–1906), who became a genre painter much fêted by the social elite.

The close relationship between French and Belgian artistic life hinted at by these few observations would certainly repay further study. That a certain understanding existed between the artistic circles of the two countries, at any rate, is quite clear. And just as France absorbed Belgian artists, some French artists felt particularly at ease in Belgium; to a few it was virtually a second home. In the 1880s Les XX forged close ties between Brussels and Paris, and we can be sure that the 1860s generation of Realists had prepared the ground.

Favourable circumstances and contacts do not provide the only explanation for the speed with which Realism conquered Belgium. The country also had a highly receptive artistic tradition of its own. It is often said (and not only in relation to Belgian art) that external impulses can awaken latent potential within a country, or activate existing ideas. In the present context, the French style of landscape, particularly Courbet's Realism, helped the Belgians to discover themselves. Observations of this kind often have the hollow ring of nationalism, yet the resolute way in which Realism became entrenched in Belgian art was definitely related to a national sensitivity. It is widely accepted that Belgian art, possibly in response to the country's new-found status as a nation-state after 1831, experienced a process of national consciousness-raising in the nineteenth century. In the first half-century, an imported Neoclassicism had to contend with a strong Romantic school whose roots lay in the Flemish baroque. And at the same time, French artists such as Géricault and Delacroix, in their search for greater emotional and representational verisimilitude, found the Flemish baroque a source of inspiration. The English painter John Constable, the progenitor of Realist landscape painting, owed a great deal to Rubens, whose landscapes he admired all his life. The mid-century Realists too, especially Courbet, admired the same baroque tradition.

There is nothing startling about these affinities. Anyone who views the portraits, landscapes, still lifes and genre pieces of artists such as Rubens, Jordaens, Snyders, De Vos and Siberechts will immediately see that they supplied powerful examples for anyone willing to jettison superfluous academic ballast, look around, and express unadorned reality in a direct and unpretentious style. Numerous quotations could be supplied to demonstrate the awareness among Belgian artists and critics of their kinship with the national pictorial tradition. Perhaps one will suffice. An article published in *L'Art moderne* in 1881 claimed roundly: 'It is Courbet who is responsible for this return to the roots of the Flemish school'.[8] A deeply entrenched Realism would continue to dominate Belgian art right through the period covered by this exhibition, and well into the twentieth century, when the Flemish version of Expressionism – in the work of someone like Constant Permeke (1886–1952) – was still imbued with the Courbet-esque Realism that has been referred to as an expression of 'the genius of the North'.

LANDSCAPE PAINTING

The most important Belgian landscapist was undoubtedly Hippolyte Boulenger (1837–1874). Influenced above all by Théodore Rousseau, he was a committed artist who sought the solitude of the natural world and enjoyed confronting the elements. His works are as much a record of his observations of that world as of his emotional response to it. Although Boulenger did not actually take on pupils, he was nevertheless the central figure in what is known as the Tervuren School, and may be regarded as the prototypical Belgian Romantic-Realist landscape painter. Allowing for individual stylistic differences, his art displays all the features that characterize the entire Belgian school in the 1860s and 1870s: a preference for an overcast landscape (in tune with the Belgian climate) charged with emotion, a tendency to favour a grand, imposing vista, and broad, spontaneous brushwork using a heavy impasto. There is a virtual absence of pure colour, but the works display a rich variety of shades, with grey often the dominant tone [fig. 1].

The 1881 article in *L'Art moderne* quoted above referred to Boulenger as 'the finest contemporary exponent of landscape painting in Belgium'. The key to his originality, the writer continued, was his workmanship: 'What is it, above all, that attracts and seduces us? It is not the location itself, however fine that may be, nor – for all its depth of vision – the artist's expression of nature. No. It is the lively, ingenious, unexpected disposition of the lines, or the vibrant hues with their masterly nuances, arranged harmoniously, now contrasted, now mixed together with a boldness that is ever felicitous. The whole is a blend, a bouquet, a unique virtuosity. At every point we can sense the hand, the active, adroit and nervous grasp, making a brushstroke and lifting the brush again, adding light or an accent where it is needed, swiftly describing a feature, following it with a wonderful sureness of hand, above all distinguishing the different types of foliage with superb finesse. It is this combination of suppleness and fluidity in craftsmanship in the highest and noblest sense of the word, this verve, this ardour in colouring and brushstroke, that makes Boulenger a peerless artist'.[9]

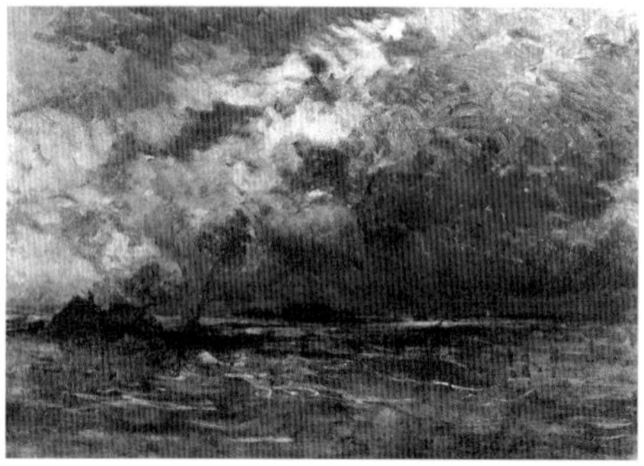

fig. 1 HIPPOLYTE BOULENGER, The Flood, 1871, Musées royaux des Beaux-Arts de Belgique, Brussels

It is important to dwell briefly on Boulenger and the admiration of craftsmanship recorded by the critic of *L'Art moderne* since his work was so typical of this era. It describes what was regarded in the early 1880s – certainly in landscape painting – as an outstanding example of the modern style. Whereas the intuitive style favoured by the French Realists evolved at this time into the light brushwork and clear tones of Impressionism, Belgian Impressionists remained committed to painting with a heavy impasto and a relatively subdued palette.

SOCIAL REALISM

When Charles Baudelaire was living in exile in Belgium (1864–1866), making the notes he would later use to write his satire 'Poor Belgium', he too found himself confronting an all-pervasive Realism. At one point he too implied a direct relationship between Belgian Realists and Courbet when he referred to: 'the philosophy of Belgian painters, the philosophy of our friend Courbet'.[10] As an advocate of an elevated form of art which sought the ideal that lay beyond the mundane world of description and experience, he viewed with disfavour the Belgian artists with their radical focus on the material world: 'In France I am thought too much of a painter. Here I am thought too literary. Whatever passes the comprehension of these painters, they refer to as literary art.'[11] Baudelaire immediately understood that the country had been conquered by Realism, and he too saw Realism as a continuation of the Flemish pictorial tradition, in which he emphasized the aspect of materialism: 'Flemish painting shines only through those qualities which are not intellectual – it has no *esprit*, but it sometimes possesses a richness of colour, and almost always an astonishing sureness of hand.'[12]

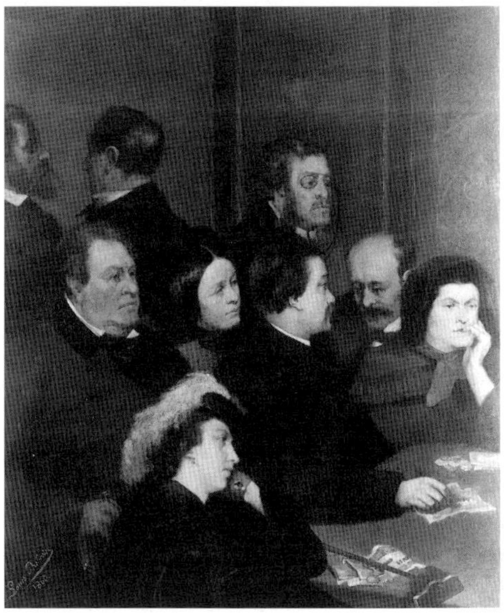

fig. 2 LOUIS DUBOIS, The Roulette Table, 1860, Musées royaux des Beaux-Arts de Belgique, Brussels

It is certainly true that Realist aesthetics which demanded the truthful record of the world as it presented itself to the artist, was immediately applied with the utmost rigour. Louis Dubois (1830–1880), a follower of Courbet and one of Realism's main spokesmen in Belgium, painted still lifes 'without content', and one of his most ambitious works, *The Roulette Table* [fig. 2], does not at first glance display a great deal of *esprit*. It presents a nihilist view of the middle classes. Around the same time, Alfred Verwee (1838–1895), also acquainted with Courbet, was painting cattle and horses in the Flemish pastures, with a detachment not encountered even in French animal pieces of this period. And many practitioners of Realist portraiture, such as Vanaise, Stevens and Agneessens (1842–1885), confront the viewer with objectively rendered recordings of their sitters, devoid of emotional charge but executed as splendid 'belle peinture'.

fig. 3 CHARLES DE GROUX, The Coffee Roaster, c. 1875, Koninklijk Museum voor Schone Kunsten, Antwerp

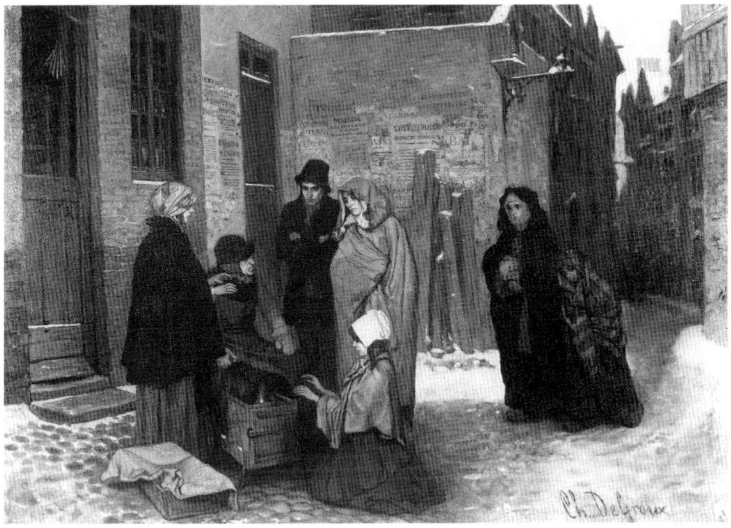

Baudelaire's view that Belgian Realism was uniquely concerned with the neutral representation of the external world was, however, an incomplete analysis. The leading Belgian Realists, such as Félicien Rops (q.v.), Charles de Groux (1825–1870) and Joseph Stevens, took a profound interest in society, and were not content with presenting objective images of their times stripped of any moral or social comment. In the late 1840s Joseph Stevens was already rendering the oppressed lives of dogs, whether strays or draught animals yoked to carts, whose near-human characters permitted them to become representations of the down-trodden labouring poor. Charles de Groux was the first artist in Belgium to paint realistic representations of the urban proletariat and the lower middle class [fig. 3]. Likewise, in his paintings, and even more in his prints, Félicien Rops set himself up as a Hogarth or Daumier. In contrast to the compassion that dominated the work of De Groux and Stevens, he took a more denunciatory, even embittered view of life [fig. 4] in which the vices of capitalism were seen to create untold misery and moral degeneration.

Confronted with the social realities of rapidly industrializing towns or of rural poverty, these artists, each in his own way, drew attention to diseased parts of Belgian middle-class society. Their work won recognition outside Belgium, notably in Paris. That those works by Courbet which contained a more overtly critical social comment should have fallen on such fertile soil in Belgium is easy to understand since the country possessed a nucleus of socially committed artists and intellectuals who had been active long before the founding of Les XX. It was in these Brussels circles, for example, in 1868, that the Société Libre des Beaux-Arts had been founded, which had endorsed the tenets of Realism as a legitimate commentary on the age. This society counted all the major Realists among its members. The periodical *L'Art libre* became the mouthpiece of the group, with the naturalist writer Camille Lemonnier its main art critic.[13] This Société can be regarded as the first organized expression of the avant-garde in the Belgian art world.

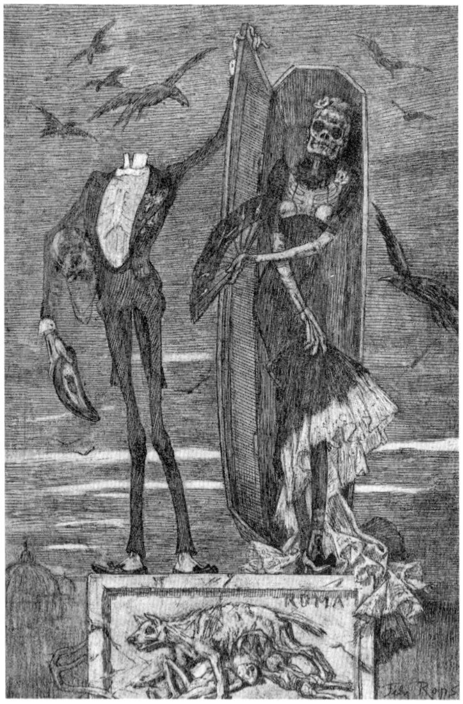

fig. 4 FÉLICIEN ROPS, 'Le Vice suprême', 1883, heliography, Private Collection

Landscape painting remained the prime focus of Belgian Realism in the 1860s and 1870s, although works which contained social comment were only relatively less celebrated.[14] Both elements, serious landscape and arresting scenes of everyday life, imbue the Belgian art of this period with a moral weight, a certain earnestness that could perhaps be singled out as an intrinsically Belgian trait. The Flemish pictorial tradition has already been identified as a determining factor in Belgian art. Perhaps we should also look at another constant factor, more related to content: its tendency to moralize. Sixteenth- and seventeenth-century Flemish art was concerned to project a moral message; satire lay beneath apparently trivial subject matter and highminded moral seriousness was enclosed within often ebullient or extravagant forms.

HENRI LEYS AND MEDIEVALISM

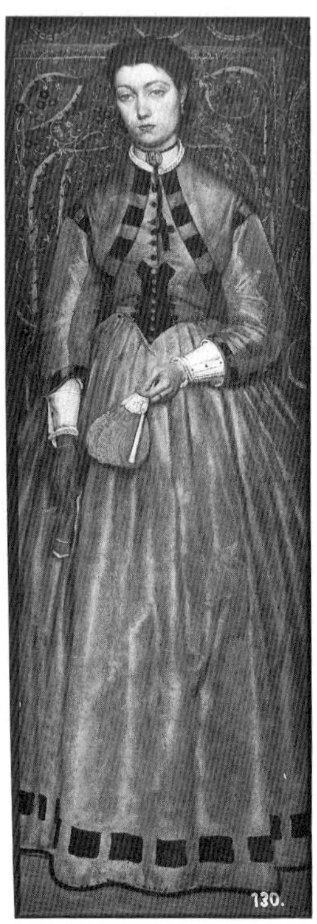

fig. 5 HENRI LEYS, Portrait of the Artist's Daughter, Lucie, 1865, Koninklijk Museum voor Schone Kunsten, Antwerp

The art of the period preceding the time-span of this exhibition, notably Romantic-Realist landscapes, a middle-class Realism with rich painterly qualities as its idiom, and a significant core of social criticism and satire, has been dwelt upon at some length because it contains the seeds of the modernism of the 1880s. But one essential ingredient is missing from this list of antecedents. Certain artists with a Realist orientation looked further back than the Flemish baroque, seeking a point of departure in early sixteenth-century and even medieval art. The Antwerp painter Henri Leys (1815–1869), for instance, followed a route which ran counter to the neo-baroque, painterly bravura of his contemporaries. Contemporaneously with French Realism, Leys devoted himself to a historical realism that was inspired far more by examples of the German Nazarenes and perhaps also the English Pre-Raphaelites. Leys mainly painted meticulous reconstructions of medieval scenes, works that were much imitated. It is in his portraits that his innovative vision appears most clearly, for instance in that of his daughter [fig. 5] in which he draws on the medieval tradition of intense focus upon physiognomic detail, thereby evoking an atmosphere laden with psychological overtones. Subtle works of this kind already point forwards to the portraits of Khnopff.

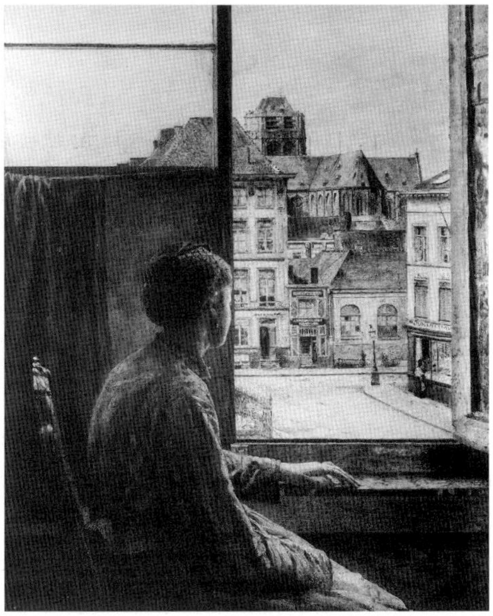

fig. 6 HENRI DE BRAEKELEER, Teniersplaats, Antwerp, 1878, Koninklijk Museum voor Schone Kunsten, Antwerp

One of Leys's pupils, Henri de Braekeleer (q.v.), infused a similar spiritual power into his interiors and still lifes [see cat. 5]. Drawing his formal inspiration from seventeenth-century examples, his preoccupation with a motionless atmosphere and the inner life of objects creates an intensely intimate art which accorded him a special place among the Realists [fig. 6]. He was also a source of inspiration to younger artists such as Ensor, Khnopff and Mellery (q.v.).

Leys and De Braekeleer shared a fascination with the past, a nostalgia that rebelled against the dominant *modernité* that reigned supreme especially in the avant-garde circles of Brussels and Paris. They combined a quest for substance with an interest in the past. Strangely enough it was above all in Antwerp, where the baroque tradition was still at its liveliest, that the presence of both Leys and De Braekeleer ensured that this reaction first made its appearance. Furthermore, despite an apparent contradiction in terms, such a reaction was able to incorporate a landscape painter. The Antwerp artist François Lamorinière (1828–1911), having already moved to Barbizon in 1848, could be considered a member of the Belgian School of Realist landscape painters. However, an accurate observation of detail which recalled the approach of Leys imbued his landscapes with a static, timeless quality more closely aligned to the Pre-Raphaelite approach to landscape, or the German naturalist tradition, than to that of France.

The tendencies to revive the art of the Medieval Age in Belgium were not confined to the interests of a few artists; in some circles they were of central concern. In general, too little attention is paid to the development of Neo-Gothic architecture, design and monumental art in Belgium. Yet, supported by the examples of the German Nazarenes and the English Gothic Revival, an indigenous Gothic Revival, running parallel to the official taste sanctioned by the salons and the State, inspired the architecture and mural decorative cycles of churches and public buildings. This alternative style fed a sensibility that would ultimately triumph over Realism. While the interest in the Middle Ages remained of secondary importance for Belgian painting and sculpture during much of the nineteenth century, in the modernist circles of the 1880s – especially in Symbolism – it emerged as an important primary source of inspiration.

THE 1880s: IMPRESSIONISM AND NEO-IMPRESSIONISM

Many of the works in this exhibition derived from the Realist tradition described above. In the 1880s, Realism evolved into an approach to the external world which, while being broadly defined as 'Impressionism', nonetheless retained a commitment to the technical tradition of picture making. This was expressed in a local variant of the French Impressionists' short brushstroke known as 'tachisme' (from the French *tache*, i.e. 'blob') – a style in which the painterly qualities of artists such as Boulenger, Artan (q.v.) and Dubois were given full rein. It is in this context that we should place the work of Vogels (q.v.), Van Strydonck (q.v.), Mertens (q.v.), Larock (q.v.), Verstraete (q.v.), Baertsoen (q.v.), Hens (q.v.), and the early work of Finch (q.v.), Van Rysselberghe (q.v.) and Ensor, and, to a certain extent, also the work of Evenepoel (q.v.).

Some artists took 'tachisme' to extremes. Vogels, for instance, recorded his impressions of towns and landscapes using an extremely loose technique [see cat. 80]. In keeping with the predominantly more subdued palette of these Belgian artists, Vogels, barring a few sea-pieces, never adopted the bright colours and relatively spare use of paint of the French Impressionists. Instead, he gravitated towards a rich variation of hues and a complex painted surface, with a combination of thick impasto and translucent glazes.

There were also artists, however, who radically changed their style under the influence of French Impressionism. One such was Emile Claus (q.v.), the most French-oriented of Belgian Impressionists. Taking realistic country scenes as his point of departure, he evolved by way of the sun-drenched Realism of the French artist, Jules Bastien-Lepage, towards a systematic application of Impressionist broken brushstrokes and a palette utilizing much brighter colours. His new technique is somewhat reminiscent of the mature Impressionist technique of Camille Pissarro and Alfred Sisley. Claus never adopted as loose an approach as his French counterparts, however, and he never allowed form to dissolve in the dynamic interaction of light and colour. His landscapes have a clear topography and structure, and his animals and human figures always retain their plastic form. Claus's version of Impressionism, sometimes referred to as Luminism, was immensely influential in Belgium (see Goyens de Heusch).

When Belgian art circles first encountered Seurat's pointillism, in 1886–1887, certain 'tachistes' seized on the new technique as a way of escaping from a virtuoso style of painting that some had come to see as a threat to the integrity of form. We can watch this evolution taking place almost simultaneously in the work of Van Rysselberghe, the Dutchman Jan Toorop (1858–1928) (who worked in Belgium), Willy Finch (q.v.) and Henry van de Velde (q.v.), all of whom became committed pointillists in the space of a very few years. The case of Théo van Rysselberghe provides a good illustration of this transformation; his style evolved almost from one year to the next, as he experimented with virtually every possibility that was available.

As a young man, Théo van Rysselberghe painted heavily laid in landscapes and portraits [see cat. 69] similar to those of Vogels and Ensor. He became highly skilled as a portraitist and a painter of orientalist scenes, his work marked by an austerity and depth of analytical description. In his *Portrait of Octave Maus* [cat. 70] and other portraits produced in the years 1886–1887, such as the double portraits of the sisters Camille and Marguerite van Mons (1886; Museum voor Schone Kunsten, Ghent, and Niedersächsisches Landesmuseum, Hanover), the square-brush technique and subdued tones of Realism in the early 1880s gave way to a softer, more subtly blended technique and a brighter, but carefully modulated palette which brings these works close to those of Khnopff and Whistler. This phase came to an abrupt end, however, in 1887 when he succumbed to the influence of Seurat and Signac and took to painting in dots. He applied the pointillist technique in ightly-composed landscapes and sea-pieces, and even more in stately portraits and ingeniously constructed portrait groups. His achievement was that he succeeded in dovetailing the new technique with the lofty status of the old forms of portrait and conversation piece.

Pointillism was not a faddish trend in Belgian art, although it may on the surface appear to have been so. It is true that Van Rysselberghe, Finch, Lemmen (q.v.) and others practised a strict form of divisionism for only a few years, later gravitating towards a less radical Impressionism or – in the case of Finch and Van de Velde – to a different style altogether. But in the case of every one of these artists, their pointillist works are so outstanding as to rank among their greatest achievements, guaranteeing that the Belgian contribution to pointillism was of great significance. It should be remembered that even in France, pointillism in its purest manifestation was something of an ephemeral phenomenon.

JAMES ENSOR

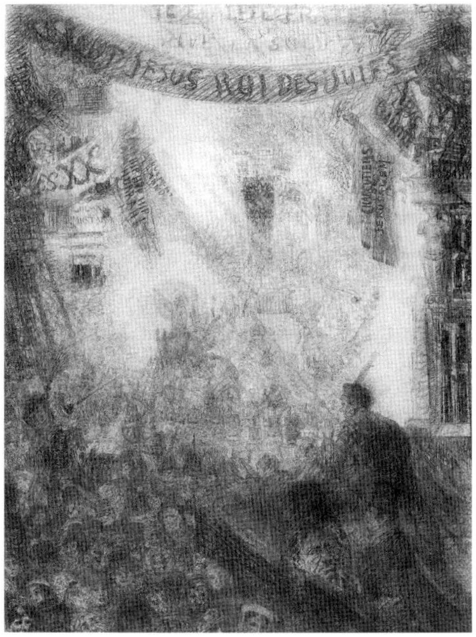

fig. 7 JAMES ENSOR, The Entry of Christ into Jerusalem, 1885, conté crayon, brown and black chalk on paper, Museum voor Schone Kunsten, Ghent

James Ensor too took 'tachisme' as his point of departure, but he was soon exploiting the expressive scope of the free technique to the full, arriving at an Expressionist 'matière' form of painting. In his landscapes and marine paintings Ensor started with vigorous dabs of paint reminiscent of Courbet, but these were imbued with such energy that they gradually acquired a life of their own. In the years 1885–1887, Ensor painted truly visionary landscapes, clouds and seas. The other traditional subjects too, such as middle-class interiors, social themes or portraits, underwent a complete metamorphosis in Ensor's hands that places him more in the twentieth century, as it were, than in the nineteenth. When set beside works such as *Christ's Entry into Brussels* (J. Paul Getty Museum, Malibu), *Intrigue* (Koninklijk Museum voor Schone Kunsten, Antwerp), *Lady with Masks* (Museum voor Schone Kunsten, Ghent) or *Man of Sorrows* (Koninklijk Museum voor Schone Kunsten, Antwerp), the civilized world of Khnopff and Van Rysselberghe suddenly appears past and buried, and the social themes of Fréderic (q.v.) and Meunier (q.v.) – even Rops's satire – seem almost irrelevant.

Drawings played a major role in the development of James Ensor. He initially used a chiaroscuro technique, common at the time, to record fragments of his everyday surroundings. But while drawing he became obsessed with the expressive possibilities inherent in the medium itself, and began to exploit them. In 1887, he showed a large number of drawings at Les XX collectively entitled *Les Auréoles du Christ ou les sensibilités de la lumière (The Halos of Christ or the Sensibilities of Light)* [fig. 7]. They displayed an exceedingly complex style of draughtsmanship with allusions to the etchings of Rembrandt, applying the latter's complex graphic suggestion of light to a large format. Now, it was no longer his everyday surroundings that captivated him, but a fanciful crowd, or a biblical story blown up into grotesque proportions; in these he allowed an almost malevolent imagination to run riot in the creation of oddly shaped and caricatural creatures. He saw himself, in the midst of the hostile crowd, as a rejected Christ figure. It was in these drawings that Ensor's fantasy world was born, a world that would later become so distinctive an aspect of his work. After 1887 he drew far less, but he devised a curious world peopled by masks and skeletons, in paintings produced in bright colours rich in contrasts [see cat. 17], with a psychologically charged technique that would be equalled only by Emil Nolde. At the apex of this creative intoxication, he also came to revile his own earlier works. In this period, a large number of drawings and paintings were reworked into fantastic, almost dadaist representations. However, it was characteristic for someone as contradictory as Ensor that, in the same period that gave birth to his most fantastic creations, he also applied his expertise as a draughtsman to create etchings. But these do not record the fantastical world but rather carefully observed landscapes and marine pieces whose subtlety recalls Whistler's work in the same medium. Ensor's are small etchings and dry-points that belong to the best graphic art of the day.

SYMBOLISM

The almost proto-Expressionist character of Ensor's work stands in sharp contrast to the apparently nostalgic, timeless worlds constructed by Fernand Khnopff. And it is true that the art of this Symbolist draughtsman and painter is in effect a splendid *fin-de-siècle* synthesis of the themes and styles of the previous hundred years. Khnopff refined the middle-class portrait and interior to their ultimate statement, with his sophisticated theatrical poses and compositions, the disposition of props and the stage-managing of glances, poses and gestures [fig. 8]. After the bold technique of his predecessors, Khnopff's painting appears to express a somewhat diffident application of precious materials. This becomes clear if *Listening to Schumann* [cat. 28] is compared to one of Ensor's interiors [cat. 11]. In Ensor there is much unresolved energy, even in the diaphanous *Children washing* [cat. 16]. In Khnopff, on the other hand, painterly realism has been rendered static in a delicate sfumato, somewhere between restrained tension and fatigue. Khnopff's Ardennes landscapes likewise typify this distinction [see cat. 34]. While their origins lie in the rich Belgian Romantic-Realist school already referred to, they seem to fix the natural world at the moment at which life, as it were, is being drained from it.

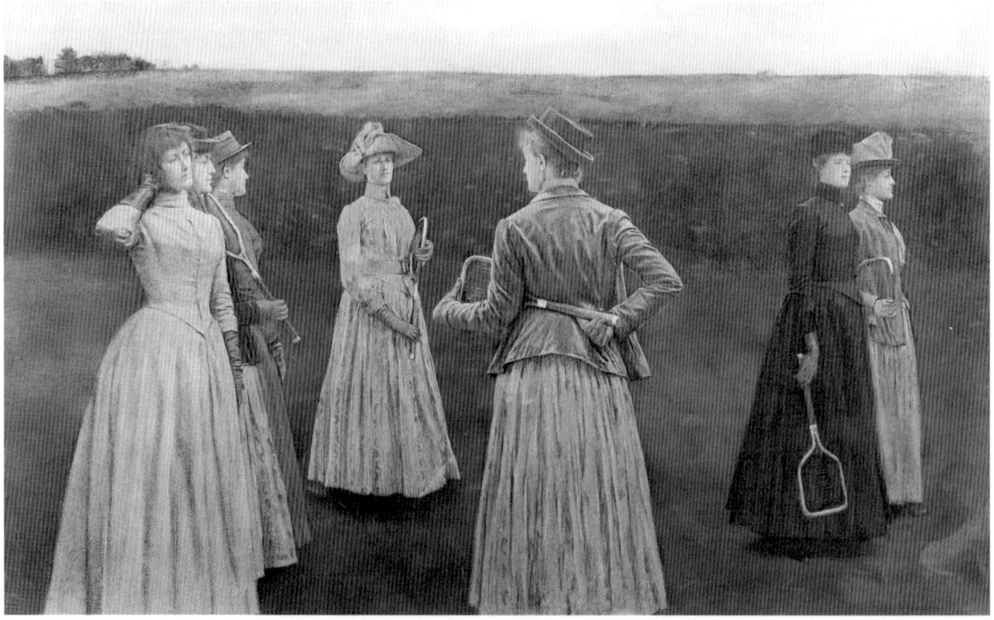

fig. 8 FERNAND KHNOPFF, Memories, 1889, pastel on paper on cardboard, Musées royaux des Beaux-Arts de Belgique, Brussels

Khnopff's particular mode of Realism as evidenced in his portraits of the 1880s and his Ardennes landscapes [see cats. 28, 29, 34] constitutes a high point in Belgian art of the *fin-de-siècle*. The dominant trend in his work, however, remains his application of a personal Symbolist aesthetic. Provoked as a reaction against the domination of 'truth to the material world', Symbolism had its roots in the late Romanticism of Baudelaire and the nostalgic reconstruction of the Middle Ages by the Nazarenes and the Pre-Raphaelite Brotherhood. Symbolism fell on fertile soil in Belgium, possibly as a reaction against the realism that seemed to many artists to be a preoccupation with banal materialism rather than with matters of the spirit. While Symbolism took on many different guises, from the radical non-naturalism of Paul Gauguin (1848–1903) to the esoteric idealism of Sâr Péladan, it was this latter manifestation, proclaimed through a programme published in 1891 and made manifest in a series of annual exhibitions, the Salons de la Rose+Croix (1892–1897) held in Paris, that appears to have appealed to several Belgian artists, notably Khnopff. Instead of reality, the 'initiated' followers of Péladan focused on allegory; rather than grappling with current conditions and problems, they preferred either to take refuge in an ideal beauty or to descend, generally in a mood of deep melancholy, to the innermost depths of their being.

While Khnopff's life and work embodied this idealist vision, both were also greatly influenced by the ideas and forms of the English Pre-Raphaelites; indeed, Khnopff was a close friend of Burne-Jones. With its synthesis of these two spheres of influence – French and English – his work fundamentally enriched European Symbolism.

Khnopff succeeded in uniting in his work two divergent routes within Symbolism – the more esoteric side, and the more poetic-realist side. He was virtually the only Belgian versatile enough to do so. Another 'initiate', Jean Delville (q.v.), who focused exclusively on allegory, soon degenerated into eccentricity and dogmatism, often proclaimed on a monumental scale. The remaining Belgian Symbolists are less important for their allegorical works than for their more modest transmutations of everyday life. Xavier Mellery (q.v.), originally a Realist, largely confined his art to richly atmospheric black-and-white drawings of interiors such as those of his own home [cats. 43–45]. He himself aptly summarized the inner meaning of such scenes when he showed a group of seven drawings at Les XX in 1890 under the collective title of 'la vie des choses' ('the inner life of things'). In addition to interiors, however, he also made decorative allegorical compositions with figures intended to adorn public spaces, whose theatricality seemed to be at odds with the spirituality of his drawings. William Degouve de Nuncques (q.v.) is another artist who is at his most convincing in his simplest compositions: they are wondrous landscapes, usually produced in pastels [see cats. 7, 8]. He would eventually abandon these dreamlike scenes, painting nothing but simple, somewhat naïve landscapes.

This form of intimate Realism imbued with poetic resonance which found its purest expression in the drawings of Mellery occupied an important place in Belgian Symbolism around the turn of the century. In various parts of the country, artists adopted this simplicity and intimacy as their keynote. They worked in seclusion, at some distance from the more thrusting urban circles. They hoped to find in village life an unspoilt spirituality that would nourish their art. In the Ardennes villages where Khnopff liked to work we also find the artists Donnay [cat. 11] and Le Brun [cat. 39]. Jacob Smits (1855–1928) worked in the remote Kempen region (La Campine), and in Sint-Martens-Latem on the River Lys near Ghent, the first 'Latem group' was established, with Valerius de Saedeleer (1867–1941), Albijn van den Abeele (1835–1918), Albert Servaes (1883–1966) and Gustave van de Woestijne (1881–1947). The Symbolist poet Karel van de Woestijne (1878–1929) and the sculptor George Minne (q.v.) were the inspiring forces behind this 'school'.[15]

Léon Spilliaert (q.v.), while deriving his initial pictorial inspiration from these Symbolists' transmutations of the real world into one with inner spiritual meaning, pushed such imagery to the edge where nightmare and reality meet. Like them, this artist, who worked in Ostend, portrayed his own surroundings, such as the sea, the dykes, the seashore, the interior of his house and himself. However, he was not averse to theatrical exaggeration and special pictorial effects, which gives him a unique place in Belgian art somewhere between Symbolism and Surrealism [see cats. 63, 64].

The name of George Minne has already been mentioned. Minne was a highly original artist whose full significance has only recently been recognized. As a young sculptor emerging in the 1880s, he found himself confronting on the one hand a strong Neo-Classical style and on the other hand a somewhat pompous monumental sculpture, in which artists such as Egide Rombaux (1865–1942) and Jef Lambeaux (1852–1908) pitted themselves against the apparently superhuman power of Rodin, the latter deriving in part from the fact that Rodin had worked for some time in Belgium, and had many contacts there; in 1889 he joined Les XX. In the period 1886–1887, taking Rodin's example as his starting-point, Minne developed an unusual, expressive idiom, by 'reducing' (a key concept in Minne) the baroque plastic energy in sculpture to a restrained modelling, and by departing from correct anatomical form and harmony to convey feelings of fear and despair. His quest for a primitive form of expression led Minne to study Gothic sculpture, and he was one of the first artists to conceive his pieces in natural materials such as granite and untreated wood [see cat. 56]. After a series of emotionally charged works [see cats. 54, 55], he evolved towards an increasingly stylized formal language creating his kneeling and self-absorbed youthful figures. These captured perfectly the introverted, spiritually expressive concerns of Symbolism, enclosed as they were within the elegant forms of Art Nouveau.

THE ART OF SOCIAL RECORD AND REFORM

Most Symbolists, and George Minne was no exception, had a keen, if implicit, interest in social reform. In this they continued the tradition of social involvement which had been initiated by the Realists of the previous generation, although often in a less overtly combative way. Even those whose art appeared wholly divorced from such a politically topical concern, such as Khnopff and Lemmen (q.v.), played some part in the social struggle that marked the last few years of the nineteenth century in Belgium. Some of them contributed materially to the educational programmes of the labour movement, and in general Belgium's progressive artists at the close of the nineteenth century had a clear leftist orientation.[16]

Although, as has been pointed out earlier, different lines of force are discernible in Belgian art during this period, the relative significance of each affiliation (from Symbolism to Luminism, Neo-Impressionism and Social Realism) depends on one's vantage-point. Although Symbolism may be pinpointed as the dominant trend, it is also valid to see social involvement, the preoccupation with the lot of the ordinary man, as a unifying factor, a thread that runs through the work of most of the progressive artists.

Constantin Meunier (q.v.) is of course the figure who best exemplifies this social commitment, and who created an almost universal iconography for it. His sculptures and paintings record the daily lives of miners – an important topical subject not only in Belgium, but also in France and England. But in the final analysis, his work goes beyond that. His sculptures, like the slender figures of Minne, are quite simply about the despair and heroism in any human life [see cats. 48–53]. In the oeuvre of Léon Fréderic, too, it is the realistic works that prove most arresting. As an 'idealist', Fréderic also painted allegorical scenes that strike us as somewhat contrived and naïve. More important are his boldly drawn and incisive images of peasants and workers, whose hard lives and utopian futures he imbued with an almost ritualistic significance. Finally, someone who is often neglected in this context – presumably because of the unevenness of his work – is Eugène Laermans (1864–1940). As a child this artist became deaf, which isolated him from the surrounding world. He depicted country life in a heroic mode, in much the same way as Meunier had portrayed the miners. Using a large format, he displayed processions of beggars, outcasts and wanderers filing past motionless trees and rivers beneath tragic cloudscapes [fig. 9]. In his best works, Laermans has a highly expressive style, which heralds the Expressionism of Kollwitz and Barlach.

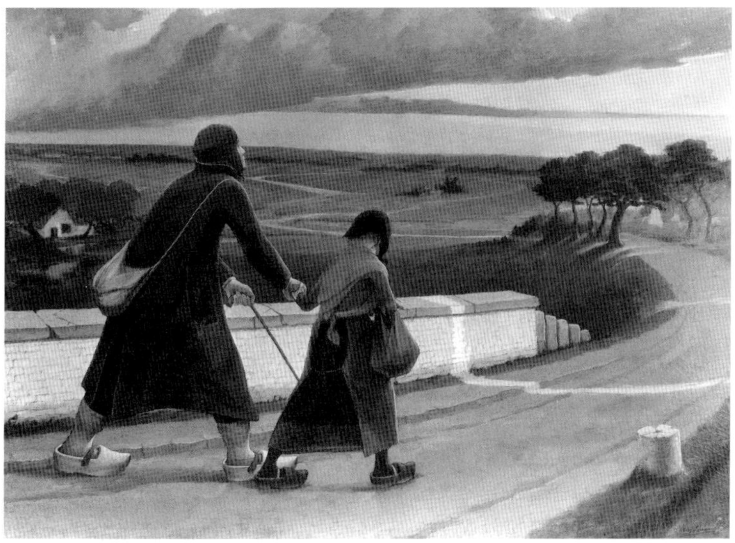

fig. 9 EUGÈNE LAERMANS, The Blind Man, 1898, Koninklijk Museum voor Schone Kunsten, Antwerp

THE BELGIAN FIN-DE-SIECLE

In the 1860s and 1870s there was a certain homogeneity in the plastic arts, with Realism identifiable as the dominant mode. In contrast, the Belgian art of the 1880s and 1890s is strikingly varied; every trend present in *fin-de-siècle* Europe is represented, in a highly concentrated form. In an extraordinary artistic revival, we find Impressionism and Neo-Impressionism, Ensor's individualistic form of Expressionism, the esoteric Symbolism of Khnopff and Delville, the *intimisme* of Mellery and the social reflection of Minne, Meunier and Laermans all manifesting themselves within a circumscribed area. This revival coincided with an increase in activity in the world of art that looked to Brussels as its centre and its link to other European centres, notably Paris. The diversity of styles was clearly reflected in the structure of Les XX, which did not itself promulgate any artistic programme, aiming solely to gather into its ranks the most promising artistic forces from home and abroad. This made it possible for artists as different as Ensor and Van Rysselberghe, in turn, to dominate the foreground within the group.

Les XX was certainly not the only society in the arts, nor was *L'Art moderne* the only progressive journal. In Belgium, as in the rest of Europe, artists' groups and ephemeral periodicals were the order of the day. The literary counterpart to Les XX and *L'Art moderne* was *La Jeune Belgique* which focused particularly on naturalist literature. In 1893, the year in which Les XX was succeeded in Brussels by La Libre Esthétique, Antwerp witnessed the launching of the literary journal *Van Nu en Straks* (Present and Future). It was a polished publication, designed by Henry van de Velde [fig. 10] who by that time had abandoned painting for architecture and the decorative arts. Although the journal appeared for only a few years, it became a byword for the Flemish artistic and socially committed avant-garde.[17]

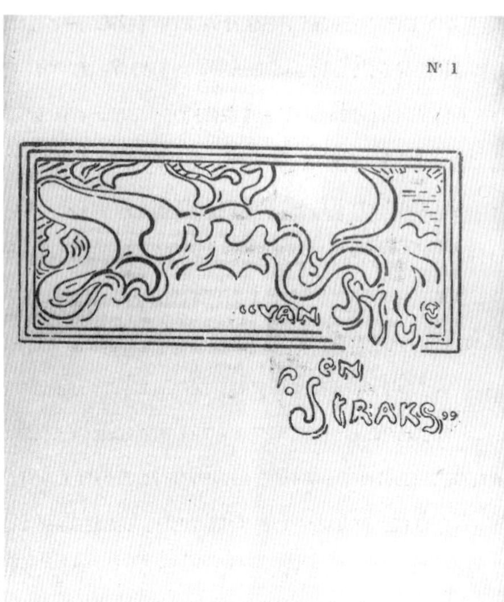

fig. 10 HENRY VAN DE VELDE
Cover for *Van Nu en Straks*, first series, 1893

The various societies and journals organized a stream of exhibitions, lectures and concerts. And within them, different artistic disciplines became closely integrated in a way that typifies Belgian artistic life at the close of the nineteenth century. Belgium experienced a veritable literary Renaissance at this time, both in French and in Dutch, the latter being the preferred language of several of the progressive Flemish writers. A strikingly large number of writers and poets ventured into print as art critics, had painters and sculptors among their closest friends, and were highly involved in the art scene. Of the Symbolist poets, Maeterlinck, Rodenbach, Le Roy and Verhaeren [fig. 11], as well as their French equivalents, notably Stéphane Mallarmé and J.-K. Huysmans, injected powerful impulses into the plastic arts. And conversely, the innovative imagery of artists such as Ensor, Minne or the pointillists inspired the writers. Social awareness was something they all had in common. In the oeuvre of many plastic artists we can trace a clear literary inspiration, and numerous examples can be given of artists and writers whose work is complementary. The Bruges townscapes of Khnopff, for instance, constituted a plastic equivalent of the city scenes in the poetry of Rodenbach – to mention only the most obvious parallel [see cat. 30]. Minne's desperate figures look as if they are either reciting Maeterlinck's laments or moving to their melancholy rhythm. In a telling comment on this intense relationship between artists and writers, Minne says of his friend Maeterlinck: 'we sometimes communicate so well that it actually seems to me that I produced *Princesse Maleine* myself, with either a chisel or a pen, I cannot remember!'[18]

In the last two decades of the nineteenth century, the close relationship between literature and the plastic arts stimulated a wave of renewal in graphic design and book-printing, with artists and writers frequently collaborating to make a literary publication into a finely crafted work of art.[19] Khnopff, Lemmen, Van de Velde and Van Rysselberghe were particularly active as Art Nouveau designers. More generally, graphic design and the production of fine books commanded positive interest within Les XX, and the catalogues of the annual exhibitions were designed by the artists themselves. This enthusiasm, initially confined to graphic art and later expanding to include other areas of applied art, would increase still further in the 1890s. It was a trend that went hand in hand with a general revival of the decorative arts within Art Nouveau, of which Brussels was an im-

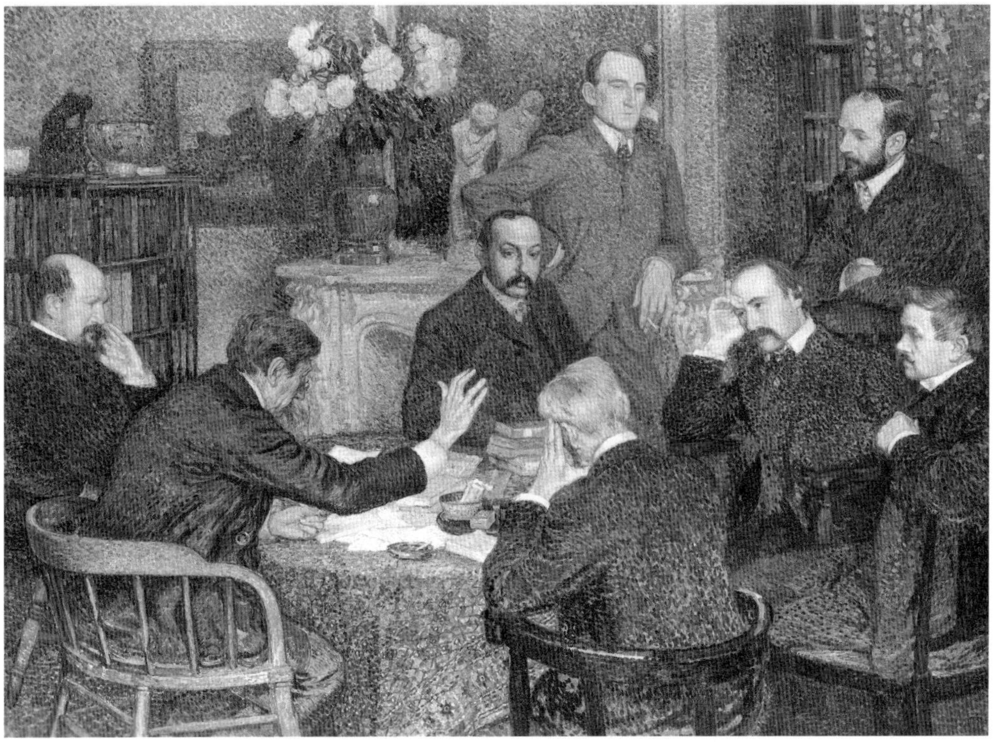

fig. 11 THÉO VAN RYSSELBERGHE
The Reading, 1903,
Museum voor Schone Kunsten, Ghent

Left to right: Félix Le Dantec (biologist), Francis Viélé-Griffin (writer), Félix Fénéon (critic), André Gide (writer), Henri Ghéon (physician, writer), Maurice Maeterlinck (writer); front left: Emile Verhaeren; seen from behind: Henri-Edmond Cross (painter)

portant centre and which the Belgian architects Van de Velde and Horta (1861–1947) helped to promote. Within Les XX itself, interest in the applied arts was already strong; moreover, socially committed members saw the promotion of craftsmanship as a means of educating the people. The society's successor, La Libre Esthétique, gave even more emphasis, in its exhibition policy, to the combination of the plastic arts with every conceivable form of modern design. Unsurprisingly in the context of this 'decorative movement', some artists gradually came to devote themselves completely to the applied arts. George Lemmen's focus shifted, in the course of time, from painting to graphic design. Finch plunged into the decorative arts around 1890, working chiefly in ceramics. Henry van de Velde stopped painting altogether, and concentrated on design and architecture.

Can Belgian art of the latter half of the nineteenth century – particularly the final two decades – be said to have an identity of its own, distinct from the French, English or German, and if so, what were its essential characteristics? Answering the first part of this question in the affirmative is easier than providing a definition. This introduction has suggested a number of features that could be considered characteristic of this period of Belgian art: the strong component of realism and naturalism, the painters' tendency to emphasize painterly quality, a strong spirit of social involvement expressed in a variety of ways from Meunier's Social Realism to the anarchist mockery of Rops and Ensor. It is impossible to go much further than this in pinpointing national features, although many writers have made bold claims in this regard. It is equally difficult to determine whether certain traits, such as humanitarianism, stemmed from the country's history, a history that was fraught, to put it mildly, with social turmoil. Despite such caveats, however, it is indisputable that the Belgian art of the period covered by this exhibition is highly distinctive. Although Belgium was almost part of French cultural territory in the nineteenth century, and the Belgian and French art worlds were seamlessly interwoven, it is curious that artists sprang up in this relationship that are impossible to imagine in a French context, whether because of the form or the idiosyncratic subject matter of their art. This applies to a certain extent to Félicien Rops, although he often worked for a French public and was strongly influenced by French satirical artists. It certainly applies to the great figures of this period such as Vogels, Ensor, Khnopff, Minne and Meunier. Even the Neo-Impressionists display a recognizably distinct approach.

It is without question significant that Belgium, lying as it were on the outskirts of Paris, made possible different and opposing influences to co-exist in such a way as to enrich the French canon. In this respect, there was first and foremost the Flemish tradition, jolted out of its slumbers by the arrival of the influences of France. There were, in addition, German and English influences which gave rise, in Belgium, to highly original combinations and syntheses.

Another question worth addressing is whether one can speak of a Flemish or Walloon identity in nineteenth-century art. This was the century, after all, of regional cultural emancipation, and one of the consequences of the principles of democracy was a new national awareness and self-respect. The processes of deepening Flemish and Walloon awareness were certainly important issues in the nineteenth century; they were expressed in literature and art criticism more than in the plastic arts. But there was as yet no question of any cultural parting of the ways, whether reflected in or caused by the linguistic division. This means that the question of whether we are dealing with Flemish or Walloon art is historically irrelevant. At the end of the nineteenth century, when the art critic Jules du Jardin published a reference book for the entire region entitled *L'Art flamand*, it was entirely uncontroversial,[20] and Flemish artists participated alongside their Walloon colleagues in the French-language avant-garde of Les XX and *La jeune Belgique* without self-deprecation. *La Légende d'Ulenspiegel*, published in 1867 by Charles de Coster and described by Lemonnier as the 'Flemish Bible', is generally regarded as one of the first expressions of the revival of French-language Belgian literature.[21]

To the artists of the nineteenth century, the emphasis on national character did not have the separatist overtones that it would acquire for many in the twentieth century. While national sentiments were felt strongly, they were part of a harmonious whole of progressive ideas and sympathies that were still so diffuse and remote from reality that they did not conflict. The progressive fountainhead could accommodate elements as disparate as a strong internationalism, anarchism and a pronounced nationalism. In the name of liberty, not only artists but also political thinkers saw many concepts as essentially reconcilable. In the same spirit, an artist could express his Flemishness in the French language (Maeterlinck and Verhaeren both wrote in French) and the Walloon artist Rops felt at home in the Flemish tradition of painting. In the modern artistic vision, apparently contradictory views such as 'art for art's sake' and socially committed art rubbed shoulders with one another, and there were many artists in whose work Realism and Symbolism stood side by side in a homogeneous oeuvre.

This communion of ideas was unique to the *fin-de-siècle* in Belgium. From it derived both an openness for the new and contradictory, and a strong awareness of tradition and identity. This complex structure may be one of the main reasons for the persistent appeal of figures such as Ensor, Khnopff, Verhaeren and Maeterlinck. It may also go some way to explaining how Brussels, for the space of two decades, came to command a centre-stage position in the history of modern art.

1 F. C. Legrand, in *Le Groupe des XX et son temps*, Musées royaux des Beaux-Arts de Belgique, Brussels / Rijksmuseum Kröller-Müller, Otterlo, 1962, 17–36; J. Block, 'Les XX: Forum of the Avant-Garde', in *Belgian Art 1880–1914*, The Brooklyn Museum, New York 1980, 17–40; J. Block, *Les XX and Belgian Avant-Gardism, 1868–1894*, Ann Arbor 1984; S. M. Canning, '"Soyons Nous": Les XX and the Cultural Discourse of the Belgian Avant-Garde', in *Les XX and the Belgian Avant-Garde, Prints, Drawings and Books ca. 1890*, ed. S. H. Goddard, Spencer Museum of Art, University of Kansas, 1992, 28–54 – also published in Belgium: *Les Vingt en de avant-garde in België, Prenten, tekeningen en boeken ca. 1890*, Museum voor Schone Kunsten, Ghent 1992, 11–31.

2 The original 'twenty' were: Achille Chainaye, Frantz Charlet, Jean Delvin, Dario de Regoyos, Paul Dubois, James Ensor, Willy Finch, Charles Goethals, Fernand Khnopff, Jef Lambeaux, Pericles Pantazis, Willy Schlobach, Frans Simons, Gustave Vanaise, Théo van Rysselberghe, Guillaume van Strydonck, Piet Verhaert, Theodoor Verstraete, Guillaume Vogels and Rodolphe Wytsman. During the first few years the group acquired a more clearly progressive identity. Several artists of a more conservative bent resigned, including Lambeaux, Verhaert, Delvin, Vanaise and Verstraete. Modernists such as Henry de Groux, Georges Lemmen, George Minne, Auguste Rodin, Félicien Rops, Paul Signac and Henry van de Velde only joined at a later stage.

3 See esp. P. Roberts-Jones, *Du Réalisme au Surréalisme* (Belgique, L'Art du temps), Brussels 1969, 6–24.

4 *Letters of Gustave Courbet*, ed. and transl. by P. Ten Doesschate-Chu, Chicago, London 1992, 67–69, 72–74. See also the biographical information in R. Fernier, *La vie et l'oeuvre de Gustave Courbet*, 2 vols., Paris 1977–1978.

5 *Letters of Gustave Courbet* (*op. cit.* note 4), 67.

6 Courbet's Antwerp address was published in *Le Précurseur* (22 August 1861); see F. C. Legrand, in *De realistische stroming in België van de 19de eeuw tot heden*, Musées royaux des Beaux-Arts de Belgique / Koninklijke Musea voor Schone Kunsten van België, Brussels 1963–1964, 8–9. For Courbet's participation in the Ghent Salon, see R. Hoozee, 'Gustave Courbet op het Gentse salon van 1868', in *De wagenmenner en andere verhalen. Album discipulorum Prof. Dr. M. de Maeyer*, State University, Ghent 1986, 82–89.

7 R. Hoozee, 'Barbizon en België', in *De school van Barbizon. Franse meesters van de 19de eeuw*, ed. J. Sillevis and H. Kraan, Museum voor Schone Kunsten, Ghent / Haags Gemeentemuseum, The Hague / Institut Néerlandais, Paris, 1985–1986, 112–126.

8 'Ce retour au principe de l'école flamande, c'est à Courbet qu'on le doit'. 'Exposition des œuvres de Courbet', in *L'Art moderne* 1 (3 July 1881), 139.

9 'Qu'est-ce qui attire, qu'est-ce qui séduit surtout? Ce n'est pas le site, quoiqu'il soit, ni l'expression de la nature, quoiqu'elle ait de la pénétration. Non, c'est l'arrangement dans les lignes, vives, spirituelles, imprévues, ou dans les tons, vibrants, adroitement nuancés, harmonieusement agencés, tantôt opposés, tantôt confondus avec une hardiesse toujours heureuse. Il y a là un ragoût, un bouquet, une virtuosité singulière. Partout on sent la main, on sent la patte, active, habile, nerveuse, posant le coup de brosse, enlevant la touche, accrochant aux bons endroits la lumière ou l'accent, décrivant prestement le trait, le dirigeant avec une sûreté qui ravit, dessinant notamment la physionomie des divers feuillages avec une merveilleuse finesse. C'est cet ensemble de qualités souples et déliées, tenant au métier compris dans sa plus haute et sa plus noble signification, c'est cette verve, cette fougue dans le coloris et le pinceau, qui placent Boulenger hors de pair.' Hippolyte Boulenger, in *L'Art moderne* 1 (10 July 1881), 146.

10 'Philosophies des peintres belges, philosophie de notre ami Courbet'. *Œuvres complètes*, II, ed. Claude Pichois, Paris 1976, 933.

11 'En France on me trouve trop peintre. Ici on me trouve trop littéraire. Tout ce qui dépasse la portée d'esprit de ces peintres, ils le traitent d'art littéraire'. *Ibid.*

12 'La peinture flamande ne brille que par des qualités distinctes des qualités intellectuelles. Pas d'esprit, mais quelquefois une riche couleur, et presque toujours une étonnante habileté de main.' *Ibid.*, 931.

13 Members included Louis Artan, Théodore Baron, Charles de Groux, Louis Dubois, Constantin Meunier, Félicien Rops, Eugène Smits, Camille van Camp and Alfred Verwee. As far as we know, however, neither a charter nor an accurate membership list exists. See also A. A. Moerman's introduction to *Réalisme et liberté. Les maîtres de la 'Société Libre des Beaux-Arts' de Bruxelles*, Musées royaux des Beaux-Arts de Belgique, Brussels 1969.

14 Cf. *Arbeit und Alltag. Soziale Wirklichkeit in der belgische Kunst 1830–1914*, Neue Gesellschaft für bildende Kunst, Berlin 1979.

15 Cf. *Le premier groupe de Laethem-Saint-Martin, 1899–1914*, Musées royaux des Beaux-Arts de Belgique, Brussels 1988.

16 Cf. S. Levine, 'Politics and the Graphics of the Belgian Avant-Garde', in *Les XX and the Belgian Avant-Garde* (*op. cit.* note 1), 55–74.

17 For groups and journals, see S. M. Canning, *op. cit.* (note 1), 30–32.

18 'Parfois, je communie si bien avec lui, qu'il me semble vraiment que c'est moi qui ait fait *Princesse Maleine*, avec l'ébauchoir ou la plume, je ne sais plus moi-même!'. Franz Hellens, 'Les dessins de George Minne', in *Sélection* (15 July 1921).

19 J. Block, 'Book design among the Vingtistes: The Work of Lemmen, Van de Velde and Van Rysselberghe at the Fin-de-siècle', in *Les XX and the Belgian Avant-Garde* (*op. cit.* note 1), 98–125.

20 6 vols., Brussels 1896–1899.

21 Cf. A. Gerlo, in *Nationaal Biografisch Woordenboek* 3 (1968), 218–222: 'Alles is bij hem Vlaams, uitgenomen de taal' ('Everything about him is Flemish except his language'; p. 221).

Impressionism, Neo-Impressionism and Luminism in Belgium

SERGE GOYENS DE HEUSCH

The struggle to liberate landscape painting from the confines of the studio in order more accurately to depict external nature in all its variety marked the evolution of the genre during the nineteenth century. In Belgium, as in the rest of Europe, but particularly in France, the impulse was one informed by a new definition of 'truth to Nature', a new 'realism'. This, in its turn called for a reassessment of earlier schools of landscape painting, most notably those of the Low Countries during the sixteenth and seventeenth centuries. Likewise it both transported the artist beyond the studio to a direct confrontation with the subject – the landscape – and demanded of him a more direct transcription of that external world in which light and atmosphere dominated its physical forms and hence required translation onto the canvas through a relatively brighter palette and freer brushwork.

From around 1860, a generation of Belgian painters laid the foundations for those successors who were to become the standard bearers of a nationally identifiable form of Impressionism: Hippolyte Boulenger (1837–1874) in Tervuren [fig. 12],[1] Heymans (1839–1921) in the Kempen (La Campine),[2] Louis Artan de Saint-Martin (q.v.) and Félicien Rops (q.v.) on the North Sea coast. To be sure, Belgian Impressionism was in part inevitably touched by the developments of its counterpart in France, accessible through both the ready passage of these younger artists to Paris, and the inclusion of works by the latter's major exponents at the exhibitions both in Brussels at Les XX from 1884, and, to a more limited extent, in Antwerp. However, a distinct group of landscape painters, led by Guillaume Vogels (q.v.) and James Ensor (q.v.), and including the youthful Van Rysselberghe (q.v.), observed the more sombre tones of the Belgian climate, translating them onto canvas with a distinct application of technique which reflected in part the painterly tradition of Flemish art, whose major exemplar was still deemed to be Rubens. While their French counterparts favoured pure colours applied with short, broken brushwork, the Belgian artists tended to adopt more muted tones which they applied in broadly laid in strokes to create richly textured surfaces. Their tonal range, in particular, earned the sobriquet of the 'Grey School' *('l'ecole du gris')*.[3]

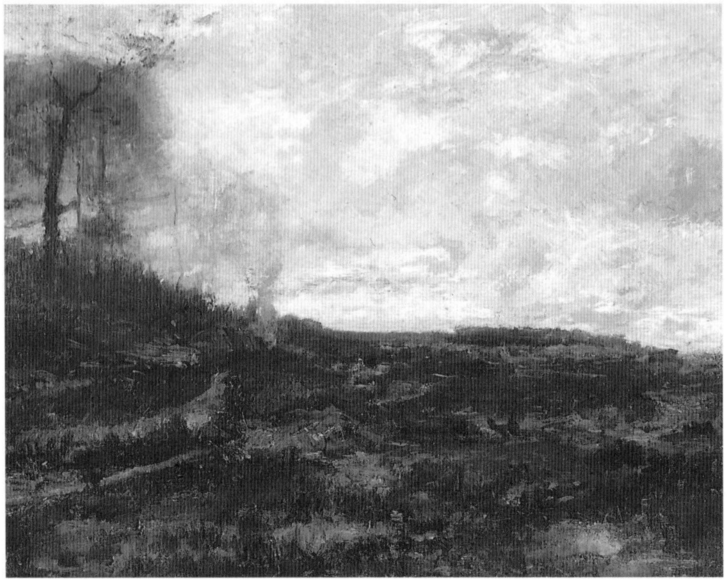

fig. 12 HIPPOLYTE BOULENGER, Horizon (Edge of the Wood), c. 1870, Musée de l'Art Wallon, Liège

THE BIRTH OF BELGIAN IMPRESSIONISM

This innovative approach to landscape painting in Belgium coincided with the sweeping social and cultural changes which marked the country during the closing two decades of the last century. Indeed, the new approach to landscape formed part of an emergent avant-garde in literature, painting and music. These developments were paralleled by rapid economic growth which in turn brought with it social unrest and political realignments. Within this new political reality was to be found an active minority of young intellectuals and artists, some of whom were from working-class backgrounds and had gained access to culture for the first time, others from those sections of the bourgeoisie who had a strongly-developed social conscience. Socialist ideals and Socialism marked many of the artists who, in 1883, formed the Groupe des XX. The association between radical politics and innovative painting had already been underlined by some of the founder members of Les XX, whose work, when shown over the previous few years at the alternative exhibiting bodies such as La Chrysalide[4] and L'Essor,[5] had created considerable critical debate. Indeed, a dispute within the Brussels group L'Essor, which was considered by some to have become too bourgeois for some of its younger members such as James Ensor, led to the establishment of the Groupe des XX.[6] Masterminded by the lawyer, Octave Maus [fig. 13], Les XX united the plastic arts, music and literature. In its successor body, La Libre Esthétique, Maus would bring together fine art and the applied arts, Realist painters and young Impressionists and, before very long, exponents of Symbolism. Several of the founder members of Les XX were either suspended or resigned on the grounds that the group was too catholic in its affiliations.[7] The banner for innovation within Les XX was initially raised by the presence of Impressionist paintings shown in their exhibitions, whether from Belgium or from France, although this subsequently passed to Neo-Impressionism and a modified form of international Symbolism.

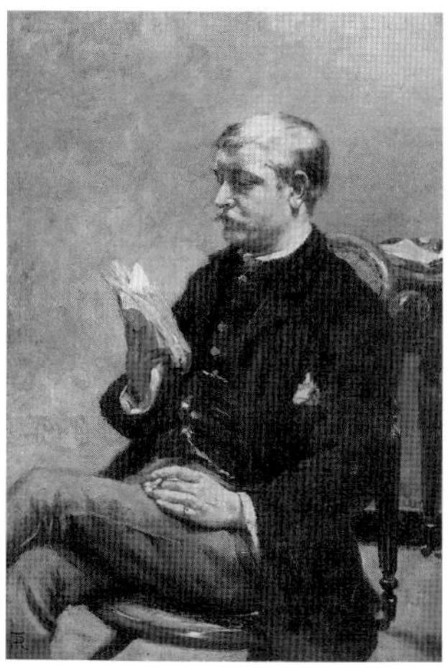

fig. 13 THÉO VAN RYSSELBERGHE
Portrait of Octave Maus, c. 1883,
Musée d'Ixelles, Brussels

The boldest of the founder members of Les XX was incontestably James Ensor. Less marked by French influences than many of his colleagues, he introduced a completely new way of looking at light, in particular that light which has been filtered into sombre, often somewhat claustrophic, domestic interiors. In 1880, the year generally considered to mark the birth of a national Impressionist school of painting in Belgium, Ensor was aged twenty and had just left the Acadamy of Fine Arts in Brussels. He returned to his studio in the attic of his parents' home in Ostend and started painting his magnificent series of bourgeois interiors. He did not make a complete break with realism, but rather his treatment of light caused him to paint figurative subjects as if they were weightless and transparent. Having devined the secrets of Rubens, he revived certain of his techniques, using glazes in areas of shadow to increase the density of the darker tones. His highlights on the other hand are laid in thickly. His disdain for outline, for conventional modelling and for perspective was seen as evidence of grave negligence, and at first earned him severe criticism. It took Emile Verhaeren, the Belgian critic and writer, to come to the defence of the young man from Ostend and to hail his *Oyster Eater* (Koninklijk Museum voor Schone Kunsten, Antwerp), painted in 1882, as the first painting to celebrate light to be executed in Belgium. Given the fact that it is unlikely that Ensor would have been familiar with French Impressionism at the time, his conviction concerning the dominant force of light within a composition emanated from indigenous examples and direct observation. Fresh though his palette may be it is not yet as bright as that of Monet; it comes closer to Manet, whose paintings Ensor could certainly have seen, if only at the Antwerp Triennial Exhibition of 1882. Such comparisons with French prototypes, however, are not very productive within the particular case of Ensor's handling of light. He puts his colour to quite different use. In his work colour represents an explosion of the imagination rather than simply the rendering of the effects of light. This removes the great Anglo-Flemish painter from the Impressionist school; his *Christ's Entry into Brussels* (J. Paul Getty Museum, Malibu), painted in 1888, is the most striking painting ever produced in Belgium. Though his symbolism separated him from the Impressionist movement, his painterly technique and exploration of light within confined interior spaces continued to influence some of his *vingtiste* fellow-artists such as Guillaume van Strydonck (q.v.), the Dutchman Jan Toorop (1858–1928), Frantz Charlet (1868–1928), Willy Finch (q.v.) and even the most senior of all, Guillaume Vogels (q.v.).

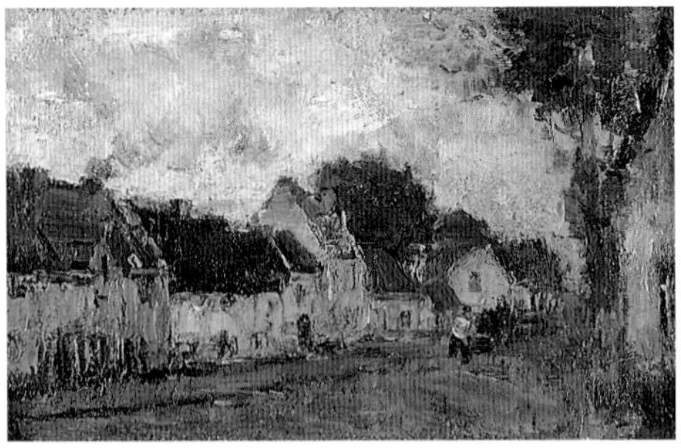

fig. 14 GUILLAUME VOGELS, 'Mother Lambic', c. 1880, Hôtel Charlier, Brussels

Vogels is related to Ensor through his treatment of light; both convey the multiple highlights of reflected light in a combination of tones and half-tones. But Guillaume Vogels's brushstrokes are much more energetic [fig. 14]; he took a powerful sensual pleasure in his material, expressing himself lyrically but with bravura. Like Ensor, but with even greater commitment, Vogels was attracted by the soft humidity of trees and roads. The damp atmosphere however does not destroy the basic structure of his compositions. If anything his preferred subjects of rainy or snowy views contain the dramatic ingredients for his light. He retained a kind of northern melancholy and expressed it in a subtle range of greys, with the occasional burst of brighter colour. Traditionalists certainly criticized what was in fact the mainstay of his Impressionism, the sketchiness and roughness of his work, but in fact the directness of his interpretation was highly influential amongst his young colleagues. One painter in particular, Pericles Pantazis (1849–1884), a Greek who had come to Brussels from Paris, participated in this liberation of the landscape until his untimely death in 1884. He painted the play of light in the Forest of Soignes and the changeable skies of the North Sea coast more subtly and more truthfully than Vogels.

It was the North Sea above all that drew Théo van Rysselberghe and some of the other *vingtistes* to Impressionism. The ever-changing light of the sea made their painting more fluent; their studio colours, ochres and dark greys, were blown away by the summer breezes. Some of them also went south to brighten up their palettes. Van Rysselberghe, from Ghent, made several trips to Spain and Morocco, and found his excuse there for abandoning the dark colours that had characterized his earlier figurative work. At the same time Whistler's painting helped to lead some of the members of Les XX away from their more ponderous, sombre form of realism.

Octave Maus included paintings by Whistler in the Salons des XX of 1884, 1886 and 1888, even before showing Monet and Renoir. His paintings attracted the attention of some of the younger Belgian artists, who were eager to make his acquaintance. In 1885 Frantz Charlet and Théo van Rysselberghe met the artist during a trip to Holland, and

Willy Finch and Willy Schlobach (q.v.) saw him on more than one occasion in London. Before they had any contact with French Impressionism these young Belgians came under the influence of the Anglo-American painter, and learned to appreciate his individual use of colour and his finely graded tones. Whistler was a cosmopolitan and a passionate admirer of things Japanese. He taught the Belgians an important lesson in sophistication, and they, including Georges Lemmen (q.v.) and even James Ensor,[8] also learned from him new methods of composition, a freer use of colour and an attention to light which paved the way to Impressionism. In fact the kind of Impressionism that Whistler was leading them towards was closer to that of Degas than to that of Monet; this was the Impressionism of his *Nocturnes*, in which he wanted, in his own words, to 'omit form and, using only colour, to emulate the musician who uses only sound'.[9]

THE INFLUENCE OF FRENCH IMPRESSIONISM THROUGH THE GROUPE DES XX FROM 1886

No sooner had they absorbed the influence of Whistler than the young members of Les XX were confronted by French Impressionism. It is interesting to observe the response of the painters whom I have called 'native Impressionists' when confronted by this double influx from Paris: first, in 1886, Monet and Renoir took part in the salon, then in 1887 Pissarro, Morisot and Seurat. Add to this the new names exhibited in 1888 (Caillebotte, Cross, Lautrec, Dubois-Pillet and Signac) and the importance accorded by Octave Maus to this revolutionary aesthetic which had just begun to make its mark in artistic circles in Paris is evident. The title given by Octave Maus to the essay accompanying the catalogue to the 1888 exhibition: 'Painting and the search for light' comes as no surprise. Once and for all the aesthetics of light swept through Les XX and would eventually persist beyond the group's disbandment; La Libre Esthétique, established in 1894, contained an appraisal of their progress to date.

At first the Belgian press greeted French Impressionism with sarcasm and a complete lack of understanding. A number of painters on the other hand expressed their interest by turning dramatically to much lighter colours, and this was to be the most important and most durable effect of the influence of French Impressionism. Light was the goddess to idolize. This explains the wholesale conversion of painters such as Van Rysselberghe, Schlobach, Finch, Lemmen, Van de Velde (q.v.), Jan Toorop, all practitioners of Belgian Impressionism, to the new French aesthetic, and shortly after to Neo-Impressionism. Their discovery of Impressionist colour encouraged them to look more closely at the effects of light on natural objects, and this led to a lightening and whitening of the tones they used, rather than to the adoption of any of the techniques of composition proposed by Monet and his friends. Emile Verhaeren wrote: 'From now on, light is in control of every painting, determining the appearance and the shape and structure of each object, by turns gnawing away at it, changing its shape, exaggerating its structure. Light creates colour, then breaks it up into an infinite variety of separate shades'.[10] Other Belgian painters who adopted the tenets of French Impressionism included: Frantz

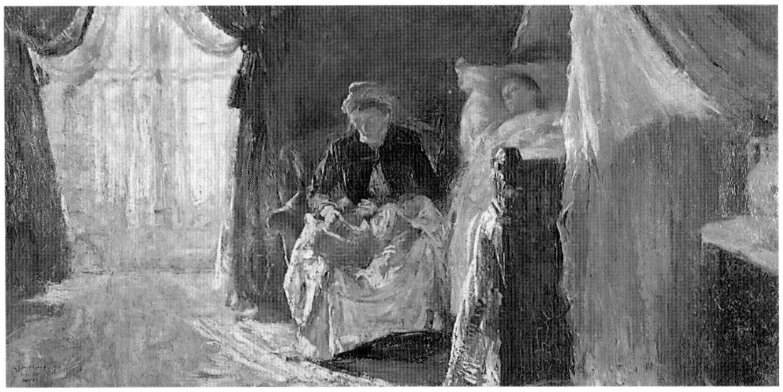

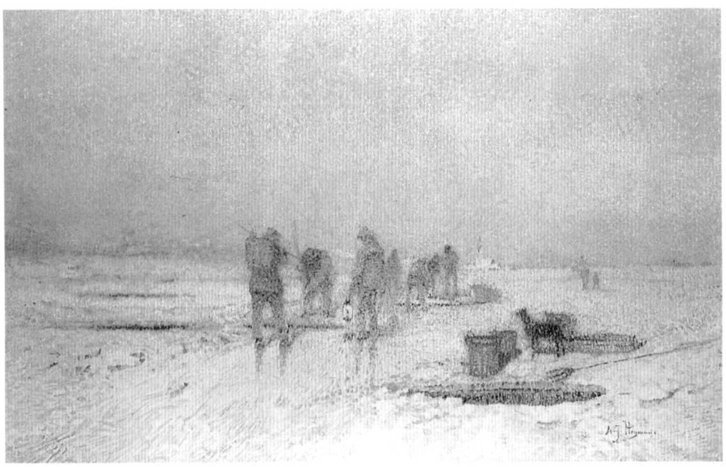

fig. 16 ADRIEN-JOSEPH HEYMANS
The Eel Catch, c. 1893, Private Collection

fig. 15 GUILLAUME VAN STRYDONCK
Sick Child, 1887, Musée des Beaux-Arts, Tournai

Charlet, who had close ties with Paris anyway; Anna Boch, Maus's cousin, who adapted her technique to accommodate paintings of the landscapes observed during her travels in the South of France, Brittany and Spain; Guillaume van Strydonck, whose style loosened when he made trips to Florida and India [fig. 15]; and A.-J. Heymans, an older painter from Antwerp who moved to Brussels and gradually eliminated definite outlines from his landscape paintings in favour of softer contours, suppler brushstrokes and much more fluid paint [fig. 16].

In Antwerp the landscape painters met with even greater hostility from the academic world (see Buyck). Henry van de Velde, one of the future leaders of the Belgian Art Nouveau in both architecture and design, tried to put an end to this hostility. He was at this time a painter and a member of the avant-garde, soon to be attracted to Neo-Impressionism; he was also active in setting up various groups and associations along the same lines as the Groupe des XX. Some of the artists from around Antwerp responded even more strongly than their fellow artists in Brussels to effects of light, even if the light were a uniform grey, and they invented new ways of painting it which are closer to Belgian Impressionism than to the version imported from France. Among these Richard Baseleer (1875–1951), Frans Hens (q.v.) and their colleagues fixed their gaze on the mists and spray of the estuary of the River Scheldt. Unlike the French Impressionists, they rendered elements like air and water in solid colour, without breaking the colour into shades, and their preferred atmosphere was a damp grey haze. If their use of colour had been brighter, with stronger contrasts, they might have been dubbed *fauves*. Sometimes their contrast of light and shade was on an epic scale, as when they painted the huge hulls of the red and black ships criss-crossing the estuary.

In Ghent and Liège landscape painters also abandoned their studios to celebrate the melancholy charms of old towns and the pleasures of the countryside, blurring the outlines in the shimmering effects of light screened through a limpid, damp air. In Ghent there was Albert Baertsoen (q.v.) and Ferdinand Willaert (1861–1938); their sturdy professionalism, taciturn natures and enjoyment of the melancholic and the silent created a certain reservation in their commitment to the tenets of Impressionism. Another Flemish painter, Evariste Carpentier, went to teach at the Liège Academy of Fine Arts and there disseminated the new style of landscape painting. The most significant member of the 'School of Ghent', however, was undoubtedly Emile Claus (q.v.), whose contribution to the spread of late Impressionism, subsequently designated 'Luminism' in Belgium, was crucial. Luminism will be discussed below.

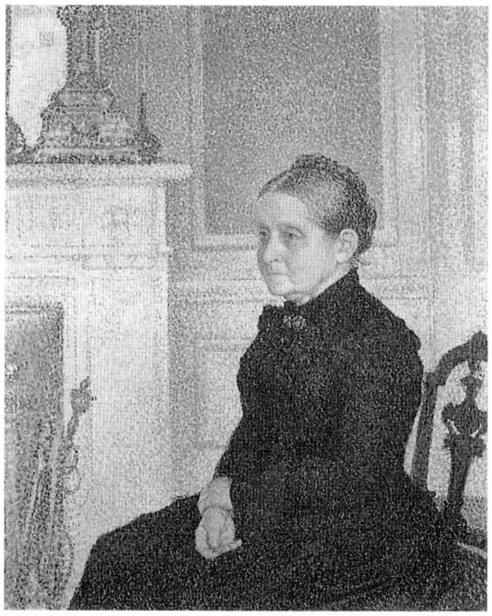

fig. 17 THÉO VAN RYSSELBERGHE
Portrait of Mme Charles Maus, 1890,
Musées royaux des Beaux-Arts de Belgique, Brussels

In May 1886 Emile Verhaeren was in Paris for the publication of his collection of poems, *Les Moines*. While there he visited the 8th and final Impressionist Exhibition and was bowled over by George Seurat's first Neo-Impressionist paintings; he immediately conveyed his enthusiasm to his friend Théo van Rysselberghe. A few months later *Sunday Afternoon at La Grande Jatte* (1884–1887; Art Institute of Chicago) was exhibited again at the second Salon des Indépendants. It was on the subject of this exhibition that Félix Fénéon sent an important article to *L'Art moderne* in Brussels, in which the term Neo-Impressionism was used for the first time. The writer spelt out the difference between traditional Impressionism and this new technique of painting. In traditional Impressionism light was broken up in an arbitrary fashion and its translation into colour on to the canvas undertaken through a certain element of chance. Seurat on the other hand broke light into its constituent hues, then applied small spots of pure colour to the canvas, according to the rules of complementary colours, and in measured proportions; this made for subtle shading and modelling that was both fluid yet incisive. Théo van Rysselberghe was disconcerted at first by this new way of painting light, but within two years he became its most ardent advocate in Belgium. He arranged with Octave Maus for *La Grande Jatte* to come to the Salon des XX in 1887. Although it caused a scandal, as might have been predicted, comparable to that created in Paris the previous year, Seurat would very soon have Neo-Impressionist followers in Belgium. Both Seurat and Signac were present at the opening of the Salon and took part in discussions with some of the members of the group.

Willy Finch was Belgium's first convert to Neo-Impressionism, attracted by an aesthetic that suited his more speculative nature. Just after the Salon des XX in 1888, in which the new tendency was represented by Seurat, Signac, Pissarro and Finch, Van Rysselberghe (who had just returned from a trip to Morocco) began using divisionist techniques, with scientific precision, in his portraits. He remained committed, however, to a degree of realism and continued to need to catch the psychological likeness of his subject, with the result that he adopted Seurat's technique without incorporating his hieratic stylization. Van Rysselberghe varied the size of his dots, using large ones for the background and smaller ones for the hands, the face and important anatomical details [fig. 17]. The first attempts at pointillism by Henry van de Velde, at almost the same time, imply a much deeper understanding of Seurat's intentions. During the summer of 1888 the young painter from Antwerp, in a quandary about the direction his art was taking, painted several pointillist canvases, including the radical *Beach at Blankenberghe with Beach Huts* [cat. 65] which earned him membership of Les XX, along with Georges Lemmen who was himself in the process of joining the Neo-Impressionists. After Jan Toorop, a Dutchman living in Belgium, had joined the fray, Georges Lemmen was the fifth member of Les XX to change his painting technique, which had been strongly indebted to Whistler, in favour of the revolutionary methods of Seurat and Signac. Lemmen was attracted by the objectivity of a technique that satisfied his intelligence and his taste for experimentation; more particularly, however, he was attracted by the depth of inquiry which Seurat had brought to Neo-Impressionism. He was interested in the heart and soul of his subjects more than in physical verisimilitude [fig. 18].

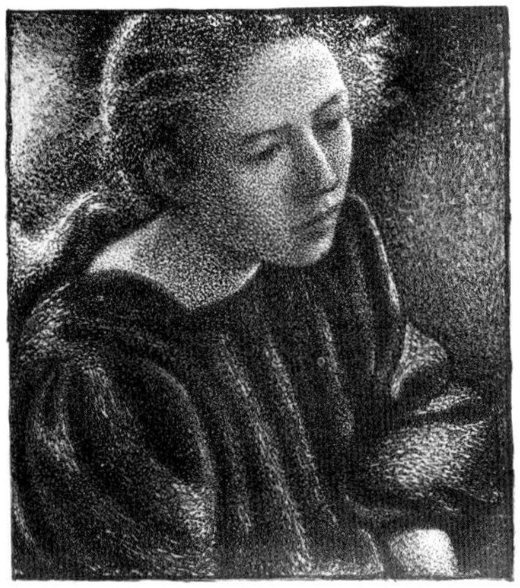

fig. 18 GEORGES LEMMEN Portrait of the Artist's Wife, c. 1892, lithograph

In 1891, Seurat's untimely death caused considerable consternation amongst the Groupe des XX.[11] Some of the members at this time, Symbolists and Neo-Impressionists alike, were turning their attention to the new wave of decorative art coming from England. Artists such as Van de Velde, Lemmen, Finch and Van Rysselberghe began to admit the need for some kind of parity between different art forms. At the Salon of 1891 French posters were shown for the first time, as were book illustrations by Walter Crane; Finch presented his first attempts at ceramics, and there were three vases and a statue in enamelled stoneware by the *invité*, Paul Gauguin. Shortly after, Van de Velde and Lemmen turned their attention to the decorative arts. Meanwhile the infatuation with Neo-Impressionism was already waning; interest in the decorative arts apparently distanced these painters from Seurat's teachings, about which Lemmen was later to express strong reservations.

Van Rysselberghe remained faithful to Neo-Impressionism for a while, though gradually modifying his use of the technique, and several other painters flirted with it briefly: Dario de Regoyos, a Spaniard who became a member of Les XX during his stay in Brussels, George Morren, Willy Schlobach, Frantz Charlet, Anna Boch (Van Rysselberghe's disciple), Franz Gailliard (1861–1932) and of course Emile Claus and his followers in and around Ghent, who viewed the technique as a justification for achieving greater brilliance of effect by a daring juxtaposition of complementary colours.

LUMINISM: THE SECOND WAVE OF IMPRESSIONISM IN BELGIUM

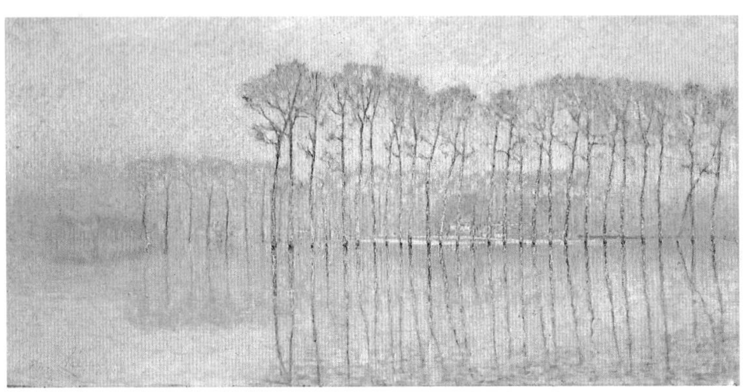

fig. 19 EMILE CLAUS, Trees along the River Lys, c. 1900, Private Collection, Antwerp

During the 1880s Emile Claus returned to his birthplace at Astene, on the banks of the Lys, and concentrated on painting in the open air [fig. 19]; his analytical figurative painting kept alive the rural subject matter of Millet and Bastien-Lepage, imbuing them with an acute concern for recording the pastoral mood of such scenes. The artist's growing interest in lighter, nimbler brushwork and brighter colours is increasingly apparent in the works of this period, yet these innovations could not entirely dispell the sense that they remained essentially studio works. His permanent conversion to Impressionism occurred shortly after 1890, following the winter trips which he made to Paris in three successive years. Under the influence of pointillism he modified Monet's comma brushstroke to a finely hatched one of variable length. He managed to disperse the grey and gloomy fog favoured by the School of Dendermonde (see Hoozee), and henceforth the banks of the Lys became bathed in sunlight. Although he and some of his followers became enthusiastic supporters of Impressionism, their paintings lacked the ardour and experimental, spontaneous character of much French Impressionist paintings, where the colours seem to have been chosen at random, where the brushstrokes have the strength of sabre thrusts. Claus's

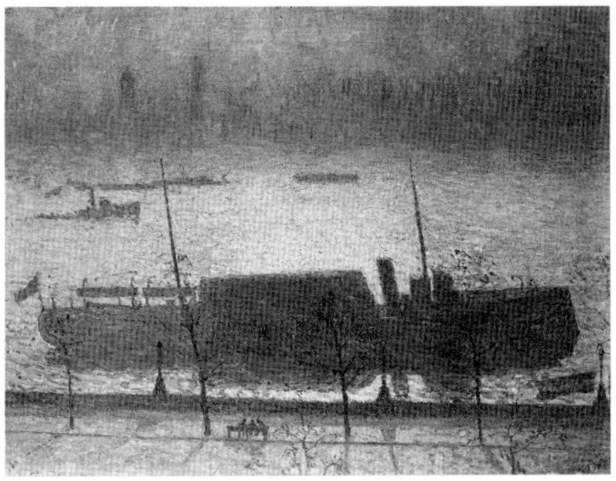

fig. 20 EMILE CLAUS, The Thames, c. 1916–1918, Musées royaux des Beaux-Arts de Belgique, Brussels

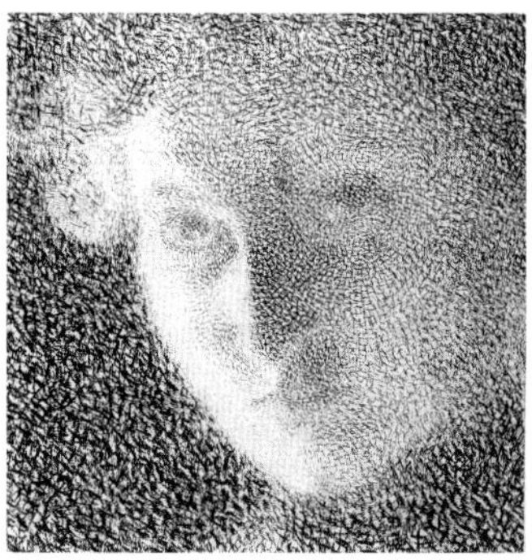

fig. 21 JENNY MONTIGNY
Self-portrait, c. 1900, drawing, Private Collection

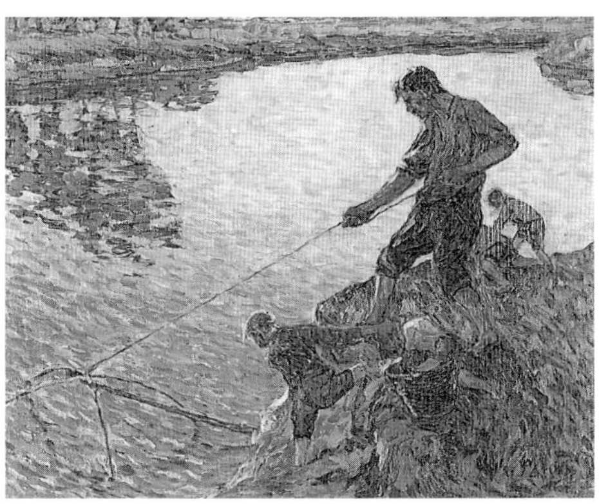

fig. 22 MODEST HUYS, The Eel Catch, c. 1921, Private Collection

careful compositions and his laborious style bear no relation to the improvised, spontaneous quality of Monet's painting. During the 1890s Emile Claus was greatly admired; his affable and eccentric nature, as well as his painting, attracted a number of followers in the Ghent region. They would see Flanders through the light-filled eyes of the master of Luminism. His reputation was so great that even young Japanese and American art students, in Paris to study Impressionism, came to seek his advice. His favourite followers included Jenny Montigny (1875–1937), Anna de Weert (1867–1950), Modest Huys (1875–1932): when they painted the valley of the Lys they used a heightened palette, to celebrate the quality of light, and a controlled tangle of small brushstrokes.

The belated success of Impressionism in Belgium was confirmed by the huge interest aroused by the Salons held by La Libre Esthétique[12] in 1904 and 1905. In 1904 the whole of Europe converged on Brussels to see the extraordinary collection of French Impressionists assembled by Octave Maus: more than twenty leading exponents of Impressionism in all its varied manifestations. Faced with the triumph of French Impressionism, Belgian critics, in particular Octave Maus's erstwhile colleague, the lawyer Edmond Picard, reproached him for his avowed aim to exclude all but French artists, completely ignoring his fellow Belgians. News of the controversy reached Paris, and the French art world, as may be imagined, followed the affair with undisguised glee. The following year, Octave Maus continued to concentrate on Impressionism but now invited representatives from all over the western world. The Salon of 1905 was entitled 'L'Evolution externe de l'impressionnisme' (the external development of Impressionism), and included work by some twenty artists from Germany, England, Spain, Holland, Russia, the United States and, of course, Belgium.

By the time of the 1905 Libre Esthétique exhibition, most of the Belgian Impressionists had re-grouped under a new banner, Vie et Lumière, recently formed under the leadership of Emile Claus [fig. 20], George Morren and A.-J. Heymans. In addition to these three artists, the group consisted of a number of former *vingtistes* such as James Ensor, Georges Lemmen and Anna Boch, some disciples of Emile Claus (Georges Buysse [1864–1916], Edmond Verstraete [1870–1956], Jenny Montigny [fig. 21], Anna de Weert) and Heymans. Apart from Lemmen, by now close to the Nabis, and Ensor of course, rightly considered the leading light of Belgian Impressionism,[13] all of these followed the techniques (some more slavishly than others) of French painters such as Monet, Pissarro and Sisley. Some of the younger members of the group, devoted followers of Emile Claus, prolonged their pursuit of Impressionist values up to and after the First World War [fig. 22].

The obsessional interest shown by these painters in light and its effects, and their search for ways of depicting it on canvas led art critics and commentators to dub their style 'Luminism'. The neologism apparently was only applied in Belgium and it marks an attempt to distinguish between the concept behind traditional and typically French Impressionism, Neo-Impressionism and Post-Impressionism. Luminism was the result of a combination of French Impressionism and Seurat's pointillism, both of which arrived in Belgium at the end of the century; this combination was ingested through, and modified by, native Belgian Realism. The most active centre of Luminism was in and

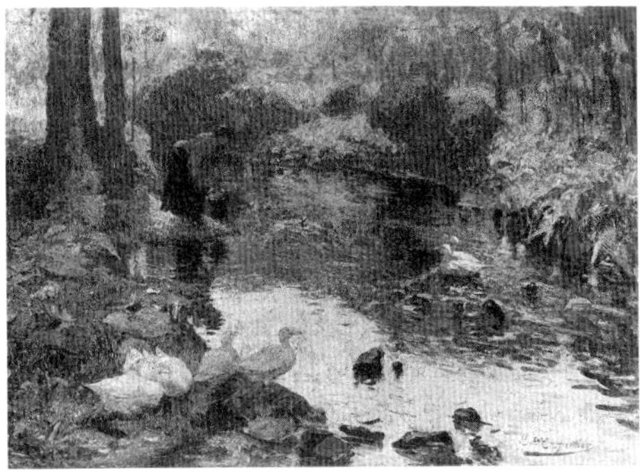

fig. 23 EVARISTE CARPENTIER, The Ducks, c. 1890, Musée des Beaux-Arts, Liège

around Ghent, where Emile Claus enjoyed a distinguished reputation and Jean Delvin, a breakaway from Les XX, turned out a stream of young luminist painters from the Academy of Fine Arts in Ghent. In Flanders, 'schools' of luminists formed in the region of Sint-Niklaas, in Dendermonde where *plein-air* realism had traditionally been the dominant mode of painting, and in the Kempen region near Antwerp. In the valley of the Lys for a time, before Expressionism took over, artists like Gustave de Smet (1877–1943), Frits van den Berghe (1883–1939) and Constant Permeke (1886–1952) practised Luminism for some years, and Leon de Smet (1881–1966) in particular gave the genre a very individual charm. If the development of some of these Luminists is examined closely, however, the traces of a sound academic training can be found lurking behind a chromatically audacious exterior. As time went by Ensor was not the only person to denounce the spectacular but superficial effects achieved by the Luminists. Some exponents of the style were turning out clichés. They were fecklessly combining the style of Monet and his followers with Neo-Impressionism, unaware of the guiding principles lying behind the latter. Unsurprisingly the most original of the Luminists began to turn inexorably towards a simpler, more primitive and much more deeply felt mode of expression. This marked the birth of Flemish Expressionism.

In Liège, from 1900 to 1905, there was also a sudden interest in the painting of light, and the individual brushstrokes of the Impressionists, under the leadership of Evariste Carpentier (1845–1922), who taught at the Academy of Fine Arts in Liège [fig. 23]. His influence produced Albert Lemaître (1886–1975), Armand Jamar (1870–1946), André Hallet (1890–1959) and especially Richard Heintz (1871–1929), the eulogist of the Ardennes and the Meuse valley and instigator of a more excitable version of Impressionism. Like many of his fellow artists, notably Paul Leduc from Louvain, Richard Heintz was in the habit of going south to paint the Mediterranean light. In Brussels too it would be difficult to list all the painters won over to Luminism; their style was more influenced by Ensor than by Claus. In Brabant the progression was through Impressionism to, for some painters, Fauvism, before the artists of Sint-Martens-Latem had turned to Expressionism. Painters of the Luminist persuasion operated with the audacity of all followers: exonerated from the need to invent a new language, and to cope with any painful reactions such a new language would arouse, they plagiarized ideas and forms from the innovators with the greatest ease. An example of this is their facile recourse to the depiction of days bathed in spectacular sunshine.

fig. 24 HENRI EVENEPOEL, Sunday Walk at Saint-Cloud, 1899, Musée de l'Art Wallon, Liège

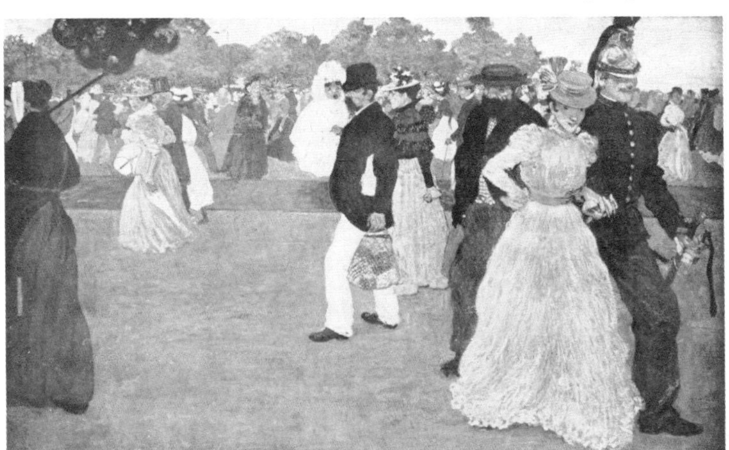

While some of the landscape painters lost themselves too fully in the French notion of Impressionism, others frankly acknowledged their debt to the French Impressionists but managed to do so without abdicating their own personalities. One of these, and a very special case, was Henri Evenepoel (q.v.) who, having received his training in Paris, retained the set of themes and the flexibility of form of the French Impressionists; his frothy, audacious ornamentation recalls Toulouse-Lautrec and Degas while his *tachiste* use of colour presages Fauvism [fig. 24]. At the beginning of the century George Morren and Marcel

Jefferys (1872–1924), both with close links to France, painted works that were redolent of Impressionism [fig. 25]. They presided over the final years of the landscape revival that burgeoned from the end of the nineteenth century into the first decades of this century; the revival had first been fuelled by the admirable Dutch-Flemish tradition of landscape painting, the pride of the northern provinces (see Hoozee). Later it absorbed the daring lightening of the palette and the technique of painting with individual brushstrokes taught by the French Impressionists, to depict and encapsulate the strength and beauty of the natural world.

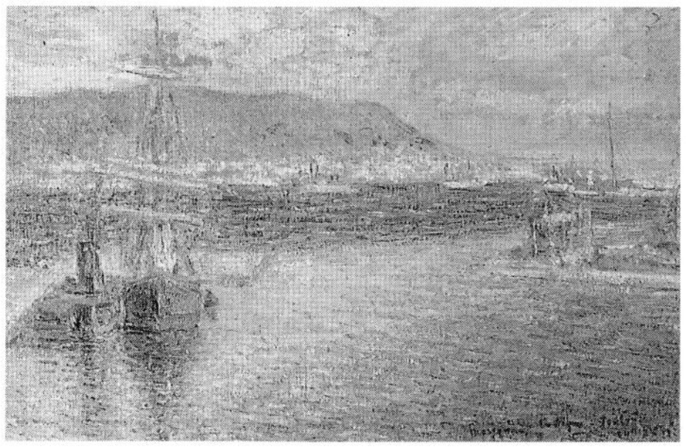

fig. 25 GEORGE MORREN, Toulon, 1913, Collection Crédit Communal de Belgique, Brussels

1 In 1864 Hippolyte Boulenger (1837–1874) moved to Tervuren, a village on the edge of the Forest of Soignes, near Brussels, and painted there in the company of the landscape artists Joseph Coosemans and Alphonse Asselbergs. When he exhibited landscapes at the Brussels Salon of 1866, partly as a joke and partly to make an allusion to the Barbizon School, he had himself described in the catalogue as an 'artist of the School of Tervuren'. Eventually the name caught on, and was used to describe the small colony of artists who wanted to paint the natural world in as realist a manner as possible, according to the tenets of the Société Libre des Beaux-Arts.

2 Adrien-Joseph Heymans (1839–1921) spent some time in Paris and discovered the naturalism of the Barbizon School; he was familiar with Théodore Rousseau, Corot, Daubigny and Millet. During the 1860s he dedicated his time to *plein-air* painting in the Kempen, near Antwerp, in the company of artists such as Jacques Rosseels, Florent Crabeels and Isidore Meyers; they formed the School of Kalmthout. A loosening of technique can be observed in their work at this time which would lead some of them to an early form of Impressionism.

3 Between 1860 and 1880 a number of landscape artists led by Théodore Baron (1840–1899), one of the leading members of the Société Libre des Beaux-Arts, depicted desolate and wintry landscapes in colour schemes devoid of any brightness or any contrast. They favoured greys and silvery ochres, the colours of sand and mist; as a result these painters working in the country around Kalmthout and Dendermonde were dubbed the 'Grey School', *'l'école du gris'*.

4 Founded in 1875 at the instigation of Félicien Rops, La Chrysalide was a more youthful version of the Société Libre des Beaux-Arts. Members included Louis Artan, Louis Dubois, Théodore Baron, Constantin Meunier, Alfred Verwee, Guillaume Vogels; the younger members included Willy Finch, Pericles Pantazis and Ensor. Ensor, exhibiting for the first time, showed his *Lampiste* (1880; Musées royaux des Beaux-Arts de Belgique, Brussels) at their final Salon in 1881.

5 L'Essor was established in 1876 by former students of the Academy of Fine Arts. It was an eclectic group, only moderately attached to modernism and keen to defend objective realism. Newcomers to the group such as Albert Baertsoen, Frantz Charlet, Willy Finch, Fernand Khnopff, Théo van Rysselberghe, Guillaume van Strydonck, Willy Schlobach, Jan Toorop and Ensor brought fresh ideas into the group and eventually provoked its split into two separate camps.

6 Octave Maus and the founding painters met on 28 October 1883 at the Taverne Guillaume, Rue du Musée. The founders were: Frantz Charlet, Jean Delvin, Dario de Regoyos, James Ensor, Willy Finch, Charles Goethals, Fernand Khnopff, Pericles Pantazis, Willy Schlobach, Frans Simons, Gustave Vanaise, Théo van Rysselberghe, Guillaume van Strydonck, Piet Verhaert, Theodoor Verstraete, Guillaume Vogels, Rodolphe Wytsman and the sculptors Achille Chainaye, Paul Dubois and Jef Lambeaux (see Block).

7 When some of the original members resigned, were expelled or died, the Groupe des XX enrolled Félicien Rops, Anna Boch, Henry van de Velde, Georges Lemmen, Jan Toorop, Paul Signac, Auguste Rodin and George Minne.

8 Although Ensor admired Whistler's painting, as can be observed particularly in his *Children washing* [cat. 16], he was opposed to his election to Les XX when some of the members put forward the name of the Anglo-American painter.

9 Quoted in: Dictionnaire Bénézit.

10 'C'est elle désormais qui commande le tableau; elle détermmine l'apparence des objets, leur forme, leurs arêtes, que tour à tour elle ronge, infléchit, exagère; elle fait la couleur, l'émiette en tons variés à l'infini.' *La Jeune Belgique*, 182–188; quoted by M. J. Chartrain, in *Les Jeux de la lumière dans la peinture belge de Boulenger à Rik Wouters*, Musées royaux des Beaux-Arts de Belgique, Brussels 1964–1965.

11 The Salon des XX in 1892 included a retrospective homage to Seurat. With help from Signac and Van Rysselberghe, Brussels exhibited (before Paris) eighteen canvases, twelve sketches and ten drawings by Seurat.

12 In 1893, when Les XX decided to disband themselves, Octave Maus established a new association which he planned to direct single-handedly, under the name of La Libre Esthétique. Under this new guise Octave Maus continued to organize annual Salons, in which the most innovative Belgian and foreign artists continued to be invited to exhibit, more or less up to 1914.

13 In the introduction to the exhibition Octave Maus made a point of emphasizing James Ensor's role as precursor, stating that he 'was the point of departure for investigations that would soon absorb a whole group of painters; an uninterrupted series of ten annual exhibitions between 1884 and 1893 accurately charted their developments and showed their commitment'.

Belgium's laboratories for new ideas

Les XX and La Libre Esthétique

JANE BLOCK

Les XX (Les Vingt, i.e. The Twenty; 1884–1893) and its successor, La Libre Esthétique (The Liberal Aesthetic; 1894–1914), were revolutionary art groups whose annual exhibitions in Brussels recorded three decades of prolific activity in the history of modern art. At the centre of the groups' credo was the rejection of traditional embodiments of authority as manifested in the Triennial Salons in Belgium – a system of government-sponsored annual shows that rotated among Brussels, Antwerp and Ghent – and their passionate endorsement of the power of the individual. Before the first exhibition of Les XX, an artistic career in Belgium without recognition through official shows was unthinkable; by the last showing of La Libre Esthétique, such a course had long since ceased to be an issue.

The concept of an avant-garde art society, of course, did not originate with Les XX. The history of art in the second half of the nineteenth century abounds with challenges to traditional academic authority. As artists struggled to use their art financially to support themselves without official or aristocratic commissions, they increasingly needed to band together to create an independent market of collectors who, rather than continue to dictate to artists, were now willing to follow the artists' lead. The story of Les XX is an important and integral part of these independent movements; but it is certainly not the whole story. A decade before the first Les XX exhibition in Brussels, the Impressionists had shown their work collectively in Paris for the first time in the studio of the photographer Nadar in order to do battle with the official Salon. In 1884, three months after the opening of the first Les XX show (2 February 1884), a group of artists, the Groupe des Artistes Indépendants, made another gesture against the art establishment by holding their first exhibition. United solely by the common cause of official censure, the Indépendants instituted a jury-free society that awarded neither prizes nor medals. Les XX was a combination of the two. Like the Impressionists, it defined itself as a particular group of artists, yet it adamantly refused to be defined by style or aesthetic credo. At the same time, it was not simply a jury-free society, thus setting itself apart from the more *laissez-faire* policy of the Indépendants.

The goal of Les XX and La Libre Esthétique was certainly more ambitious and overtly confrontational than that of the Impressionists. It sought to supplant the academic canons sanctioned by the Salon and by that bastion of conservative officialdom, the Academy of Fine Arts, with its own brand of artistic freedom. In order to defeat the stranglehold of establishment taste, the two groups actively sought the engagement of the

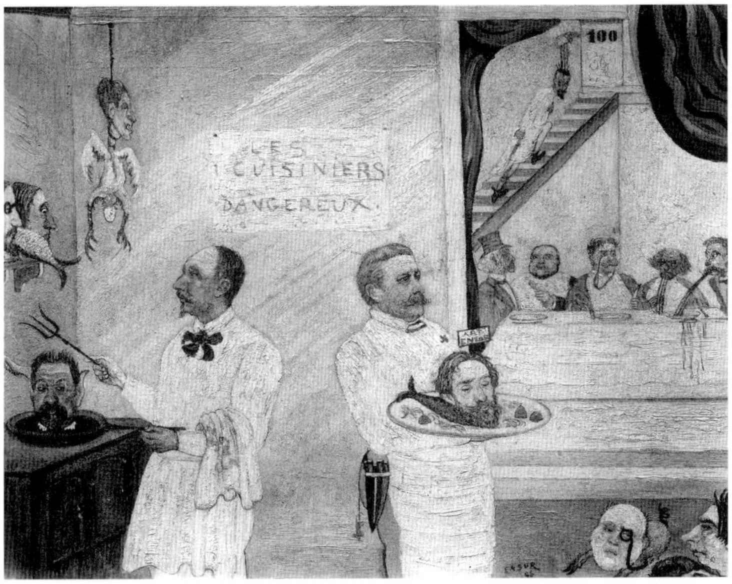

fig. 26 JAMES ENSOR, Dangerous Cooks, 1896, Private Collection

Two cooks shown: Picard (l) tending to the head of Guillaume Vogels; on the shelf above sit the heads of Georges Lemmen and Théo van Rysselberghe. Suspended above, Anna Boch, as a plucked chicken. Maus (r) holds the head of James Ensor. At the right: the monocled pig, Charles van der Stappen, and the lobstered Henri de Groux. In the next room from left to right, writers and critics: Edouard Fétis, Eugène Demolder, Camille Lemonnier, Max Sulzberger and Emile Verhaeren. Climbing the stairs, Ensor's good friend, Théo Hannon

most radical artists both at home and abroad, many of whom were virtually unknown at the time, including James McNeil Whistler, Odilon Redon, Paul Gauguin, Georges Seurat, Henri de Toulouse-Lautrec, Vincent van Gogh and the younger generation of Maurice Denis, Edouard Vuillard and Pierre Bonnard. The organizers of Les XX and La Libre Esthétique were adamant that this struggle be not only international but also serve all aspects of art. Thus, the writers Villiers de l'Isle-Adam, Paul Verlaine and Stéphane Mallarmé, the composers César Franck, Vincent d'Indy, Gabriel Fauré and Ernest Chausson and the violinist Eugène Ysaÿe were engaged to participate in this concept of a new and all-encompassing art (a 'Gesamtkunstwerk'), and to perform in the very rooms displaying the successive waves of Impressionism, Neo-Impressionism, Symbolism and the decorative arts.[1] The longevity and success of the Belgian avant-garde exhibition societies can in large part be attributed to two lawyers, who were passionate and volatile men of letters and patrons of art – Edmond Picard (1836–1924) and Octave Maus (1856–1919). Together they selected and mixed the ingredients that produced the triumphs of Les XX and La Libre Esthétique, although their methods were sometimes unpalatable to artists like James Ensor (q.v.), who bristled under the will of these 'dangerous cooks' [fig. 26]. In 1881, Picard and Maus founded the weekly review devoted to modern art and appropriately entitled, *L'Art moderne,* that served as the backbone for the two groups during their entire existence; but the lawyers' combative personalities were formed long before that. In 1865, Picard[2] [fig. 27] helped found a liberal paper, *La Liberté*,[3] whose progressive platform called for greater freedom of the press, compulsory instruction for the working class and electoral reform. In 1870 Picard began a series of unsuccessful bids for Parliament (he finally garnered a seat as a Socialist representative in 1894). In 1878 he began work on the monumental *Pandectes belges,* an encyclopaedia of law numbering over 100 volumes, while in 1880 he published his first novel, derived from his experience of the law, *Le Paradoxe sur l'avocat*. It was said that his rapier wit was matched only by his fencing arm.

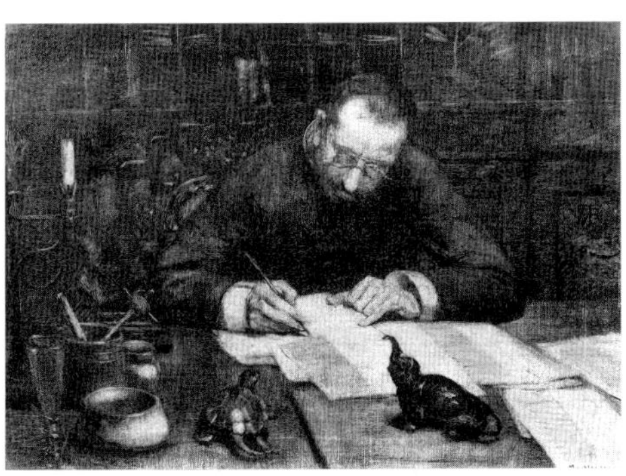

fig. 27 THÉO VAN RYSSELBERGHE
Portrait of Edmond Picard, 1883, grisaille on canvas, Private Collection

In 1877, the celebrated Picard met Octave Maus [fig. 28], an eager young lawyer beginning an internship.[4] Four years later Maus and Picard, now fast friends, joined two of Picard's former collaborators from *La Liberté* to found *L'Art moderne*. This new venture, whose first issue appeared on 6 March 1881, was to last until 9 August 1914, and thus presented thirty-three years of uninterrupted coverage of Belgium's artistic life. Although Belgium was its focal point, the review attempted to be international in scope. Its stated goal was to 'concern itself with Art in all fields: literature, painting, sculpture, prints, music, architecture, furniture, apparel, etc., and to publish reviews according to no preconceived artistic or philosophical programme.'[5] The quarto-sized periodical, with eight pages of double columns in each issue, appeared every Sunday. If its 'Petite Chronique' provided news of artistic, literary, musical, and theatrical events, the inflammatory reviews became the weekly's hallmark.

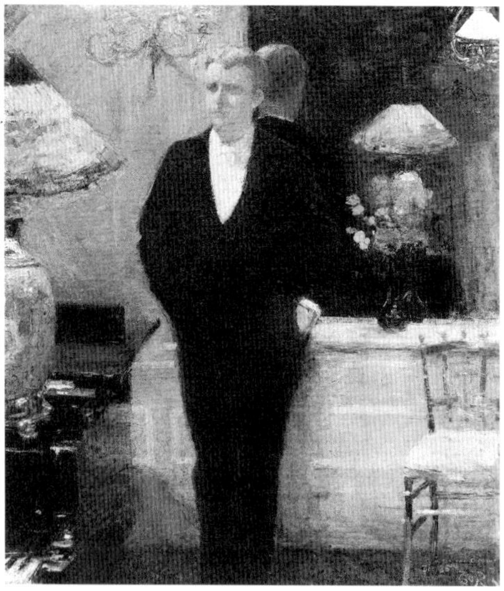

fig. 28 THÉO VAN RYSSELBERGHE
Portrait of Octave Maus, 1885 [cat. 70]

The majority of *L'Art moderne*'s articles were not signed and its masthead gave no clues as to the composition of its editorial board. Although the editors confided that 'our resolutions rarely express the opinion of one – they are examined, discussed and decided in committee',[6] nevertheless the board wisely agreed to present a cohesive and united viewpoint in print, realizing that it could not hope to wage a successful campaign against entrenched critics if internal squabbles were made public. In fact, although the board members' names were revealed on 8 April 1883, articles remained unsigned until 1898.[7]

Backed by its powerful editorial board, *L'Art moderne* became the self-proclaimed mouthpiece for all avant-garde tendencies in Belgian art, literature and music. Defining the struggle as nothing less than artistic freedom, Picard and Maus identified the enemies as the Salon system, official patronage, the conservative press and a hostile public. Their emphatic sharpening and heightening of the conflict in the pages of *L'Art moderne* forced artists and collectors to choose sides and, it was hoped, to play active roles in the transformation of Belgian art and society. In this way, and through Maus and Picard's considerable political, social and artistic contacts, an immediate coterie came into being capable of supporting a radical organization of artists. The review's importance to the survival of such a group was inestimable; its existence meant that a critical apparatus was already in place that could protect a new organization and its emerging artists.

And in the autumn of 1883 such a group appeared. It was formed when a group of dissidents broke away from an exhibition society called *L'Essor* ('Soaring'), itself established in opposition to the official Belgian Salon. Rejecting L'Essor's constitution that regimented exhibition activities and its hieratic make-up of a president and governing committee of twenty which served as a jury, the new organization sought to keep institutional bureaucracy to a minimum. Embodied in its very name – Les XX – was a renunciation of the twenty Essorians who comprised the old governing committee.[8] This 'new' Twenty would be free from stifling regulations that further symbolized the conservatism of the official Salon. Instead, Les XX operated only with a secretary and a rotating committee of three who were charged with the task of organizing exhibitions. Artists would play key roles in the hanging of their own works. To complement the twenty member-artists, twenty invited artists (*invités*) from within and outside of Belgium would exhibit alongside the *vingtistes* in a show of international fraternal support.

Naming Maus as their secretary, thirteen of the future *vingtistes*, including James Ensor, Fernand Khnopff (q.v.) and Théo van Rysselberghe (q.v.), linked their names with his on 28 October 1883.[9] Several days later, Maus confided to his cousin, the artist Eugène Boch, his distress at the artistic conditions in Belgium: 'Everything that is beautiful, free and sincere is stifled by a coterie of octopuses who suck up all the money, esteem and reputation for themselves.' Yet he immediately revealed his own delight in changing this situation through the new society: 'We propose to topple everything and put our poor bourgeois country back on the map.'[10] Maus left no doubt that he found the energy and zeal of Les XX's cause appealing and that he was to be fully engaged in this artistic warfare: 'It is a proud and independent art they wish to create, and, as it's a matter of turning everything upside down and doing battle, I'm for it.'[11]

Maus quickly assumed the role of impresario, writing letters to prospective *invités*,

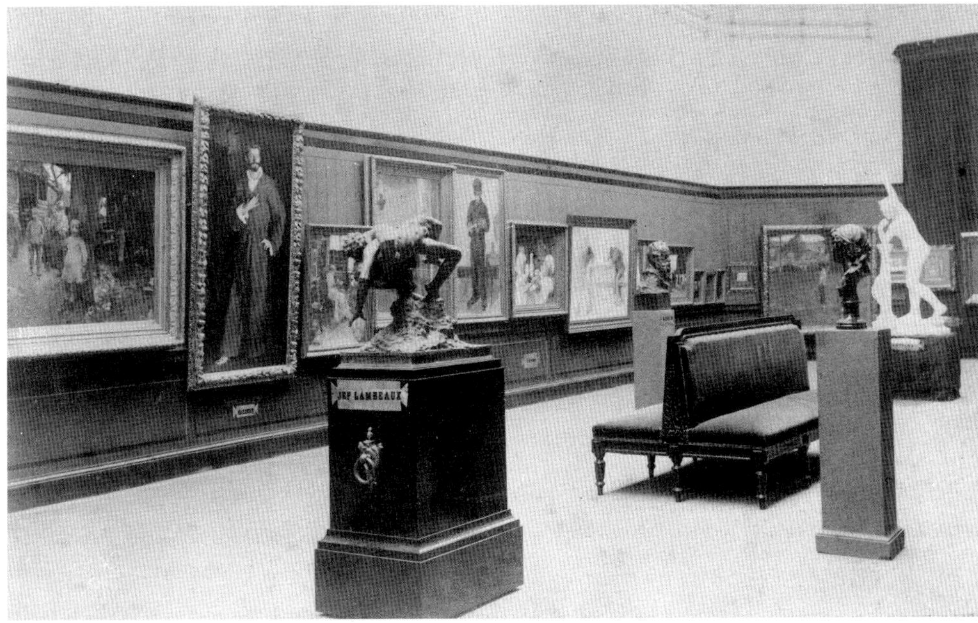

fig. 29 The 1884 Salon des XX, Palais des Beaux-Arts, Brussels (wall with Sargent and Ensors)

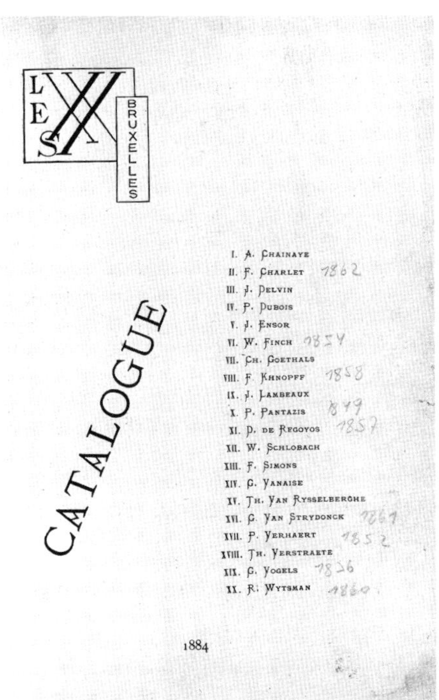

LES XX BRUXELLES

CATALOGUE

I. A. CHAINAYE
II. F. CHARLET
III. J. DELVIN
IV. P. DUBOIS
V. J. ENSOR
VI. W. FINCH
VII. CH. GOETHALS
VIII. F. KHNOPFF
IX. J. LAMBEAUX
X. P. PANTAZIS
XI. D. DE REGOYOS
XII. W. SCHLOBACH
XIII. F. SIMONS
XIV. G. VANAISE
XV. TH. VAN RYSSELBERGHE
XVI. G. VAN STRYDONCK
XVII. P. VERHAERT
XVIII. TH. VERSTRAETE
XIX. G. VOGELS
XX. R. WYTSMAN

1884

fig. 30 Page from the 1884 Les XX catalogue, listing the members of Les XX, with logo by Fernand Khnopff

issuing press releases, and securing a place to show. The first exhibition opened on 2 February 1884 at the Palais des Beaux-Arts (the present-day Musée de l'Art ancien). Despite the group's claim that it would be devoted to 'an independent art free from all official ties', it was granted permission to exhibit there by the government.[12] This situation later led one famous *invité*, Paul Gauguin, to search in vain for the location. Maus was delighted with the irony that 'Gauguin could not conceive that his canvases would be exhibited in an official building'.[13]

For the first exhibition, the twenty *vingtistes* were joined by twenty *invités* from Belgium, France, Holland, England, Germany, Sweden and the United States.[14] To our lasting good fortune, the affair was preserved on film. One of the photographs [fig. 29] reveals an innovation common to Les XX's exhibitions: the aesthetic arrangement of the objects. The works are hung with care above the rail level, arranged by artist in an order chosen by lot, as opposed to the hodgepodge and cramming characteristic of installations at the official Salons. Each artist's work bears an identifying plaque, visible under Sargent's *Portrait of Dr Pozzi* and Jef Lambeaux's sculpture, *Les Lutteurs*. James Ensor's six paintings hang between works by Sargent and Khnopff (q.v.).[15] The group's logo, designed by Khnopff, also appeared on the exhibition walls, and was reprinted on the exhibition catalogues [fig. 30] and on the advertising posters. The look of Les XX exhibitions changed somewhat in 1890, and was apparently perpetuated by La Libre Esthétique. It is recorded in a photograph of an installation of the latter's exhibition of 1908 [fig. 31]. Following a suggestion from Van Rysselberghe, the walls at Les XX were covered with an olive green fabric, held in place with tiny nails, upon which the group's logo was stencilled.[16]

From the first exhibition, Les XX hosted a lecture and concert series. At the inaugural lecture of 9 February 1884, Edmond Picard launched the first of many salvoes. He established credibility for the new group by tracing its artistic lineage to the first Belgian group to attempt to establish an alternative exhibition mechanism to the Salon – the old

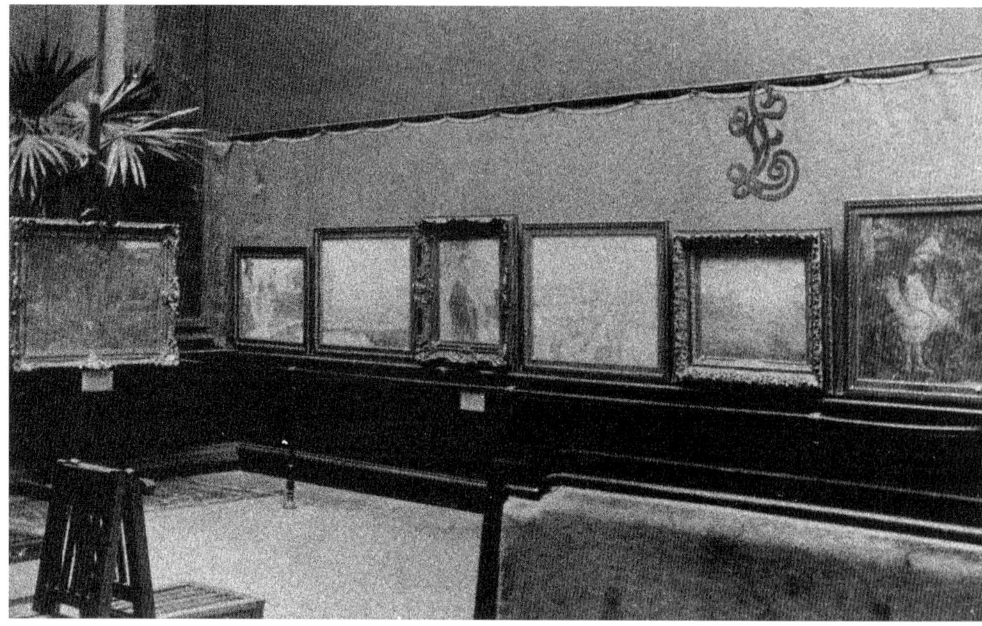

fig. 31 Installation at La Libre Esthétique, 1908

Société Libre des Beaux Arts, formed in 1868 – and particularly to the art of three of its respected members, Louis Dubois (1830–1880), Charles de Groux (1825–1870) and Hippolyte Boulenger (1837–1874). Picard then lashed out at the press and the stupidity of the public who generally perpetuated the paralysis in art.[17] Calling for a 'social art' that would combat conservatism and signify an integration of art and society, Picard declared that art's mission was to 'fortify everyone, to enrich them through feeling, and to improve them'.[18] The critic for *Le National Belge* wholeheartedly agreed, writing of the *vingtistes* on 14 February: 'All of them practise a young, new art, as free of formulae as their personalties are free from official exigencies'. Picking up the military imagery that was becoming prevalent, he continued: 'They affirm that art is constantly changing, that it participates in profound revolutions; that, even without barricades and musketry, it changes the social state of nations and, sometimes rising above movements, exerts over them its share of influence....'[19]

Les XX instituted an entry fee for the public, and a modest membership fee from each *vingtiste*, which would allow it to be relatively free from monetary constraints. These arrangements were in contrast to its rival L'Essor, where entry to its exhibitions was free but works of art were raffled to the public through a lottery, a circus that disgusted many *vingtistes*. At Les XX, art would never be merely a commodity. And the system worked: in its initial two weeks some 5,000 visitors streamed through the exhibition, which eventually turned a profit, and produced several outright sales and even a few commissions.[20] Once fully established in the public's mind, the annual exhibitions became so successful that they marked one of the social events of the year. As a critic noted in 1887: 'One month in advance, people chatter about it, are preoccupied with it, fight over it: Young ladies have new costumes made for that day, the hunt for invitations begins. All of artistic Brussels is in attendance, people who know painters, who love Wagner and put the latest novel from Paris on their table.'[21]

Despite its name (which as we have seen was largely symbolic), Les XX's membership did not remain at a constant twenty. Indeed, just before the first opening, one of the members, Greek-born Pericles Pantazis (1849–1884), died. Shortly after, two others, Jef Lambeaux (1852–1908) and the painter, Piet Verhaert (1852–1908), resigned, disconcerted by the progressive spirit that was allied to the new freedom at Les XX. The way in which replacements were chosen was openly democratic: members put forward suggestions for a group vote.[22] A run-off exhibition for Pantazis's spot pitted Isidore Verheyden (q.v.) against the young Javanese-Dutch artist, Jan Toorop (1858–1928). The critically acclaimed Verheyden won out, eliciting a response mixed both with envy and incredulity from one of the *vingtistes*: 'Imagine that! A decorated, medalled, successful man, with a painting in a museum' – who was now a member![23] Yet Toorop did not have to wait long. In December 1884 he also became one of the *vingtistes*.

If the group itself was run democratically, *L'Art moderne* ruthlessly served as judge and jury for members who did not live up to its expectations. In subsequent years the more conservative members of Les XX, including Simons (1855–1919), Verstraete (q.v.), Delvin (1853–1922) and Vanaise (1854–1902), resigned after harsh criticism by the periodical. Clearly Maus's two hats – secretary and board member – produced more than a little of what we might call 'conflict of interest'.

Discussions about membership *within* the group were also not always amicable. Charles Goethals's death in November 1885, which left a vacancy to be filled after the 1886 show, led to a heated discussion within Les XX dealing with nationality. When James McNeil Whistler was put forward by his friend, the anglophile Willy Finch (q.v.), although he had exhibited as an *invité* in 1884 and 1886, Maus argued that he should be denied membership on the grounds that 'he was not only foreign, but lived abroad'.[24] This additional criterion reflected the existing membership of two non-Belgians – the Spaniard, Dario de Regoyos and Jan Toorop. However, these two artists had impeccable Belgian credentials: both had studied at the Brussels Academy of Fine Arts, both were exhibitors at L'Essor and both were then resident in Belgium. The majority agreed with Maus, and the vacancy went to the Belgian Henri de Groux (1866–1930), son of the Realist painter Charles de Groux.[25] This policy remained in place for several years, the two remaining vacancies being set aside for young Belgians, and ultimately being filled by Georges Lemmen (q.v.) and Henry van de Velde (q.v.) in the autumn of 1888.

By this date, however, the attitude towards foreign members residing abroad had dramatically changed. The French sculptor Auguste Rodin became a *vingtiste* in 1889, and he was joined by his fellow countryman Paul Signac in 1891. Although one of Les XX's primary goals was to resuscitate art in Belgium and to provide a hospitable climate for avant-garde artists to flourish, *L'Art moderne* vehemently argued for a more unabashedly international approach. Faulting the overwhelming nationalism of Antwerp artists who were mired in the past and enslaved to tradition (see Buyck), the review argued in favour of an avant-garde art that had no boundaries, that was constantly in a state of evolution and flux. It was through its exhibition instrument, Les XX, that Belgium was opening its doors to *les apporteurs du neuf* ('the bearers of the new'), regardless of nationality.

Vingtistes not only controlled who would be elected to their ranks but also who among foreign and Belgian artists would be invited to show alongside them. During its ten years of existence, 126 *invités* exhibited at Les XX, fifty-seven coming from France alone. Belgium itself supplied a fifth of the total at twenty-four. The remaining group consisted of fifteen artists from Holland, twelve from Great Britain, six from the Scandinavian countries of Sweden, Norway and Denmark, four from America, four from Italy, three from Germany, and one from Switzerland.

From the first these *invités* included well-known artists such as Whistler, Rodin and Max Liebermann, and their Belgian equivalents Artan (q.v.), Heymans (1839–1921) and Rops (q.v.), who all showed at the 1884 exhibition. Among its guests (as opposed to its own members), the *vingtistes* continued this policy, inviting artists who at the time were relatively unknown, such as Odilon Redon, Vincent van Gogh and Paul Gauguin, even as it welcomed the *eminences grises* Félix Bracquemond, Henri Fantin-Latour, Frémiet and the more established members of the avant-garde, notably Renoir, Monet, Sisley, Pissarro and Sargent. By walking a fine line between tradition and revolution – that is, by inviting artists in both camps – Les XX broadened its appeal and increased its attendance. This was of crucial importance; in seeking to reform taste and topple the Salon system, it first had to attract a broad public to its exhibitions. Achieving this involved a number of tactics: lively discussions in *L'Art moderne* to generate a response in the Belgian press; provocative lectures and concerts of contemporary music held in the same rooms as the exhibitions; and an explicit tolerance towards certain 'older' masters. Maus was fully aware that this would produce eclectic results. Indeed, he seemingly revelled in this probability, announcing before the 1887 show: 'There will be something for every taste: the "tight" and the "loose", the "Impressionists" and the "intentionists", and even the "impossibilists"!...'[26]

As Les XX became more international in outlook, Maus relied on his growing network of contacts to recruit new and promising artists. Chief among his 'talent scouts' were the artists Van Rysselberghe, Signac, Lautrec and Eugène Boch (1855–1941), and the critic Téodor de Wyzéwa. Mirroring *L'Art moderne*, Les XX's commitment to openness and individuality of style, as opposed to any affirmation of a group or national identity, provided Les XX with its chameleon-like nature. Nonetheless, certain stylistic tendencies flourished within Les XX. Of particular significance was its role in the development of Neo-Impressionism. One of the great events at Les XX was the display of – and ensuing furor over – Seurat's *L'Après-midi à la Grande Jatte* (1884–1887; Art Institute of Chicago) in 1887. One of the six other Seurats shown, *L'Hospice et le phare, Honfleur* (1886; Washington, National Gallery of Art) was already owned by the Belgian writer and critic Emile Verhaeren; Henri van Cutsem, an owner of hotels and wealthy patron of the arts, bought another, *La Grève du Bas-Butin, Honfleur* (1886; Musée des Beaux-Arts, Tournai). These were Seurat's first sales anywhere – and serve to indicate the extent to which Brussels was becoming a safe haven for many French *apporteurs du neuf.* Over the next few years, nine French artists overtly committed to Neo-Impressionism showed at Les XX, including Seurat, Dubois-Pillet, Henri-Edmond Cross, Maximilien Luce, Camille Pissarro, Louis Hayet, Charles Angrand, Léo Gausson and Hippolyte Petitjean. Within a few years a rival group of divisionist *vingtistes* emerged, among them Anna Boch, Finch (q.v.),

Lemmen (q.v.), Regoyos, Willy Schlobach (q.v.), Toorop, Van Rysselberghe and Henry van de Velde. By 1889, the Salon des XX was announced with a blue-and-white pointillist poster designed by Van Rysselberghe [fig. 32].

In 1888 *L'Art moderne* identified another movement co-existing among the *vingtistes*: Symbolism. Odilon Redon's works were already championed by Belgium's Symbolist poet and playwright, Emile Verhaeren, who had lent some of his Redons to the 1886 exhibition, and by Picard, who had commissioned Redon to illustrate his monodrama *Le Juré*, in 1887.[27] By 1888, when Redon and Paul Gauguin were invited to exhibit, they were joined by what was now a mighty handful of Belgian Symbolists, including Henri de Groux, Fernand Khnopff, Xavier Mellery (q.v.), George Minne (q.v.) and Félicien Rops. In 1889, although he had not made a sale at Les XX, Gauguin briefly entertained the idea of establishing a studio in Antwerp with Vincent van Gogh. As he confided to his friend Vincent, he was heartened by the prospect that, 'because our names are somewhat known through the *vingtistes*, it would be a possible thing.'[28] Again, Les XX provided not only a welcome marketplace for many a foreign *invité*, but also a substantial measure of solidarity and friendship for a shared artistic vision.

Picard, Maus, and *L'Art moderne* never defined what style or stylistic attributes constituted *l'art social*, genuinely intending to foster a climate of openness in which all styles could flourish. The deliberate refusal of Les XX and *L'Art moderne* to define themselves artistically extended to their refusal to take an overt political stance; yet politics were inextricably intertwined with both. Indeed, Verhaeren argued that in Belgium the artistic and political struggles were inseparable in the seething cauldron of the 1880s. For him Les XX's efforts at reform were 'ardent, youthful, bitter, violent', and they encountered 'the same attitudes, the same enemies, the same hopes, the same goal, the same obstacles' as were found in the political arena.[29] As Belgium continued its pace of rapid industrialization, it experienced massive social upheaval caused by inequities in the political, economic and linguistic spheres, while a monied and cosmopolitan upper middle class flourished.

Anarchy, Socialism and Revolution were in the air. While the majority of the portraits, land- and seascapes shown at Les XX carried no overt Socialist or political themes, individual works, such as Ensor's 1885 drawing, *The Entry of Christ into Jerusalem* [see p. 21, fig. 7], with its inclusion of banners bearing the messages 'Vive la Sociale', 'Amnestie', and 'Le Mouvement flamand', often created a disproportionate stir. But *vingtistes* came to realize, as *L'Art moderne* had warned, that membership itself of the group constituted a revolutionary act. As Paul Signac wrote: '... the anarchist painter is not he who does anarchist paint-

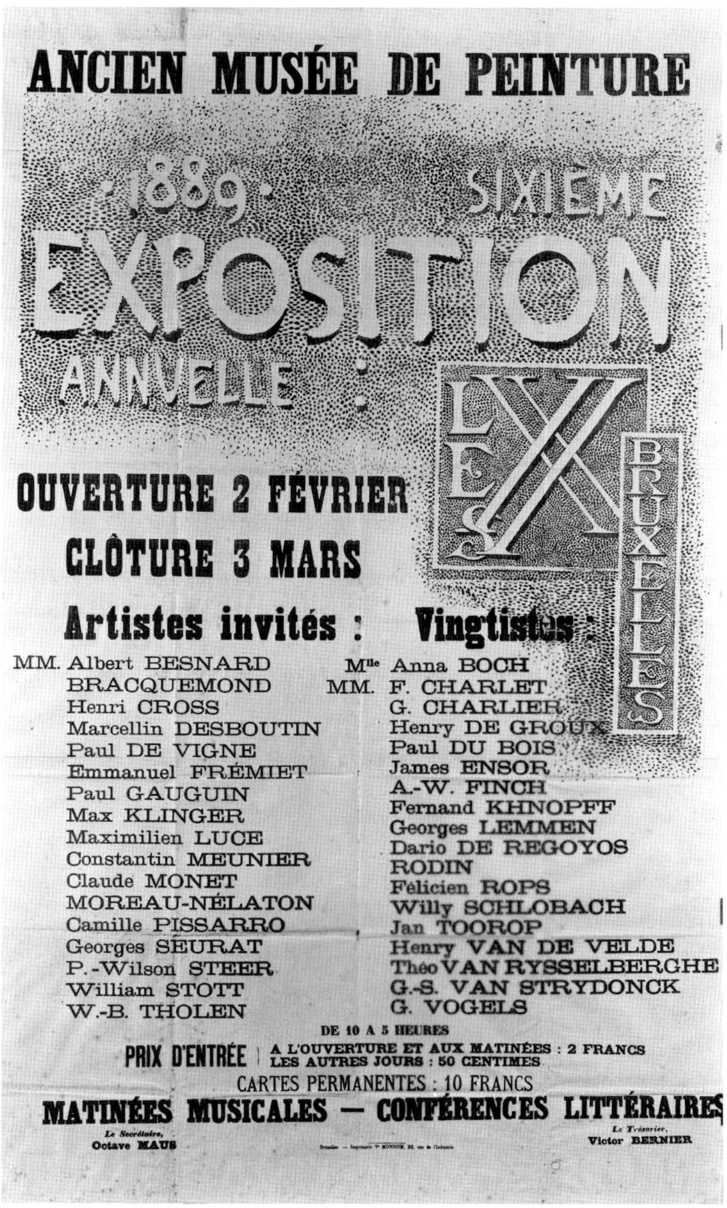

fig. 32 THÉO VAN RYSSELBERGHE
Poster for the 1889 Salon des XX, lithograph, Brussels, Archives de l'art contemporain

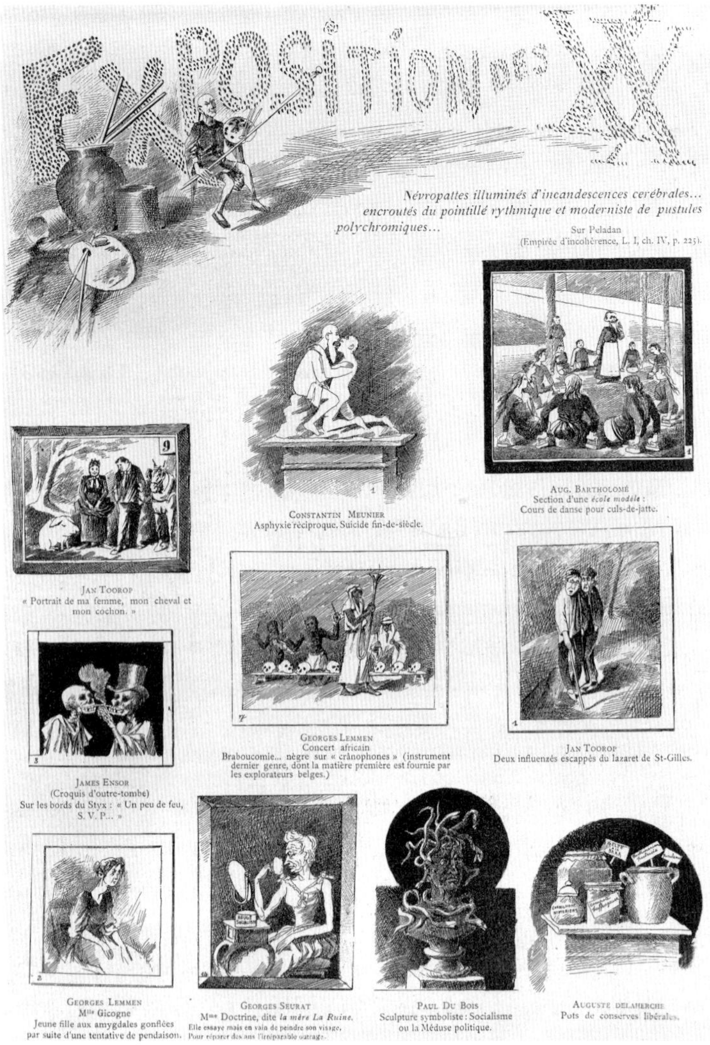

fig. 33 'Exposition des XX', *Le Patriote Illustré*, 21 February 1892

ing but he who without caring for money, without desire for recompense, struggles with all his individuality against bourgeois and official conventions….'[30]

During an age which had come to view exhibitions as 'political' statements, those of Les XX were surrounded by an aura of revolution. In 1888, the very catalogue itself could be seen as a rebellious challenge: 'The catalogue is red, a blood red, a red of combat and of carnage', bawled an incensed newspaper critic.[31] Picard's columns defending *l'Art social*, coupled with Les XX's promotion of *l'Art jeune*, clearly tainted Les XX as 'anarcho-socialist'. Thus, *Le Patriote Illustré*, equating the art of Les XX with ruinous Socialism, transformed Seurat's *Young Woman powdering Herself* into an old hag powdering her face with 'la rouge socialiste' [fig. 33]. Suspicious also of Meunier, it lampooned his *Puddler* [cat. 48] as a work of decadence. Edmond Picard, Les XX's Socialist conscience, did nothing to quell this critical equation. Exhorting artists to become involved with the society in which they lived in order to transform it, he warned that 'the hour has arrived to dip one's pen into red ink'.[32]

The artists and the exhibitions continued their rapid evolution. English graphic design and book arts exerted a growing influence on several *vingtistes*. Lemmen's cover to the 1891 catalogue [fig. 34], printed in reddish orange and black, revealed a debt to Arthur Mackmurdo, Walter Crane and Selwyn Image. Lemmen presented the radiance of the sun's rays as a pictorial equivalent of Les XX's vitality and nurturing effect on Belgium. Again in 1892, Lemmen's dynamic and bold design [fig. 35] recalls English precedents such as Selwyn Image's cover for the periodical *The Hobby Horse*: the banner of Les XX, victoriously unfurled before a tree whose roots reveal not only the force of its artistic mission but also its diversity.

At the 1891 Salon des XX a new class of objects made its appearance alongside the

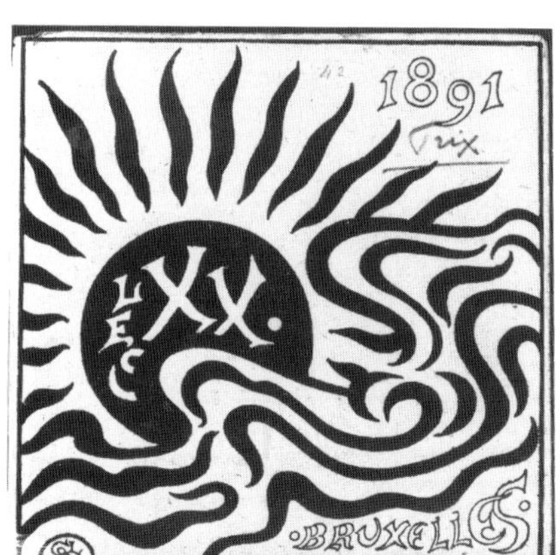

fig. 34 GEORGES LEMMEN
Catalogue cover for Les XX, 1891, photomechanical reproduction

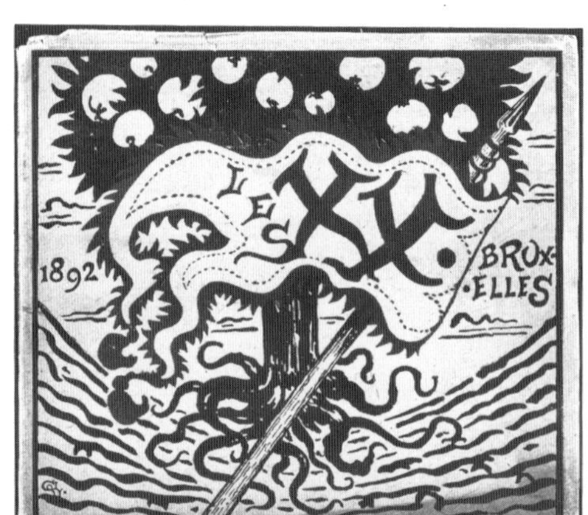

fig. 35 GEORGES LEMMEN
Catalogue cover for Les XX, 1892

paintings and sculpture. Now Willy Finch sent not paintings, but ceramic panels. Jules Chéret exhibited a series of posters and Georges Lemmen loaned his copies of Walter Crane's children's books. The Decorative Arts movement had arrived. Lemmen paid homage to Crane in a two-part article in *L'Art moderne*, in which he put Crane's book illustrations on an equal footing with the paintings of Burne-Jones, Watts, Leighton and Whistler.[33] In 1892 an even greater prominence was given to the new subject. Toulouse-Lautrec's posters were shown with pottery by Auguste Delaherche, Finch's ceramic tiles, decorative designs by Selwyn Image, samples of Herbert Horne's book decorations, and the project for a tapestry by Henry van de Velde. In 1893 two entire rooms were reserved for the decorative arts, where Willy Finch exhibited a tea table and Anna Boch [see cat. 71] a screen that complemented one that she had commissioned from Emile Bernard and which was also exhibited in the same year. Delacherche reappeared with his plates, Lautrec with his posters, and Van de Velde exhibited the influential embroidery *La Veillée des Anges* (*The Angels' Watch*) (Museum Bellerive, Zurich).

This expansion of the definition of fine art to include the decorative arts once again reflected Les XX's Socialist leanings. By raising objects of everyday life to the status of the Fine Arts, artists declared that rugs, furniture, wallpaper, glass, ceramics, books and doorknobs – one's complete environment – could serve as a means of improving daily life. And this enrichment was now available to all people, not just to the wealthy few who could afford to own an easel painting or a piece of sculpture. At the same time, this democratization of the art object bestowed on the artist a crucial role as an agent of reform in society. In 1891, when the decorative arts made their first appearance at Les XX, the Parti Ouvrier Belge (Belgian Labour Party) formed a 'Section d'Art'. This new wing of the party espoused the importance of art in attaining its goal of social equality. Like Les XX, the Section d'Art sponsored lectures and concerts, and could count upon Picard, Maus and Verhaeren to support and advertise its activities in the pages of *L'Art moderne*. These three also presented lectures at the party headquarters, which eventually occupied Victor Horta's Maison du Peuple, completed in 1899. In addition, the *vingtistes* Khnopff and Van de Velde lent their support to the Section d'Art by lecturing and by supplying graphic images for its activities.[34]

On 26 February 1893 in *La Nation*, Verhaeren declared: 'The influence of Les XX has been so profound and successful that tomorrow it could cease to exist, without great harm – its goal seems already attained.'[35] Although this idea may have come to Maus earlier, this was the first public suggestion that Les XX should end. Several months later, Van de Velde urged his fellow *vingtistes* 'to think about the hour of death!',[36] arguing that the group had achieved its goals and should disband before it became outmoded. Indeed, one week later, *L'Art moderne* carefully published compilations of all artists, lecturers and musicians who had participated in Les XX's annual salons, as if recording the group for posterity.[37] The tenth exhibition held from 19 February to 26 March was, indeed, Les XX's last.

Immediately, Octave Maus began dreaming about Les XX's successor. His vision now was one of a society backed by benefactors who, in contrast to the power exercised by artists within Les XX, would relinquish control to an organizing committee, led by none other than himself. Many years later Maus reflected on the contrasting systems used at Les XX and La Libre Esthétique, which he identified as Anarchy and Autocracy respectively: 'During the anarchic period, the exhibitors fought among themselves, all the while exchanging blows with the public; under the autocrat that I became, they only fought against the incomprehension of the crowds. It was altogether an improvement.'[38] Maus sought the more autocratic route to avoid the internal quarrels that he felt had plagued Les XX's democratic process. Van Rysselberghe approved of Maus's plan, rationalizing that artists were 'ill-equipped for such partnerships and for conducting business'.[39]

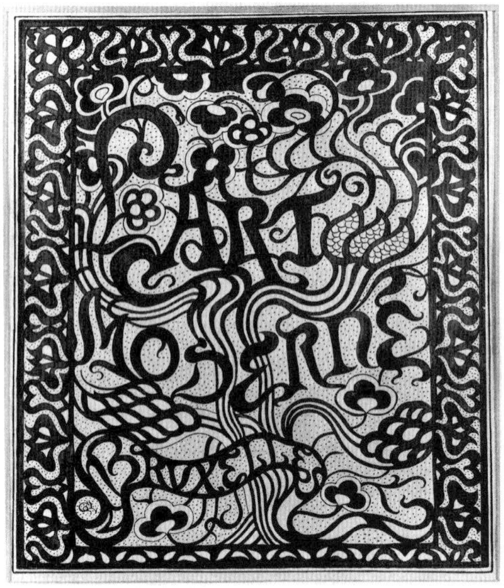

fig. 36 GEORGES LEMMEN, Cover design for *L'Art moderne*, 1894, ink on paper, Musée d'Ixelles, Brussels

In its first public announcement, which appeared on 16 July 1893 in *L'Art moderne*, the new group endorsed the independence of the artist, the renunciation of formulae and pastiche, and vowed to continue the work of Les XX. Adopting the slogan 'Pro Arte' as its rallying cry, its governing committee would exclude artists and be composed of aestheticians, men of letters and collectors.[40] Several months later 'La Libre Esthétique' was publicly baptized in the columns of *L'Art moderne* and was identified as 'the inevitable expansion and development of the Vingtistes Salonnets.'[41] Signaling this new beginning, a new cover for *L'Art moderne* designed by Georges Lemmen appeared on 7 January 1894 [fig. 36]. Expressed in an electrifying Art Nouveau style, the cover reveals Lemmen's interest in the power of line and his continued commitment to graphic design.

Eventually 104 founding members of La Libre Esthétique were listed in the pages of *L'Art moderne*. Among these were the former editors of *L'Art moderne*, Arnould and Robert, and two current editors, Picard and Verhaeren. Many were lawyer-friends of Picard and Maus, such as Alexandre Braun and Georges Schoenfeld, or lawyers who had abandoned legal careers for literary ones, including Jules Destrée, Eugène Demolder and Maurice Maeterlinck. Among the other founding members were the editors of several Socialist newspapers and reviews: Jean Volders of *Le Peuple*, Max Hallet of *La Justice* and Fernand Brouez of *La Société nouvelle*.

La Libre Esthétique promised in its general declaration of October 1893 that special importance would be given to the decorative arts.[42] In 1894, it kept its promise with a vengeance. Among the host of exhibitors of such objects was C. R. Ashbee, whose display of twenty-eight pieces designed by him and executed by The Guild and School of Handicraft marked his first entry in a European exhibition.[43] But there was a seemingly endless quantity of such work, including Aubrey Beardsley's illustrations for Oscar Wilde's *Salomé*, Jules Chéret's decorative panels, Dalpayrat & Lesbros's earthenware, pewterware by Paul Dubois, posters by Toulouse-Lautrec, Eugène Grasset's posters, title pages and book covers, a Selwyn Image lithograph lent by Georges Lemmen and published by The Fitzroy Picture Society, rugs by Lemmen and Wytsman, Aristide Maillol's tapestry and embroidery, Marius Michel's book bindings, three of William Morris's Kelmscott books, Heywood Sumner's frontispieces, and the sensational installation of the Liège architect, Gustave Serrurier-Bovy.[44]

For the exhibition, Serrurier created a complete environment, a 'cabinet de travail', by taking over one of the small rooms for the exhibition. He installed a false window and wooden beams, added brick trim dividing the wall-panels that also served to form the dado moulding, covered the walls and ceiling with English paper of large poppies, and placed rugs on the floors. The transformation of a museum room into this complete domestic environment did not come easily, and Serrurier informed Maus that he would need about two weeks to effect the change.[45] The furnished room was described as 'a fortunate application of all styles resulting in a new purified style where worldliness is linked to rusticity and restraint to comfort.'[46]

The 1894 Salon de La Libre Esthétique was a resounding success by all accounts. Not only had it received an official visit from the king and queen, but a strong Parisian contingent attended its opening, including exhibiting artists such as Berthe Morisot, Paul Signac and Toulouse-Lautrec, the Inspector of Fine Arts, Roger-Marx, and the writers Henri de Régnier, Téodor de Wyzéwa and Joséphin Péladan. Almost immediately, many artists found buyers for works displayed at La Libre Esthétique, among them Heymans's *L'Avenue des sapins*, Toorop's Symbolist *L'Annonciation du nouveau mysticisme*, and decorative art objects by the Frenchman Charpentier and the Belgian Paul Du Bois. Private collectors were not the only buyers. The curator of the Museum of Decorative Arts in Belgium, the baron de Haulleville, purchased works by Charpentier, George Frampton, Delaherche, Emile Gallé and Ashbee for his museum.[47] The popular show was prolonged by two weeks, closing on 1 April instead of 15 March. Writing in *Gil Blas*, the French critic, Jean Ajalbert, impressed with the group, claimed they had converted Brussels into a 'laboratory for new ideas' and hailed their capital as 'the centre of intellectual internationalism'.[48]

The following year, 1895, Serrurier presented a new installation called a 'chambre d'artisan', and issued a brochure denouncing an art that served only wealth. Restating the arguments of Ruskin and Morris concerning the causal relationship between aesthetic environment and moral character, he declared: 'the majority must participate in artistic life'.[49] In his exhibition lecture, Picard reinforced this imperative of the social significance of art, and stated: 'Artists through their works must play the role of apostles',[50] while in an adjoining exhibition room were large, coloured lithographs intended for school rooms and missions that were designed by the English artists Sumner, Image and Louis Davis, and published by The Fitzroy Picture Society. Artists who formerly consecrated their careers to one of the 'higher arts' found themselves universally called upon to adopt Morris and Crane's ideals of the artist as reformer of society.[51]

With Octave Maus successfully reigning as the 'autocrat' of La Libre Esthétique, Edmond Picard yearned for his own artistic realm. The raging passion for decorative art objects set in artistic installations proved irresistible. Picard created a personal 'laboratory for new ideas' by converting his sumptuous mansion at 56, avenue de la Toison d'or into a gallery called 'La Maison d'art'.[52] Based on the two groups that were its progenitors, the gallery was open to painting, sculpture and architecture, but also featured ceramics, iron, glasswork, wallpaper, rugs, bindings, and furnishings displayed in a domestic setting. In addition, like La Libre Esthétique, the gallery was to serve as a major link between artists, industrialists and collectors. In its first six months the society undertook an ambitious programme of ten exhibitions, eleven lectures, seven concerts and three plays.[53] *L'Art moderne* praised Picard's venture, where 'for the first time, art objects are exhibited in their environment, in the light for which they were created with their expressed purpose: instead of a merchant's display or a marketplace of trinkets, a modern house, furnished, decorated and ornamented as it should be.'[54] Among the visitors was Siegfried Bing, a Parisian dealer in Japanese art, who was directly inspired by La Maison d'art to remodel his shop into one of the most famous nineteenth-century galleries, L'Art nouveau.

Picard kept close ties between La Maison d'art and Maus's La Libre Esthétique by displaying works by many of the same artists, by lecturing frequently at La Libre Esthétique, and by hosting receptions in the Maison d'art on the inauguration of La Libre Esthétique Salons.[55] The Maison d'art even served as the setting for the fourth and closing concert given at La Libre Esthétique in 1896. Eugène Ysaÿe and his quartet performed in the rooms where an installation of 75 works by the French artist, Raffaëlli, were on display.[56]

La Maison d'art was not the only precocious progeny of La Libre Esthétique. Gustave Serrurier, fresh from his two triumphs in Brussels, organized an exhibition called 'L'Œuvre artistique' that opened in May of 1895 in his native Liège. This decorative arts extravaganza was not a Picard-styled showing of a few objects, hand-picked by an aesthete, but was more in accord with the vast scheme of La Libre Esthétique. One hundred participants exhibited 606 items![57] Many of the contributors had shown some of the same works only months earlier at La Libre Esthétique; but Serrurier also included the work of Hector Guimard and Paul Hankar, architects who had not shown at La Libre Esthétique. Activities at L'Œuvre artistique ranged from a performance of Ibsen's *Solness the Builder*, performed by the French Symbolist avant-garde Théâtre de l'Œuvre founded in 1893 by Lugné-Poë, to lectures by Fernand Khnopff on Walter Crane and by Henry van de Velde on the 'Renaissance of the Decorative Arts'. Of course, *L'Art moderne* heartily approved of Serrurier's attempt to spread the gospel of the new art to Liège and exclaimed: 'One must loudly praise the group of unselfish artists and aesthetes who have so courageously undertaken the shaking up of their fellow citizens from their indifference.'[58]

In 1894, for the first time, the pages of *L'Art moderne* carried line drawings and photographs of important objects and posters to commemorate the first exhibition of La Libre Esthétique and to reach those who could not make the trip to Brussels themselves to see the 'laboratory' at work. The foreign press followed suit and began to document the Salons of La Libre Esthétique with photographs and drawings. In 1898 *L'Art moderne* proudly announced that three reviews, *The Studio* (London), *Art et Décoration* (Paris) and *Dekorative Kunst* (Munich) had sent the directors of these magazines to study and photograph important objects from the fifth exhibition. Clearly the annual pilgrimage to Brussels was now obligatory for the international modern art press. Already in 1897, the Parisian *Revue des Arts Décoratifs*, in a xenophobic pique, urged French artists to resist the allures of these new glossy magazines and to 'remain French!', asking rhetorically: 'Is it not the moment to make this appeal to artists and to the public when, after several years of servitude to English art and its derivatives, an invasion of Belgian art is now being attempted....'[59]

These massive displays, featuring upwards of 500 works, continued into the new century, with the decorative arts continuing to play a prominent role among the paintings, prints and sculpture. Among the painters, Maus paid special attention to his friend Théo van Rysselberghe, a founding veteran of Les XX. When Van Rysselberghe showed a substantial number of portraits and landscapes in 1898, after a three-year absence from La Libre Esthétique, his submission was hailed by *L'Art moderne* as 'the principal entry' in the exhibit.[60] Not only was most of the article devoted to the artist, but one week later Van Rysselberghe garnered an entire review for himself.[61] And Van Rysselberghe played a role in the later history of La Libre Esthétique. In 1901 his pointillist portrait of his wife and daughter was purchased by the Brussels Musées royaux des Beaux-Arts de Belgique, Brussels [fig. 37]. Maus, in a thinly veiled 'anonymous' review in *L'Art moderne*, hailed the entry of the first Neo-Impressionist canvas in the Brussels museum as the ultimate vindication of the policies of Les XX and La Libre Esthétique which had finally opened academic doors to modern art. It waxed poetic as Van Rysselberghe claimed his rightful place in the museum alongside the pioneers of Belgian modernism Henri de Braekeleer (q.v.), Louis Artan (q.v.) and Hippolyte Boulenger. Like Emile Claus (q.v.), Georges Lemmen, James Ensor and Fernand Khnopff, Van Rysselberghe 'personified the struggle of painters of the present generation who strove for freedom of thought and the affirmation of an original, personal and sincere art....'[62]

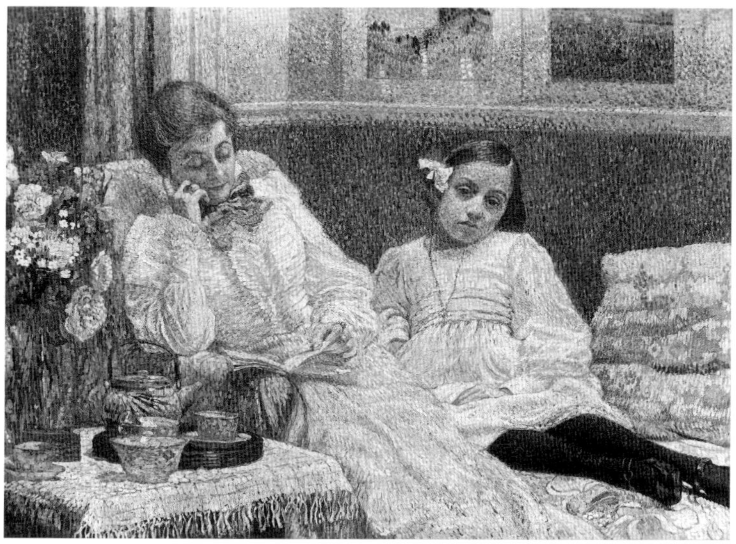

fig. 37 THÉO VAN RYSSELBERGHE
Portrait of the Artist's Wife and Daughter, 1899, Musées royaux des Beaux-Arts de Belgique, Brussels

With this palpable victory, Maus felt free to refashion the focus of the exhibitions at La Libre Esthétique. As the 1902 and 1903 shows diminished in size by a third, he began to dream of yet another exhibition strategy. In 1903, on the occasion of the tenth exhibition of La Libre Esthétique, Maus declared that the group had attained its goals. He announced his plan to arrange forthcoming shows thematically, in a systematic manner, and concluded: 'To the cycle of initiation [at Les XX] would follow a series of openly educational exhibitions.'[63]

fig. 38 THÉO VAN RYSSELBERGHE, Poster for the 1904 Salon de La Libre Esthétique, lithograph

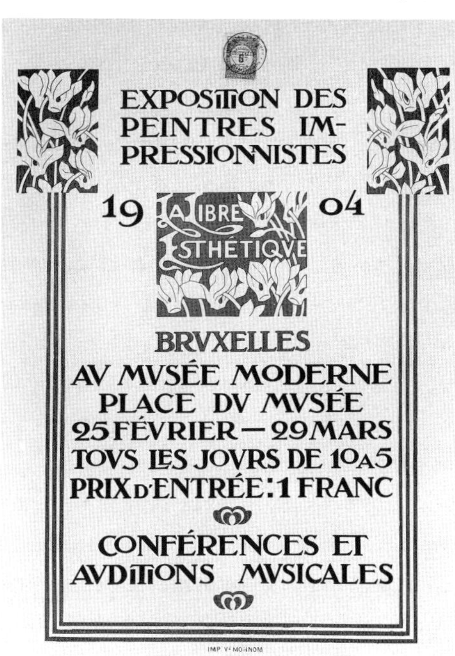

The 1904 exhibition was a retrospective of Impressionism, broadly defined, and consisted of twenty-five French artists and one Belgian [fig. 38]. The 195 pieces (which returned the installation to the size of Les XX) were all borrowed from more than thirty Parisian collectors and dealers, including the venerable Durand-Ruel and Messieurs Bernheim-Jeune. Eight of the painters were no longer living (C. Pissarro, Manet, Sisley, Morisot, Gauguin, Van Gogh, Seurat and Lautrec). Maus included four French Neo-Impressionists (Seurat, Cross, Luce, Signac) and the Belgian Van Rysselberghe (who now lived in Paris), and four Nabis (Denis, Vuillard, Bonnard, and K. X. Roussel). Four concerts, including works by Debussy and César Franck, attempted to suggest the 'parallel evolution' in music, while all was made clear by four lectures, covering art (by André Mellerio), literature (Médéric Dufour), theatre (André Gide) and music (Louis Laloy). Maus's twelve-page essay tracing the history of the Impressionist movement was used as the preface to the catalogue.[64]

The choice of nearly all French exhibitors, save the ex-patriot Van Rysselberghe, by a *Belgian* group in a *Belgian* museum, particularly raised the ire of Edmond Picard who launched a vehement campaign against Maus in the press. If Picard had been a peripheral player in the first incarnation of La Libre Esthétique, he was at least able to create his own version at the Maison d'art. Now he found himself completely removed from a situation that he considered wholely objectionable. Picard, who had left the editorial board of *L'Art moderne* in 1901, launched his first attack in the Belgian Socialist newspaper, *Le Peuple*, with 'L'Ostracisme des maîtres belges au salon de la Libre Esthétique'. Here, Picard argued that his former confrère had done a great injustice to Belgian art by excluding Belgian artists.[65] Maus replied several days later in the same newspaper, defending his right to show Belgian artists 'an expression of art different from theirs that is not familiar to them'. He lamely accused Picard of deliberately ignoring his stated intent to create an exhibition at a later date that treated Impressionism beyond France's borders.[66]

This was not the end, however. The two warriors, having initially won their artistic battles through close collaboration, now turned on each other. Furious exchanges continued in the press, with Maus enlisting the aid of Georges Lemmen, who defended the exhibition and even declared: 'The predominance of the French contemporary school is incontestable.'[67] Maus began garnering the support of Belgian artists who, one by one in the pages of *L'Art moderne*, seemed to vindicate his inquiry into the important role played by Impressionism in the evolution of their art.[68] Picard then demanded a chance to make his points known at La Libre Esthétique. Maus refused, claiming that the schedule of lectures and concerts was immutable. Picard was unstoppable, however, and sponsored his own lecture in the Hôtel Ravenstein in Brussels on 17 March 1904, in which he railed that the deliberate exclusion of Belgian artists would lead to the 'disparagement of our national art'. Picard also attacked the sponsoring of four French lecturers who had the affront to lecture to Belgians on the struggle of the avant-garde, as though they were not major protagonists.[69] Picard even pressed his campaign in the Senate, where on 22 April he delivered an impassioned speech to the assembled politicians attacking Maus's conception of the Impressionist exhibition held at La Libre Esthétique![70]

If Maus was ever actually hesitant about investigating Impressionism outside of France, this furor forced him to keep his promise. The 1905 exhibition explored 'L'Evolution externe de l'impressionnisme'. In his preface to the catalogue, Maus explained that he was entrusting the newly formed Belgian group, Vie et Lumière ('Life and Light'), to represent the Belgian Impressionist movement. Vie et Lumière, headed by George Morren, consisted of the former *vingtistes* Anna Boch, James Ensor and Georges Lemmen, as well as Georges Buysse, Emile Claus, Degouve de Nuncques (q.v.), Aloïs de Laet, Alfred Hazledine and A.-J. Heymans, all of whom had exhibited with Les XX or at La Libre Esthétique.[71]

Subsequent exhibitions continued to be organized around a general theme; for example, 1909 dealt with portraits and 1910 with landscapes. As Maus increasingly looked backward in time instead of forward, retrospective tributes to fallen artists who had valiantly fought with the group became a staple of the exhibitions, including Rops (1899), Evenepoel (q.v.) (1900), Toulouse-Lautrec (1902), Isidore Verheyden (1906), Eugène Carrière (1907), Alexandre Charpentier (1910), Henri Edmond Cross and Charles van der Stappen (1911), and Dario de Regoyos (1914). Although the group had opened its doors to Fauvism through the work of Matisse and his circle, and invited an occasional German Expressionist, in the end Maus was unable to accept the early work of Picasso or most of the modern 'isms' of the first fifteen years of the twentieth century – Cubism, Futurism, Expressionism, or other experiments in Russia and France. Indeed, by 1912 the spirit of novelty and adventure in some measure had been taken over by the private Brussels gallery of Georges Giroux, where the Italian Futurists first made their appearance in Belgium that June. And in 1913 Maus failed to take stock of his organization after its second ten exhibitions – as he had done in 1893 and 1903.

However, the twenty-first exhibition of La Libre Esthétique in 1914 turned out to be the last. Maus's great experiment of establishing a laboratory for all that was new in Belgium came to an end – as did so much else in Europe – with the outbreak of World War I in August 1914. Indeed, the German occupation led to the self-imposed exile to Holland and England of some of Belgium's brightest stars of the future, among them the pillars of Belgian Expressionism – Frits van den Berghe, Rik Wouters, Gustave and Léon de Smet, Edgard Tytgat, Valerius de Saedeleer and Gustave van de Woestijne. Maus's parting advice, delivered to a devoted audience at the Société d'Etudiants de Belles-Lettres in Lausanne (where he was part of the Belgian delegation to the Embassy), could serve as the credo for his remarkable career as an artistic impresario to his beloved Belgium: 'Love Art, Strive to Serve It, and to Promulgate It.'[72]

If by the end La Libre Esthétique in some ways resembled more the Salon it worked so hard to overthrow, perhaps its failure to identify what constituted the new avant-garde after ten of its twenty-one exhibitions is not so surprising. Still the dogged determination and dedication to art of its members and leader is moving, for Les XX and La Libre Esthétique had broken the back of the Salon system and had won the right of the artist to be independent from this official government machine. The heroic battles waged by Les XX and La Libre Esthétique placed art at the centre of society and the artist as the principal agent of societal reform. It is due to their courageous fight and international impact that they earn a place not only in the history of Belgian art, but in the larger tale of modern art in Europe.

1 This essay focuses on the artistic rather than musical or literary events that occurred at Les XX and La Libre Esthétique. For more on the music, see Albert Vander Linden's 'Octave Maus et la Vie musicale belge (1875–1914)', *Mémoires, Académie royale de Belgique, Classe des Beaux-Arts* 6:2 (1950), and the study by Serge Goyens de Heusch, *'L'Invitation au Voyage': La musique aux XX et à La Libre Esthétique* (Brussels 1990). For extensive coverage of all events, see the fundamental study by Madeleine Octave Maus, *Trente années de lutte pour l'art* (Brussels 1916). This seminal work was reprinted in 1980 by Editions Lebeer Hossmann.
All modern scholarship on Les XX and La Libre Esthétique owes a debt of gratitude to Francine-Claire Legrand who, as director of the Musée d'Art moderne in Brussels, curated the groundbreaking exhibition, *Le groupe des XX et son temps*, Brussels, Otterlo 1962. Under her aegis Albert Vander Linden donated the archives of Les XX and La Libre Esthétique to the Archives de l'Art contemporain (hereafter referred to as AAC). Thanks to her direction, the letters preserved in the AAC from James Ensor, Théo van Rysselberghe, Paul Signac and Jan Toorop to Octave Maus have been published in the *Bulletin des Musées Royaux des Beaux-Arts de Belgique* (Ensor by Legrand, in 1966, no. 1–2; Van Rysselberghe and Signac by Marie-Jeanne Chartrain-Hebbelinck, in issues 1966, no. 1–2, and 1969, no. 1–2 respectively, and Toorop by Phil Mertens in 1969, no. 3–4). The publication of these archival sources and Legrand's catalogue led to two American scholars preparing doctoral dissertations on Les Vingt: Jane Block's 1980 work, published as *Les XX and Belgian Avant-Gardism, 1868–1894* (Ann Arbor 1984) and Susan M. Canning's *A History and Critical Review of the Salons of 'Les Vingt': 1884–1893*, Pennsylvania State University, 1980. These studies could not have been completed without the gracious assistance of Francine-Claire Legrand, and the staff of the AAC, Micheline Colin and André Godart.
About this time, two different exhibitions, one held at the Royal Academy of Arts and the other at the Brooklyn Museum of Art, paid homage to Belgian art of the period. The former, *Post-Impressionism: Cross-Currents in European Painting*, 1979–1980, attempted to deal with the entire period and included an insightful essay by MaryAnne Stevens, *Belgian Art: Les XX and the Libre Esthétique* (252–254). Organized by Sarah Faunce, *Belgian Art: 1880–1914* concentrated on developments in Belgium and included essays by two of the contributors to the present catalogue, Jane Block on Les XX (17–40), and Jean F. Buyck on Antwerp (71–80).
More recently, there has been a revived interest in Les XX and La Libre Esthétique as witnessed by two exhibitions: Steve Goddard's *Les XX and the Belgian Avant-Garde, Prints, Drawings and Books ca. 1890* (1992–1993) and Gisèle Ollinger-Zinque's *Les XX, La Libre Esthétique, Cent ans après* (1993–1994). The former catalogue includes essays by an American team of literary scholars, historians, and art historians treating subjects such as history (Murphy/Strikwerda), politics (Levine), Les XX (Canning), Print culture (Goddard), Book design (Block) and Symbolism (Friedman); the latter was limited to works shown at Les XX and La Libre Esthétique now held by the Musée d'Art moderne. Its catalogue contains a useful chronology of key events from 1883–1914 written by Anne Adriaens-Pannier and Micheline Colin.

2 For Picard, see the substantial entry by René Warlomont in the *Biographie Nationale*, vol. 34, 644–658, as well as the following: François Vermeulen, 'Edmond Picard et le Réveil des Lettres Belges (1881–1888)', *Mémoires, Académie Royale de Langue et de Littérature françaises de Belgique* 9 (1935); Albert Licart, *L'Œuvre d'Edmond Picard*, Brussels 1937; and A. Pasquier, *Edmond Picard*, Brussels 1945. More recently, Paul Aron has treated Picard's Socialist ideas on art in *Les Ecrivains belges et le socialisme (1880–1913)*, Brussels 1985. There is no modern biography of Picard.

3 Other colleagues of the bar who helped found the newspaper were Charles Graux, Xavier Olin (whose sister, Adèle, married Picard in 1864), Eugène Robert, Paul Janson and Victor Arnould.

4 There is still no biography of Octave Maus, nor even an entry for him in the standard Belgian *Biographie Nationale*. Information on his life and service to the arts can be gleaned from M. Octave Maus, Albert Vander Linden's *Octave Maus et la vie musicale belge*, Maus's numerous articles and the published and unpublished letters of the AAC.

5 '… s'occuper de l'Art dans tous les domaines: littérature, peinture, sculpture, gravure, musique, architecture, ameublement, costume, etc.' and 'sans parti-pris d'école, sans préoccupation aucune de règle, de code ou de formule', both from *L'Art moderne* (6 March 1881), 2.

6 'Qu'il s'agisse pour nous d'écrire ou de nous abstenir, nos résolutions expriment rarement l'opinion d'un seul: elles sont examinées, discutées et arrêtées en comité', *L'Art moderne* (6 December 1881), 116.

7 Exceptions to this were articles supplied by collaborators, including the writers, Camille Lemonnier, Maurice Maeterlinck, and the artists Georges Lemmen and Henry van de Velde. In 1888 the board's composition changed with the departure of Robert and Arnould, and the adhesion of the poet and art critic, Emile Verhaeren.

8 This idea was first presented by Block, 'What's in a Name: The Origins of "Les XX"', *Bulletin des Musées royaux des Beaux-Arts de Belgique* (1981–1984), 135–141.

9 The other ten were Frantz Charlet, Jean Delvin, Paul Du Bois, Charles Goethals, Pericles Pantazis, Frans Simons, Gustave Vanaise, Guillaume van Strydonck, Theodoor Verstraete and Guillaume Vogels (AAC, no. 4608).

10 'Tout ce qui est beau, libre, sincère est étouffé par une coterie de pieuvres, qui pompent à elles la finance, la considération, la réputation'; and 'Enfin, nous nous proposons de tout casser pour remettre notre pauvre bourgeois de pays la place qu'il devrait occuper'; both taken from a letter, Maus to E. Boch, 1 November 1883 (AAC, Fonds Bouquelle, 3900).

11 *Ibid.*, 'C'est de l'art fier et indépendant qu'on veut faire et comme il s'agit de bousculer et de batailler, j'en suis.'

12 'un art indépendant dégagé de toute attache officielle,…'; 'Les Vingt', *L'Art moderne* (11 November 1883), 361.

13 'En son ingénuité, Gauguin ne pouvait concevoir qu'on exposât ses toiles dans un édifice officiel'; O. Maus, 'La Lanterne Magique', lecture delivered to the Société d'Etudiants de Belles-Lettres de Lausanne, *Revue de Belles-Lettres* 55 (1927), 207. The exhibitions from 1884–1886 were held at the Palais des Beaux-Arts in the building on rue de la Régence designed by Alphonse Balat. After 1887 (when Gauguin exhibited), they were held at the Ancien Musée Royal de Peinture, or at the Musée d'Art moderne, Place du musée. These rooms were formerly the gallery of ancient

art which moved to the Balat building. In 1959 the Musée d'Art moderne was closed and the space was given to the Bibliothèque Royale.

14 Chainaye, Charlet, Delvin, Dubois, Ensor, Finch, Goethals, Khnopff, Lambeaux, Pantazis, De Regoyos, Schlobach, Simons, Vanaise, Van Rysselberghe, Van Strydonck, Verhaert, Verstraete, Vogels and Wytsman.

15 From left to right: *Une Coloriste, Les Masques, Le Lampiste, Chinoiseries, Les Pochards*, and *La Dame en détresse*, partially obscured by Rodin's *Portrait of Victor Hugo*.

16 Van Rysselberghe to Maus (AAC, no. 5352). This letter is reproduced in the *Bulletin des Musées royaux des Beaux-Arts de Belgique* (1966) no. 1–2, 71–72, edited by Marie-Jeanne Chartrain-Hebbelinck, as 'Les lettres de Van Rysselberghe à Octave Maus'. The 1908 photo shows the monogram designed by poster artist Léo Jo.

17 E. Picard, 'L'Art Jeune', *L'Art moderne* (10 February 1884), 41–43.

18 'fortifier l'homme, de l'aggrandir par *l'émotion* en le rendant meilleur'. E. Picard, 'L'Art Jeune', *L'Art moderne* (9 March 1884), 73.

19 'Tous, ils pratiquent un art jeune, neuf, dégagé des formules comme leurs caractères sont détachés des exigences officielles ... ils affirment que l'Art se transforme sans cesse, qu'il participe aux révolutions profondes, qui, même sans barricades et sans mousqueterie, modifient l'état social des nations, qu'il domine parfois ces mouvements et exerce sur eux sa part d'influence....' Yves Didier, 'La lutte pour l'art', *Le National Belge* (14 February 1884). Joining Picard in the lecture series that season were his fellow Belgians Georges Rodenbach and Albert Giraud, and the Frenchman Catulle Mendès.

20 'Petite Chronique', *L'Art moderne* (4 May 1884), 150.

21 'un mois à l'avance on en jacasse, on s'en préoccupe, on en dispute; de jeunes femmes font faire des toilettes neuves pour ce jour-là; la chasse aux cartes d'invitation commence,... C'est le Tout-Bruxelles artiste, les gens qui connaissent les peintres, qui aiment du Wagner et mettent sur leur guéridon le dernier roman de Paris.' G.[eorges] R.[odenbach], 'Têtes de Vingtistes', *Le Progrès* (10 February 1887).

22 As Bruce Laughton explained: 'Les XX must have been one of the most amiably run societies of artists in the nineteenth century, and perhaps there has been none like it in this century', in 'The British and American contribution to Les XX, 1884–1893', *Apollo* 86 (November 1967), 372.

23 'Pensez donc ... un homme arrivé, décoré, médaillé, tableau au musée, etc....' (AAC, undated letter, Goethals to Maus, 4693).

24 'C'est qu'il est étranger et qu'il habite à l'étranger' (Glasgow University Library, Maus to Finch, B.P. II 11/101, 21 November 1886). See also Canning's 'Soyons Nous': Les XX and the Cultural Discourse of the Belgian Avant-Garde', in *Les XX and the Belgian Avant-Garde, Prints, Drawings, and Books ca. 1890*, 39–41.

25 The incident masked other feelings as well: the most virulent attack on Whistler emanated from James Ensor, who felt that Whistler was not just too foreign, but too established and too old (AAC, 4784, Ensor to Maus, November 1886, published in the *Bulletin des Musées Royaux de Belgique* [1966] 1–2, 25–26).

26 'Il y en aura pour tous les goûts, des 'serrés' et des 'lâchés' des 'impressionnistes' et des 'intentionnistes' et des 'impossibilistes'...' (Maus to Eugène Boch, AAC, Fonds Bouquelle, 3914, 29 December 1886).

27 Redon also supplied the frontispieces to Verhaeren's *Les Soirs* and *Les Debâcles*, both published by Edmond Deman in 1888, Brussels. In addition, Redon created frontispieces to works by Jules Destrée, *Les Chimères*, and Iwan Gilkin's *La Damnation de l'Artiste* and *Ténèbres*.

28 'notre nom un peu connu par les vingtistes, ce serait chose possible'; Gauguin to Vincent van Gogh, ca. 28 January 1890, as cited in Douglas Cooper, *Paul Gauguin: 45 Lettres à Vincent, Théo et Jo van Gogh*, The Hague, 298–299.

29 'ardente, jeune, âpre, violente ... elle rencontre mêmes tendances, mêmes ennemis, mêmes espoirs, même but, mêmes obstacles' (E. Verhaeren, 'La lutte pour l'Art', *Le National Belge*, 10 February 1884).

30 Cited in Eugenia Herbert, *The Artist and Social Reform*, New Haven 1961, 190, note 38.

31 'Le catalogue est rouge, d'un rouge sang, d'un rouge de combat et de carnage....' ('Chronique de la Ville', *L'Etoile Belge*, 5 February 1888).

32 'L'heure est venu de tremper la plume dans de l'encre rouge' (E. Picard, 'L'Art et la Révolution', *L'Art moderne*, 18 July 1886, 225).

33 G. Lemmen, 'Walter Crane', *L'Art moderne* (1 March 1891), 67–69; (15 March 1891), 83–86.

34 For more on the Section d'Art, see Sura Levine, 'Politics and the Graphic Arts of the Belgian Avant-Garde', in: *Les XX and the Belgian Avant-Garde: Prints, Drawings, and Books ca. 1890*, Spencer Museum of Art, 1993, 55–74; and Paul Aron, *Les Ecrivains belges et le socialisme (1880–1913): L'Expérience de l'art social: d'Edmond Picard à Emile Verhaeren*, Brussels 1985.

35 'L'influence des XX a été tellement profonde et triomphante que demain, ils pourraient cesser de former un ensemble, sans grand dam, puisque leur but semble atteint.'

36 'Songez à l'heure de la mort!' ('Les XX', *Floréal*, 1 April 1893, 51).

37 'Les XX: Dix années de campagne, un peu de statistique', *L'Art moderne* (9 April 1893), 115–117.

38 'Pendant la période anarchique, les exposants se chamaillaient entre eux, tout en échangeant des coups avec le public; sous l'autocrate que je devins, ils ne se battaient plus que contre l'incompréhension des foules. C'était, somme toute, un progrès' (Maus, in *Revue de Belles Lettres*, 210). However, Maus could not manage all aspects of the new society on his own and enlisted the aid of Eugène Ysaÿe to supervise the concerts, Léon de Lantsheere for the lectures, and faithful Victor Bernier who, having served as treasurer of Les XX, would continue in that capacity at La Libre Esthétique. For the list of founding members, see 'La Libre Esthétique', *L'Art moderne*, (26 November 1893), 379–380, and additions in 'Petite Chronique', *ibid.* (3 December 1893), 390.

39 'les artistes sont ... peu faits pour s'associer et monter des "affaires"' (AAC, 6332, published in Chartrain-Hebbelinck, 'Les lettres de Van Rysselberghe à Octave Maus', 77).

40 'Pro Arte', *L'Art moderne* (16 July 1893), 225–226.

41 'expansion inévitable et épanouissement des Salonnets vingtistes' ('Le Salon', *L'Art moderne* 24 September 1893, 306).

42 'La Libre Esthétique', *L'Art moderne* (29 October 1893), 345–346.

43 Alan Crawford, *C. R. Ashbee: Architect, Designer & Romantic Socialist*, New Haven, Conn., 1985, 410.

44 It was partly the imported Liberty of London fabric and Japanese objects that could be found in Serrurier's shop in Liège that inspired Henry van de Velde, searching for his own modern style, to move towards the decorative arts. Van de Velde's high regard for Serrurier presumably led to his invitation to La Libre Esthétique. The key work on Serrurier is Jacques-Grégoire Watelet's 'Gustave Serrurier-Bovy: architect, décorateur, 1858–1910', *Mémoires: Académie Royale de Belgique* 14 (1975). A more popular version of this work was issued for the exhibition, 'Gustave Serrurier-Bovy, à l'Aube de l'Esthétique Industrielle', titled *Serrurier-Bovy: de L'Art Nouveau à l'Art Déco*, Centre Wallonie-Bruxelles de Paris, 1989.

45 AAC, 6918, 6 January 1894.

46 Florestan, 'La Journée à Bruxelles', *L'Express*, 20 February 1894.

47 See 'Petite Chronique', *L'Art moderne* (25 February 1894), 63; and (1 April 1894), 105.

48 Jean Ajalbert, 'Aimons les Belges', *L'Art moderne* (11 March 1894), 76.

49 'Il faut que la grande masse participe à la vie artistique' (as cited in Watelet, *Gustave Serrurier-Bovy, architecte et décorateur 1858–1910*, 36). He continued: 'Une habitation construite, meublée et décorée d'une manière logique et rationnelle ne peut abriter des habitants vivant d'une vie fausse, pleine de prétention et de luxe hypocrite...'.

50 'Les artistes, par leurs œuvres, doivent jouer le rôle des apôtres...' (E. Picard, 'La Socialisation de l'Art', *L'Art moderne*, 14 April 1895, 116).

51 This idea of beautification of one's environment was tried on an urban scale in 1894, when the organization, Art appliqué à la rue, sponsored local competition in order to beautify Brussels. The plan was to create artistic civic monuments such as public light fixtures, signs, fountains, stamps and even coins. The experiment was doomed to failure since it did not have the support of the progressive artists of the day to whom competitions was anathema.

52 He named his middle son, William, as director; see J. Block, 'La Maison d'Art: Edmond Picard's Asylum of Beauty', in: *Irréalisme et Art Moderne; Les voies de l'imaginaire dans l'art des XVIIIe, XIXe, et XXe siècles; Mélanges Philippe Roberts-Jones*, Brussels 1991, 145–162.

53 In its brief six-year existence, it featured works by Dalpayrat & Lesbros, Charpentier, Finch's ceramics from Virginal, glass of Tiffany, Daum, Gallé, Clément Massier, crystal from Val-Saint-Lambert. Some of the initial backers of the gallery were also patrons of La Libre Esthétique, including Maus, Georges and Edmond Picard, Pierre Olin, Verhaeren and Paul Otlet. In addition, the Maison d'art could count among its founders the former *vingtistes* Finch, Du Bois, Khnopff, Lemmen, Van de Velde and Van Rysselberghe.

54 'Pour la première fois, on exhibera les objets d'art dans leur atmosphère, sous le jour pour lequel ils ont été créés, avec leur destination spéciale. Au lieu d'un déballage de marchand ou d'une halle aux bibelots, une maison moderne, meublée, décorée et ornée comme il convient' ('Les Industries d'art', *L'Art moderne*, 21 October 1894, 332).

55 The Maison d'art was the setting for a buffet dinner commemorating the inauguration of the 1896 Salon. Among those in attendance were Eugène Carrière, Alexandre Charpentier, Camille Mauclair, Constantin Meunier (q.v.), Toulouse-Lautrec, Gustave Serrurier, Auguste Donnay (q.v.), Armand Rassenfosse, Charles Doudelet, Fernand Khnopff (q.v.), Emile Claus (q.v.) and Charles Van der Stappen. Eugène and Théo Ysaÿe played Fauré's violin sonata with the festivities lasting until 1.00 a.m!; see 'Petite Chronique', *L'Art moderne* (1 March 1896), 71.

56 'Concerts de la Libre Esthétique', *L'Art moderne* (19 April 1896), 125.

57 Serrurier sought diversity by including both Belgian and foreign artists. In addition, he prominently featured his fellow Liège artists, Rassenfosse, Berchmans and Donnay (q.v.). Maus served as advisor to Serrurier, who wished to borrow the wall fabric that was used at La Libre Esthétique exhibitions and even some of the mirrored armoires. Like its Brussels model, the group was backed by enlightened protector-members.

58 'Il faut hautement louer le groupe d'artistes et d'esthètes désintéressés qui ont si courageusement entrepris de secouer la torpeur de leurs concitoyens' ('L'Œuvre artistique', *L'Art moderne*, 12 May 1895, 145).

59 'Soyons Français!... N'est-ce pas le moment de jeter cet appel aux artistes au public, alors que, après quelques années de servitude à l'art anglais et à ses dérives, une invasion d'art belge est tentée...' (Charles Genuys, 'A propos de l'Art nouveau: Soyons Français!', *Revue des Arts Décoratifs* 17 [1897], 1).

60 'Le Salon de la Libre Esthétique', *L'Art moderne* (6 March 1898), 75.

61 'Théo van Rysselberghe', *L'Art moderne* (13 March 1898), 85–87.

62 '... il personnifie la lutte des peintres de la génération actuelle pour l'emancipation de la pensée et l'affirmation d'un art original, personnel, sincère...' ('La Libre Esthétique et le Musée de Bruxelles', *L'Art moderne*, 31 March 1901, 106).

63 'Au cycle d'initiation succéderait une série de démonstrations hautement éducatrices' (O. Maus, 'La Libre Esthétique', *L'Art moderne*, 1 March 1903, 68).

64 The essay also appeared as 'L'Art Impressionniste', *L'Art moderne* (21 February 1904), 57–60.

65 The column appeared on 28 February 1904.

66 'Divulguer aux artistes belges une expression d'art différente de celle qui leur est familière...' (O. Maus, 'Invitation', *Le Peuple*, 3 March 1904). Maus's letter is actually dated 29 February 1904.

67 'La prédominance de l'école française contemporaine est incontestable...' (G. Lemmen, 'Propos d'Actualité', *L'Art moderne*, 6 March 1904, 75).

68 The responses of the artists, among whom were Albert Baertsoen (q.v.), A.-J. Heymans, Fernand Khnopff (q.v.), Xavier Mellery (q.v.), Georges Morren (q.v.) and Armand Rassenfosse, were published under the rubric, 'Enquête sur l'Impressionnisme'. For the complete series see 13, 20, 27 March; 3, 10, 17, 24 April; 8 and 15 May, and 5 June 1904.

69 '... dénigrement de notre art national' (Jean Bar, 'Entre Artistes', *La Chronique*, 18 March 1904).

70 Annales parlementaires de Belgique: Sénat, Legislative Session of 1903–1904, 367–371. The debate continued also on 29 April, 3 and 4 May 1904.

71 Only Mme Anna de Weert, Mlle Jenny Montigny, Rodolphe de Saegher and Edmond Verstraeten were newcomers. Among the foreign exhibitors were Curt Herrmann and Emile Nolde (Germany); George Clausen and Roderic O'Connor (England); J.W. Morrice (Canada); the *vingtiste* Dario de Regoyos and Santiago Rusiñol (Spain); Childe Hassam and Alexander Charles Robinson (USA); F. Hart-Nibbrig and Toorop (Netherlands); Nicolas Tarkhoff (Russia).

72 'Aimez l'art, efforcez-vous de le servir et de le répandre' (Maus, in *Revue de Belles-Lettres*, 227).

'Vingtisme' and its opponents in Antwerp

JEAN F. BUYCK

The position accorded to James Ensor as the 'forerunner' of the twentieth century has tended to mean that his name, alone of all Belgian nineteenth-century artists, has received international attention. In recent years however, the revival of interest in the art of the *fin-de-siècle,* including Art Nouveau, Symbolism and Neo-Impressionism, has focused attention on art centres which lay beyond those main European cultural capitals where dominant stylistic movements were shaped. Among them, Brussels, with the art association Les XX has received special attention (see Block). A generation of young American scholars has contributed to its international renown as a major centre of the avant-garde through both publications and exhibitions. It was almost inevitable that Antwerp, as an art centre, from early on, positioned as the 'rival' of Brussels, be accorded a secondary status to the 'progressive' capital. By comparison, it was deemed to have been its more conservative, retrograde, provincial counterpart. Compared with the wealth of innovative accomplishments in Brussels, Antwerp had but little to offer. To use a military metaphor: the Brussels 'avant-garde' was confronted with the 'bastion' of the reactionary Metropole. I intend to give a survey of how the conflict between 'tradition and innovation' took shape in the 'City on the Scheldt'.[1]

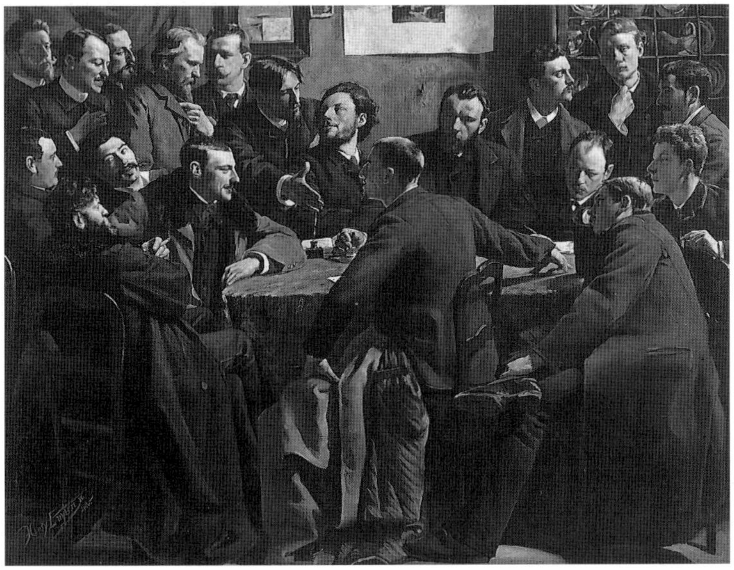

fig. 39 HENDRIK LUYTEN, Meeting of the Art Circle 'Als Ik Kan' in 1885, 1886, Koninklijk Museum voor Schone Kunsten, Antwerp

In 1886, Hendrik Luyten (1859–1945) gathered together some of his young, fellow artists in the monumental group portrait, *Meeting of the Art Circle 'Als Ik Kan' in 1885*[2] [fig. 39], whose composition is somewhat reminiscent of the seventeenth-century militia company paintings by Frans Hals in its representation of the more than life-sized full-length figures. The art circle was founded on 25 October 1883 by some nine students of Charles Verlat (1824–1890), at that time professor in charge of the painting class at the Antwerp Academy of Fine Arts. The name of the group was taken from Jan van Eyck's device 'As I may', demonstrating that, in part, the young artists were eager to pay tribute to the glorious tradition of Flemish painting. By so doing, they certainly did not position themselves as revolutionaries, but rather as proud defenders of the values that the Antwerp School of Gustaaf Wappers (1803–1874), Nicaise de Keyser (1813–1887) and Henri Leys (1815–1869) was assumed to have preserved in direct line of succession from the illustrious 'Flemish School' of

Rubens. As was the case with the Brussels group, Les XX, founded within the same month,[3] the basic purpose was the formation of a collective in order to offer its members an alternative venue for exhibitions outside of the official Triennal Salons.

Unlike the Brussels XX, Als Ik Kan was a relatively homogeneous association as regards the age and social origin of its members. They were all born around 1860 and were in their early or mid-twenties at the time they joined the group. With the exception of Hendrik Luyten, a Dutchman born in Roermond, they all originated from places in the vicinity of Antwerp[4] and none had received an artistic education outside Antwerp. By contrast, among the members of Les XX, there were some artists of an older generation like Guillaume Vogels (q.v.), or slightly older, like Theodoor Verstraete (q.v.), while some of the younger artists already had some experience abroad at the time they joined the group: Fernand Khnopff (q.v.) had studied in Paris in 1879–1880 and Théo van Rysselberghe (q.v.) had travelled in Spain and Morocco in 1882–1883 as beneficiary of a grant. In Antwerp, only Henry van de Velde (q.v.) would soon be travelling to Paris (1884–1885) to study with Carolus Duran; this journey, however, only occurred after he joined the group.[5] Apart from this, none of the other members have been considered sufficiently successful to merit even an honorable mention in the History of Art, neither on an international nor on a national level. At best, they were celebrated as local heroes, 'des gloires de clocher', as was reiterated on the pages of the Brussels avant-garde art magazine, *L'Art moderne*. To be sure, although Henry van de Velde was to emerge as a fully fledged modernist from the ranks of Als Ik Kan, he did so by joining the Brussels *vingtistes*. Aside from this 'ultra' – as Van de Velde was labelled in pro-Flemish periodicals due to his application of Seurat's pointillism – several other members of Als Ik Kan were contemporaneously abandoning the 'poncifs' of the local tradition. Some of them did not remain untouched by international currents that led them to abandon academic practices without even attempting a more radical break with tradition as was demanded by the avant-garde. *Plein-airism* and a local, modified form of Impressionism, would mark the approach of many Antwerp painters until far into the twentieth century. Such was the case of Richard Baseleer (1867–1931), a painter with a love for the waters of the River Scheldt in its changing moods, which he rendered in delicate pastel tones. There were also, of course, some adherents of a popular Naturalism, painters of scenes from everyday life in a Realist vein, though sometimes touched by Impressionist moods and brighter colours. Artists such as Louis van Engelen (1856–1940) [fig. 40] or Edgard Farasyn (1858–1938) [fig. 41] treated themes from the life of the city without however transgressing the stylistic standards of a tempered modernism. How difficult it was for these moderately innovative artists to be accepted by the Antwerp public, can be demonstrated by the case of Charles Mertens (q.v.); he was initially acclaimed for his remarkable skills in painting traditional genre scenes, but as soon as he made the representation of light a dominant concern, the conservative public turned against him.[6]

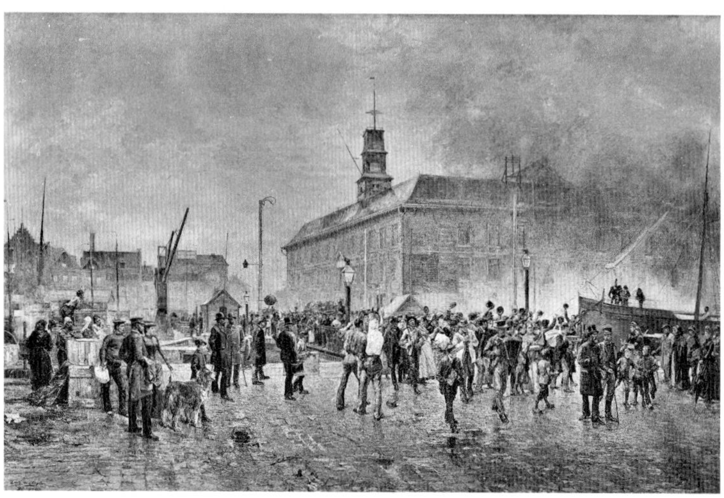

fig. 40 LOUIS VAN ENGELEN, Belgian Emigrants, 1890, Koninklijk Museum voor Schone Kunsten, Antwerp

From early on in the last quarter of the nineteenth century, critical and historical discussions of the current situation reigning in the art world of Antwerp tended to become shaped by a desire to argue a cause rather than by a concern to provide a balanced assessment of actual developments or innovations. Thus, for example, as the question of the 'old-fashioned School of Antwerp' was raised and discussed, most notably by *L'Art moderne*,[7] the Brussels periodical edited by Octave Maus and Edmond Picard, there was a tendency to weigh all Antwerp art against the innovative achievements of *L'Art moderne*'s main protagonist, Les XX. In its columns, Antwerp artists were marginalized or, worse still, dismissed without consideration. And it is this attitude which has tended to colour all subsequent accounts of the art scene in that city.

At the beginning of the 1880's, *L'Art moderne* was not unfavourably disposed towards Antwerp. The merit of a local tradition preserving the heritage of the past while keeping up the standard of a solid painting technique, was fully recognized and appreciated. At the Brussels Salon of 1881 there was even an appraisal of Antwerp as a place where constructive organizational changes in the visual arts were being initiated.[8] One can hardly get a more succinct idea of the differences that existed around 1900 between the progressive circles of the capital and the conservative milieu of the provincial centre, than by comparing *L'Art moderne* with the Antwerp magazine, *De Vlaamsche Kunst* (Flemish Art). The latter was founded in 1855 to propagate Romantic nationalism as the style best suited to the defence of the Flemish spirit in Belgian culture, a central element in reinforcing a sense of conservatism. One of the principal themes running through its articles was the rejection of French ideas, considered to be a pernicious influence upon the national character. In the end, this defensive attitude closed the door on all threatening innovations from the South. Pride for the past, triumphalism in regard to the 'Glory of the Flemish School of Painting from Van Eyck to Rubens', and, finally, the conviction that true pictorial genius had been revived in the art of Wappers and De Keyser, were all mobilized to arouse native self-consciousness, while at the same time reinforcing a conservatism which was far stronger than elsewhere in Belgium. In the 1880s and 1890s, conservatism dominated the Antwerp press. If the various types of Realism appeared to be increasingly accepted as as valid style, their more 'excessive' manifestations were viewed with the greatest of reserves. The concept of 'realism' was acceptable only to the point that it could be reconciled with the principles of a national style. Realism, it was argued, could be an ahistorical quality, an intrinsic element within the national character, innate within the artists who expressed a natural disposition for an 'authentic experience of reality', rather than as a gesture of adherence to a topical movement. If idealistic Romanticism initially rebuffed Realism for its trivial aspects, a more positive attitude slowly developed. In an article of 1888 on 'Realism and Impressionism', P. Buschmann, editor of *De Vlaamsche School*, declared appreciation for Realism as a protest against academic rigour and idealistic exaggeration, but criticized Impressionism for its blank rendering of nature. As a

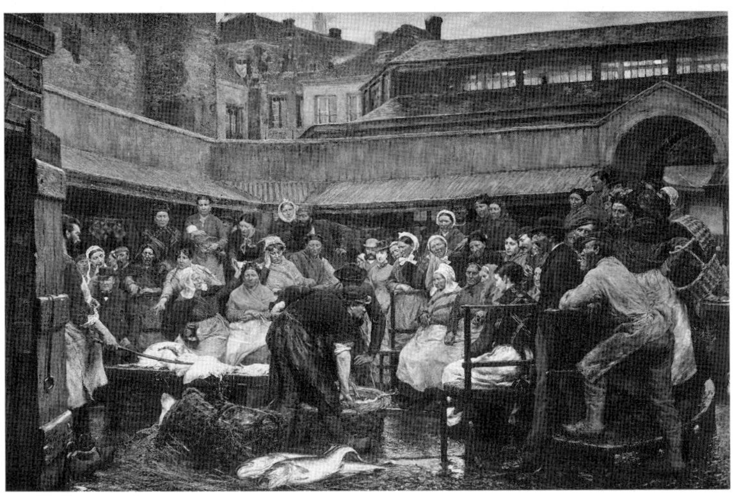

fig. 41 EDGARD FARASYN, The Old Fish Market in Antwerp, 1882, Koninklijk Museum voor Schone Kunsten, Antwerp

(typically conservative) preacher of the *juste milieu*, he considered 'truth' located 'in between all those extreme theories', claiming that artists should be occupied with adopting a middle course, 'rendering the character of nature as well as preserving its finer aspects, while taking good care of the importance of technical proficiency and beauty. Why should they pick dreadful characters and turn their debased scenes into a course of anthropology?'[9] Significantly, the author opposes the identification of specific 'schools', thus dissociating himself from the modernist movements of his time. A few years later, he dealt extensively with 'Modernism in painting', once again claiming to remain sceptical about naturalism, luminism and pointillism: 'there is no *vingtist* art, no *modernist* art, no *thirteen's* art, no *Circle's* art, but simply *art*, good or bad art, depending on the talent of the artist. No wonder that in the end he asks himself: "What is the aim of the modernists, or don't they have any?" Maybe modernism in painting is the same as nihilism in politics?'[10] This critic's position may explain why modernist art was so slow to develop and be accepted in Antwerp. We can assume that such opinions as expressed by the leading Antwerp art magazine, were a fair reflection of the attitudes of the local public concerning modernist art.

Antwerp's *De Vlaamsche School* did not rate the most important modernist movement in Brussels, namely Les XX. In 1888 Domien Sleeckx mentioned the 5th Salon des XX at which Belgian artists such as Finch (q.v.) and Van Rysselberghe had presented their new essays in Seurat's Neo-Impressionism, as being 'an exposure of the strangest digressions'; he regretted the waste of time involved in probably copying some sixth-rate French artist in order to master the latter's unfortunate 'vibrations'.[11] J. M. Brans repeated this sentiment later in the same publication when he castigated 'the dogmatic, only true church of the new… with its complete lack of technical skill, especially when they use totally non-existent colours… this downright nonsense stemming straight from France, that in the end results in a servile mimicry.'[12] The author descended to a rather worrying level when one year later his criticism degenerated into downright scolding.[13] The first appreciative note about Les XX in *De Vlaamsche School* was written by August Vermeylen in his review of their 8th Salon in 1891. With much greater sensitivity the critic of the *Van Nu en Straks* movement struck a polemical note when fustigating 'the inimical stupidity of the crowd, the sniggering of the crippled and the impotent, the barking of the newspaper yappers'.[14] Of course, disapproval of Les XX was not the exclusive domain of the nationalistic *De Vlaamsche School*. Rather it was also pursued by generally held conservative and provincial attitudes, pronounced equally by the francophone press.[15] If *De Vlaamsche School* provided a sure touchstone of the attitudes of a predominantly conservative public in Antwerp towards innovation, we should keep in mind that there were also other reactionary agents at work which were also instrumental in maintaining the *status quo*.

First, there was the Academy of Fine Arts which was a prime force in sustaining the provincial, accepted view on modernity and innovation. During the last two decades of the nineteenth century, it was subject to extensive discussions concerning the restructuring of the educational curriculum. These led to the establishment of the Higher Institute of Fine Arts in 1885. There were also considerable debates over the Government's policies towards the appointment of the director of the institution. That the Academy could be presented as a 'bastion' of conservatism can be exemplified by the incident of Vincent van Gogh's short sojourn there. By the end of 1885 Van Gogh arrived from Nuenen (Netherlands), having completed his *Potato Eaters* (Vincent van Gogh Museum, Amsterdam), and inscribed at the Antwerp Academy. His teacher relegated him to a lower degree class for lack of drawing skills![16]

The role of both contemporary and subsequent commentators on the art of Antwerp at the end of the nineteenth century has been critical in reinforcing the entrenched view of Brussels as avant-garde and Antwerp as retardataire. Take, for example, the case of Henri de Braekeleer, whose genius lay largely unrecognized by his Antwerp critics, but who was celebrated as an underestimated outsider, a victim of his infamous colleagues, by such collectors in Brussels as Henri van Cutsem and Gustave Coûteaux or by the critics of *L'Art moderne* and the members of Les XX.[17] Such support, at the same time, could relegate most other Antwerp artists to purgatory or worse, with the exceptions of Jan Stobbaerts (1838–1914) or Adrien-Joseph Heymans (1834–1921), both of whom left Antwerp for Brussels, where they subsequently made their reputations. Yet another case of bias on the part of critics can be seen in the relative treatments given to Charles Verlat (1824–1890) and Jean Portaels (1818–1895). They were directors of the Academy of Fine Arts in Antwerp and Brussels respectively but, whereas Jean Portaels, himself an orientalist painter,[18] was presented as quite a liberal-minded educator who greatly stimulated his young students (somewhat the role Gustave Moreau played in Paris with regard to his pupils),[19] Verlat was pictured as the prototype of the reactionary artist. This view is too simplistic. Max Rooses, for example, estimated his position rather differently, praising him as 'generous and charitable without limits', as a man with a sharp mind, sarcastic and obstinate.[20] Verlat was certainly a dominant personality in the Antwerp of the 1880s, in part due to his involvement with the educational reforms of the Academy, but also as a guide for the younger artists who founded Als Ik Kan;[21] however, he also published *Causerie artistique* (1883), which contained a strong defence of the Flemish tradition in painting, a view that was certainly not favourably received by modernist-minded artists. While in this book Verlat blamed the younger artists for imitating French art, he explicitly spoke in defence of absolute artistic freedom with regard to the organization of non-official exhibitions. But this liberal-mindedness was not sufficient to satisfy the Brussels cohorts. *L'Art moderne*, for example, declared (without naming him) that: 'We don't want to mention the cases where we've seen an academy or a conservatory stop producing anything valuable from the unholy moment on when local interests or political support have appointed some mediocre artist without merit or notoriety or authority.[22] And on Verlat's death Henry van de Velde published these terrible words: 'The painter Verlat died of the disease he was teaching as the head of that hospital.'[23]

Despite such harsh judgements, Verlat ran a studio which nurtured a kind of regional 'Secessionism'. As in the main art centres of Europe, younger artists assembled to oppose the system of the official salons that offered few opportunities to the newcomers.[24] The pragmatic aim of gaining their place 'in the sun' had priority over artistic principles, a point which was duly observed by contemporary critics in respect of both Als Ik Kan

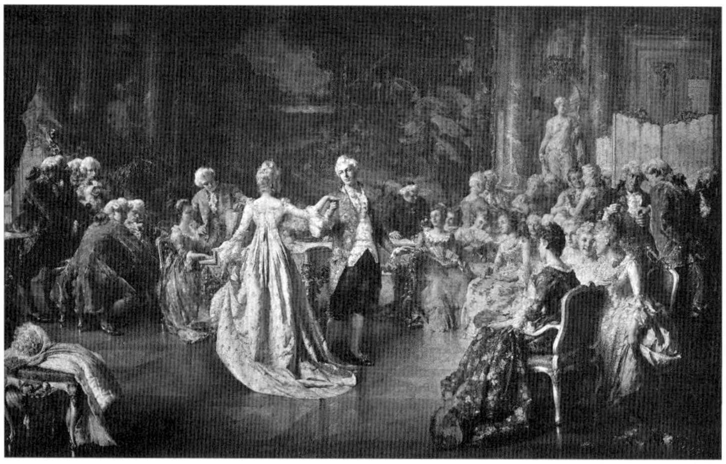

fig. 42 JAN WILLEM ROSIER, The Menuet, 1891, Koninklijk Museum voor Schone Kunsten, Antwerp

and Les XX. As regards its artistic views, Als Ik Kan was a catholic association. Extreme conservatives, such as Jan Willem Rosier (1858–1931), painter of neo-rococo genre scenes [fig. 42], and a modernist like Henry van de Velde made strange company, and the group essentially lacked the coherence necessary to establish and prosecute an innovative programme. Later on, some of its members were to figure in similar groups that had greater affinities with the innovative intentions of Brussels' Les XX, for example, L'Art Indépendant, in 1887, and L'Association pour l'Art, in 1892.

In their fight against (or maybe rather their rivalry with) the official salons, the young artists of Antwerp had no single, clearly defined goal. During the 1880s, or even the 1890s, the triennial exhibitions still were more prestigious in Antwerp than in Brussels or Ghent. When Antwerp organized its Triennial of 1882, there seems to have been a desire to present a complement to the Brussels 'Historical Exhibition' of 1880, where Antwerp artists had been in a minority within the Belgian section. 'Correcting' that 'national reunion', Antwerp offered a grandiose show of some 940 participants exhibiting some 1600 works, including 175 Antwerp-based artists as if to demonstrate their predominance. The 1882 Salon was equally prestigious through the presence of important numbers of foreign artists, Germans (mainly members of the 'Düsseldorfer Schule' like A. Achenbach, E. Bendemann, C. Jungheim and F. Kaulbach), but there were also French and Dutch. Aside from Fantin-Latour, the presence of Manet was certainly noteworthy, as he presented his famous painting *Un Bar aux Folies-Bergère* (Courtauld Institute Galleries, London).[25] Even more remarkable was the participation at the Salon of a number of Brussels artists who would, somewhat later, participate in Les XX: Anna Boch, James Ensor, Willy Finch, Léon Fréderic (q.v.), Théo Hannon, Fernand Khnopff, Xavier Mellery (q.v.), Constantin Meunier (q.v.), Pericles Pantazis (1849–1884), Théo van Rysselberghe, Guillaume van Strydonck (q.v.), Guillaume Vogels (q.v.) and Rodolphe Wytsman (1860–1927). *L'Art moderne* reacted with condescension: 'Antwerp remains ... faithful to the great memory and the imperishable glory of Rubens. It feels obliged to stay worthy of that past history and glorifies itself as the artistic Metropolis. It tries to legitimate that pretence through the presence of a considerable number of artists and also through the self-indulgence of its inhabitants who consider themselves to be more knowledgeable in art matters than the majority of our little nation.'[26] Then follows a long diatribe about the insignificance of the majority of participants at the Salon, treated as 'an artistic Babylon because of the anarchy of its failed artists as was cruelly formulated by Daudet'.[27]

Three years later the Antwerp World Fair took place, where not only 'all civilized peoples of the earth expose the rich products of their industry',[28] but where once again the opportunity was seized by a grandiose concentration of power with no less than 1526 participants who showed 2750 works. Apart from its international scope, with delegations of various foreign countries, this manifestation is interesting because it caused a storm of protest against the exclusions imposed by the members of the jury. A 'salon libre' (free

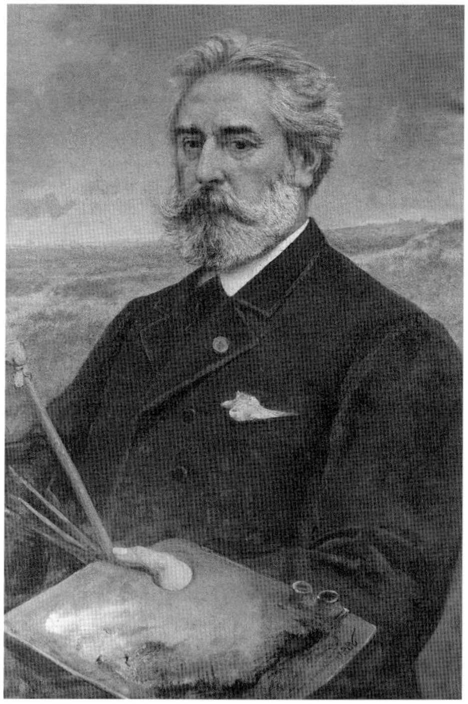

fig. 43 CHARLES VERLAT, Portrait of the Landscape Painter François Lamorinière, 1886, Koninklijk Museum voor Schone Kunsten, Antwerp

salon) was organized to offer an alternative to the official event. This 'salon des refusés' was stigmatized by *L'Art moderne* as 'the extension of some known showrooms of art dealers eager to benefit from the presence of foreigners by catching them in their traps.'[29] On this and other occasions we may notice a common criticism of the 'Antwerp School' as being polluted by commercial interests. Despite the fact that it was praised for its attachment to values of the past, Antwerp was consistently lambasted for its mercantilism. Indeed, commercial priorities as the cause for the degeneration of art was an accusation often found in the articles of *L'Art moderne*.[30] What is most important to notice about the exhibition of 1885, was the resolute stance that the hard-line conservatives were taking about this time, as if the appearance of the younger artists at the 1882 Salon and their newly formed associations, Als Ik Kan and Les XX in its aftermath, forced them to reaffirm their position. Conservatives almost simultaneously pledged their allegiance to the values of tradition. Not only elderly artists like Verlat or François Lamorinière [fig. 43] (1828–1911) – both members of the exhibition jury – declared their adherence to the past, but also an artist of the younger generation like Piet Verhaert (1852–1908) professed his loyalty to 'art and tradition'. Like the sculptor Jef Lambeaux and the painters Frans Simons (1855–1919) and Theodoor Verstraete, Verhaert belonged to the group of Antwerp artists who were co-founders of Les XX, though he resigned early in 1884 after having been heavily attacked in the press. The same happened to his companions, whose tradition-bound work did not correspond with the artistic intentions of the innovators.[31]

During the years following the World Fair of 1885, the conflict between conservatives and modernists intensified. While the old guard seemed to gather its forces at the Salon, the establishment of the Higher Institute of Art was also considered a reinforcement of a traditionalist stance. Soon thereafter, in 1887, some of the younger artists tried once again to make a stand against the establishment. The founding of the association L'Art Indépendant was clearly intended to emulate Les XX. In 1886 Henry van de Velde, after returning from Paris in 1885, contacted Les XX's secretary, Octave Maus, through the mediation of his friend Heymans, with whom he had spent some time, together with Jacob Rosseels (1828–1912) and Florent Crabeels (1829–1896), in Wechelderzande.[32] Not surprisingly, the organization of the first (and only) Salon de L'Art Indépendant, which took place in March–April 1887, was copied from Les XX. Besides the members themselves, other artists were invited, mostly recruited from the ranks of L'Essor and Les XX.[33] The catalogue introduction was written by the prominent critic Camille Lemonnier, whose noncommittal rhetoric stated (in a footnote), that the group '[of L'Art Indépendant] does not aspire to enlarging the battlefield while bringing more radical solutions, it only decentralizes in order to make more radiant the truth that Les XX had previously formulated. Its ambition lies in the hope of bringing fraternal support to their predecessor, their equals in valour, their friends in their apostolic mission.'[34] One can hardly think of a more elegant formulation for locating the relationship between Brussels and Antwerp. *L'Art moderne* reinforces the idea when stating: 'Their only claim is to play – with a charming modesty – their role as propagators and apostles, for in Antwerp, stronghold of academic art, the battle is harder and victory more difficult to achieve than

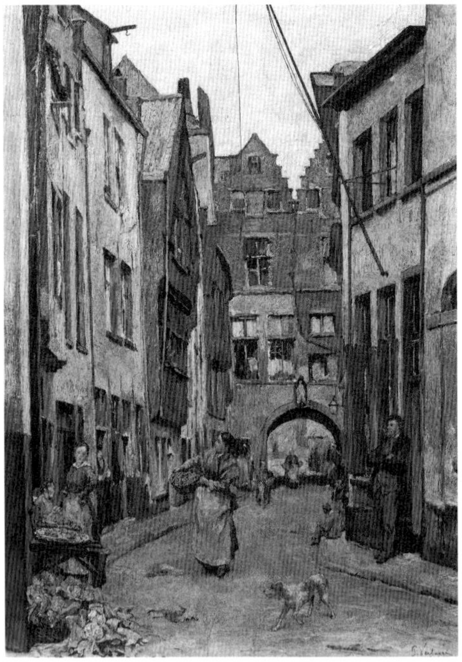

fig. 44 PIET VERHAERT, Palingbrugstraat, Antwerp, 1880, Koninklijk Museum voor Schone Kunsten, Antwerp

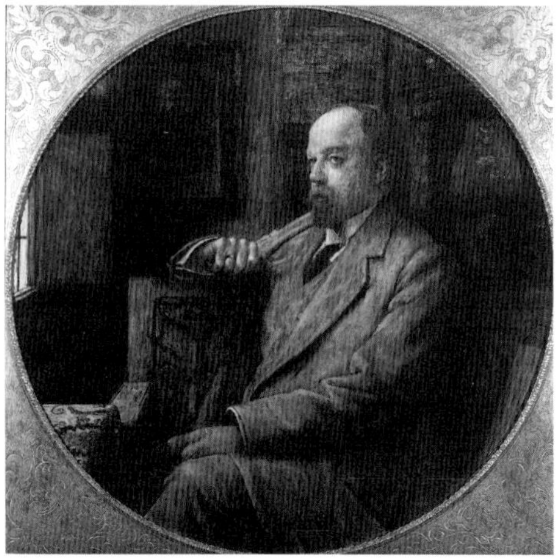

fig. 45 CHARLES MERTENS, Portrait of François Franck, Koninklijk Museum voor Schone Kunsten, Antwerp

in Brussels.'[35] Although there were, of course, some accusations of 'smudgy art', the Antwerp press was not exclusively critical; the local newspaper *Het Handelsblad* (Journal of Commerce) assumed that Antwerp 'no longer allowed itself to be taken in by Brussels' bragging.'[36]

The 'old wigs' (as conservatives were named) once again made themselves felt at the Antwerp Salon of 1888. The sectarianism of the hanging committee caused Jan Stobbaerts – who left Antwerp for Brussels in 1886 – to protest against the discrimination against himself and his Brussels colleagues.[37] As in 1885 – though with less grandeur than at the World Fair – local authorities wanted to celebrate the centennial of the Society for the Encouragement of the Fine Arts. A considerable number of Belgian artists (388) was invited, together with an impressive number of foreigners, notably Austrians, Italians, Swedish, Norwegians, Hungarians, but most of all Germans (171), French (151) and Dutchmen (101). It goes without saying that the 'Schools' of Düsseldorf and Munich were mainly present, though it was also noticeable that France had sent its 'peintres pompiers', as if calling upon their support for the provincial 'old guard' in order to sustain the pressure on the aggressive innovators. Those participating included Jules Breton, William Bouguereau, Alexandre Cabanel, Jean-Louis Gérôme, Georges Rochegrosse and Alfred Roll.[38] Some more 'progressive' artists were also shown, such as Fantin-Latour, Lovis Corinth and, for the Hague School, J. Israëls, A. Mauve, W. Mesdag and W. Roelofs. For *L'Art moderne,* the whole Salon was of a profound insignificance, with the foreigners in particular being castigated as 'the Teutonic horrors paired with the French banalities.'[39]

In 1890 *L'Art moderne* tolled the funeral bell of the Brussels Salon.[40] More attention was now being paid by the public to the Salons of Les XX or, even more so after 1894, to those of La Libre Esthétique which implemented a less combative programme. One has the impression that the groups of artists and exhibiting bodies founded around 1900 (such as Vie et Lumière, in 1904) were generally much less aggressive.

In the city on the River Scheldt the agony of the official Salon dragged on. In 1891 the spectacle is somewhat colourless, notwithstanding a special tribute paid to the deceased Verlat. *L'Art moderne*'s critical stance over the vicissitudes of the hanging committee seemed to be somewhat exaggerated. The journal's characterization of the Salon as 'The Very Holy Temple of the Very Saintly Nullity', where 'a horrifying exposure of all varieties of pictorial diseases' took place, can only provoke a vague smile.[41] In 1894 Antwerp repeated the experience of a World Fair with – significantly – a memorable evocation of 'Old Antwerp'. Around 1900 modernist organizational practices had subverted the official Salon and its end was considered to be imminent. In Antwerp the new association Kunst van Heden (Art now), founded in 1905, was gradually to gain dominance as the presenter of 'living art'. On the other hand, exhibitions tended increasingly to present 'art in retrospect',[42] a formula with a great future since the artistic heritage was continuously filtered according to criteria which reflected the changes of taste.

In the mean time, various attempts to further the progress of innovative art had been initiated at the beginning of the 1890s. After the short-lived group of L'Art Indépendant, the circle of the XIII was founded in 1891. In *De Vlaamsche School,* the critic Pol de Mont

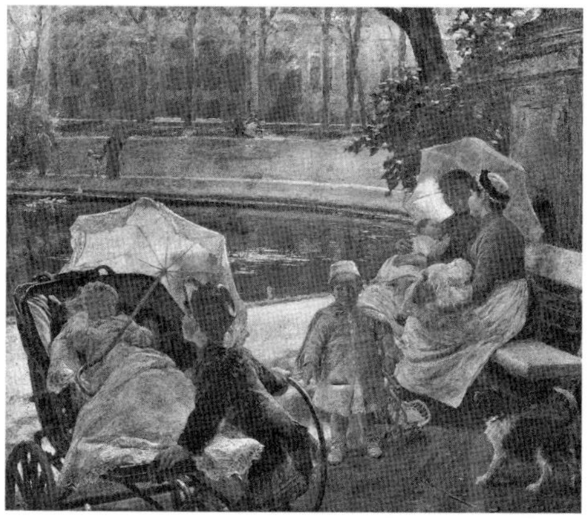

fig. 46 EDGARD FARASYN, In the Park, Groeningemuseum, Bruges

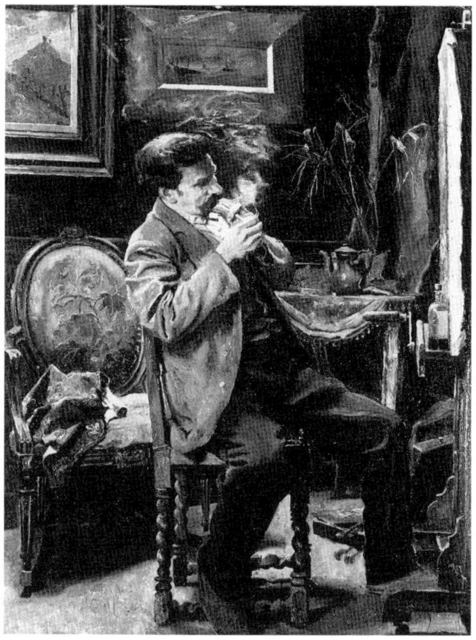

fig. 47 HENRI DE SMETH, The Smoker, Musée des Beaux-Arts, Tournai

noticed that there were actually but twelve members: Emile Claus, Edward de Jans (1855–1919), Henri de Smeth (1865–1940) [fig. 47], Edgard Farasyn (1858–1938) [fig. 46], Frans Hens (q.v.), Romain Looymans (1864–1914), Hendrik Luyten (1859–1945), Charles Mertens [fig. 45] (q.v.), Léon van Aken (1857–1904), Louis van Engelen, Piet Verhaert [fig. 44] and Theodoor Verstraete (q.v.).[43] In the following years, the manifestations of the newly-founded group were met with tolerance and even acclaim. Critics observed that realism was the dominant style of the newcomers and they also mentioned with great precision how different they were from the Brussels XX. There is no doubt that the tenor of their art was far from being strictly 'avant-garde'.[44] Strictly local by vocation, its adherents did not precisely belong to the 'younger generation'. The participants in its exhibitions were successors to Als Ik Kan, without sharing the progressive intentions of the *vingtistes*. Henry van de Velde was merciless in his condemnation. He refused to acknowledge them as inheritors of the legacy of L'Art Indépendant, since they were mere representatives of 'le juste milieu': 'The child will grow as a weakling, but nevertheless will last. The Good Fairy of the "Juste Milieu" will take care of this meagre person, painstakingly supported by dissembling members, who mutually praise each other – with what right! – as being "indépendants"!'[45]

The foundation of L'Association pour l'Art in 1892, brought to Antwerp a short-lived but intense breakthrough of *Vingtisme*. Max Elskamp and Henry van de Velde were once again the driving forces,[46] though the participation of George Morren – he was occupied in Paris with the selection of the foreign guests – should not be underestimated. They organized two Salons (1892 and 1893) with a resolute modernist and international tenor, whereby Neo-Impressionism and Symbolism were favoured, but attention was also given to the decorative arts. As before, their effort was not appreciated by the local critics and public. Not only a chauvinistic rejection of foreign elements, but also the limitations of a provincial milieu and its cultural nationalism were responsible for this conservative reaction.

At the turn of the century signs of change were noticeable in the city. The initiative of some eminent art lovers and artists created more favourable conditions for the development of a progressive cultural climate, a power centre that could stimulate innovative ambitions. Mainly through the efforts of the young interior decorator François Franck and his brother Louis Franck, who was a lawyer, leading figures from different social backgrounds – commercial, political, intellectual and artistic – came together in a fertile alliance. The painters Charles Mertens and Richard Baseleer, the authors Emmanuel de Bom, Lode Baekelmans and Jef van Overloop, the composer Lodewijk Mortelmans, the publisher-journalist Victor Resseler met with the brothers Franck in a lively circle, open to a wide range of philosophical or ideological viewpoints, Socialist, Liberal, anarchistic or militantly nationalistic (i.e. pro-Flemish), and also to all kinds of people, middle class as well as labourers, dockers and craftsmen. In the hospice Lantschot they formed the group of De Kapel (The Chapel), where exhibitions took place (Evert Larock [q.v.], Richard Baseleer), concerts (César Franck, Robert Schumann, or Russian composers) and lectures by prominent Belgians such as Emile Vandervelde, Edmond Picard, Julius Mac Leod, August Vermeylen, or writers such as Stijn Streuvels, Prosper van Langendonck, Emile Verhaeren, Georges Eekhoud, Camille Lemonnier or Frederik van Eeden. In this context two new initiatives were taken that would become of great significance for the artistic future of Antwerp. In 1903 the New Concert Society was founded by François Franck. In 1905 Kunst van Heden (Art Now) was founded in order to promulgate the plastic arts. This association would dominate artistic life in the city until the Second World War through the organization of an energetic series of exhibitions. However influential its activities may have been, it has to be noted that conservative tendencies were soon to take hold of the prestigious association. In the aftermath of World War I, only a short intermezzo of radical avant-garde art occurred in Antwerp, with the poet and critic Paul van Ostaijen, and the magazine *Het Overzicht* (The Survey), soon to be pushed to one side by the reactionary tendencies that washed over Europe and turned the tide on Antwerp's 'art now'.[47]

1 The following presents an abridged adaptation of my introduction to *Antwerp 1900*, Koninklijk Museum voor Schone Kunsten, Antwerp 1985 (exhibition catalogue by J. F. Buyck, D. Cardyn and H. Todts).

2 Oil on canvas, 190 x 246 cm. Signed and dated: *H. Luyten 86 Antw.*. Purchased at the Triennial Exhibition in 1894, Koninklijk Museum voor Schone Kunsten, Antwerp, inv. no. 1275.

3 The foundation of Les XX was announced in *L'Art moderne* on 7 October 1883. On 28 October, 13 *vingtistes* met to sign the founding charter (see Brussels 1993, 19).

4 Charles Mertens was born in Calverley, England, but he did not belong to the founding members.

5 Van de Velde was one of the founding members of Als Ik Kan on 25 October 1883, but withdrew on 29 December 1886. He did not mention his membership of the association in his memoirs.

6 J. F. Buyck, Introduction to *Als Ik Kan*, Koninklijk Museum voor Schone Kunsten, Antwerp 1975.

7 This magazine was published from 1881 and propagated Social Realism in art, following the ideas of Edmond Picard, a radical liberal who joined the Parti Ouvrier. After 1886 the new tendencies of Neo-Impressionism and Symbolism were adopted. Most unsigned leading articles of the bimensual magazine in the early period were written by Picard. Henry van de Velde was the Antwerp correspondent and editor from 1890 to 1894 (L. Tibbe, 'Art Nouveau en Socialisme. Henry Van de Velde en de Parti Ouvrier Belge' [Kunsthistorische Schriften 5], Amsterdam 1981; P. Aron, *Les écrivains belges et le socialisme (1880–1913). L'expérience de l'art social: d'Edmond Picard à Emile Verhaeren*, Brussels 1985).

8 *L'Art moderne* (21 August 1881), 195.

9 *De Vlaamsche School* (1888), 161–164.

10 *Ibid.* (1892), 91–99.

11 *Ibid.* (1888), 32–33.

12 *Ibid.*, 40–42.

13 *Ibid.* (1889), 48–50.

14 *Ibid.* (1891), 85–86. Concerning the relation of the magazine *Van Nu en Straks* to the plastic arts, see: *Van Nu en Straks. Belle Epoque in Vlaanderen*, St. Pietersabdij, Ghent 1983, 19–25.

15 S. M. Canning, *A History and Critical Review of the Salons of 'Les Vingt': 1884–1893*, Ph. D. diss. Pennsylvania State University, 1980.

16 Reading Dr Mark Edo Tralbaut's study of Van Gogh's brief Antwerp period (February 1886 he left for Paris), one cannot but question the trustworthiness of his – mainly oral – sources concerning the incident (M. E. Tralbaut, *Vincent Van Gogh, Antwerpsche periode*, Amsterdam 1948). The same author attributed likewise the role of a martyr of the Antwerp art establishment to Henri de Braekeleer ('De Braekeleeriana', XVII and XVIII, *Antwerpen* 16:4 (1970) and 17:1 (1971).

17 See *F. Lamorinière 1828–1911*, Koninklijk Museum voor Schone Kunsten, Antwerp 1974 ('Kroniek van F.L.', sub 1855), and *Gustaf Wappers en zijn School*, Koninklijk Museum voor Schone Kunsten, Antwerp 1976, 16ff (catalogue by J.F. Buyck). Also: R. Hoozee, 'Barbizon en België', in: *De School van Barbizon. Franse meesters van de 19de eeuw*, Museum voor Schone Kunsten, Gent 1885, 114ff); *Henri De Braekeleer 1840–1888*, Koninklijk Museum voor Schone Kunsten, Antwerp 1988.

18 In 1847–1850 Portaels was director of the Ghent Academy of Fine Arts, from 1858 he led a free workshop before becoming a teacher in 1863–1865, then (1874) director of the Brussels Academy.

19 See Ph. Roberts-Jones, *Van Realisme tot Surrealisme*, Brussels 1969, 57.

20 *De Vlaamsche School*, 1890, 169–171.

21 See J. F. Buyck, Introduction in *Als Ik Kan*, Koninklijk Museum voor Schone Kunsten, Antwerp 1975.

22 'Nous ne voulons pas citer ici les cas où l'on a vu une académie ou un conservatoire ne plus rien produire à partir du jour néfaste où des intérêts de clocher ou des appuis officiels ont mis à sa tête un artiste médiocre, sans portée, sans notoriété de bon aloi et sans autorité' ('Les Académies de province', *L'Art moderne*, 26 December 1886, 409–410).

23 'A la tête de cette clinique, le peintre Verlat est mort de la maladie qu'il y enseignait' (*L'Art moderne*, 2 November 1890, 348–349).

24 P. Paret, *The Berlin Secession. Modernism and its enemies in imperial Germany*, 1980.

25 Painted in 1881–1882. The Salon catalogue (Flemish edition) mentions the painting with the title 'Een boer ['a peasant'!] in de Folies Bergères [sic]' (no. 903). Henri de Braekeleer is supposed to have seen the painting at that Salon. See *Album gewijd aan Henri De Braekeleer en zijn werk*, Koninklijk Museum voor Schone Kunsten, Antwerp 1956, 19.

26 'Anvers reste… fidèle aux grands souvenirs et à l'impérissable éclat que lui a donnés la gloire de Rubens. Elle se croit obligée à rester digne d'un tel passé et elle s'arroge volontiers le titre de métropole artistique. Ce n'est pas seulement par un groupe considérable d'artistes

qu'elle cherche à légitimer cette prétention, mais encore par les préoccupations de ses habitants dont la plupart se croient, assez complaisamment, mieux doués au point de vue du goût que le surplus de notre petite nation ...' (*L'Art moderne* [1882], 283–285, 289–291; 297–300).

27 '... la Babel artistique par cette anarchie où pullulent ce que Daudet a cruellement nommé les ratés' (*Ibid.*, 300).

28 *De Vlaamsche School* (1885), 84.

29 '... le prolongement des vitrines de quelques marchands de tableaux conns qui ont eu l'idée de profiter du grand passage des étrangers par Anvers pour tendre leur lacets sur leur route' (*L'Art moderne* [1885], 264).

30 E.g. 'Les grandes fortunes et l'art' (*L'Art moderne*, 1 September 1889); 'Agiotage artistique' (*L'Art moderne*, 10 April 1892); 'Dividendes intellectuels' (*L'Art moderne*, 27 October 1895). Concerning the importance for Picard's concept of 'l'art social', see P. Aron, *op. cit.*. The influence of Proudhon and Saint Simon on Picard is well demonstrated by the author.

31 J. Block, *Les XX and Belgian Avant-Gardism 1868–1894* (Studies in the Fine Arts: The Avant-Garde, 41), Ann Arbor 1981, 28ff.

32 *Les XX et leur temps*, Musées Royaux des Beaux-Arts de Belgique, Brussels 1962, 125–127. Van de Velde becomes a member of Les XX in 1889. On 29 December 1886 he resigned from Als Ik Kan.

33 Invited artists were: Louis Artan (q.v.), O. Dierickx, James Ensor (q.v.), Léon Fréderic (q.v.), Adrien-Joseph Heymans, Fernand Khnopff (q.v.), Jules Lagae, Henri Le Roy, Hendrik Luyten, Constantin Meunier (q.v.), Louis Philippet, Félicien Rops (q.v.), Jacob Rosseels, Théo van Rysselberghe (q.v.), Guillaume Vogels (q.v.). Ensor exhibited *L'après-dîner, La dame en détresse* and *La convalescente*, and the series *Les Auréoles du Christ ou les sensibilités de la lumière*. Khnopff exhibited *En écoutant Schumann* [cat. 28], and Van Rysselberghe the *Portrait of Octave Maus* [cat. 70]. Van de Velde did not exhibit for the first time at this Salon, as was claimed by R. L. Delevoy (*Ensor*, Antwerp 1981, 308). This error was based on Van de Velde's *Geschichte meines Lebens*, which kept silent about his adherence to Als Ik Kan (see *Als Ik Kan* [*op. cit.* note 6], 18; and H. Van de Velde, *Récit de ma vie*, edited and annotated by A. van Loo, Brussels 1992, 75, note 2).

34 '... n'aspire pas à étendre le terrain de la lutte en y apportant des solutions plus radicales; il le décentralise seulement pour faire rayonner davantage les vérités que les XX, avant lui, ont affirmées. Son ambition n'excède pas le ferme espoir d'apporter une aide fraternelle à leurs ainés en date, à leurs égaux en vaillance, à leurs amis en apostolat' (p. XIV).

35 'Avec une modestie charmante, ils ne revendiquent qu'un rôle de propagateurs et d'apôtres, alors qu'à Anvers, redan de l'art académique, la bataille est plus chaude encore et la vistoire plus difficile à conquérir qu'elle ne l'a été à Bruxelles' ('Le Vingtisme à Anvers', *L'Art moderne*, 20 March 1887, 89–90).

36 *Ibid.*, 90.

37 'L'Incident Stobbaerts', *Ibid.* (30 September 1888), 316–317.

38 Several works of these artists were bought for the Antwerp Museum.

39 'Les horreurs teutones y voisinent avec les banalités françaises' (*L'Art moderne*, 2 September 1888, 282).

40 'Le Salon défunt', *Ibid.* (23 November 1890), 369–370. *De Vlaamsche School*, however, devoted extensive attention to the Salon, be it in purely descriptive terms.

41 'Le Très Saint Temple de Très Sainte Nullité ... un horrifiant étalage de toutes les variétés de maladies picturales' (*L'Art moderne*, 16 August 1891; 30 August 1891; 27 September 1891).

42 E.g. *Exposition rétrospective de l'art belge 1830–1905*, Brussels 1905, or, in 1908, Berlin.

43 *De Vlaamsche School* (1891), 45.

44 *Ibid.* (1892), 44–64.

45 'Le poupon grandira malingrement: néanmoins durera. La bonne Fée du Juste Milieu veillera sur cette mince personne laborieusement échafaudée de membres dissemblables, se vantant eux-mêmes – et de quel droit! – d'être 'INDÉPENDANTS'! (*L'Art moderne*, 8 March 1891, 79).

46 M. Daloze, 'Henri Van de Velde en l'Association pour l'Art', in *Henry Van de Velde. Een Europees kunstenaar in zijn tijd*, Museum voor Schone Kunsten, Ghent 1993, 81–91.

47 J. F. Buyck, 'Modernist tendencies. The Critical Debate', in F. Suyckens *et al.*, *Antwerp. The New Spring*, Antwerp 1991, 182–318; J. F. Buyck, 'Het Interbellum: "Kunst van Heden" en het debat omtrent het Vlaamse expressionisme', in *In dienst van de kunst*, Koninklijk Museum voor Schone Kunsten, Antwerp 1991, 129–142.

CATALOGUE

Louis Artan de Saint-Martin

THE HAGUE 1837 – NIEUWPOORT 1890

Artan's father was born in France and served as an officer in the Dutch army. His mother belonged to the high Portuguese nobility. The family moved to Brussels when Artan was a child, but after the death of his father, they moved to the fashionable town of Spa in the Ardennes. The talented Louis was given painting lessons by Edouard Delvaux (1806–1862) and Henri Marcette (1853–1929). The first documented painting by Artan is a *Landscape with Sunset near Spa* (Salon of Ghent, 1856).

We do not know the details of his life between 1858 and 1863. He sojourned for a considerable time in Paris, where he worked by the Seine and visited Barbizon and Fontainebleau. He appears to have been in contact with Corot and Courbet. Artan spent most of his summers in Spa, working in the Ardennes or Luxembourg. He primarily painted landscapes in this period.

He moved to Etterbeek near Brussels in 1863, and maintained close contacts with Louis Dubois (1830–1880) with whom he shared a strong admiration for Courbet. He was a co-founder in 1869 of the Société Libre des Beaux-Arts, a group which sought to provide a progressive counterbalance to the more academic art favoured by the Academy of Fine Arts and the official Salon in Brussels.

It was around this time that a major change occurred in Artan's subject matter: having visited Brittany in 1867–1868, he began to concentrate on painting seascapes. He often worked at Blankenberghe, Ostend and the Channel coastline down into France. In 1872–1873, he temporarily shifted his activities to Antwerp, where he took a studio in the harbour area. The River Scheldt was the principal theme of his paintings in this period. The Antwerp period was followed by another extended stay in Paris (1874–1876), during which Artan also worked at the fishing port and fashionable resort of Honfleur.

He was chiefly interested between 1876 and his death in 1890 in the Channel coast between Dunkirk and Westende. He spent a considerable time at Ostend where he lodged in the hotel run by Willy Finch's (q.v.) parents. It is thus possible that he played a formative role in the early artistic concerns of both Finch and Ensor (q.v.), two young Ostend men, both with British roots, who lived near to one another and were doubtless already acquainted by that time.

It was in his final period that Artan developed a particularly loose, spirited technique. This brought him closer to pure, atmospheric painting in the impressionist manner, in which all secondary details are suppressed. He was much admired for that reason by the members of Les XX, who invited him to participate as guest exhibitor at their Salons of 1884 and 1887.

Artan worked obsessively in the final decades of his life. He had a house built on stilts on the beach at De Panne as an observation post, and he kept a *pied-à-terre* in Oostduinkerke in addition to his Brussels home. He paid increasingly scant attention to his appearance and comfort, and, although wealthy, lived like a pauper. His tomb in the graveyard at Oostduinkerke was designed by the Art Nouveau architect Victor Horta, and bears a relief portrait of the artist by Charles van der Stappen (1843–1910). | NH

SUMMARY BIBLIOGRAPHY

G. Vanzype, *Louis Artan*, Brussels 1929; N. Hostyn, 'Louis Artan', *Nationaal Biografisch Woordenboek* 10 (Brussels 1983); P. and V. Berko, N. Hostyn, *Marines des peintres belges nés entre 1750 et 1875*, Brussels 1984; S. Goyens de Heusch, *L'Impressionnisme et le Fauvisme en Belgique*, Antwerp 1988; *L'Impressionnisme et le Fauvisme en Belgique*, Musée d'Ixelles, Ixelles [Brussels] 1990.

1 Morning

De morgen – Matin, c. 1885
Oil on canvas, 37 x 57 cm
Koninklijk Museum voor Schone Kunsten, Antwerp, inv. no. 1943

Artan concentrated in the early part of his career on landscapes, with only the occasional seascape. It was not until 1867–1868 that he began to produce a large series of maritime paintings. Artan was one of the earliest Belgian artists to opt resolutely for *pleinairisme*. He was an innovator in Belgium in the genre of Realist seascape. Paul-Jean Clays (1819–1900) was the only artist before him to break with Romantic maritime painting. Although there was already a touch of Impressionism in his style, Clays kept within certain limits so that his work remained acceptable to a wider public. Artan's aesthetic was of a different, more daring and progressive order. He was not worried about how his work would be received.

Morning is probably one of Artan's later works, produced shortly before his death at the age of 54 in 1890. It is a nature study in which the delicate interplay of air, light and water at early morning are suggested. The work is constructed very informally in the characteristically impulsive and self-confident style which the younger generation of Impressionists so admired in the work of the older Artan. A typical appreciation was provided by Camille Lemonnier *(L'Ecole belge de peinture,* p. 153): 'An essential characteristic of his work is refinement combined with vigour. His colours are free and the surface of his paintwork unyielding. The boldness of execution is tempered by the delicacy of the colours. He explores attenuated tones – faded blues, diluted greens, dull pinks – a chord of muted harmonies. Like that of all the fine painters of the Art Libre group, the execution of Artan's work is alive: the brushstrokes fly, strike and caress; the whole field of the canvas vibrates, giving it the tangible activity of an organism.' | NH

PROVENANCE Sale Louis Artan Bequest, Brussels 1893; sale André Toussaint, Brussels, Galerie Georges Giroux, 18 December 1923, no. 8; purchased by the Museum.
EXHIBITION Brussels 1932, no. 59 (as 'c. 1885–1890, former coll. André Toussaint, Brussels').

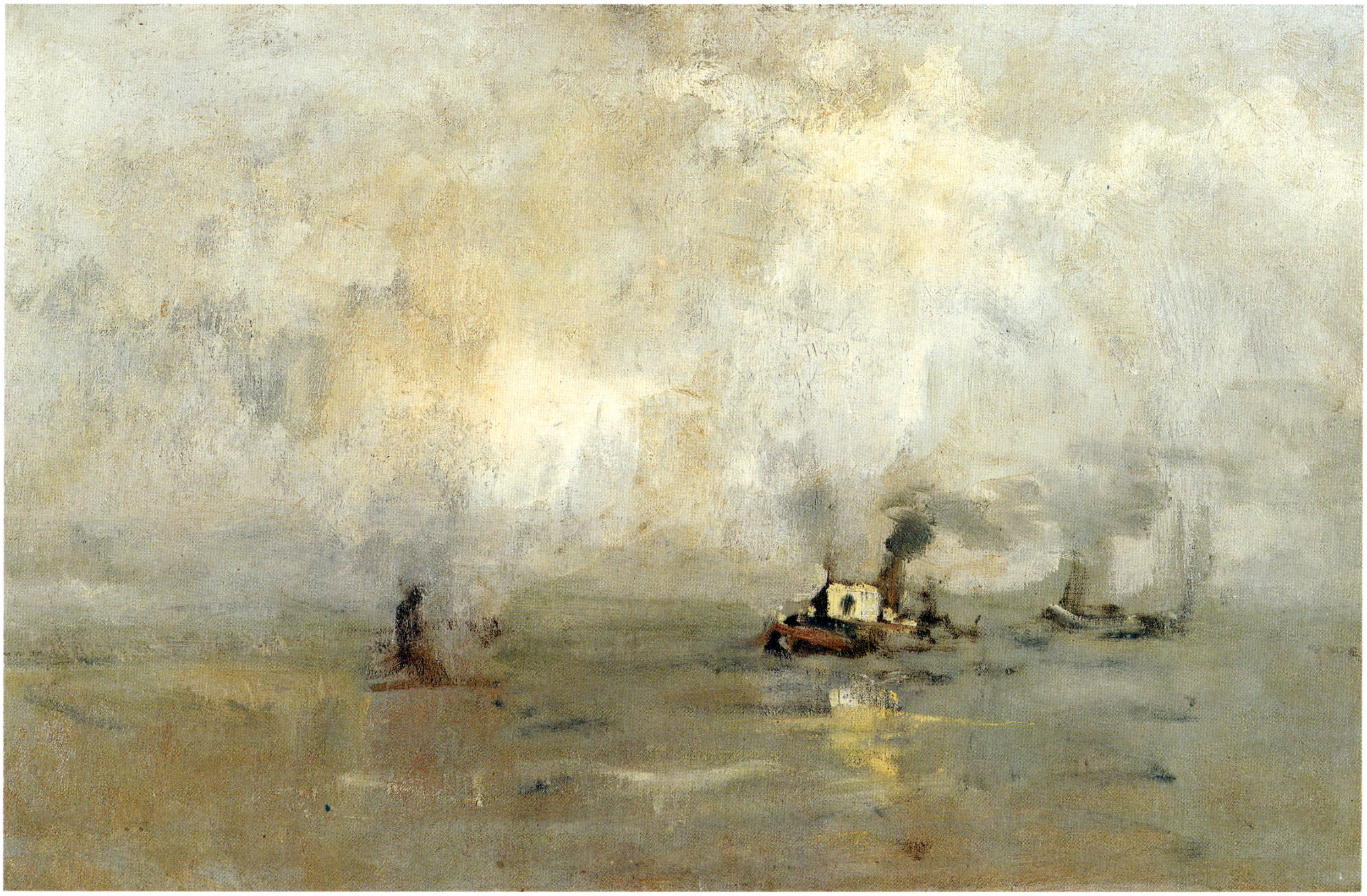

Albert Baertsoen

GHENT 1866–1922

Albert Baertsoen came from a wealthy and cultured industrial family in Ghent and showed artistic leanings from a very early age. Having been introduced to the art of drawing by the painter Gustave den Duyts, Baertsoen attended Jean Delvin's classes at the Academy of Fine Arts in Ghent. In 1885–1886 he made his artistic début at L'Essor in Brussels. At the age of 20 he was painting at Kastel on the Scheldt and was mixing with landscape painters of the School of Dendermonde such as Isidore Meyers (1836–1917), Jacques Rosseels (1828–1912) and Franz Courtens (1854–1943). In 1888 he exhibited for the first time at the Paris Salon and won a gold medal at Antwerp. He spent time in Paris in 1888 and 1889, attended Alfred Philippe Roll's studio, and came into contact with the work of Monet and Sisley. From a trip to London in 1890, he brought back a view of the Thames which was exhibited at the Brussels Salon and which prefigures the works he was to execute in London during the First World War. Baertsoen established himself as the painter of the towns of Flanders, particularly Ghent, but also Bruges, Nieuwpoort, Dixmude and Courtrai. In 1898 he travelled by canal in a floating studio to Zealand (Netherlands) in order to paint. Between 1905 and 1908 he sought – without much success – a new mode of expression in studies of the industrial landscape and the region around Liège, returning eventually to the old quarters of Ghent. During the First World War, he joined his son in London and worked in the studio of the painter John Singer Sargent.

Baertsoen was a meticulous painter and made numerous preliminary studies, mostly in charcoal, for each of his paintings. He used the technique of squaring up the drawing before transferring it to the canvas. He also destroyed a number of his paintings. Although some of his works have a luminosity that allies him to the Impressionists, Baertsoen remained essentially a highly individual painter who escaped particular influences and categorizations. | BV

SUMMARY BIBLIOGRAPHY

H. Fierens-Gevaert, *Albert Baertsoen*, Brussels 1910; G. Vanzype, 'Notice sur Albert Baertsoen', *Annuaire de l'Académie royale des Sciences, des Lettres et des Beaux-Arts de Belgique* (Brussels 1926), 79–105; S. Houbart-Wilkin, 'Baertsoen (Albert)', *Biographie nationale (Académie royale des Sciences, des Lettres et des Beaux-Arts de Belgique* XXXII:1) (Brussels 1964), cols. 23–29.

2 Barges in the Snow

Chalands sous la neige, 1901
Oil (formerly with pastel) on canvas, 140 x 192 cm
Signed and dated bottom right: alb. Baertsoen / Gand / ..01
Musées royaux des Beaux-Arts de Belgique/Koninklijke Musea voor Schone Kunsten van België, Brussels, inv. no. 3583

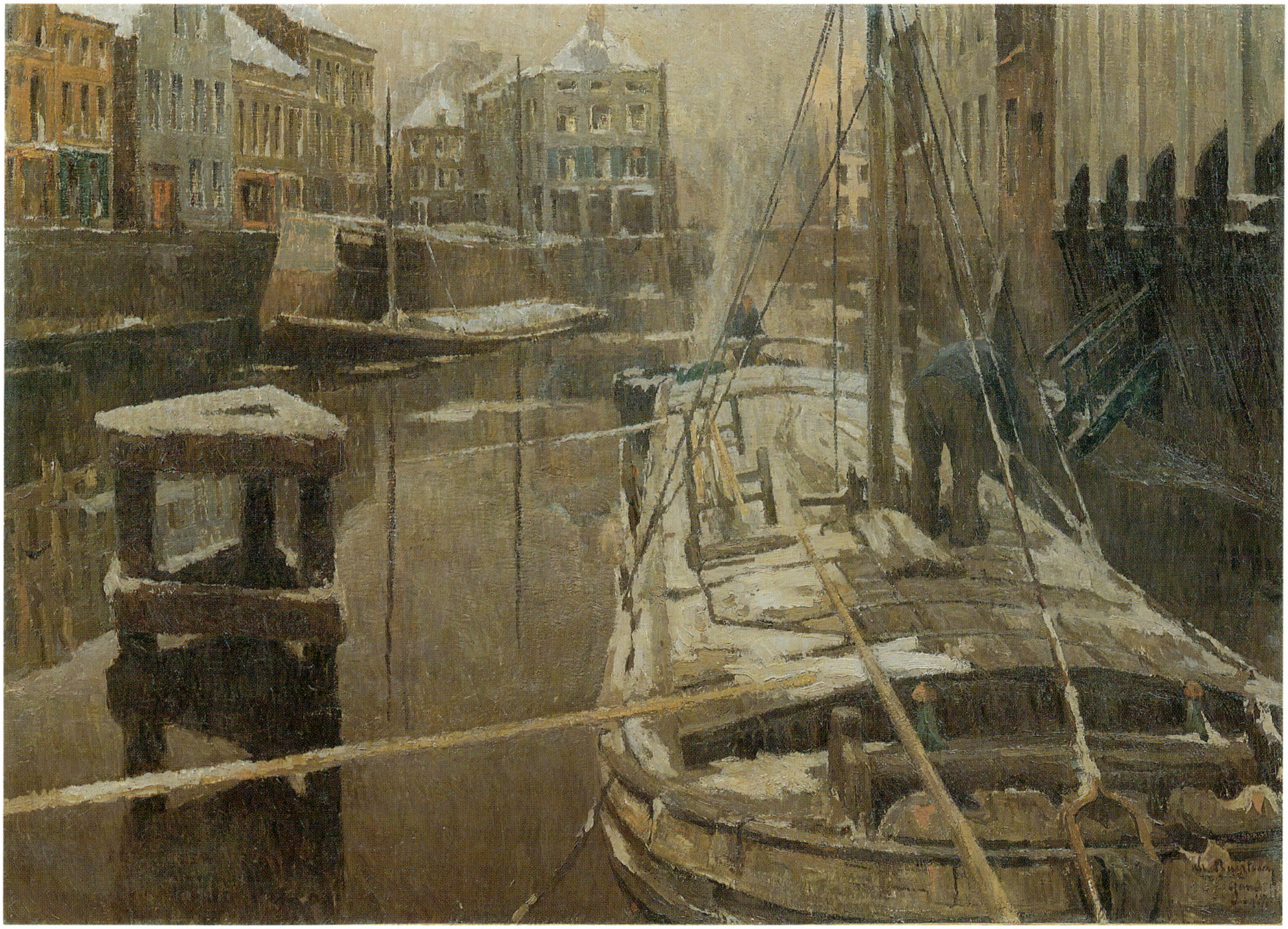

Painted in 1901, *Barges in the Snow* was accepted at two major exhibitions that year: at the Internationale Kunstausstellung *Münchener Secession* at the Königliches Glaspalast in Munich, where it won a gold medal, and then at the eighth exhibition of La Libre Esthétique at the Musée Moderne in Brussels, from where it was purchased by the Musée de Bruxelles (the future Musées royaux des Beaux-Arts de Belgique): 'At the Salon de La Libre Esthétique of 1901, the Musée de Bruxelles acquired the truly masterful *Barges in the Snow*, in which the artist seems to have asserted all his talents as a painter and poet. It is a poignant scene, traced in broad, luscious strokes, conveying all the sorrow of the mournful snow on the canals, the grieving winter skies over the silent cities, and the harsh beauty of the chill season in typically Northern landscapes' (*L'Art moderne*, 20 October 1901, 349). Baertsoen was allowed to keep the painting temporarily in order to exhibit it the following year at the Paris Salon, where it aroused considerable interest: 'Albert Baertsoen, whose *Chalands sous la neige*, lent by the Musée de Bruxelles, reveals a certain sadness of vision and a very personal faculty of interpretation' (*The Studio*, August 1902, 192).

Barges in the Snow was originally a mixed media painting, combining paint with pastel. It would appear that the artist normally placed glass on the work in order to protect it, for, in an undated postcard sent from Ghent to the museum in response to their inquiry of 30 August 1902, Baertsoen replied: 'I can do no more than repeat to the members of the commission that my painting is highlighted in pastel; it is easy to establish this, and I would willingly show them the highlights in question. Removing the glass would therefore inevitably make the pastel disappear and thus change the look of the painting' (Archives Musées royaux des Beaux-Arts de Belgique, Dossier 4937). The artist's advice was apparently not followed.

Baertsoen found great difficulty in completing his large-scale works. He is reported to have confided to Gustave Vanzype that 'I made several attempts at this painting.' And Vanzype wrote: 'I saw three or four versions of his *Barges in the Snow*' (Vanzype 1903, 18–19). One of these versions was exhibited at the Exposition internationale des Beaux-Arts organized by the Cercle des Beaux-Arts in Ostend in 1894, appearing as no. 4 in the catalogue. Another version, smaller than the one shown here, which may be the same as the preceding one, was evidently kept in the painter's studio until his death since it appeared as no. 102 in the catalogue of the auction of the Albert Baertsoen Studio (Galerie Georges Giroux, Brussels, 7 March 1932).

Baertsoen was the artistic chronicler of the city of Ghent, of its ancient stones laden with history, and of the charms of its alleyways and dark canals. In his *Barges in the Snow*, which takes up the frequently treated theme of barges and water, Baertsoen depicts the Kraanlei on the Lys. Of broad and solid construction, in a range of deep, muted tones, *Barges in the Snow* is one of the finest works by Albert Baertsoen, painter of solitude and silence, melancholy and immutability. | BV

PROVENANCE Bought by the Museum from the artist at the Salon de La Libre Esthétique, 1901 (no. 71).

EXHIBITIONS Munich 1901, no. [135]; *La Libre Esthétique* 1901, no. 71; Paris 1902, s.n.; Liège 1905, no. 11; Paris 1923 (Section d'Art moderne), no. 7, ill.; Berlin 1933, no. 7; Ghent 1972–1973, no. 29, pl. XVI; Brussels 1993–1994, no. 1, ill.

BIBLIOGRAPHY Mourey 1901, 349; Mourey 1902, 192, 200, ill.; Vanzype 1903, 11, 13, 15, 19, 20, ill.; Fierens-Gevaert 1904, 289; Maus 1905, 391; Fierens-Gevaert 1910, 27, 39, 44, 45, 46, 50, 51, 81, ill.; Vanzype 1926, 89, 92, 102; Fierens-Gevaert, Laes 1928, 47; Roelandts 1928, 26, pl. X; Houbart-Wilkin 1964, cols. 24, 26.

Emile Claus

SINT-ELOOIS-VIJVE 1849 – ASTENE 1924

Emile Claus was the twelfth of thirteen children born in a village on the Lys in West Flanders. In 1869, at the instigation of the composer Peter Benoit, Claus enrolled at the Antwerp Academy of Fine Arts, which was then run by Nicaise de Keyser. Most of Claus's time there was spent under the tutelage of the romantic landscape painter Jacob Jacobs (1812–1879). Claus left the Academy in 1874, having won its second prize, and he went on to make his début at the Ghent Salon. The following year he took part in the Exposition générale des Beaux-Arts in Brussels. He lived in Antwerp until 1882, painting portraits and genre scenes in the realist narrative style typical of the Academy. His first contribution to the Paris Salon des Artistes français of 1882 (*Cockfighting in Flanders*, Private Collection) attracted considerable attention. From then on, Claus visited Paris with great regularity, sometimes spending the whole winter there; these contacts with France encouraged him to produce a sequence of highly-finished, realist scenes of rural life, often set in the open air, which permitted him to pursue a persistent interest in light effects and atmosphere (e.g. *Sunny Lane*, 1893, Musées royaux des Beaux-Arts de Belgique, Brussels). From 1883 Claus worked at Astene, near Deinze, on the banks of the Lys, in an old hunting-lodge evocatively dubbed 'Zonneschijn' (Sunshine). This became a meeting-place for pupils and friends – painters, sculptors, poets and men of letters, such as the writer Camille Lemonnier, under whose influence Claus fell. In 1886 Claus married Charlotte Dufaux, of whom he painted a number of portraits. In Paris, during the winters from 1889 to 1892, encouraged in particular by contact with Henri Le Sidaner (1862–1939), he discovered the works of the Impressionists. In 1904 he was one of the founders of the Vie et Lumière circle, whose members, moved by a common ideal, a common desire 'to paint light', organized exhibitions. Claus visited Spain, Algeria and Morocco, and made several trips to France and Zealand (Netherlands). He paid a brief visit to Pittsburgh and travelled twice to Venice. During his period of exile in Britain, from 1914 to 1919, he painted views of the Thames in London. A celebrator of country life and a painter of sun-filled scenes, Claus came to be viewed as the master of Luminism, that home-grown and rather belated form of Impressionism. Frequently working on a fairly monumental scale, his work came to combine a generally recognizable impressionist technique with an often fairly strident colour range which he applied to subjects that confirmed a poetic-realist approach to landscape and scenes of rural life. | BV

SUMMARY BIBLIOGRAPHY

G. Vanzype, 'Notice sur Emile Claus', *Annuaire de l'Académie royale des Sciences, des Lettres et des Beaux-Arts de Belgique* (Brussels 1929), 1–33; A. Sauton, *Un Prince du Luminisme, Emile Claus (1849–1924)*, Brussels 1946; P. Eeckhout, G. van Severen, *Rétrospective Emile Claus, 1849–1924*, Museum voor Schone Kunsten, Ghent 1974; B. Velghe, 'Emile Claus en Grande-Bretagne: 1914–1919', *Bulletin Musées royaux des Beaux-Arts de Belgique. Miscellanea Philippe Roberts-Jones* (1985–1988), 353–369, nos. 1–3.

3 Summer

Zomer – Eté, 1893
Oil on canvas, 59 x 91 cm
Signed bottom left: Emile Claus; dated and signed on reverse: Junij 1893 / E.C.
Koninklijk Museum voor Schone Kunsten, Antwerp, inv. no. 1836

By 1893 Emile Claus had attained complete maturity as a painter. He had travelled the long road from anecdotal academicism via rural realism to triumphant luminism. As early as 1890, the year of execution of *The Beet Harvest* (Museum van Deinze en Leiestreek, Deinze), which may be regarded as marking a turning-point in his career, he had found his feet as an artist. The canvas entitled *IJsvogels* (Museum voor Schone Kunsten, Ghent), dating from 1891, is the first important work of this period, during which the desire to convey a tangible atmosphere gradually supersedes concentration on the figure. Two things prompted this development in Claus's work. The first was the formation, during the 1880s, of Claus's close and highly significant friendship with the naturalist Belgian writer Camille Lemonnier (1844–1913), author of *La Belgique*, an important work for which Claus provided a number of drawings. Lemonnier was a forceful personality, a man of letters who had served his apprenticeship in the artistic circles of Paris. He encouraged Claus to emancipate himself from academic constraints, to give up the studio for the open air, and to clean up and lighten his palette: 'Don't paint nature as you think it is but as you would like it to be ... You have to combine honesty with independence. Your palette will never be light enough to convey the impression of air or of the vitality of things' (Lemonnier 1908, 17–18). The influence was mutual: in 1897, as a result of his contact with the painter, the writer embarked on a naturalist path and became, in his turn, a celebrator of the grandeur of nature. The second influence on Claus was that of the French Impressionists, whose bright, luminously vibrant work he discovered in Paris during the winters from 1889 to 1892. He was fascinated in particular by the painting of Claude Monet (1840–1926), and went on to adopt some of the latter's techniques, modifying them to suit his own style. He also studied the work of Camille Pissarro made after his rejection of Neo-Impressionism, available both for study in Paris and in Les XX in 1891 (nos. 1 and 2). Although Claus used the technique of juxtaposing tiny, nervous brushstrokes of pure colour, of allowing colour to invade the shadow, and of eliminating black and the earth colours that muddied his palette, he never adopted the dilution of form beloved of the French Impressionists. He always adhered in some degree to reality, and in this he was following one of the constants of Belgian art.

The theme of the seasons, which made a tentative appearance in Claus's work during the 1880s, became a regular subject from the 1890s. Summer, autumn, winter and spring served as felicitous pretexts for Claus to indulge in the pleasure of, as it were, painting variations on a theme. The fact that the work shown here is not the only one to bear the title of *Summer* makes it difficult to document the various exhibitions at which it may have appeared. Only those where the picture is specifically listed as belonging to the Museum of Antwerp have therefore been cited. This only applies after 1922, the year in which the widow of the Antwerp collector Edmond Wappers donated the painting to the museum. A letter dated 28 February 1922 (Archief Koninklijk Museum voor Schone Kunsten, Antwerp, sub Schenkingen 1922) announces Mrs Edmond Wappers's wish to donate to the museum the landscape entitled *July* (!).

Summer depicts the familiar Clausian universe, namely a rural setting, often featuring the labours of working people but without any hint of the tragic. Claus's world is one of sun-filled landscapes, fertile fields, healthy, tranquil beings, cloudless hours and joyful atmospheres; a world in which man and nature live in perfect harmony. | BV

PROVENANCE Mrs Wappers, widow of Edmond Wappers, Antwerp, who donated it to the museum in memory of her late husband, 1922.
EXHIBITIONS Helsinki 1948a, no. 11; Oslo 1948–1949, no. 11; Prague 1949, no. 9, ill.; Antwerp 1952, no. 23; Belgrade 1953, no. 12; Ghent 1974, no. 54, pl. xv; Ghent 1975, no. 147; Antwerp 1990, no. 39, ill.
BIBLIOGRAPHY Maret 1949, 15, pl. 16; Buyck (ed.) 1977, 97 (as dated and signed on reverse: 'Januarij 1893 E.C.'), ill.

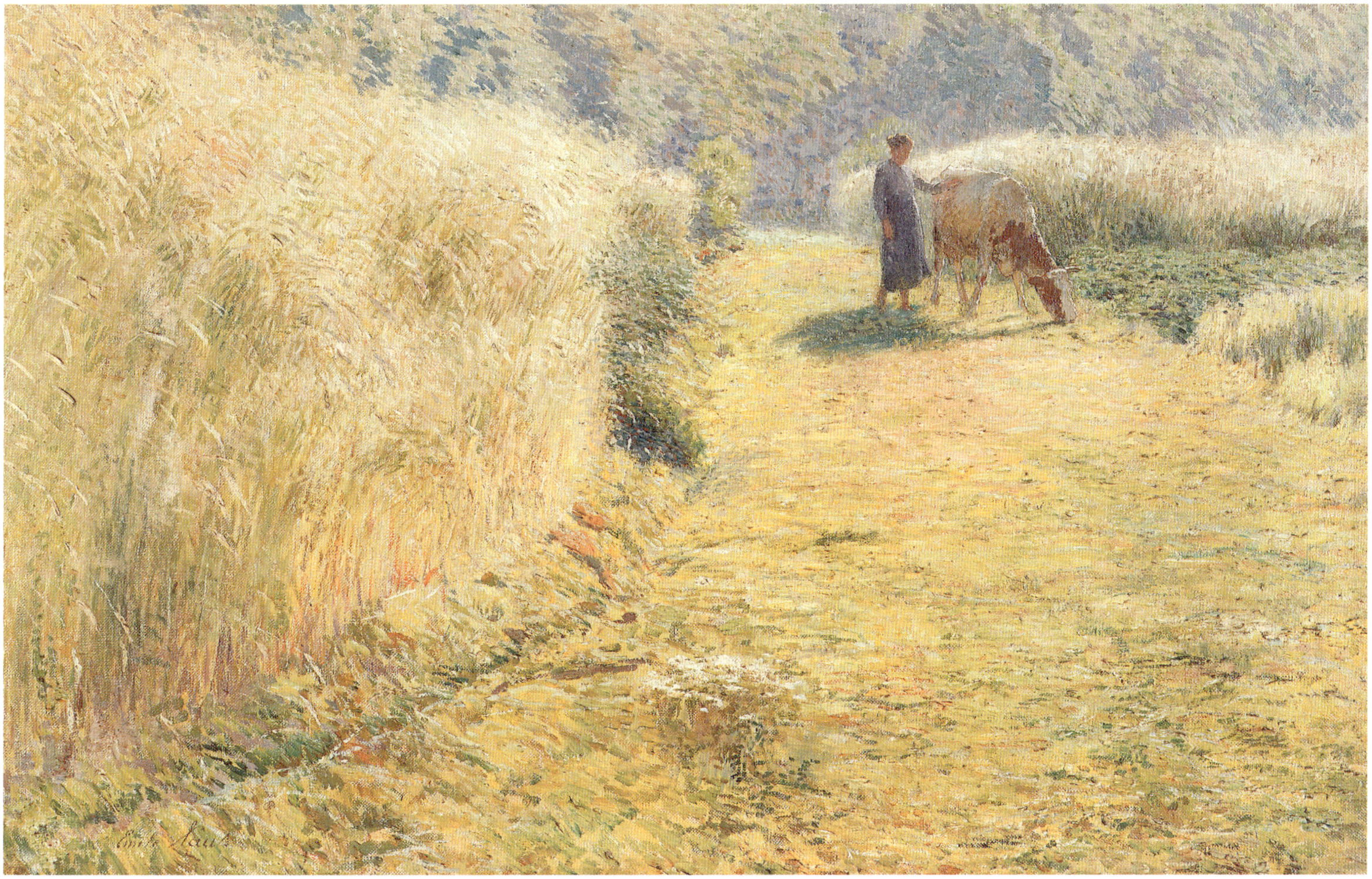

4 First Communion

Les Communiantes, 1893
Oil on canvas, 82 x 117 cm
Signed bottom left: Emile Claus; signed and dated on reverse: Emile Claus April 1893
Collection Crédit Communal de Belgique / Collectie Gemeentekrediet van België, Brussels

Dated April 1893, this picture was exhibited in the same year at the Exposition générale des Beaux-Arts in Brussels under the title *Pâques* (Easter). This salon took place from 16 September to 31 October in the temporary structure of the Musée Moderne, dubbed the 'Baraque des Beaux-Arts' ('the Fine Arts Shed'; *L'Art moderne*, 24 September 1893, 309). In 1893 [see cat. 3] Claus had already been initiated into Impressionism, having seen the work of such artists as, in particular, Monet and Pissarro, both in Paris and in Brussels. Even at this date, the particular interpretation given to Impressionism by Claus, in which form is not dissipated by the fall of light, permits his work to be described as 'luminist'. In *First Communion*, for example, there are echoes of work from his earlier period, c. 1883–1889, which followed the subject matter and technique of artists such as Jules Bastien-Lepage (1848–1884) and of photographically inspired realism. The art of photography had made enormous strides during the nineteenth century and the appearance of the gelatino-bromide plate in 1880, which gave birth to the snapshot, made it possible to capture fleeting effects and to focus attention on chance congruences of light and shade. As regards *First Communion*, Lemonnier gave a wonderful description of the future discoveries and developments which the picture contains in embryonic form: 'In that picture, on a sunny April day, little country girls in their white veils, off to make their communion, looked like flowers in a mystical garden. You could feel that he [Claus] was already preoccupied with conveying the pattern of transparent shadow on bright surfaces, heralding a whole new output. It signalled the awakening of a spirit in search of unexpected effects, subtle perceptions, and expressive momentary images' (Lemonnier 1908, 27).

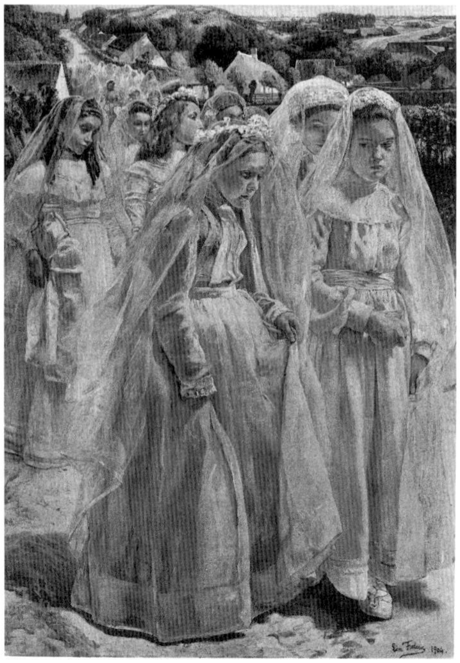

fig. a LÉON FRÉDERIC, Return of the Procession, 1904, Musées royaux des Beaux-Arts de Belgique, Brussels

Indeed, *First Communion* contains a subtle balance between the need to retain a firm sense of structure, denoted in the recession of wall and path, the gently rounded forms of the girls clothed in white, and the fleeting effects of light and shade. These latter are not only conveyed through the shimmer of small dots of colour placed within areas of shadow, but also in the rhythmic pattern of horizontal shadows cast by the unseen trees which lie beyond the right edge of the canvas. This latter device also extends the space of the painting in order to allow the spectator to establish a supplementary zone of space. Such manipulations of spatial definition through colour rather than specific descrip-

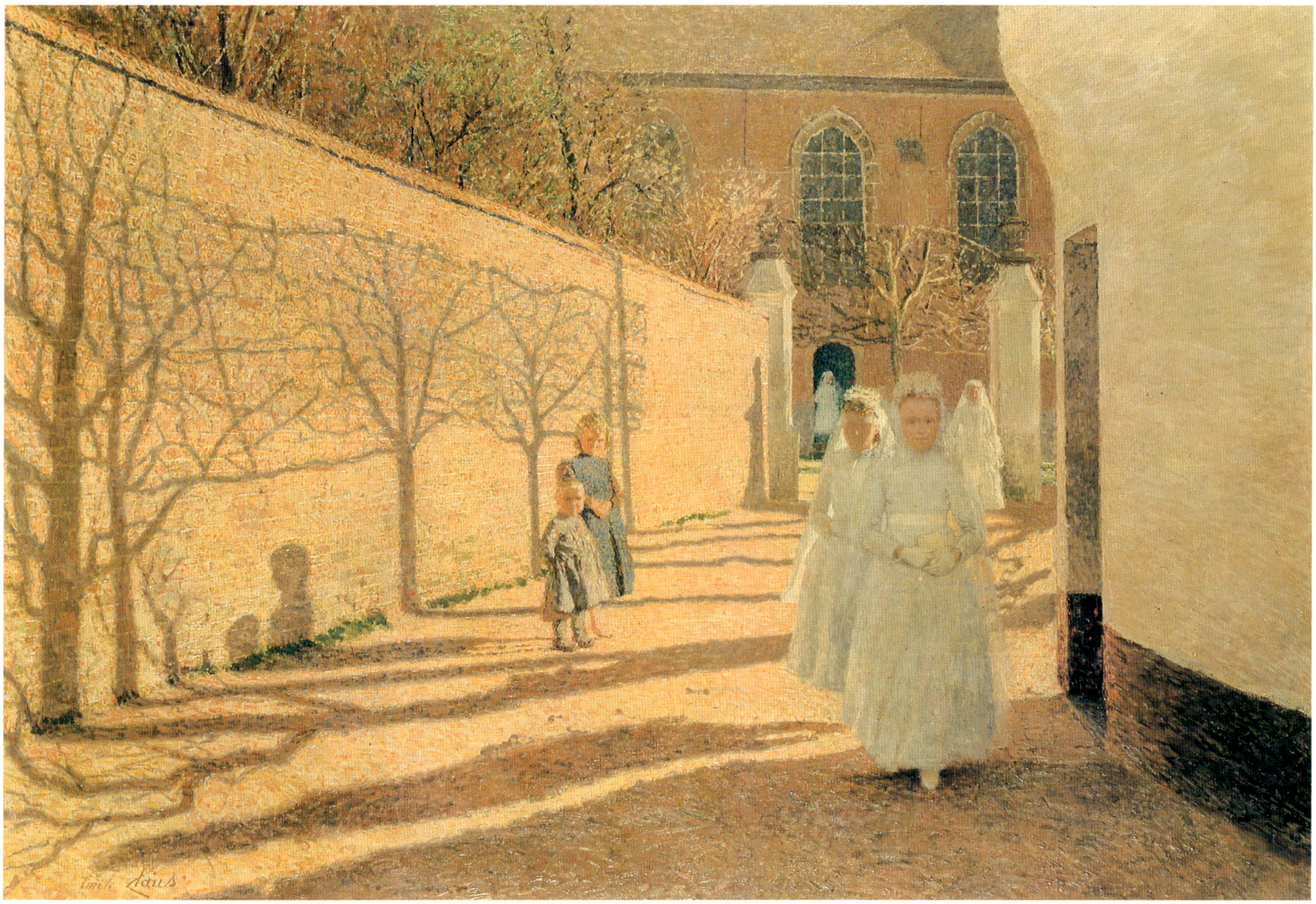

tion are found in a number of Claus's later works, for example *The Tree* (Museum voor Schone Kunsten, Ghent).

In a world of rationalism and materialism, religious themes took on various guises in nineteenth-century art. In most cases a motif was used as a pretext for formal creation rather than as an expression of actual faith: 'The opening-up to transcendence is almost always lacking in a great many realist religious scenes ... The nearer one gets to the Impressionists, the more often events are set out of doors: pilgrimages, processions, funeral cortèges ... Plants and trees, mist, rain and blazing sun become the most important features, and, despite their titles, the works must be regarded as entirely secular.'[1] The communion theme, sometimes located within the 'setting' of a procession, fits naturally into this context, and was a frequently treated subject. Examples are: *La Communiante* (1875; Musée des Beaux-Arts, Tournai) by Jules Bastien-Lepage (1848–1884); *Les Communiantes* (1884; Museum and Art Gallery, Perth, Scotland) by Jules Breton (1827–1906); *Return of the Procession* [fig. a] by Léon Fréderic (q.v.). Emile Claus was unable to resist the appeal of the subject and the delight of reproducing the reassuring image of one of the many rituals that mark out the rhythm of the seasons and of life. | BV

PROVENANCE Mr Stern, Berlin; purchased by the Crédit Communal de Belgique at sale Antwerp, Campo, 2 April 1974, no. 61 (as 'De kommunicanten / Les communiantes, dated 1893').

EXHIBITIONS Brussels 1893, no. 95 (as 'Pâques / Paaschzonnenschijn'); Ghent 1974, no. 56 (as 'Les Communiantes' or 'Pâques'); Liège 1981, no. 9, pl. III (as 'Les Communiantes'); Brussels 1983–1984, no. 32, ill. (as 'Pâques' or 'Les communiantes'); Waregem 1985, no. 25, ill. (as 'Paaszonneschijn' or 'De Kommunikanten'); Pontoise 1990, no. 8, ill. (as 'Les Communiantes. Soleil de Pâques'); Paris 1990a; Luxembourg 1993, no. 22, ill.

BIBLIOGRAPHY Lemonnier 1908, 18, 23, 27, 28, 56; Marcel 1910, 326 (as 1892), ill. (lithograph, as 'Pâques'); Biermé 1924, 73 (as 'Les Premières Communiantes'); Sauton 1946, 24, 52 (as 'Pâques, dated 1892'); Goyens de Heusch 1988, ill. 145.

1 L. M. A. Schoonbaert, *La Thématique religieuse dans l'art belge de 1875 à nos jours*, Galerie CGER, Brussels 1986, 21.

Henri de Braekeleer

ANTWERP 1840–1888

Henri de Braekeleer's earliest works betray the influence of his father Ferdinand, the famous and successful painter of amusing and melodramatic scenes. De Braekeleer studied at the Antwerp Academy of Fine Arts between 1854 and 1861. He also made studies of the interiors and corners of old Antwerp for his uncle, the history painter Henri Leys (1815–1869), to use in his pictorial reconstructions of Antwerp's past. De Braekeleer made his début at the 1858 Antwerp Salon, and took part regularly in the triennial exhibitions in Brussels and Antwerp.

His early works consisted of genre scenes of women working and children playing in the backstreets on the edge of the city and pictures of walled gardens and church interiors. Pictures of craftsmen in cramped interiors bear witness to his receptiveness to French Realism. They received a mixed reception. Some critics rejected them for their banal subject matter, while others praised them for their striking characterization of the people and settings, and for their colouristic qualities.

De Braekeleer signed a contract in 1869 to supply the Brussels banker and art-dealer Gustave Coûteaux with paintings. This agreement gave rise to a certain amount of commercial as well as social success. De Braekeleer's contract with Coûteaux lasted until 1876, and the works which he made for him are amongst the most highly prized in his oeuvre. In paintings such as the *Man at the Window* (1873; Musées royaux des Beaux-Arts de Belgique, Brussels), he declared his commitment to recording the introverted, often unpretentious members of society, many of whom, as in this painting, he placed before windows, absorbed in mundane occupations. He did not endow his subjects with social or political meaning. Rather he concentrated on either carefully analysing or rapidly recording the light and the substance of things. He also painted nature studies on the coast and in the countryside around Antwerp.

The ending of De Braekeleer's contract with Coûteaux coincided with a creative block, which might have been due either to psychological or to artistic reasons. During the 1880s he sought to diversify his output, with landscape and still life most prominent. Despite his obstinate attitude towards artistic innovation, as illustrated in his adamant refusal to participate as an invited artist at the Salon des XX in 1887, De Braekeleer was revered by the younger generation of Belgian avant-garde artists, both for his neutral, contemplative interiors and for his increasingly exploratory handling of paint in his later years. | HT

SUMMARY BIBLIOGRAPHY

Retrospectieve Leys-De Braekeleer, Kunst van Heden, Antwerp 1905; G. Vanzype, *Henri De Braekeleer*, Brussels 1923; U. van de Voorde, 'Henri De Braekeleer of de Romantiek', in *Vorm en geest*, Louvain 1939; W. Vanbeselaere, 'Henri De Braekeleer', *Jaarboek Koninklijk Museum voor Schone Kunsten Antwerpen* (1939–1941), 101–136; E. de Bom, *Henri De Braekeleer en Antwerpen*, Antwerp 1941; M. Gilliams, *Inleiding tot de idee De Braekeleer*, Antwerp 1941; A. J. J. Delen, *Henri De Braekeleer. Een keuze van 48 tekeningen*, Antwerp *s.d.*; *Album Henri De Braekeleer*, Antwerp 1956 (Catalogue by W. Vanbeselaere, M. Gilliams, J. Broeckx, *et al.*); M. E. Tralbaut, 'De Braekeleeriana. Archivalia, rariora en curiosa in verband met leven en werk van de Antwerpse kunstschilder', I–XXI, *Antwerpen* (1964–1971); *Henri De Braekeleer*, Koninklijk Museum voor Schone Kunsten, Antwerp 1988 (Catalogue by H. Todts).

5 Still Life

c. 1880
Oil on panel, 28 x 38 cm
Signed bottom right: Henri De Braekeleer
Private Collection

Henri de Braekeleer's artistic output declined markedly from c. 1880, due, it has been suggested, to bouts of depression which inhibited his creativity. However, in the last eight years of his life he continued to participate in major exhibitions in Belgium and abroad, showing paintings which he had supplied to the Brussels art-dealer Gustave Coûteaux between 1869 and 1876. He also received admirers and connoisseurs at his studio, finding amongst them ready sales of small nature studies and still lifes. The latter are not dated, but can be placed between 1882 and 1887 on the basis of documentary evidence.

These still lifes depict the accoutrements of a simple meal, a more luxurious dessert, flowers, or an assemblage of antique objects. The artist often used the title 'accessoires' for these works, without further distinction. The motifs are, indeed, set out like props from the studio of a traditional still life painter.

The nature studies painted by De Braekeleer in the open air in the course of the 1870s and 1880s reveal his interest in rapidly recording fleeting atmospheric phenomena. These aspects are exhaustively analysed – with infinite patience – in his still lifes. The images seem painfully detailed, yet, thanks to a multiplicity of subtle nuances, tiny brushstrokes and highlights, they above all evoke the play of light. The execution enables us, as it were, to follow the concentration and sensibility of the artist himself.

De Braekeleer's still lifes, with their calculated arrangement of constituent parts, found an echo in the approach to the same subject matter in James Ensor's highly contrived compositions [e.g. cat. 13], and the relative freedom of his brushwork after 1880 rang a common chord with the exploratory painting techniques of Van Rysselberghe (q.v.), Vogels (q.v.), and, again, James Ensor. | HT

PROVENANCE A. Janssens, Antwerp, who sold it to P. Brusseleers, Antwerp, in 1946.
EXHIBITIONS Antwerp 1905, no. 222; Antwerp 1988, no. s52.
BIBLIOGRAPHY Antwerp 1988, 162–170.

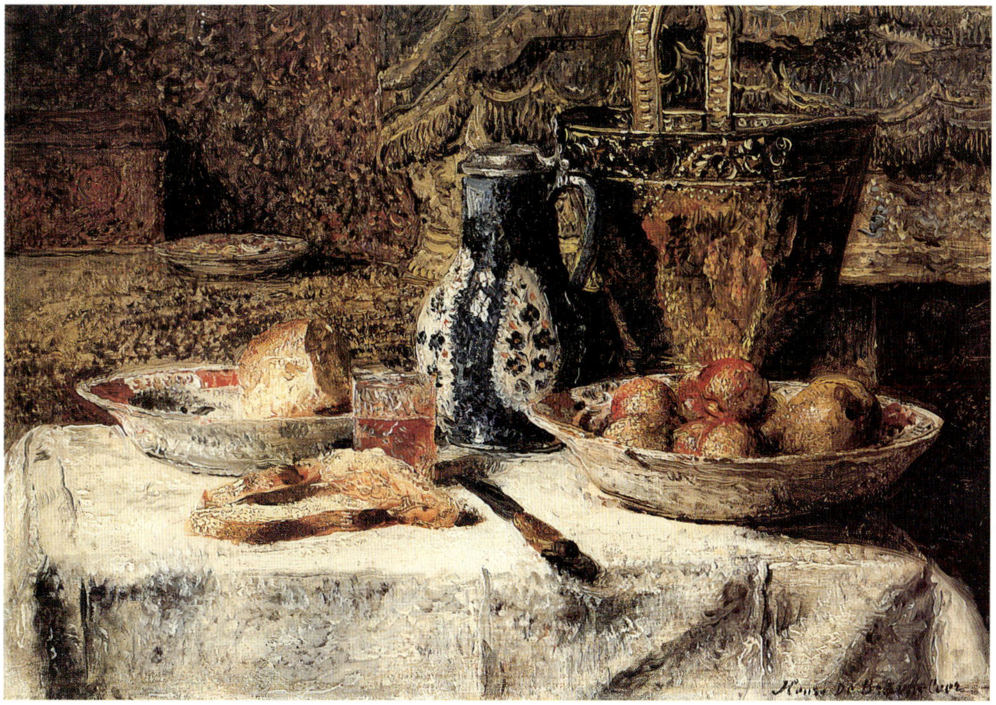

William Degouve de Nuncques

MOTHERMÉ (FRANCE) 1867 – STAVELOT 1935

Degouve de Nuncques came from an ancient, ennobled French family which had traditionally been associated with the arts. When he was three, the family moved from the French Ardennes to Belgium, settling first in Spa and then in Brussels. His father, a highly cultured man for whom Degouve had a lifelong admiration, encouraged his son's interest in philosophy, science and music, as well as in art and literature. A quiet, introspective child, Degouve de Nuncques determined on an artistic career; he briefly studied, for a few months, at the Academy of Fine Arts in Brussels, but was largely self-taught. Friendships with the Dutch-Javanese artist, Jan Toorop (1858–1923), with whom he shared a studio in Brussels in 1883, and with Henry de Groux, whom he met c. 1890, as well as contacts established in Paris with Pierre Puvis de Chavannes, Maurice Denis, Auguste Rodin and the Norwegian artist Fritz Thaulow all contributed to the evolution of his own particular approach to subject matter and technique. Encouraged by Rodin, he exhibited for the first time at the Exposition générale des Beaux-Arts in Brussels in 1890, and again in 1894 at the Salon du Champ-de-Mars in Paris, where he made his first sale. He married Juliette Massin, a painter and the sister-in-law of the poet Emile Verhaeren, who brought him into contact with the Symbolist poets of *La Jeune Belgique*. In search of new sources of inspiration, Degouve travelled widely in Italy, Austria, Switzerland, Germany, and France. From 1900 to 1902 he lived in the Balearics. During the First World War, he sought refuge in Holland. He returned to Brussels, but the death of his wife in 1919 plunged him into deep depression. He set up home in Stavelot, in the Belgian Ardennes, and gradually regained a taste for life and painting, devoting himself exclusively to depictions of the Ardennes landscape. His Symbolist period, from about 1892 to about 1900, is his most important and most interesting. It is marked by a particular atmosphere that sometimes prefigures Surrealism. | GOZ

SUMMARY BIBLIOGRAPHY

L. and P. Haesaerts, *William Degouve de Nuncques*, Brussels 1935; A. de Ridder, *William Degouve de Nuncques*, Brussels 1957; G. Ollinger-Zinque, 'William Degouve de Nuncques', in *William Degouve de Nuncques et les intimistes verviétois*, Musée d'art religieux régional et de l'ancienne Abbaye, Stavelot 1990, 19–23.

6 Child with Owl

L'Enfant au hibou, 1892
Pastel on paper, 41 x 35 cm
Signed top left: W D / de / N; dated bottom left: 1892
C & R, Antwerp

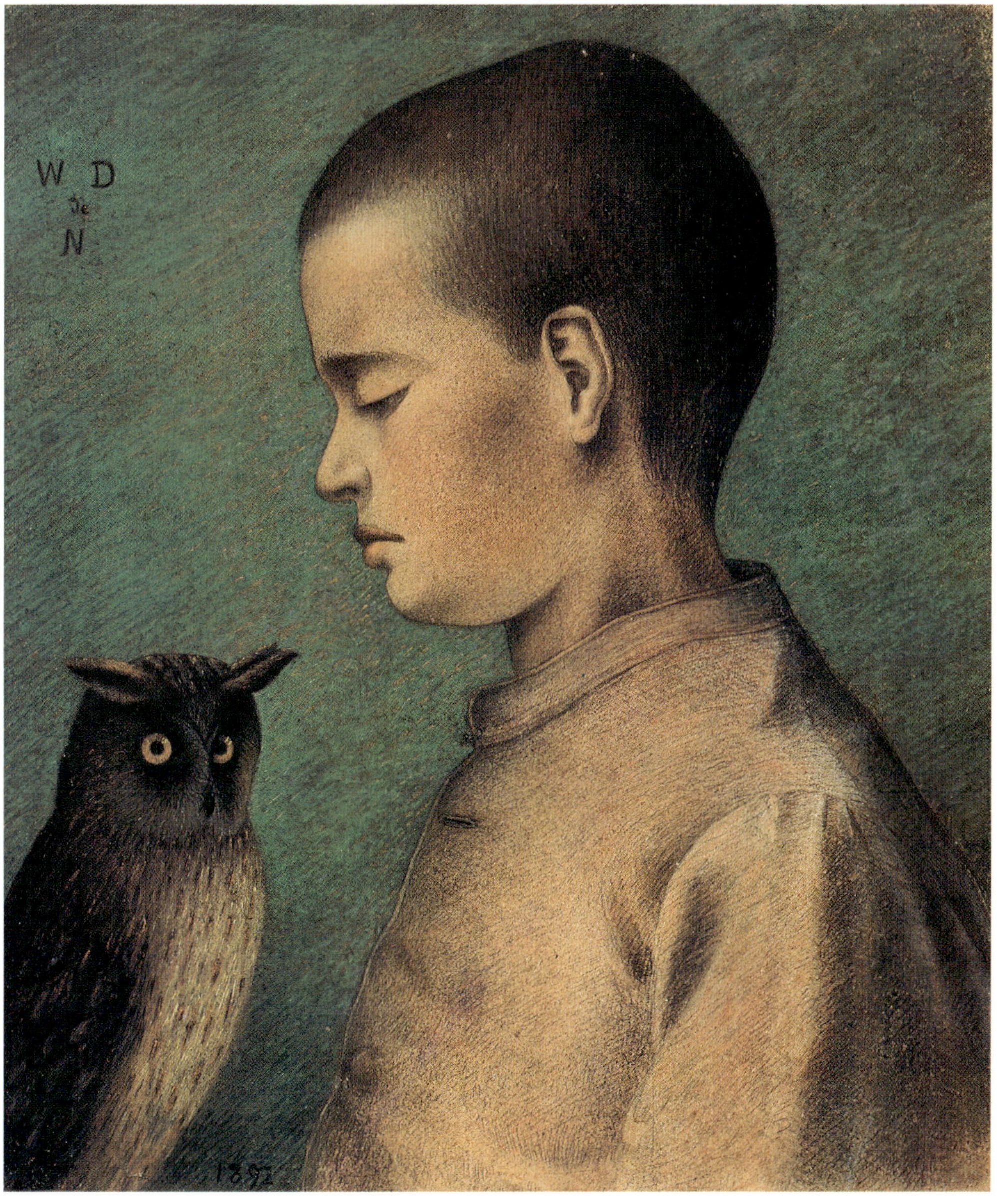

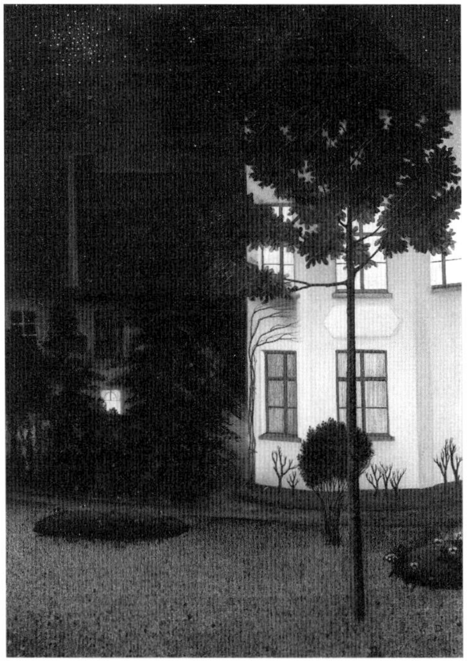

fig. a WILLIAM DEGOUVE DE NUNCQUES
House of Usher, 1892,
Rijksmuseum Kröller-Müller, Otterlo

Child with Owl is a rare example of a figure subject in Degouve de Nuncques's oeuvre. It appears not so much to be the representation of a young child accompanied by an owl than the sense of complicity between the two beings. What is going on between the bird, looking out at us and seemingly calling on us as witnesses, and the austere and already adult-looking child, his eyes lowered and seemingly unseeing of the bird? The composition is simple but intense; everything turns on the strange and ambiguous relationship between the two protagonists. The forms, pushed up claustrophobically onto the surface of the picture, are deliberately pared down, linear, yet intensely realistic in their rendering: Degouve's vision is always synthetic, he retains only those lines that will capture the distinctive aspect of things which he wishes to convey. Is the child a symbol of innocence, of hope for the future, who is perhaps being confronted with the mystery of its fate? Is the owl, an omen of darkness, melancholy and sadness, not also, as in Greek mythology, the emblem of Atropos, the one of the three Fates whose function was to cut off the thread of life? Through a combination of specific emblematic forms, Degouve de Nuncques has sought to give representation to a mood of anxiety, uncertainty and apprehension of the unknown. In this respect, the work may reflect Degouve's own psychological condition which was marked by melancholy and bouts of intense depression.

Degouve's oeuvre is concerned with the portrayal of the inner life. It reveals the artist's spirit, which, though calm, harmonious and shrouded in silence, is also capable of great fluctuations, given to sudden changes of mood, veering from the tranquil and serene to the agitated, though always retaining its silence. *Child with Owl* signals Degouve's affinities with the Symbolist movement. Symbolist painters and writers rejected materialism and fled the vulgarity of everyday life. Using the refinements and subtleties of the imagination, they sought refuge outside reality and enclosed themselves in the bizarre or the hermetic. In Belgium, which already enjoyed a long tradition of the fantastical, Symbolism found the ideal soil in which to flourish. From Maeterlinck to Verhaeren, by way of Rodenbach, Van Lerberghe and Le Roy, or again, from Fernand Khnopff (q.v.) to Degouve de Nuncques, and also in the work of Montald (1862–1944) and Delville (q.v.), the common rule was to follow the precept of one of the major propagandists for Symbolism in France, Jean Moréas, and 'clothe the idea in a tangible form'. Although he mapped out a very individual approach to the Symbolist programme, Degouve found inspiration in certain specific literary figures, namely Shakespeare and Edgar Allan Poe. Affected by their concerns with the tragic and the fantastic, Degouve was especially drawn to Shakespeare's depiction of the madness of King Lear; and the short stories of Poe provided the source for such works as his *House of Usher* [fig. a] and *Maelström*, as well as informing the general atmosphere of a work such as *Child with Owl*. | GOZ

PROVENANCE Enrique Mistler, Antwerp; A. de Glas, Mortsel (Antwerp).
EXHIBITIONS *Les XX* 1893, no. 4; Brussels 1926a, no. 87; Antwerp 1936, no. 14; Schaerbeek (Brussels) 1954, no. 13; Brussels, Otterlo 1962, no. 17; Stavelot 1963, no. 5; London 1965, no. 7; Paris 1972, no. 1; New York, Houston 1974, no. 2; Knokke-Heist 1974, no. 55.
BIBLIOGRAPHY Verhaeren 1893, 74; Biermée 1911, 15; Haesaerts 1935, pl. 40; De Ridder 1957, pl. 1; Legrand 1971, 191, pl. XIX.

7 Night in Venice

Nuit à Venise, 1895
Signed and dated bottom right: W D / de / N 95
Oil on canvas, 60 x 34 cm
Groeningemuseum, Bruges, inv. no. 85.1.1

Much of Degouve de Nuncques's life was nomadic, as he sought out the less well-known and frequented corners of Europe. He was fascinated by entomology, and his greatest love was nature and the creatures that inhabit it. He never ceased to be haunted by the idea of far-off realms, sunny lands whose fairy-tale landscapes became enveloped in mystery when darkness fell. Although in c. 1900, his vagabond's spirit prompted him to pay a long and very fruitful visit to the Balearics, this was not before he had already travelled through France, Austria and, in particular, Italy, where he produced some haunting nocturnal images of Venice. The dilapidated yet radiant physical environment of this unique city, with its coloured stone and shifting waters, fascinated and enchanted him. Under his brush, the features of the City of the Doges acquired a new status, their distant and legendary forms shrouded in the vagueness of the night. It was not Venice the Beautiful that tempted Degouve, but the melancholy of its lagoons, the mysterious ancient courtyards where the shadows of conspirators hover and the stairways lead away to some unknown destination. Degouve liked to observe the dark waters, over which unseen gondolas glided. Venice recalled Degouve's own work, where life and death, light and shadow rub shoulders with one another, and where mystery is ever present. In Venice, as everywhere else, Degouve was pursued by the dark obsessions that peopled his dreams. Verhaeren, who used to call him 'he who reveals the soul of things', also said of him that 'his intellectual art soars beyond reach, into the disquieting realms of unreality and dreams. He is more a poet than a painter. That is why his hermetic art is accessible only to men of letters' (*L'Art moderne*, 24 March 1895). The whole of Degouve's oeuvre displays not only a profound sense of poetry, but also an absolute sincerity. He never makes any concession to fashion or artificial conceit.

Although executed in a different medium, the essentially monochromatic, strongly two-dimensional presentation of the brooding façade of a Venetian palazzo suspended above the dark waters of a canal recalls similar compositional procedures for the same subject matter in James McNeil Whistler's *Venice* etchings. Commissioned by the Fine Arts Society London in 1880, three of them were shown in the first Salon des XX in 1884 (nos. 5–7), where Degouve could have studied them.

Night in Venice was initially in the collection of the distinguished Belgian violinist, leader of the quartet which bore his name, and friend of Octave Maus, Eugène Ysaÿe. Maria Biermé, in her study of Degouve de Nuncques, drew up a rudimentary catalogue of his oeuvre in 1911 in which two paintings entitled *Night in Venice* are listed. One belonged to the Ninauve Collection in Brussels, the other to Ysaÿe. There has been no subsequent detailed study of the work of this mysterious and solitary artist since that date. | GOZ

PROVENANCE Feltkamp, Brussels; acquired by the Museum through the Vrienden van de Stedelijke Musea, 1985.
EXHIBITION Brussels 1896, no. 112.

BIBLIOGRAPHY Joly 1896, 92; [Verhaeren] 1896, 74; Biermé 1911, 15, 90; X., *Stedelijke Musea Brugge. Informatiebulletin* (1985), 1.

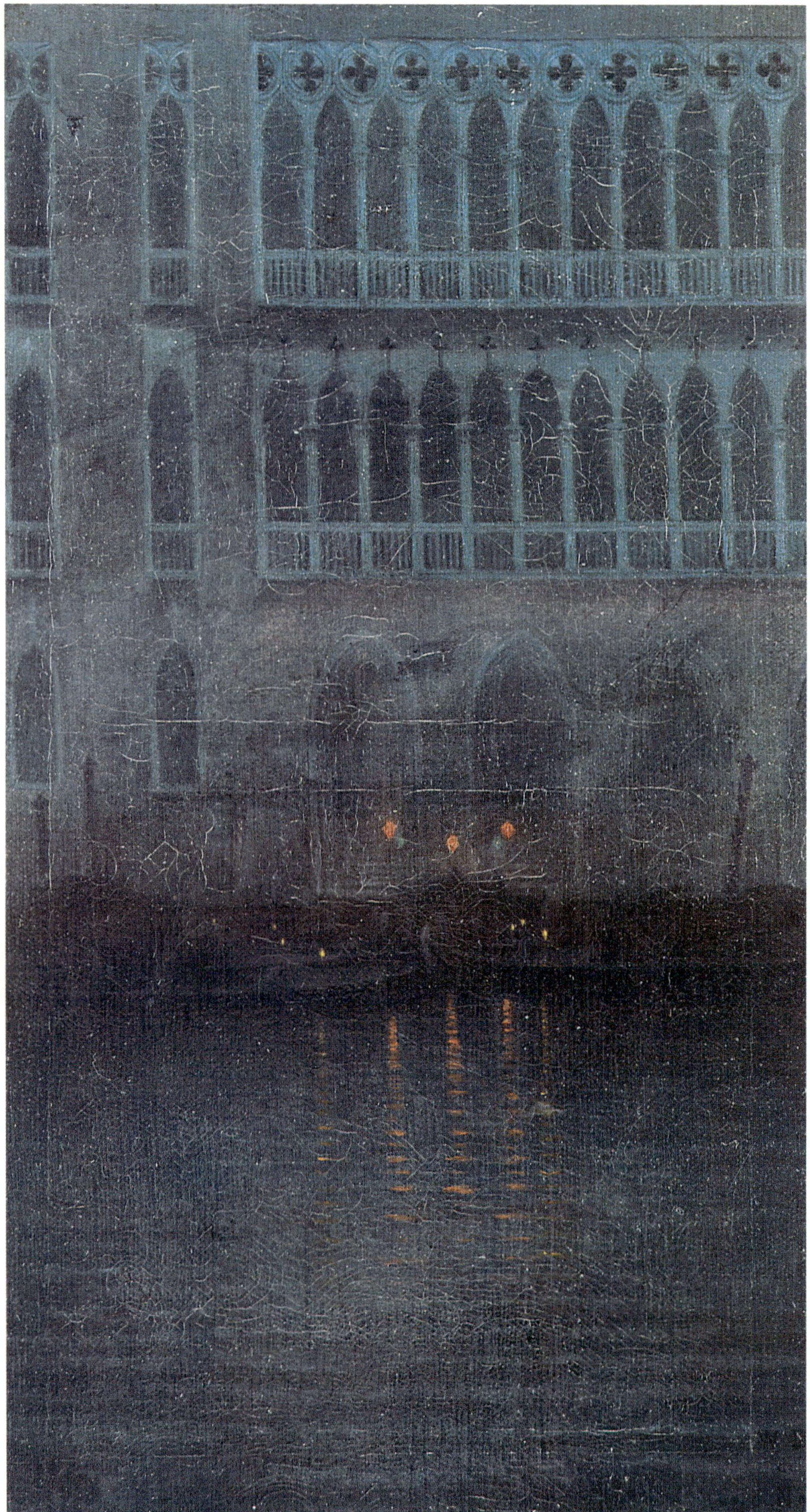

8 Nocturnal Impression

Effet de nuit, 1896
Signed and dated bottom right: W. D / de / 1896 N
Pastel on paper, 49.2 x 66.7 cm
Musée d'Ixelles, Brussels, Octave Maus no. 44

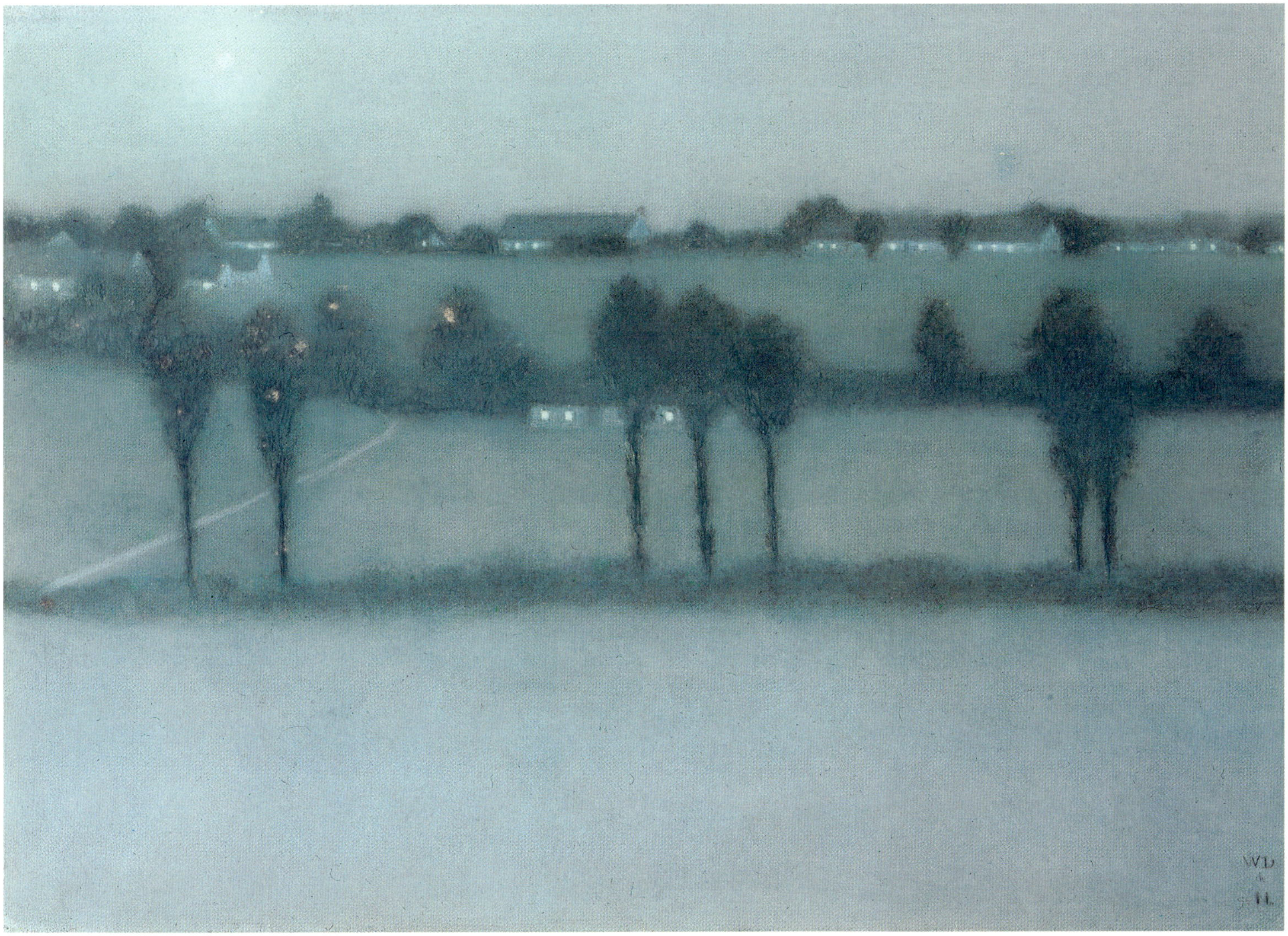

fig. a WILLIAM DEGOUVE DE NUNCQUES
Night Scene in the Parc Royal in Brussels, 1897, pastel, Musée d'Orsay, Paris

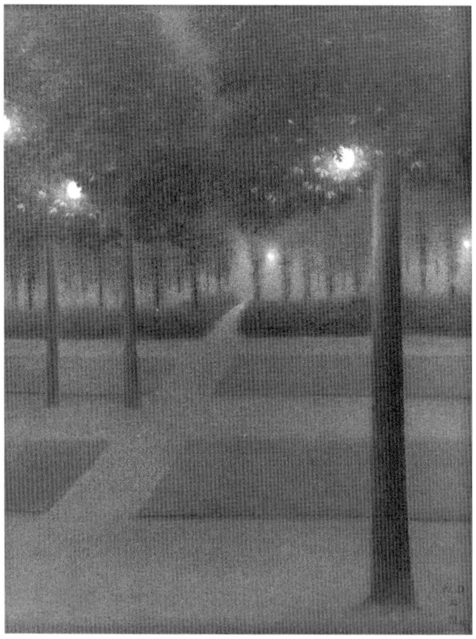

Degouve de Nuncques was largely self-taught. Of his art he declared: 'To make a painting, all you need to do is take some paints, draw some lines, and fill the rest up with feeling.' *Nocturnal Impression* aptly demonstrates this point. Having drawn his initial inspiration from nature, Degouve sought to imbue the scene with a particular atmosphere. He favoured those phases of the day when the world took on a more tranquil aspect, either under the charms of twilight or in the embrace of night. His fondness in particular for the night found expression in many of his works, notably those of parks enveloped in the mysteries of darkness. The theme of solitude tends to be conveyed through silent, uninhabited landscapes whose contained stilness transforms them into visions of dreams.

The technical problems of picture-making, such as composition and medium, held little interest for him. However, his mastery of pastel, which he handled with a lightness of touch, was well-suited to the depiction of his dream-reality images. Some of these works, notably *Nocturnal Impression*, appear to be monochromatic, and yet they are veritable symphonies of colour: like a musician, the artist achieves extraordinary harmonies using only a small number of tones. His choice of tone is always subordinated to the feelings that he is trying to express, and his predilection for blue, a colour associated with dreams, is obviously no accident. Blue is the colour of the night, but it is also the colour of gentleness – which in Degouve's case always has a slight hint of melancholy. Even in those cases where his compositions have titles which suggest the representation of a specific location, *Park in Milan*, for example, or *Night Scene in the Parc Royal in Brussels* [fig. a], the absence of detail, of specific anecdote transforms them into fairy-tale landscape. In the case of *Nocturnal Impression*, not only is it impossible to give a specific geographic location to the landscape, but also such specificity is rigorously eschewed by the artist through the arrangement of the landscape into parallel horizontal bands of foreground, horizon and silhouetted forms of trees, thus deliberately reinforcing the two-dimensionality of the composition. In addition, the rendering of the entire scene in different tones of blue allows it to move into the realms of timelessness. In all the artist's works, the dominant feeling is one of a deep and contemplative tenderness, an indeterminate aspiration towards a sacred Beauty. This ultimately found its translation in the last phase of Degouve de Nuncques's life in works inspired directly by the Holy Gospels. | GOZ

PROVENANCE Octave Maus, Brussels, who donated it to the Museum in 1906.

EXHIBITIONS Schaerbeek (Brussels) 1954, no. 8 (erroneously as 'Nocturne en Brabant, 1901'); Stavelot 1963, no. 28; Brussels 1977, no. 21; Ghent 1980, no. 262; New York 1980, no. 9; Tokyo, Hyogo, Sapporo 1982–1983, no. 81; Antwerp 1985, no. 50; Milan, Rome, Caserta 1986, no. 43; Hokkaido, Tokyo, Fukuoka, Itami 1988, no. 53; Stavelot 1990, no. 2 (erroneously as 'Effet de nuit aux Baléares, 1903'); Brussels 1991, no. 19; Ghent, Lawrence, Williamstown, Cleveland 1992–1993, no. 4.

BIBLIOGRAPHY Mathieu 1990, 134; Norman 1990, 13.

Jean Delville

LOUVAIN 1867 – FOREST (BRUSSELS) 1953

Jean Delville was born on 19 January 1867. He spent his childhood in Brussels, studied at the Academy of Fine Arts from 1879 to 1884, and attended Jean Portaels's (1818–1895) studio.

Delville started his career as a realist, exhibiting for the first time at L'Essor in 1885. In 1887 he was drawn to Symbolism and became an *habitué* of esoteric circles. He published his first poems in 1888 in the periodical *La Wallonie*, and in about 1890 he came into contact with Sâr Péladan, the author, critic and advocate of an aesthetic programme which called for a return to the ideal Beauty derived from the Renaissance that was expounded in his Salon de la Rose+Croix established in Paris in 1891. In 1892 Delville founded the Salon Pour l'Art in Brussels, which consisted primarily of Idealist artists, but also included Auguste Rodin, Eugène Laermans (1864–1940) and Henri Evenepoel (q.v.) among its members. Having become Péladan's chief disciple in Belgium, Delville embarked on large-scale compositions with philosophical connotations (*The Treasures of Satan, The School of Plato*); he wrote numerous theoretical texts, and worked for various periodicals. In 1894 he won the Prix de Rome for his *Christ glorified by the Children* and spent some time in Italy, first in the Eternal City and later in Florence. In 1896 and 1897, he organized annual salons of Idealist Art, in which, among others, Albert Ciamberlani, Léon Fréderic (q.v.) and Constant Montald (1862–1944) took part. He also edited the periodical of the same name. From 1900 to 1905 he taught at the Glasgow School of Art, of which he briefly became head. Having returned to Belgium, he taught at the Belgian Royal Academy of Fine Arts from 1900 to 1937, and also at the Academy in Mons, of which he became director. After the war, in 1920, he joined with Emile Fabry, Constant Montald, Emile Vloors, and Albert Ciamberlani to found the group L'Art monumental. With his colleagues he devoted his time to the decoration of a small number of public buildings, including the arcades of the Cinquantenaire hemicycle in Brussels. Grandiloquent allegorical compositions were popular with public bodies at that time. Gradually Delville began to devote more time to portraiture and sometimes also landscape; but he also wrote a great number of essays on philosophy and aesthetics, for presentation to the Académie royale des Sciences, des Arts et des Lettres, of which he had been a member since 1924. He died at Forest on 19 January 1953. | BF

SUMMARY BIBLIOGRAPHY

A. Ciamberlani, 'Notice sur Jean Delville, membre de l'Académie', *Annuaire de l'Académie royale des Beaux-Arts de Belgique* CXX (Brussels 1954), 181–191; F.C. Legrand, *Le symbolisme en Belgique*, Brussels 1971, 75–93; C. Piérard, 'Jean Delville, peintre poète, esthéticien 1867–1953', *Mémoires et Publications de la Société des Sciences, des Arts et des Lettres du Hainaut* 84 (1971–1973), 209–247; O. Delville, *Jean Delville, peintre*, Brussels 1984; B. de Clerck, 'Jean Delville', in *Académie royale des Beaux-Arts de Belgique, 275 ans d'enseignement*, Musées royaux des Beaux-Arts de Belgique, Brussels 1987, 160–161.

9 Death

La Mort, c. 1890
Signed: Jean Delville
Charcoal and pastel on paper mounted on cardboard, 66 x 38 cm
Private Collection, Belgium (Represented by Leodico, Liège)

There is no documentation for this work, which recently reappeared at a public sale[1] under the title *La Mort*. It may be the same drawing as *La Camarde (The Grim Reaper)*, which formerly belonged to Omer Coppens and was exhibited at the Salon Pour l'Art in 1892.[2]

Various iconographical details, such as the hands on the clock indicating midnight, the cadaverous face and the shroud soiled with blood, allude to Edgar Allan Poe's short story *The Masque of the Red Death*, which had been translated into French by the poet Charles Baudelaire in 1855. The scene is traced out in charcoal, applied with varying degrees of intensity: the drawing-room with walls covered in black velvet, the ebony clock. A few highlights in red pastel suggest the scarlet window-panes and the purple marks of the plague. This literary reference, which probably derived from Delville's links with Villiers de l'Isle-Adam, who himself drew inspiration from the American writer, allows the work to be dated to about 1890, at the start of the artist's career. The composition bears some resemblance to an engraving entitled *Les Aveugles*,[3] the subject of which is borrowed from a play of the same name by Maurice Maeterlinck, and to a *Christ in the Garden of Olives*[4] which bears a signature and a date of 1888. In this period, there are affinities between Delville's work and the haunting world of Odilon Redon. Redon had exhibited several times at the Salon des XX in Brussels (in 1886, 1887 and 1890) and several works by him were in Belgian collections by the end of the 1880s, including a charcoal drawing of a decapitated head which was owned by Edmond Picard, a fervent champion of this idealist painter.

In this case Redon's influence is confined to the choice of medium (charcoal), the haunting image, and the contrast between areas of shadow and the whiteness of sheeting or the bloody gleam of a halo – a technique which Delville borrowed from, amongst other works, *Apparition* of 1883. The density of the blacks and the vigour of the line, both unusual features in Delville, gradually softened into a more academic style, and this characterizes the whole of his oeuvre. Moreover, there is, in Delville's work, no deviation from classical canons of form.

Literary influence in the broad sense remained a dominant feature in Delville's work, as in that of many of his contemporaries. His influences included Poe, Villiers de l'Isle-Adam and Maeterlinck, but also Wagner and Dante. It was from the latter that Delville borrowed the theme for his *Cycle of the Passions* in 1890. All that now remains of this is a small number of sketches of figures.[5] These document a slow stylistic development: the contrasts of light and shade that give the livid mask in *Death* its structure make way for a line based entirely on curves and countercurves, as developed in Art Nouveau.

Delville's interest in Theosophy and religious studies – proof of which is offered, in this drawing, by the hermetic triangle in which the skull is enclosed – occasioned an iconographical renewal in his work. His meeting with Péladan in about 1890 prompted him to translate the esoteric theories of the Sâr into pictorial form and was the cause of the creative exhaustion that becomes obvious in his work in the 1920s.

The tragic face of *Death*, with its bulging eyes, records a moment of aesthetic hesitation, when Delville moved to the brink of a more internalized form of Symbolism and rejected it in favour of his grand idealist vision. | BF

PROVENANCE Collection Omer Coppens (?); sale Brussels, Palais des Beaux-Arts, 15 February 1991; Private Collection, Sint-Martens-Latem.

1 Sale Brussels, Palais des Beaux-Arts, 15 February 1991, no. 725.
2 *Pour l'Art* [catalogue of the first annual exhibition], Musée d'Art moderne, Brussels, November 1892, no. 7.
3 Only one copy of this youthful work is currently known to exist (Private Collection, Brussels).
4 Sale Brussels, Palais des Beaux-Arts, 12 November 1991, no. 355.
5 This monumental work, executed in about 1890 in charcoal on red cardboard and intended as a decoration for the 'Round Table' room at the Town Hall in Louvain, disappeared during the First World War. A few preparatory sketches have survived, including two that are now in Brussels (Musées royaux des Beaux-Arts de Belgique).

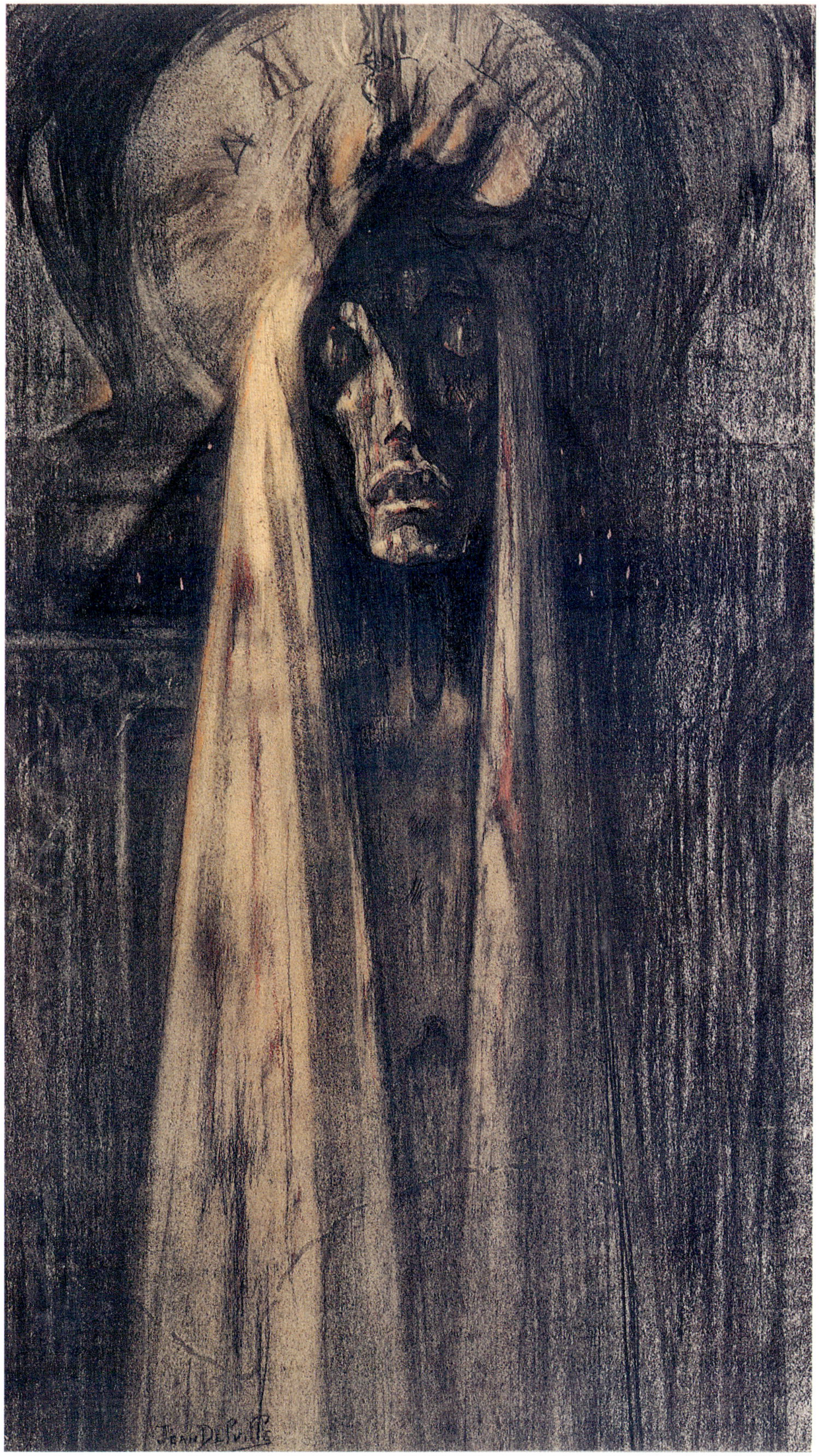

10 Head of a Woman

Tête de femme, 1897
Signed and dated bottom right: Jean Delville Florence 1897
Charcoal and blue pencil ('bleuïne') on paper, 37 x 26 cm
Private Collection, Belgium

In 1894 Jean Delville, then aged 27 and in straitened financial circumstances,[1] took first prize in the Prix de Rome, with a grandiloquent academic composition on the set theme of *Christ glorified by the Children*. When the painter set off for Italy that year,[2] he already had a number of important works strongly influenced by Symbolism to his credit: the *Cycle of the Passions* (1890; destroyed, formerly Town Hall, Louvain), *Head of Orpheus* (1893; Private Collection, Brussels), and *The Treasures of Satan* (1895; Musées royaux des Beaux-Arts de Belgique, Brussels). These works display some of the distinctive features that were to characterize the artist's oeuvre as a whole: an emphasis on line, a taste for a monochrome palette, and a choice of subject derived from philosophical concepts and occultism. Delville's stay in Italy gave him the opportunity both to study at first hand those masters whom he already revered and to consolidate his own aesthetic tendencies. In his Rome studio he began work on his *School of Plato*, a huge canvas which he intended to exhibit at the Salon in Paris[3] and which he completed in Brussels in 1898. True to the principles of Mme Blavatsky's Theosophical programme, Delville represented Plato, the Greek philosopher with the attributes of Christ in this painting.

On his way home, Delville spent some time in Florence,[4] and it was here that he executed this drawing in blue pencil. The woman's delicately traced profile is reminiscent of virgins by Botticelli and Lippi, from whom he borrowed the elaborate hairstyle; by virtue of this very borrowing, the work also displays close affinities with the works of the English Pre-Raphaelites, notably Burne-Jones. The pensive features, deprived of their obvious femininity, recall the hermaphrodites in Delville's *School of Plato*. An Egyptian-style jewel made up of flower-buds echoes the foliage encircling the figure.

The importance accorded to the colour blue in Delville's work after 1893 reflects the development of the artist's ideas on the relationship between art and Theosophy. Although this drawing of the head of a woman is less overtly imbued with obvious classical, theological and Theosophical associations, the cast down eyes and the reference to Florentine Quattrocento sources suggest the influence of the Idealist aesthetics of Sâr Péladan, and the blue tonality, achieved through the use of a blue-toned pencil, to which Delville gave the name *bleuïne*, reveals the influence which the speculative writings of Edouard Schuré (*Les Grands Initiés*[5] [1893]) and of Helena Blavatsky, the founder of the Theosophical Society, had on the painter's work. In the texts on colour theory published by followers of Mme Blavatsky, for example that of Charles W. Leadbeater, which appeared in 1902,[6] and in the writings of Kandinsky,[7] blue, a celestial colour associated with religion, is regarded as a symbol of profundity. It was these qualities that prompted Delville to make intensive use of blue over a number of years, even going so far as to paint the little room in his house where he went to meditate in this colour.[8] | BF

PROVENANCE Sale London, Christie's, 1 December 1989.
EXHIBITION Brussels 1991, no. 51.

1 Piérard 1971–1973, 213.
2 Delville, *Mon autobiographie* (curriculum vitae), unpublished autograph manuscript (Delville Family Collection, Brussels).
3 *Ibid.*
4 Piérard 1971–1973, 215.
5 E. Schuré, *Les grands initiés, esquisse de l'histoire secrète des religions* [1889], Paris 1949, 219–263.
6 C. W. Leadbeater, 'Key to the Meanings of Colors', in *Man Visible and Invisible*; see S. Ringbom, 'Transcending the Visible: the Generation of the Abstract Pioneers', in *The Spiritual in Art: Abstract Painting 1890–1985*, County Museum of Art, Los Angeles, November 1986–March 1987, 131–153.
7 W. Kandinsky, *Ueber das Geistige in der Kunst*, Munich 1911; English trans. *Concerning the Spiritual in Art*, 1947.
8 Delville 1984, 14.

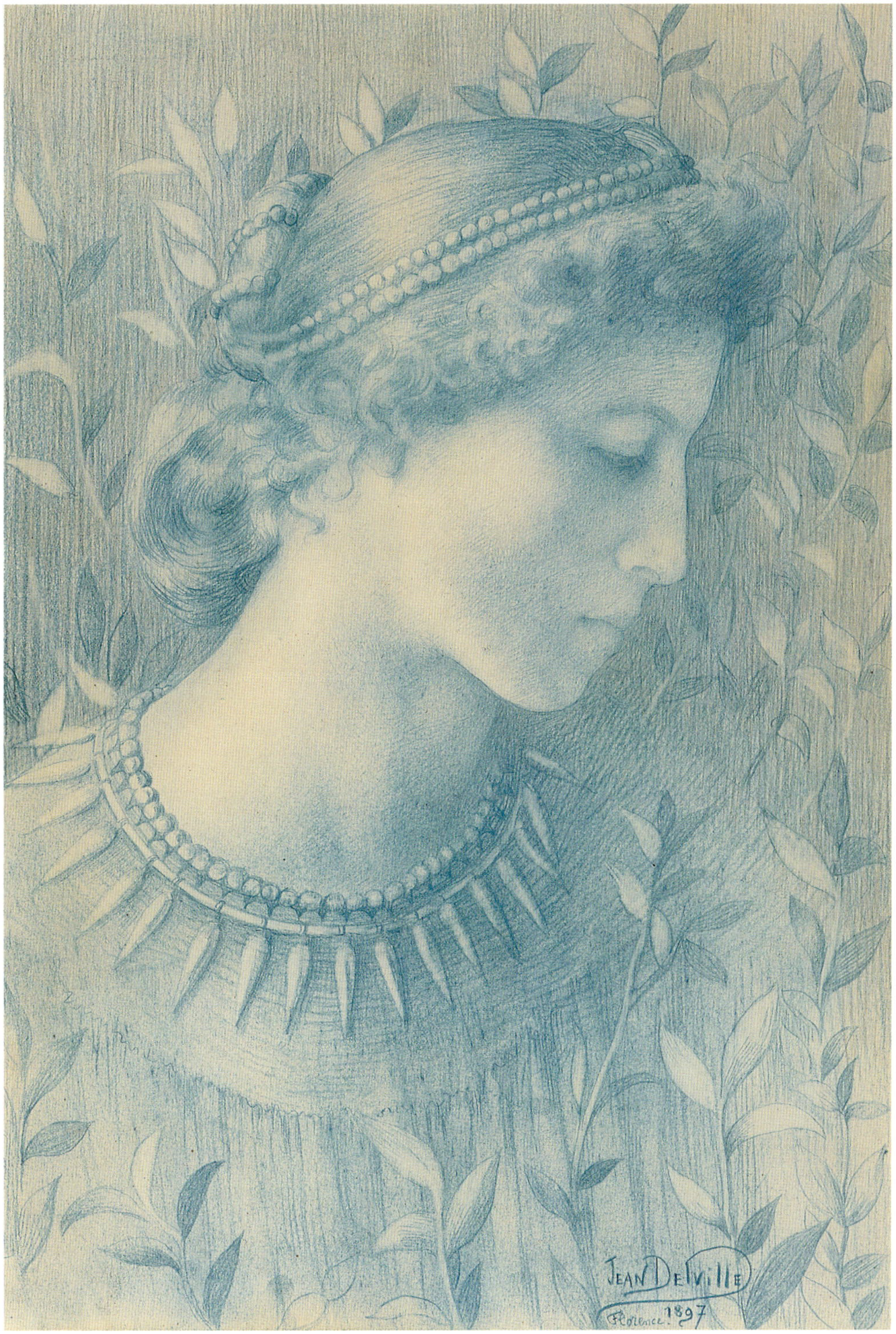
JEAN DELVILLE
Florence 1897

Auguste Donnay

LIÈGE 1862 – JETTE/SAINT-PIERRE 1921

Auguste Donnay was born in Liège on 22 March 1862. His mother died shortly after his birth, and he was brought up by his grandmother, an old servant-woman, who, the artist was later to say, was 'haunted by popular fantasies' and 'smelled of mystery'. From a very early age he learned to seek out the transcendent dimension of even the most humble of objects or actions.

A timid, conscientious child, Donnay determined on a career as a painter-decorator. He was apprenticed to Delbecque and attended evening classes at the Liège Academy of Fine Arts under Adrien de Witte de Limminghe (1850–1935). In 1886, to his astonishment, he won first prize in a competition and was awarded a five-month trip Paris in what proved to be a highly influential journey. Donnay visited museums and exhibitions, and was fascinated by Tanagra figurines, Egyptian and Japanese art, and the Italian Primitives.

Donnay's meeting with Albert Mockel, co-editor, with Henri Regnier, of the important Symbolist periodical *La Wallonie*, was decisive. In 1887, Mockel put him into contact with the periodical's main contributors who had been influenced by the English Pre-Raphaelites and by the French proto-Symbolists, Gustave Moreau, Puvis de Chavannes and Odilon Redon.

Donnay subsequently provided illustrations for the works and periodicals of his literary friends, including ones for *Floréal*, *Wallonia*, *L'Almanach des poètes*, and, most importantly, *La Vie wallonne*. However, as a painter, Donnay was primarily committed to landscape. He showed at the Salon de La Libre Esthéthique in 1894. He also exhibited with Levêque (1866–1921), Delville (q.v.), Fréderic (q.v.) and Montald (1862–1944), at the exhibitions of the esoteric group Kumris. In 1896 his works figured at the Salon de L'Art indépendant, together with those Rops, Redon and Denis, and also those of his colleagues from Liège, Emile Berchmans (1866–1921) and Armand Rassenfosse (1862–1934). His work was subsequently shown in Italy, France, Britain, the Netherlands and Sweden.

He was appointed to the Liège Academy of Fine Arts in 1901 where he introduced a course on ornamental composition. In 1905, he settled at Méry-sur-Ourthe, and in the same year, at the first Congrès wallon, he presented a report on Walloon sentiment in painting which attracted considerable attention. He also enjoyed the admiration of a group of artists known as the 'Intimists of the School of Verviers', which included Georges Le Brun (q.v.).

Despite national and international recognition, Donnay became increasingly the victim of depression. He was badly affected by the First World War (in 1898 he had married Louise Leitz, a native of Mannheim), and on 18 July 1921 he took his own life. He was accorded a major retrospective exhibition by Liège in 1922. | LS

SUMMARY BIBLIOGRAPHY

A. Mockel, *Auguste Donnay, souvenirs et réflexions*, Liège [1922]; M. Kunel, *Aug. Donnay. Peintre de Wallonie*, [Liège 1923]; J. Bosmant, *La Peinture et la Sculpture au Pays de Liège de 1793 à nos jours*, [Liège] 1930, 181–191; J. Bosmant, *Auguste Donnay* (Monographies de l'Art belge), Bruxelles 1967; J. Parisse, *Auguste Donnay, un visage de la terre wallonne*, Editions du Crédit Communal, 1991; *Rétrospective des œuvres d'Auguste Donnay*, Liège 1922; *Rétrospective Auguste Donnay*, Université de Liège, Château de Colonster, 1968; *Auguste Donnay, un visage de la terre wallonne*, Musée de l'Art Wallon, Liège 1991 (Catalogue by J. Parisse).

11 The Blue Door

La Porte bleue, c. 1895
Mixed media on cardboard, 44.5 x 69 cm
Signed centre lower edge: Aug Donnay
Musée de l'Art Wallon, Liège, inv. no. AW 464

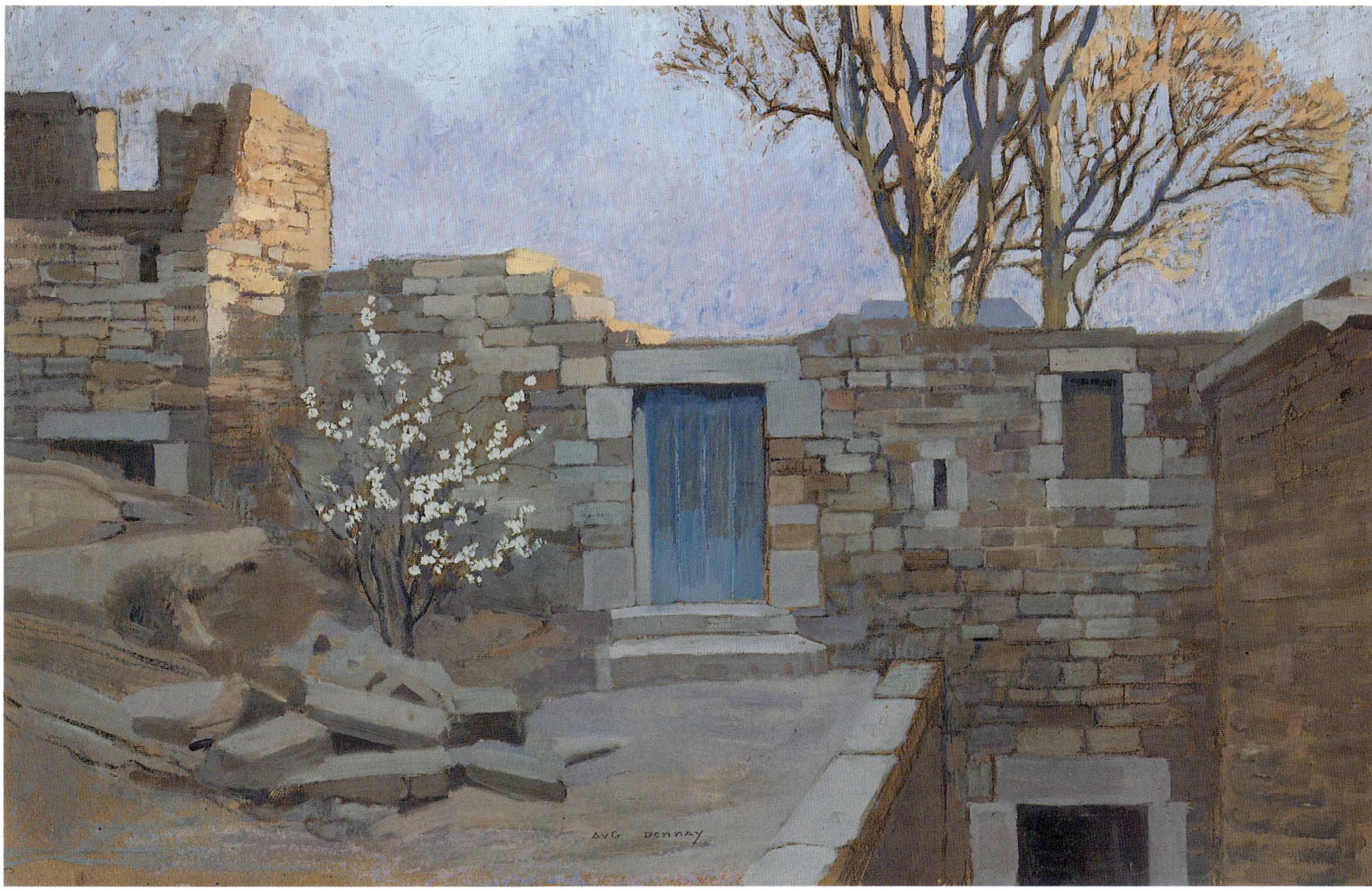

Donnay approached landscape in order to extract from a given location the underlying structural elements and essential atmosphere which he rendered in simple outline and a dominant tonality. In his hands, the landscape of the Ourthe and Amblève valleys underwent constant refined and subtle variation, as they became the messengers of the artist's meditation upon Nature: 'Each one [of his landscapes] is hallowed with tenderness and respect: there is not one detail of landscape ... that he cannot adapt to follow hidden, venerable purposes; the woods and the old walls are full of supernatural spirits; legends prowl around every dwelling; everything is charged with memory and times past' (Richard Dupierreux). *The Blue Door* well illustrates this process of transformation. The crumbling stone wall and ancient doorway are set in contrast to the branches of the trees, lit by the residual rays of te setting sun. The simplified forms, delineated with a minimal black line, are cast in an overall blue tonality, which imbues the composition with a sense of meditation and silence. Such an application of a dominant tone to a landscape invites parallels with the French proto-Symbolist painter, Pierre Puvis de Chavannes, who employed dominant tonalities to establish the mood of a given subject, as, for example, in the impoverished greyness which envelopes *The Poor Fisherman* (1881; Musée d'Orsay, Paris). While *The Blue Door* contains no figures, some of Donnay's landscapes do include discreet narrative groups such as an Annunciation or a Flight into Egypt, which confer supplementary religious meaning to a given scene. | LS

PROVENANCE Auguste Donnay Bequest, 1922.
EXHIBITION Paris 1987–1988.

James Ensor

OSTEND 1860–1949

Born in Ostend, the son of an Anglo-Belgian father and a Flemish mother, James Ensor was painting and drawing reproductions by the age of thirteen. He enrolled at the Ostend Academy in 1876, where he drew from plaster casts of the Antique and life models; he also made small studies on pink card, depicting the town and the surrounding area, the dunes and the sea which were cherished throughout his life. From 1877 to 1880 he studied at the Brussels Academy of Fine Arts, but the drawings, life studies and history compositions he produced there met with scant approval. He reworked several of these academic pieces a few years later. In Brussels, Ensor met the critic and amateur painter Théo Hannon, who introduced him to the liberal circle of Ernest Rousseau, a professor at the city's Université Libre, and his young wife Mariette (Ensor's 'unattainable love'), a talented scientist. The artist returned to Ostend in 1880, moving into the attic studio of his parents' house-cum-souvenir and curiosity shop on the corner of Vlaanderenstraat and Van Iseghemlaan. He made his début in Brussels at the first exhibition of the progressive society, La Chrysalide, in 1881, where he showed *The Painter* and the *Bourgeois Drawing Room* (both 1881; Musées royaux des Beaux-Arts de Belgique, Brussels, and Koninklijk Museum voor Schone Kunsten, Antwerp, respectively). He was rapidly acknowledged to be one of the leading and boldest exponents of 'Belgian Impressionism' or 'tachisme'. In 1882, *Woman eating Oysters* (Koninklijk Museum voor Schone Kunsten, Antwerp) was rejected by the Antwerp Salon, but two interiors were accepted by the Salon des Artistes français in Paris. One year later, he deflected with a number of artists from L'Essor and set up Les XX. Between 1885 and c. 1888 he concentrated on drawings and engravings, strongly influenced by the work of Rembrandt. He resisted French Impressionism and Symbolism, choosing to explore the expressive possibilities of light, line and colour in the service of a highly personal, symbolic visual vocabulary. He produced crowd scenes like *The Halos of Christ or the Sensibilities of Light* (1885–1886; Musées royaux des Beaux-Arts de Belgique, Brussels; Museum voor Schone Kunsten, Ghent; and various private collections), which he first showed at Les XX. Ensor developed a grotesque metamorphosis of reality which culminated in his famous mask paintings and the monumental *Christ's Entry into Brussels* (1888–1889; J.P. Getty Museum, Malibu). It was at this time that he met the eighteen-year-old Augusta Boogaerts with whom he formed a life-long relationship, although they continued to live apart. Ensor was much concerned with family affairs and the well-being of his mother, his aunt who lived with him, his sister 'Mitche' and her daughter Alexandrine, 'la Chinoise'.

From the 1890s onward, he increasingly tempted art-lovers with engraved or painted reprises, variations and brighter versions of his 'heroic' works, which he sold with mounting success at numerous one-man exhibitions from 1891 (Galerie Dietrich, Brussels). Hailed as a pioneer, his art was promoted at home and abroad after 1905 by François Franck and other members of the Antwerp exhibition society Kunst van Heden. He himself claimed precedence in numerous speeches and articles in the evolution of Luminism, Fauvism, Expressionism, Futurism and Surrealism. He was made a baron in 1929, and became a naturalized Belgian, giving up his British nationality. | HT

SUMMARY BIBLIOGRAPHY

E. Demolder, *James Ensor*, Brussels 1892; 'James Ensor, peintre et graveur', *La Plume* (special issue), Paris 1898; E. Verhaeren, *James Ensor*, Brussels 1908; L. Tannenbaum, *James Ensor*, New York 1951; P. Haesaerts, *James Ensor*, Brussels 1958; H. de France, *James Ensor, essai de bibliographie commentée*, Brussels 1960; H. T. Piron, *Ensor, een psychoanalytische studie*, Antwerp 1968; F. C. Legrand, *Ensor, cet inconnu*, Brussels 1971; J. D. Farmer, *Ensor*, New York 1976; R. L. Delevoy, *Ensor*, Antwerp 1981; *Ensor*, Koninklijk Museum voor Schone Kunsten, Antwerp 1983; D. Lesko, *James Ensor. The creative years*, Princeton 1985; X. Tricot, *James Ensor. Catalogue raisonné des peintures*, Antwerp 1992, 2 vols.

12 Russian Music

La Musique russe, 1881
Oil on canvas, 133 x 110 cm
Signed and dated bottom left: James Ensor 1881
Musées royaux des Beaux-Arts de Belgique / Koninklijke Musea voor Schone Kunsten van België, Brussels, inv. no. 4679

The composition of this work is closely related to that of the *Bourgeois Drawing Room* (Koninklijk Museum voor Schone Kunsten, Antwerp) which was exhibited in May 1881 at La Chrysalide under the title 'Le Salon (impression)'. In both works, Ensor uses a diagonal perspective with slightly elevated viewpoint and a combination of profile and back views for the figures.

Russian Music was shown at the Brussels Salon that summer under the title 'Chez Miss', to emphasize the rather anecdotal intent of the picture, in which a gentleman visits a young lady who entertains him by playing the piano. The painting belongs thematically to a group of works in which Ensor captured – with no hidden agenda – the vicissitudes of a young bourgeois woman's life. Unlike his popular contemporary Alfred Stevens, Ensor was not interested in obvious anecdote or the psychology of his subjects, but in sketching a situation. He is concerned with the way light reveals and affects the identity of things and the overall mood. The interior is not intended as a mere setting for the depicted action, but instead complements the protagonists: it is the intimate microcosm of their existence.

Ensor almost invariably painted the rooms of his parents' house in Ostend, usually incorporating members of his family or friends (the figures shown here are the painter Willy Finch [q.v.] and Ensor's sister Mariette ['Mitche']). There are numerous drawings in which Ensor offers a pictorial record of his intense relationships with Théo Hannon, Willy Finch and Mitche. But the precise nature of the bond between Ensor's sister and his inseparable friend Finch is not known to us. In addition, there are no motifs or features that enable us to interpret these interiors as autobiographical statements of Ensor's dislike or fear of an oppressive family and provincial milieu.

The painting was shown at Les XX in February 1886 under the title *Russian Music*. A concert held in Brussels the previous January had caused a major stir. Organized by Madame de Mercy-Argenteau, it was the first occasion that the music of the young Russians Borodin and Rimsky-Korsakov had been performed in Belgium.[1] We do not know whether Ensor attended the concert and renamed his painting out of admiration for Russian music, but the title might be seen as characteristic of Ensor's alert but superficial attitude towards the cultural fashions of his time. The same exhibition of Les XX included Fernand Khnopff's *Listening to Schumann* [cat. 28], and Ensor was furious when *L'Art moderne* subsequently dedicated three articles to Khnopff's work. In a letter to Octave Maus, the secretary of Les XX, he accused Khnopff of plagiarism, and referred to Emile Zola's novel *L'Œuvre* (Paris 1886), comparing himself to Claude Lantier, the unacknowledged artist, and Khnopff to Fagerolles, the servant who takes advantage of his master's suicide to plagiarize his work.[2] | HT

PROVENANCE Anna Boch, Brussels, who donated it to the Museum in 1927.
EXHIBITIONS Brussels 1881, no. 300 (as 'Chez Miss'); Paris 1882, no. 980 (as 'Chez Miss'); Ghent 1883, no. 349 (as 'Chez Miss'), *Les XX* 1886, no. 13 (as 'Musique russe'); *La Libre Esthétique* 1905, no. 175; Ghent 1913, no. 190; Brussels 1920a, no. 40; Brussels 1929a; no. 100; Paris 1932, no. 29; London 1946, no. 29; Chicago, New York 1976–1977, no. 8.
BIBLIOGRAPHY Verhaeren 1908, 107 (as 1880); Le Roy 1922, 173; Haesaerts 1957, 249; Heusinger von Waldegg 1991, 57–61; Tricot 1992, 181.

1 'Le premier concert populaire', *L'Art moderne* 6 (1886), 19–20.
2 F. C. Legrand, 'Les Lettres de James Ensor à Octave Maus', *Bulletin Musées royaux des Beaux-Arts de Belgique* 15 (1966), 24.

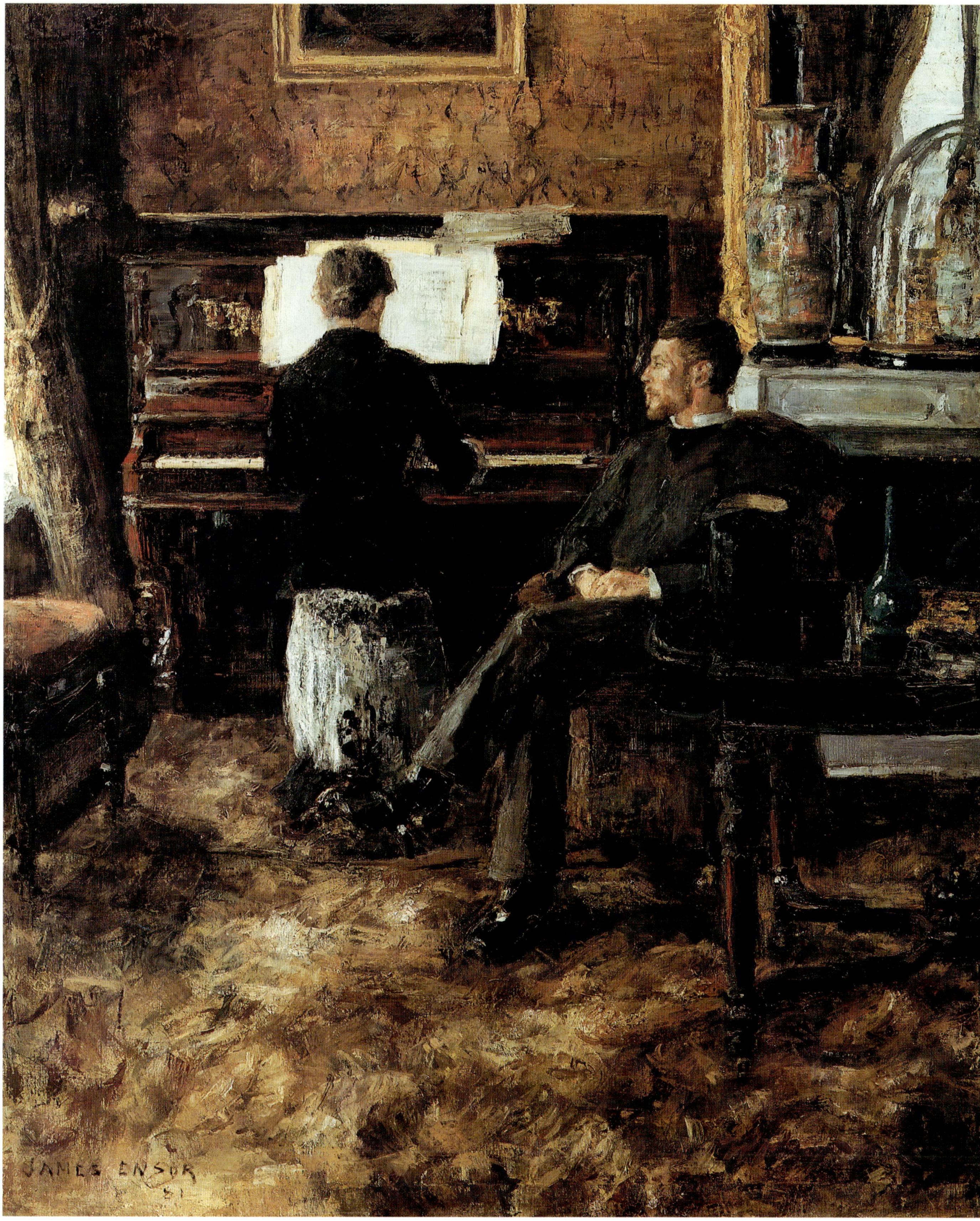
JAMES ENSOR
81

13 Still Life with Vegetables

Nature morte aux légumes, 1882
Oil on canvas, 80 x 100 cm
Signed bottom left: Ensor
Musée d'Art moderne et d'Art contemporain, Liège, inv. no. AM505/269

Still life remained a secondary genre throughout most of the nineteenth century. A handful of specialists, who remained true to the precepts of Neo-Classicism, showed still lifes at the Salons, but it was not until the final decades of the century that something of a resurgence (measurable quantitatively) occurred in the genre. The revival began in France in the 1860s in the work of artists such as Philippe Rousseau, Antoine Vollon, Théodule Ribot, François Bonvin, Adolphe-Félix Cals, and the Belgian Louis Dubois (1830–1880). Ensor's first biographer, Eugène Demolder (1892), was the first to remark upon Dubois's influence on Ensor in this regard.

Ensor was always more interested in still lifes than, for example, landscape painting [cats. 14, 18]. His efforts in this field were, moreover, generally given a favourable reception by the critics. During the early part of his career, he painted still lifes of flowers, oriental porcelain and fans and numerous pictures of food piled up on the corner of a tabletop. Ensor exhibited these still lifes with vague, non-specific titles, such as 'Nature morte (impression)', 'Accessoires' or 'Le Hochepot'.

His 'kitchen still lifes' are generally reminiscent of the Baroque market and kitchen scenes of Frans Snyders, reflecting a revival of interest in the seventeenth-century precursors of the Realist still life. Compared to Snyders's abundance, however, Ensor's kitchen pieces possess a simplicity that is almost banal and impoverished. If it is true that the wealth displayed in the earlier still lifes was inversely proportional to the subsistence economy of the *Ancien Régime*, Ensor's 'poverty' might equally be seen as inversely proportional to the sharply improved prosperity of industrialized, bourgeois society. The composition is always seemingly simple, providing the artist with the latitude and freedom to subordinate motifs and specific forms to the interplay of light and colour, the sensuality of tactile values and the solid monumentality of shapes, stressed throughout the canvas by the application of thick paint with a palette knife. | HT

PROVENANCE Bought from the artist by the Museum in 1905.
EXHIBITIONS Brussels 1929a, no. 103; Paris 1932, no. 32; Paris 1939, no. 11; Antwerp 1951, no. 46; New York, Boston, Cleveland, St Louis 1951–1952, no. 17; London 1960, no. 27; Ostend 1960, no. 30; Stockholm 1970, no. 21; Stuttgart 1972, no. 15; Stavelot 1976, no. 3; Chicago, New York 1976–1977, no. 11; Zurich 1983, no. 41; Antwerp 1983, no. 45; Hyogo 1984, no. 31.

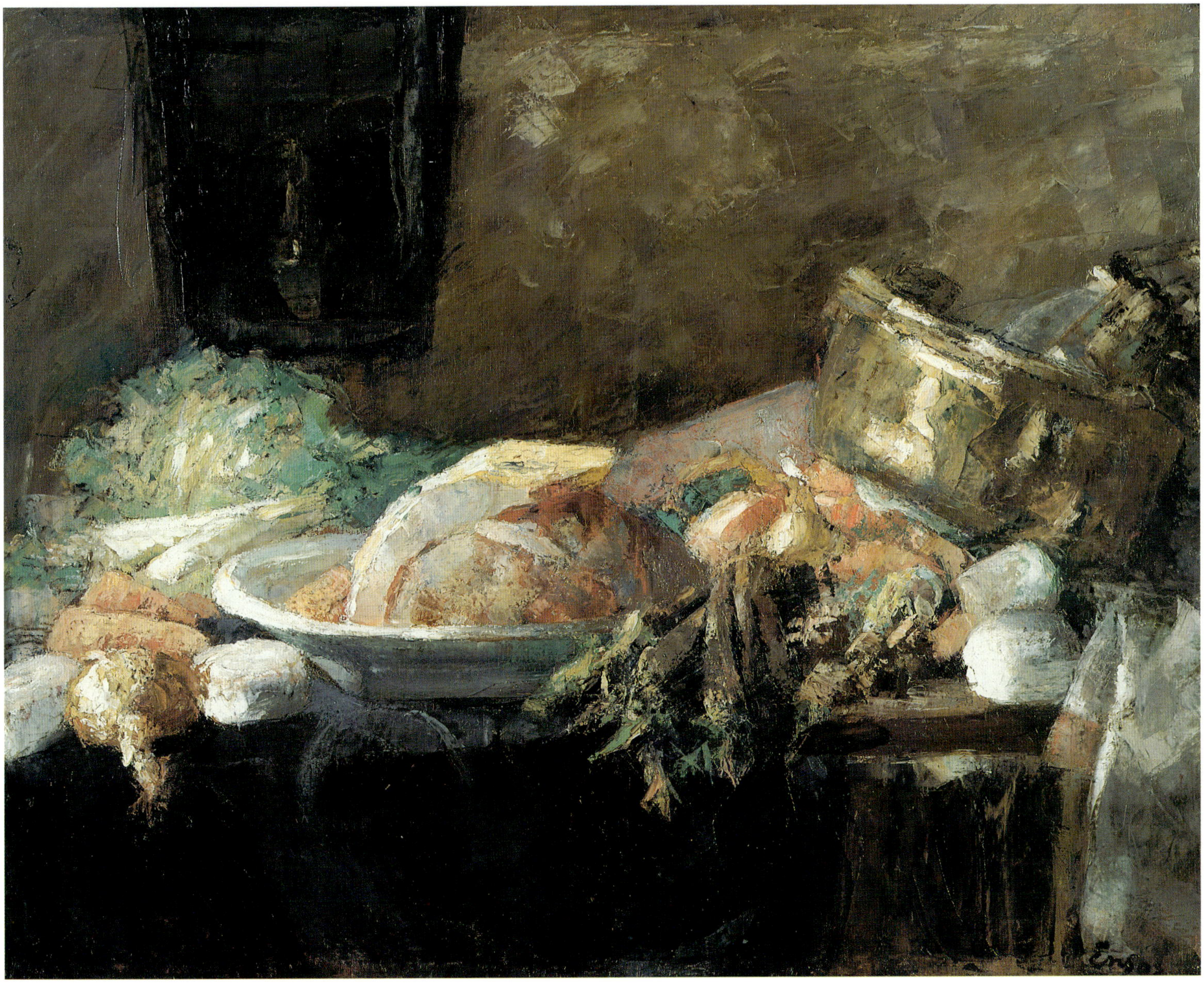

14 The White Cloud

Le Nuage blanc, 1884
Oil on canvas, 80 x 99 cm
Signed and dated bottom right: Ensor 84
Koninklijk Museum voor Schone Kunsten, Antwerp, inv. no. 2175

Like an ecologist *avant la lettre*, Ensor frequently sang the praises of the sea in his later writings. However, he only concentrated intensively on marine painting for a few years – in his prints of 1887 to 1891, and the oil paintings characteristic of his previous, so-called 'dark period' (1880–1885).

The radical reduction of a seascape to little more than parallel strips of dry and wet beach, surf, water and an infinite sky recall certain empty seascapes painted by Gustave Courbet and J. M. Whistler in the mid-1860s. We do not know whether Ensor discovered Courbet's elemental vision independently, or whether he came to it through the example of Eugène Boudin, Pericles Pantazis (1849–1884), Louis Dubois (1830–1880), Louis Artan (q.v.) or Guillaume Vogels (q.v.). Like Courbet, Ensor strove to give material form, as it were, to the different substances of the sand, the waves and the clouds. And like Courbet, he used the palette knife to achieve this end. However, he went much further than Courbet in both conception and execution.

Ensor painted dozens of seascapes in the first half of the 1880s, with an unusually large variation in colour and handling of paint: refined, monochromatic works exist side by side with expressionistic, chromatic evocations of the sea. This variation makes it difficult to identify the seascapes listed in older exhibition catalogues, and to trace the relative chronology within this group of works. While also reflecting changing weather conditions at sea, the same variation is primarily the fruit of Ensor's extraordinary talent as a colourist. A highly developed sense of nuance brings him to the boundaries of Impressionism in certain works. He was thus able in 1887 effortlessly to transform two of these seascapes into the entrancing *Carnival on the Beach* (Musées royaux des Beaux-Arts de Belgique, Brussels, and Private Collection). But *The White Cloud*, which casts a surprisingly dark shadow onto the surface of the water, is there to remind us that Ensor wished above all to remain true to the representation of the motif. | HT

PROVENANCE François Franck, Antwerp, who donated it to the Museum in 1930.

EXHIBITIONS Antwerp 1913, no. 5; Brussels 1920a, no. 22; Antwerp 1921, no. 59; Hanover, Berlin, Dresden 1927; Mannheim, Leipzig 1928 (as 'Seestück, 1882'); Brussels 1929a, no. 133; Antwerp 1951, no. 60; Paris 1954, no. 32; Otterlo, Rotterdam 1961, no. 27; Basel, Münster 1963, no. 32; Zurich 1983, no. 48; Antwerp 1983, no. 53.

BIBLIOGRAPHY Verhaeren 1908, 112; Le Roy 1922, 178; Haesaerts 1957, 308 (as c. 1882); H. Todts, in Utrecht 1993, 60–61; Tricot 1992, 224.

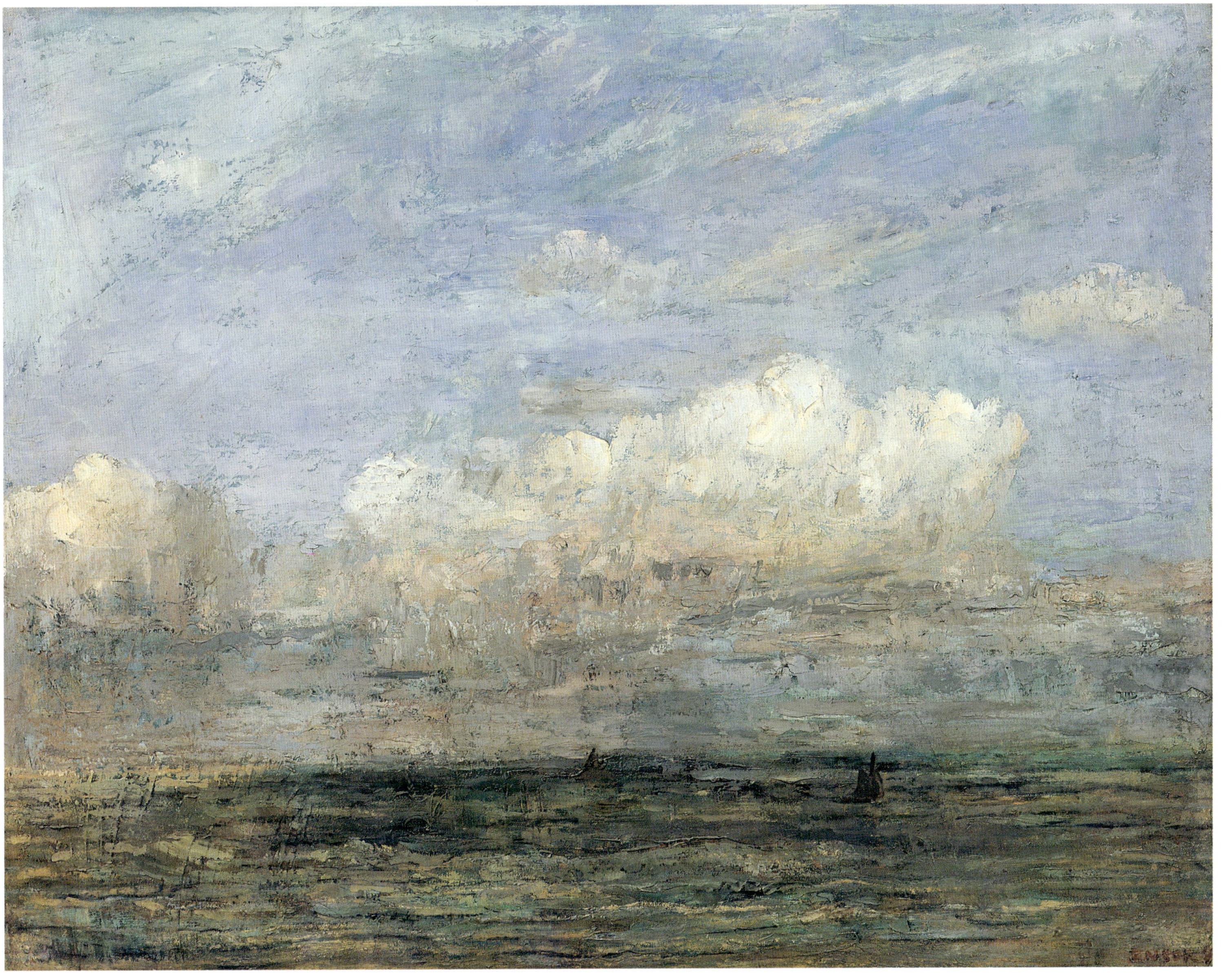

15 Brussels Town Hall

Hôtel de Ville de Bruxelles, c. 1885
Oil on canvas, 100 x 81 cm
Signed bottom left: Ensor
Musée d'Art moderne et d'Art contemporain, Liège, inv. no. AM64/268

Ensor filled many sketchbook pages with records of Ostend street life observed from the attic studio in his parents' house. There are several paintings with general views of Vlaanderenstraat and Van Iseghemlaan. But his life was not confined to the coastal town. Having completed his studies at the Brussels Academy of Fine Arts, he stayed on several occasions at the home of the Rousseau family in the capital. He also rented a room in Brussels for several months at a time. This view of the tower of Brussels town hall was done during one of these temporary sojourns in the city.

Views of a town or a landscape seen through a window began to appear in art in the late eighteenth century. The bird's eye perspective was the traditional means of conveying topographical information. As the urban experience became increasingly complex, such cityscapes tended to stress the fragmentary, arbitrary nature over the strictly topographical in order to evoke the city in a synecdochic way. Ensor's painting demonstrates this transformation, showing a striking but in no way essential or recognizable view of Brussels: only those who recognize the Gothic towers will realize that this is a picture of the town hall of that city. Instead, the precipitous viewpoint, the roofs with their odd geometric patterns which extend beyond the chance boundaries of the picture plane, create a new, anti-picturesque view of the urban scene.

Panoramic city views of this kind were common in the nineteenth century, possibly with the addition of a figure before the window which could accentuate the dramatic potential. Impressionist artists were quick to exploit panoramic street and town views to capture fleeting atmospheric effects in an expansive sky. Figuration – the silhouettes of fleeting presences – could also be set against the high, even surface of the road. The street, with its hurried, fashionable and anonymous passers-by, thus offered a perfect cross-section of modern life.

Although Ensor concentrated in other paintings on shifting weather conditions and light effects, this particular work lacks the 'sunny pulse' of modernity. He focuses instead on the interplay of the façades and roofs. The sun rises behind the tower of the town hall, while a handful of people hurry through the early morning winter cold. The overcast, sombre mood is alleviated by the red and blue advertisements treated as almost abstract patterns within the composition.

The painting is not dated. It was first shown in 1887, but has been ascribed to 1885 by Emile Verhaeren and Gregoire Le Roy; this date is also given in the catalogue of Ensor's 1929 retrospective. | HT

PROVENANCE Purchased by the Museum in 1902.

EXHIBITIONS Antwerp 1887, no. 49; Brussels 1929a, no. 148 (as 1885); Antwerp 1951, no. 66; New York, Boston, Cleveland, St Louis 1951–1952, no. 23; London 1960, no. 35; Ostend 1960, no. 43; Otterlo, Rotterdam 1961, no. 31; Basel, Münster 1963, no. 34; Stockholm 1970, no. 40; Stuttgart 1972, no. 22; Stavelot 1976, no. 5; Chicago, New York 1976–1977, no. 19; Zurich 1983, no. 51; Antwerp 1983, no. 56; Hyogo 1984, no. 35; Munich 1989, no. 20; Paris 1990b, no. 81.

BIBLIOGRAPHY Verhaeren 1908, 112 (as 'Vue de Bruxelles, 1885'); Le Roy 1922, 179 (as 'Vue de Bruxelles, 1885'); Haesaerts 1957, 277; H. Todts, in Paris 1990b, 144; Tricot 1992, 236.

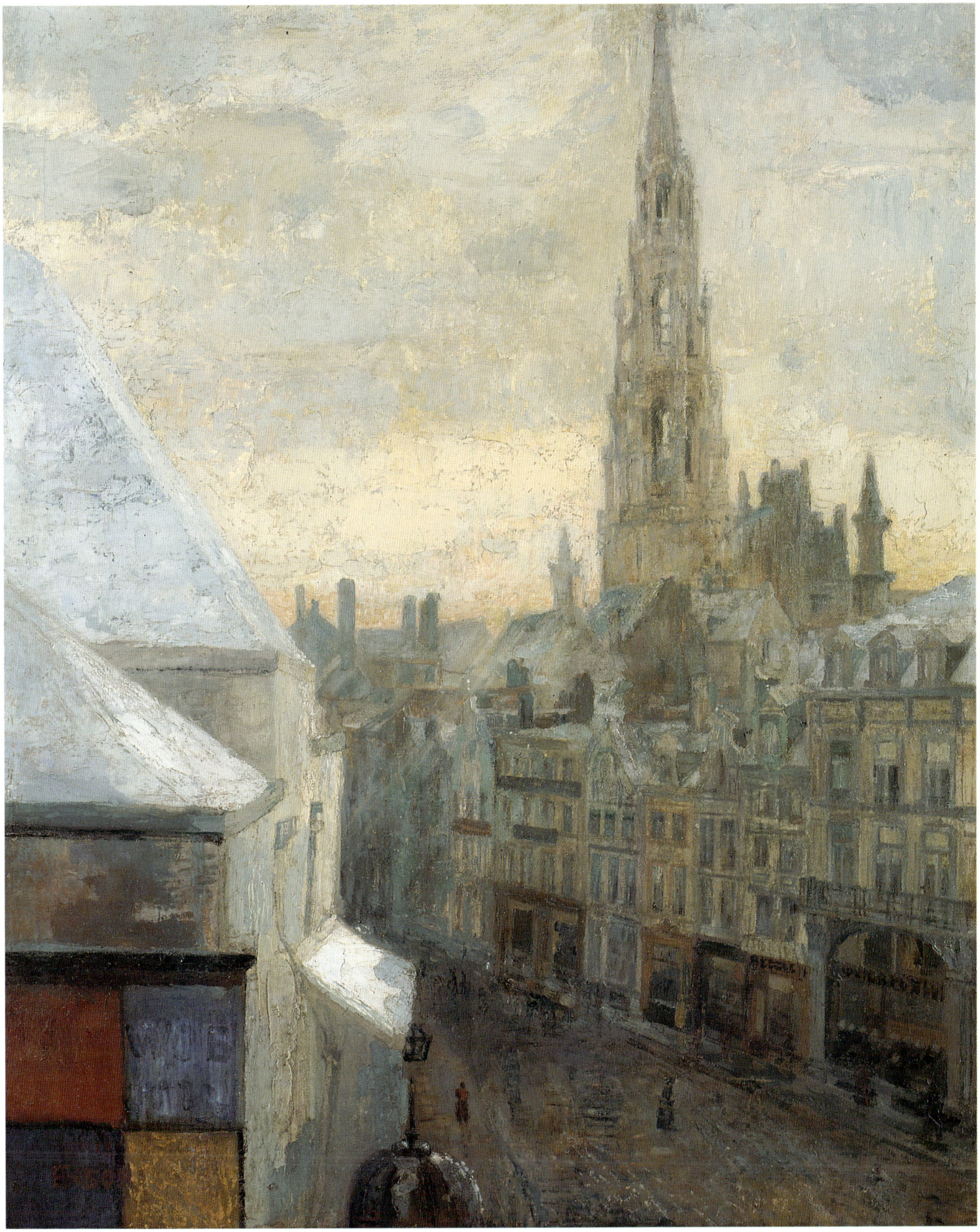

16 Children washing

Les Enfants à la toilette, 1886
Oil on canvas, 135 x 100 cm
Signed and dated bottom left: Ensor 1886
Private Collection

A major shift occurred in James Ensor's work after 1885. Following the triumphant reception of French Impressionism at Les XX of 1886, Ensor's palette brightened and he abandoned the loaded 'tachiste brush'. He also began to concentrate almost exclusively on drawing and print-making, a change of emphasis that was to last for several years. The results of this shift are apparent in the painting *Children washing.* The conception of the motifs is interwoven with the dominance of the light. Ensor later christened the work *Etude de lumière* to show his younger colleagues, especially those followers of Vuillard and Bonnard, that he too had been the author of pioneering work. Most commentators since Vanbeselaere have pointed to the tonal relationship between Ensor and the late work of Turner. Thus far, however, it has not been possible to document any visit by Ensor to London in 1886 or 1887.

The painting shows two girls washing. As Lesko has pointed out, the washbowl that belongs with the pitcher is missing. The bowl was, however, discovered by De Maeyer through analysis of the paint structure and photographs taken under raking light. The foot of the child on the chair was originally placed in the bowl, which was later painted out by the artist. The picture began as an original interpretation of a popular contemporary motif. Numerous sculpted and painted representations of innocent, naked children were produced in the second half of the nineteenth century, often in mundane or amusing circumstances. As in this case, the nudity of these young figures becomes a kind of attribute, enabling us to distinguish boy from young man and Lolita from harlot. The moral innocence of the children makes good their lack of manners. This reading is altered by Ensor's removal of the bowl, which transforms an innocent genre scene into a rather erotically charged and intriguing portrayal. The distant, slightly elevated viewpoint favoured by Ensor now forces the viewer into the distasteful role of voyeur. The artificial poses of the children are emphasized and become much more reminiscent of examples in classical sculpture such as the *Spinario* or the contrapposto figures of Praxiteles.

Contrary to Diane Lesko's claim, presentation and execution show no sign of allegorical, symbolist or autobiographical intent. Her identification of the children as Ensor's mother and sister is based purely on wishful thinking. Indeed, the same anonymous sitters which are seen washing in the painting are found in several drawings made in the same period [see fig. a]. Their features cannot be those of Ensor's mother or his sister. | HT

PROVENANCE A. Lambotte, Esneux, Antwerp; Galeries Breckpot, Antwerp; C. Jussiant, Antwerp.

EXHIBITIONS *Les XX* 1888, no. 4; *La Libre Esthétique* 1908, no. 80 (as 'Etude de lumière'); Antwerp 1909, no. 170; Antwerp 1910, no. 19; Rotterdam 1910, no. 19; Ghent 1913, no. 188; Antwerp 1921, no. 94; Brussels 1929a, no. 153; Paris 1932, no. 49; Paris 1939, no. 20; Brussels 1945, no. 46; Antwerp 1951, no. 67; New York, Boston, Cleveland, St Louis 1951–1952, no. 24; Antwerp 1955, no. 34; London 1960, no. 47; Ostend 1960, no. 47; Otterlo, Rotterdam 1961, no. 32; Basel, Münster 1963, no. 39; Paris 1970, no. 49; Stuttgart 1972, no. 24; Kamakura, Nagoya, Fukuoka, Kyoto 1972–1973, no. 13; Tel Aviv 1981, no. 21; Antwerp 1983, no. 61; Zurich 1983, no. 55; Brussels, Paris 1985–1986, no. 16; Munich 1989, no. 23; Paris 1990b, no. 93.

BIBLIOGRAPHY Verhaeren 1908, 113; Le Roy 1922, 179; W. Vanbeselaere, in Antwerp 1951, 14–16; Haesaerts 1957, 265; Lesko 1985; L. Schoonbaert, in Paris 1990b, 154; Tricot 1992, 242.

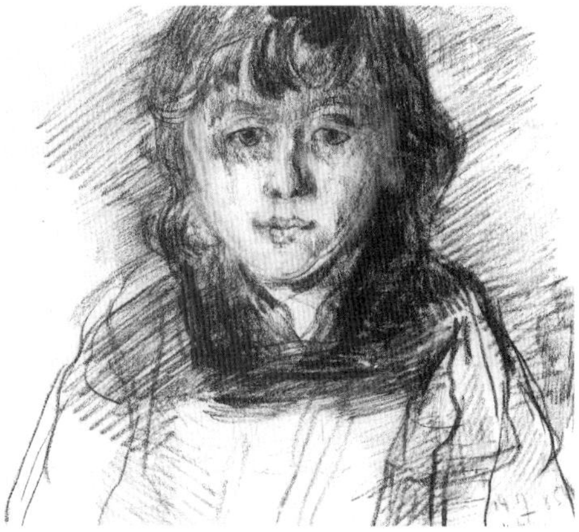

fig. a JAMES ENSOR
Portrait of a girl, 1885,
pencil and conté crayon on paper,
Koninklijk Museum voor Schone Kunsten, Antwerp

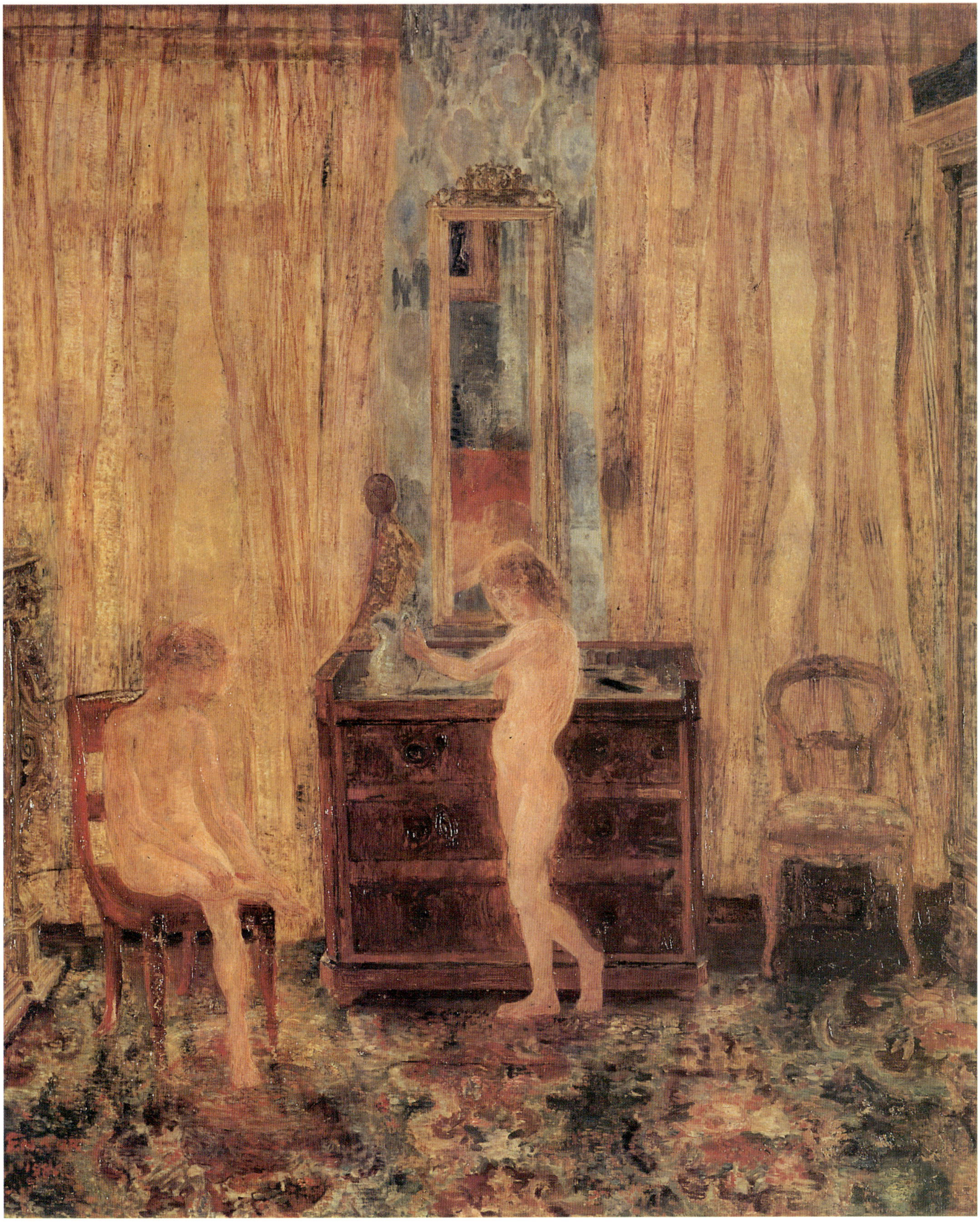

17 Skeletons warming Themselves

Squelettes voulant se chauffer, 1889
Oil on canvas, 74.8 x 60 cm
Signed and dated bottom left: Ensor 89
Kimbell Art Museum, Fort Worth, Texas, inv. no. AP 1981.20

Although motifs of mask and skeleton occur in Ensor's work as early as 1886, they take on a far more prominent role in his oeuvre in the period following the creation of the drawing *Satan et les Légions fantastiques tourmentant Le Crucifié (Satan and the Fantastic Legions tormenting the Crucified Christ*, 1886; Musées royaux des Beaux-Arts de Belgique, Brussels), part of the series entitled *Les Auréoles du Christ (The Halos of Christ)*. In this respect, Ensor is in part responding to the contemporary interest of both decadent and Symbolist writers and artists in images of artificiality and death.

Ensor identified himself with death in a number of drawings, paintings and prints. According to the psychoanalyst Henri Piron, such an unconcealed, relentless obsession with morbidity is evidence of an unusual anxiety on Ensor's part of losing his identity and creativity. This castration anxiety was said by Piron to have been exacerbated by the initial lack of recognition shown to Ensor's genius both by the art world and by his own family. In adopting the imagery of death, Ensor sought unsuccessfully to exorcize these fears, notably in the period following the death of his father and confidant in 1887. Although open to certain fundamental, and factual, objections, this interpretation has tended to be accepted, albeit with certain reservations, by most critics.

Diane Lesko followed Tannenbaum in interpreting this picture as an allegory of the demise of art, religion and the artist. Music (the skeleton with the violin), Truth (the one with the extinguished lamp) and Painting (Ensor's alter ego with a palette at his feet) stand around a stove trying to warm themselves. As indicated by the inscription, *'Pas de feu / en trouverez-vous demain?'* (No heat / Will there be some tomorrow?) the skeletons' task is in vain and could well be so again the next day. Not only is the heat from the stove, that emblem of the heat of the imagination which fires the creative process, absent and hence unable to ensure the current production of painting and music, but the very intimation that a skeleton is capable of being warmed contains the profoundly pessimistic view that no art is any longer able to possess creative power or resources.

This interpretation, however, can also be rejected for absence of evidence. Every attempt to interpret the characteristic Ensorian iconography of masks and skeletons is, moreover, rendered hazardous by the fundamentally grotesque character of these works. The grotesque reverses the logical and natural order of things, creating an incredible, paradoxical situation. The result is surprising, amusing, strange and sinister. Some of the skeletons are highly animated, while others lie on the floor, lifeless or stupefied. The stove glows, its door is open and there is coal to burn, but the skeletons cannot warm themselves. The figure entering the scene at the rear looks like a priest, but he is not in a religious stance. He holds a piece of knitting in his hands. The sinister character of the skeletons is offset by the hilarious accent provided by the musician with the overly large top hat and carnival-like costume.

Marcel de Maeyer (1963) demonstrated how the grotesque appearance of works like this is inherent to their process of execution. Around 1886–1890, Ensor deliberately destroyed the realistic aspect of many of his drawings and paintings by adding theatrical costumes, masks, skeletons and other related motifs. Thus this painting was derived from a study of a ship's lamp placed at the base of the little stove in his Ostend attic studio, which probably dates from 1880–1882. A few years later, he drew a ghost with a top hat next to the stove [fig. a]. | HT

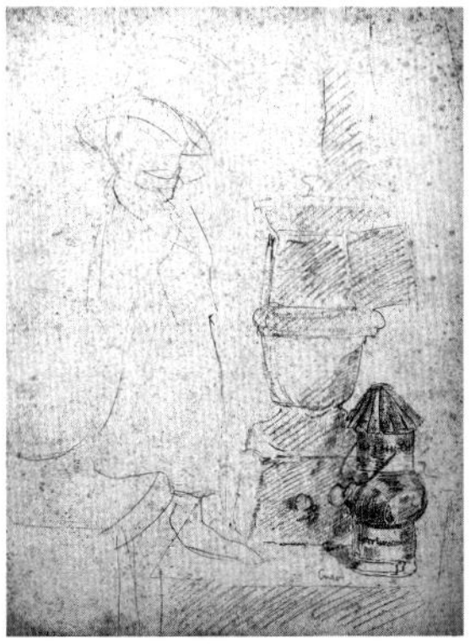

fig. a JAMES ENSOR
Skeleton warming Himself, 1889, crayon on paper, Koninklijk Museum voor Schone Kunsten, Antwerp

PROVENANCE Vicomte de Lantsheer, Brussels; Baron Gendebien, Brussels; Anne Burnett Windforth Tandy, Fort Worth; bequeathed to the Museum.

EXHIBITIONS *Les XX* 1890, no. 6; Antwerp 1910, no. 26; Rotterdam 1910, no. 27; Brussels 1929a, no. 169; Paris 1932, no. 57; Paris 1937; Brussels 1945, no. 52; London 1946, no. 20; Paris 1948b, no. 3; Antwerp 1951, no. 76; New York, Boston, Cleveland, St Louis 1951–1952, no. 33; Antwerp 1983, no. 75; Zurich 1983, no. 67.

BIBLIOGRAPHY Verhaeren 1908, 115; Le Roy 1922, 181; Tannenbaum 1951, 82–83; Haesaerts 1957, 171; Piron 1968; Lesko 1985, 90–92; H. Todts, 'Le grotesque dans l'œuvre d'Ensor, in Paris 1990b, 43–50; Tricot 1992, 269; V. Adolphs, *Der Künstler und der Tod. Selbstdarstellungen in der Kunst des 19. und 20. Jahrhunderts*, Cologne 1993, 143–150.

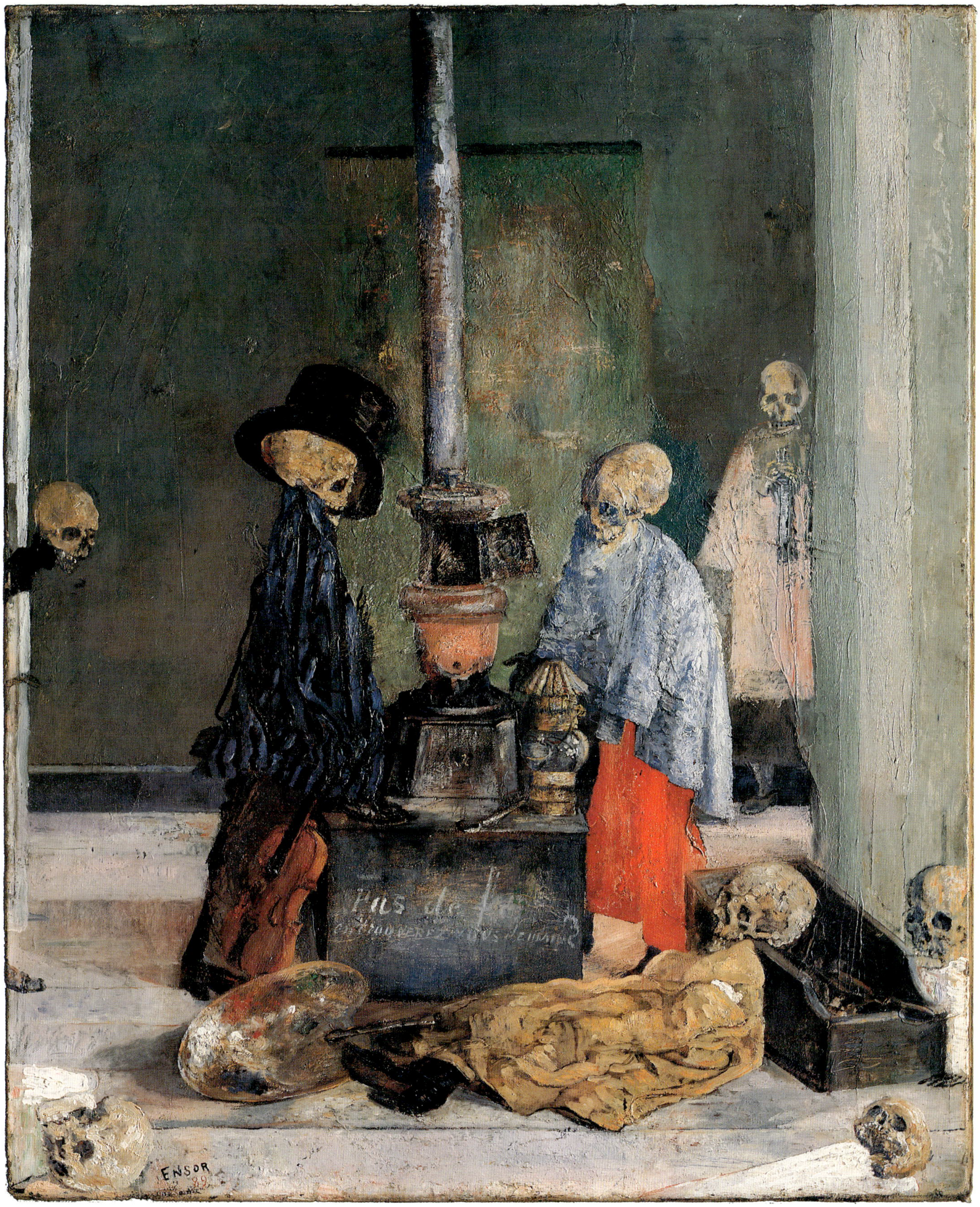
ENSOR

18 Tower of Lissewege

Tour de Lissewege, 1890
Oil on canvas, 61 x 73 cm
Signed bottom right: Ensor
Fondation Socindec, Berne

Between 1886 and 1891 Ensor etched dozens of landscapes. These views of harbours and countryside account for over a third of his entire graphic output. In these prints, and drawings made during the same period, Ensor discovered and developed the potential of light and line as expressive tools which could be used simultaneously to record the direct observation of a specific motif and to transform such a realist description into a visionary scene.

The few landscapes which were also made during this period share this process of transformation. In some, such as *Les Tribulations de Saint Antoine* (*Tribulations of Saint Anthony*, 1887; Museum of Modern Art, New York), *La Chute des anges (The Fall of the Angels)* and *Adam et Eve chassés du Paradis (The Expulsion of Adam and Eve from Paradise)* (1887 and 1889; both Koninklijk Museum voor Schone Kunsten, Antwerp), the presence of figures provokes the translation from objective representation of nature into a vision of often apocalyptic intent. The absence of figures, however, does not imply that the landscapes of this period should be any less visionary. In the *Tower of Lissewege*, a work which has at the central point of its composition the early Gothic church tower in a village between Ostend and Bruges, the topographical information is virtually obliterated by the explosion of expressively handled paint in both sky and land. Indeed, the 'impressionistic' palette and rendering of weather conditions and light effects have been made subordinate to an overwhelming, hallucinatory effect. In this respect, this landscape is closely related to *The Domain of Arnheim* (c. 1889; Private Collection). | HT

PROVENANCE Edgar Picard, Jemeppe; Galerie Georges Giroux, Brussels; François Franck, Antwerp; L. Franck, Antwerp, London, Gstaad.
EXHIBITIONS Brussels 1920a, no. 34; Paris 1926, no. 21; Hanover, Berlin, Dresden 1927; Brussels 1929a, no. 162 (as 1888); Antwerp 1931, no. 191; Ostend 1931, no. 16; Paris 1932, no. 53; Chicago, New York 1976–1977, no. 27 (as 1888); Tel Aviv 1981, no. 23 (as 1888); Antwerp 1983, no. 66 (as 1888); Zurich 1983, no. 59 (as 1888); Paris 1990b, no. 124 (as 1888).
BIBLIOGRAPHY Verhaeren 1908, 116 (as 1890); Le Roy 1922 (as 1890); Haesaerts 1957, 310 (as 1888); Tricot 1992, 299 (as 1890 [1888?]).

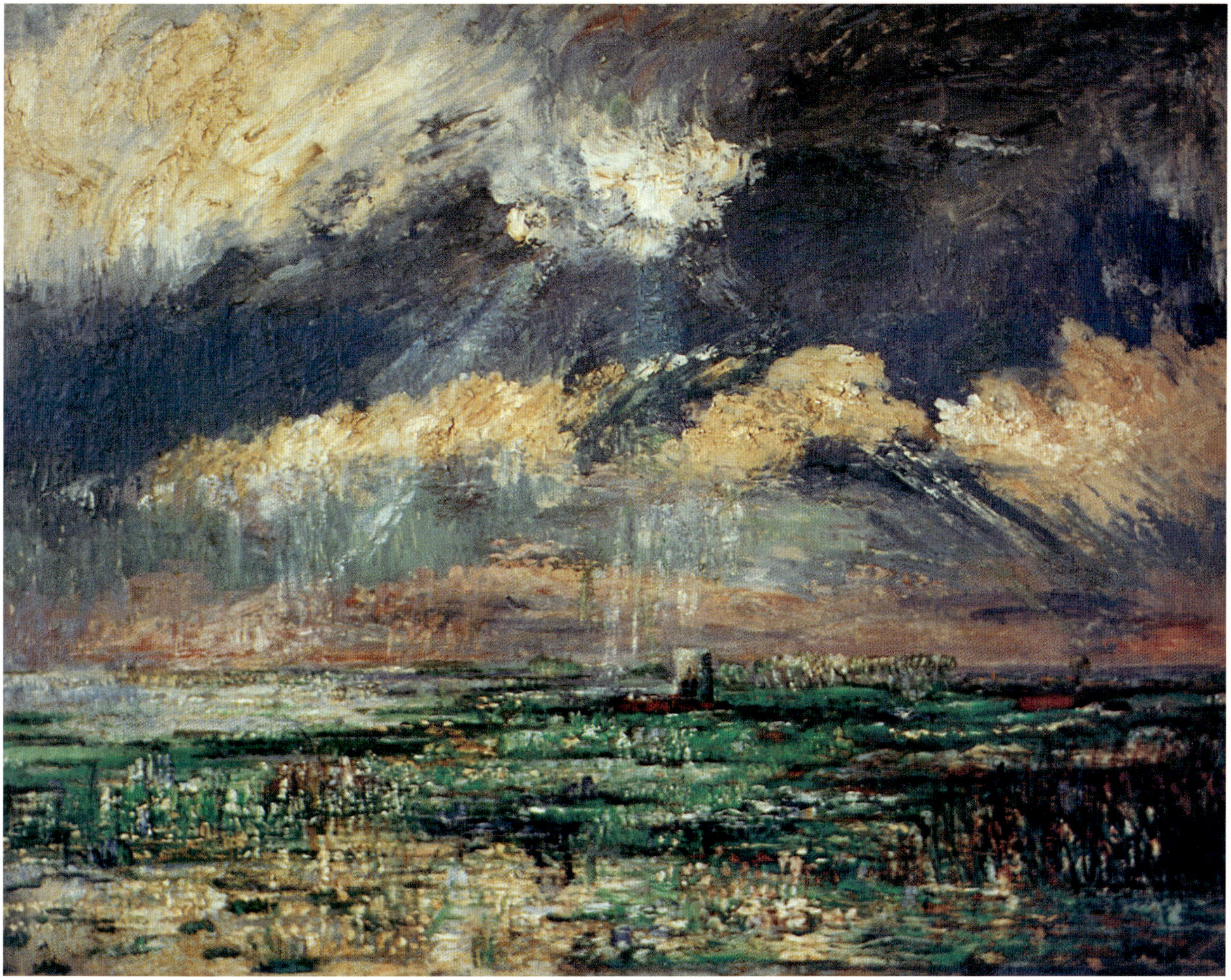

19 Melancholy Fishwives

Les Poissardes mélancoliques, 1892
Oil on canvas, 100 x 80 cm
Signed and dated bottom right: Ensor 1892
Inscribed: A mort! Elles ont mangé trop de poisson
Fondation Socindec, Berne

The familiar iconographical motifs of late-nineteenth-century Naturalism [see cats.47, 59] are found in Ensor's early, realistic works. His large charcoal drawings of around 1880 feature many different local Ostend figures, some of which were incorporated into a number of paintings made c. 1883, including *Les Pochards* (*The Drunkards*, Private Collection), from which *Melancholy Fishwives* takes both the general disposition of the two figures and the sparse, impoverished interior.

The fishwives in the present painting are identified by their characteristic costume and the exaggerated articulation of their faces and hands. One holds a snuffbox, the other an empty coffee bowl. They share a pot filled with hot coals which is placed between them, in order to provide a modicum of warmth. Ensor makes the transition from naturalistic rendition of the condition of one segment of the labouring poor by overlaying the figures of the two old women and their domestic interior with a number of additional elements. Caricature is introduced in the exaggerated features of the fishwife with the black hair and in the details of the still life in the foreground consisting of a herring and a crab. The presence of the exaggerated aggressive skeletons seen at the back of the composition, either as reflected in a mirror or placed physically in an opening in the wall, suggests that the women, their baskets empty and the detritus of their meal strewn at their feet, may indeed have been condemned to death for their gluttony. However, as in so many of Ensor's highly personal works, any interpretation of the painting's meaning must probably remain ambiguous. For the presence of an admittedly rather carelessly drawn cat (possibly added at a later date) at the feet of the two fishwives raises the question as to whether it was they, or the cat, who consumed the herring and the crab. If it was the cat, then the women's plight is precarious: with empty baskets and the remnants of the cat's meal, they are indeed condemned to death, but this time, through starvation. The message of the skeletons behind remains, however, constant.

From c. 1891 Ensor began to rework both figure subjects and still lifes made in the previous decade in order to supply a gradually growing market for his work. The somewhat bald handling of the pink background, with the large simplified dark forms of the figures set against it, looks forward to a style of painting which Ensor was to use for such thematic and compositional reprises made from c. 1897 onwards. | HT

PROVENANCE F. Buelens, Ostend; C. Franck, Antwerp; P. Colin, Brussels; M. Motte, Brussels; A. Burnett Tandy, Fort Worth; L. Franck, Antwerp, London, Gstaad.

EXHIBITIONS *Les XX* 1890, no. 6; Antwerp 1910, no. 26; Rotterdam 1910, no. 27; Brussels 1929a, no. 169; Paris 1932, no. 57; Paris 1937; Brussels 1945, no. 52; London 1946, no. 20; Paris 1948b, no. 3; Antwerp 1951, no. 76; New York, Boston, Cleveland, St Louis 1951–1952, no. 33; Antwerp 1983, no. 75; Zurich 1983, no. 67.

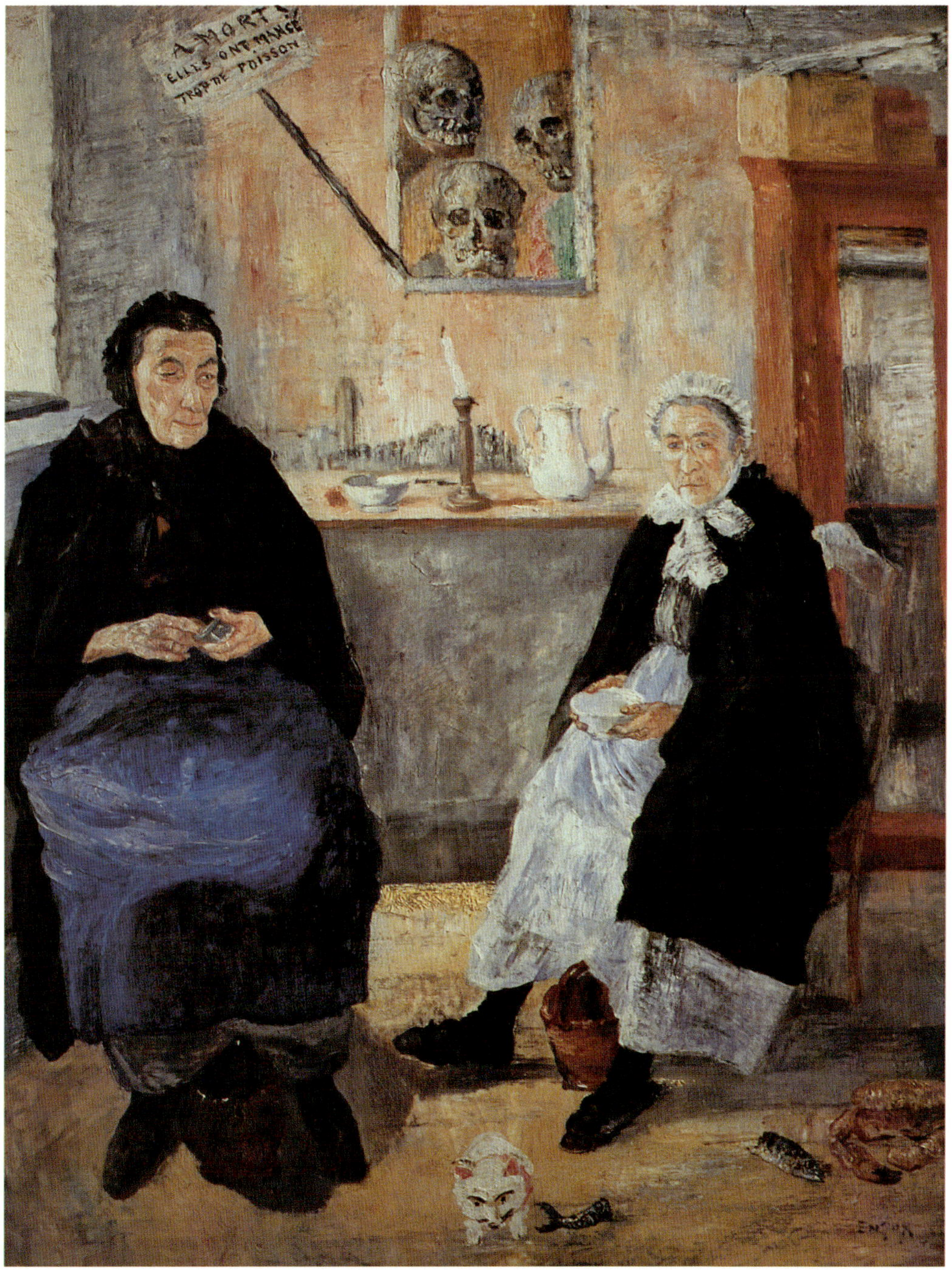
A MORT!
ELLES ONT MANGE
TROP DE POISSON
ENSOR

Henri Evenepoel

NICE 1872 – PARIS 1899

Henri Evenepoel was born in Nice on 3 October 1872 and died of typhus in Paris on 27 December 1899. His life and work were greatly influenced by the early death of his mother (in 1874), by the strict but highly cultured bourgeois milieu to which he belonged and in which liberal opinions mingled with a refined Wagnerianism, by his meeting with Gustave Moreau, and by his passion for his first cousin Louise de Mey-van Mattemburgh, with whom he had a son, Charles. Evenepoel studied first in Brussels, under Ernest Blanc-Garin, Ernest Acker, and Adolphe Crespin, and later in Paris; it was his father's intention that he should become a decorative painter. The death of Pierre-Victor Galland shortly after Evenepoel's arrival in Paris at the Ecole des Beaux-Arts (1892) gave the latter the opportunity to enrol in Gustave Moreau's studio, which he did on 14 March 1893. While there, he showed great admiration for Rouault and established close links with Baignères (*The Man in Red*, 1895; Musées royaux des Beaux-Arts de Belgique, Brussels), Milcendeau, Bussy, Hoffbauer, and Matisse. Until his departure for Algeria in October 1897, where he spent several months producing a number of remarkable works imbued with a nascent Fauvism, he formed close ties with Moreau. The older artist was a demanding master, who appreciated Evenepoel's sensitivity, his innate feeling for pigment and colour, and, above all, his continual struggle to outreach himself, his frenzied desire to paint. Having made his artistic début with *Louise in Mourning* (Koninklijk Museum voor Schone Kunsten, Antwerp) at the Salon des Artistes français (Salon des Champs-Elysées) in 1894, he became a regular exhibitor of the Salon du Champ-de-Mars. In December 1897 he presented his first one-man exhibition at the Cercle artistique et littéraire in Brussels. Evenepoel was a remarkable portraitist (*Charles in a Striped Jersey*, 1898, Private Collection; *The Spaniard in Paris*, 1899, Museum voor Schone Kunsten, Ghent): he was concerned with veracity and has a wonderful ability to convey the candour and depth of childhood, the anguish of passion, or the serenity of friendship and mutual trust. He was equally interested, however, in translating everyday themes onto canvas, at the same time employing colour, pigment, line and composition in a resolutely modern fashion (*Fête at Les Invalides*, 1898, Musées royaux des Beaux-Arts de Belgique, Brussels; *Sunday Walk in the Bois de Boulogne*, 1899, Musée d'Art moderne, Liège). | DDC

SUMMARY BIBLIOGRAPHY

P. Lambotte, *Henri Evenepoel*, Brussels 1908; L. and P. Haesaerts, *Flandre*, Paris 1931; L. and P. Haesaerts, *Henri Evenepoel*, Brussels 1932; Ph. Jones, 'Evenepoel ou La Vie mesurée', *Les Arts plastiques* (7 September 1953), no. 4, 273–282; F. E. Hyslop, *Henri Evenepoel, Belgian Painter in Paris 1892–1899*, s.l. 1975; M.-J. Chartrain-Hebbelinck, 'Henri Evenepoel', *Biographie nationale* XXXIX:1 (1976), col. 343; D. Derrey-Capon, Ph. Roberts-Jones, G. Ollinger-Zinque *et al.*, *Henri Evenepoel*, Brussels 1994 [with catalogue raisonné of the paintings by D. Derrey-Capon and complete bibliography]; H. Evenepoel, *Lettres à mon père*, ed. D. Derrey-Capon, Brussels 1994, 2 vols.

20 Lady with a Green Hat

La Dame au chapeau vert, 1897
Oil on canvas, 134 x 61 cm
Signed and dated bottom left: h. evenepoel/97
Musée de l'Art Wallon, Liège, Donation Jaumain-Jobert, inv. no. AW 2167

This fine portrait of Evenepoel's cousin and lover, Louise de Mey-van Mattemburgh, was painted at the beginning of 1897 and exhibited at the Salon du Champ-de-Mars. Although compositionally similar to his structurally forceful large-scale male portraits (e.g. *Portrait of the Lawyer Charles Didisheim*, 1896, Private Collection), the painting can more usefully be compared with a work dating from spring 1894: *Portrait of Mme D. or Louise in Mourning* [fig. a]. Both portraits position the sitter's right hand on a furled umbrella placed to the left of the model, which gives a slight rotation to the body, and hence a rhythm to the picture as a whole. The black veil and high collar in *Louise in Mourning* throw into relief the oval of the face, with its profoundly sad and weary expression; the resultant impression is one of a mask simply set atop an elongated silhouette. The background – a sort of creamy yellow, slightly grey-green panelling or straw fabric – is intended to brighten the whole scene, at the same time acting as a counterbalance to the dark mass of the dress. The portrait, which shows the influence of Goya, not of Manet, whom Evenepoel only really discovered the following May, at Durand-Ruel's, was painted shortly after the artist had written these words: 'How wonderful to be able to follow one's vocation, to let oneself be guided by one's tastes; I feel I am beginning to see the way ahead more clearly: I have a liking for certain things that particularly interest me. As regards the human figure, my concern, my obsession is to search out the character, the essential character, the distinctive, unexpected dimension. So, painting portraits would make me truly happy: of course, I would paint them as I saw them – I would find it impossible, unnatural, to embellish a face, any face. I feel a real delight when I plot a profile and work feverishly to tighten it up: it's the same delight you yourself feel when you hear a particular theme emerge from the jumble of the orchestration, when you hear it emerging clear and rhythmical' (*Lettres à mon père*, 19 January 1894, Brussels 1994, II:257).

But the face of Evenepoel's one and only love was not just any face, and he remained true to his declaration, although idealizing it. The metamorphosis of Louise – the mother of his two 'models' Henriette and Sophie, and later of his son Charles, born in 1894 – may already be observed in an 1895 painting entitled *In the Studio or The Cup of Tea* [fig. b]. In this transitional work, the background is deliberately allowed to become a more dominant ingredient within the composition; the model,

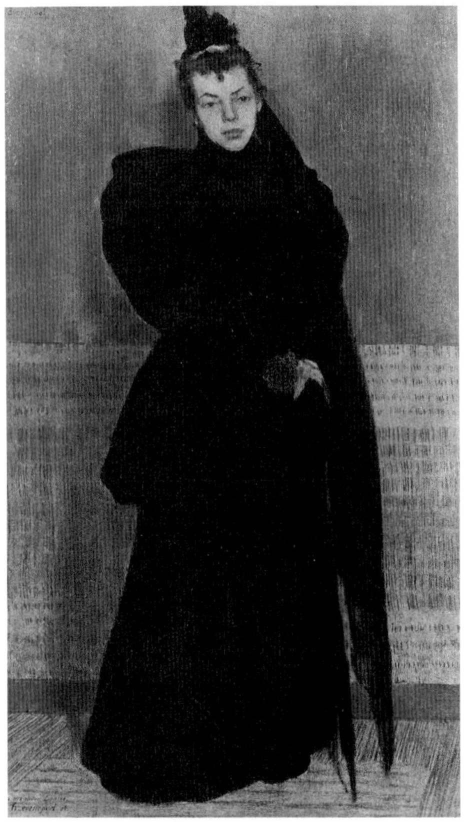

fig. a HENRI EVENEPOEL
Portrait of Mme D. or Louise in Mourning, 1894,
Koninklijk Museum voor Schone Kunsten, Antwerp

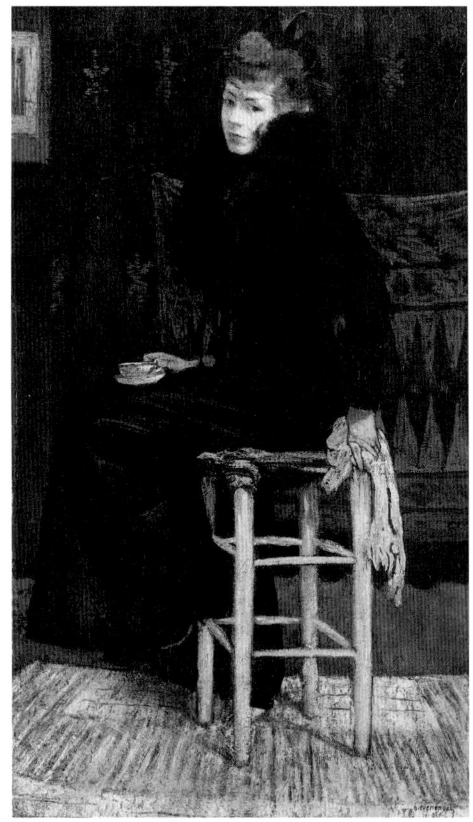

fig. b HENRI EVENEPOEL
In the Studio or The Cup of Tea, 1895,
Gouvernement provincial du Brabant, Brussels

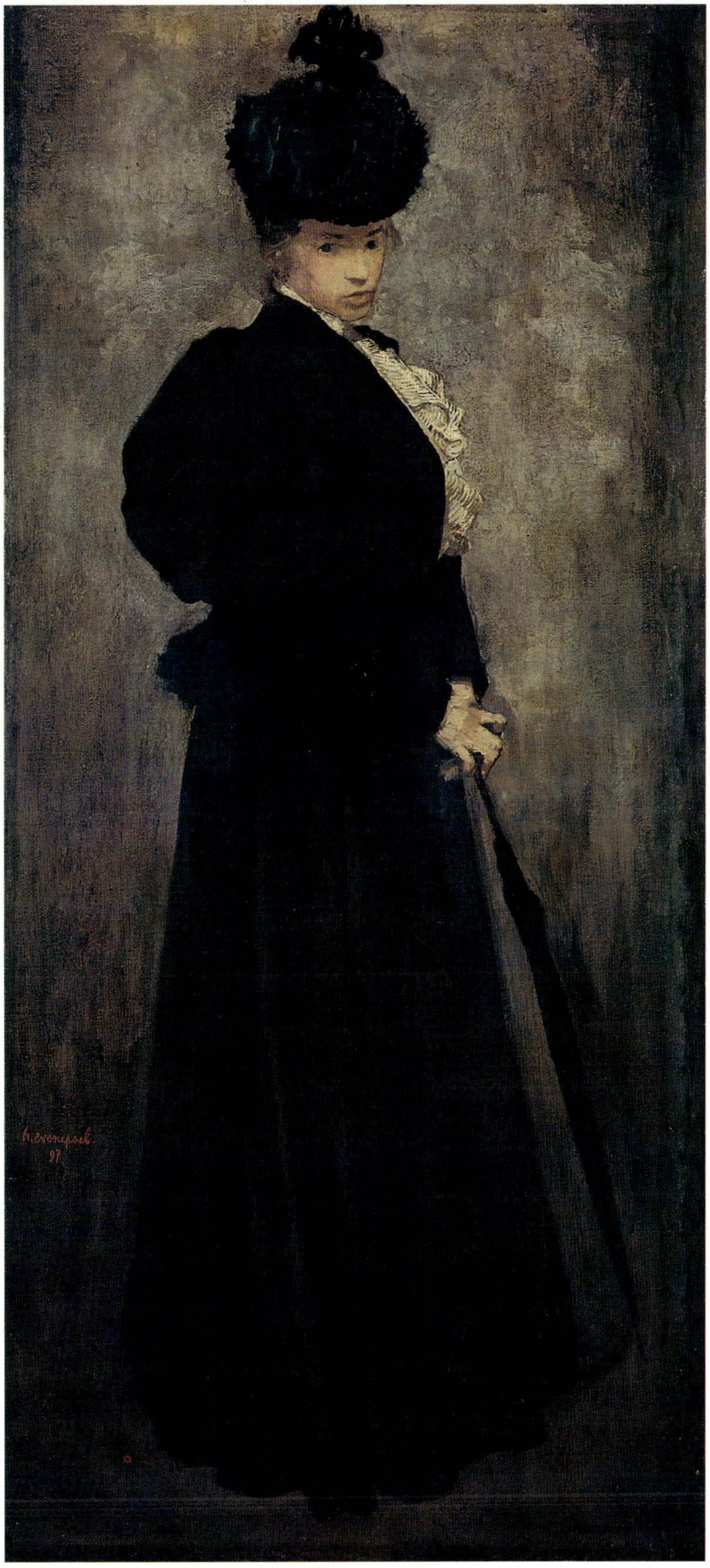

wearing a small red hat, her cheek caressed by a fur collar, conveys a more markedly *femme fatale* image. The *Lady with a Green Hat* shows that the artist has here absorbed the teachings of Manet and Degas, incorporating them intelligently into a work that is actually very personal, and resolutely modern. The absence of any spatial recession, the subtle play of light on a muted palette, the unctuous pigment and the harmonious proportions combine to accentuate the elegant set of the head, the questioning expression and the diaphanous modelling of the face, all of which give the portrait a timeless quality. Louise has become unrecognizable, having been invested with all the other female presences that inhabit the artist's mind: she is at once mother, sister and lover, unique and yet legion, sensual and yet artless, furnished with an indefinable charm; she is as he saw her, as she was required to be – concealing strength beneath a fragile exterior. | DDC

PROVENANCE Louise van Mattemburgh, Brussels; Dr Jaumain; Désiré Jaumain–Ada Jobart Donation, 1974.

EXHIBITIONS Paris 1897, no. 479; London 1897, *s.n.*; Brussels 1897–1898, no. 12; Vienna 1907, no. 176 (?); Brussels 1913, no. 93; Liège 1920, no. 3; Brussels 1923–1924, no. 98; Copenhagen 1931, no. 112; Brussels 1931, no. 35; Brussels 1932b, no. 73; Brussels 1935, no. 155; Brussels 1942a, no. 27, ill.; Brussels 1942–1943, no. 30; Amsterdam 1945–1946, no. 34; Bern 1946, no. 34; Paris 1946, no. 32; Brussels 1947, no. 31; Cairo 1947, no. 14; Ostend 1952, no. 38; Antwerp 1953, no. 64, ill. no. 18; Charleroi 1960, no. 18; Liège 1978, no. 12, ill.; Moscow 1985, no. 10; Oviedo 1985, no. 8; Brussels 1994b, no. 32.

BIBLIOGRAPHY *(selected)* Lambotte 1908, 83, ill.; Haesaerts 1931, 420 (ill. detail), 430 (ill.), 501; Haesaerts 1932, 17, pl. 16; Haesaerts 1942, 29; Fierens 1947–1948, 23, 24, 29; Jones 1953, 278; Poirier 1953, 129; Haesaerts 1960, 87 (ill.), 88; Vanbeselaere 1961, 161 (ill.), 168; Dasnoy 1965–1966, no. 27, ill.; Hyslop 1975, 60, 61 (ill.), 142; Chartrain-Hebbelinck 1976, col. 343; R. L. Delevoy 1981, 360; Roberts-Jones 1981, 212; Derrey-Capon 1994, 43, 68 (ill.), 275 (ill.), 276–277, no. 176; Evenepoel 1994, 2:113, 114 (ill.), 116, 155–157, 178, 191, 207, 208, 221, 280 (ill.).

Alfred William Finch

SAINT-JOSSE-TEN-NOODE 1854 – HELSINKI 1930

Alfred William (Willy) Finch was born in Saint-Josse-ten-Noode, a suburb of Brussels, on 28 November 1854. His family, originally from Exeter, had settled in Belgium in about 1818, and Finch spent his youth in Ostend, where there was a sizeable British community. In 1878 he joined Joseph van Severdonck's class at the Academy of Fine Arts, Brussels, and two years later he made his artistic début at Ghent's Salon Triennal, after which his work adopted a more avant-garde stance. He was a member of the Chrysalide group, and of L'Essor, and in 1883 he was involved in the founding of Les XX, to which he invited Whistler, whom he much admired, to exhibit in the first exhibition the following February. Finch's discovery of Monet (1886) steered him, like his friend Ensor, towards a very personal form of Impressionism, with a marked emphasis on realism. The following year, excited by the work shown at the Salon des XX by Georges Seurat, Finch immediately applied himself to the study of divisionist principles. These he adopted in his own painting, becoming the prime Belgian exponent of the style [see cats. 22–25]. Converted to the ideas of John Ruskin, William Morris and the Arts and Crafts Movement, the development of which he was able to observe during his frequent trips to England, Finch soon began to shift his attentions to the decorative arts, notably ceramics, a craft which he practised first at La Louvière and later at Virginal and Forges-lez-Chimay. He moved to Finland at the request of the industrialist Louis Sparre, to direct the ceramics department of the Iris company at Borgå (1897–1901). Later he settled in Helsinki, where he died on 28 April 1930. Finch's creativity and rigorous approach, and his teaching at the School of Decorative Arts from 1902 – pursued in tandem with his career as a painter – established him one of the pioneers of modern European design. He promoted Impressionism and Neo-Impressionism in Scandinavia, championing, in particular, the work of Signac. His name has been linked with that of Magnus Enckell and Sigurd Frosterus as the protagonists of a renewal of Finnish painting, manifested, in 1912, in the formation of the Septem group. | DDC

SUMMARY BIBLIOGRAPHY

D.D.C [D. Derrey-Capon], 'A. W. Finch', in *Académie royale des Beaux-Arts de Bruxelles. 275 ans d'enseignement*, Musées royaux des Beaux-Arts de Belgique, Brussels 1987, 172–175, ill; *Alfred William Finch 1854–1930*, The Art Museum of Ateneum, Helsinki 1991 – Musées royaux des Beaux-Arts de Belgique, Brussels 1992 (Catalogue by D. Derrey-Capon, A. Lindström *et al.*) [First monograph on the artist with complete biography and bibliography].

21 Box at the Theatre

La Loge, c. 1886
Mixed media, pastel and watercolour on paper mounted on canvas, 100 x 80 cm
Signed bottom right: Willy Finch
Collection Crédit Communal de Belgique / Collectie Gemeentekrediet van België, Brussels

Claude Monet's dominant presence at the 1886 Salon des XX, when as an 'invité' he showed ten canvases, including *La Manne-Porte (Etretat)*, then in the collection of Georges Petit, and the *Bridge at Argenteuil* from the Faure collection, prompted Finch to adopt his own personal variant of Impressionism. While retaining the realist traditions of Belgian art, he introduced tonal division, fragmented brushwork and a lightened palette. Several works dating from the period immediately after February 1886 and before January 1887 (on the basis of signature or style), document the artist's development: they range from *Seascape, Low Tide* (Whitford & Hughes Collection, London), once owned by the painter Willy Schlobach (q.v.), through an *Interior*, completed shortly after this (Turku Art Museum, Nils Dahlström Collection), and a similarly handled still life (Private Collection, Paris), to *Snow in a Suburb* (Josefowitz Collection), and this intriguing *Box at the Theatre*. Possibly set in the Théâtre de la Monnaie in Brussels, this work is the only example of such a detailed treatment of the human figure in Finch's work, and we are left with the puzzle as to whether it was done as a commission or as a technical or stylistic exercise. The frontal, somewhat closely placed figures in the composition suggest a certain affinity with the presentation of Mme Charpentier and her two daughters in Renoir's portrait shown at Les XX in 1886 (no. 2). However, the absence of any identifiable details of the architectural setting give this work a far more claustrophobic atmosphere than that described in Van Rysselberghe's virtually contemporaneous portrait of *Mme Edmond Picard in a Box at the Théâtre de la Monnaie* (c. 1886; Private Collection).

From a technical point of view, this work is particularly elaborate: the artist uses several media to create the impression of depth and render the subtlety and intensity of the tones and gradations of colour. A combination of vivacity and precision, together with a delicate touch that is varyingly tight, undulating and fragmented, give the composition its rhythm; light is captured by a judicious juxtaposition and superimposition of coloured strokes. This undeniably enigmatic picture has the merit of being the only one of its kind in an oeuvre otherwise entirely devoted to landscape – and of succeeding admirably in holding its own among these other works. | DDC

PROVENANCE Private Collection, Brussels; sale Paris, Hôtel Drouot, 25 November 1977, no. 73; David Hughes, London.
EXHIBITIONS London 1983, no. 7, ill.; Albi 1985, no. 22, ills.; Brussels 1987a, no. P35, pl. VIII; Pontoise 1990, no. 23, ill.; Charleroi 1990, no. 23, ill.; Helsinki 1991, no. 12, ills.; Brussels 1992, no. 12, ills.
BIBLIOGRAPHY D.D.C [Derrey-Capon] 1987, 172–175, ill.; Derrey-Capon 1992, 38, 168, ills.

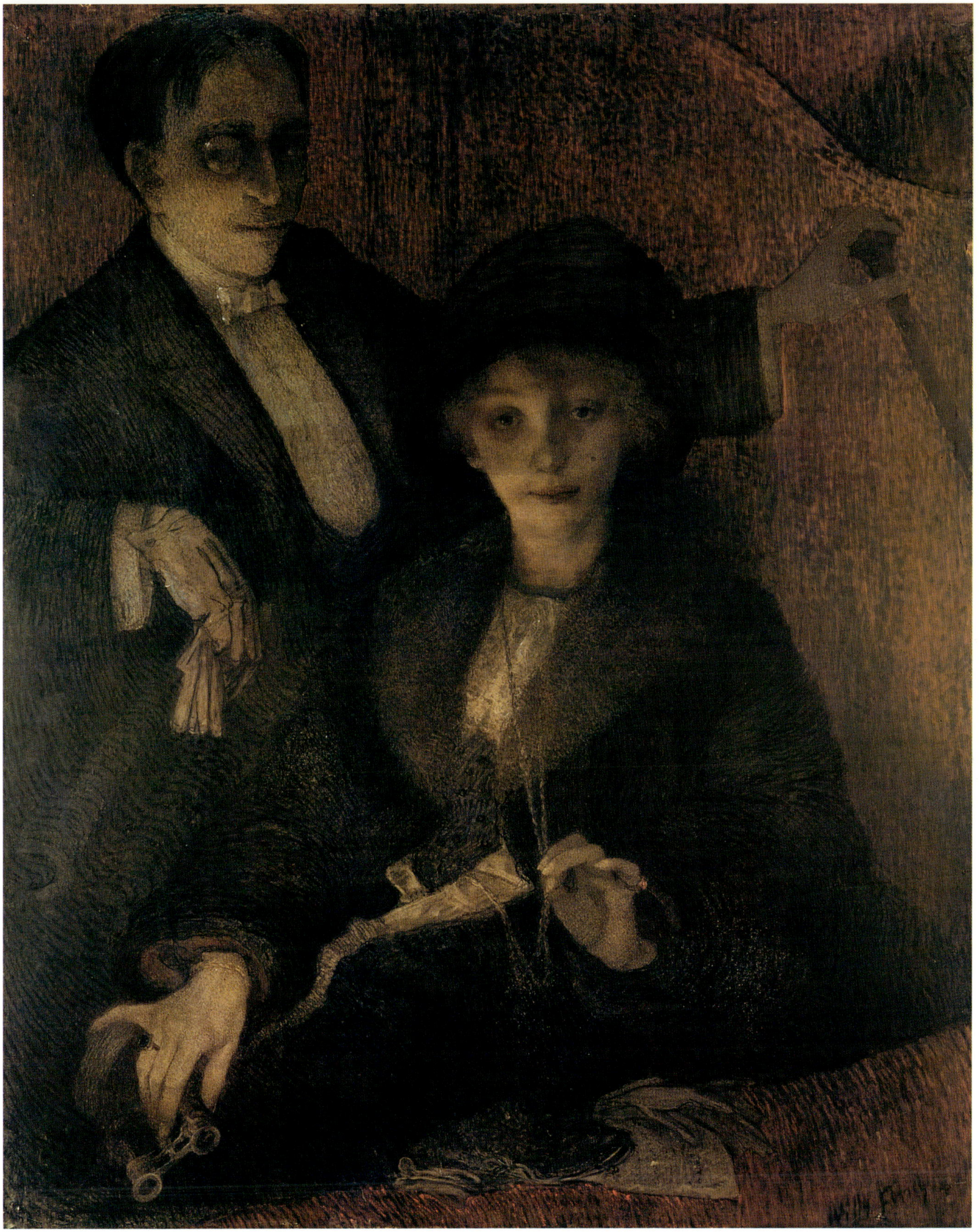

22 Country Road near the North Sea

Route de campagne près de la Mer du Nord, 1888–1889
Oil on canvas, 65.5 x 77 cm
Initialled bottom left: A.W.F.
Turku Art Museum (Finland), Nils Dahlström Collection, inv. no. ND33

From early in 1887, Finch became increasingly committed to the principles of divisionism. On 5 January 1888, he wrote to Octave Maus: 'I shall be sending [to the 1888 Salon des XX] four paintings (and a few watercolours) done in a quite personal style, but I fear that unschooled eyes will not spot the technical differences between ourselves and our friends in Paris. They will come down hard on us! This time we've had it, as Napolion [*sic*] said.' The critics did indeed react harshly, describing the works submitted by Finch and Willy Schlobach as grotesque, raving, eccentric, like boil-infested mosaist pastiches. In contrast, *L'Art moderne* of 5 February 1888 (probably in the person of Emile Verhaeren) lent encouragement to Finch and Schlobach, backing the former's assertion of individuality and at the same time praising his talents as a colourist: 'And here we have M. Finch, the first of the Belgians to move decisively into the ranks of the Neo-Impressionists, adopting division of tone, rejecting mixture on the palette, allowing only the colours of the spectrum and using only these ... His paintings can be analysed, decoded; and yet regardless of all this scientific predictability, his refined Northern painter's spirit shines through and asserts itself. Those who maintain that all paintings done in the stippled style [*au pointillé*] look as if they have emerged from the same "factory" should compare the very individual approaches of the three artists mentioned. And if they are prepared to look a little further, they should consider the distance covered and the progress made, in the present-day study of colour and light, from the time of MM. Guillaumin and Caillebotte to the time of MM. Signac, Dubois-Pillet, and Finch.'

These comments give an idea of the atmosphere of permanent polemic in which Finch pursued his divisionist work between 1887 and 1892. *Country Road near the North Sea* – possibly the painting entitled *Route de Mariakerke*, which was shown at the Panorama Society's exhibition of May 1889 in Amsterdam and in the 1890 Salon des XX (no. 3) – was certainly one of the first dozen or so works which Finch painted using the pointillist method, a technique that necessitated great meticulousness in both design and execution. It shows some technical affinity with *The Haystacks* [fig. a], a small-scale painting dated 1889. The composition, with its untrammelled foreground that literally forces the viewer to step back in order fully to enjoy the work, is reminiscent of the vacant foreground in Van de Velde's *Beach at Blankenberghe with Beach Huts* [cat. 65] which was exhibited at Les XX in 1889 (no. 1) and to some extent of some of Seurat's seascapes, such as *La Grève du Bas-Butin, Honfleur* (1886; Musée des Beaux-Arts, Tournai), exhibited at Les XX in 1887 (no. 6). Indeed, such a radical, anti-picturesque treatment of the composition endows Finch's work with an obvious sense of the 'new' and the modern. | DDC

PROVENANCE Private Collection, Belgium; Louis Camu, Aalst; sale London, Sotheby's, 12 December 1970 (no. 25, ill.); Nils Dahlström, who donated it to the Museum in 1973.
EXHIBITIONS Turku 1973, no. 18, ill. no. 75; Finland 1973, no. 18; Helsinki 1991, no. 16, ill.; Brussels 1992, no. 16, ills.
BIBLIOGRAPHY [Turku] 1984, 71; D.D.C [Derrey-Capon] 1987, 173; Derrey-Capon 1992, 104, 171, ills.

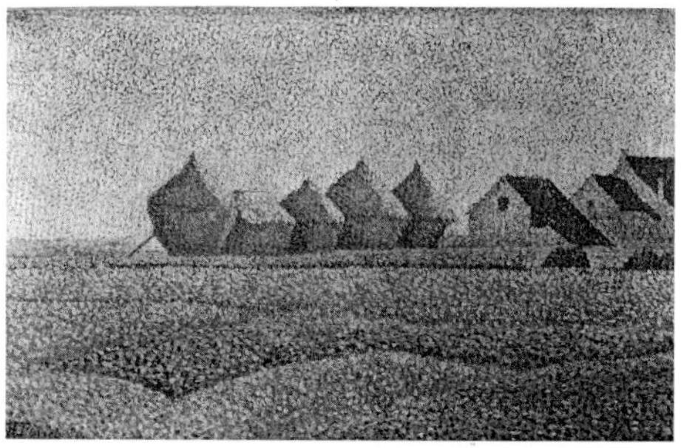

fig. a ALFRED WILLIAM FINCH
The Haystacks, 1889,
Musée d'Ixelles, Brussels

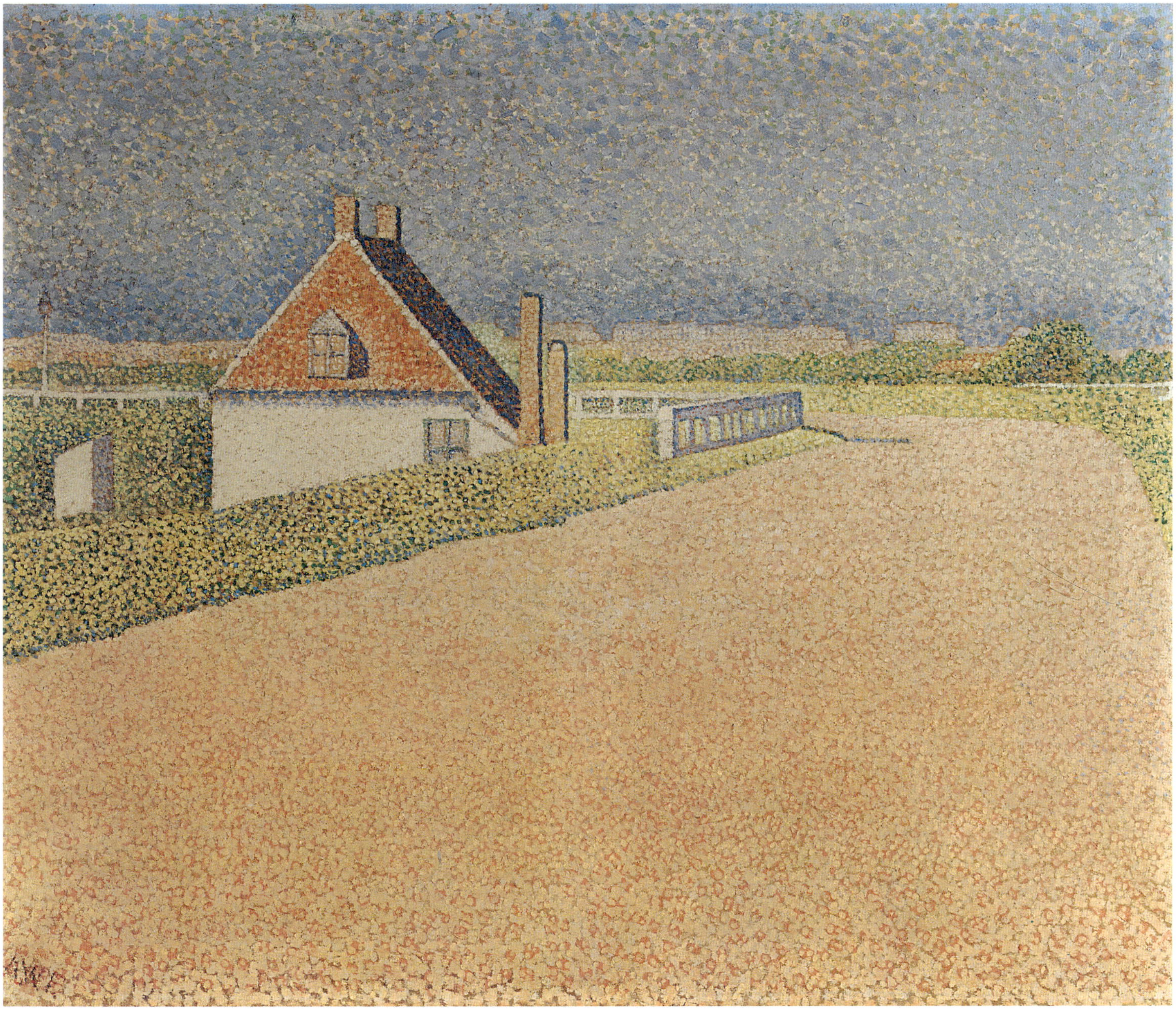

23 Orchard at La Louvière

Verger à La Louvière, 1890
Oil on canvas, 54 x 67 cm
Signed bottom right: A. W. Finch
The Finnish National Gallery, Helsinki, Collection Antell, inv. no. A IV 2958

In January 1890, Finch decided to leave Mariakerke and move to La Louvière, where local records show him living from 24 April 1890 to 30 January 1893. It was undoubtedly Anna Boch [see cat. 71], a member of Les XX whose father was in charge of the Kéramis pottery works in the town, who arranged employment for Finch at the works as a *peintre-décorateur*. While he probably spent much time copying Delft-style decoration, then very much in fashion, he also acquired the rudimentary technical skills for the making and decorating of ceramics which were to prove so useful to him in his later experiments with the medium. During his frequent visits to England, Finch had developed not only a keen interest in the aesthetic theories of John Ruskin and William Morris, with their advocacy of 'art for every one, art in everything', but also knowledge of the relatively new Arts and Crafts Movement. This interest in the decorative arts and principles of good design he was to pass on to his fellow Neo-Impressionists, Georges Lemmen and Henry van de Velde. However, Finch's involvement in the decorative arts did not prevent him from pursuing his divisionist paintings: 'My dear Maus', he wrote on 23 January 1891, 'I am late! My panel came out of the kiln yesterday morning and I have now decided to exhibit 1. Landscape at Seneffe, 2. Orchard at La Louvière, 3. and 4. decorative landscapes, ceramic panels, 5. drawings. Not much, you see, but there will be one or two new things. I am very much looking forward to seeing you' (Archives de l'Art contemporain, Musées royaux des Beaux-Arts de Belgique, Brussels, inv. no. 5731). The press reviews of the 1891 Salon des XX accused Finch of resorting to producing ceramic tiles which were bizarre and of paintings which were fantastical and lacking in 'accuracy and a proper mastery of light'. Despite these adverse comments, *Orchard at La Louvière* is an effective exposition of divisionist principles: the composition is rigorously denoted by the diagonals of light and shadow, recorded in strictly Neo-Impressionist complementary tones of the luminous yellows, for the sun's rays, running over the greens and lilacs of the fields and pathways.

Given Finch's close affinity with the procedures of Seurat, it is not surprising that he reacted emotionally to the news of the latter's death on 29 March 1891, broken to him by Theo van Rysselberghe two days later. 'I am devastated,' he wrote to Paul Signac, 'It is a great loss! He was a boon to modern ideas. I should like very much to join with you in any event, however small, that may be held to commemorate Seurat' (typed copy, Suomen taitailijaseuran arkisto, Helsinki).

The presence of a significant phalanx of Neo-Impressionists at the Salon des XX for 1891 prompted several of the more conservative critics, Georges Verdavainne included, to deplore this invasion of the Group by those committed to 'anti art': 'The pointillist Vingtistes, carried along by science, wish to discover order in the laboratories. Often chemists, sometimes obscurantists, but never artists!...' | DDC

PROVENANCE Bought from the artist at the opening of 1910 exhibition (University of Helsinki) by the Hörhammer Gallery, where it was acquired by the Museum in 1955 with funds from the Antell Collection.

EXHIBITIONS Les XX 1891, no. 2; Antwerp 1892a; Helsinki 1910, *s.n.*; Helsinki 1943, no. 19; Helsinki 1946, no. 2; Helsinki 1948b, no. 33; Helsinki 1955, no. 10, ill; Rome 1955, no. 2059; Brussels 1967, no. 95; Ghent 1980, no. 214, ill.; Stockholm 1981, no. 4, ill.; Helsinki 1991, no. 19, ills.; Brussels 1992, no. 18, ills.

BIBLIOGRAPHY Hintze 1966, 14 (ill.), 42; Lindström 1966, 38; Herbert 1968, 168; Sutter 1970, 235, ill.; [Antell] 1975, no. 76, ill.; Kelder 1986, ill.; D.D.C. [Derrey-Capon] 1987, 174; Derrey-Capon 1991–1992, 21, 69 (ill.), 105, 108, 112, 172–173 (ill.).

cat. 23

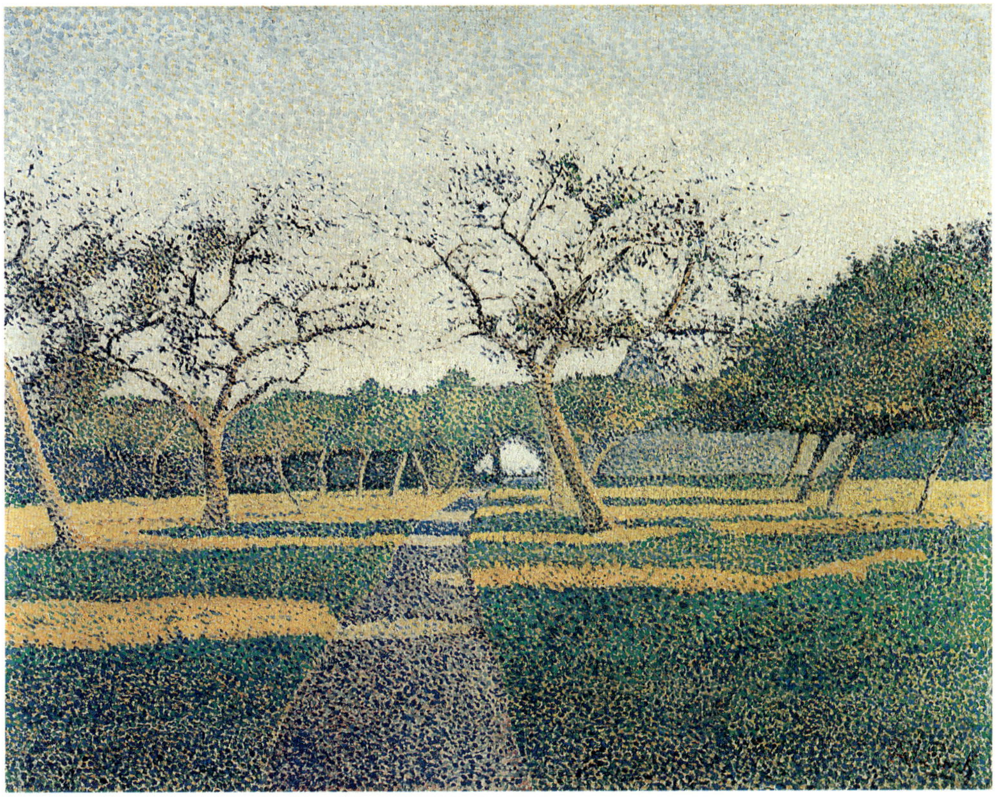

cat. 24

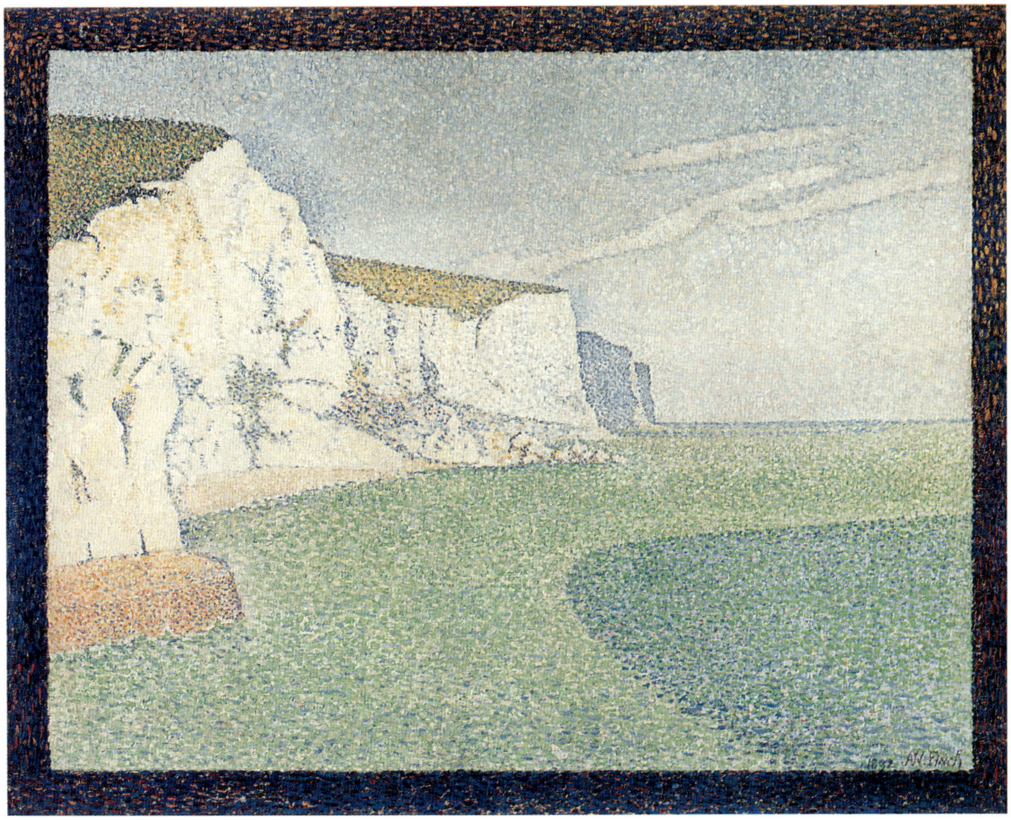

24 The Cliffs at South Foreland

Les Falaises de South Foreland, 1892
Oil on canvas, 66.5 x 80.5 cm
Dated and signed bottom right: 1892 AW Finch
The Finnish National Gallery, Helsinki, inv. no. A II 1700

This painting, together with *Orchard at La Louvière* [cat. 23], are Finch's most highly developed works in terms of divisionist theory. It was sketched in summer 1891, painted in the artist's studio during the following winter, and exhibited, from February 1892, at the Salon des XX, at which Octave Maus had recommended that only 'previously unshown' works be displayed. Originally the picture had not only a painted border but also a large painted frame *à la Seurat*, which has subsequently disappeared. However, a photograph of the pictures exhibited at the 1892 exhibition of the Association pour l'Art provides the only indication of just how far Finch had gone in applying the knowledge and precepts of his master.[1]

The Cliffs at South Foreland, like all strictly pointillist works, conveys a certain coldness. This is due not only to the stiffness produced by the necessarily tightly measured application of small dots of colour in order to obtain the effects of optical mix, but also to the use of a palette in which blue dominates. At the same time, however, the painting conveys an impression of tranquillity and freshness, and defies any obvious tendency to focus on the surface plane by drawing the eye towards the back of the picture, where it can either wander along the horizon-line or, if it opts for the vertical lines of the cliffs, move up towards the clouds, reminiscent of large white birds. In this painting, as in *Landscape, Sunset* [cat. 25] – where, in contrast, Finch uses a warm, blazing palette that makes the painting more accessible – the artist succeeds in imposing with impressive rigour his precise, measured and 'intelligent' stroke, and his systematic composition, based on strict principles. At the same time, the overall impression provokes sufficient disquiet to cause us want to look a little longer. The same fascination is exerted by *Breakwater at Heyst* (dated 1891 but probably painted in 1890) [fig. a], a masterpiece of Japanese-style wave-painting, in which the waves are composed of hundreds of tiny iridescent patches. It is undoubtedly this capacity to fascinate which distinguishes Finch from other Pointillists in whose works the technical process is often too explicit and 'laborious'. | DDC

PROVENANCE Bought from a private collection in 1928.

EXHIBITIONS *Les XX* 1892, no. 1; Antwerp 1892a; The Hague 1892, no. 5 or 6; Helsinki 1901, no. 62; Helsinki 1910, *s.n.*; Helsinki 1928, no. 72; Helsinki 1929, no. 4; Helsinki 1930, no. 58; Helsinki 1955, no. 12; Brussels 1967, no. 98, ill.; New York 1968, no. 124, ill.; Düsseldorf 1977, no. 40, ill.; Brooklyn 1980, no. 27, ill.; Stockholm 1981, no. 6, ill.; Tokyo, Kyoto 1985, no. 56; Amsterdam 1988, no. 51, ill.; Helsinki 1991, no. 22, ills.; Brussels 1992, no. 20, ills.

BIBLIOGRAPHY Frosterus 1907; Saarikivi 1949, 47 (ill.); Rewald 1956, 121; Hintze 1966, 10 (ill.), 15, 42; Lindström 1966, 38; Dorival 1969, 418; Sutter 1970, 235, ill.; Stevens 1979, 266; Goyens de Heusch 1988, 168, 169, ill.; D.D.C. [Derrey-Capon] 1987, 174; Derrey-Capon 1991–1992, 21, 82 (ill.), 108, 112, 174 (ill.).

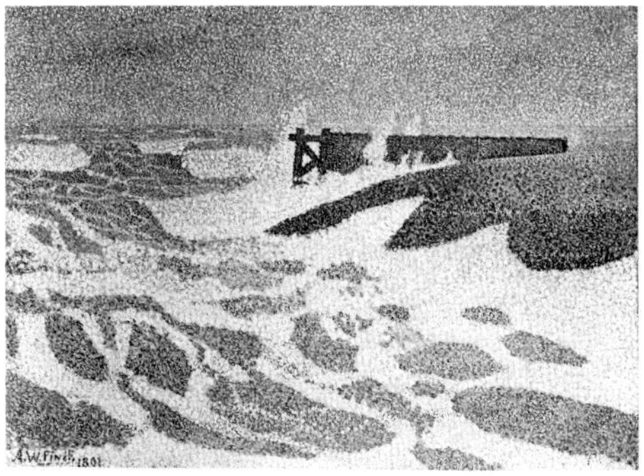

fig. a ALFRED WILLIAM FINCH
Breakwater at Heyst, 1891,
Private Collection, Finland

1 On this, see D. Derrey-Capon, *A. W. Finch*, exhibition catalogue, Brussels 1992, 174–175.

25 Landscape, Sunset

Paysage, soleil couchant, 1892
Oil on canvas, 54 x 67 cm
Signed bottom right: A. W. Finch
Turku Art Museum (Finland), Nils Dahlström Collection, inv. no. ND 15

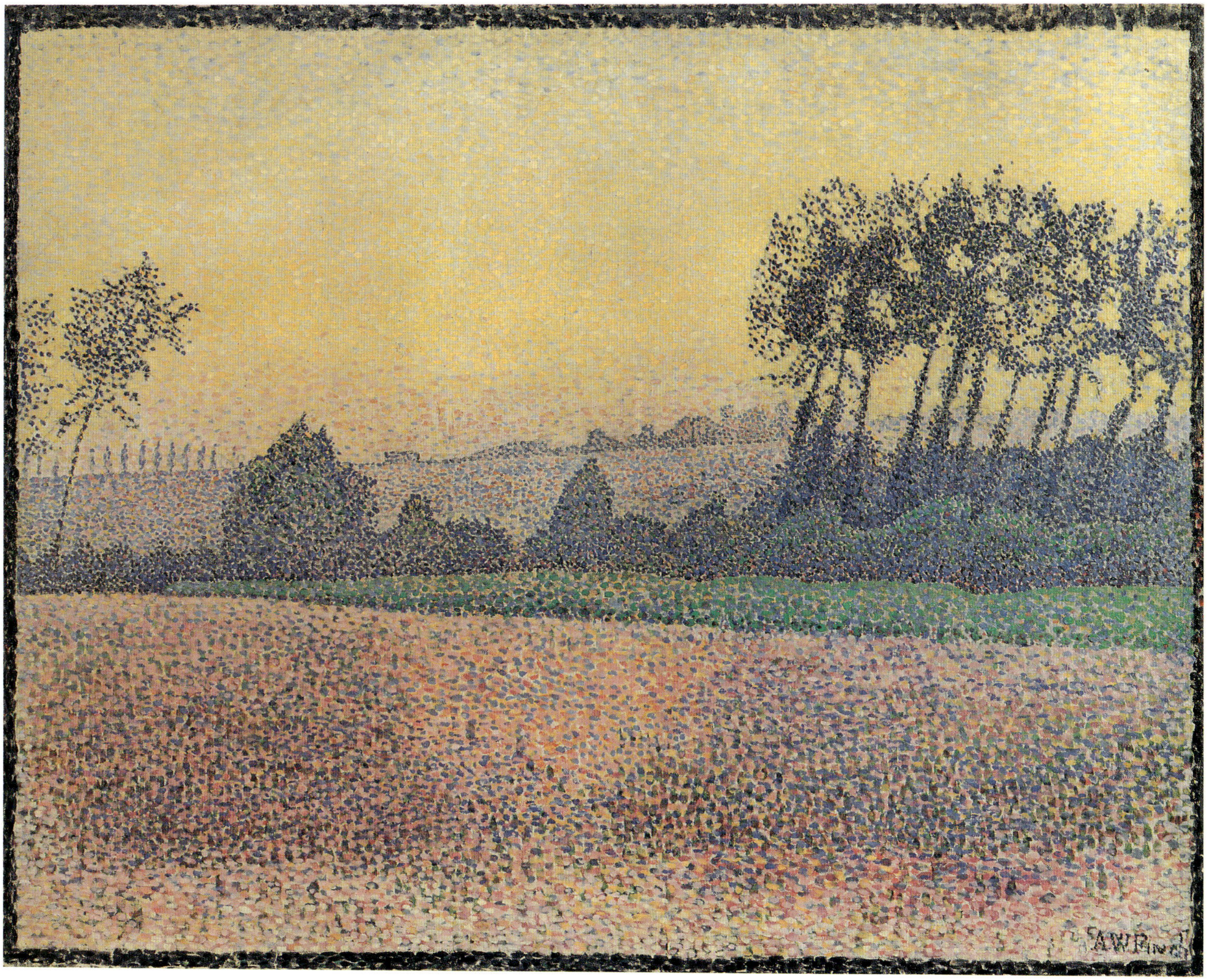

Landscape, Sunset was the last work painted by Finch before he decided to devote himself exclusively to the practice of ceramics, with which he was already involved at La Louvière from 1890 [see cat. 23]. It was exhibited at the Salon des XX in February 1893. It has consistently been confused with another pointillist work by Finch, which has still not been identified, entitled *Road to Nieuwpoort*.

Like *The Cliffs at South Foreland* [cat. 24], *Landscape, Sunset* originally had not only a border but also a painted frame. The picture forms part of the series of divisionist works by Finch, which, although their brushwork, palette and rhythm bear the hallmarks of the artist, none the less derive directly from the theories of Seurat. The combination of the light, the interplay of complementaries, the flexible pointillist technique, and a structure based on three horizontal planes punctuated by diagonals in the central section, give the painting an unusual impression of 'time standing still'. These same features are already to be found in Finch's striking small-scale works such as *The Haystacks* (1889) [see cat. 22, fig. a], *Channel at Nieuwpoort* (1889; Josefowitz Collection), and *Orchard at La Louvière* [cat. 23]. On the other hand, *Landscape, Sunset* also heralds the works of the Finnish period. When Finch took up the brush once again in Porvoo/Borgå, after an interval of five years, his manner was more spontaneous, emancipated from the constraints of Seurat's divisionism; the more ample style, richer impasto, and more 'aggressive' palette – cool and rosy under the influence of the Nordic light which Finch struggled to master – resulted in works that stand out from the local artistic output of the time, dominated as it was by a nationalist Romanticism. From these works, it is easy to see why Finch soon came to play a decisive role in the development and renewal of Finnish art. | DDC

PROVENANCE Bought from the artist's family in England by Mr Nils Dahlström, who donated it, together with other works by Finch, to the Museum in 1973.

EXHIBITIONS *Les XX* 1893, no. 1; Brussels 1967, no. 92, ill.; Turku 1973, no. 19, ill. no. 76; Finland 1973, no. 19; Helsinki 1991, no. 23, ill.; Brussels 1992, no. 21, ills.; Paris 1993, no. 36, ill.

BIBLIOGRAPHY Hintze 1966, 11, pls. 7, 8; Herbert 1968, 163; *Les XX* 1981, ill.; [Turku] 1984, 81; D.D.C. [D. Derrey-Capon] 1987, 173; Derrey-Capon 1991–1992, 21, 83 (ill.), 112, 175 (ill.); D.D.C. [D. Derrey-Capon], in Paris 1993, 140–141, ill.

Léon Fréderic

BRUSSELS 1856 – SCHAERBEEK 1940

Léon Fréderic was the son of a jeweller. He was educated at a Jesuit boarding school near Ghent and at fifteen was apprenticed to the painter-decorator, Charles Albert. He studied at the Brussels Academy of Fine Arts and under J. F. Portaels (1818–1895). Failing to win the Prix de Rome, he visited Italy at his father's expense. During his time there, he copied works of art and drew and painted from nature. At an early stage he favoured the predominance of line over colour. His admiration for the Flemish Primitives, with whom he shared a sense of the spiritual and a love for detail, led him to an interest in the work of the English Pre-Raphaelites. Fréderic was attracted to the timeless rituals of rural life. He initially recorded this interest in naturalistic compositions painted in the manner of Bastien-Lepage. Some of these works were made on a large scale and arranged as polyptychs or as serial paintings, such as *Les Ages du paysan* (*The Ages of the Peasant*, 1885–1887, Musées royaux des Beaux-Arts de Belgique, Brussels) and *Les Ages de l'ouvrier* (*The Ages of the Worker*, 1895–1897, Musée d'Orsay, Paris). His pursuit of the unsullied rural existence led him to discover Nafraiture, an isolated village in the Ardennes where, from 1883, he spent almost every summer. He began to contribute to the Triennial Salons in 1878 and to L'Essor, which he joined in 1880. After the triptych *Le Ruisseau* (*The Stream*, 1890–1899, Musées royaux des Beaux-Arts de Belgique, Brussels), Fréderic began to produce religious and allegorical compositions which paralleled his social and realistic work. These made him an important figure in Belgian Symbolism, and were first shown at the Salons d'Art Idéaliste in 1896. He spent time in the Netherlands and travelled to Britain and Germany. The official approval he enjoyed enabled him to exhibit abroad regularly, and he received a number of honours, including membership of the Academy in 1904 and the rank of baron in 1929.

His work remained popular for a long time, despite its generally cold, thin and occasionally acidic, discordant tones. This popularity derived not only from his precise and true-to-life technique and strange symbolism, but above all from his striking naturalistic scenes. If the latter are not always free of sentimentality, they often combine genuine compassion with objectivity. | ML

SUMMARY BIBLIOGRAPHY

F. Khnopff, 'A Belgian painter Léon Fréderic', *The Studio* 40: 169 (1907), 171–181; *Rétrospective Léon Fréderic*, Palais des Beaux-Arts, Brussels 1948 (Introduction by M. Sulzberger); L. Jottrand, *Léon Fréderic*, Antwerp 1950; *Rétrospective Léon Fréderic*, Hôtel Charlier, Saint-Josse-ten-Noode 1973.

26 Funeral Wake

Le Repas de funérailles, 1886
Oil on canvas, 124 x 176 cm
Signed bottom right: L. [?] Fréderic 1886
Museum voor Schone Kunsten, Ghent, inv. no. 1886–D

Funeral Wake was painted some four years after Fréderic's first masterpiece, *Les Marchands de craie* (*The Chalk Sellers*, 1882–1883; Musées royaux des Beaux-Arts de Belgique, Brussels), while he was working on one of his most important projects – the series *Les Ages du paysan* (*The Ages of the Peasant*, 1885–1887). Nevertheless, the work still displays certain technical imperfections that make it seem earlier than the two more famous paintings. Problems with the handling of space are still apparent, for instance, not only in the details, like the positioning of the objects on the table, but also in the awkward setting of the people against the less sharply delineated, more loosely brushed background. An exaggerated depth is suggested by the planks of the tabletop and the jump in scale between the figures at the front and those towards the rear, but this clashes abruptly with the landscape, which remains as flat as a naïvely painted theatre backdrop. It is difficult to find an explanation for this, especially when we compare the work with another table scene in a similarly sized canvas, *Christmas at the Old People's Home* (1884) [fig. a], in which satisfactory solutions are found for problems of the same type. However, the differences serve also to reveal the special character of *Funeral Wake*.

The composition of both works may be compared with that of another table scene, namely Millais's *Lorenzo and Isabella* (1849; Walker Art Gallery, Liverpool), in which the figures are strung behind one another in a similar manner. Fréderic had already been linked to Millais by Hymans in 1906, and strong echoes of the latter are certainly to be found in his work. Like the Englishman's painting, *Christmas* is animated and easily accessible to the viewer. *Funeral Wake*, by contrast, is closed to us: the two monumental figures and the horizontal elements of the furniture at the front close the scene off, and as the eye seeks a way in, it is repelled by the jug placed in the middle. This, and the fact that the motionless figures take up two-thirds of the width of the image, causing their heads to form a horizontal straight line, suggests a tendency to keep the scene parallel to the picture plane, despite the foreshortening of the table. A similar frontality is the dominant characteristic of *Les Ages du paysan*, where it is applied more radically. The group is there given a greater unity, and despite the sometimes overly visible combination of the components, it comes over as a single entity – a company united in prayer and thought, compared to which the naturalism of *Christmas* is reduced to the banality of an anecdotal genre painting. The avoidance of anecdote in the present painting also removes the drama that was heightened by Millais to generate a subtle tension. It is replaced by stillness and silence. The meticulous individualization of the facial features is also tempered – again unlike Millais – by the action of the shadows which unite the mourners in an almost mystical way. This spirituality is reinforced by the sparing, yet clearly present light between the dark, cool colours: its artificiality seems to conjure up the presence of the deceased. It reflects off the table in the middle of the mourners, blurring and internalizing the facial features of the people furthest away, and linking them in the closest imaginable way with the deceased. The figures on the left, whose posture recalls the works of the Flemish Primitives, further underscores the sacral overtones of the scene.

Funeral Wake shares its sense of reverence and restraint, stripped of any element of pathos or sentimentality, with works such as the Finnish painter Edelfelt's *Funeral of a Child* (1879; Ateneumin Taidemuseo, Helsinki). There too, simple farmers are lifted by the composition and the action of the light into a silent, yet grandiose, mythical and almost supernatural happening. | ML

PROVENANCE Purchased by the Museum in 1886.
EXHIBITIONS Brussels 1886; Ghent 1886, no. 227; Vienna 1888; Brussels 1948; Saint-Josse-ten-Noode 1973, no. 12; Berlin 1979, 249; Charleroi 1980, no. 44.
BIBLIOGRAPHY Poirier 1953, 215.

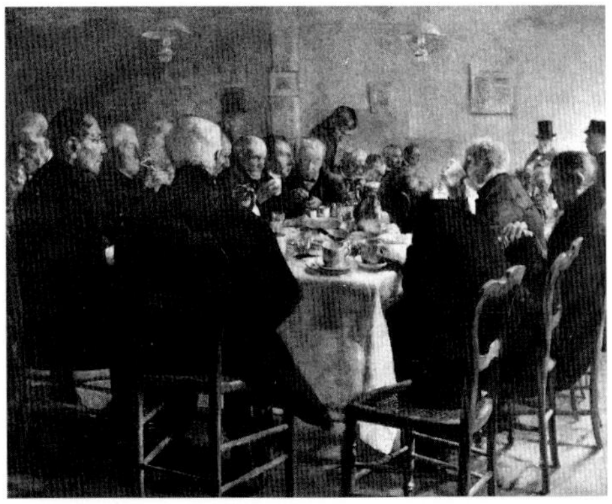

fig. a LÉON FRÉDERIC
Christmas at the Old People's Home, 1884, Musée des Beaux-Arts, Mons

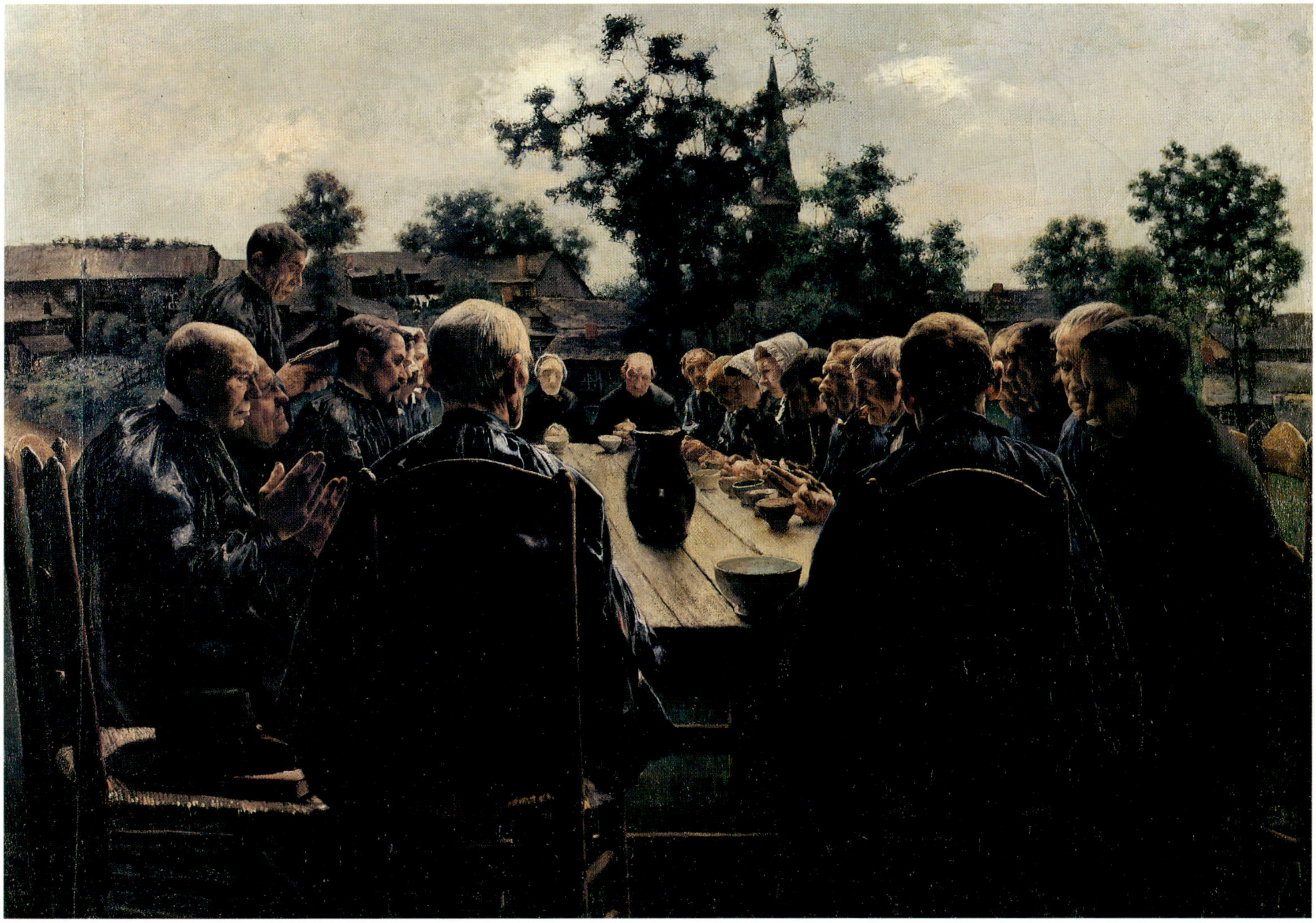

Frans Hens

ANTWERP 1856–1928

Frans Hens, the son of a butcher, was attracted to drawing and painting from an early age. His earliest impressions were formed in the area around Antwerp harbour and along the River Scheldt. He studied at the Academy of Fine Arts in Antwerp between 1871 and 1876. His teacher was Jacob Jacobs (1812–1879), a romantic landscape and marine painter. Hens was not satisfied by his academic studies, but they did bring him into contact with two similarly minded, progressive artists: Theodoor Verstraete (q.v.) and Eugeen Joors (1850–1910). His training was followed by a period of travel and adventure: sojourns in North America (1873–1874), and in Germany as a circus acrobat (1874–1875).

He made his début as an artist with an exhibition in Dendermonde (1875), where he showed views of Germany and the area around Buffalo in the United States. He returned to America in 1876, where he visited the World Fair in Philadelphia. His attempt in 1877 to join an expedition to the coast of East Africa, organized by King Leopold II's recently set-up Association Internationale Africaine, proved unsuccessful.

In the subsequent period he produced a series of Scheldt landscapes. Like Artan (q.v.), Hens wished to experience these river subjects as intensely as possible. To this end, he set up a studio on board a boat moored off the Vlaams Hoofd. He was co-founder in 1883 of the Weest U Zelve (Be Yourself) circle of artists. Other members included Emile Claus (q.v.), Theodoor Verstraete, the sculptor Jef Lambeaux (1852–1908) and several writers.

Hens tried again in 1884 to find sponsorship for a trip to Africa. He intended to collect material there for a panorama to be shown at the 1885 World Fair in Antwerp. He contacted the Association Internationale du Congo, another organization patronized by King Leopold II, but was again refused. This time he decided to make the journey on his own initiative. He spent several months in the Lower Congo in 1886. In addition to paintings and sketches, he returned from his expedition with numerous botanical, zoological and ethnological specimens. A second journey to the Congo in 1887 took him deeper into the country. He was back in Antwerp by December 1888, and exhibited work produced during these visits to the Congo on a variety of occasions in Brussels and Antwerp in the subsequent years. Despite his apparent eligibility, Hens lost the commission for a Congo diorama at the 1894 World Fair in Antwerp to two other painters, Robert Mols (1848–1903) and Piet van Engelen (1863–1924). His efforts to join Adrien de Gerlache's Antarctic expedition also failed.

The River Scheldt, however, continued to inspire him. He observed the river and the multifarious activities plied along the waterway, working repeatedly from his floating studio. He also translated these scenes into etchings.

He was one of the founders in 1891 of the XIII and in 1919 he became a teacher at Antwerp's Higher Institute of Fine Arts. | NH

SUMMARY BIBLIOGRAPHY

M. Luwel, 'Frans Hens', *Nationaal Biografisch Woordenboek* 2 (Brussels 1966); P. and V. Berko, N. Hostyn, 'Marines de peintres belges nés entre 1750 et 1875', Brussels, Knokke 1984; S. Goyens de Heusch, *L'Impressionnisme et le Fauvisme en Belgique*, Antwerp 1988; *L'Impressionnisme et le Fauvisme en Belgique*, Musée d'Ixelles, Brussels 1990; *Fin de siècle. Dessins, pastels et estampes en Belgique de 1885 à 1905*, Galerie CGER, Brussels 1991.

27 View of the Scheldt

Gezicht op de Schelde, 1894
Oil on canvas, 38.5 x 30 cm
Signed and dated bottom left: Frans Hens 94
Koninklijk Museum voor Schone Kunsten, Antwerp, inv. no. 2856

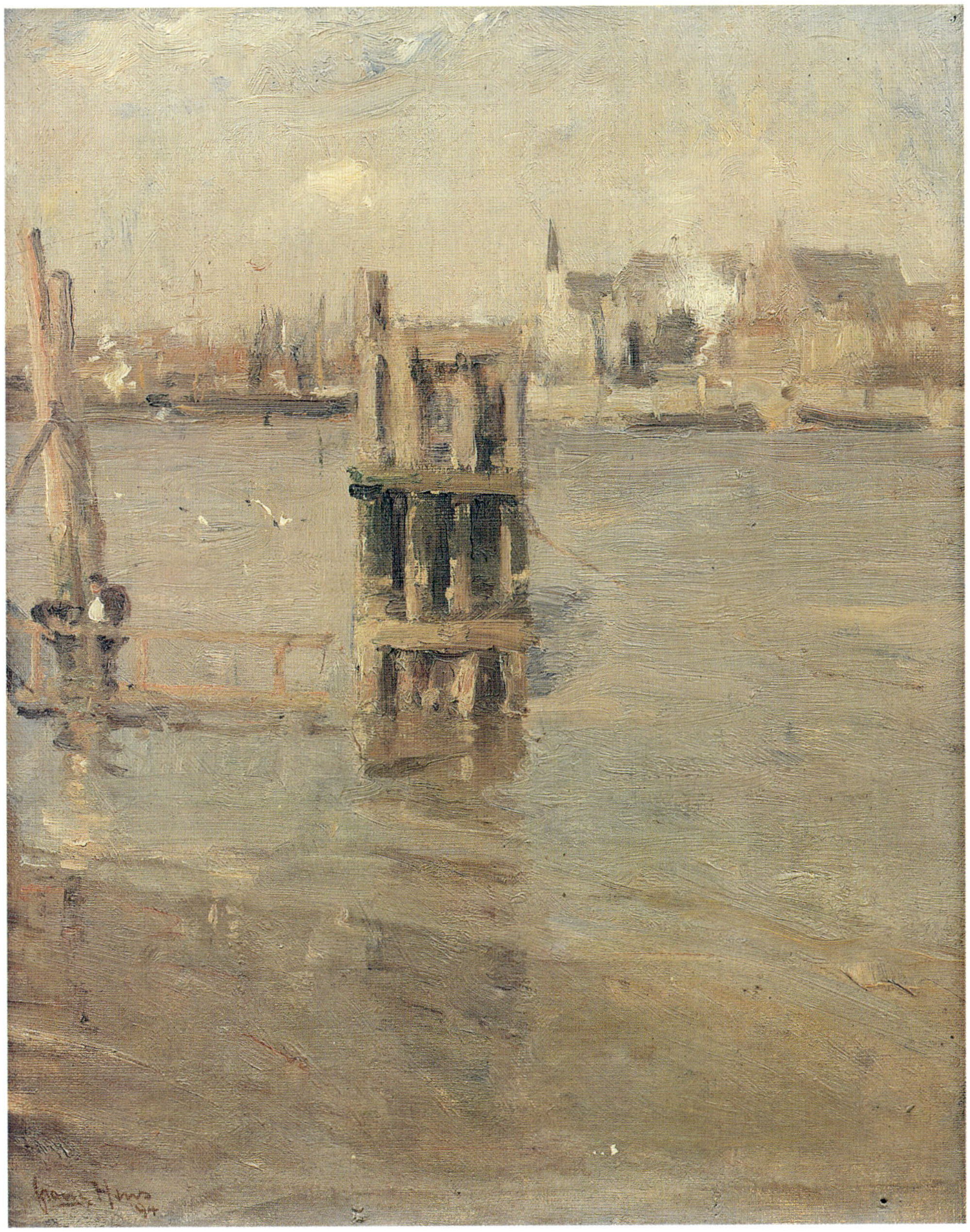

Frans Hens's early seascapes employed a restrained impressionistic style influenced by Theodoor Verstraete (q.v.) (see, for example, *The Sint-Anna Ferry Boat*, 1885, Koninklijk Museum voor Schone Kunsten, Antwerp). They gradually became richer in technique, in keeping with a painterliness much practised by his fellow Antwerp landscape painters, for example James Ensor [see cats. 14, 15], and finally evolved into an almost expressionistic style, with boldly applied, thick masses of paint (e.g. *Clear Night on the River Scheldt*, 1925; Musées royaux des Beaux-Arts de Belgique, Brussels). Hens's preferred subject was the River Scheldt at Antwerp, his native city. He generally showed it in fog, rain or at evening time, which explains the somewhat subdued range of his palette. Hens was extremely skilful at conveying the atmosphere of the landscape, which he achieved through simple compositions with recognizable features like tugboats, sailing boats and ferries at their moorings. A sturdy mooring post features at the centre of the exhibited painting. | NH

PROVENANCE J. Wollants Bequest, 1957.
EXHIBITION Antwerp 1985–1986, no. 108.

Fernand Khnopff

GREMBERGEN NEAR DENDERMONDE 1858 – BRUSSELS 1921

Khnopff came from an upper middle class Belgian family whose members traditionally pursued their careers in the law. From 1859 to 1864, he lived in Bruges. The town, known as the Venice of the North and celebrated in Rodenbach's novel *Bruges-la-Morte* (Paris 1892), made a lasting impression on him. In 1875 he began law studies at the University of Brussels, but his true passion was literature. He read Flaubert, Baudelaire and Leconte de Lisle, and mixed with the young writers of the day: Max Waller, Iwan Gilkin, Georges Rodenbach and Emile Verhaeren. It was not long before he gave up university and began studying art under the painter Xavier Mellery (q.v.). From 1876 to 1879 he was enrolled at the Academy of Fine Arts in Brussels, where one of his fellow students was none other than James Ensor (q.v.). He also made many trips to Paris where he visited the museums, displaying a special interest in Rubens, Veronese, Rembrandt, Ingres, Giorgione, and Delacroix. It was in Paris, at the Exposition Universelle of 1878, that he discovered Moreau, Millais and Burne-Jones. In 1879, he attended Jules Lefèbvre's open studio and worked in the Académie Julian. Khnopff made his artistic début in 1881, at the Brussels salon held by the group L'Essor. In 1883 he was a founding member of Les XX and later also of La Libre Esthéthique. From 1885, he came into contact with Joséphin Péladan, by whom he was held in high regard. Khnopff exhibited at the 1892, 1893, 1894, and 1897 Salons de La Rose+Croix in Paris. In 1889 he established his first links with England, where he was to become a regular exhibitor; Hunt, Watts, Rossetti, Ford Maddox Brown, and Burne-Jones became his friends. In 1895, he became a correspondent for the periodical *The Studio,* and he edited its 'Studio-Talk-Brussels' column until 1914. From 1900, Khnopff devoted all his energies to building his house, a veritable temple to the 'self', for which he himself drew the plans. | GOZ

SUMMARY BIBLIOGRAPHY

L. Dumont-Wilden, *Fernand Khnopff*, Brussels 1907; N. Eemans, *Fernand Khnopff*, Antwerp 1950; *Fernand Khnopff 1858–1921*, Musée des Arts Décoratifs, Paris / Musées royaux des Beaux-Arts de Belgique, Brussels / Kunsthalle, Hamburg 1979–1980 (Catalogue by C. de Croës and G. Ollinger-Zinque); R. L. Delevoy, C. de Croës, G. Ollinger-Zinque, *Fernand Khnopff*, Brussels 1979 (2nd revised and enlarged edition, 1987).

28 Listening to Schumann

En écoutant Schumann, 1883
Oil on canvas, 101.5 x 116.6 cm
Signed upper left: Fernand Khnopff
Musées royaux des Beaux-Arts de Belgique /
Koninklijke Musea voor Schone Kunsten van België, Brussels, inv. no. 6366

This bold, essentially modern painting, dated 1883, was exhibited twice in the year of its creation and provoked a stormy debate. In particular, it was criticized for being too impressionist and for having a curious composition in which the main figure, the pianist, is not visible, the body of the picture being occupied by a woman sunk deep in thought in an armchair. It is one of Khnopff's youthful works and depicts an interior, a *salon bourgeois*, comparable to that in James Ensor's *Russian Music* [cat. 12] of 1881. Indeed, when Khnopff exhibited the painting at the 1886 Salon des XX, Ensor, who was showing *Russian Music* at the same salon, took offence at the similarity between the two works, comparing his own fate to that of Claude Lantier, the hero of Emile Zola's novel *L'Œuvre*: Lantier, an unacknowledged pioneer, ends up committing suicide, whilst Fagerolles, whom Ensor identified with Khnopff, enjoys popular esteem despite being no more than a common plagiarist. Ensor attacked all those who backed Khnopff and wrote to the Secretary of Les XX, Octave Maus, in the following terms: 'The future will decide, and award each the place he deserves ... It is written that he who humbles himself shall be exalted.' After this incident, there was deep dissension between the two artists, each of whom, in any case, went on to pursue totally different paths. It was Emile Verhaeren who, in 1886, took up the cudgels in favour of Khnopff's work, publishing several laudatory articles in the Brussels periodical, *L'Art moderne*. Of the present painting, which found a purchaser at the 1886 Salon des XX in the person of the senator Henri Lafontaine, Verhaeren wrote: 'This is an important canvas ... The painting commands attention both by its severity and by its great distinction. The lady listening – it is she who makes the whole painting, raising it to the status of a spiritual study – has a rare power. She is the embodiment of concentrated attention, impression materialized, aesthetic anguish made reality. Through her we feel passion, and experience the nature of musical life; her attitude, fraught with tension, has about it something indefinably austere and painful ... *Listening to Schumann* is the only purely modern work by Fernand Khnopff which I find pleasing' (*L'Art moderne*, 10 October 1886, 322).

The woman in the chair, enclosed in her own private universe, is none other than the artist's mother. She is detached from the world, lost in her memories; a sort of intellectual charm emanates from this closed interior. Khnopff was very fond of his mother and would talk about her with affectionate pride. In his portraits of her (*Portrait of Mme Edmond Khnopff*, 1882, Musée des Beaux-Arts, Liège), she is always depicted with fine, regular features, and her whole attitude expresses intelligence, goodness, distinction and energy. | GOZ

PROVENANCE Henri Lafontaine, Brussels; acquired in 1945.

EXHIBITIONS Brussels 1883, no. 110; Ghent 1883, no. 547, *Les XX* 1886, no. 1; Antwerp 1887, no. 83; Paris 1907, no. 103; *La Libre Esthétique* 1908, no. 111; Berlin 1908, no. 106; Brussels 1912b, no. 65; Brussels 1922, no. 106; Paris 1923, no. 49, pl.; London 1927, no. 423; Brussels 1930, no. 222; Brussels 1932a, no. 14; Brussels 1957, no. 805; Brussels 1961, no. 55; Brussels, Otterlo 1962, no. 56; Vienna 1962, no. 55; Brussels 1966, no. 19, ill.; Brussels 1967–1968, no. 31, Brussels 1968, no. 22; Brussels 1970b, no. 28; Brussels 1971a, no. 23; Paris 1972, no. 30, ill.; Paris, Brussels, Hamburg 1979–1980, no. 5, ill.; New York 1980, no. 33, ill.; Brussels 1980–1981, no. 142, ill.; Brussels 1981, no. 12; Brussels 1987a, no. P42, pl. IX; Tokyo, Himeji, Nagoya, Yamanashi 1990, no. 4, ill.; Brussels 1994a, no. 37, ill.

BIBLIOGRAPHY Verhaeren 1886, 322; Lemonnier 1887, 320, 340; De Mont 1891, 270; De Taeye 1894, 742, 745, 749; Du Jardin 1900, 67; De Mont 1901, 150; Pica 1902, 188; Lemonnier 1906, 170, 182; Dumont-Wilden 1907, 14, 22, 48, 69; Verhaeren 1908, 22; Pica 1909, 170; Bénédite 1910, 307; Biermé 1911, 1; De Mont 1921, 82; Vanzype 1923, 76, 116; Delville 1925, 22; Maus 1926, 42; Pica 1927, 246; Colin 1930, 22; Vanzype 1930, 59, pl. XXXV; Fierens 1939, 498; Fierens 1943, 16; Eemans 1950, 6, 10; Legrand, Ollinger-Zinque 1966, 24–26; Jullian 1969, 150–151; Legrand 1971, 69; Milner 1971, 108; Haesaerts 1973, 18; Carluccio 1974, 57; Laclotte 1976, 192; Delevoy, De Croës, Ollinger-Zinque 1979, 219–220, no. 52; Goldwater 1979, 34, 205, 207, ill. 34; Boenders 1979–1980, 84–85; Metken 1979–1980, 33–34; Roberts-Jones 1980, 46–47, ill. 5; Van Kerckhoven 1980, 237–238; Delevoy 1981, 304–306; Van Kerckhoven 1981–1984, 165–176, ill. 1; Howe 1982, 5–6, 121–122, 149–150, pl. 37; Metken 1983, 99; Block 1984, 62–63, 71, ill. 25; Dufey 1985, 60; Goyens de Heusch 1985, 75; Wangermée 1985, 61, 63; Dalemans 1986, 104 (ill.); Delevoy, De Croës, Ollinger-Zinque 1987, 219–222, 413, no. 52; G.O.Z. [Ollinger-Zinque] 1987, 166; Ollinger-Zinque 1990, 72–73, ill. 4; Koyanagi 1990, 13 (pl. 2), 60; Leppert 1993, 230-232.

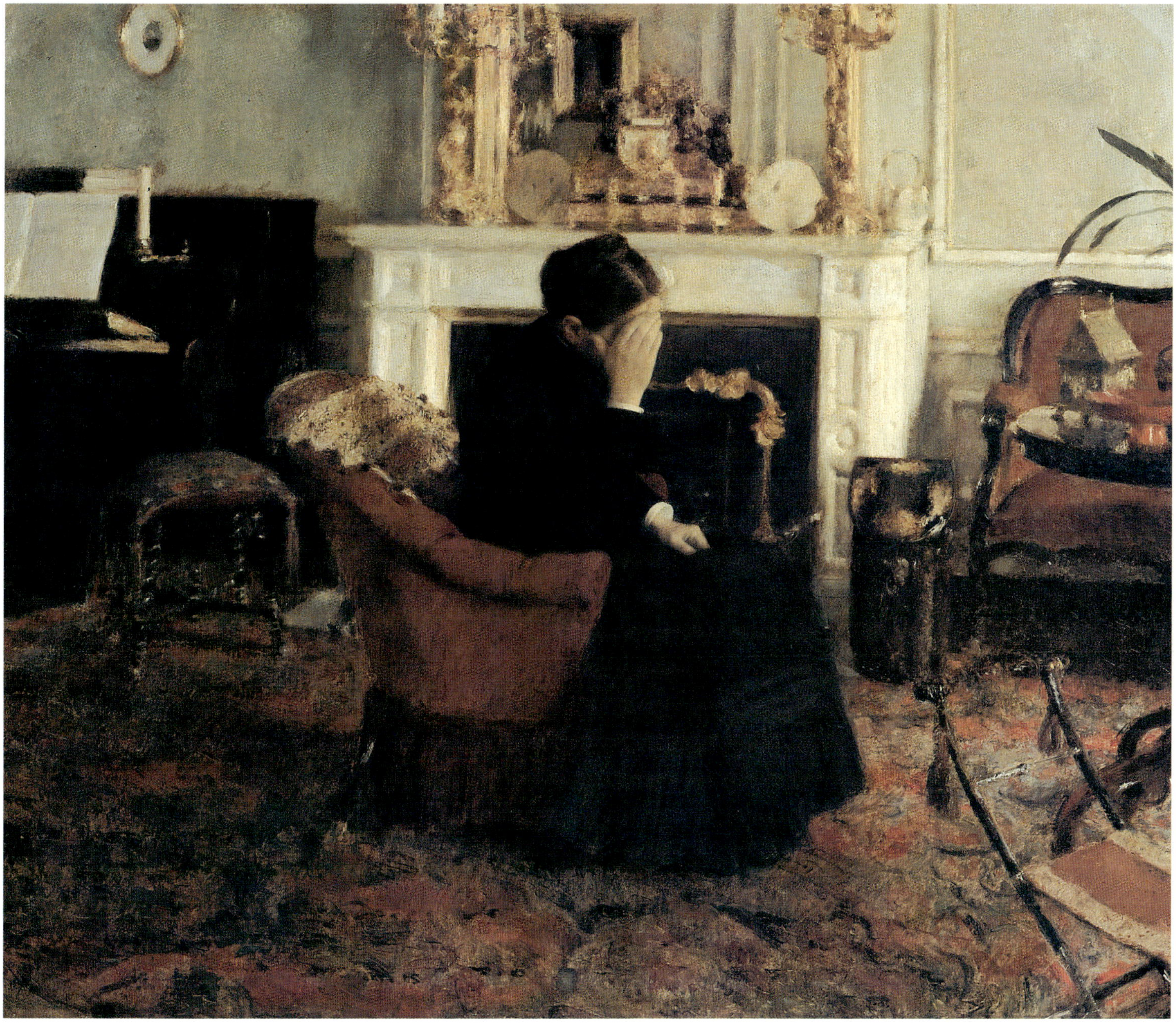

29 Portrait of Jeanne Kéfer

Portrait de Jeanne Kéfer, 1885
Oil on canvas, 80 x 80 cm
Signed bottom centre: Fernand Khnopff 1885
Private Collection, Sweden–Norway

Jeanne Kéfer was the daughter of the pianist and composer Gustave Kéfer, whose portrait Khnopff also painted in 1885, together with that of Kéfer's friend, the violinist Achille Lerminiaux (Delevoy, De Croës, Ollinger-Zinque 1987, nos. 74 and 75). Both musicians played an extremely important role, not only in the world of music, but also in the world of art. In 1881 the quartet to which Kéfer belonged began giving concerts in artists' studios; and two years later, Kéfer and his friend Lerminiaux founded the Union instrumentale, which made regular appearances in the avant-garde circles of Brussels: L'Essor, Les XX and La Libre Esthétique.

When Khnopff began his artistic career, it was towards the portrait that he gravitated. He found ready models in his immediate entourage, and his sketchbooks for the years 1879 to 1882 are full of precisely recorded profiles and poses. In a letter written to his friend Paul Schultze Naumburg in 1889, he explained his method of working: 'When I am working on a picture, I do very few sketches but a lot of studies. I imagine the whole life my figures have lived in their own settings, up to the moment when that life is to be depicted in a work of art. It is these prior details that give the work its complexity' (quoted in Delevoy, De Croës, Ollinger-Zinque 1987, 26–27). Having completed portraits of his mother and father, Khnopff turned his attention to children, and after 1885 he became the regular portrait-painter to all the great noble families and the *haute bourgeoisie*.

The works which Khnopff produced were commissions – quasi-official ones, since his models were often famous people (*Portrait of the Empress Elizabeth of Austria*, 1899, Österreichische Nationalbibliothek, Porträtsammlung, Vienna) – and yet he always managed to give his own personality full rein within them. They display all the major traits of his style: modernity, a taste for the hermetic and the mysterious, elegance, and an element of aristocratic breeding. Khnopff also took special care over framing and layout, very often chosing the image of a closed door, against which he makes his model lean, as if irrevocably shutting out that which cannot exist beyond physical appearance.

Here, Khnopff transfixes the young girl for eternity. With his remarkable scene-setting talents, he creates a theatre-like backdrop, intentionally cutting off the top of the door and centring his picture on the girl, as a film-maker or professional photographer might do. Although descriptive, Khnopff has excluded the external world, enveloping and isolating the figure itself. This is a more radically modernist approach than the isolation of subject found in the portraits of both Manet and Whistler. Thus, despite obvious affinities in terms of muted, tonally harmonious palettes and carefully constructed compositions between Khnopff and Whistler, it is possible to understand the astonished reaction to Khnopff's portraits by his contemporaries, used as they were to more realistic, conventional portraits.

The present painting was exhibited for the first time at the 1886 Salon des XX. It intrigued the critics, and one of them, Georges Verdavainne, wrote: 'Consider this young girl with her gleaming blond hair and her eyes wide open with surprise, looking as if she is waiting for the camera's click. The meticulous, tight execution does nothing to diminish the charm of the picture.' | GOZ

PROVENANCE Gustave Kéfer, Brussels; Hugo Engel, Paris; Rapps Konsthandel, Stockholm 1957; Private Collection, Sweden; sale London, Christie's, 30 November 1990, no. 80.

EXHIBITIONS *Les XX* 1885, no. 3; *Les XX* 1886, no. 4; Antwerp 1887, no. 85; London 1892, no. 166; Florence 1896–1897, no. 44; Munich 1898, no. 100; Brussels 1987b, no. 24; Tokyo, Himeji, Nagoya, Yamanashi 1990, no. 5

BIBLIOGRAPHY De Taeye 1894, 749; Schultze Naumburg 1900, 447; Pica 1902, 173; Sarfatti 1906, 64; Dumont-Wilden 1907, 22, 70; Biermé 1911, 2; Lambotte 1913, 125; Delville 1925, 22; Delevoy, De Croës, Ollinger-Zinque 1979, 231–232 no. 82; Van Kerckhoven 1981–1984, 168; Delevoy, De Croës, Ollinger-Zinque 1987, 231–232 no. 82, 417 no. 82.

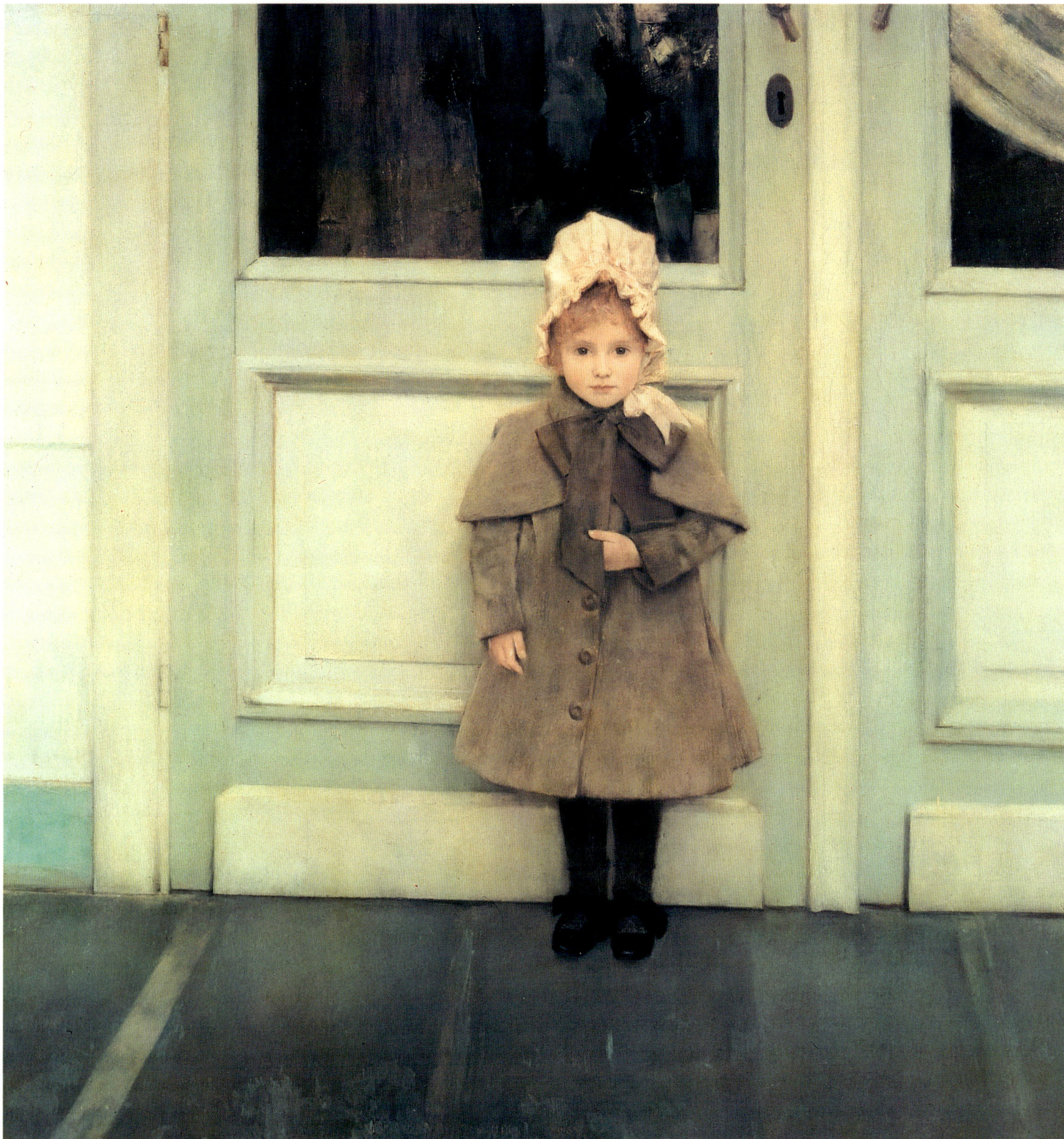

30 With Georges Rodenbach. A Dead City

Avec Georges Rodenbach. Une ville morte, 1889
Pastel and ink on paper, 26 x 16 cm
Signed bottom left: Fernand Khnopff
The Hearn Family Trust

The theme of womanhood is an inexhaustible one, and its manifestations in the work of the Symbolists were legion. Charles Baudelaire, one of the most influential writers on the Symbolist generation, in his poems defines various kinds of women: 'I am as beautiful, o mortals, as a dream of stone and my breast where each person has, in his own time, been killed, is made to inspire in poets an eternal, silent love as well as the substance.' The androgynous quality of the women depicted by Fernand Khnopff did not surprise his contemporaries. The soul has no gender, and Khnopff painted only souls.

In this work, Khnopff evokes time, always considered as infinite rather than finite in his oeuvre. It is a time whose pace is other than that of daily life; of so vast a duration that one cannot see it pass. This impression of eternity, of never-endingness, was a central concern for Symbolism and is expressed specifically in this work through the suggestion that the immobilized and transfixed female figure is operating in a realm separated from the material world.

The drawing is dedicated to Georges Rodenbach (1855–1898) and was completed three years before the publication of the novel *Bruges-la-Morte*, one of Rodenbach's major literary successes, for which Fernand Khnopff provided a frontispiece [fig. a]. Rodenbach set his story in the old quarters of Bruges. His hero, a young widower, projects his grief on to the town, thus making it the symbol of his emotional distress. In Bruges he discovers a double of the woman whose death he mourns, but she proves unable to replace her. The novel embodies that sense of the mysterious which was celebrated in both Symbolist literature and visual art. The poet's voice is audible in the very first lines of the Foreword: the book is a study in emotion; it depicts the city as a living person, linked to particular moods – advising, warning, determining: 'Bruges, on which our choice has fallen, seems almost human.'

In *A Dead City*, Khnopff appears to have anticipated in pictorial form everything that the poet was to seek to express in words. This capacity to encapsulate the ideas that lay behind the novel led the German Symbolist poet Stefan George (1868–1933) to reproduce this pastel drawing in the August 1894 issue of *Blätter für die Kunst*.

Bruges acquired universal fame as a result of Rodenbach's novel, in which it is depicted as having an atmosphere of foreboding comprising elements of silence, mysticism and death. Khnopff attempted to convey this strange beauty in many of his works. He had left the city at the age of six, but its image persisted in his memory and, after 1900, became a rich source of inspiration [cat. 36, 37]. Khnopff was passionately interested in literature, and his friendship with Georges Rodenbach had a profound influence on his work and on the themes he tackled. The close links between the two men are unmistakable: the 'dead city' figures in the works of both, and in both, silence is a sought-after and essential element. This affinity between the poet and the artist also has to do with certain basic obsessions, such as the women who were the object of their passions, the mournfulness of the urban landscape, of human beings doomed to destruction, and a yearning for the unobtainable and the inaccessible. | GOZ

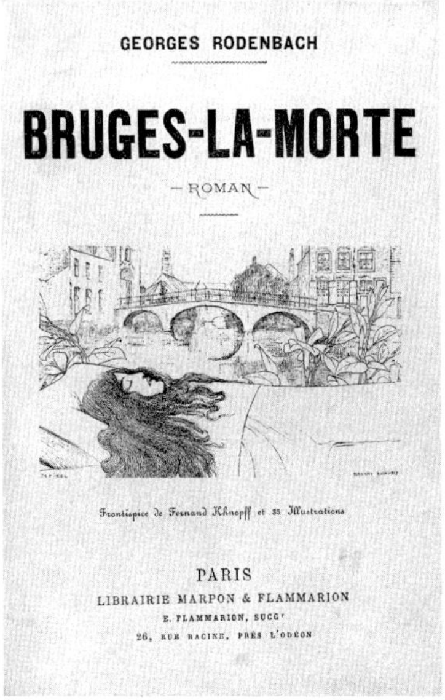
GEORGES RODENBACH

BRUGES-LA-MORTE

— ROMAN —

Frontispice de Fernand Khnopff et 35 Illustrations

PARIS
LIBRAIRIE MARPON & FLAMMARION
E. FLAMMARION, SUCC^r
26, RUE RACINE, PRÈS L'ODÉON

fig. a FERNAND KHNOPFF
Frontispiece of George Rodenbach's *Bruges-La-Morte* (Paris 1892)

PROVENANCE Horwitz, Brussels; Galerie Mietke, Vienna; Private Collection, London; The Piccadilly Gallery, London; Barry Friedman Ltd, New York.

EXHIBITIONS *Les XX* 1890, no. 7; London 1890, no. 7; Brussels 1891; Louvain 1894, no. 169; Munich 1894, no. 338; Berlin 1914, no. 2111; Marbach 1968, no. 85; Paris, Brussels, Hamburg 1979–1980, no. 32, 118 (ill.); Tokyo, Hyogo, Sapporo 1982–1983, no. 35, 65 (ill.); Chicago, New York, Wilmington 1984, no. 9, ill.; Tokyo, Himeji, Nagoya, Yamanashi 1990, no. 19, ill.

BIBLIOGRAPHY De Taeye 1894, 749; Dumont-Wilden 1907, 49, 70; Siösteen 1909, 363; Biermé 1911, 2; Delville 1925, p. 23; Guenther 1968, 214–221; Kluncker 1974, 70–71; Delevoy, De Croës, Ollinger-Zinque 1979, 246, no. 125; Howe 1980, 126, ill. 2; Benedetti 1981, 265, ill. 2; Howe 1982, 24, 30, 65, 115, pl. 1; Delevoy, De Croës, Ollinger-Zinque 1987, 246, 424 no. 125; Koyanagi 1990, 19 (pl. 11), 62; Bonneure, Van Houtryve, Puype 1992, 32–34, ill. (frontispiece).

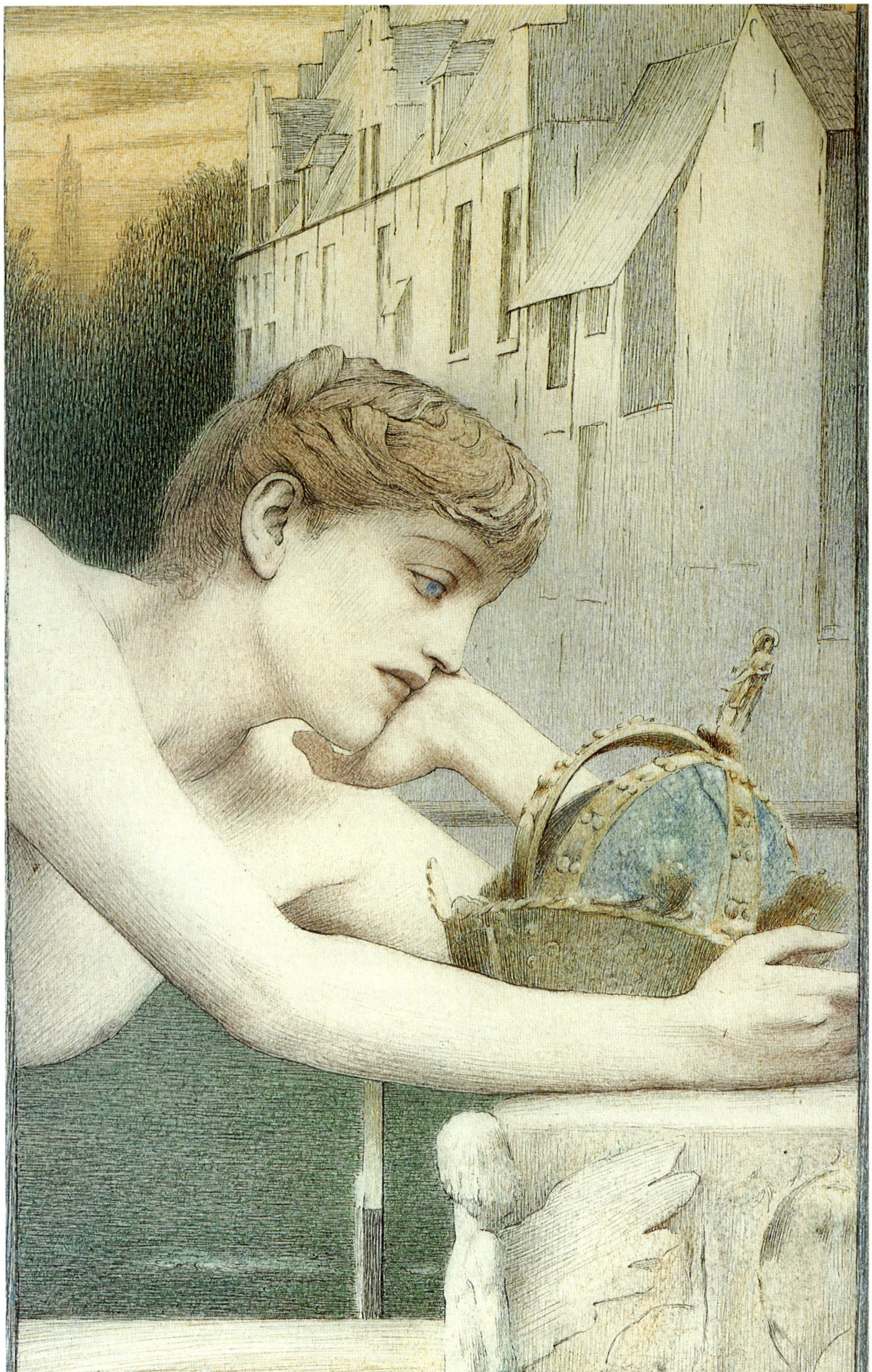

31 With Grégoire Le Roy. My Heart cries for the Past

Avec Grégoire Le Roy. Mon cœur pleure d'autrefois, 1889
Pencil, coloured pencil and white chalk on grey-blue paper, 25.5 x 14.5 cm
Monogrammed bottom right: FK (intertwined)
The Hearn Family Trust

Dedicated to Khnopff's friend, the poet Grégoire Le Roy (1862–1941), this view of Bruges, with the Begijnhof Bridge, gleaming water, and the narcissistic image of a young woman, was used as a frontispiece to *Mon cœur pleure d'autrefois,* a collection of poems by Le Roy published by the Paris editor Vanier in 1889. In this book, the poet takes as his theme – as did so many other Belgian writers, notably Georges Rodenbach [see cat. 30] – the atmosphere in those silent cities so beloved of the Symbolists, places inhabited by dreams, langour and the search for the soul. It was through Emile Verhaeren that Khnopff met and established a close rapport with Le Roy, the poet. Khnopff took great care in titling the work. In keeping with other works which derived their inspiration from literature, Khnopff tended to adopt the word 'with' ('avec') rather than appending either the literary title on its own or adopting the more reverential phrase 'to' ('à') followed by the name of the author and the literary work. Thus, work inspired by Gustave Flaubert's *Tentation de Saint Antoine* becomes 'With Flaubert. The Temptation of St Anthony'. This specific designation within a title suggests that the artist wished to imply that he was not alone on his creative journey but was travelling *with* the poet, and that they were both following the same spiritual path.

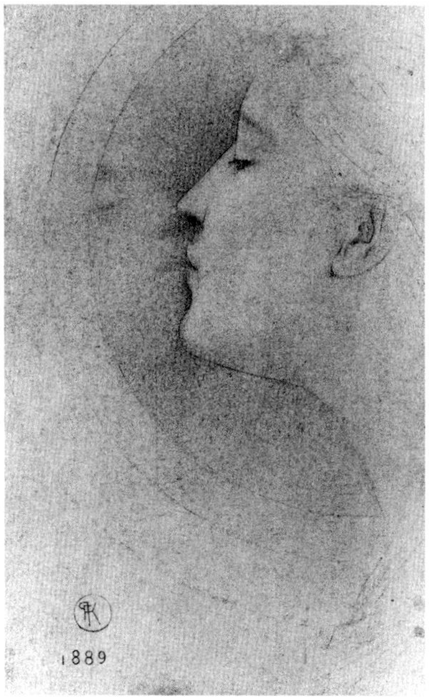

fig. a FERNAND KHNOPFF
With Grégoire Le Roy. My Heart cries for the Past, 1889, crayon on paper, Collection Marcia and Martin Werner, Philadelphia

My Heart cries for the Past was the first collection of poetry published by Grégoire Le Roy, and the only one that bears a truly Symbolist stamp. It was dedicated to Villiers de l'Isle-Adam, whom Le Roy greatly admired. The theme of reflection, the narcissistic theme *par excellence,* greatly appealed to Khnopff, and he devoted much time to it. To date, six different versions of *My Heart cries for the Past* have been identified; some of these are reproduced in the catalogue raisonné of Khnopff's work, others have only just been discovered and have not yet been published (Delevoy, De Croës, Ollinger-Zinque 1987, nos. 121 [fig. a], 126, 126a, 127, 127a [the version discussed here], 127b). They all differ slightly in tone or in the framing of the view of Bruges. In some, the view fades into the mist, leaving a greater focus on the figure of the woman, who, with eyes closed, is kissing the reflection contained in a circular mirror. Khnopff regarded the circle as a symbol of perfection. He had a golden circle painted on the floor of his studio, and he was always careful to place his easel exactly in the middle of it before beginning any kind of work. The mirror provides a reflection of self, but it is also, and most importantly, a turning-in on the self. The face here keeps its secrets to itself, holds its feelings in. The woman betrays nothing. Her look is veiled; she plumbs the depths of her soul in search of some kind of knowledge to which the mirror is perhaps privy.

Khnopff began his career as an illustrator in 1883, with *The Kiss,* executed for the book *Le Baiser* by Max Waller, published in Brussels and Paris (1883). He went on to make illustrations for numerous authors, notably Emile Verhaeren, Edmond Picard, Lucien Solvay and Joséphin (Sâr) Péladan. The latter held Khnopff in great regard, describing him as 'the subtle one, so intense'. | GOZ

PROVENANCE Sale Lokeren, Galerie De Vuyst, 22 May 1982, no. 222; Barry Friedman Ltd, New York.
EXHIBITIONS Chicago, New York, Wilmington 1984, no. 28; Brussels 1987b, no. 71; Tokyo, Himeji, Nagoya, Yamanashi 1990, no. 21; Ghent, Lawrence, Williamstown, Cleveland 1992–1993, no. 56, pl. 16 and cover.
BIBLIOGRAPHY De Taeye 1894, 749; De Mont 1901, 153–154; Dumont-Wilden 1907, 67, 70; Biermé 1911, 2; Delville 1925, 23; Legrand 1971, 12, 70; Delevoy, De Croës, Ollinger-Zinque 1987, 424 no. 127bis; Koyanagi 1990, 8, 21 (pl. 14), 63; Marechal 1992, 378–379.

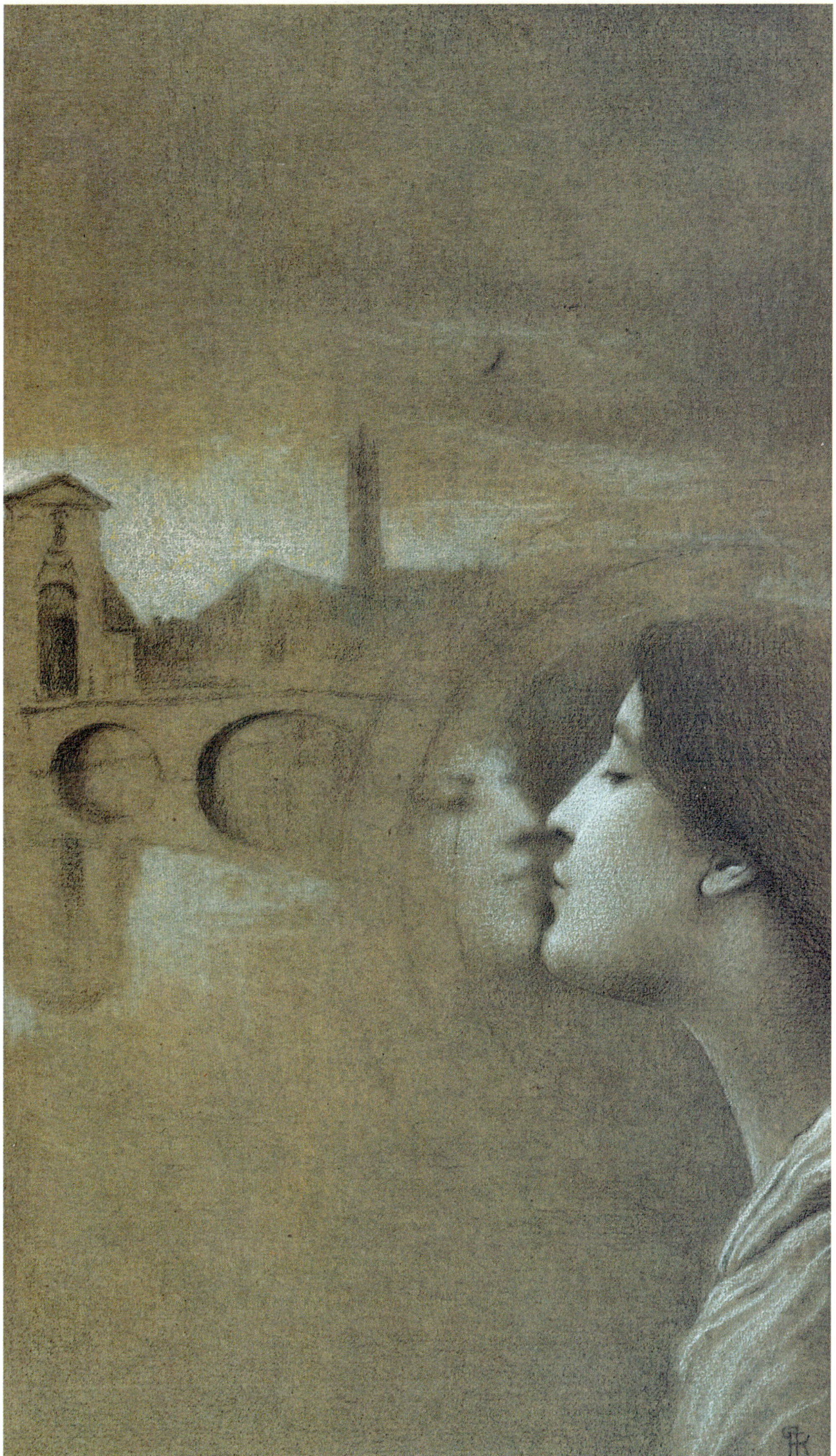

32 By the Sea

Près de la mer, 1890
Coloured pencil on paper, 17 x 44.5 cm
Signed top left: Fernand Khnopff
Private Collection

Khnopff is the painter of Woman *par excellence*, the delineator of her mystery and duality. She appears by turns as angel, muse, sister and friend, flying to the aid of man; but she is also temptress, perverse *femme fatale*, the embodiment of *Supreme Vice*, as described by Péladan and illustrated by Khnopff (1885). In the present picture, Khnopff conveys an impression of mysterious beauty, conjuring up an imaginary ideal woman. Jean Delville said of the women created by Khnopff that they were: 'imaginary examples of womanhood, simultaneously displaying traits of the Idol, the Chimera, the Sphinx, and the Saint'. Here, the face, turned slightly towards the onlooker, with a questioning expression, is impenetrable, idealized and sad. The gaze is fixed, focused on a distant point; the sibylline expression evokes that line in Baudelaire's sonnet: 'I hate the movement that moves the lines and never do I cry, never do I laugh.'[1] The woman is alone, isolated from the world, set in a mysterious and unreal landscape. She communicates with no one but herself, with her own soul, seemingly embodied in the weightless sphere that floats like a bubble near her luxuriant hair. We know that Khnopff regarded the circle as having mythical significance and as being a symbol of perfection. Here it assumes even greater importance, as a personification of thought and of the inexpressible. In a gesture replete with elegance, the young woman brushes aside her hair, as if the better to listen to, and understand, the tumult going on inside her, and to the voice of the emotions, unable to express themselves. With its blue tones, the painting seems suffused with gentleness and calm. The water – a prominent element in Khnopff's work – is visible through the openings in the building, adding a nostalgic touch; it washes away everything, it soothes like a fresh spring. Khnopff's modernity is fully apparent in this work; even the choice of format is deliberate and studied. It recurs in *I lock My Door upon Myself* (1891; Bayerische Staatsgemäldesammlungen, Munich). Khnopff assimilates tradition after his own fashion, isolates the motifs that interest him, and rearranges them like props on a stage. The woman, a young and melancholy Venus, radiates a strange and seductive magic. This highly enigmatic work exerted a lasting fascination on the Belgian Symbolist painter Jean Delville, who described the woman's face as 'hypnotizing by its distant dreaminess, more like that of a Siren-made-angel, the boundless look in her translucent eyes conveying a yearning for the music of the waves'. | GOZ

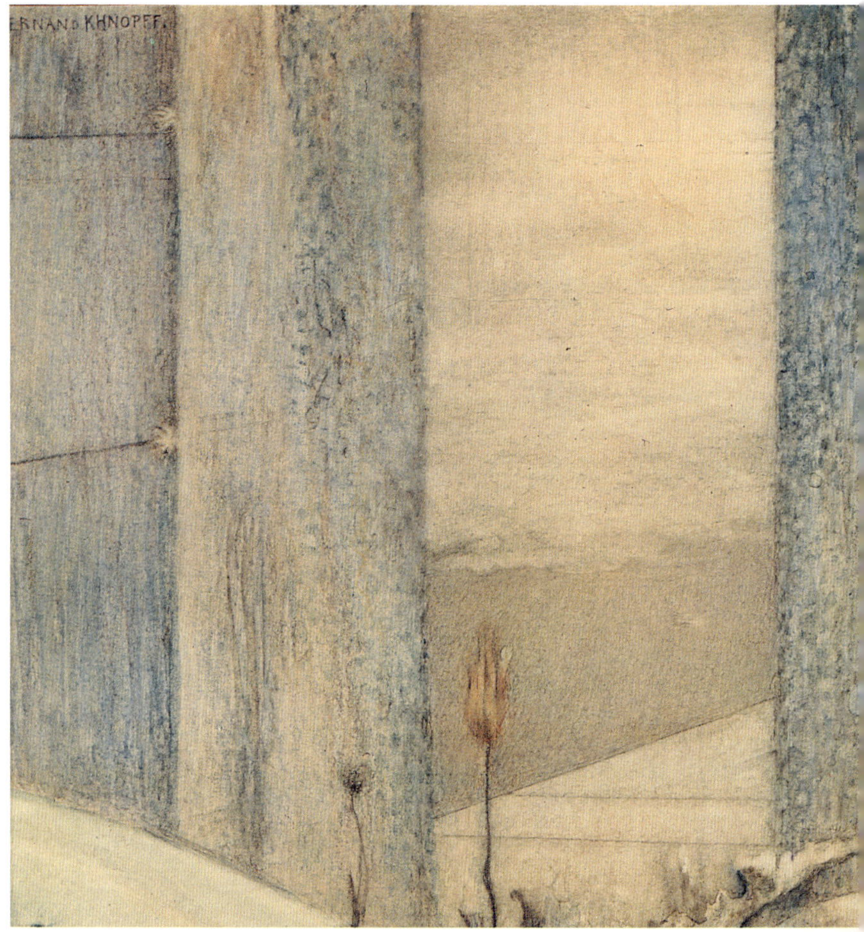

PROVENANCE Franz Philippson, Brussels.
EXHIBITIONS *Les XX* 1891, no. 6; Liège 1912, no. 36; Brussels 1971b (ex-catalogue); Paris 1972, no. 34; New York, Houston 1974, no. 14; Knokke-Heist 1974, no. 26; Paris, Brussels, Hamburg 1979–1980, no. 38; Tokyo, Hyogo, Sapporo 1982–1983, no. 37; Antwerp 1985, no. 19; Milan, Rome, Caserta, 1985–1986, no. 17; Marcq-en-Baroeul 1986, no. 67; Tokyo, Himeji, Nagoya, Yamanashi 1990, no. 27.
BIBLIOGRAPHY De Taeye 1894, 749; Dumont-Wilden 1907, 34, 70; Biermé 1911, 2; Neter 1914, 345, 347; Delville 1925, 20, 23; Legrand 1971, 70–72, pl. 28; Delevoy, De Croës, Ollinger-Zinque 1979, 254 no. 147; Roberts-Jones 1980, 52; Delevoy, De Croës, Ollinger-Zinque 1987, 254, 427 no. 147.

1 'Je hais le mouvement qui déplace les lignes et jamais je ne pleure, jamais je ne ris.'

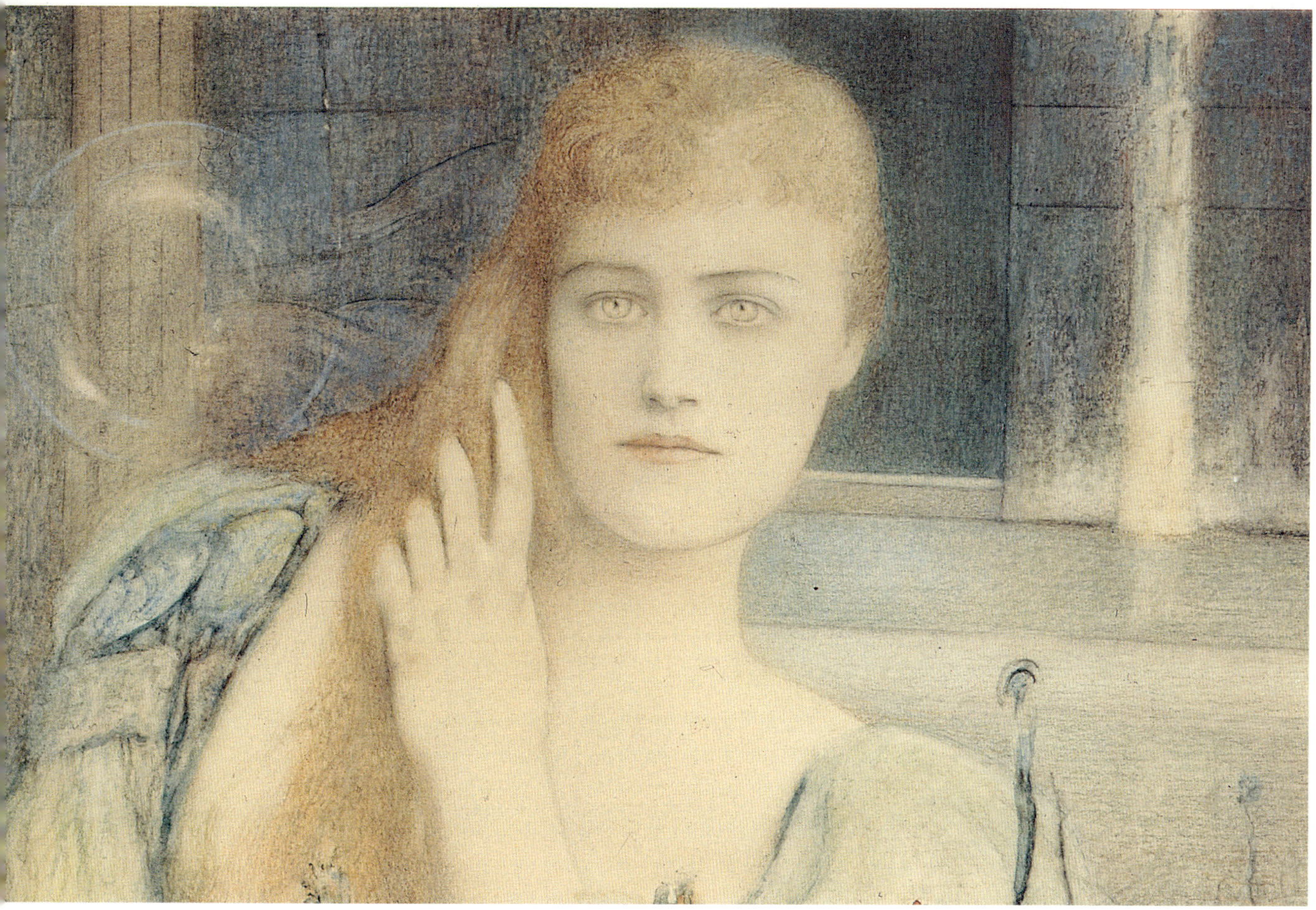

33 Stéphane Mallarmé's Poetry (Listening to Flowers)

La Poésie de Stéphane Mallarmé (En écoutant des fleurs), 1892
Pencil and pastel on paper, 21 x 10.5 cm
Monogrammed bottom right: FK (intertwined)
Private Collection

Khnopff is the painter of the invisible; for him, the image is merely the physical expression of the philosophical objective he has set himself, namely to seek out ideal beauty. Louis Dumont-Wilden (1907, 11) called him the 'painter of intellectual emotion'. His art is dreamlike but is founded on scrupulous observation of human beings and their inner lives; it tends towards the representation of ideas and the symbolic expression of purely cerebral feelings and emotions. Hence it generates elusive images of womanhood pursuing their own subconscious existence. Silence is omnipresent in Khnopff's works, as is secrecy, the keeper of knowledge and of the troubles of the heart. In life, it is not what is revealed that is important, but what is suggested. In this respect, his work had certain close affinities with that of the poet and leader of literary Symbolism in France, Stéphane Mallarmé. Already familiar with Mallarmé's poetry and his literary philosophy through his circle of Belgian Symbolist friends, notably Emile Verhaeren, Khnopff may have met Mallarmé during the latter's lecture tour of Belgium in February 1889. In 1892 Khnopff was asked to create a pictorial equivalent to the poetry of the person whom he described as 'his favourite poet'. His pastel *Stéphane Mallarmé's Poetry* is a delightfully poetic and tender work; as an illustrator, Khnopff had a wonderful gift for identifying the essence of a literary work and expressing it symbolically, while still managing to respect the writer's philosophical intent. In this picture, a woman leans over to listen to the murmuring of some flowers. Her dress is furled like a corolla, her long hair is a series of arabesques – she is a flower among flowers. The drawing, which was often referred to by alternative titles such as *Listening to Flowers* or *Tenderness*, expresses very well the close relationship that developed between the Symbolist poet and Fernand Khnopff.

As in the case of *With Grégoire Le Roy. My Heart cries for the Past* [cat. 31], Khnopff made several versions of this work (see Delevoy, De Croës, Ollinger-Zinque 1979 and 1987, nos. 205, 206, 255). One of these was used as an illustration for Mallarmé's sonnet *A la nue accablante tu*, which appeared in the April/May issue of the Berlin periodical *Pan* in 1895. The drawing in that version is more complete and the size somewhat larger. The other version was given by Khnopff to the German art critic Paul Schultze Naumburg, who published a complimentary article about Khnopff in the periodical *Die Kunst für Alle* of 1 July 1900. | GOZ

PROVENANCE Theodor Suse, Hamburg; Heinrich Stinnes, Germany; H. Bünemann, Munich; Michael Hasenclever, Munich.

EXHIBITIONS Munich 1894, no. 339; Munich 1964, no. 220; Munich 1973, no. 27; Paris, Brussels, Hamburg 1979–1980, no. 68; Chicago, New York, Wilmington 1984, no. 13; Brussels 1987b, no. 73; Tokyo, Himeji, Nagoya, Yamanashi 1990, no. 43.

BIBLIOGRAPHY De Taeye 1894, 749; Dumont-Wilden 1907, 71; Biermé 1911, 3; Delville 1925, 24; Schmutzler 1962, 71; Haas 1967, 114; Tschudi Madsen 1967, 211–212; Jullian 1969, 202; Delevoy 1977, 88; Delevoy, De Croës, Ollinger-Zinque 1979, 275 no. 206; Benedetti 1981, 266; Howe 1982, 66–69; Gibson 1984, 16; Delevoy, De Croës, Ollinger-Zinque 1987, 275, 436 no. 206; Koyanagi 1990, 30 (pl. 25), 64; Bonneure, Van Houtryve, Puype 1992, p. 50; Draguet 1992, 161–163, ill. 2.

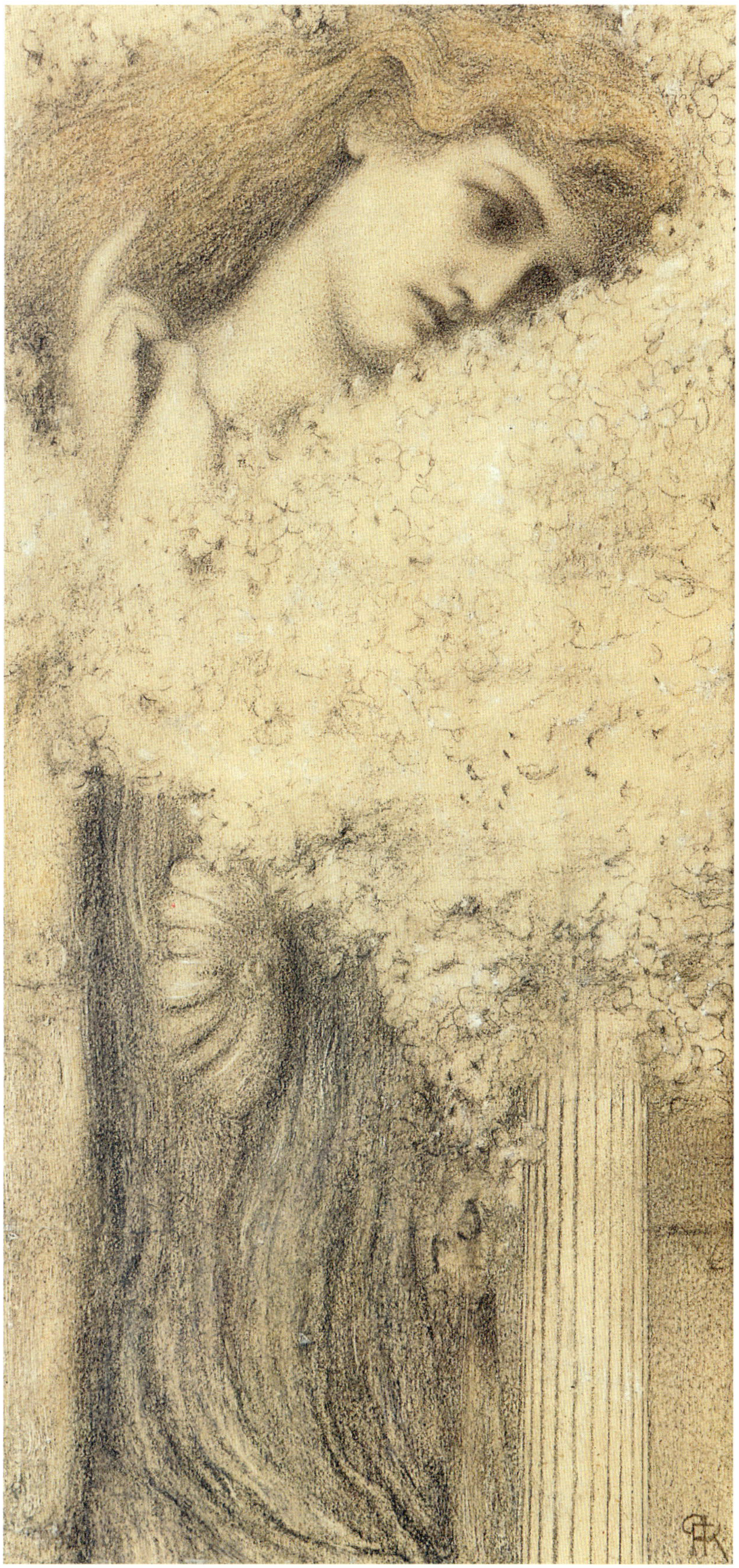

34 At Fosset. Under the Fir Trees

A Fosset. Sous les sapins, 1894
Oil on canvas, 65.5 x 44 cm
Signed bottom right: Fernand Khnopff
Galerie Patrick Derom, Brussels

This is the most interesting and most enigmatic of the landscapes painted by Khnopff. He showed relatively little interest in nature, and when he did so, his highly personal choice of composition conferred a new meaning on the finished work. His landscapes are most often views of Fosset, a village in the Ardennes where he spent the summer months on the family property.

Referring to *At Fosset. Under the Fir Trees,* Philippe Roberts-Jones rightly points out the affinities between this work and a painting by René Magritte entitled *The Leader of the Band,* completed in 1955 [fig. a]. The painting does indeed depict a very similar forest interior, haunted by the same feeling of mystery and with the same arrangement of trees, with their foliage missing and with attention focused on the trunks and roots. The latter plunge deep into the soil, as if drawing their life-force from it. In both paintings, there is a total absence of any attempt to charm, and the highly original framing retains only that part of the forest which provides a response to the artist's questioning. Khnopff was certainly not attempting to 'do a landscape'; on the contrary, he was trying to tell us something about the mystery of life. The human being has no place in the natural world which Khnopff depicts. In contrast to the practice of his day, which focused on the human presence, Khnopff's landscapes are always silent and uninhabited. Although Magritte does people his forest interior, he does so with a squirrel, not a human being. Magritte greatly admired Khnopff, and when he visited the Musée d'Art Moderne in Brussels, although he was wont to look only at a very few works, Fernand Khnopff's *Memories,* which he found fascinating and enchanting, was always one of them. It is easy to see why Symbolists and Surrealists had such an affinity: they were both painters of ideas, haunted by the great existential mysteries. | GOZ

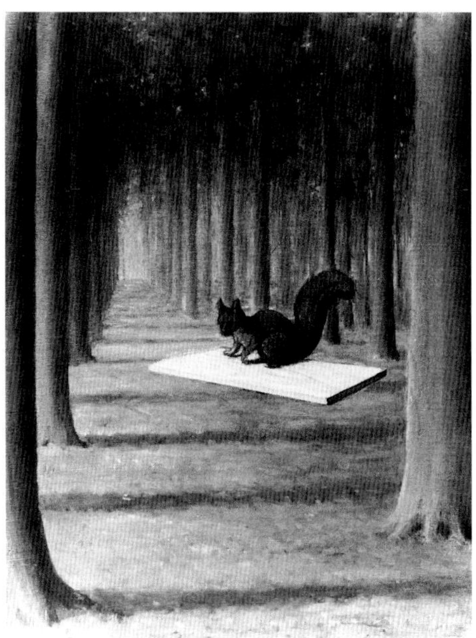

fig. a RENÉ MAGRITTE
The Leader of the Band, 1955,
Private Collection

PROVENANCE Marguerite Freson-Khnopff, Liège; Thibaut de Maisières Family, Seneffe; The Piccadilly Gallery, London; Galleria del Levante, Milan, Munich; Galerie Jan Krugier, Geneva; Galerie Isy Brachot, Brussels; Barry Friedman, New York; sale *Les Symbolistes Collection Barry Friedman,* Enghien, Hôtel des ventes, 25 October 1987 (no. 53).

EXHIBITIONS *La Libre Esthétique* 1895, no. 333; Paris 1895–1896, no. 118; London 1897, no. 252; Vienna 1898, no. 141; Venice 1899, no. 58; Budapest 1902, no. 6; Brussels 1912a, no. 177; Munich 1913, no. 1568; Brussels 1915, no. 349; London 1968, no. 52; Milan, 1970, no. 2; Florence 1973, *s.n.*; Paris, Brussels, Hamburg 1979–1980, no. 79.

BIBLIOGRAPHY Y., *L'Art moderne* (1895), 107; Hevesi 1906, 94; Boenders 1979, 94; Delevoy, De Croës, Ollinger-Zinque 1979, 286 no. 242; Adams, 1980, 94; Roberts-Jones 1980, 45; Van Kerckhoven 1980, 237; Howe 1982, 9; Delevoy, De Croës, Ollinger-Zinque 1987, 286, 440 no. 242; Koyanagi 1990, 39 (pl. 30), 65.

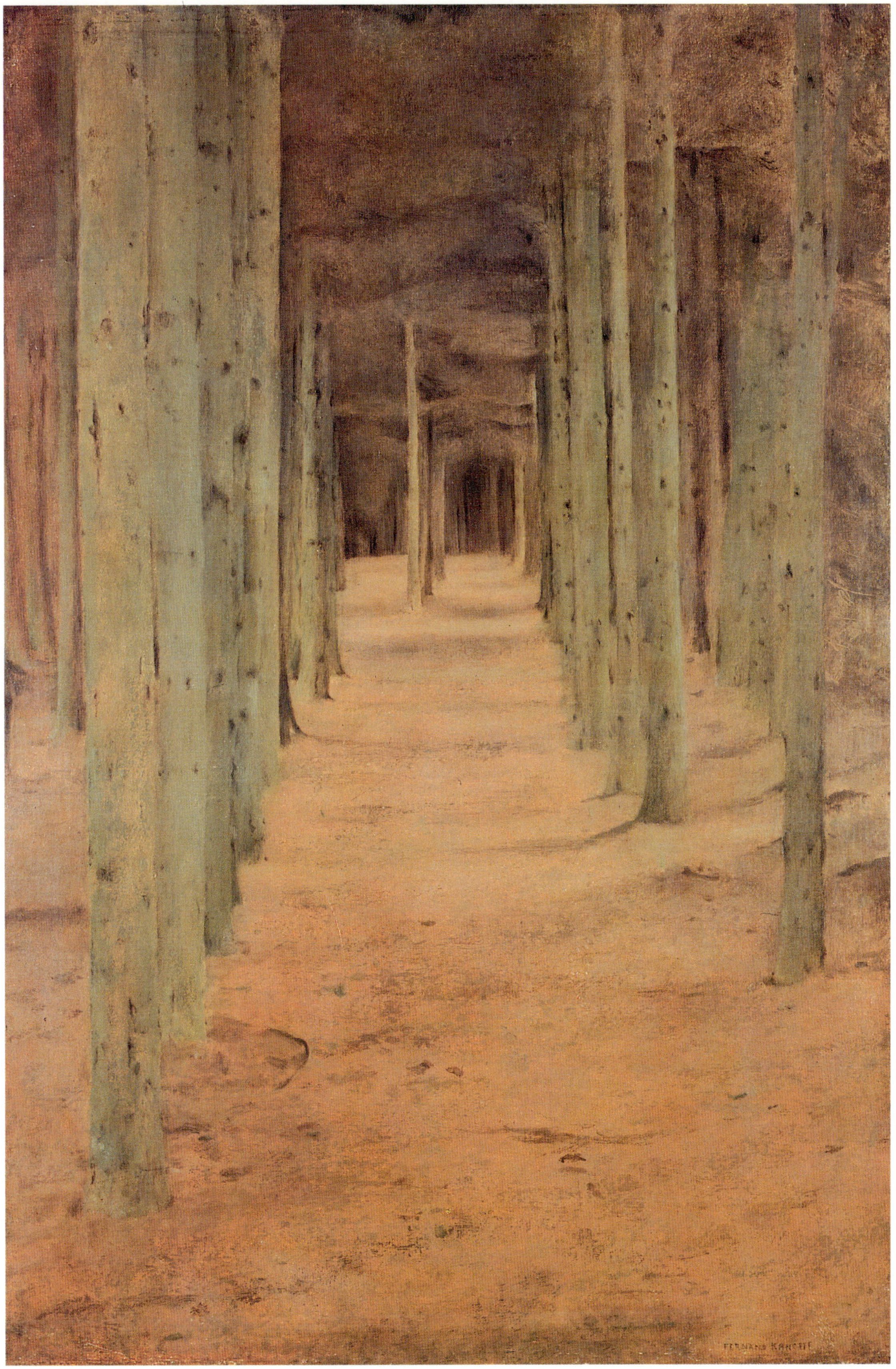

35 White, Black and Gold

Blanc, noir et or, 1901
Charcoal, pastel, watercolour, gouache, and gold dust
on paper mounted on canvas, 90 x 30 cm
Musées royaux des Beaux-Arts de Belgique / Koninklijke Musea
voor Schone Kunsten van België, Brussels, inv. no. 3707

Khnopff was profoundly affected by the philosophical works he read, and he made disenchantment and sadness the keynotes of his life and work. According to Dumont-Wilden, one of his earliest biographers, 'His goal is to raise up the ivory tower of pessimism'. Khnopff took delight in a form of hermetic symbolism which imbued his works with a deliberate isolation. In this work, a woman – half angel, half demon – embodies the feminine ideal that haunted the artist. She is a strange kind of muse, a heartbroken being. Is she perhaps the priestess of Hypnos, the god of sleep to whom Khnopff set up an altar in his own house? The theme is not a new one: in 1894 the artist had completed a work entitled *A Blue Wing* [fig. a], the proportions and subject-matter of which are almost identical to those of *White, Black and Gold*. In fact, the two works were often confused in the critical literature. And yet they differ in certain details, notably the head of Hypnos that appears in the foreground. In addition, the techniques used are different: *White, Black and Gold* is a pastel, whereas *A Blue Wing* is an oil on canvas. There are also a number of photographs highlighted with pastel and coloured pencil on the same theme as that of *A Blue Wing*. One of these is preserved in the Print Room at the Bibliothèque Royale in Brussels.

The three colours which Khnopff uses here as a title for the work were not chosen at random. In the house which he had built for himself in 1900 at 41 avenue des Courses in Brussels, white, blue and gold were the only colours he permitted inside the building, whilst the external doors, windows, and other woodwork were painted black, thus assuring the master of the impregnability of his fortress, a veritable temple to the self.

Khnopff had stated that 'Sleep is the most perfect thing in our existence.' In creating his Hypnos, he drew inspiration directly from a small bronze sculpture about 20 cm in height, attributed to Scopas and dating from the first half of the fourth century BC [fig. b]. In about 1900 he had made a bronze *Head of Hypnos* (Delevoy, De Croës, Ollinger-Zinque 1987, 327–328, fig. 363), copied from the one by Scopas and clearly marked with the artist's initials: an intertwined 'FK'. Work in this medium is unusual for this artist, and there is no mention of the sculpture in the literature of the period. He probably made the piece not as an original work but as a copy intended for his own house: a photograph of his studio shows a household altar surmounted by a head of Hypnos similar to that just described. The god of sleep's head appears for the first time in the picture entitled *I lock My Door upon Myself* (1891; Bayerische Staatsgemäldesammlungen, Munich), painted after a poem by Christina Rosetti. This work prompted Félicien Rops (q.v.) to observe that Khnopff 'had sunk himself into Burne-Jones's boots up to his neck'. | GOZ

PROVENANCE Bought from the artist in 1904.

EXHIBITIONS Brussels 1901–1902, no. 80; Copenhagen 1931, no. 131; Zurich 1952 (ex-catalogue); Brussels 1964, no. 49; Ostend 1967, no. 52; Brussels 1968, no. 26; Brussels 1970a, no. 79; Rotterdam, Brussels, Baden-Baden, Paris 1975–1976, no. 73; Paris, Brussels, Hamburg 1979–1980, no. 121; Brussels 1987b, no. 42; Tokyo, Himeji, Nagoya, Yamanashi, 1990, no. 76.

BIBLIOGRAPHY Maus 1901, 413; Louis 1901, 82–83; X., *L'Art moderne* (1902), 14; Lemonnier 1906, 168; Dumont-Wilden 1907, 51, 73; Biermé 1911, 4, 31; Fierens 1922, 97, ill.; Joly 1924, 6; Delville 1925, 26; Eemans 1950, pl. 22; Langui 1961, 128, pl. 110; Ollinger-Zinque 1969, 288, ill. 570; Houbart-Wilkin 1970, n.p.; Roberts-Jones 1978, 89–90, ill. 76; Delevoy, De Croës, Ollinger 1979, 328–329 no. 365; Goldwater, 1979, 266, note 41; Marmori 1979, 107; Adams 1980, 95; Roberts-Jones 1980, 50; Micha 1980, 40; Howe 1982, 111–115, 147, pl. 34; Delevoy, De Croës, Ollinger-Zinque 1987, 328–329, 455 no. 365; De Croës 1990, 152–153.

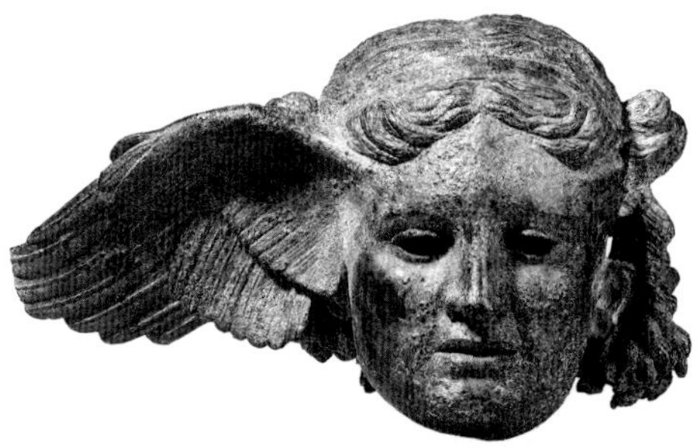

fig. b Attributed to SCOPAS
Head of Hypnos, fourth century BC
British Museum, London

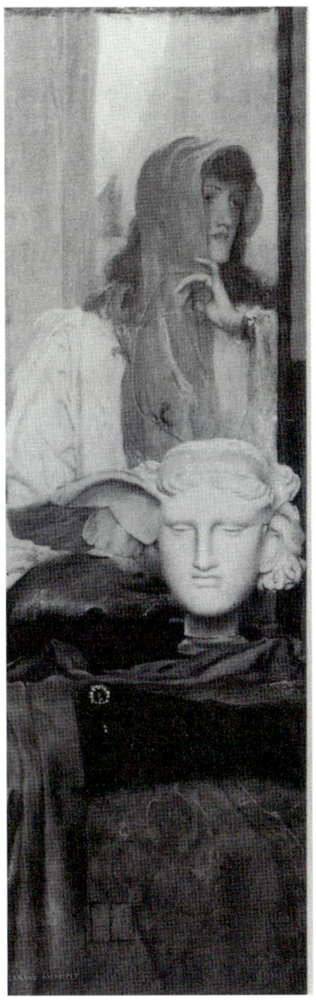

fig. a FERNAND KHNOPFF
A blue Wing, 1894, Private Collection

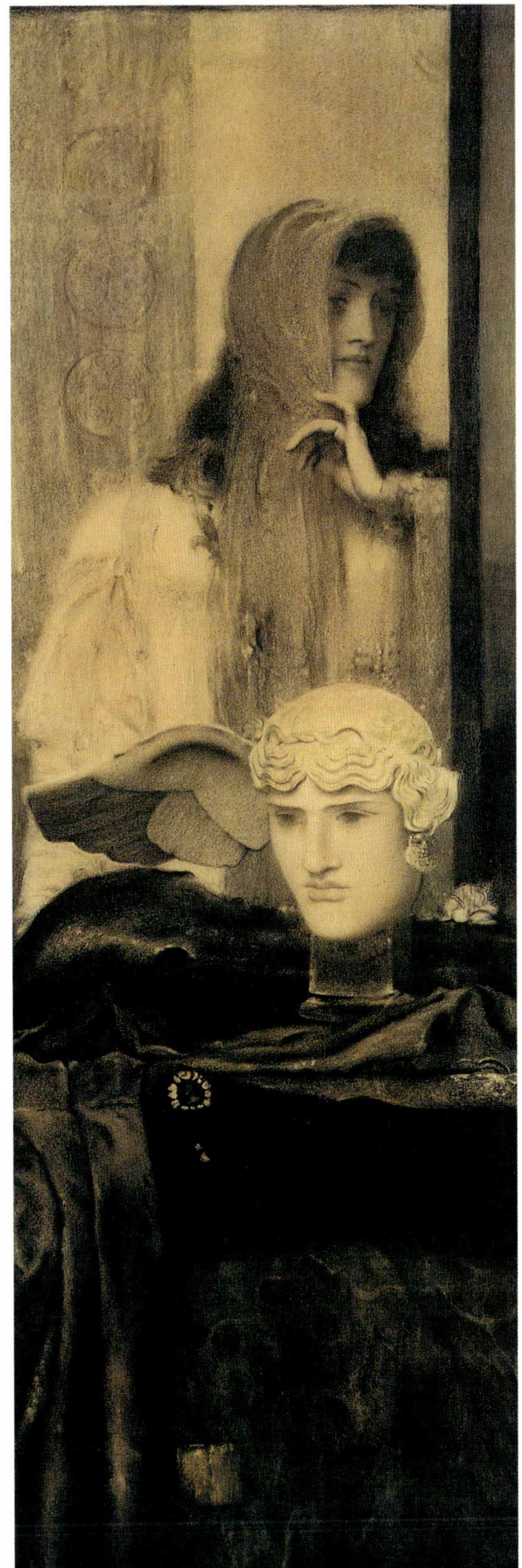

36 Bruges (The Lac d'Amour)

A Bruges (Le Lac d'Amour), 1904
Pencil and pastel on paper, 47 x 101 cm
Signed bottom right: Fernand Khnopff
The Hearn Family Trust

In 1904 Khnopff completed the most important series of drawings [see cat. 37] inspired by Bruges and by the memories, distant yet very accurate, which he had of the city in which he had spent his childhood – and to which he remained deeply attached. In the present work, he offers us a view of the Minnewater (Lac d'Amour), which once again prompts us to point to the predominance of water in Khnopff's oeuvre. A notable feature of these works is the constant duality between water and reflection, between the buildings and their reflected doubles in the canals, and, in the case of the more overtly literary inspired works, between the woman and the figure she kisses [cat. 31]. These are meditations, aspirations towards unfathomable depths, a love of self, expressed without shame. The works are also imbued with an ambiguous poetry that exalts the hidden, the secret, the profoundly silent. The views of Bruges are dreams caught in stone, and often the reflections are more substantial, more real than the originals. Many Symbolist artists were interested in the 'Venice of the North' and came to visit it, lured by its unusual atmosphere, at once mystical and decadent. Rossetti wrote a number of poems there; Ford Maddox-Brown spent some time in the city, even studying for a year at the Academy; William Morris and Holman Hunt were also visitors. Baudelaire, on the other hand, did not like the city, and talked of a ghost town, a mummified place that smelled of death and the Middle Ages. As far as he was concerned, Bruges was Venice in Black (Marechal 1992, 377). The *fin-de-siècle* enthusiasm of Georges Rodenbach, however, won over all his friends: Mallarmé came to lecture in Bruges in 1889, and the French writer Péladan expounded his esoteric theories there. In this fascinating city, each person found – as no doubt Khnopff did – what they were unconsciously seeking deep within themselves. After all, did Rodenbach not credit the city with a human personality and passions of the most intense kind?

There are two versions of this work. One is quite modest in its dimensions (28 x 62 cm; Delevoy, De Croës, Ollinger-Zinque 1987, no. 392), the other is the larger version shown here. | GOZ

PROVENANCE Sale London, Sotheby's, 17 November 1993, no. 207.
BIBLIOGRAPHY Dumont-Wilden 1907, 73; Bierme 1911, 4; Delville 1925, 26; sale cat. Sotheby's, London 1993, no. 207.

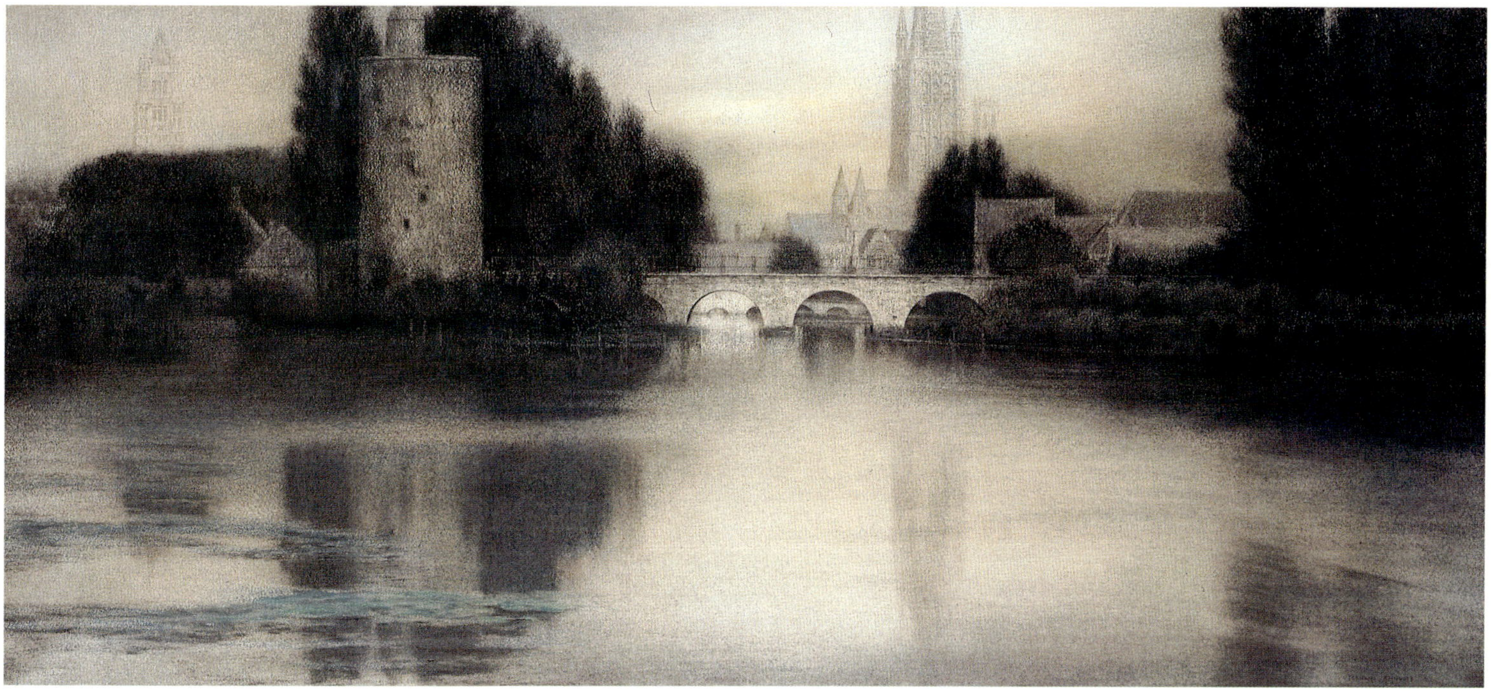

37 Memories of Flanders. A Canal

Des Souvenirs de la Flandre. Un canal, 1904
Pencil, charcoal and pastel on paper, 25 x 41.5 cm
Signed bottom left: Fernand Khnopff
The Hearn Family Trust

In the majority of the works by Khnopff which are inspired by memories of Bruges, water plays a central role as a symbol not only of this forgotten city, but also of the soul, of doubles and reflections of the self. There are two very similar versions (Delevoye, De Croës, Ollinger-Zinque 1979, nos. 399 and 399a; Tokyo, Himeji, Nagoya, Yamanashi 1990, nos. 85 and 86) of the theme of a Bruges canal. Both are of similar dimensions, show the same buildings and use the same mixed media. We know that Khnopff habitually made multiple versions of works [see cat. 31] – indeed, this is a modernist approach that is worth highlighting. But it is rare to find versions as similar to one another as is the case here.

This pastel shows a view of Bruges, where Khnopff spent the early years of his childhood, from 1859 to 1864. More specifically, it is a view of the canal that runs alongside the Groenerei, near the Basilica of the Holy Blood, with views of the backs of the Town Hall and the Law Courts. Khnopff was greatly influenced by the time he spent in the 'Venice of the North'. In 1899 he commented to Paul Schultze Naumburg that it was 'at Bruges, which at that time was truly a dead city, unfrequented by visitors, that I spent my childhood – of which I cherish distant but very precise memories' (Delevoy, De Croës, Ollinger-Zinque 1987, 26–27). In about 1904 Khnopff completed a large number of works inspired by Bruges. That he did this from memory, entirely on the basis of his recollections, reworked with the aid of the imagination, is beyond doubt, since he never wanted subsequently to see Bruges. He used to say that when he was absolutely obliged to go there, he would travel by train, take a taxi at the station, and wear dark glasses in order not to see what had become of his city. Many of the works recalling Bruges were directly inspired by half-tone engravings in Georges Rodenbach's novel *Bruges-la-Morte* (1892). The present drawing is based on the illustration on page 81, but in order to accentuate the feeling of mystery and strangeness, Khnopff has framed the view differently. He has intentionally cut off the tops of the buildings – just as he cuts off the tops of his models' heads – eliminating the sky and the roofs in order to focus on the water and on the reflections of the buildings in the canal. | GOZ

PROVENANCE Sale Antwerp, Campo, 23 October 1979, no. 121; Maurice Tzwern, Antwerp; Barry Friedman Ltd, New York.
EXHIBITIONS Brussels 1904, no. 58; Paris 1906, no. 55 or 58; Venice 1912, no. 52; New York 1980, no. 39; Tokyo, Hyogo, Sapporo 1982–1983, no. 48; Chicago, New York, Wilmington 1984, no. 25; Brussels 1987b, no. 75; Tokyo, Himeji, Nagoya, Yamanashi 1990, no. 85.
BIBLIOGRAPHY Dumont-Wilden 1907, 73; Biermé 1911, 4; Delville 1925, 26; Delevoy, De Croës, Ollinger-Zinque 1979, 339–340 no. 399; Friedman 1984, 12; Delevoy, De Croës, Ollinger-Zinque 1987, 339, 461 no. 399; Koyanagi 1990, 66; Draguet 1991, 242; Bonneure, Van Houtryve, Puype 1992, 33.

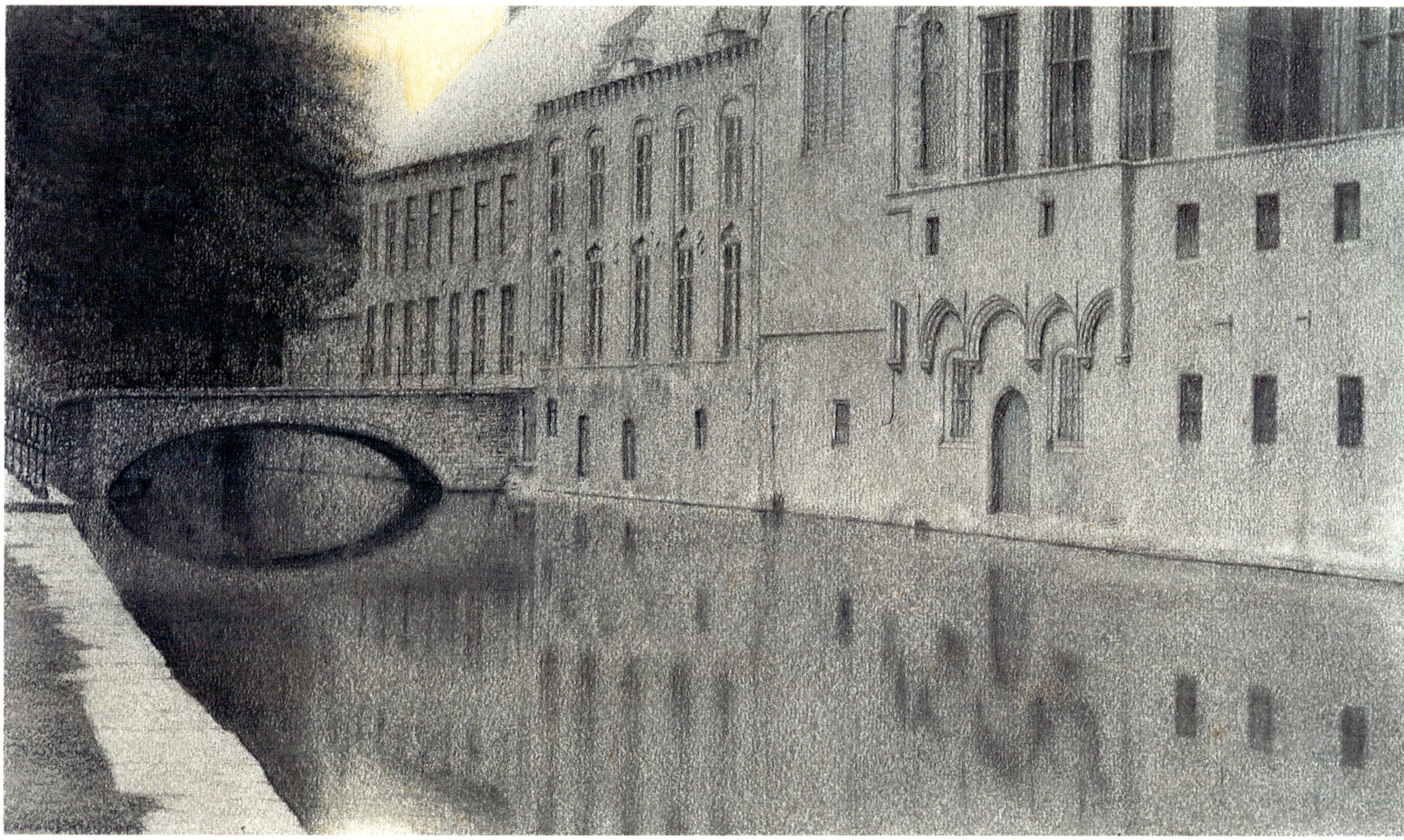

Evert Larock

KAPELLE-OP-DEN-BOS 1865–1901

Evert Larock studied at Mechelen and followed evening classes at the Academy of Fine Arts before finding work as a scene painter in Antwerp. He took a three-year evening course at the Antwerp Academy of Fine Arts, and became a full-time pupil of Charles Verlat (1824–1890), the institution's director, in 1885. His painting career was repeatedly interrupted by a lung disorder contracted during his brief military service (1883), and he was obliged to spend months at a time in a nursing home in Bokrijk, Limburg (1895). The illness eventually cost him his life at the age of 36. He worked chiefly in Brasschaat and Kalmthout (Antwerp Kempen), and finally in Kapelle-op-den-Bos. He joined the society Als Ik Kan (founded in Antwerp in 1883 as a more traditionally oriented counterpart to Les XX in Brussels) on 4 April 1890, and made his début with fourteen works at one of the group's exhibitions in 1891. The young writer and critic Emmanuel de Bom (1868–1953) immediately became his most fervent champion. The painter and critic Pol de Mont (1857–1931) also lauded Larock's talent. These two *hommes de lettres* continued to promote Larock, even after his death, at Kunst van Heden (the exhibition group backed by the Antwerp collector, François Franck), where his paintings were included in seven exhibitions. In 1891, Evert Larock joined the XIII, and participated in at least four of its exhibitions (1893, 1895–1897). An exhibition was organized shortly before the artist's death by François Franck and Larock's friend, the painter Frans Hens (q.v.). Sixty of his works were shown at De Kapel, an almshouse on the Falconrui in Antwerp which had been established as a centre of progressive ideas and art. | LDJ

SUMMARY BIBLIOGRAPHY

E. de Bom, 'XXVe tentoonstelling', *De Vlaamsche School* (1892), 1–13;
P. de Mont, 'Het Salon van 1894', *De Vlaamsche School* (1894), 132–133;
E. van Offel, 'Evert Larock', *De Vlaamsche School* (1901), 185–189;
H. van de Ven, *Evert Larock*, Zemst 1969.

38 The Village Idiot

De onnozele – L'Idiot du village, 1892
Oil on canvas, 148 x 121 cm
Signed and dated bottom left: E. Larock Junij 1892
Koninklijk Museum voor Schone Kunsten, Antwerp, inv. no. 1274

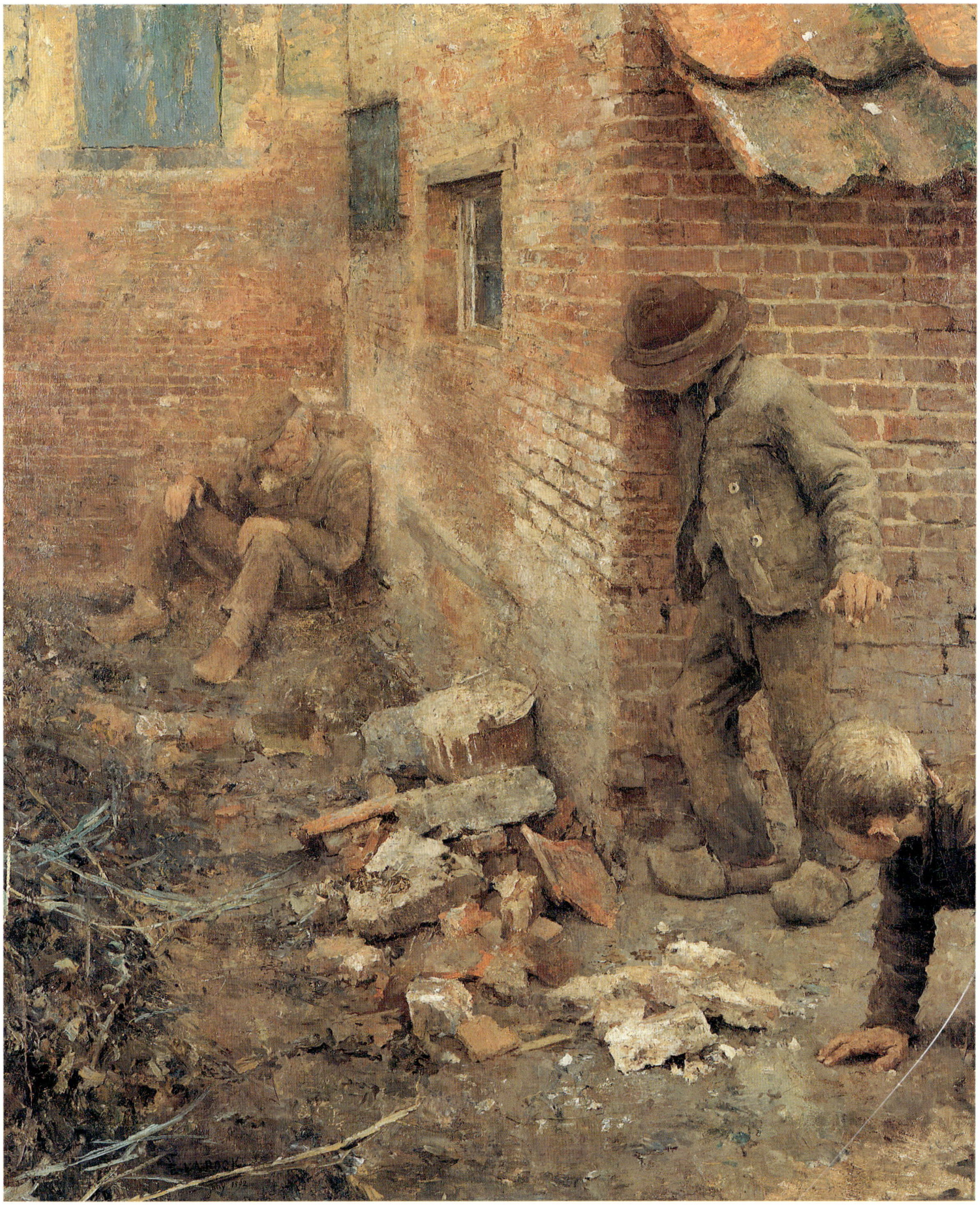

The Village Idiot was first shown at the Ghent Salon in 1892. Pol de Mont wrote in *De Vlaamsche School* (1892, 168): 'The *Idiot* by the young Antwerp artist Evert Larock is dull in colour in some places, and strident in others. Frightened as a hunted and tormented animal, the poor, threadbare idiot shelters in the grime between two lonely red brick walls. The two urchins in the foreground are spirited, but insolent and merciless'. *The Village Idiot* was a great success when exhibited at the Antwerp World Fair in 1894. Again in *De Vlaamsche School* (1894, 132–133) Pol de Mont wrote that 'Larock's *Idiot* is laden with compassion for these poor wretches, especially those living outside institutions, and the torments to which they are subjected. All the misery of their brutalized existence screams out at us from this figure. The colour is all it should be: pale, meagre, sick, painful.' The work was purchased by the Koninklijk Museum voor Schone Kunsten in Antwerp, which put the final seal on its fame: after Larock's retrospective exhibition held at De Kapel in Antwerp in 1899–1900, Edmond van Offel wrote in *De Vlaamsche School* (1901, 189): '*The Village Idiot*, Larock's masterpiece, is the work into which he poured all his individuality, soul and genius as a colourist.'

The painting owes its reputation to three principal elements: the psychological impact of the confrontation between the old man and the two children, the architectural framing of the scene and the work's intense red tonality. It is a wretched little scene that reveals Larock's empathy for the outcasts of society. The dilapidated walls, windows and roof open outwards like a stage setting. And the colours are striking because of their granularity and strident contrasts. Larock has orchestrated the narrative, the composition and the colours into a visual and emotional symphony.

The Village Idiot is a pivotal work by Larock. The artist's career was very short, stretching from 1891 until only 1901, yet a clear evolution – cautious and discontinuous – may be discerned in his style, which moves from traditional genre pieces to more lyrical exteriors, and from a grey realism to a more experimental use of colour (e.g. *The Studio* and *Morning*, Koninklijk Museum voor Schone Kunsten, Antwerp). His handling of form and space gain in structure, and anecdote gives way to the evocation of atmosphere. | LDJ

PROVENANCE Purchased by the Museum at the Antwerp World Fair in 1894 (F 2,500).

EXHIBITIONS Ghent 1892, no. 448; Antwerp 1894, no. 174; Antwerp 1975, 38–39; Antwerp 1985–1986, no. 164; Munich 1989, 228–229; Antwerp 1990, no. 25.

BIBLIOGRAPHY H. Todts, in Antwerp 1985–1986, n.p.

Georges Le Brun

VERVIERS 1873 – STUYVENKERKE 1914

Georges Le Brun was born in Verviers on 16 June 1873. After two years in Russia, from 1881 to 1883, he returned to his native town and attended the local secondary school, where he received his first lessons in drawing and watercolour. Fascinated by this latter technique, he worked independently to master it, with the aid of a theoretical treatise on the subject.

In 1893 he enrolled at the Faculty of Sciences at the Université Libre de Bruxelles. Five months later, in March 1894, he abandoned his medical studies, devoted himself to painting, and settled in the Ardennes village of Xhoffrais, where he spent long periods of time, interrupted by brief trips to Brussels and a few journeys abroad.

In 1895 he briefly attended Jean Portaels's studio in Brussels, departing after only a few days because he found the style of teaching to be too academic. He then became a member of the Patte de Dindon circle, where he drew from life and came into contact with Eugène Laermans (1864–1940), with whom he became friends. In 1897 he travelled through Holland, developing a deep admiration for the work of Rembrandt and of the *petits maîtres* of the seventeenth century, especially Pieter de Hooch. In 1900, a lengthy Italian tour took him from Milan to Naples by way of Florence, Pisa and Rome. In the course of this journey he spent time in particular in studying the masters of the Quattrocento, whose simplicity and compositional rigour greatly impressed him.

From the time of his return, a slow stylistic change is observable in his works: the initial realism loses its sharpness in favour of a poetic approach more reminiscent of Mellery (q.v.), in the case of the interiors, and of Symbolism. In 1900 he also travelled to Paris, and began to attend Blanc-Garin's free studio in Brussels. In the same year, and again in 1903, Le Brun exhibited at the Salons of La Libre Esthétique and wrote a number of articles for *L'Art moderne*. After a stay of two years at Limburg an der Lahn, he settled at Theux, where he remained until the outbreak of hostilities in 1914. He volunteered for service in the First World War and died in action on 26 October 1914 at Stuyvenkerke on the Yser front. | BF

SUMMARY BIBLIOGRAPHY

M. Pirenne, *Georges Le Brun, sa vie de peintre*, Verviers 1920; E. Desprechins, *Georges Le Brun, peintre de la Fagne*, Paris, Brussels 1925; *Georges Le Brun, 1873–1914*, Musée d'Ixelles, Ixelles [Brussels] 1976.

39 Interior. The Man who passes

L'Intérieur. L'Homme qui passe, 1900
Initialled bottom right: GLB
Charcoal on paper, 47 x 63 cm
Musées communaux, Verviers

Georges Le Brun's move, in March 1894, to Xhoffrais, a tiny Ardennes hamlet a few kilometres from La Baraque Michel, had a decisive influence on his artistic career.[1] The discovery of an unchanged rustic setting and of a style of life untainted by the superficiality of urban taste was as important to him as was the Breton village of Pont-Aven to artists who, like Paul Gauguin, Emile Bernard and Paul Sérusier, took refuge there in order to escape the artificiality of life in Paris.

In his quest for a form of primitivism, Le Brun lived amongst the local population, translating the characteristic rhythms of life in studies which sought to extract the essence of those patterns rather than recording them in a direct, anecdotal or descriptive form. This work was executed at Xhoffrais shortly after Le Brun's return from Italy (1900). The Italian sojourn of several months had presented him with a variety of striking artistic experiences which seemed to confirm his earlier aesthetic tastes rather than to undermine or transform them: 'I remain convinced that being able to draw consists not so much in not making any mistakes, but rather in revealing the individual, psychological character of people and things by a judicious accentuation of every typical irregularity. There is more art, more feeling and more poetry in a realist work done in the style of the primitives or of the minor Dutch artists than in the stuffy compositions of the so-called great masters.'[2]

The present work, which is a combination of various influences, derives its unity, and also a certain poetic aura, from the use of charcoal on stippled paper, in a manner not unlike that of Seurat's *noirs*. The use of a succession of rooms receding deep into the composition derives from the perspective technique found in the works of the Dutch artist Pieter de Hooch, to whom Le Brun often referred.[3] The attention to detail, the rigour of the composition, and the inclusion of a figure half masked by the doorway betrays an affinity with the Flemish Primitives and the Italian masters of the Quattrocento. Within this framework, the artist creates intimist scenes similar to those of Xavier Mellery [see cats. 43–45], in which ordinary, everyday objects are the only token of the human presence. Le Brun's enclosed and silent rooms, sometimes traversed by a furtive silhouette, are a translation onto paper or canvas of a feeling of confinement and a turning-in on oneself. This meditative atmosphere comes within the orbit of Symbolism, to which Le Brun intuitively adhered both in his interiors and in his views of the Ardennes. Towards the end of his life, the latter became reminiscent of the cosmic landscapes of Friedrich and Carus. | BF

PROVENANCE Bought from the artist by Emile Peltzer; donated by his widow to the Museum in 1920.

EXHIBITIONS Verviers 1904, no. 9; Verviers 1936, no. 76; Verviers 1973, no. 60; Verviers 1975, no. 11; Ixelles 1975, no. 11; Berlin 1979, no. 85; Cologne 1981, no. 4; New York 1980, no. 43; Charleroi 1980, no. 60; Tokyo 1983, no. 100; Paris 1988, no. 38; Stavelot 1990, no. 50; Brussels 1991, no. 16.

1 Pirenne 1920, 9–13.
2 Le Brun in a letter to his mother (Milan, 20 March 1900), manuscript, Private Collection, Brussels.
3 On this subject, see Le Brun's correspondence (Private Collection, Brussels).

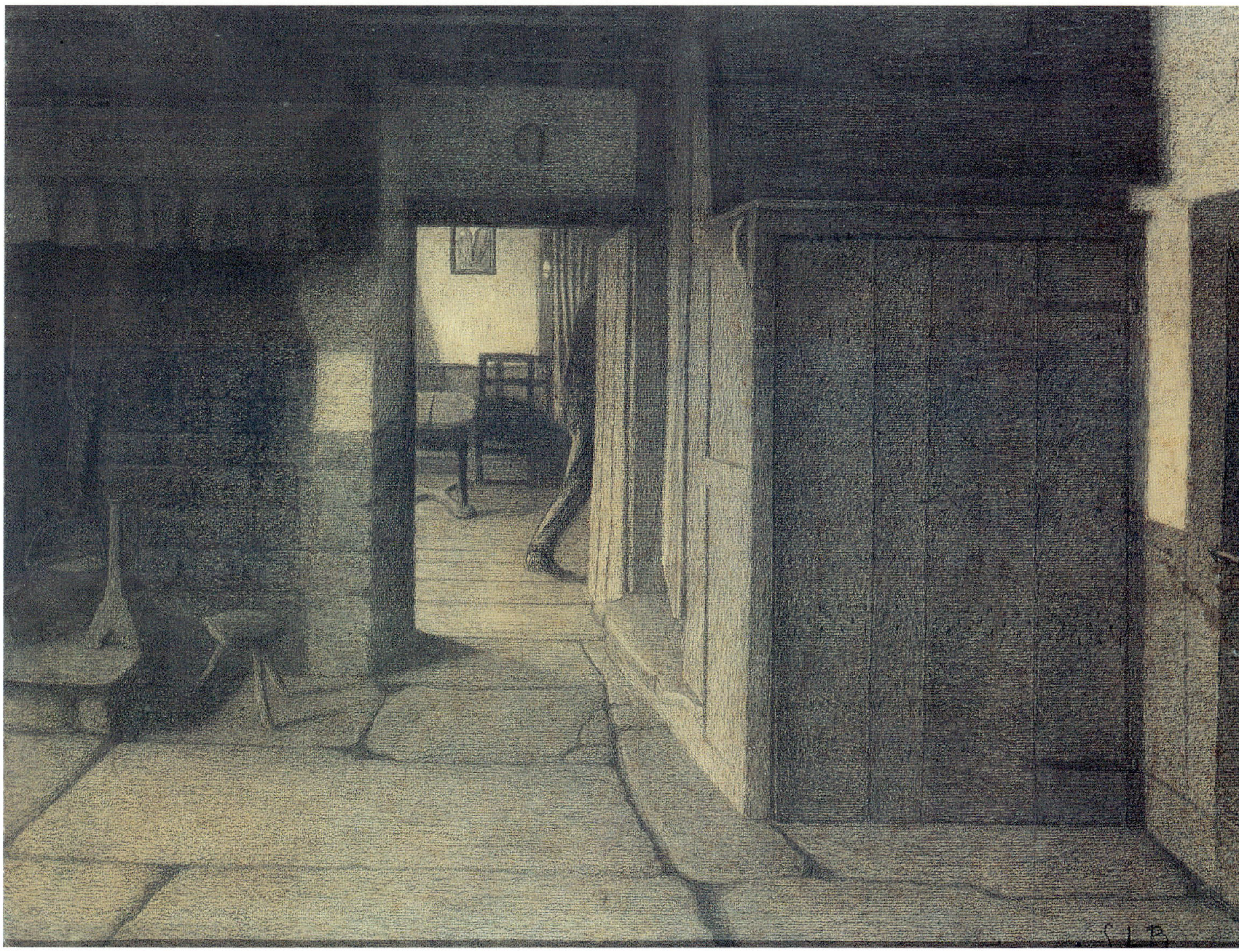

Georges Lemmen

SCHAERBEEK 1865 – UCCLE 1916

After an initial period of study at the Academy of Fine Arts in Saint-Josse-ten-Noode (Brussels), Georges Lemmen came under the influence of Fernand Khnopff (q.v.), the English Pre-Raphaelites and J.-K. Huysmans's novel *A Rebours* (1884, *Against the Grain*), an essay in literary Decadence. However, this concern with an art inspired by literature and the imagination was replaced in 1888 by confrontation with works by Degas and Henri de Toulouse-Lautrec, both of whom drew their inspiration primarily from the observation of the external world. Around the summer of 1890 Lemmen was converted to Neo-Impressionism, which he applied to landscapes (The Thames, The River Meuse) and the seaside, and to subjects drawn from modern life (fairs, the dancer Loïe Fuller), as well as to intimist scenes and portraits. The painstaking meticulousness required in the application of the pointillist technique led him to abandon it four years later.

From 1895 to 1899, in keeping with several of his contemporaries, for example Finch (q.v.) and Henry van de Velde (q.v.), Lemmen devoted himself primarily to the applied arts, notably the decoration and design of two-dimensional objects such as book-covers, billboards, posters, carpets, fabrics, wallpaper and endpapers. In this he made an important contribution to the contemporary revival of the art of the book in Belgium. His commitment to the art of the book and design led to important collaboration with Henry van de Velde.

In 1900, Lemmen returned to painting. Close to the second generation of French Symbolist painters, the Nabis (Vuillard, Bonnard, Denis) both in style and subject matter, Lemmen depicted quiet scenes of intimate domestic interiors, presented through the application of carefully balanced blocks of muted colours which build up to create a surface which is both descriptive and patterned.

Lemmen participated in the exhibitions organized by the group L'Essor from 1883, and exhibited regularly with Les XX (of which he was elected a member in 1888), La Libre Esthétique, and at the Salon des Indépendants in Paris (between 1889 and 1908). Individual exhibitions of his work were organized by Galerie Druet in Paris in 1906 and 1908, and by Galerie Giroux in Brussels in 1913. | RC

SUMMARY BIBLIOGRAPHY

O. G. Destrée, 'Die Schmuckkünstler Belgiens: Georges Lemmen', *Dekorative Kunst* 1:3 (December 1897), 105–111, ill.; O. Gerdeil, 'Georges Lemmen', *L'Art décoratif* 12 (September 1899), 229–261, ill.; [J. Meier-Graefe], 'Georges Lemmen', *Dekorative Kunst* 4:12 (September 1899), 209–241, ill.; M. Nyns, *Georges Lemmen* (Monographies de l'art belge), Antwerp 1954, ill.; J. Block, 'A Study in Belgian Neo-Impressionist Portraiture', *The Art Institute of Chicago Museum Studies* 13:1 (1987), 36–51, ill.; R. Cardon, *Georges Lemmen 1865–1916, Monographie générale suivie du Catalogue raisonné de l'œuvre gravé*, Antwerp [1990], ill.

40 View of the River Thames. The Elevator

Vue de la Tamise, 1892 or 1894
Oil on canvas, 61 x 85 cm
Museum of Art, Rhode Island School of Design, Providence, Anonymous Gift, inv. no. 57.166

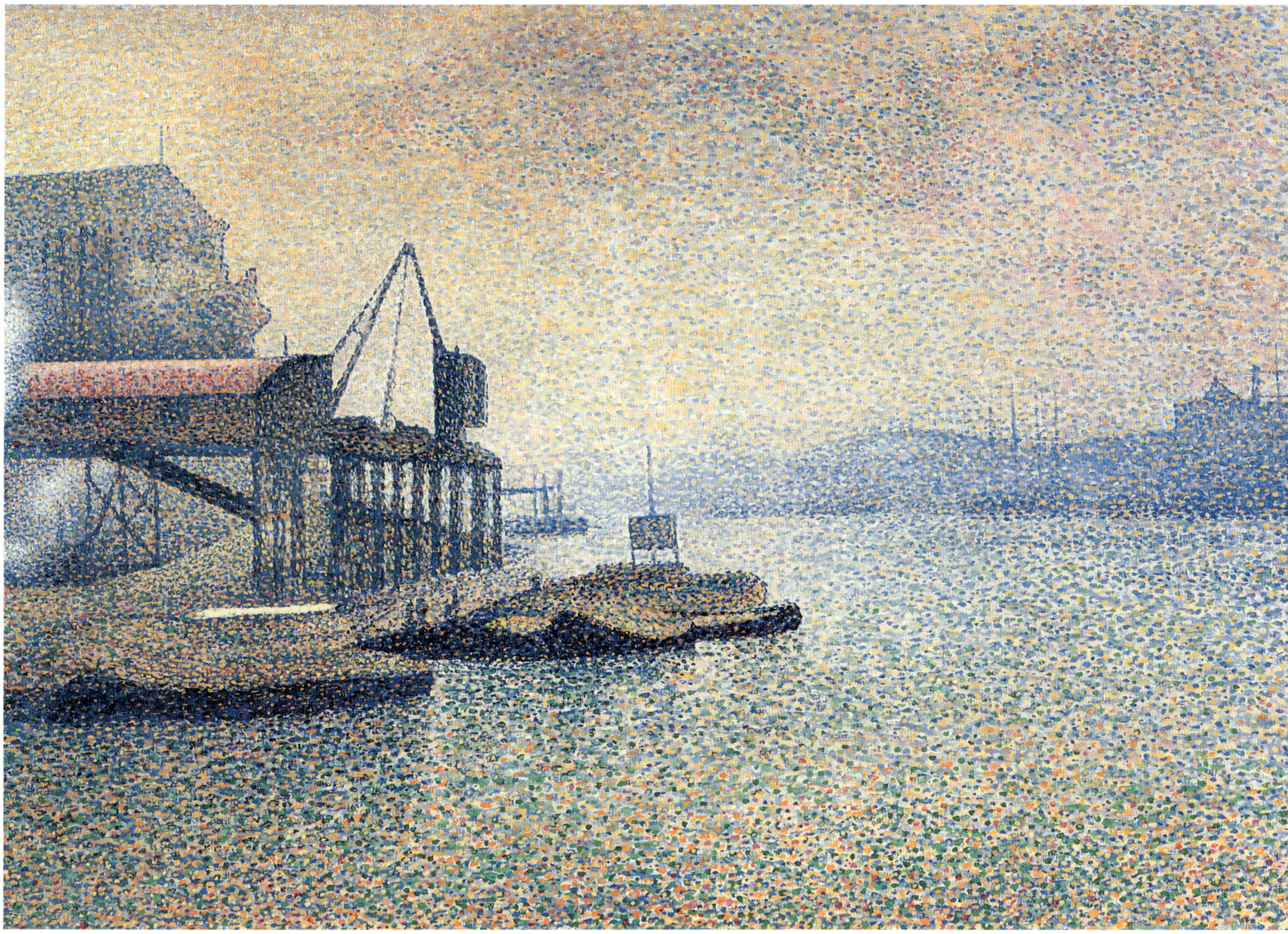

In order to give a more vivid impression of the misty atmosphere of England, Lemmen appears to have deliberately toned down the simultaneous contrasts between large areas of colour in *View of the River Thames*. However, residual, more subdued colour contrasts are retained, the green of the river and the blue of the horizon contrasting with the red and orange of the sky. The overall effect tends to emphasize the more impressionist procedures of local contrast and vibrancy. Only the industrial buildings on the left provide clear-cut oppositions and enhance the solidity of the picture. The overall atmosphere of the work is one of great tranquillity, resulting from the essentially horizontal structure of the subject. However, this serenity is tempered by the vertical lines of the crane platform, which, as well as offsetting the horizontals, introduce a feeling of mystery; the inverted V-shape of the crane also adds a note of melancholy. Finally, the position of the onlooker, deliberately set by the painter in the middle of the water, conveys a chill which is reinforced by the ambient green hue. Lemmen's choice of an industrial subject is in keeping with similar interests found in the work of his French Neo-Impressionist colleagues, notably Signac, Maximilien Luce and Seurat. It is given added significance through Lemmen's personal engagement with social movements in Belgium at that time. Indeed, he designed a poster for the 1 May celebrations in 1892 in Brussels and a membership card for the Brussels Maison du Peuple (People's Palace) in June 1897.

Lemmen visited London twice: in June–July 1892, and in July 1894. His growing interest in the decorative arts had encouraged a deep admiration for England, for the Arts and Crafts Movement and, in particular, for the artist, designer and theorist Walter Crane, about whom Lemmen had published an article in *L'Art moderne* in March 1891. Once he had embraced the decorative arts, Lemmen's graphic output in particular displayed obvious English influences, notably that of Mackmurdo.

View of the River Thames was made during one of the two trips to London. There is a preparatory oil-sketch on wood (16 x 24 cm), now in the Musée d'Orsay in Paris. There is also, in the Rijksmuseum Kröller-Müller at Otterlo, a large pointillist oil-painting on a similar theme, *Factories on the Thames*, which again was executed during one of the artist's two trips to the city. | NH

PROVENANCE Linje Collection; Galerie Georges Giroux, Brussels, 1956; T. P. Grange, London.

EXHIBITIONS Atlanta 1962, no. 56; New York 1968, no. 130, ill.; Greenwich 1977, no. 103, ill.; New York 1980, no. 49, ill.; Brussels 1990a, no. 61, ill.

BIBLIOGRAPHY David E. Stark, in Rosenfeld 1991, 176–178, ill.; Cardon 1990, 134, ill.

41 Portrait of Emile Verhaeren

July–December 1891
Oil on panel, 51 x 45.9 cm (with painted frame)
Monogrammed top left
Historical Museums, Plantin-Moretus Museum, Antwerp, inv. no. v.v.603.29

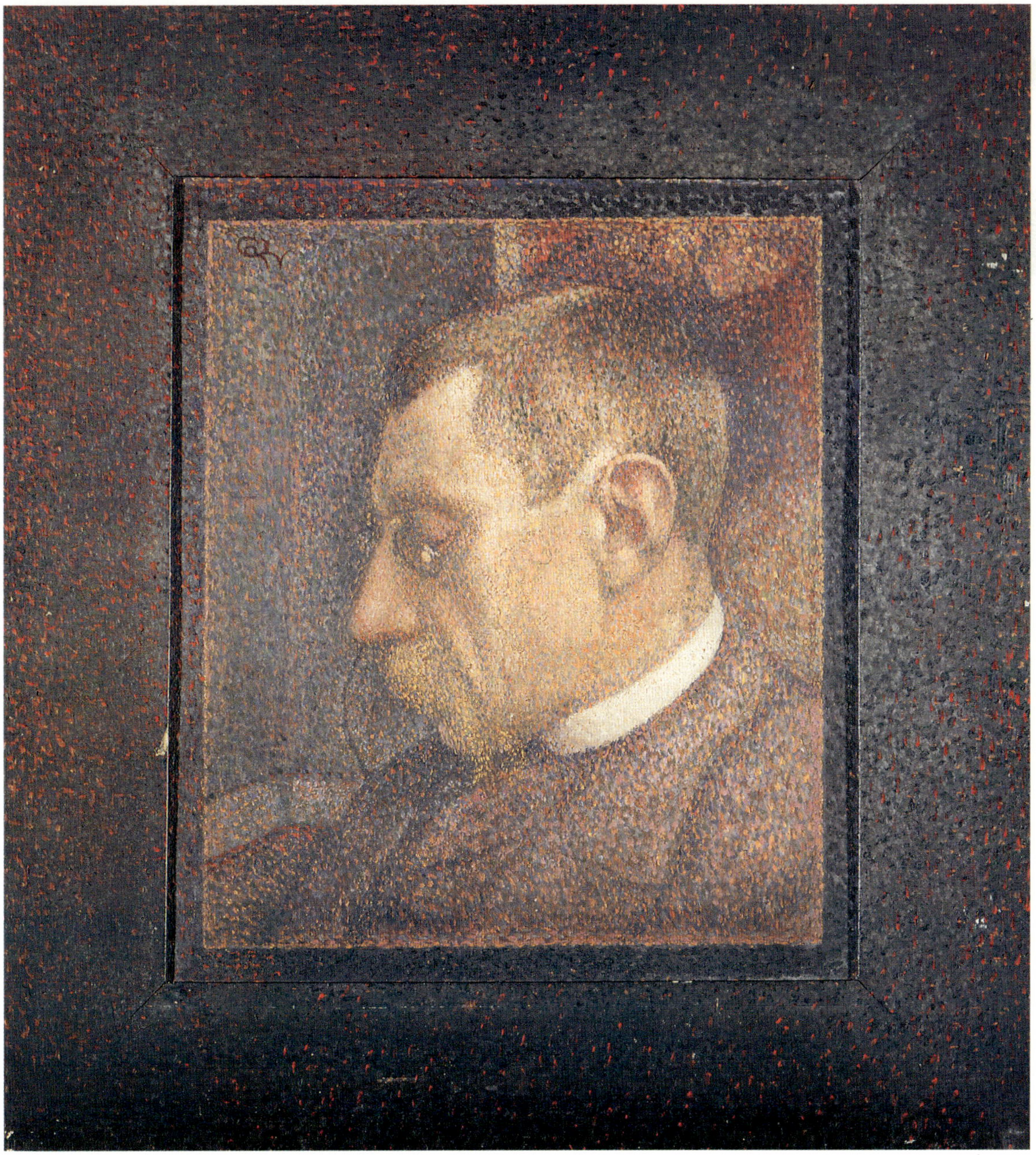

During the summer of 1890, Georges Lemmen followed the example of Willy Finch (q.v.), Théo van Rysselberghe (q.v.), Anna Boch [see cat. 71] and Henry van de Velde (q.v.), and joined the little group of Belgian *vingtistes* who had adopted Neo-Impressionism. His 'conversion' to the ideas of Seurat was based first and foremost on particularly deeply rooted affinities with the latter's sober, rational style. In addition, Lemmen's youthful interest in decadent and proto-Symbolist aesthetics made him receptive to those essential elements in Seurat's art which sought out the inherent structure within a given subject, be it a figure composition or a landscape, and gave expression to particular emotional and psychological states through the use of specific combinations of line and colour.

Of all the subjects attempted by Lemmen in this style, his portraits, together with those of Van Rysselberghe [see cats. 71, 72], constitute the most specifically Belgian contribution to Neo-Impressionism. However, while both artists demonstrate the compatibility of pointillism with the art of the portrait, those of Van Rysselberghe cast in serene harmonies of light, contrasting hues, are primarily concerned with the physical attributes of the model, whereas those of Lemmen, cast in sharper harmonies set in a more sombre gamut of tones, seek to project the inner movement of his sitters' souls. Lemmen did not produce many portraits. Lacking in specific commissions, he selected his models from among his close circle of friends, the procedure which he followed for this portrait of Emile Verhaeren.

Emile Verhaeren (1855–1916) was a Flemish-born French-speaking poet, playwright and art critic, who had initially trained as a lawyer under Edmond Picard. As a leading exponent of Belgian Symbolism, he both established links with the Parisian literary avant-garde of the 1880s, and collaborated on two of the most important innovative literary and artistic reviews in Belgium, *La Jeune Belgique* and *L'Art moderne*. He formed links with most of the *vingtistes*, whose innovative ideas and art he passionately defended in his articles. He also shared with many of them a commitment to create a socially oriented type of art.

Lemmen probably met Verhaeren in September 1890, at the house of Theo van Rysselberghe. He began work on this portrait in the following July when the poet was just emerging from a long period of depression, alleviated by his meeting with Marthe Massin, whom he was to marry on 24 August. By choosing to depict Verhaeren in virtual profile, a pose which provides a most lasting, stable angle from which to view the human face, Lemmen sought to focus attention upon the essence of his model. The slight downwards tilt of the head towards the lower left-hand corner of the canvas, accentuated by the line of the collar, would seem, according to Neo-Impressionist theory, to indicate an excess of energy being painfully contained, a degree of suffering. The blue halo surrounding the back of the head, created through the application of the theory of complementary colours in which the yellow-orange lines of the face and hair are complemented by blue, reinforces the sense of confined space within the composition. Following Seurat's example, the work is enclosed in a dark border and frame painted by the artist, which together establish systematic contrasts with the dominant colours in the adjacent areas of the painting as well as isolating the work from its immediate environment. Lemmen's insect-shaped monogram recalls Whistler's signature of a butterfly.

There is a preparatory study for this portrait executed in watercolour (22 x 18.5 cm) and dated August–December 1891 (Private Collection).

This portrait of Emile Verhaeren was exhibited for the first time at the Salon des XX in Brussels in February 1892. The exhibition also included, as a posthumous tribute to Georges Seurat who had died the previous spring, a selection of twenty-nine of his works, of which nineteen were paintings. These were lent by, among others, the French Symbolist poet and critic, Gustave Kahn, the Belgian writer and lawyer, Edmond Picard, Lemmen (three drawings), and Verhaeren, who had been on close terms with Seurat since autumn 1886 and who contributed a painting, *L'Hospice et le phare, Honfleur* (*The Hospice and the Lighthouse, Honfleur*, no. 6) and a drawing, *Café-Cabaret* (no. 24). | RC

PROVENANCE René Vandevoir Donation.

EXHIBITIONS *Les XX* 1892, no. 3; Paris 1892, no. 696; Antwerp 1892a, no. 3; The Hague 1892, no. 18; Brussels 1990a, no. 63, ill.

BIBLIOGRAPHY Cardon 1990, 91, ill.

42 The Serruys Sisters

Les Deux Sœurs ou les Sœurs Serruys, August–September 1894
Oil on canvas, 60 x 70 cm (with painted frame 68.1 x 79.8 cm)
Stencilled monogram bottom left of canvas and bottom right of frame, dated August–September 1894 on upper stretcher bar
Indianapolis Museum of Art, Indianapolis, The Holliday Collection, inv. no. 79.317

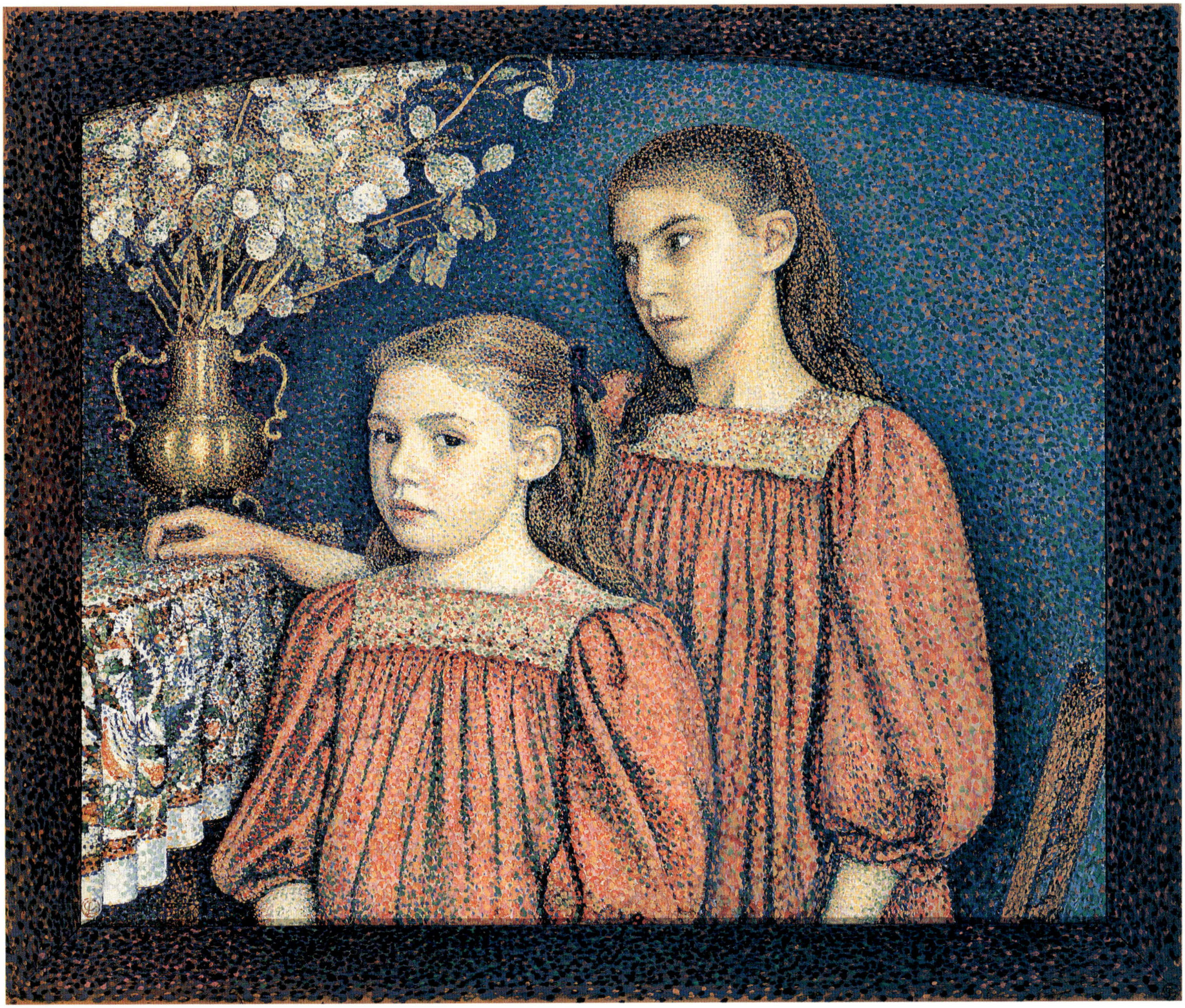

The double portrait of the *Serruys Sisters* provides a particularly rigorous example of Neo-Impressionist principles applied to figure painting. This is achieved primarily through the use of colour contrasts: the simultaneous contrasts between the coppery yellow of the vase or the orange of the chairback with the surrounding blue, and of the orange-stippled red of the clothes with the green-stippled blue of the background; the projection of the orange-red of the dress on the right into the blue ground and, conversely, the echoes of the green of the background in the dresses, thus setting up new internal oppositions; the concentration of strokes of complementary hues, producing a halo effect on either side of the lines that separate the large areas of colour, illustrating the law of successive contrasts. In addition, Neo-Impressionist principles are applied in the use of both emotionally charged colours and psychologically charged directional lines in the composition. The warm orange-red of the clothes suggests the open, youthful vitality of the two young girls, as opposed to the coldness and hostility of the surrounding world, which is denoted by the blue of the background. The lines ascending to the right of the lower edge of the tablecloth, of the curve of the bouquet and of the chairback embody the dynamism and vigour of youth, whilst the gaze of the elder of the two models, falling away as it does towards the left, already subtly expresses the confusion and doubts of adolescence. The design on the tablecloth, the symmetrically positioned handles of the vase, the choice of flowers, and the brushwork pattern on the chairback accentuate the two-dimensionality of the work and its decorative aspect; at the same time, the angle formed by the divergent cast of the eyes of the two figures restores a measure of depth, which could be interpreted as a half-open door onto the inner world of childhood.

This highly structured composition is enclosed in a frame painted by the artist. The upper, curved part counterbalances the ascendant rhythms of the picture. The work is dated August–September 1894 and was perhaps the last pointillist work to be done by Lemmen, before turning, albeit temporarily, to the applied arts. Apart from responding to the influence of, in particular, the English Arts and Crafts Movement for this change of direction in his career, he also felt inadequate in his execution of the Neo-Impressionist technique, believing that no-one other than Seurat was truly able to master it and to express his personality fully through it.

Jenny and Berthe Serruys (1886–1983; 1882–1926) were the daughters of Edmond Serruys, a progressive Catholic company manager from the Menin region and a personal friend of the socialist leader Emile Vandervelde. Berthe Serruys married Fernand Grenard, a future ambassador to France; Jenny's husband, William Aspenwall Bradley, promoted American literature in France, and French literature in America, in the interwar years. The girls' older sister, Yvonne Serruys (1873–1953), took painting lessons with Lemmen c. 1892–1894, before turning to sculpture. She later exhibited at La Libre Esthétique.

There is a Conté drawing by Lemmen which is related to this oil painting and depicts Berthe Serruys (Art Institute of Chicago). | RC

PROVENANCE Serruys family, Menin; Jenny Serruys Bradley, Paris; René de Gas and Daniel Malingue Gallery, Paris; Kaplan Gallery, London, 1966; Hammer Galleries, New York, 1967; W. J. Holliday, 1969.

EXHIBITIONS Indianapolis 1983, 44–47, ill.; Amsterdam 1988, no. 58, ill.

BIBLIOGRAPHY Block 1987, 36–51, ill.; Cardon 1990, 126, ill.

Xavier Mellery

LAEKEN 1845–1921

The son of a gardener at the Royal Palace at Laeken, Xavier Mellery initially worked with the painter-decorator Charles Albert before attending the Brussels Academy of Fine Arts from 1860 to 1867. There his teachers included Portaels (1818–1895). In 1870 he won the Prix de Rome, enabling him to visit Italy where he studied the works of the Renaissance masters as well as developing a refined sense of the potential of the medium of drawing. In 1878, Mellery was commissioned by Charles de Coster to illustrate an article on Holland, and to this end he journeyed to the island of Marken (off the Dutch coast), then a simple, traditional fishing community. His experiences there not only reinforced his tendency towards introspection but also helped define his lasting preference for a sober and quiet realism that rapidly infected the mood of his paintings and drawings. Or, as he himself put it: 'He who will manage to have us forget colour and form at the price of emotion will achieve the highest goal of all.' It was in his drawings above all that this realism attained a rare degree of poetry, revealing *l'âme des choses* (the soul of things), the invisible behind the visible in the familiar, day-to-day world of his house and garden. The elements of silence and secrecy, together with his internalized perception of the world had a crucial influence on Fernand Khnopff (q.v.). In a less introverted, more public domain, Mellery sought to create an allegorical art in which classically-inspired figures, set against flat, golden backdrops and frequently accompanied by texts, expanded universal ideas or truths. Such works, greatly informed by his visit to Italy in 1871 and a subsequent trip to Germany, Switzerland and Austria in 1887, were generally conceived on a monumental scale as programmes for major public decorative cycles. While Mellery never realized this ambition, these works were exhibited in reduced version, both at Sâr Péladan's Salon de la Rose+Croix in Paris in 1897, and in Brussels.

Mellery exhibited regularly at Les XX as an invited artist from 1885 (1888, 1890, 1892), and he subsequently contributed four times to La Libre Esthétique (1894, 1895, 1899, 1908). He was a founding member of Pour l'Art, and a member of Kunst van Heden, the Société Royale Belge des Aquarellistes and the Belgian Académie Royale. Mellery also produced book illustrations, such as those for Lemonnier's *La Belgique* (1888), and executed designs for sculpture, including the small bronze statuettes personifying various trades for the park of Le Petit Sablon in Brussels in 1882, and, a few years later, symbolic figures on the façade of the Palais des Beaux-Arts, now the Musée d'Art Ancien in Brussels. | ML

SUMMARY BIBLIOGRAPHY

A. Goffin, *Xavier Mellery*, Brussels *s.d.*; *Xavier Mellery*, sale catalogue Brussels, Galerie Royale, 1922 (Introduction by A. Goffin); J. Potvin, *Xavier Mellery*, Brussels 1925; A. Goffin, 'Xavier Mellery', *Revue d'Art* 25: 5–6 (1925), 161–183; G. Vanzype, *Notice sur Xavier Mellery*, Brussels 1929; F. Hellens, *Xavier Mellery*, Brussels 1932; *Xavier Mellery*, Palais des Beaux-Arts, Brussels 1937 (Introduction by L. and P. Haesaerts).

43 My Hallway, Light Effect

Mon vestibule, effet de lampe, c. 1889
Black chalk and ink and wash on paper, 54 x 76 cm
Signed bottom left: X. Mellery
Private Collection, Belgium

My Hallway is one of the best-known and finest examples of that more intimate aspect of Mellery's oeuvre, in which he sought to express the 'âme des choses'. Better represented by his drawings than his paintings, the most successful of these works tended to be concentrated in the earlier part of his career. This work is no exception. It was exhibited in 1889 with *The Stairway* [cat. 44] and a third drawing, now lost. The subject is the hall of Mellery's parents' home (subsequently demolished in 1898), which was depicted by Mellery on several occasions from a number of different viewpoints. These include the painting, *L'Antichambre avec masque (Anteroom with Mask*, Musées royaux des Beaux-Arts de Belgique, Brussels), and an almost identical, painted version of this drawing, though somewhat reduced, which formed part of a triptych that has since been broken up (Collection L. Dohmen, Antwerp). The large sculpture, *La Poverella*, by his friend Paul de Vigne (1843–1901) [fig. a], appears in several works, including a drawing in Antwerp (Koninklijk Museum voor Schone Kunsten), in which it is shown at the bottom of a staircase in the artists' second home.

My Hallway is more accessible than some of Mellery's other works, and seems less laden with *Weltschmerz:* it does not share the weariness with life that sets the tone in *After Evening Prayers* [cat. 45]. The drawing, no matter how hallucinatory, might appear at first sight to be a mere study of the effects of light. Whereas the light source in many of his works cannot be identified, in this case it clearly emanates from behind *La Poverella*, whose location seems to have been deliberately chosen to provide the focus for the most intense area of tonal contrast. The result is direct, emphatic, spectacular and theatrical. It is as if Mellery were being more concrete, almost illustrative (in contrast with his later work) in the interpretation of what really interests him: the world as seen through the eyes of a child, at a time of day when everything inanimate reveals its hidden, inner life. *L'Art moderne* wrote in 1889 (p. 203): '[These drawings] only show empty interiors, yet they are haunted by something that lives.' In 1895, when the drawing was shown again at La Libre Esthétique, the same periodical reported (p. 89): 'The soul of things? There it is flowing from the walls, at once pensive and familiar. For a moment this is a hallway filled with plaster casts and illuminated by a lamp. But the light is *waiting*. Something is watching. There is a mysterious voice in these shadows and highlights.' The everyday surroundings of the familiar corridor are thus transformed into a place between concrete reality and dream – a zone of transition to a reality that resides behind the visible, behind the appearance of things. And in the process they reveal the mystery of the world. It is no mere chance that the light shines from behind *La Poverella's* head: her eyes are closed, motionless and cut off from the visible. Her gaze is instead directed inwards, towards dreams and secrets. | ML

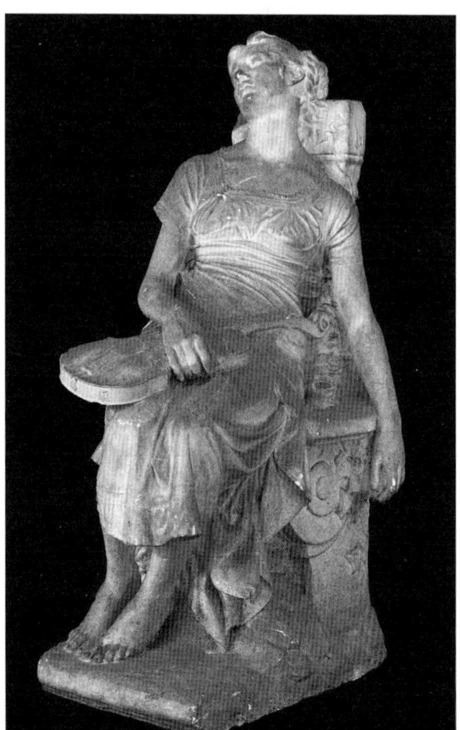

fig. a PAUL DE VIGNE
La Poverella, marble,
Musées royaux des Beaux-Arts de Belgique, Brussels

PROVENANCE E. Burthoul; sale Brussels, Galerie Giroux, 1923, no. 75 (as 'Studio of the Sculptor'); Meert, Sint-Niklaas; H. Vanderhaegen, Ghent.

EXHIBITIONS Brussels 1889, no. 89; Namur 1889, 22; *Les XX* 1890, no. 2; *La Libre Esthétique* 1895, no. 394; Brussels 1937, no. 137; Ghent 1979, no. 31 (as 'Corridor to the Studio'); New York 1980, no. 54 (as 'Entrance to the Studio'); Antwerp 1985, no. 7 (as 'Corridor to the Studio'); Frankfurt 1988, no. 131 (idem); Brussels 1991, no. 13 (idem).

BIBLIOGRAPHY *L'Art moderne* (1889), 139; *L'Art moderne* (1895), 89; S. Houbart-Wilkin, in Legrand 1979, n.p.; S. Houbart-Wilkin, in New York 1980, 122; M. Lambrechts, in Brussels 1991, 38.

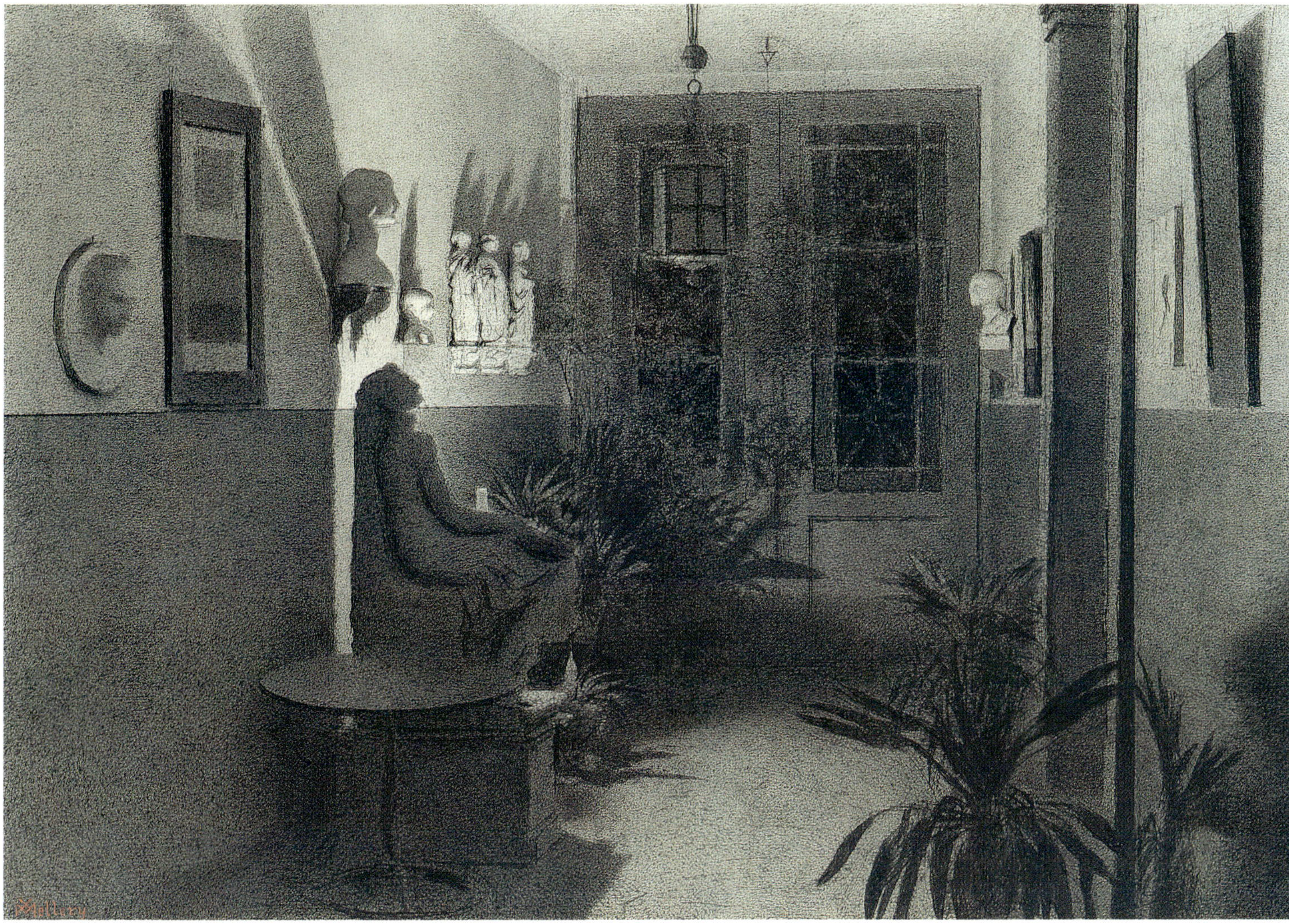

44 The Stairway

L'Escalier au pot blanc, c. 1889
Chalk on paper, 57 x 45 cm
Signed top left: X. Mellery
Koninklijk Museum voor Schone Kunsten, Antwerp, inv. no. 2095

The Stairway, like *My Hallway, Light Effect* [cat. 43] and five other drawings, belongs to a series which Mellery exhibited at Les XX in 1890 under the collective title *La Vie des choses (The Inner Life of Things)*. The two works had already been shown as part of a group of three with the same title at the Salon of the Société Royale Belge des Aquarellistes in 1889, and so must date from that year or a little before. Both are large in size and minutely worked out, both in terms of composition and observed detail. Nevertheless, they already convey the same concern with the immaterial that was to mark Mellery's later, mostly smaller drawings, in which the visible becomes dissolved through the application of a considerably looser graphic technique. In *The Stairway* the reflections and shadows created in thin and transparently applied chalk render the tangible surfaces translucent. When the drawing was exhibited again, this time as part of a group which included *My Hallway* [cat. 43] at La Libre Esthétique in 1895, the group bore the corporate title of *Emotions d'Art. L'Ame des choses*. Symbolist literature and criticism makes frequent reference to 'the soul of things'. Hector Chainaye, for instance, published an anthology of the same name in 1890, and Jules Destrée used the expression in connection with an exhibition at Les Aquarellistes (*La Jeune Belgique* 1889, 211). Virtually all the drawings had been sold by the end of the 1895 exhibition. *The Stairway* was bought by the sculptor Charles van der Stappen (1843–1910).

A shiny, bulbous pot and a woman emerge (in that order) from the complex and rectilinear structure of a stairway. Like the figure in Le Brun's *Interior, The Man who Passes* [cat. 39], the woman is on the point of disappearing out of the composition: the human element makes way for the world of things. Mellery used the motif of a staircase on several occasions in his oeuvre, including *After Evening Prayers* [cat. 45]. Stairs must have given him a heightened sense of the mystery of space. The gloomy depths and striking shadows in particular create a strong sense of menace. Together with the calm rhythm generated by the surface pattern, this transforms concrete space into Mellery's inner landscape, an image of his soul: 'For the mystery and foreboding of the shadows, the meditation turned in upon itself and the silence are the very forms your thought takes on' (Lemonnier to Mellery, January 1899).

Works like *The Stairway* recall the somewhat later, equally geometrical, quasi-abstract interiors of the Danish painter, Hammershøi (1864–1916). These, too, are replete with silence, and use strange effects of light, or include a solitary, introspective figure often seen from behind. Hammershøi's melancholy is, however, more humane than the apparent desolation of Mellery's interior spaces. It also lacks the other-worldliness that emanates from the familiar, intimate setting of some of Mellery's best works. | ML

PROVENANCE Ch. van der Stappen, Brussels; Galerie Le Roy, Brussels 1911, no. 52; Ch. Franck, Antwerp, who donated it to the Museum in 1927.

EXHIBITIONS Brussels 1889, no. 89; Namur 1889, 22; *Les XX* 1890, 11 (no. 3); *La Libre Esthétique* 1895, no. 394; Antwerp 1922a, no. 115; Paris 1923, no. 67; Brussels 1937, no. 97; New York 1980, no. 55; Frankfurt 1988, no. 126; Antwerp 1991, no. 131.

BIBLIOGRAPHY *L'Art moderne* (1889), 139; S. Houbart-Wilkin, in New York 1980, 123.

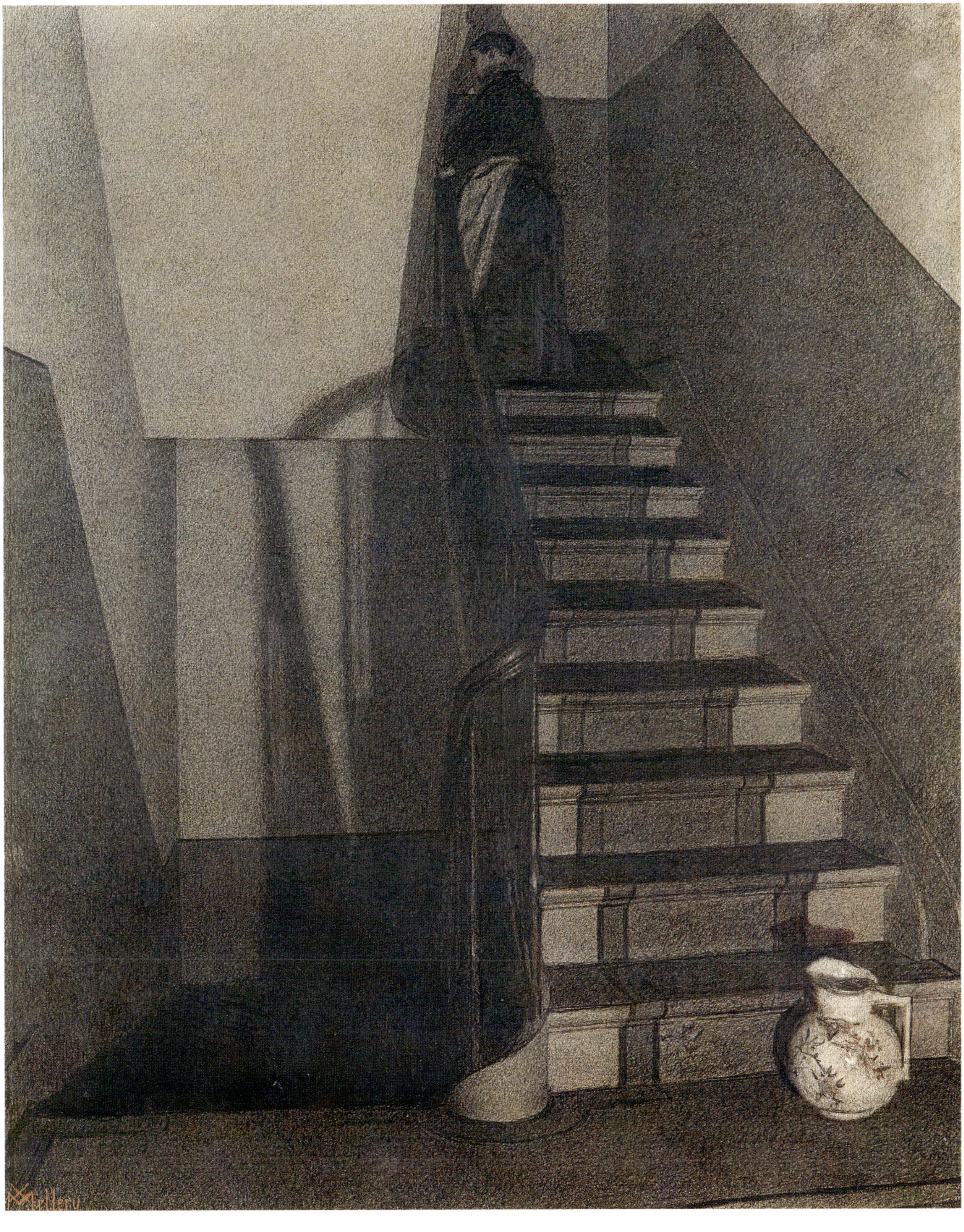

45 After Evening Prayers

Après la prière du soir, c. 1910?
Chalk with ink and wash on paper mounted on canvas, 100 x 70 cm
Signed bottom right: X. Mellery
Musée d'Ixelles, Brussels, inv. no. 326

This drawing is first recorded at the 1912 exhibition of the Société Royale Belge des Aquarellistes, when it was sold to the Musée d'Ixelles, Brussels. It is customarily dated to around 1890 or 1900. This earlier date, however, cannot be tenable since the existence of a photograph proves that the staircase depicted in the drawing was no other than that in the house in Laeken which Mellery had built in 1898. In addition, the artist's habit of repeating earlier themes in his later career, including his Marken motifs accumulated during his visit to the island in 1879, makes much of Mellery's work difficult to date. However, titles with religious connotations tend to appear mostly in exhibition catalogues dating from after 1910. A drawing at the Museum voor Schone Kunsten in Ghent represents the same landing with similar shadow effects, but without the figures, while another one depicts an empty stairwell (Collection J. Schroeder, Brussels); still other drawings are separate studies of the figures.[1]

The scene is bathed in twilight, its source seemingly emanating simultaneously from an unseen skylight above and from a dully glowing lamp. These in turn illuminate the high veils of the nuns, which thus become supplementary sources of illumination within the space. As in the other drawings by Mellery [cats. 43–44], this manipulation of light sources, with its concomitant patterns of chiaroscuro, create a strong spatial effect, in which light falling upon the treads of the stairs and the bannister emphasises the twisting movement of the diagonal of the staircase, while the darkened balusters and their shadows establish a rhythmic sense of movement upward and through the space which is punctuated at regular intervals by the sudden flash of light reflected from the nuns' veils. The nuns – a favourite theme of Mellery's, and one that was also used by Minne (q.v.) – evoke the idea of a mystical existence oriented towards the inner world, a denial of the self and the contemplation of the supernatural: these nuns appear to have no solid corporeal form; even their faces cannot be seen. This reclusive negation of femininity is a recurrent feature in Mellery's work, although a certain sensuality is retained in the more substantial female figures of his decorative allegorical works.

Intimate scenes of the kind conveyed in *After Evening Prayers* appear to be the pictorial counterpart of the themes and moods in the work of the Belgian Symbolist writer Georges Rodenbach [see cat. 30], the author of *Le Règne du silence* (1891) and *Le Musée des béguines* (1894). It is tempting, therefore, to find parallels between the writer's aesthetics and the slow cadence and the repetition of the figures which mark this drawing. A more immediate comparison, however, can be made with a painting of women on a staircase, namely the *Golden Stairs* by Burne-Jones (1872–1880; Tate Gallery, London), for which just one woman was the model. Unlike Mellery's subjects, the identical women in Burne-Jones's work represent the different stages of a single movement. The canvas deals with the rhythmic progress of time. Mellery's work also has movement, but the restrained number of figures and the measured distance between them make them appear weary to the point of being deprived of all sense of movement. As a result, *After Evening Prayers* simultaneously has motion and is motionless, has rhythm and is silent. If there is a sense of time in addition to that of space in *After Evening Prayers*, then it is the absence of time, the frozen moment of a memory. This suggests an even more pertinent comparison: with Khnopff's *Memories* (1889; Musées royaux des Beaux-Arts de Belgique, Brussels), exhibited at the Salon des XX in 1890 (no. 5). This work also features the multiple representations of the same woman holding a tennis racket, who turns in different poses within a timeless setting. In Khnopff's work, however, the repetition of the figure reveals and hence confirms the individuality of the model, whereas in Mellery's drawing such a repetition effaces all sense of individual identity. These shrouded, faceless figures are interchangeable apparitions which merge into the shadows and are only included as components of a particular, strongly felt mood. | ML

PROVENANCE Bought from the artist by the Museum in 1912.
EXHIBITIONS Brussels 1912a, no. 107; Antwerp 1922, no. 10 (as 'Beguinage. Return from the Divine Service'); Brussels 1930, no. 277 (as 'After the Divine Service'); Brussels 1937, no. 98; New York, Houston 1974, no. 39; Knokke 1974, no. 23; Brussels 1978, no. 13; London 1979–1980, no. 405; New York 1980, no. 57; Tokyo *et al.* 1981, no. 58; Antwerp 1985, no. 9; Tokyo, Hyogo, Hokkaido 1992–1993, no. 13.
BIBLIOGRAPHY M.A. Stevens, in London 1979–1980, 268; S. Houbart-Wilkin, in New York 1980, 125.

1 See Ghent 1985, no. 90; Frankfurt 1988, no. 136; Hellens 1932, fig. 25; Brussels 1937, no. 125.

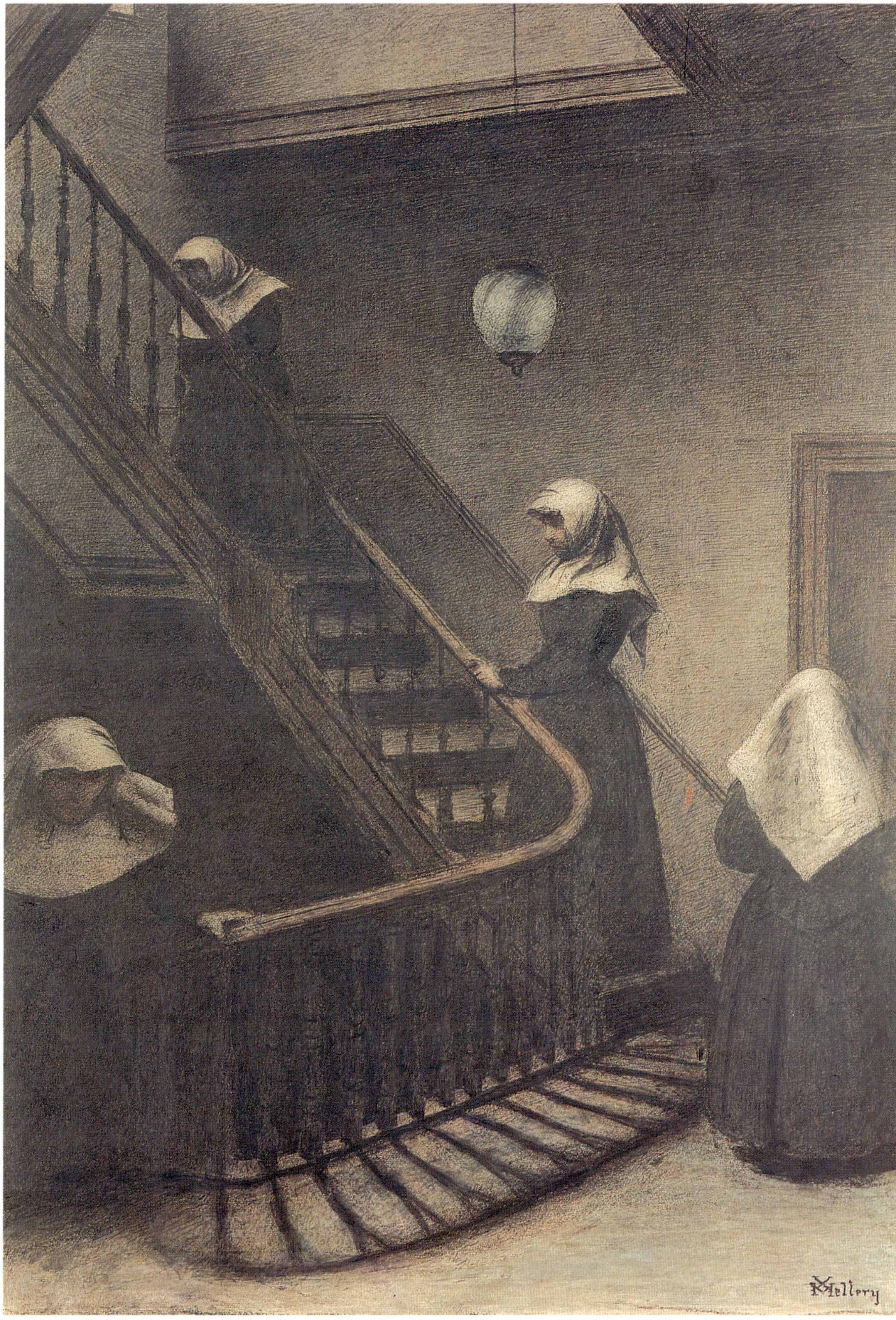
Mellery

Charles Mertens

ANTWERP 1865 – CALVERLEY (YORK) 1919

Charles Mertens, a goldsmith's son, was a student at the Antwerp Academy of Fine Arts from 1876 to 1885. From 1881 onwards, he studied under the genre, history and portrait painter Charles Verlat (1824–1890). He first exhibited at the triennial Ghent Salon in 1883. On 23 November that same year, Mertens became a member of Als Ik Kan, a group of moderately progressive artists in Antwerp, to whose exhibitions he was a regular contributor. He was given a teaching post at the Antwerp Academy in 1885, at the age of only twenty.

Charles Mertens was no revolutionary. He co-founded the somewhat traditionalist society of the XIII in 1891 and even joined the distinctly conservative group Eenigen. The Zaal Verlat in Antwerp organized an exhibition of Mertens's work in 1897, which included thirty-two paintings and eight drawings. Like many other Belgian, German and Dutch painters, he worked in Zealand (Axel) around 1898 (see Verstraete, q.v.). In 1902 he visited Italy, and Spain in 1907. Having made the acquaintance of the lawyer, and patron of the arts, François Franck, he was invited to exhibit at De Kapel (an almshouse on the Falconrui in Antwerp), where the focus was on the art, literature and music of young artists. This led to his co-founding Kunst van Heden in 1905, where again Franck was the driving force. He exhibited at six of the group's shows during his lifetime. After his death in 1919, Kunst van Heden organized a retrospective show, and his paintings were regularly exhibited by the group until 1935. Mertens also gained considerable official acclaim; he was made a member of the Academisch Corps in Antwerp in 1911, and the Koninklijke Vlaamse Opera commissioned him to decorate its ceiling. The theme of this work, installed in 1910, was rhythm as the foundation of cosmic and human harmony.[1]

Charles Mertens was also a member of the Société Royale Belge des Aquarellistes and Pour l'Art. Like many other painters, including Albert Baertsoen (q.v.), Gustave van de Woestyne (1881–1947) and Constant Permeke (1886–1952), he fled to England on the outbreak of the Great War, and settled in Calverley near York, where he died. He was buried in Antwerp. | LDJ

SUMMARY BIBLIOGRAPHY

P. de Mont, 'Karel Mertens', *De Vlaamsche School* (1897), 137–144; P. de Mont, *Vlaamsche meesters der 19de eeuw*, Antwerp, Ghent 1902; P. de Mont, *Schilders van hier en nu*, Antwerp 1929; W. Koninckx, 'Trois peintres anversois, Ch. Verlat, P. Verhaert, Charles Mertens', in *Conférences 1943–44*, Musées royaux des Beaux-Arts de Belgique, Brussels 1944.

1 After Alfred Hegenscheidt, 'Belijdenis', in *Van Nu en Straks*, 1892–1894.

46 The Trio

Trio, 1891
Oil on canvas, 72 x 91 cm
Signed and dated bottom right: Charles Mertens An. 91
Koninklijk Museum voor Schone Kunsten, Antwerp, inv. no. 2657

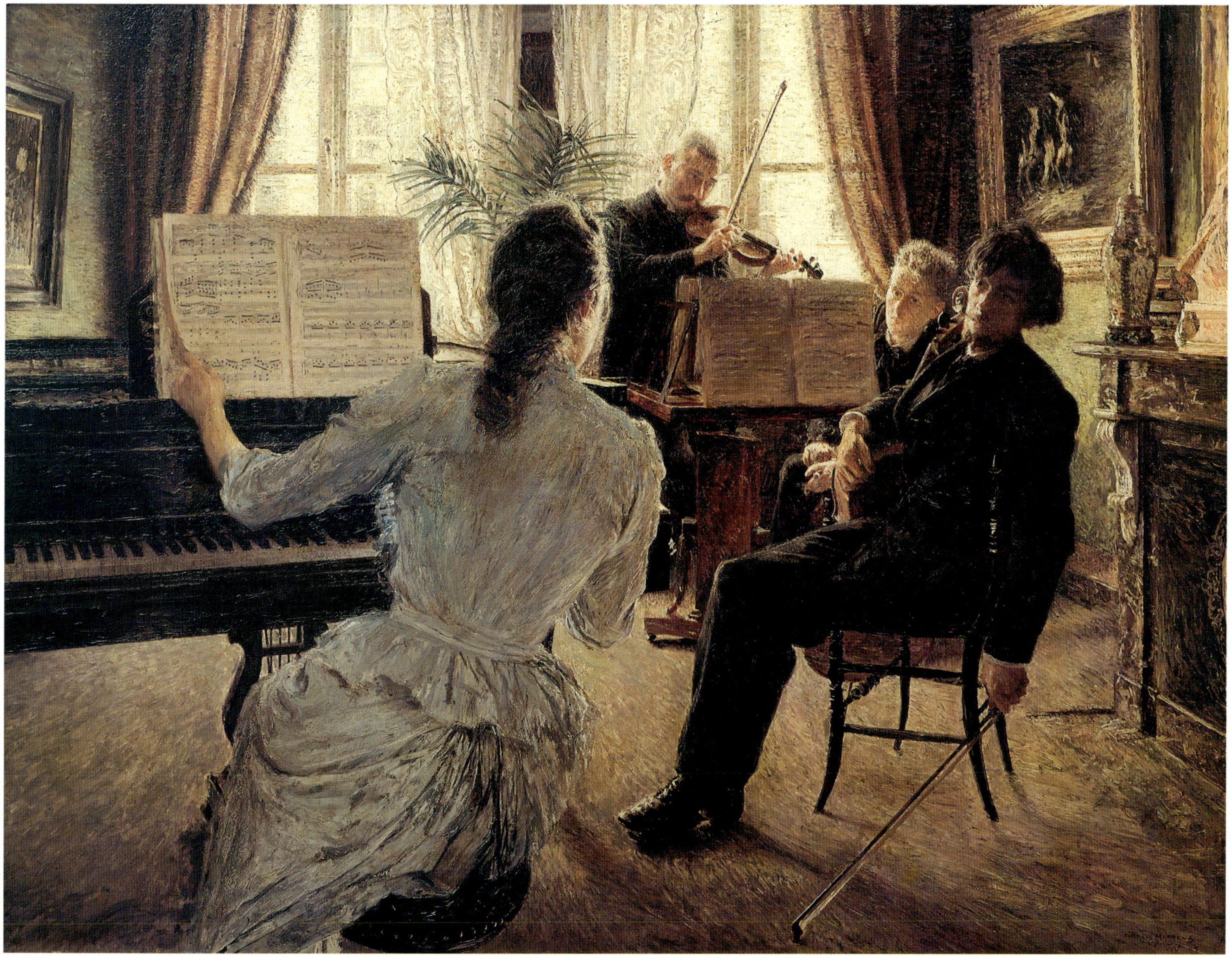

This painting is known by several titles, *The Quartet, Quatuor, Trio* and the *First Reading,* but judging from the score on the piano, it must be a trio. Set firmly in *contre-jour,* the musicians pause during rehearsal for a discussion: the string players listen to the pianist, who is seen from the rear. The woman at the piano is painted in a variety of white tints, contrasting with the three men who are dressed in black and lit from behind. Half of the canvas is taken up by the woman in the foreground, and the other half by the men in the background. The oblique angle of the figures, the intimacy of the space and the delicacy of the lighting are all evidence of Charles Mertens's sharp observation.

The painting marks the end of a stage in Mertens's career in which he had concentrated on genre paintings of craftsmen and workshops in the style of Henri de Braekeleer (q.v.). Max Rooses wrote in *De Vlaamsche School* in 1889 (p. 187): 'Mertens continues to paint quiet, motionless, yet striking interiors in his fine, quiet tones.' Elsewhere in the same publication, it was noted that: 'Mertens remains a fine, discerning colourist, who is as still and wise as a seventy-year-old gentleman fond of neat, doll-like things.'[1]

Mertens's paintings open up after 1890, taking on a more modern flavour achieved through the impressionistic handling of light, conveyed through short dabs of colour and the naturalistic settings of the genre scene. While the figure set against the light is a current motif in Belgian art at this time, for example Van de Velde's *Woman at a Window* (1889; Koninklijk Museum voor Schone Kunsten, Antwerp), Van Strydonck's *Crackers* (Hôtel Charlier, Brussels) [see also cat. 76] and *Portrait of Friends* [cat. 77], the setting and subject matter of *The Trio* demand that it be compared directly with James Ensor's *Russian Music* of 1881 [cat. 12], and Fernand Khnopff's *Listening to Schumann* of 1883 [cat. 28]. All these works celebrate the performance of music, a reminder of that art's central role within the Belgian avant-garde of the day. However, whereas both Ensor and Khnopff present the art of music making to a listener already described within the painting, Mertens involves the spectator as the passive auditor of the musical event.

Mertens's new subject matter and technique turned the highly conservative Antwerp public against him, yet he continued to be ignored by the Brussels avant-garde. This was despite the rather grudging approval expressed by *L'Art moderne* in 1888, which described the Antwerp Salon in the following terms: 'The only Antwerp exhibitors to win us over were Messrs Mertens and Desmeth. Our praises would surely have been hedged about with many reservations, were it not for the desperately mediocre company in which they appeared, and which helped them stand out all the more.'[2] | LDJ

PROVENANCE Family of the artist until 1948; bought from Miss Juliette Mertens by the Museum in 1948 (F 50,000).
EXHIBITIONS Antwerp 1891, no. 411; Antwerp 1892b; Antwerp 1975, 44; Antwerp 1985–1986, no. 138.
BIBLIOGRAPHY J. F. Buyck, in Antwerp 1975, 17–18; Antwerp 1985–1986, n.p.

1 'Tentoonstelling Als Ik Kan', *De Vlaamsche School* (1889), 99, 187.
2 'Au Salon d'Anvers', *L'Art moderne* (1888), 282.

47 Fisherman in the Moonlight

Pêcheur au clair de lune – Visser in de maneschijn, 1897?
Oil on canvas, 115 x 150 cm
Signed and dated bottom left: Charles Mertens 1897 (date poorly legible)
Koninklijk Museum voor Schone Kunsten, Antwerp, inv. no. 2109

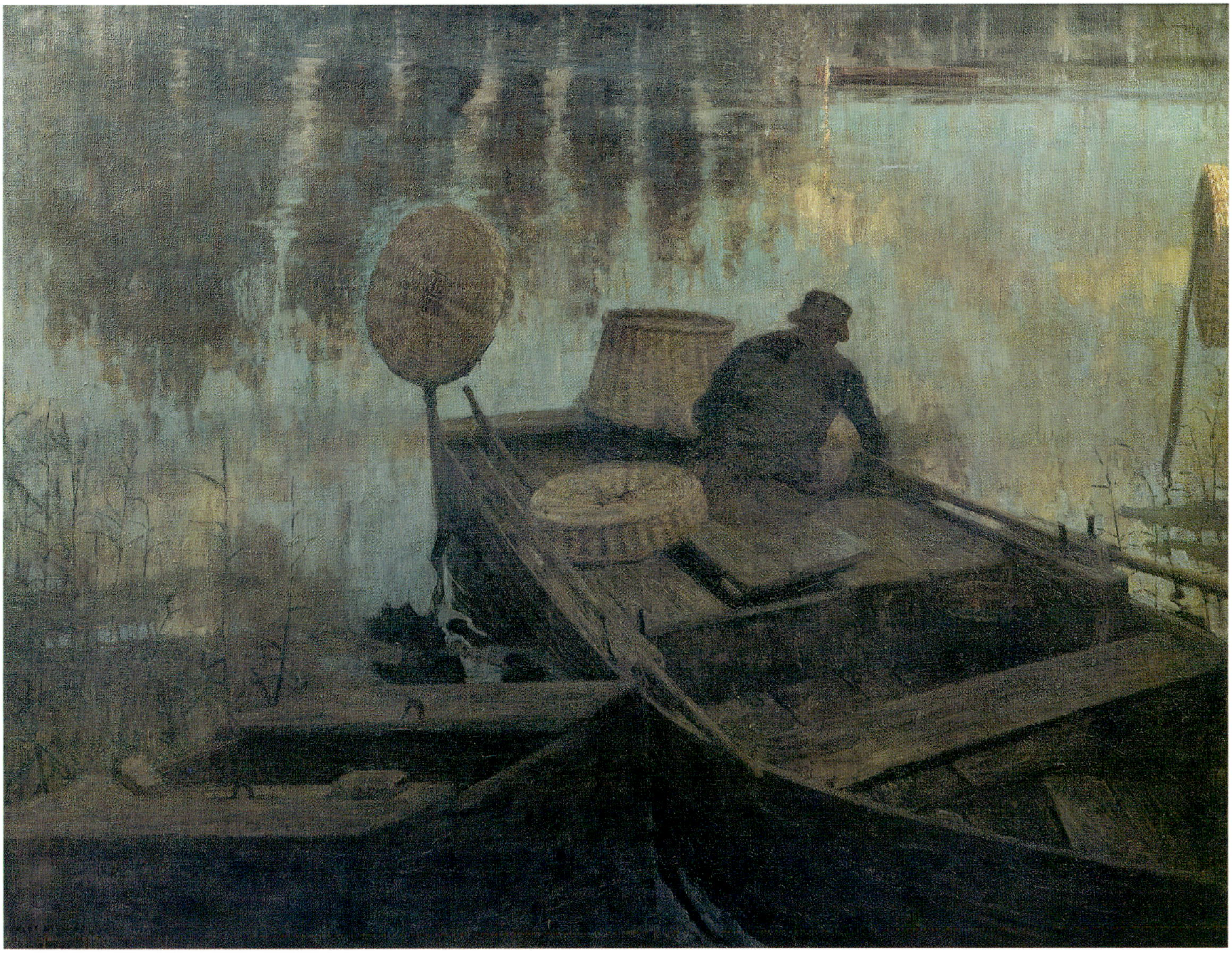

Charles Mertens was fascinated throughout his career by the life of fishermen and sailors. He painted boats on the River Scheldt, mussel-fishermen at work, fishermen mending their nets or hauling their boats onto the quayside, the fisherfolk of Zealand, and canal scenes in England. The *Fisherman in the Moonlight* sits with his baskets in a little rowing boat on a lake. He has his back to us, and seems to be daydreaming, as he is neither rowing nor fishing. Perhaps he is emptying his nets. Mertens's attention is concentrated on the water: blue-green and full of shadows, with purple and orange highlights. The light of the moon colours the water and envelops the foreground action in semi-darkness. Mertens's sensitivity for the technique and conception of Impressionism are at their most developed in this work. The visitors to the 1897 exhibition seem, however, to have been unmoved. Pol de Mont wrote in *De Vlaamsche School* (1897, 144): 'They do not know what to make of that strange water, in which the summer clouds are reflected so harshly.' True Impressionism, with its systematic analysis of light and colour, and informal compositions, never quite penetrated Antwerp artistic circles, nor the work of Charles Mertens. To quote Pol de Mont once again: 'Mertens is working increasingly from the spirit, and not merely the pictorial sensibility of his eyes. Works like the *Fisherman* are poems' (*De Vlaamsche School* 1897, 144). De Mont evidently approved of Mertens's restraint. Despite the naturalism, we detect a hint of Symbolism in his work from around 1900, although once again there is no genuine allegiance to the movement. Mertens preferred to work in pastels at this point in his career, as he did during his English period (1914–1919). The works produced in Calverley are softer in tone and intimate in atmosphere, but are hardly innovative within his own artistic output.

Fisherman in the Moonlight has been given several titles over the years, including 'Visser in zijn schuit' (Fisherman in his Boat) and 'Miroitements' (Reflections). Another work in Mertens's estate, entitled *L'Etang (The Pond)*,[1] strongly recalls this painting. | LDJ

PROVENANCE Family of the artist until 1922; donated to the Museum by Cléomir Jussiant through Artibus Patriae in 1928.

EXHIBITIONS Antwerp 1897; Antwerp 1922b, 46, no. 39; Antwerp 1975, 43; Antwerp 1985–1986, no. 144; Antwerp 1991, no. 134.

BIBLIOGRAPHY P. de Mont, 'Karel Mertens', *De Vlaamsche School* (1897), 137–144; Antwerp 1922b, 46, no. 39.

1 *Catalogue des tableaux, pastels, dessins, eaux-fortes composant l'atelier du feu Charles Mertens*, Antwerp [1922], 30, no. 22.

Constantin Meunier

ETTERBEEK (BRUSSELS) 1831 – IXELLES (BRUSSELS) 1905

Having studied sculpture at the Academy of Fine Arts in Brussels from 1845 to 1852, Meunier abandoned this discipline, which was then still too constrained by tradition, and turned instead to painting. He became friends with Charles de Groux (1825–1870), Louis Dubois (1830–1880), Félicien Rops (q.v.) and several other future founders of the Brussels-based Société Libre des Beaux-Arts, thus involving himself in the realist avant-garde.

From 1857 to 1875 he mainly painted religious works, later turning to subjects drawn from the recent history of Flanders. However, in 1878 he discovered the industrial landscapes of the steelworks, coal-mines and factories near Liège. In 1880 he began to exhibit works devoted to the theme of industry, and soon after this, in the company of Xavier Mellery (q.v.) and the writer Camille Lemonnier, he travelled round Belgium's coal-mining area – the Borinage, Le Pays Noir.

From October 1882 to April 1883 he spent time in Seville, having been sent there by the Belgian government to make copies of the works of a Flemish-born artist. His experience of Spain helped him to complete the task of self-discovery.

In 1884 he took up sculpture again, and two years later he submitted to the Salon de Paris the work entitled *The Hammerman*, where it caused considerable critical reaction.

In 1887 he became a teacher at the Académie de Louvain, a move which finally assured his material security. It was in Louvain, in the period up to 1894 – the date at which he returned to Brussels – that a number of his masterpieces were created. It was also at this time that the idea of a monument to Work began to develop in his mind. In 1896, at the behest of Henry van de Velde (q.v.), Siegfried Bing organized a retrospective of Meunier's work at his new gallery, the 'Salon de l'art nouveau', in Paris. It was a considerable success. The following year, Meunier was given a triumphal welcome in Germany, first in Dresden and then in Berlin. In spring 1898 he presented a set of his works at the Vienna Secession. In 1900 he moved into the house-cum-studio which he had had built for himself in Ixelles, a suburb of Brussels.

The *Monument to Work*, which was ultimately purchased by the Belgian State, occupied the last years of Meunier's life, as he searched – notably with Victor Horta – for the best architectural setting for the work.

In 1903, although entirely taken over by this project, he still accepted a commission for a monument to Emile Zola, whom he admired greatly. This was left unfinished on his death two years later. | PB

SUMMARY BIBLIOGRAPHY

C. Lemonnier, *Constantin Meunier, sculpteur et peintre*, Paris 1904; M. Devigne, *Constantin Meunier*, Turnhout 1919; A. Fontaine, *Constantin Meunier*, Paris 1923; L. Piérard, *Constantin Meunier*, Brussels 1937; A. Behets, *Constantin Meunier – L'homme, l'artiste et l'œuvre*, Brussels 1942; P. Baudson, *Les trois vies de Constantin Meunier*, Brussels 1979.

48 Puddler

Un Puddleur, c. 1884
Bronze, 37.3 x 21 x 24.5 cm
Signed right side of chair: C. Meunier; inscribed reverse of plinth: B. Verbeyst. Fondeur/Bruxelles
Musées royaux des Beaux-Arts de Belgique / Koninklijke Musea voor Schone Kunsten van België,
Musée Constantin Meunier, Brussels, inv. no. 10.000/87

It was in 1884 that Constantin Meunier, well over 50, returned to sculpture, a discipline that he had abandoned in favour of painting shortly after his studies at the Academy of Fine Arts in Brussels thirty years before. For some years, the artist had been exploring, at first alone, and then in the company of his friend Xavier Mellery (q.v.) and the writer Camille Lemonnier (to whom he was now related by marriage), the industrial regions around Liège and later those of the Borinage, Le Pays Noir. The impact upon the artist was profound. From 1880 he had begun to exhibit works inspired by this world of labour at the Salons of Ghent and Paris.

From a trip to Spain, which lasted from October 1882 to April 1883 and which no doubt rounded off his introduction to his new life, he brought back a superb painting, *The Tobacco Factory at Seville,* in which his mastery of colour is displayed. He exhibited the painting at the Ghent Salon of 1883 and then at the Brussels Salon of 1884, together with another great work celebrating an aspect of industrial life, *The Removal of a Broken Crucible (Glassworks at Val Saint-Lambert,* Musée Constantin Meunier, Brussels). Following an invitation from Octave Maus some months later, Meunier took part in the 1885 Salon des XX. On 4 December he wrote to Maus: 'I shall be sending works made specially for this exhibition. I am even planning to exploit the invitation to exhibit some sculpture, on which I am actively engaged.' In addition to a number of paintings, his submission did indeed include, amongst others, two small wax casts that appear as the prototypes of two major future creations: *Puddler* and *Stevedore.* 'Constantin Meunier is not just a great painter; he is well on the way to becoming one of our finest sculptors', wrote Max Waller immediately, adding that: 'His *Puddler* and his *Stevedore,* one standing in a superb pose, the other seated in the weary attitude in which Meunier is fond of depicting his workers, heralds a new and uncharted art.... Up to now, there has been little representation of the worker in sculpture.'

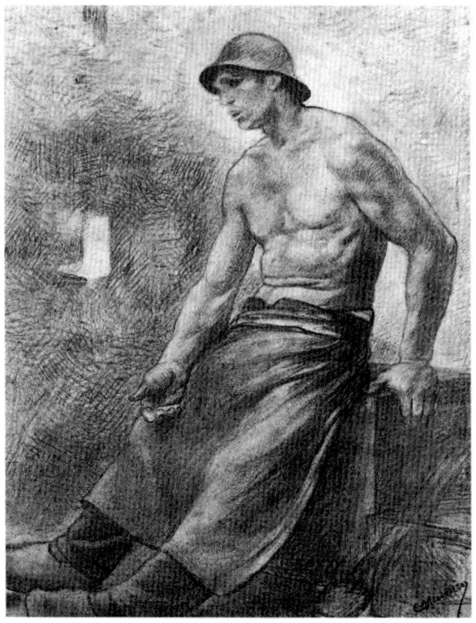

fig. a CONSTANTIN MEUNIER
Weariness, c. 1879–1880,
charcoal on paper, Musées royaux des Beaux-Arts de Belgique, Musée Constantin Meunier, Brussels

A charcoal drawing entitled *Weariness* [fig. a] was undoubtedly the source for the *Puddler,* his first sculptural enterprise, and it was probably drawn, no doubt from life, in 1879 or 1880, at the Cockerill works at Seraing. Meunier used it first as the basis for a painting, which appeared at the Brussels Salon under the same title in 1881. The drawing has several features in common with the sculpture. Despite a difference of pose, the model, his form, his dress, his expression, are identical. Furthermore, in both works the arm weighs down upon the thigh so wearied by its labour as to be no longer able to raise the hand.

This small version of the *Puddler* is found in the background of the portrait of Meunier painted by his friend Isidore Verheyden (q.v.) in 1887 (Musée Constantin Meunier, Brussels). Was it perhaps included because in that year, following the triumph of his *Hammerman* at the 1886 Paris Salon, Meunier exhibited – again in Paris, and later at the Triennial Salon in Brussels – a plaster *Puddler at Rest,* which was a life-sized extrapolation of the small wax of 1884? Verheyden seems to be recording the beginnings of Meunier's mature sculptural activities.

The *Puddler* was acquired by the State and cast in bronze the following year. Thus monumentalized, the work highlights the development, within the space of a few years, of a 'new kind of statuary, passionate and seditious in its quietness,' as Camille Lemonnier put it. A year before this, in 1886, Lemonnier had published his novel *Happe-chair,* set in the world of the iron foundries, which he had discovered partly through the eyes and drawings of Constantin Meunier. | PB

PROVENANCE Bought from Mr and Mrs Charles Jacques-Meunier, son in-law and daughter of the artist, Brussels, 1936.
EXHIBITIONS Les XX 1885, no. 1; Brussels 1905, no. 685; Louvain 1909, no. 88; St Louis 1914, no. 58; Ghent 1924, no. 29; Bochum 1970–1971, no. 5; Berlin 1971, no. 5; Berlin 1979; Charleroi 1980, no. 110; Brussels 1993–1994, no. 141.
BIBLIOGRAPHY M. W. [Max Waller] 1885; Sulzberger 1937, 48–49; Baudson 1985–1988, 296–297; Baudson 1990, 216–217.

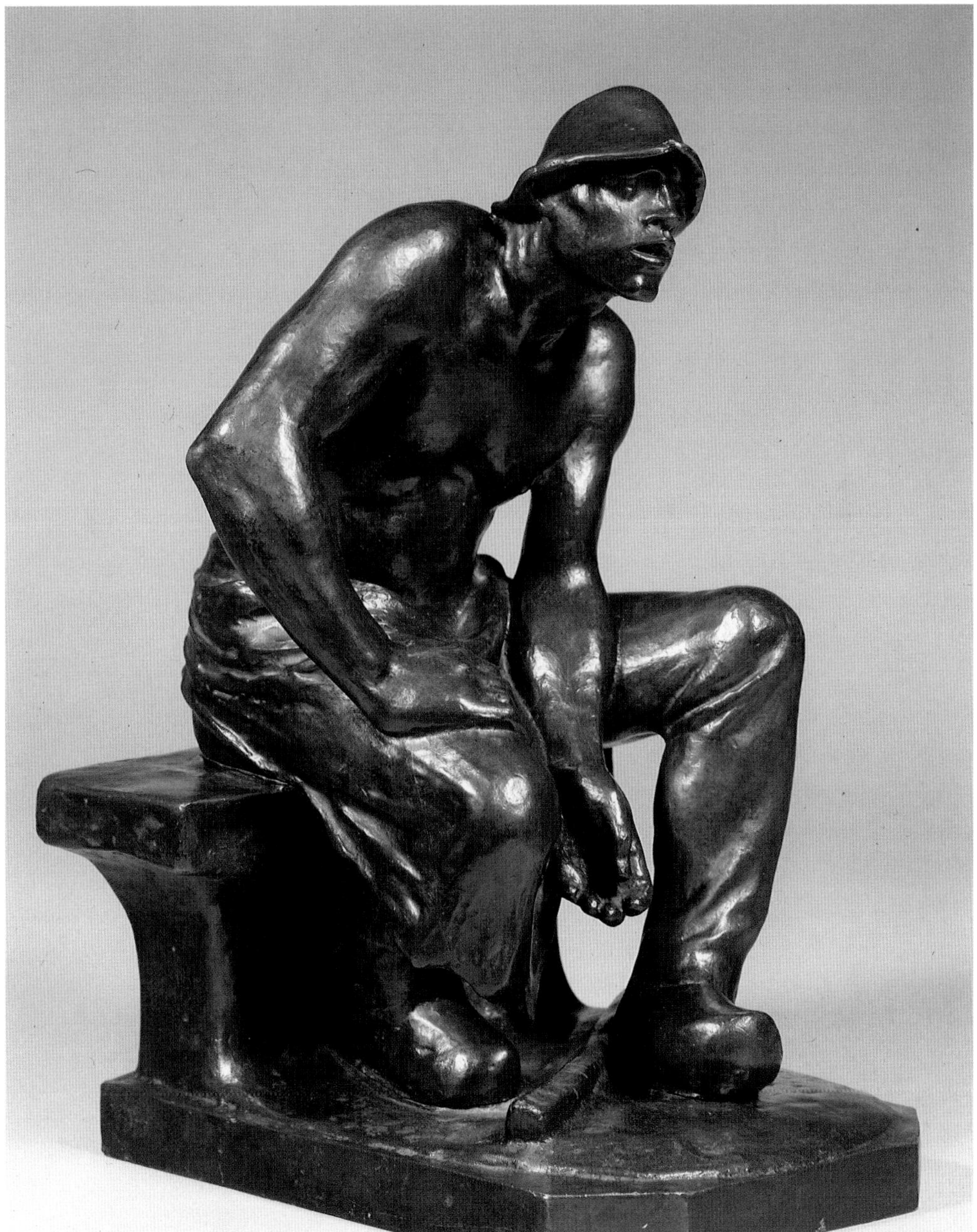

49 Ostend Fisherman

Pêcheur ostendais, 1890
Bronze, 80.7 x 28.9 x 24.5 cm
Signed behind right foot: C. Meunier; inscribed on left side of base: Fondu par B. Verbeyst / Pour l'Atelier Constantin Meunier Bruxelles
Musées royaux des Beaux-Arts de Belgique / Koninklijke Musea voor Schone Kunsten van België, Musée Constantin Meunier, Brussels, inv. no. 10.000/100

In May 1890 Meunier sent this work, already cast in bronze, to the Salon du Champ-de-Mars, Paris. *L'Art moderne* of 25 May 1890 commented: 'On a plinth just by the entrance, five figures by Constantin Meunier, one of the undisputed successes of the Salon. Rough, nervous bronzes in a grand style, with realistic gestures, powerfully synthesized musculature; the pose of an astonishing Stevedore, the extended slenderness of a Glassblower, small versions of the *Hammerman* and the *Puddler*, a superb *Boulogne Fisherman*.' The French government bought the *Hammerman* and the *Stevedore* for the Musée du Luxembourg, making Meunier the first Belgian sculptor considered worthy of such an honour.

The modern title, replacing 'Boulogne' with 'Ostend', only began to be used immediately after the artist's death. Treu in 1898, and Lemonnier in 1904, both talked of the *Boulogne Fisherman*, who 'standing in his great boots, under his stiff gummed pea-jacket, with his sou'wester on his head, exhibits all the oddity in dress and pose of a hieratic Japanese statue'. This apparent confusion may have arisen from the fact that – as confirmed by a very fine preparatory drawing [fig. a] – although it was at Ostend that the vigorous pose of this rough figure, with its gaunt features, lively eye, and swinging arms, ready to launch into action, was captured, the model was a sailor from Boulogne.

Meunier regularly spent part of the summer on the Belgian coast. In 1889 he wrote from Mariakerke, near Ostend, to his friend Camille Lemonnier: 'I am working a little bit. At the harbour I discovered some magnificently characterful teams of French fishermen from Boulogne, and I have an idea for a statue that I may make. The unfortunate thing is that these chaps fly off like sea-gulls and come back without warning. So for 8 days I've been keeping a doggedly patient look-out for a boat that hasn't come back yet, and it's quite a distance from where I am to the harbour.' A number of other charcoal drawings hastily jotted on to paper during this same period in August bear the name, and in some cases even the address in Boulogne, of the seamen Meunier had met. However, the figure of the fisherman is not a very common one in Meunier's sculpted work. It makes its first appearance here – at more or less the time that another Belgian sculptor, Guillaume Charlier (1854–1925), who became a member of Les XX in 1885, began to take an interest in the port of Blankenberghe.

Whatever the geographic origins of the intense presence and the restrained form, this *Fisherman* embodies, as do the foundrymen, miners, glassworkers, and rural labourers who are his counterparts, the figure of the worker. Writing two years later, Emile Verhaeren declared that the worker had at last invaded the worlds of urban life and art: no longer 'the vague, far-off person who gets talked about when catastrophes occur; he has made his way into the town, he has set up camp in the art rooms, he has taken up residence in the museums, he has come from distant horizons to make his real, living, tragic presence felt, and he is someone with whom a number of age-old scores will soon have to be settled' (*L'Art moderne*, 21 August 1892, 269). | PB

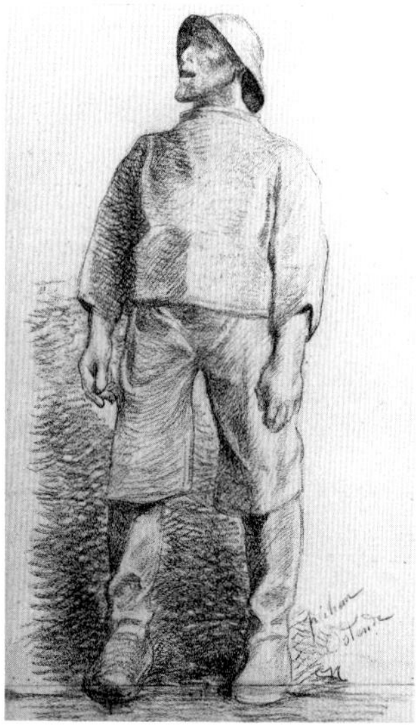

fig a CONSTANTIN MEUNIER
Ostend Fisherman, 1890,
charcoal on paper, Musées royaux des Beaux-Arts de Belgique,
Musée Constantin Meunier, Brussels

PROVENANCE Bought from Mr and Mrs Charles Jacques-Meunier, son-in-law and daughter of the artist, Brussels, 1936.
EXHIBITIONS Paris 1890, no. 1283; Brussels 1905, no. 698; Louvain 1909, no. 101; St Louis 1914, no. 71; Ghent 1924, no. 52; Brussels 1928, no. 218.
BIBLIOGRAPHY De Taeye 1894, 36; Lemonnier 1904, 62; Gensel 1907, 49–50; Fontaine 1923, 93, 101; Baudson 1990, 225.

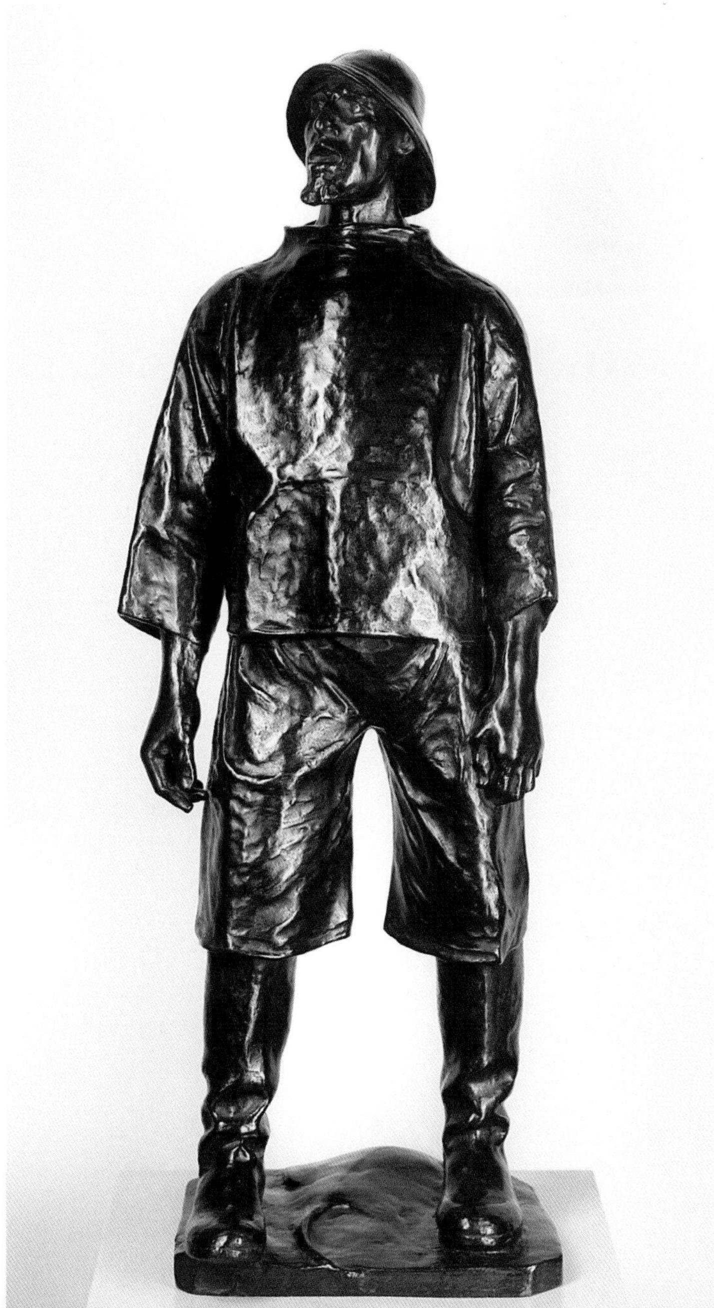

50 Old Pit Horse

Vieux Cheval de mine, 1890
Bronze, 36.5 x 48.5 x 14.5 cm
Signed on pedestal: C. Meunier; inscribed on side of base: Atelier/59 rue l'Abbaye
Musée royaux des Beaux-Arts de Belgique / Koninklijke Musea voor Schone Kunsten van België, Musée Constantin Meunier, Brussels, inv. no. 10.000/76

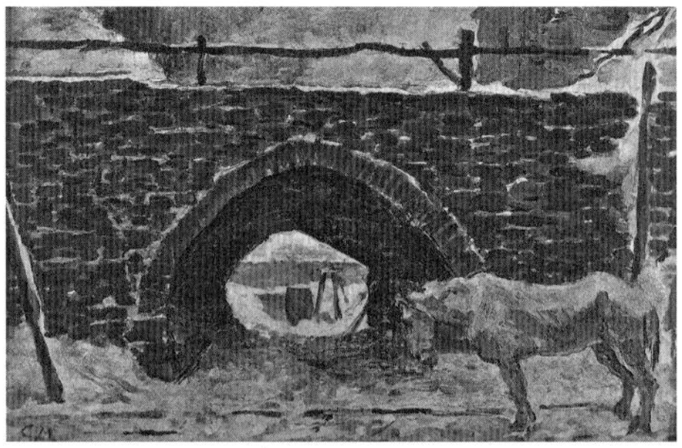

fig a CONSTANTIN MEUNIER Old Pit Horse, oil on panel, Musées royaux des Beaux-Arts de Belgique, Musée Constantin Meunier, Brussels

This work is generally dated 1890. It was first exhibited at a private show of the artist's work in Brussels in December 1891. However, this little bronze figure, often regarded as one of Meunier's masterpieces from his so-called 'Louvain period' (1887–1894, when he was a teacher at the Academy and was resident in Louvain) may have been inspired, as was his famous *Fire-damp Explosion* (started 1887), by events witnessed by the artist in March 1887. A devastating explosion occurred at the La Boule colliery, in the Quaregnon and Pâturages districts of the Borinage, not far from Mons. Together with Dr Van Hassel, a general practitioner in Pâturages and a friend of Charles de Coster, Camille Lemonnier, Georges Eekhoud and Emile Verhaeren, Meunier came upon an 'apocalyptically' thin old horse that had just been brought up from the mine, where, because of the urgency of the rescue operation, he had been forgotten for the best part of a week. 'The poor beast, half-collapsed, resigned and indifferent to everything, looked pitiful, its head bent, its backbone curved inwards, its ribs sticking out, and its legs half-bowed,' wrote Van Hassel. He continued by relating how he saw the artist stop to contemplate this lamentable anatomical construction, fill his eyes and memory with it, and finally draw it, becoming completely absorbed in his work. He then said to Van Hassel: 'In two days I shall make a model of it.'

The horse, solitary, pitiful and abandoned, is a recurrent theme in Meunier's work, particularly in his small paintings [fig. a], gouaches, pastels and charcoal drawings. The *Old Pit Horse*, whose every line spells sadness, also has literary parallels, for example, Old Bataille in Zola's *Germinal* (1885), who 'stood with his head bowed, trembling on his old legs, making vain efforts to remember the sun'.

When the work was exhibited at the Salon du Champ-de-Mars in Paris in spring 1893 and again at the first Salon de La Libre Esthétique in Brussels in 1894, it provoked a host of critical comments, including a laudatory one from Octave Mirbeau: 'What is particularly well observed is that Constantin Meunier has given this old and pitiful carcass of a horse a face. And what a moving face it is! Old, sick animals have faces like those of old people, faces composed of misery and resignation, tragic faces that recount, better than any book, the injustice that weighs on the doomed lives of lowly people.'

This striking little bronze is full of the kind of 'character' that the sculptor was fond of depicting and which was recognized by Emile Verhaeren. It also displays the spirit of synthesis that characterizes a number of Meunier's works. Most of all, however, like his *Puddler* [cat. 48], *Stevedore*, *Glassblower* and *Drinking Man*, the *Old Pit Horse* demonstrates Constantin Meunier's ability to endow a small sculpture with a sense of the monumental. | PB

PROVENANCE Bought from Mr and Mrs Charles Jacques-Meunier, son-in-law and daughter of the artist, Brussels, 1936.
EXHIBITIONS Paris 1893, no. 94; *La Libre Esthétique* 1894, no. 313; Paris 1896, no. 1; Louvain 1909, no. 76; Brussels 1905, no. 662; St Louis 1914, no. 47; Ghent 1924, no. 40; New-York 1980, no. 68; Beijing 1988.
BIBLIOGRAPHY Verhaeren 1891; Mirbeau 1893, 196–197; Shaw-Sparrow 1897, 80–83; Vermeylen 1903, 50; Lemonnier 1904, 113; Devigne 1919, 21–22; Van Hassel 1927, 152; Baudson 1985–1988, 299; Baudson 1990, 227–228.

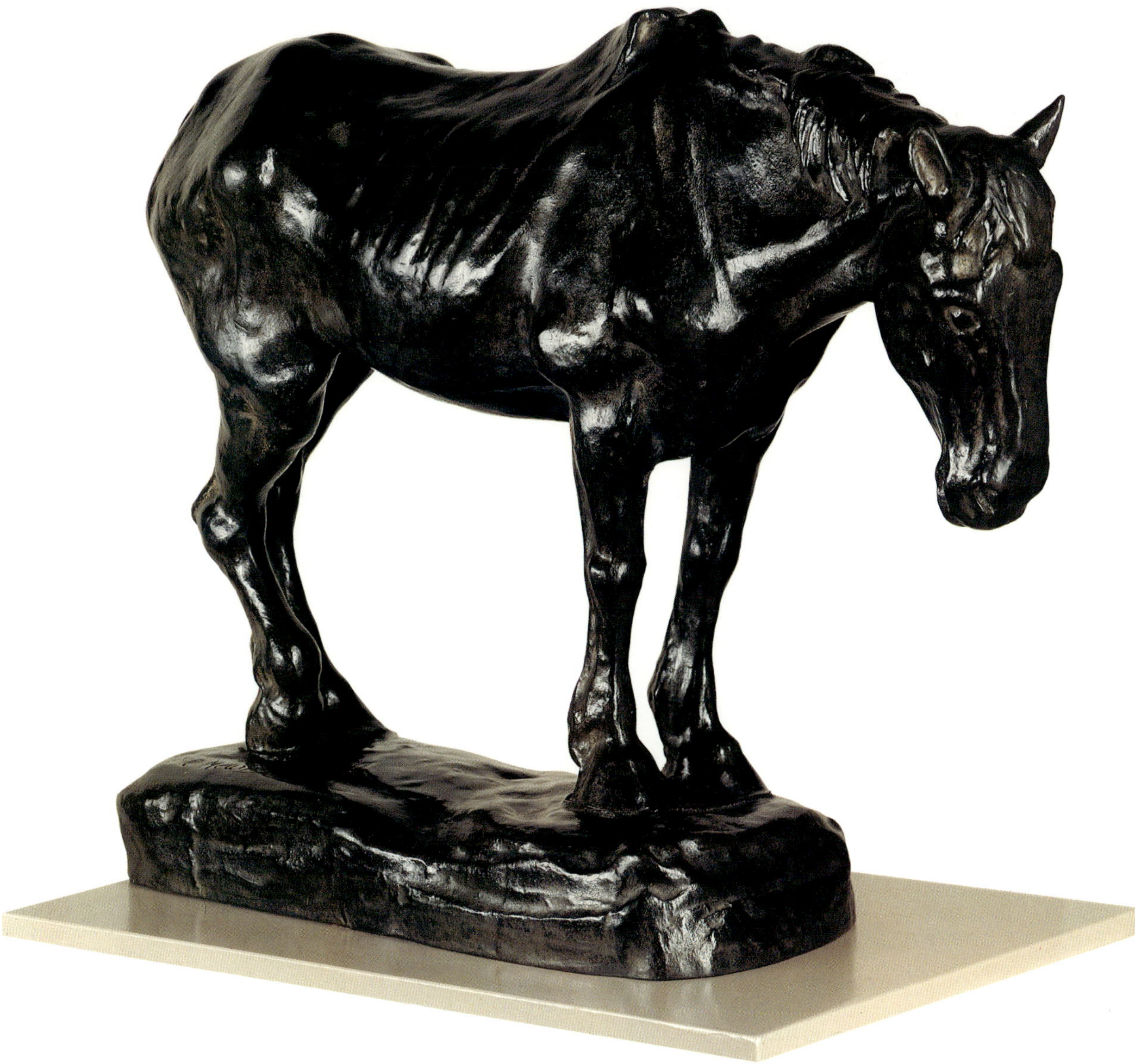

51 Truck in the Mine

Wagonnet dans la mine, c. 1890
Oil on canvas, 80 x 96 cm
Signed bottom right: C. Meunier
Musées royaux des Beaux-Arts de Belgique / Koninklijke Musea voor Schone Kunsten van België,
Musée Constantin Meunier, Brussels, inv. no. 10.000/724

This work records a scene, probably in a pit in the Borinage. A preliminary sketch, rapidly noted in charcoal and bearing a purely descriptive title, *Workers pushing a Truck* [fig. a], confirms that the scene is apparently set at the surface rather than in the mine itself, probably at the receiving station, where the trucks arrive from the bottom of the mine. This is confirmed in the painting by the view of the miners' quarters and the chimney glimpsed through the archway in the background.

The drawing was reproduced, under the title of *The Arrival*, in Camille Lemonnier's 1904 study of Meunier. Two years later, in his book on Belgian painting, Lemonnier reproduced a painting entitled *Mining Interior*, and in 1923 André Fontaine reproduced the same painting, this time under the title *The Trucks*. The latter title had already been published in July 1905, in the catalogue of the Retrospective Exhibition of Belgian art, and again in Meunier's exhibition at the Galerie Giroux in 1928, also in Brussels. However, these titles probably refer to a larger, more complex composition which included a group of more or less identical men pushing trucks in front of an opening revealing a similar industrial landscape. The direction of the action, however, is reversed, with the movement taking place towards the right rather than the left. It is possible that the painting exhibited here anticipates the large-scale composition, providing figures, action and landscape elements subsequently incorporated into the larger painting.

This process of transformation and incorporation of pictorial elements derived from different experiences is common throughout Meunier's work, and demonstrates the distance that lay between Meunier's art and that of the Realists working in the latter part of the 1880s and more especially during the 1890s [see cats. 26, 38, 47, 68, 79]. In his approach to subject matter, Meunier combined the observed with the recollected and the idealized. He was both eyewitness and interpreter, recording fact in the service of a more universal message, with that 'quiet strength' which Lemonnier identified as early as 1884. Likewise, his technique eschewed the meticulous rendition of detail. Rather he adopted a form of brushwork composed of tiny dots or complementary tones chosen within a predominantly grey-brown spectrum. Landscape, however, is treated with occasional dashes of vivid colour. The brushwork, characterized by spirited, rapid, feverish gestures, is 'Impressionist'. Writing in 1889, Eugène Demolder said: 'Do not ask him to produce highly finished, meticulous paintings; do not demand an elaborate work. No, he seems propelled by the desire to give a vivid rendering of an impression; his technique is anxious; in one stroke he seems to have determined the positioning of his subject within its frame.' And in his introduction to the Bing exhibition in Paris in 1896, Georges Lecomte added: 'And one can see that M. Meunier is a painter as well as a sculptor. In both these modes of expression he displays the same ease, an equal spontaneity ... There is no feeling of struggle to overcome a difficulty. He has the eye of a painter, the talents special to a painter, a sense of colour and of the play of light on form.'

In 1930, Paul Colin, in his survey of Belgian painting, stressed the fact that Meunier's final success as a sculptor may well have eclipsed his equally well-deserved reputation as one of the greatest painters of his day. In this respect, Colin echoed the views of both Vincent van Gogh and the French Neo-Impressionist painter, Maximilien Luce. | PB

PROVENANCE Unknown; acquired in 1963, Brussels.
EXHIBITIONS Bochum 1970–1971, no. 40; Berlin 1971, no. 43; Rome 1991–1992, no. 62.
BIBLIOGRAPHY Demolder 1889, 51–52; Baudson 1991, 228.

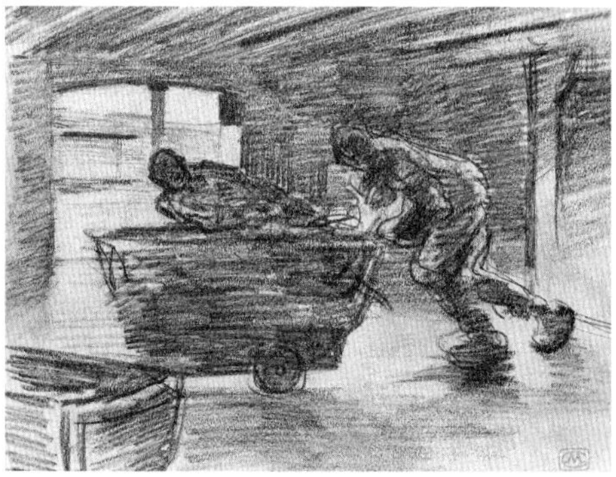

fig. a CONSTANTIN MEUNIER
Workers pushing a Truck, charcoal on paper,
Musées royaux des Beaux-Arts de Belgique,
Musée Constantin Meunier, Brussels

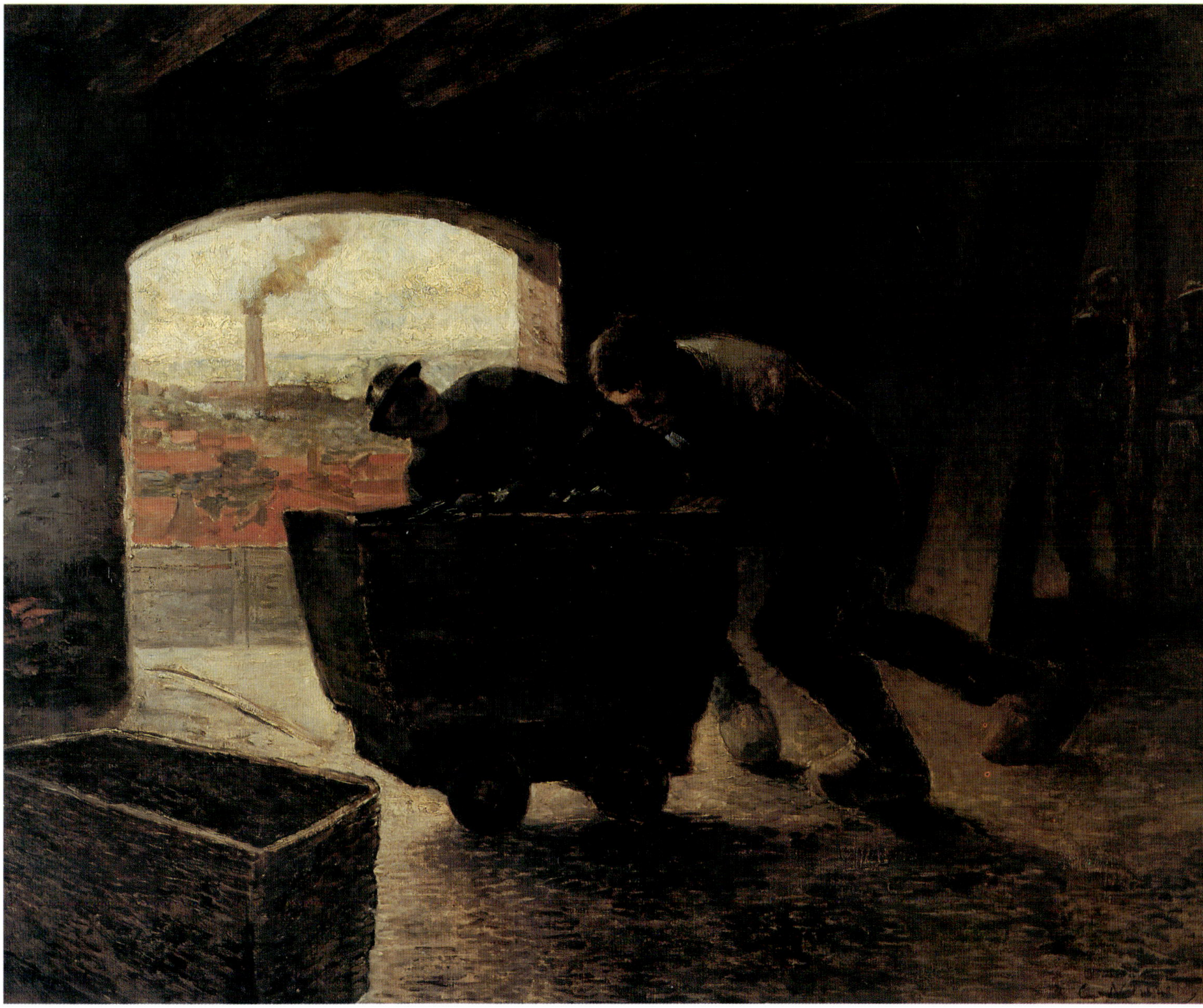

52 Industry

L'Industrie, 1890
Bronze, low relief, 64.3 x 92.4 x 14.3 cm
Signed on base, front, bottom right: C. Meunier; inscribed on base, front, bottom left: Verbeyst, Fondeur/Brussels
Musées royaux des Beaux Arts de Belgique / Koninklijke Musea voor Schone Kunsten van België,
Musée Constantin Meunier, Brussels, inv. no. 10.000/55

It was in 1879 or 1880 that Meunier witnessed a scene of industrial labour which was to haunt him until he began to work on his *Monument to Work* in c. 1894. The scene of a team of workers removing a broken crucible in a glassworks, was recorded in a large number of preliminary sketches. From these was derived a more finished drawing which was shown at the Brussels Cercle artistique in 1881. The work made a great impression due to its unusual grandeur and the originality of its celebration of a scene of industrial life which hitherto had been regarded as unacceptable within the canons of high art. It revealed the noble quality which it was possible to achieve in the depiction of scenes which up to then had been regarded as common. *L'Art moderne* commented: 'The grouping, the movement, the balance of the group, are wonderful, and one thinks of the powerful effect that would be produced by a low relief on the same lines' (8 January 1882, 12).

By 1884 the subject matter of the drawing had been transformed into a monumental painting, to be hung beside the artist's *Tobacco Factory* at the Brussels Salon of that year. Meunier made two different versions of the *Removal of a Broken Crucible (Glassworks at Val Saint-Lambert,* Musée Constantin Meunier, inv. nos. 10.000/171 and 233 [fig. a]). From a technical point of view, the painting is a critical document for the study of Meunier's subsequent development. It is also a work which suggests a sculptural treatment. Since the year of its exhibition in Brussels coincided with his decision to return to sculpture, it is tempting to suggest that Meunier may already have considered this possible transition. The translation from canvas to bronze was, however, to take a few more years.

A watercolour made shortly after 1885 reveals that Meunier was planning a monumental mantelpiece on the theme of Work. Two caryatids in the form of workers, a miner and a glassworker, support an entablature executed in high relief (Musée Constantin Meunier, Brussels). The first translation into three dimensions appeared at the Brussels Salon of 1890, in the form of the small low relief in plaster entitled *Industry*, the bronze cast of which is shown here. In its definitive monumental version of 1894, this was to form the first of the four large-scale reliefs designed by Meunier for the *Monument to Work*, which, from then on, never left his thoughts. In a letter written to Georg Treu, director of the Dresden Museum, the artist himself gave a description of the work: 'The glass is being melted in large crucibles of fireproof clay, under the action of intense heat in a furnace. Over a longish period of time, a crack develops in the crucible, the molten glass spreads out over the hearth, and the crucible has to be replaced. A team of specially trained men then arrives and brings the incandescent crucible along on a steel wagon. It is a delicate operation, given the weight of the white-hot crucible. There are several minutes of upheaval and devilish commotion, which I have tried to convey.' Over a period of ten years, this upheaval and 'devilish commotion', which had already been translated from charcoal into paint, finally took the form of a sculpted allegory, eventually cast in bronze, and later hewn from stone by the sculptor. Yet it is the preliminary model made for the 1890 Salon, with its less elaborate technique and its direct, spontaneous power, that probably remains the closest sculptural expression of the artist's initial impressions. | PB

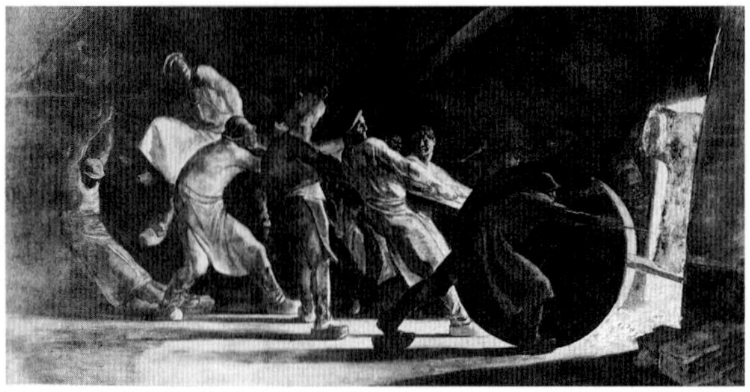

fig. a CONSTANTIN MEUNIER, Removal of a Broken Crucible (Glassworks at Val Saint-Lambert), 1884, Musées royaux des Beaux-Arts de Belgique, Musée Constantin Meunier, Brussels

PROVENANCE Bought from Mr and Mrs Charles Jacques-Meunier, son-in-law and daughter of the artist, Brussels, 1936.
EXHIBITIONS Brussels 1890, no. 1122; Dresden 1897; Brussels 1905, no. 663; Louvain 1909, no. 54; St Louis 1914, no. 32.
BIBLIOGRAPHY Treu 1898, 17; Gensel 1907, 66; Baudson 1985–1988, 298–299.

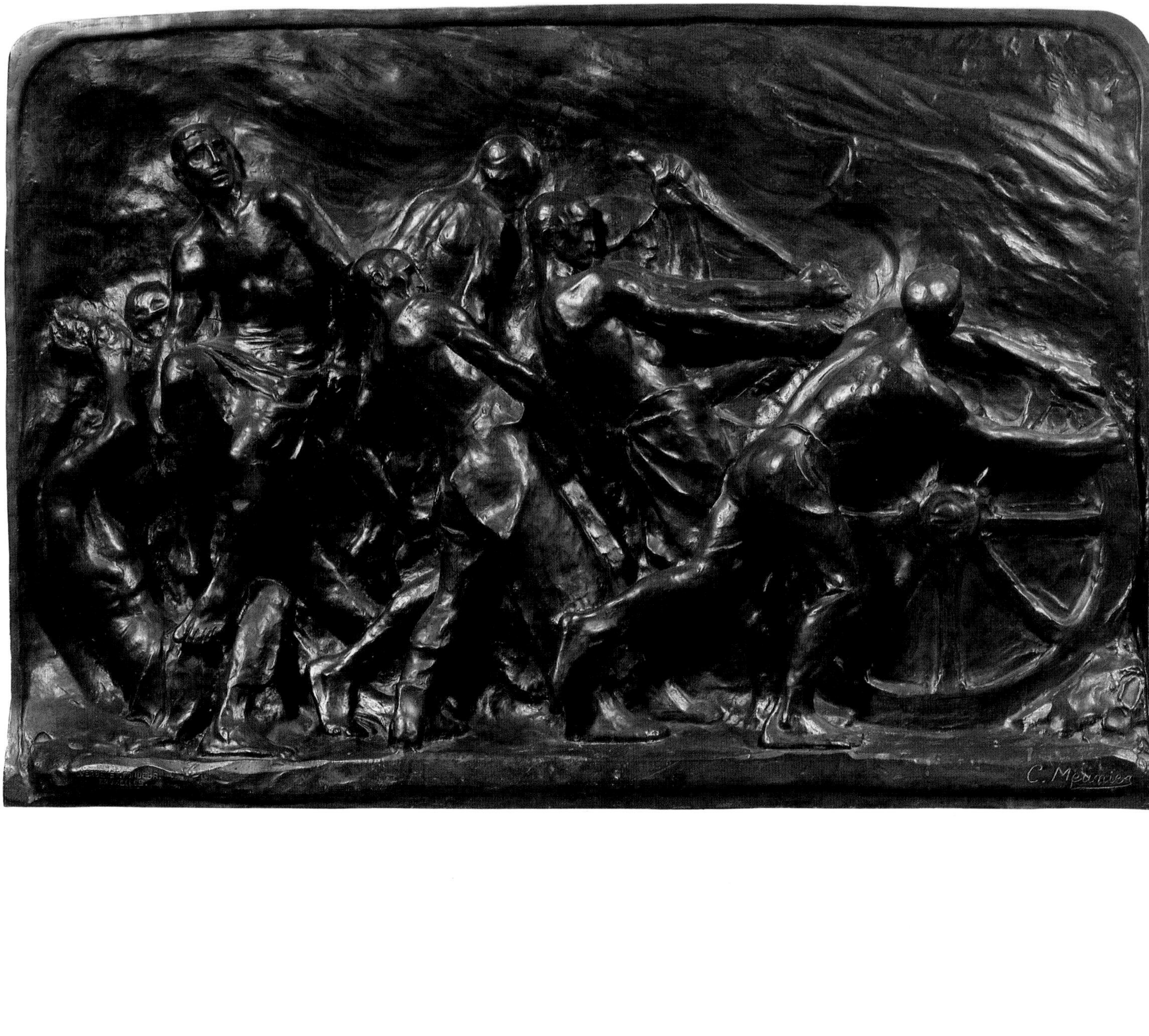

53 Return from the Mine

Retour de la mine, c. 1896–1897
Bronze, low relief, 58.7 x 82.2 x 6.3 cm
Signed on front of base, bottom left: C. Meunier; inscribed on front of base, bottom right: Atelier / 59 rue l'Abbaye
Musées royaux des Beaux-Arts de Belgique / Koninklijke Musea voor Schone Kunsten van België,
Musée Constantin Meunier, Brussels, inv. no. 10.000/57

This relief was an initial study for the panel devoted to the mining industry in the *Monument to Work*. It may have been exhibited at the 1897 Salon du Champ-de-Mars in Paris, under the title *The Miners*. In his book on Meunier, published in 1898, Georg Treu devotes a few lines to this work, describing it as one of the four reliefs – the others were *Industry, The Port*, and *The Harvest* – which eventually made up the *Monument*. He reproduced the work at the end of his book, under the title *Return from the Mine*.

The Port and *The Harvest* figured in sketch-form at the Salon de La Libre Esthétique in Brussels in February 1895. In February the following year, both reliefs were included in the major exhibition of Meunier's work held at Siegfried Bing's Salon de l'Art Nouveau in Paris. *Return from the Mine*, however, was not included in that show. The date of its execution, therefore, can probably be placed either in that year or at the beginning of 1897.

Return from the Mine has affinities with a number of drawings or paintings in Meunier's oeuvre. Among these are a huge, magnificent charcoal drawing highlighted with white chalk, *Miners going home from the Mine*, and a painting of the same title [figs. a, b]. However, the positions of the figures, the fragmentary references to landscape, the scree, the chimney, the structure on which the wagons go back and forth, and the poses of some of the figures are more reminiscent of a large-scale painting that was shown in the Belgian section of the Exposition Universelle in Paris in 1889, under the title *Return from the Pit (Evening)* (Private Collection). The latter was described by Eugène Demolder as: '... night is falling, casting a sinister pall, and out of the darkness, like immense shadowy guillotines, like huge instruments of torture, the pit-heads, with their chimneys and their strange extracting structures rise up. The

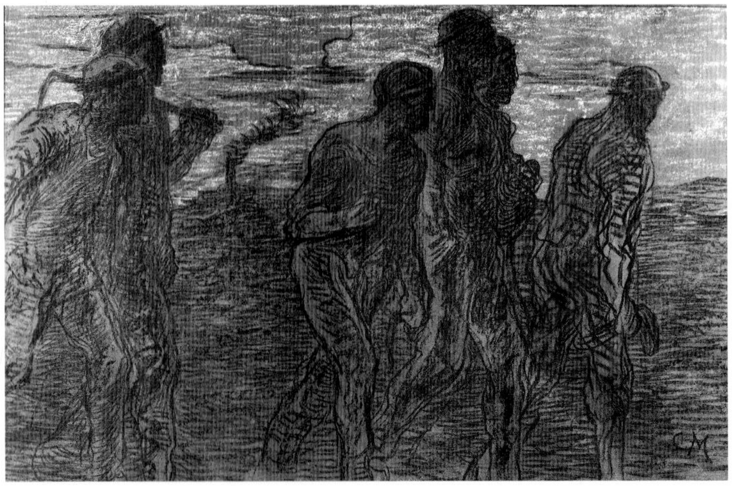

fig. a CONSTANTIN MEUNIER, Miners going home from the Mine, charcoal heightened with white chalk, Musées royaux des Beaux-Arts de Belgique, Musée Constantin Meunier, Brussels

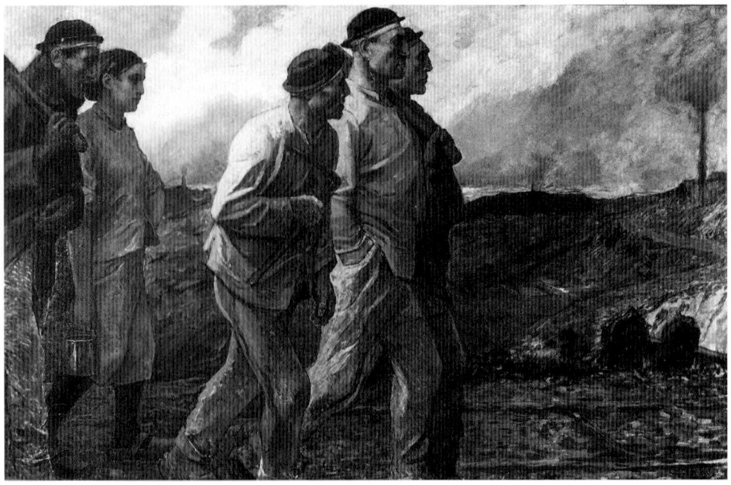

fig. b CONSTANTIN MEUNIER, Miners going home from the Mine, oil on canvas, Musées royaux des Beaux-Arts de Belgique, Musée Constantin Meunier, Brussels

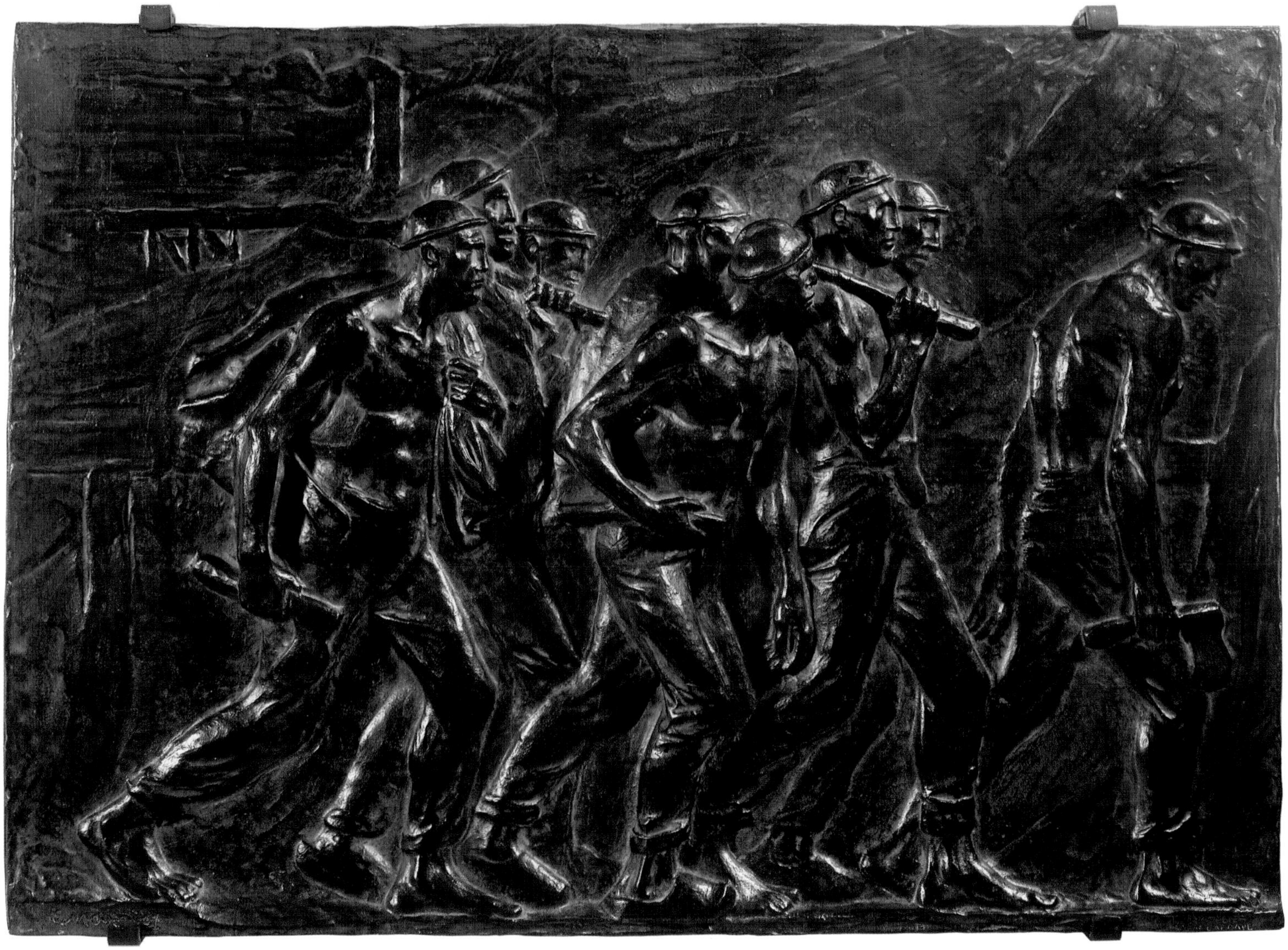

coal-tips become enveloped in shadow.... And the miners make their way down a rugged path to their huts, a sorry band, backs broken, steps heavy, tripping on the track already plunged in darkness, bearing on their shoulders, along with their pick-axes, the burden of their parlous existence.' Apart from one or two details, this description is equally applicable to this small, bronze low relief.

By playing with different scales and media in his representations of scenes from industrial life, Meunier invents and reassembles the landscapes, scenes and individuals that he had studied near Liège and in the Borinage, in combinations of both the conventional and the novel, to create a sequence of images which cast aside concern for the strictly realistic to express universal truths about labour and the condition of the labourer.

In Meunier's hands, drawing, painting and sculpture became, in the course of a few years, perfectly complementary modes of expression. Use of varied techniques enabled him, on the one hand, to create his figures and reliefs in bronze or plaster, and, on the other, to paint them on canvas or to draw them in watercolour, pastel or charcoal. And he did this in a spirit of perfect continuity as he moved between close description and the ideal forged within his own imagination. | PB

PROVENANCE Bought from Mr and Mrs Charles Jacques-Meunier, son-in-law and daughter of the artist, Brussels, 1936.

EXHIBITIONS Paris 1897, no. 105; Brussels 1905, no. 666; Venice 1905, no. 69; Louvain 1909, no. 57; St Louis 1914, no. 35; Ghent 1924, no. 37; Brussels 1969b, no. 51.

BIBLIOGRAPHY Treu 1898, 7, 17; Demolder 1901, 27; Lemonnier 1904, 69; Gensel 1907, 68–70; Thiery, Van Dievoet 1909, 86; Behets 1942, 50; Baudson 1985–1988, 299.

George Minne

GHENT 1866 – SINT-MARTENS-LATEM 1941

George Minne studied at the Ghent Academy of Fine Arts from 1879 to 1886 and then worked in Ghent (until 1895) and Brussels (1895–1899) before settling in Sint-Martens-Latem, a village near Ghent which was to become the centre for an artists' colony. His first drawings and sculptures of grieving and injured figures were produced in Ghent. The emotional power of these works was quickly recognized by Symbolist poets such as Maeterlinck, Verhaeren [see cat. 41] and Le Roy [see cat. 31], whose works Minne later illustrated.

Minne was invited to exhibit at Les XX in 1890. He was elected a member the following year, and in 1892 he was one of the Belgian Symbolists who participated in Sâr Péladan's first Salon de la Rose+Croix in Paris. In 1895 he worked at the Brussels Academy of Fine Arts under the sculptor Charles van der Stappen (1843–1910). In the ensuing five years, in Brussels and then outside the city, he was to produce his most important works, which included the evolution of the figure of a kneeling, introverted youth.

Through Henry van de Velde (q.v.) and the German art critic Julius Meier-Graefe, Minne was introduced to the international centres of Art Nouveau: Paris, various German cities and above all Vienna. He took part in numerous exhibitions, including the Vienna and Berlin Secessions and the Venice Biennale. His work was noted in Vienna by artists such as Klimt, Schiele and Kokoschka. If Minne's art was thematically and formally limited, its spiritual power was acknowledged by critics and artists alike. Although he took Auguste Rodin as his example, he did not wish to compete with his plastic strength; he chose to produce works on a less monumental scale and looked to medieval art for his source of inspiration. He developed an expressive formal vocabulary that prefigured the work of the German 'Expressionist' sculptors Ernst Barlach, Käthe Kollwitz and Wilhelm Lehmbruck.

Minne initially modelled his sculptures in clay. They were then cast in plaster from which they were rendered in bronze, stone or wood. His most important commission came from the German collector Karl Ernst Osthaus, who had invited Henry van de Velde in 1900 to design the Folkwang Museum in Hagen. In addition to several other sculptures, Minne created his masterpiece, *Fountain with Kneeling Youths,* in 1905 for the entrance hall. In this latter work, sculpted in marble after a plaster model (Museum voor Schone Kunsten, Ghent), the figure of a kneeling youth is repeated several times around a circular basin (now in the Museum Folkwang, Essen). Minne showed designs for this 'fountain' at a succession of exhibitions from 1899.

Minne received the Hagen commissions at a time when he had established a workshop in Sint-Martens-Latem, where he became the central figure of the so-called First Latem School. On their completion, he subsequently produced no further important works. He fled to Wales during the First World War with his family, where he made drawings on the theme of the mother and child and the Christ figure (principal collection, Museum voor Schone Kunsten, Ghent), themes which he continued on his return to Belgium in 1918; he also made studies of nudes and reworked earlier pieces. These late works earned him great renown in Belgium; unlike his work created pre-1900, which is inherently expressionistic in style, they are more decorative and classical in conception. | RH

SUMMARY BIBLIOGRAPHY

J. Meier-Graefe, 'Das plastische Ornament', *Pan* 4 (1898), 257–264; M. Maeterlinck, G. Chabot, P. Fierens, P. Desmedt, 'George Minne', *La Nervie* 8 (1923), 205–215; L. van Puyvelde, *George Minne,* Brussels 1930; A. de Ridder, *George Minne* (Monographies de l'Art belge), Antwerp 1947; P. Haesaerts, *Sint-Martens-Latem, gezegend oord van de Vlaamse kunst,* Brussels 1965, 92–126; A. Hünecke, 'George Minne. Der grosse Kniende', *Bildende Kunst* 28 (1980), 605–608; *George Minne en de kunst rond 1900,* Museum voor Schone Kunsten, Ghent 1982; P. Boyens, *Sint-Martens-Latem, Kunstenaarsdorp in Vlaanderen,* Tielt 1992, 234–256.

54 Mother mourning her Dead Child

Mère pleurant son enfant mort, 1886
Marble, 46 x 15 x 27 cm
Signed on base: MIN/NE
Hessisches Landesmuseum, Darmstadt, inv. no. Pl. 66:4

Mother mourning her Dead Child is one of George Minne's first sculptures, produced when the artist was twenty years old. Although he had only just completed his academic training, the piece is surprisingly devoid of any academicism. The group represents a mother crying over the body of her dead child. The theme is not unusual in late-nineteenth-century art, but it is one that Minne will undoubtedly have been confronted with personally in the working-class areas of Ghent where he lived. Unusually for his time, he used a primitive formal vocabulary to express the tragedy of the scene in as powerful a manner as possible. With little concern for anatomy or decorative form, he created a massive, angular block from the base and the mother's legs and feet which he then combined with the skeletal curve of the mother's body. The latter is almost convulsively upright, in sharp contrast to the limp, angled, little body of the dead child. A setting sun motif can be found on the side of the base.

Minne became the focus of critical attention when he first exhibited *Mother mourning her Dead Child* in Brussels in 1890. A cartoon in *Le Patriote Illustré*[1] portrayed Minne as a clown beside the sculpture. *La Revue Blanche* wrote: 'The public in the gallery stops in amazement before these strange sculpted forms: the figures all form part of a single block – angular, hieratic, with frenetic or grief-stricken gestures ... They are the work of the Ghent sculptor Georges Minne.'[2] More progressive critics admired the expressive force of Minne's groups. One of them was Eugène Demolder: 'From what primitive region do Mr Minne's plaster figures ascend? From what era of the earth's history have they been brought back? They are infinitely sorrowful, and as distressing as the mournful figures of the old Gothic stonemasons. Yet they are so simple, so fundamentally human. They still tread the moist soil left behind by the deluge – exposed, naked and defenceless against all the evils that assail such poor creatures to whom fate has given life. With their emaciated bodies and miserable hides stretched over their skeletons, they are like naive vessels of suffering. Despite their archaic air they remind me of Baudelaire's description of the human body as "l'alambic de l'éternelle douleur" ["the distillation of eternal sorrow"].'[3] Although impressed, Demolder considered the rigid poses, which he suggested had been borrowed from Egyptian statues, and the puppet-like figures to be rather overdone.

Minne showed a plaster version at the Salon des XX in 1890. After 1900, when the artist began to receive a growing number of foreign commissions, versions of the piece were made in bronze and marble by craftsmen under the sculptor's supervision. Minne first exhibited a marble version at the 1907 Venice Biennale. | RH

PROVENANCE Galerie Brockstedt, Hamburg, 1965.
EXHIBITIONS *(not necessarily the copy exhibited here) Les XX* 1890; Dresden 1901, no. 1757; Venice 1907, no. 826; Weimar 1907, no. 30; Cologne 1912, no. 620; Brussels 1920b, no. 12; Venice 1926, no. 57; Budapest 1927, no. 120; Brussels 1929b, no. 1; Brussels 1941, no. 1; Brussels 1962, no. 77; Hagen 1962, no. 1; Brussels 1969b, no. 81; New York 1980, no. 73; Ghent 1982, no. 6; Brussels 1988, no. 7; Brussels 1990b, no. 93; Ghent 1991, no. 90; Brussels 1993–1994, no. 186.
BIBLIOGRAPHY Van Puyvelde 1930, 51, ill.; Alhadeff 1982, 27–34, ill.; Boyens 1992, 237–239, ill.

1 2 February 1890, 55.
2 As quoted by A. Alhadeff, in Ghent 1982, 28.
3 *La Société Nouvelle* (1890), quoted by A. Alhadeff, in Ghent 1982, 50.

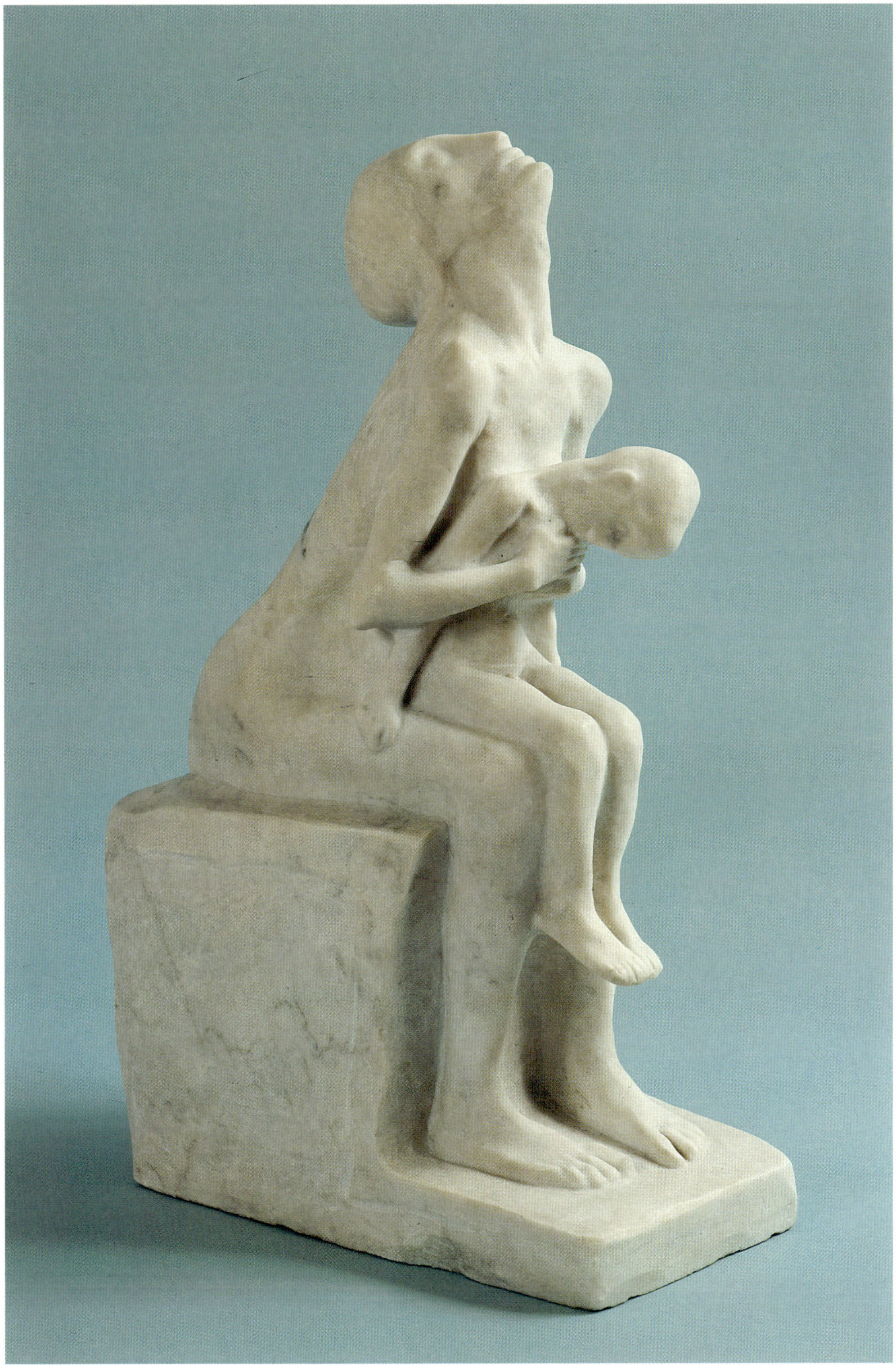

55 Sorrow. Mother weeping over her two Children

La Douleur. Mère pleurant ses deux enfants, 1888
Bronze, 65.5 x 37.5 x 56.5 cm
Signed on base: GMINNE
Musées royaux des Beaux-Arts de Belgique / Koninklijke Musea voor Schone Kunsten van België, Brussels, inv. no. 6189

This group, produced two years after *Mother mourning her Dead Child* [cat. 54] shows a grief-stricken mother figure embracing her children. One child, probably dead, is seated across her lap, while the other, slightly older child clings tightly to her. As an expression of despair, this tangle of human figures is one of George Minne's most powerful works. The image of the hunched, seated woman with long hair as a symbol of sorrow was a common one in *fin-de-siècle* art, occurring in the work of Hodler, Van Gogh and Munch, amongst others. Minne himself had previously used the figure in a drawing (Private Collection) and for his design of the cover of Grégoire Le Roy's *Mon cœur pleure d'autrefois* [see cat. 31]. A similar group, comprising a kneeling mother with long robes and flowing hair, carrying a dead child to its grave, and supported by a young girl, reappears in one of Minne's best-known drawings, *La Douleur (Sorrow)* [fig. a]. This was exhibited at the Salon des XX in 1891, and was widely reproduced from an early stage. The critic August Vermeylen described the drawing in terms that could also be applied to this sculpted group: 'A mother, enveloped in the straight folds of a long, hooded cloak, her head bowed, holds a dead child to her breast: a little girl kneels beside her, and kisses the bare feet of the body. That is all. Yet it seemed to me to be Sorrow itself. With the simplicity of a Gothic print, the group expresses all the cutting sadness of life. The ragged clothes, the lank hair, the bony hands, the emaciated, twisted bodies, the eyes dulled with sorrow, all of that wretchedness and poverty encapsulates the misery of our suffering brains and suffering flesh.'[1]

Although Minne refers in this sculpture both to the medieval tradition of the Pietà and to Rodin, as he so often did (specifically in this case to his *Death of Alcestes*), the design is wholly innovative in that it is made totally subservient to the emotion expressed. The closed character of the group, the compressed limbs, feet and heads, the simplification and exaggeration of particular elements like the large, flat hand of the mother were all aspects that Minne's contemporaries found disconcerting. Critics compared the misshapen bodies with primitive African art. Minne's work was also linked to the wooden reliefs and ceramics of Gauguin, which had been shown at Les XX in 1891. Verhaeren was one of the critics who understood and defended this primitivism on the part of the two artists: 'It seems to me that Gauguin's wooden and Minne's plaster figures are far from chance creations. They appear on the contrary to express the future. They are the step back that enables us to leap forward.'[2]

Minne showed a plaster version of the sculpture at Les XX in 1890. The work was also displayed at the Secession exhibitions in Vienna in 1900 and Berlin in 1901. A bronze version was shown at the *Internationale Kunstausstellung* in Dresden that same year. Plaster, bronze and stone versions of the work are known.

The German sculptress Käthe Kollwitz must have been familiar with this sculpture by Minne when she fashioned her *Liebespaar* (also known as *Mother and Child*) in 1913 (Nationalgalerie, Berlin). Her group is just as compact as Minne's, and we also find the characteristic pose of a figure sitting across the knees and the stress on the dangling limbs and exaggeratedly large hand. | RH

PROVENANCE Collection Elie Burthoul, Brussels, 1940.
EXHIBITIONS *(not necessarily the copy exhibited here)* Les XX 1890; Vienna 1900, no. 317; Berlin 1901, no. 1757; Dresden 1901, no. 1757; Brussels 1920b, no. 13; Rotterdam 1922, no. 1; Venice 1926, no. 57; Brussels 1929b, no. 2; Brussels 1941, no. 3; Brussels 1962, no. 78; Brussels 1969b, no. 82; Ghent 1982, no. 19; Brussels 1988, no. 8; Ghent 1990, no. 2; Brussels 1993–1994, no. 187.
BIBLIOGRAPHY Van Puyvelde 1930, 52, ill.; Alhadeff 1982, 27–34, ill.; Boyens 1992, 239–241; Hoozee *et al.* 1992, 31–32, ill.

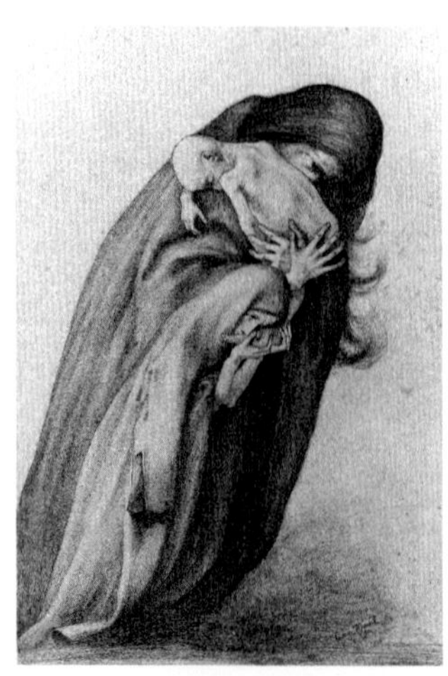

fig. a GEORGE MINNE
Sorrow, 1890, pencil on paper,
Museum voor Schone Kunsten, Ghent

1 *De Vlaamsche School* (1891), 86.
2 'Au XX', *La Nation* (20 February 1891); quoted by A. Alhadeff, in Ghent 1982, 30.

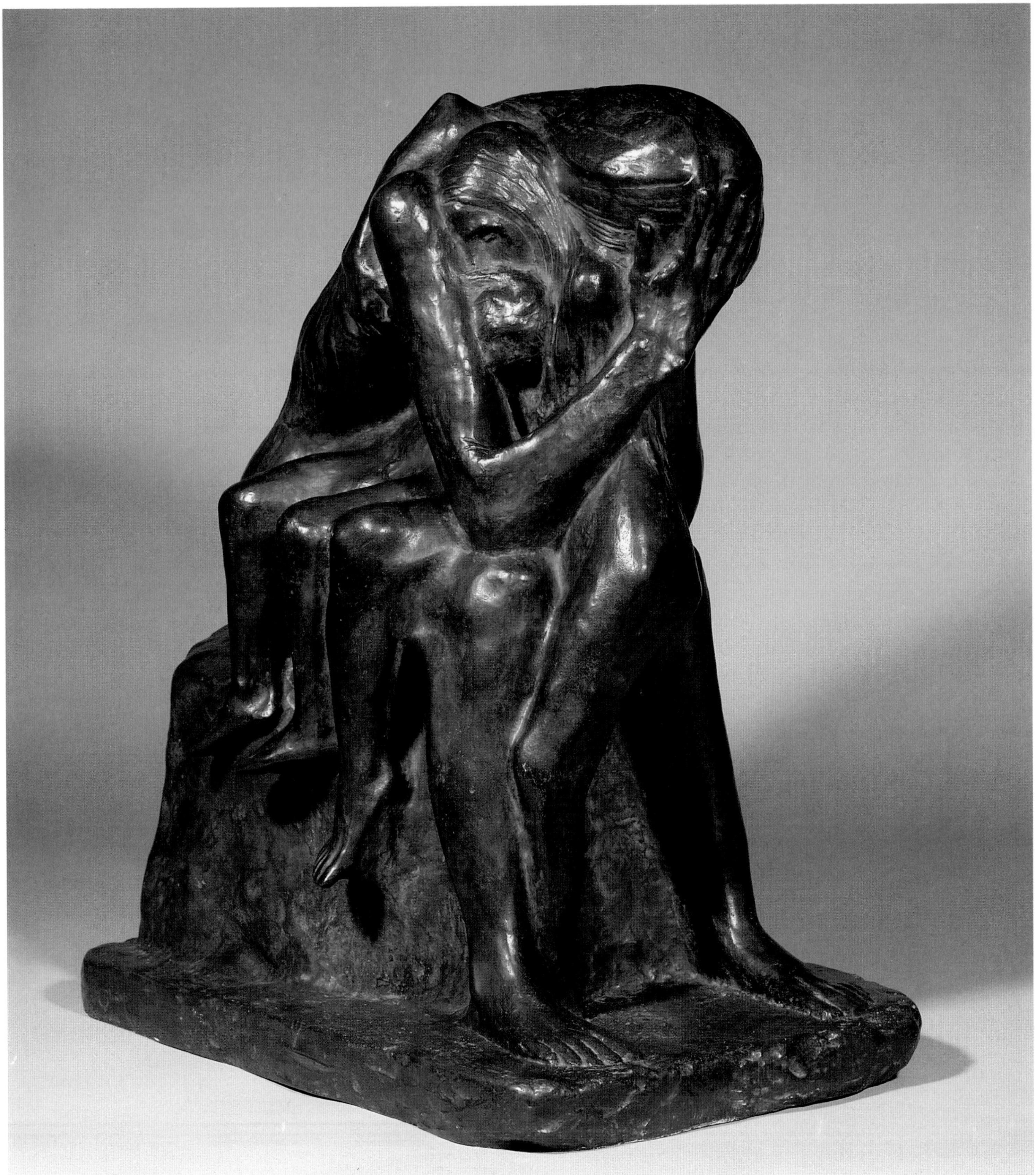

56 Three Holy Women

Les trois Saintes Femmes au Tombeau, 1896
Plaster, h. 62 cm
Private Collection

Critics referred to Minne on more than one occasion as an artist with a 'Gothic soul'. This touched on the spiritual content of his work, and the fact that he drew inspiration for themes and forms from the Middle Ages. Although the artist's entire early oeuvre is imbued with religious feeling, there are certain works in which the reference to the Middle Ages is explicit. Examples are the illustrations Minne drew for the poetry anthologies of his friends Maeterlinck, Verhaeren and Le Roy. These imitate the strong outlines and hatching of medieval woodcuts, and include images of bent figures wrapped in hooded cloaks.

The same spirit gave rise in 1894 to the sculpture, *Praying Nun*, and in 1896 to this group of three mourning women, who are entirely hidden beneath their heavy drapery. Although Minne made and exhibited both of these sculptures in plaster, the brown patina and the suggestion of the knife cutting into 'wood' on the *Three Holy Women* permit us to assume that they were conceived to be carved in wood. Minne certainly had them reproduced mainly in wood (see, for example, the group in the Musées royaux des Beaux-Arts de Belgique, Brussels), leaving the specific structure of the material clearly visible – a procedure that was later to be used frequently by the Expressionists.

Apart from Minne's book illustrations, to which this group of three holy women is related, there are virtually no other works in Minne's oeuvre that are connected to this piece. A few drawings of Pietàs (Museum voor Schone Kunsten, Ghent) are known in which similar draped figures appear, and a drawing of four nuns standing side by side and holding the body of a youth (Private Collection). The latter is probably a sketch for an illustration that was never executed. Beyond Minne's oeuvre, the group naturally refers to the *pleurants* of medieval tomb sculpture. Unlike Sluter's *pleurants,* which Minne might have known from illustrations, the robes are not developed here into a sculpturally compact ensemble. What we are given instead has more of the character of a three-dimensional drawing in which the repetition of incised lines creates a mournful rhythm.

The version shown here was made in plaster, but has been given a patina to suggest the appearance of wood. The piece comes from the collection of Grégoire Le Roy, and might be the original plaster that Minne exhibited at La Libre Esthétique in 1898. Minne subsequently sent his *Three Holy Women* to various exhibitions abroad, including the Vienna Secession in 1900, where he had already shown a version in wood. | RH

PROVENANCE Grégoire Le Roy and descendants; Galerie P. Hallet, Brussels, 1988.

EXHIBITIONS *(not necessarily the copy exhibited here)*: *La Libre Esthétique* 1898, no. 269; Vienna 1900, no. 322; The Hague 1901, no. 113; Rotterdam 1903; Weimar 1907, no. 31; Berlin 1908, no. 316; Budapest, Mücsarnok 1908–1909, no. 284; Düsseldorf 1909, no. 624; Brussels 1920b, no. 8; Rotterdam 1922, no. 18; Brussels 1929b, nos. 17, 18; Brussels 1925b, no. 84; Brussels 1941; Paris 1948a, no. 10; Brussels 1957, no. 834; Forest 1959–1960, nos. 33, 34; Hagen 1962, no. 10; Brussels 1969b, no. 83; Ghent 1982, no. 57; Brussels 1988, no. 9; Brussels 1993–1994, no. 188.

BIBLIOGRAPHY Haerens 1982, 41–48; Boyens 1992, 247, ill.

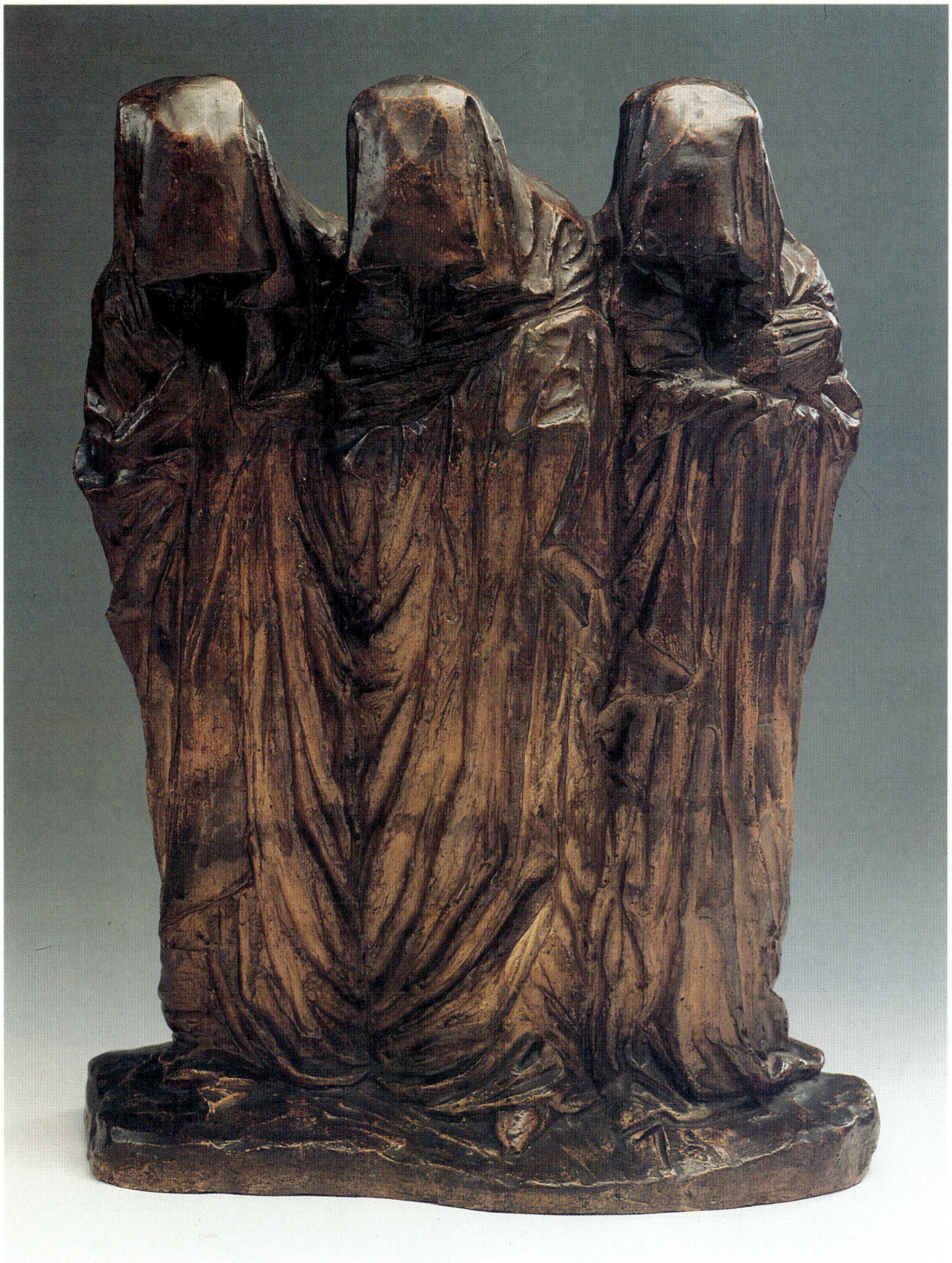

57 Boy holding a Reliquary

Le Petit Porteur de reliques, 1897
Marble, 67 x 18.5 x 38 cm
Signed on base: GMINNE
Musées royaux des Beaux-Arts de Belgique / Koninklijke Musea voor Schone Kunsten van België, Brussels, inv. no. 4789

The figure of the kneeling youth occupied Minne for several years. By 1886 he had already produced a little group comprising a kneeling man and woman, known by the titles *Adam and Eve* and *Prayer*. Kneeling and grieving figures, who often embrace or shield themselves ineffectually with their arms, appear in the sketchbooks he was using in around 1890 (Museum voor Schone Kunsten, Ghent). In 1895 Minne conceived a kneeling *St John the Baptist* [fig. a] who holds his head in both hands. This was followed by a nude, kneeling youth with crossed arms, both hands resting on his shoulders, called the *Kneeling Boy* in 1896 and this *Boy holding a Reliquary* in 1897.

Once again Minne is interpreting on a small scale, and with his characteristically delicate, fragile forms, a figure type derived from medieval art, but which demonstrates parallels with similar figures by Rodin. However, the contrast between Minne's 'caryatid' and Rodin's more muscular specimen is striking. Minne's sculpture is far more directly related to comparable representations of kneeling figures by such Symbolist painters as Filiger and Hodler, who represented kneeling figures graphically.

Minne took his exploration of the theme of the kneeling youth a stage further in 1898, when he omitted from the piece the religious afterthought of the reliquary. The resultant sculpture, Minne's famous *Kneeling Youth*, emphasises the essentially decorative, elongated form, made up of straight lines and curves. Finally, he took five identical copies of this kneeling figure and grouped them around a basin to form the *Fountain with Kneeling Youths* that he exhibited at La Libre Esthétique in Brussels in 1899, and at the Vienna Secession in 1900. A marble version was produced in 1905 for Karl Ernst Osthaus for the entrance hall of his museum in Hagen (now in the Folkwang Museum, Essen).

The various versions of Minne's kneeling youths became known in the leading artistic centres of Paris, Vienna and Berlin, through international exhibitions and dealers specializing in Art Nouveau. Their delicate physique and introspective mood are echoed in the work of Klimt, Kokoschka, Schiele, Lehmbruck and Maillol.

Versions of the *Boy holding a Reliquary* are known in plaster, bronze, marble and granite. Minne developed the habit later in his life of remaking certain earlier sculptures on a somewhat larger scale and with a greater degree of naturalism. These include a bigger version of the present sculpture, of which many bronze examples exist. This later version, however, lacks the power of its small, predecessor of 1897. | RH

PROVENANCE Acquired in 1926.

EXHIBITIONS *(not necessarily the copy exhibited here)*: Vienna 1900, no. 328; Düsseldorf 1909, no. 1169; Hagen 1912, no. 38; Brussels 1920b, no. 1; Rotterdam 1922, no. 8; Brussels 1925a, no. 51; Brussels 1929b, nos. 21, 22, 23; Brussels 1941, no. 15; Paris 1948a, no. 11; Paris 1960-1961, no. 449; Brussels 1969b, no. 84; Ghent 1979, no. 68; Ghent 1982, no. 61 en 62; Brussels 1988, no. 10; Brussels 1993–1994, no. 190.

BIBLIOGRAPHY Meier-Graefe 1898, 257–264, ill.; Van Puyvelde 1930, 57, ill.; Haesaerts 1965, 107–108, ill.; De Keyser 1972, 20–23; Elsen 1974, 29–30, ill.; Kultermann 1977, 144–152, ill.; Hünecke 1980, 605–609, ill.; Boyens 1992, 248–253, ill.

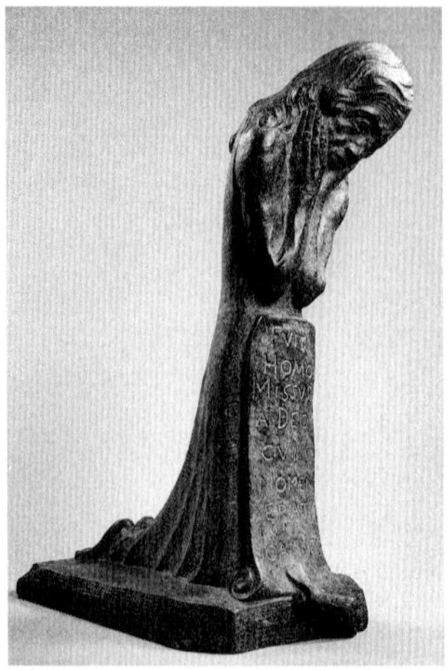

fig. a GEORGE MINNE
St John the Baptist, 1895, stone,
Museum voor Schone Kunsten, Ghent

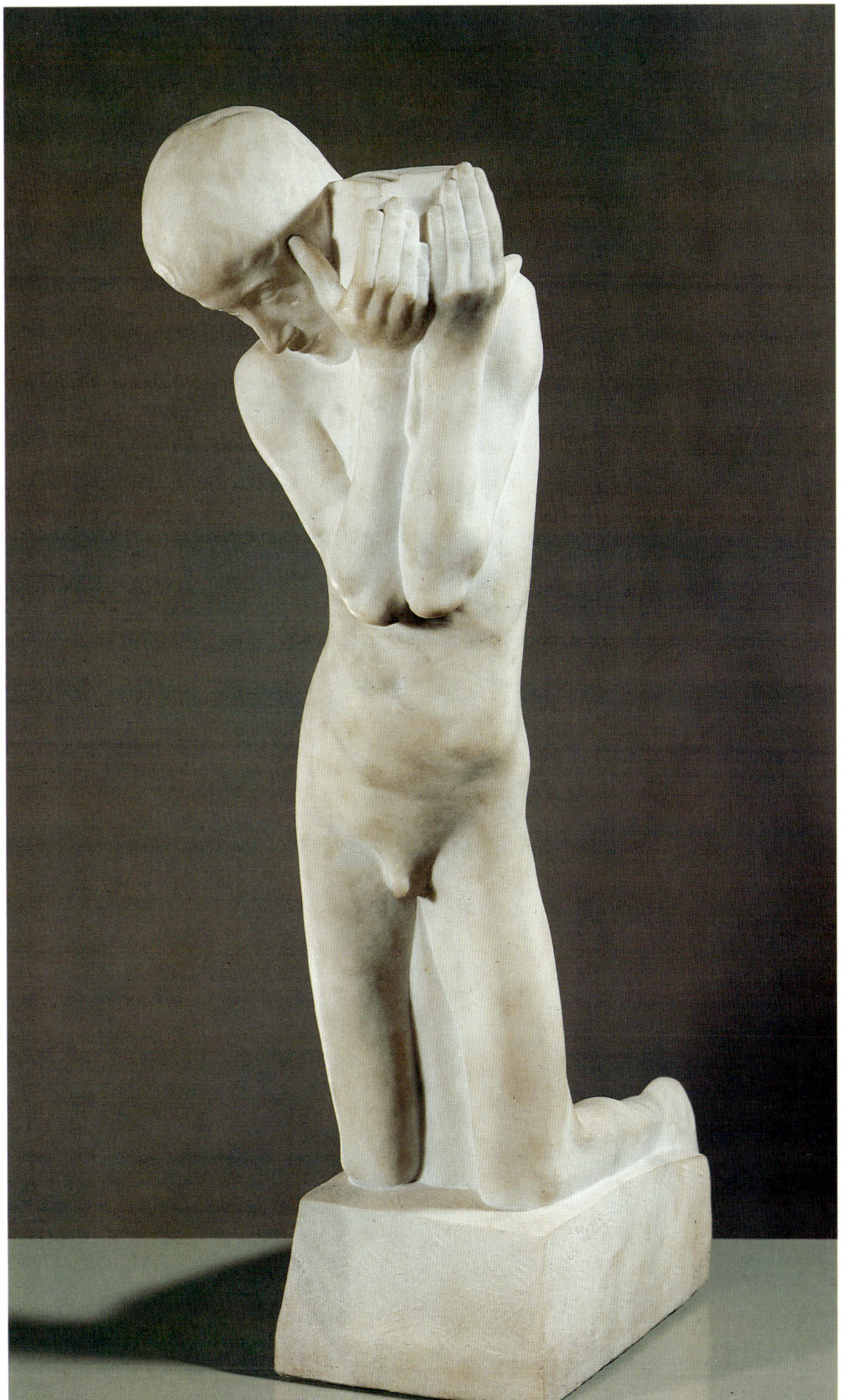

George Morren

EKEREN 1868 – BRUSSELS 1941

Born outside Antwerp, George Morren first studied painting at the Antwerp Academy of Fine Arts. He was living in Belgium when Seurat's *La Grande Jatte* (1884–1887; Art Institute of Chicago) made its Brussels début at the 1887 Salon des XX. Unlike Willy Finch (q.v.) and Henry van de Velde (q.v.), however, Morren apparently did not attempt the Neo-Impressionist technique during the late 1880s. At the suggestion of his friend Emile Claus (q.v.), Morren moved to Paris around 1888, where he studied with Alfred Roll and Eugène Carrière. Though neither of his teachers were associated with the movement, Morren probably became familiar with Neo-Impressionism during his Paris sojourn.

By January 1892 Morren had returned to Antwerp and signed the charter for the new Association pour l'Art. That year he also participated in the annual exhibition of Als Ik Kan. His first one-man show took place in 1894 at the Zaal Verlat in Antwerp. During this period Morren produced divisionist paintings, as well as some sculptures and designs for the decorative arts. Critical response during this period indicates that the young artist flirted with a variety of styles.

After 1900, however, Morren's painting was dominated by intimate, luminous interiors and portraits of young women rendered in an Impressionist manner reminiscent of Renoir. He also exhibited with La Libre Esthétique periodically from 1895 until the First World War. In 1904 Morren joined Claus, Adrien-Joseph Heymans (1839–1921), and others in founding the group, Vie et Lumière. Around 1910 Morren decided to settle in France at St Germain-en-Laye; he spent his summers in southern France. During the late 1920s Morren moved back to Belgium and continued his painting and exhibition activities in Brussels. He died in 1941 and was the subject of a memorial show at the Palais des Beaux-Arts the following year. | EL

SUMMARY BIBLIOGRAPHY

George Morren, Palais des Beaux-Arts, Brussels 1942 (Catalogue by M. P. Buyssens); *George Morren* (exhibition-related publication by C. Bernard) Galerie La Sirène, Brussels 1950; S. Goyens de Heusch, *L'Impressionnisme et le Fauvisme en Belgique*, Antwerp 1988, 266–270; E. Wardwell Lee, in *Neo-Impressionists*, Rijksmuseum Vincent van Gogh, Amsterdam 1988, 118–119.

58 Sunday Afternoon

Dimanche après-midi, 1892
Oil on canvas, 50,8 x 74,5 cm
Signed and dated bottom right: George Morren / 1892
Indianapolis Museum of Art, The Holliday Collection, Indianapolis, inv. no. 79.278

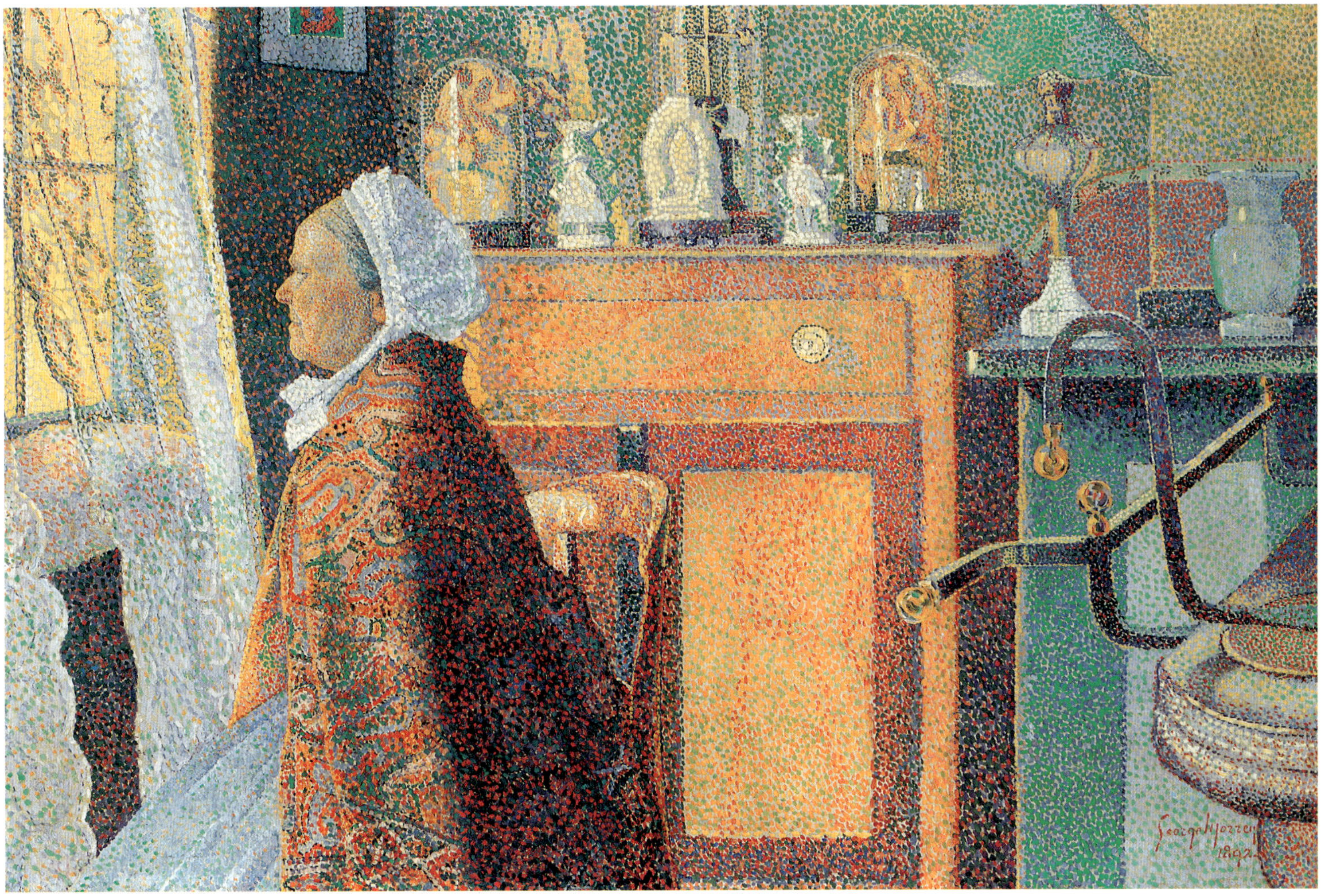

In the silent, private realm of *Sunday Afternoon*, Morren takes a traditional Belgian theme and recasts it in the language of Neo-Impressionism. With its sense of solitude and intense concentration, Morren's interior seems created in the same spirit as Khnopff's *Listening to Schumann* of 1883 [cat. 28]. Henry van de Velde provided a precedent for the Neo-Impressionist treatment of this theme in *Woman at the Window* (1889; Koninklijk Museum voor Schone Kunsten, Antwerp), which Morren could have seen in Paris in 1890. And Paul Signac applied pointillist brushwork to a comfortable middle-class interior in his painting *Breakfast* (Rijksmuseum Kröller-Müller, Otterlo) of 1886–1887. Morren also used the technique for *Dutch Interior* (Josefowitz Collection), a small watercolour of 1892 that parodies seventeenth-century genre scenes of women sewing by a window.

Since Morren was back in Antwerp by January 1892, *Sunday Afternoon* must have been among the first works created after his return from France. Its complex composition made the painting a taxing subject for divisionist treatment. As one Belgian critic warned after viewing Signac's *Breakfast* at Les XX: 'It is perilous beyond all other effort to undertake such a canvas, in full light filtered and altered and infinitely affected by the many local colours of the furniture, the clothing and the walls.'[1] Morren accepted the challenge and even set himself the ambitious task of rendering the pattern of a paisley shawl in both shadow and bright light.

In *Sunday Afternoon,* Morren employs his own very individual sense of colour rather than a strict adherence to Neo-Impressionist theories. To render the sunlight penetrating the window, he restricts his palette to variations of yellow, as if he could capture light and warmth on a pane of glass. Morren's unorthodox method of adding brilliance to shaded zones is demonstrated in the upper left corner of the room, where he pairs dots of orange with dots of blue, its complementary colours, to tint the darker wall. His dotted brushwork is similar in facture to that of contemporaneous Dutch Neo-Impressionists such as H. P. Bremmer (1871–1956) and Jan Vijlbrief (1868–1895).

Attentive to Neo-Impressionism's emphasis on stable compositions, Morren succeeded in bringing a sense of order to the array of still-life elements. The straight lines and right angles of the room interact with the curves of the woman's form and her collection of domes and porcelains. A strangely energetic effect is added to the motionless scene by the twisted rods at the right, which are the drying racks of a stove. Truncating the picture with a partial view of the stove, Morren introduces an unsettling note to the domestic scene.

Sunday Afternoon is a serious, if idiosyncratic, Neo-Impressionist effort, and the canvas is curiously absent from records of Morren's early exhibitions in Brussels or Antwerp. More than thirty years later, however, *Sunday Afternoon* was the only Neo-Impressionist work in Morren's 1926 retrospective at the Galerie Giroux, Brussels. The critics cited its historical value, viewing *Sunday Afternoon* as a point of departure for the Impressionist paintings that eventually dominated Morren's oeuvre.[2] Today *Sunday Afternoon* survives as Morren's finest Neo-Impressionist work, far more distinctive than the *intimiste* subjects that followed it. | EL

PROVENANCE Mme Dagieu-Sully, Paris; Stephen Higgons, Paris; Hammer Galleries, New York, 1963; W. J. Holliday, 1964.

EXHIBITIONS Brussels 1926b, no. 1; Paris 1955, no. 48; New York 1963–1964, ill.; New York 1968, no. 132, ill.

BIBLIOGRAPHY *L'Etoile belge*, 23 February 1926; 'La Vie artistique à Bruxelles, George Morren', *La Flandre libérale*, 28 February 1926; *Le Thyrse*, 7 March 1926; 'L'Art à Bruxelles', *Neptune*, 12 March 1926; L. Jottrand, 'Le Peintre George Morren', *Savoir et beauté* 6:7 (July 1926), 195.

1 'Le Salon des XX, L'Ancien et le nouvel Impressionnisme', *L'Art moderne* 8:6 (1888), 42 (trans.).

2 See *Le Thyrse*, 7 March 1926; *L'Etoile belge*, 23 February 1926.

Auguste Oleffe

SAINT-JOSSE-TEN-NOODE 1867 – UCCLE 1931

Auguste Oleffe began his career as a draughtsman and lithographer at a printing firm in Brussels. He attended the Academy at Saint-Josse-ten-Noode, and also followed a basic course at the Brussels Academy of Fine Arts between 1883 and 1886. Oleffe made his début at the triennial Ghent Salon in 1890. His early paintings were of social-realist subjects rendered in sombre colours. He spent some time in Paris in 1895. That same year he began to work at Nieuwpoort on the Belgian coast, where he was to return frequently. The style of the seascapes and scenes of fishermen he produced there gradually became freer in handling. Oleffe was one of the co-founders of the group Le Labeur (Brussels, 1898), together with Fernand Schirren (1874–1944), Louis Thévenet (1874–1930) and Jan Stobbaerts (1838–1914). As the name suggests, members of this group initially concentrated on naturalistic subjects, scenes of men at work, usually handled in a realist technique, although this came increasingly under the influence of Impressionism and Luminism.

The generosity of an admirer, the Brussels art-collector Henri van Cutsem [see also cat. 77], allowed Oleffe to settle comfortably in Ouderghem in 1906. His preferred subject matter at this point in his career was open-air scenes, especially sunny gardens full of light effects. He liked to work on a large scale. He also painted people, interiors and still lifes. Oleffe gradually became the mentor of several young artists, including Rik Wouters (1882–1916), Jean Brusselmans (1884–1953) and Willem Paerels (1878–1962), who came to visit him at his home. These artists later became known as the 'Brabant Fauvists'. Oleffe was first invited to exhibit at the 1906 Salon de La Libre Esthétique. In 1914 it was his turn to recommend three artists for inclusion in the exhibition: Jos Albert (1886–1981), Médard Maertens (1875–1946) and Philibert Cockx (1879–1949), all of whom were students at the free academy L'Effort with which Oleffe was closely connected.

Despite his early training as a lithographer, Oleffe only took up engraving relatively late in his career. He showed a number of etchings at the Salon des Indépendants in 1908, some of whose subjects were derived from paintings which he considered to have been successful. These works combine the classic line etching with soft-ground etching and aquatint. Some of the lines were deliberately cut to a considerable depth, which had the effect of increasing the contrast between pale and dark tones and hence enhancing the expressiveness of the print.

The later years of Oleffe's career were a period of consolidation. He was awarded the National Prize for Painting in 1926, and two important exhibitions were mounted at the Galerie Giroux in Brussels (1920) and Kunst van Heden in Antwerp (1925). Oleffe was appointed teacher of landscape art at the Higher Institute of Fine Arts in Antwerp, but died barely a year later. | NH

SUMMARY BIBLIOGRAPHY

S. Pierron, 'Auguste Oleffe', *Neptune* (19 April 1925), s.p.; M. Nyns, *Auguste Oleffe*, Brussels 1964; H. Schots, *Auderghem et ses peintres*, Brussels 1978; S. Goyens de Heusch, *L'Impressionnisme et le Fauvisme en Belgique* Antwerp 1988; *L'Impressionnisme et le Fauvisme en Belgique*, Musée d'Ixelles, Brussels 1990 (Catalogue by S. Goyens de Heusch); *Fin de siècle. Dessins, pastels et estampes en Belgique de 1885 à 1905*, Galerie CGER, Brussels 1991.

59 Fisherman's Widow in Nieuwpoort

Veuve de pêcheur à Nieuport, c. 1898–1904
Oil on canvas, 101 x 155 cm
Hôtel Charlier, Brussels, inv. no. 299/1964

Louis Artan de Saint-Martin (q.v.), together with Hippolyte Boulenger (1837–1874), was one of the first nineteenth-century Realist Belgian artists to discover the Flemish coast as a source of pictorial motifs. He was quickly followed by others, including Auguste Oleffe who started to visit the fishing port of Nieuwpoort from 1895. The latter was not merely interested in exploring the coast, but also in finding peace and isolation with his wife, far from the capital city.

Oleffe's Nieuwpoort paintings capture the grandeur of the sea. He also made portraits of his friends, often with maritime landscapes – like the harbour mouth with its moored fishing boats – in the background. He used the same setting for several monumental compositions showing fishermen and their wives, including *Twilight of Life* (1904; Hôtel Charlier, Brussels) and *Funeral in Nieuwpoort* (1901; Musées royaux des Beaux-Arts de Belgique, Brussels). *Fisherman's Widow in Nieuwpoort* belongs to a series of brooding portraits in which Oleffe expressed his deep and intense sympathy for the fisherfolk and their harsh existence.

Oleffe's obvious concern to record the harshness of the lives of this fishing community, together with his use of a predominantly monochromatic, sombre palette suggest that he was aware of the records of Breton fishing communities being created by such artists in France as Charles Cottet (1863–1925) and Lucien Simon (1881–1945). All these artists were drawn to these apparently timeless communities, wholly engaged in a battle with the sea, and all these recorded them with an intensity of observation which conveyed the sense of profound fatalism which pervaded them. Oleffe's somewhat loose, gestural application of paint possibly brings his work technically closer to that of Lucien Simon than to the dryer, more austere brushwork of Cottet. | NH

PROVENANCE Collection Van Cutsem; Guillaume Charlier.
EXHIBITIONS Brussels 1949; Knokke 1949; Ostend 1951; Charleroi 1952; Ouderghem 1972; Ouderghem 1979.
BIBLIOGRAPHY M. Vlaminck, *Een plejade kunstschilders in Nieuwpoort van 1835 tot 1938* (Dilbeekse Cahiers), Dilbeek 1990.

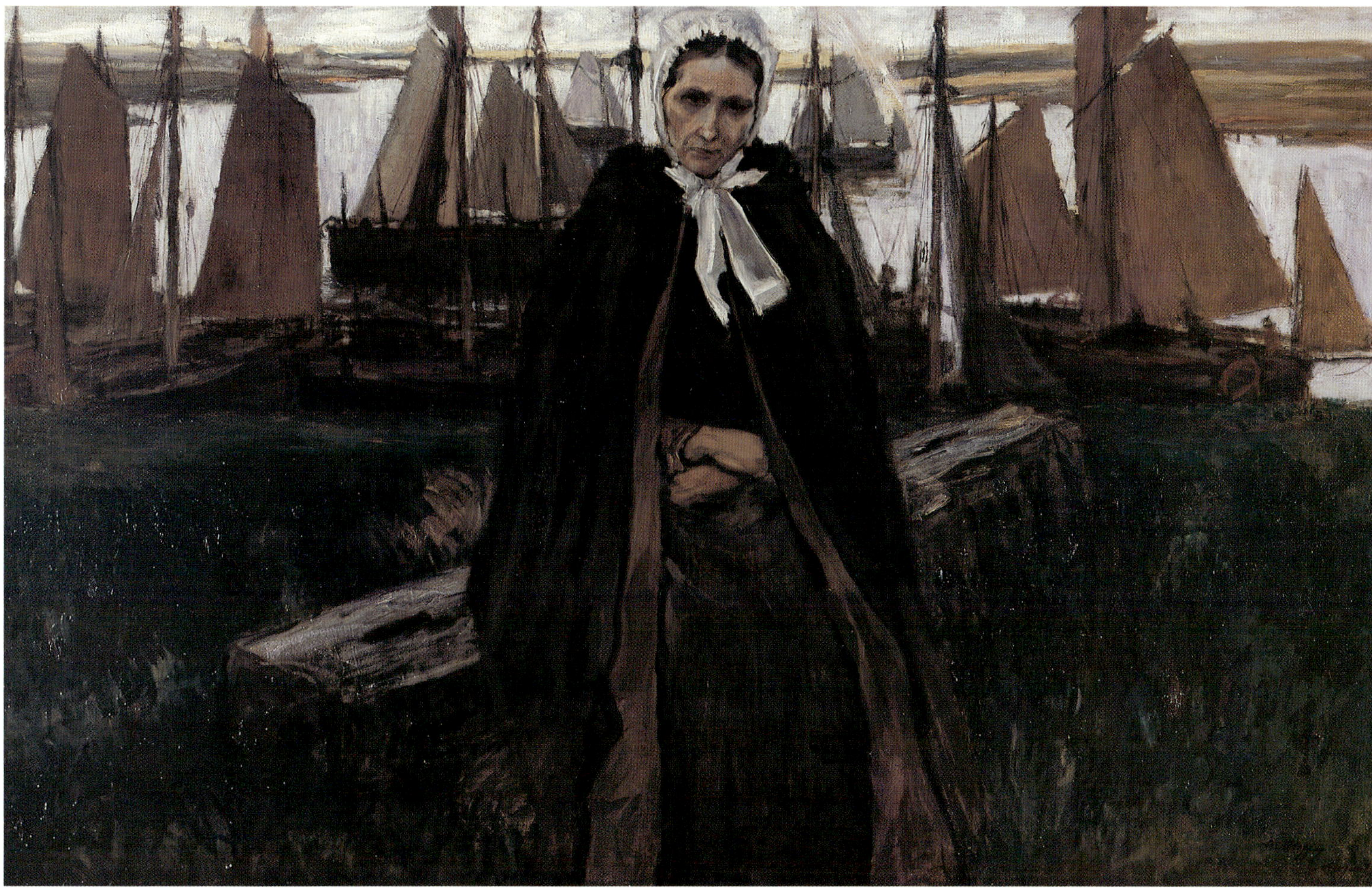

Félicien Rops

NAMUR 1833 – ESSONNES 1898

Félicien Rops was born in Namur into a middle-class industrial family on 7 July 1833. He enrolled at the Academy of Fine Arts around 1850. In 1853 he moved to Brussels and attended the Faculty of Law at the Université Libre de Bruxelles. He belonged to the bohemian student scene, and was a member of the Société des Joyeux, founded and led by the writer Charles de Coster. Rops published his first cartoons in the pamphlet put out by the Club des Crocodiles and also in the satirical magazine *Le Charivari belge.*

In 1856 Rops launched his own magazine, the *Uylenspiegel,* a 'magazine of artistic and literary frolics'. The title alluded to the hero of Flemish resistance against the Spanish occupation in the sixteenth century, whose adventures had been recounted by Charles de Coster (1867). He also supplied illustrations such as the *Médaille de Waterloo* (1858) and the *Dernière incarnation de Vautrin* (1862), for periodicals which made his name known abroad. At the same time, he produced frontispieces for a large number of literary works and engaged in *plein-air* painting in company with Louis Dubois (1830–1880) and Louis Artan de Saint-Martin (q.v.).

Rops's meeting with the French poet, Charles Baudelaire, in 1864, had a profound influence on his life and output: his iconography of political criticism and the lampooning of the bourgeoisie was replaced by a bitter-sweet vision of society dominated by Woman – frivolous, depraved or fallen – and Her two accomplices, Death, as depicted in the *danses macabres* of the seventeenth century, and the Devil. Rops settled permanently in Paris in 1874, joining his mistresses, the Duluc sisters, who owned a fashion house for which Rops made a great number of studies. It was in Paris, between 1878 and 1882, that he produced his greatest works, and these bear witness to the maturity of his talents: *The Temptation of St Anthony* (1878), *Pornocrates* (1878), *Les Diaboliques* (1879) and *Les Sataniques* (1882). From 1879 he also travelled widely – to Hungary (1879), Spain (1880), the United States (1885 and 1887) and Canada (1887), bringing back with him a number of original studies. Forever dissatisfied, doubting his talent and technical skill, Rops continued to experiment until his death, perfecting his art and studying new methods of engraving, often in the company of Armand Rassenfosse (1862–1934), with whom he invented a transparent *vernis mou* (soft-ground etching technique), 'Ropsenfosse'. During the last years of his life Rops suffered from eye problems and retired to his property 'La Demi-Lune' at Essonnes. However, he took part in countless exhibitions, including Les XX (1889, 1893) and La Libre Esthétique (1896, 1897). Félicien Rops died at Essonnes on 23 August 1898. | BF

SUMMARY BIBLIOGRAPHY

E. Ramiro, *Félicien Rops,* Paris 1905; C. Lemonnier, *Félicien Rops, l'homme et l'artiste,* Paris 1908; O. Mascha, *Félicien Rops und sein werk,* Munich 1910; L. Pierard, *Félicien Rops* (Monographies de l'Art belge) Antwerp 1952; Charles Brison, *Pornocrates, an introduction to the Life and Work of Félicien Rops (1833–1898),* London 1969; L. van Maris, *Félicien Rops, over kunst, melancholie & perversiteit,* Amsterdam 1982; *Félicien Rops 1833–1898,* Musées royaux des Beaux-Arts de Belgique and Le Botanique, Brussels / Musée des Arts Décoratifs, Paris / Musée des Beaux-Arts Jules Chéret, Nice, 1985; R. L. Delevoy, G. Lascault, J.-P. Verheggen and Guy Cuvelier, *Félicien Rops,* Brussels 1985; Th. Zeno, *Les muses sataniques. Félicien Rops. Œuvre graphique et lettres choisies,* Brussels 1985; G. Cuvelier, *Félicien Rops au Musée de Namur* (Musées vivants de Wallonie et de Bruxelles), Brussels, Liège 1987 ; *Rops et la modernité (Œuvres de la Communauté française de Belgique)*, Musée d'Ixelles, Brussels 1991.

60 Snow at Thozée

Neige à Thozée, 1885
Oil on canvas, 42 x 67.5 cm
Collection Crédit Communal de Belgique / Collectie Gemeentekrediet van België, Brussels

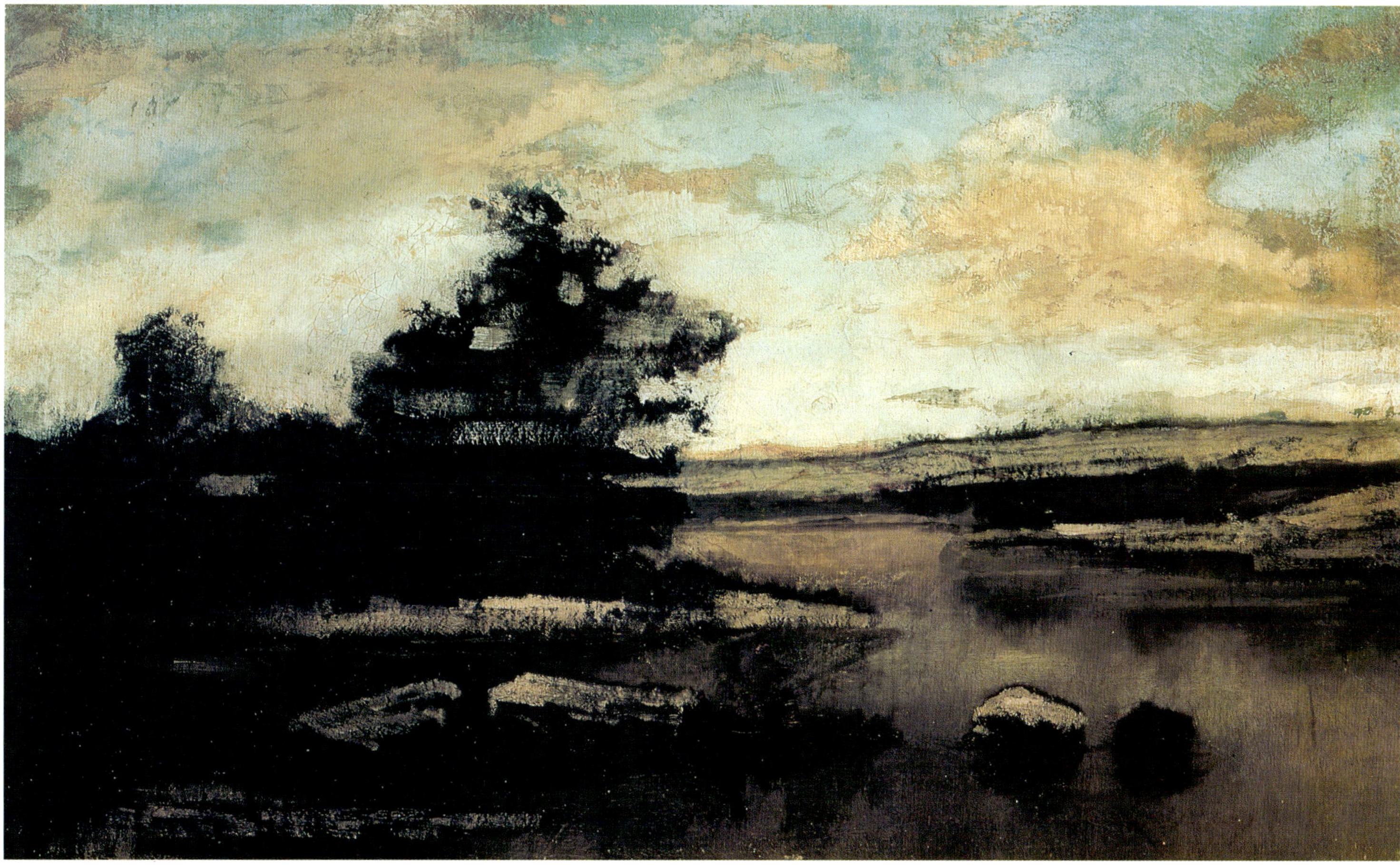

In 1857 Rops married Charlotte Polet de Faveaux, the daughter of a Namur magistrate. The Polets had a family estate in Thozée, near Mettet, where Rops liked to stay regularly until the couple's (unofficial) separation in 1874. He often painted Thozée and the surrounding area – Bambois, Molignée and Scry – and invited friends, amongst them Charles Baudelaire and his publisher Auguste Poulet-Malassis, to visit him there.

This is the context in which the present painting should be placed. The artist does not present us with a snowy landscape in the classic sense, but an impression of a setting where the snow has already largely disappeared. The horizon functions as the separating line between light and dark. The top has the cool blue of an icy winter's day, while the bottom comprises a landscape in semi-darkness with a few slightly lighter reflections of the snow on the water's edge and the big stones in the water.

Rops was co-founder of the 'Colonie d'Anseremme', which brought together artists and writers during holiday periods at the Auberge des Artistes in Anseremme between 1868 and c. 1880. The writers included such members of the literary avant-garde in the 1880s and 1890s as Eugène Demolder, Camille Lemonnier, Georges Rodenbach and Emile Verhaeren, and the artists Alphonse Asselbergs (1839–1916), Théodore Baron (1840–1899), Joseph Coosemans (1828–1904), Louis Dubois (1830–1880) and Pericles Pantazis (1849–1884).

Rops also painted frequently on the Flemish North Sea coast. He owned a villa called De Schuit in Knokke, whose walls he decorated with views of the surrounding landscape. The building was demolished in 1978. He also brought back fluently painted landscapes and seascapes from his visits to the coast on the French side of the border and his frequent foreign trips. He evolved in these works from a sombre realism, influenced by Courbet, to a bright Impressionism. It is almost impossible to believe that these beautiful landscapes are by the same man who exposed the dark side and taboos of Western society in *Pornocrates*, *Mors Syphylitica* and the series *Les Sataniques*. | NH

PROVENANCE A. Taevernier, Ghent, bt. 1964.
EXHIBITIONS Brussels 1969; Stavelot 1974; Liège 1981, no. 47; Albi 1985, no. 39; Brussels 1989, no. 5; Paris 1990; Luxembourg 1993, no. 79.
BIBLIOGRAPHY Cuvelier 1987; R. Marlier and F. Safin-Crahay, in Brussels, Waregem 1981, 61.

61 Robbery and Prostitution dominate the World

Le Vol et la Prostitution dominent le monde, c. 1880
Watercolour and pencil on paper, 24,5 x 17 cm
Signed bottom right: F. Rops; inscribed upper left: Le Vol et la Prostitution dominent le monde;
second, extremely faint inscription: en bon souvenir
Collection Patrick Derom, Brussels

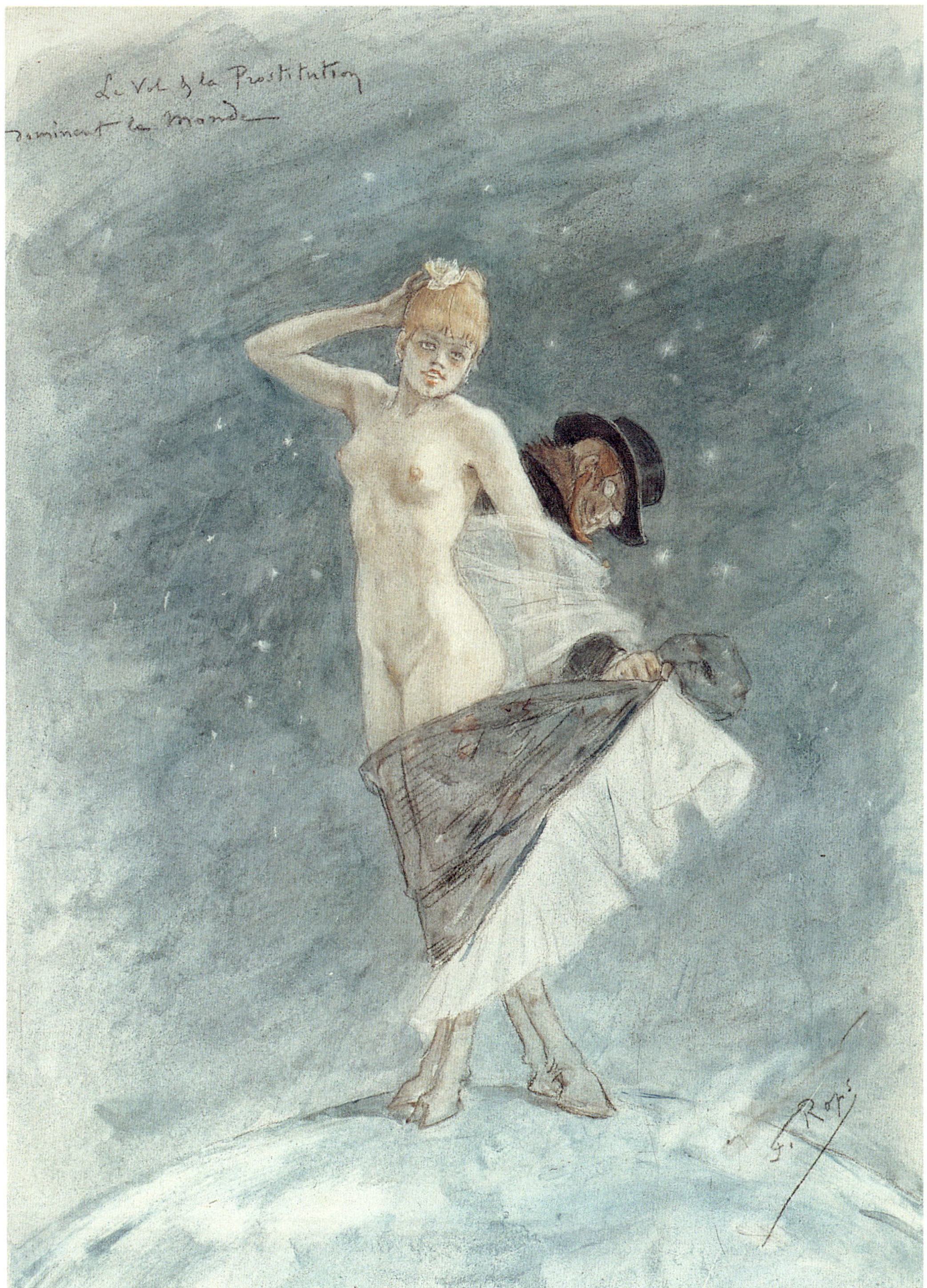

In 1879 Félicien Rops, who had been living in Paris for almost five years, began illustration of Jules Barbey d'Aurevilly's *Les Diaboliques*, the first edition of which had appeared in 1874, also in Paris. This series of illustrations – which turns out to be more of an expression of the atmosphere of the stories rather than a pictorial account of each of the episodes – is made up of one plate per story plus one preface and two postfaces.[1] The two latter pictures are variations on a single theme – *Prostitution and Madness dominate the World.* They present, in turn, a blond and a brunette girl next to a grinning figure in a clown's hat who, with a brisk gesture, uncovers the young woman's abdomen and pudenda. The tucked-up dress reveals goat's feet, thus betraying the diabolic nature of the couple. An initial set of ten little etchings[2] was published by Lemerre in Paris in 1886. Rops later produced some large-scale *vernis mous*[3] for admirers of his work, and these include a third variant of the postface, in this case, *Robbery and Prostitution dominate the World.* It features the same naked woman of easy virtue, 'bare to the thighs, proffering an ugly yet beautiful face with the provocative charm of a drunken *garçonne*, wild eyes rounded and mouth open, letting out filthy cries and jeering at the skies, and at the same time adjusting her hair with a flick of the wrist'.[4] Her cloven-footed companion, meanwhile, has exchanged the attributes of the medieval fool for a hat and pince-nez.

The watercolour presented here was probably a preliminary study for the heliography illustrating Camille Lemonnier's monograph.[5] Technically, they show similarities with the finished drawings for the collection commissioned by the art-lover and bibliophile Jules Noilly[6] and entitled *Cent légers croquis sans prétention pour réjouir les honestes gens* (One Hundred Light and Unpretentious Sketches to delight Decent People). In iconographical terms, these *pièces galantes* present the theme, drawn directly from Baudelaire, of the corrupt, perverse and destructive woman to whom man is nothing but a puppet. In the wake of this commission, the artist planned to produce a second volume, *L'Album du diable*,[7] which would have contained more powerful erotic pieces and accorded a greater place to the demoniac presence. This album never saw the light of day, especially since, from 1879, Rops was working on *Les Diaboliques*, the preface and three postfaces of which mark an important stage heralding *Les Sataniques*, this 'curious collection and rare book'[8] in which the Namur-born artist presents an extreme and very dark view of the links binding the devil to the race of women, servants but also high priestesses of his cult.

The work presented in this exhibition is thus one of the landmarks in Rops's criticism of the bourgeoisie, the victims of an evil – prostitution – which they themselves had engendered and which Rops was to study in depth throughout his œuvre. | BF

PROVENANCE Sale Antwerp, Campo, 14–15 October 1975, no. 107.
EXHIBITIONS Lokeren 1975; Frankfurt 1988, no. 194.

1 Brussels, Paris, Nice 1985, 134–139.
2 The set includes nine engravings by Félicien Rops, the preface, a plate illustrating each of the six short stories, and two postfaces, the whole being preceded by a portrait of Jules Barbey d'Aurevilly engraved by Rajon. Each plate approximately 6 x 8 x 9 cm. See M. Exsteens, *L'œuvre gravé et lithographié de Félicien Rops*, Paris 1928, III, nos. 505–513.
3 These measure approximately 16,5 x 23,5 cm. See M. Exsteens, *op.cit.*, II, nos. 425–434.
4 J.K. Huysmans, 'L'Œuvre érotique de F. Rops', *La Plume* 172 (15 June 1896) Paris, 400–401.
5 Lemonnier 1908.
6 On the bibliophile Jules Noilly, see Brussels, Paris, Nice 1985, 121; T. Zeno, *Les muses sataniques – Félicien Rops – œuvre graphique et lettres choisies*, Brussels 1985, 86–89; and V. Leblanc, *Note sur les cent légers croquis sans prétention pour réjouir les honestes gens 1878–1881*, text presented at the seminar 'Rops et la Modernité' organized at the Centre Wallonie-Bruxelles in Paris on 15 February 1992 and published in *Félicien Rops Opere grafiche*, Quaderni di Villa dei Cedri, Bellinzona 1992, 39–51.
7 Leblanc, *op.cit.*, 49–51.
8 Letter from Félicien Rops to Octave Uzanne, quoted in Brussels, Paris, Nice 1985, 216.

Herman Schlobach

BRUSSELS 1864 – NONNENHORN (BAVARIA) 1951

Herman ('Willy') Schlobach was the son of German parents. He trained at the Academy of Fine Arts, Brussels (1878–1883), and at the Academy of Saint-Josse-ten-Noode, a district of Brussels. His fellow students at the latter included Henry de Groux (1867–1930) Auguste Oleffe (q.v.) and Georges Lemmen (q.v.). His early paintings were realist in style, treated with a sombre palette. In c. 1882–1883 he met James Ensor (q.v.), Frantz Charlet (1862–1928), Jan Toorop (1858–1928) and Théo van Rysselberghe (q.v.). They exhibited together at the group salons mounted by L'Essor. He also showed *Deserted Road through the Dunes* (shown at Les XX 1884, no. 3) and *A Barge* at the Ghent Salon in 1883. Schlobach joined Les XX shortly after its foundation in October 1883. The works he showed there from 1884 to 1887 were primarily landscape subjects, portraits, genre scenes and still lifes with Japanese weaponry. Deeply affected, as were his fellow *vingtistes*, by the work of Georges Seurat, Schlobach submitted to the 1888 Salon des XX a group of works entitled *Différentes impressions de couleur et lumière* (*Different Impressions of Colour and Light*). These represented exercises in Neo-Impressionism. Signac, Seurat's principal French follower, considered Schlobach had to be the Belgian artist who had best adopted the spirit of Neo-Impressionism. However, Schlobach had abandoned the technique by 1889.

He visited London frequently between 1884 and 1887, accompanied on occasions by his friend and fellow member of Les XX, Jan Toorop. They concentrated on studying the work of J. M. W. Turner. The Pre-Raphaelites also made a strong impression on Schlobach. From 1887 he began to spend an increasing amount of time in London, and life in that city became his preferred motif, generally executed in a mixed pastel and gouache technique. Schlobach's admiration for the literary works of the 'proto-Symbolist' poet Charles Baudelaire and of the Belgian Symbolist Emile Verhaeren gave these works a Symbolist charge, through which they transcended the mere representation of everyday reality.

Schlobach exhibited at the Salons de La Libre Esthétique from 1902 to 1914, showing paintings which had adopted an Impressionist handling of paint. In c. 1910 he joined the Luminist artists' society, Vie et Lumière. He exhibited two coastal landscapes at the *Ausstellung Belgischer Kunst* at the Sezessionshaus in Berlin in 1908, when he also organized an exhibition that toured several German cities, including Leipzig (Galerie P. H. Beyer und Sohn). This included work by Finch (q.v.), Lemmen (q.v.) and himself. The following year his work also featured with that of Finch and Lemmen at the Bouté gallery in Brussels.

Schlobach remained in Brussels during the First World War, but felt obliged to leave Belgium in 1918 because of the more pronounced anti-German atmosphere. He settled in Nonnenhorn on Lake Constance in Bavaria, a picturesque setting that Schlobach painted on many occasions. He reputedly became a supporter of National-Socialism. | NH

SUMMARY BIBLIOGRAPHY

G. Le Roy, S. Boute, 'Willy Schlobach', *L'Art moderne* (31 October 1909); *Schilders van oud-Knokke*, Knokke 1981; *L'Impressionnisme et le Fauvisme en Belgique*, Musée d'Ixelles, Brussels 1990 (Catalogue by S. Goyens de Heusch); N. Hostyn, 'De zee en de kunst. Willy Schlobach', *Neptunus. Info-marine* 34 (December 1990), 5.

62 Ostend Harbour

Quai d'Ostende, 1885
Oil on canvas, 82 x 151 cm
Signed and dated bottom left: Willy Schlobach 85
Collection Crédit Communal de Belgique / Collectie Gemeentekrediet van België, Brussels

The catalogue for the 1884 Salon des XX included two addresses for Schlobach, one in Brussels and the other 'A Knocke, par Westkapelle'. This latter address suggests that Schlobach was spending considerable time on the North Sea coast at Knokke in that period, and could thus be considered to have been a member of the 'Knokke Group' of Realist and Impressionist landscape painters like Verwee (1838–1898), Wytsman (1860–1927) and numerous others, who came from the interior of the country to meet in a friendly and relaxed atmosphere at Knokke, and to paint amongst the still unspoiled polders and dunes. Like many of the landscape painters associated with Les XX, Schlobach also regularly visited Ostend, which lay not far down the coast from Knokke.

Ostend was the home of both Willy Finch (q.v.) and James Ensor (q.v.). The picturesque stretch of the town's Visserskaai shown in this painting was regularly treated by many artists. For many years Willy Finch lived a little further along with his parents, near the old lighthouse. Léon Spilliaert (q.v.) rented a room on the Visserskaai for a while, using its high vantage point to paint the wharf and the 'Trap' (the local name for the place where fish was sold), which he could see directly from his window [see cat. 64].

Schlobach also preferred a high viewpoint when recording the activity of the port. This allowed him to establish a panoramic view which provided scope for him to explore a range of different light effects: haze, vibrant skies and the bright quay with people like small, dark dots. Treated in a somewhat sombre tonality, this concern with light gives the painting an immediate affinity with the Belgian form of Impressionism, developed by such fellow members of Les XX as Ensor and Anna Boch (1848–1936) [see cat. 71]. In terms of its composition, the painting suggests parallels with some of James Ensor's etchings of the same motif, made around the same date. Schlobach later abandoned this more sombre style of painting, after coming into contact with the pointillism of Seurat. | NH

PROVENANCE Pierre Mommer, Brussels, bt. 1966.
EXHIBITIONS *Les XX* 1886; Liège 1981, no. 48; Brussels 1987a; Brussels 1990a, no. 40; Pontoise 1990, no. 20; Luxembourg 1993, no. 81.
BIBLIOGRAPHY R. Marlier and F. Safin-Crahay, in Brussels, Waregem 1981; Goyens de Heusch 1988, 76.

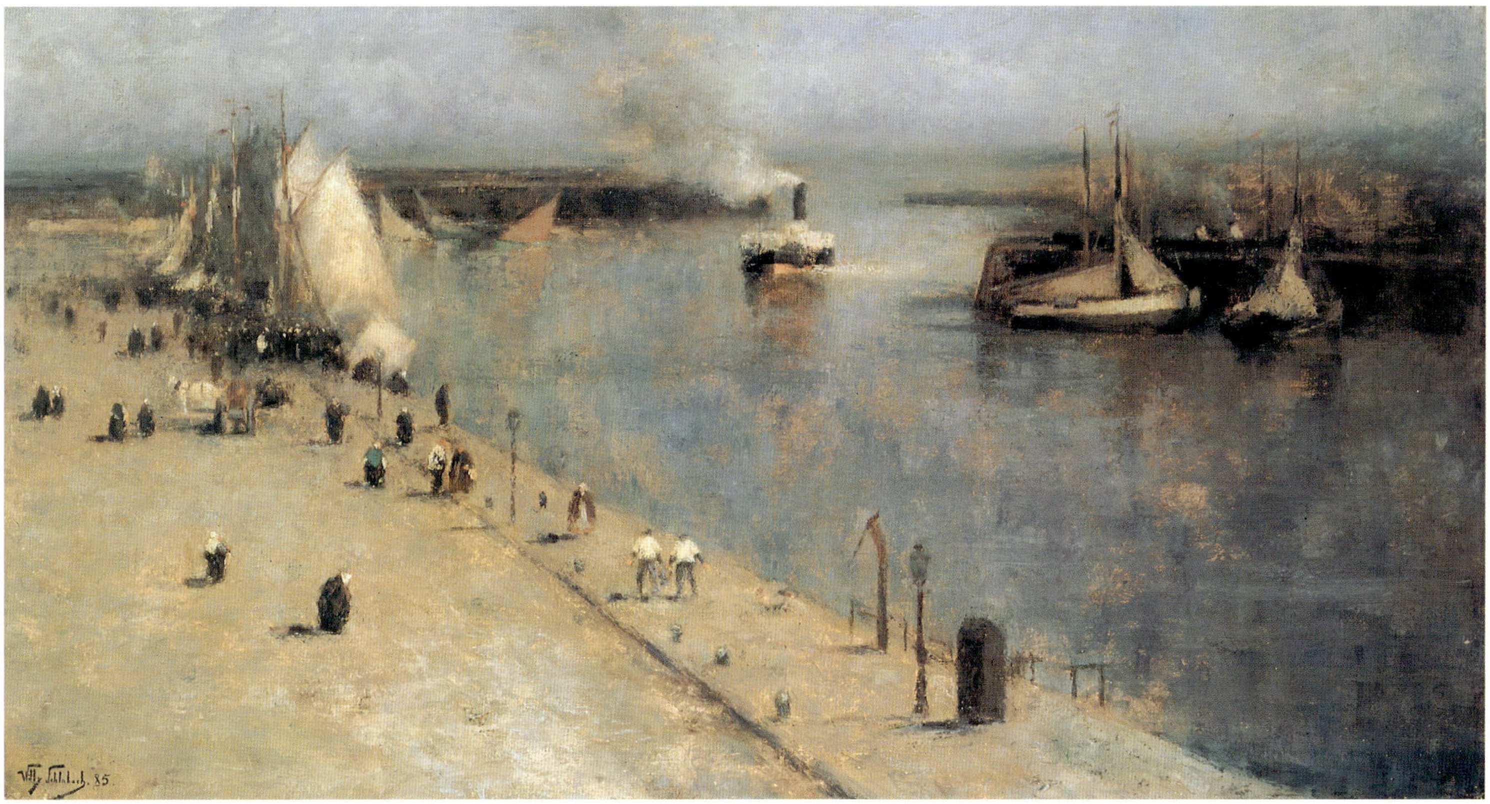

Léon Spilliaert

OSTEND 1881 – BRUSSELS 1946

Constantly experimenting with pencil, Indian ink, pastel and gouache on paper or cardboard, Léon Spilliaert's works fascinate by their sharp but mysterious images.

After a short period at the Academy of Fine Arts in Bruges, Spilliaert worked as an illustrator for the Brussels editor Edmond Deman. His passion for literature was legendary and he was an avid reader of Friedrich Nietzsche, Edgar Allan Poe, Maurice Maeterlinck, Ovidius Naso and Jan van Ruusbroeck. In 1904 the poet Emile Verhaeren introduced him to the Parisian art world. Unmoved by subject matter favoured by the avant-gardes of both Belgium and Paris, he retreated into a private world of spiritual imagery inspired by the constant presence of the sea and the peculiar aspects of the city of Ostend. Informed by the memories of his father's perfume business, he recorded the independent existences of objects, boxes and flasks. An insomniac, who wiled away the night hours in solitary walks along the seafront of Ostend, he translated onto paper the isolation of a human being confronted with the vastness of nature. In 1909, encouraged by Jean de Mot, Spilliaert participated in the Salon de Printemps and in 1911 in the Salon des Indépendants (Brussels). His friend, the poet Franz Hellens, praised his work in *Le Disque vert* and in *L'Art moderne*. He married Rachel Vergison in 1916 and moved to Brussels where he remained until 1921. Their daughter Madeleine was born in 1917. After difficulties with a contractual arrangement with Galerie Sélection (which represented the Expressionist artists Constant Permeke [1886–1952] and Gustave de Smet [1877–1943]), he became associated with Walter Schwarzenberg, the director of Galerie Le Centaure. Back in Ostend in 1922, Henri Vandeputte, the writer and director of the Kursaal, bought a lot of his work and also introduced him to Grasse (in the South of France). Spilliaert was accorded a major retrospective exhibition in 1929 at the Galerie Georges Giroux (Brussels). From now on the themes of his watercolours and ink drawings became very varied: stylized still lifes, sea and harbour scenes, landscapes, dolls. In 1935 Spilliaert returned to Brussels to give his daughter the opportunity to study the piano. Fascinated by the unspoilt nature of the region Les Fagnes, (Ardennes), his work concentrated, from 1937, on representing trees, patiently drawn with little penstrokes. In these works he expressed a rediscovered sense of spiritual quietness. | APA

SUMMARY BIBLIOGRAPHY

F. Edebau, *Léon Spilliaert* (Monographies de l'Art belge), Antwerp 1950; F. C. Legrand, *Léon Spilliaert et son époque*, Antwerp 1981; *Léon Spilliaert 1881–1946*, Galeries Nationales, Paris 1981 / Musées royaux des Beaux-Arts de Belgique, Brussels 1982 / Rijksmuseum Kröller-Müller, Otterlo 1982.

63 Self-portrait

1908

Indian ink, wash, watercolour, gouache, blue, red, green, yellow pastel on paper, 85 x 69 cm

Signed and dated bottom right corner: L. Spilliaert 08

Museum voor Schone Kunsten, Ostend, inv. no. 1953/5

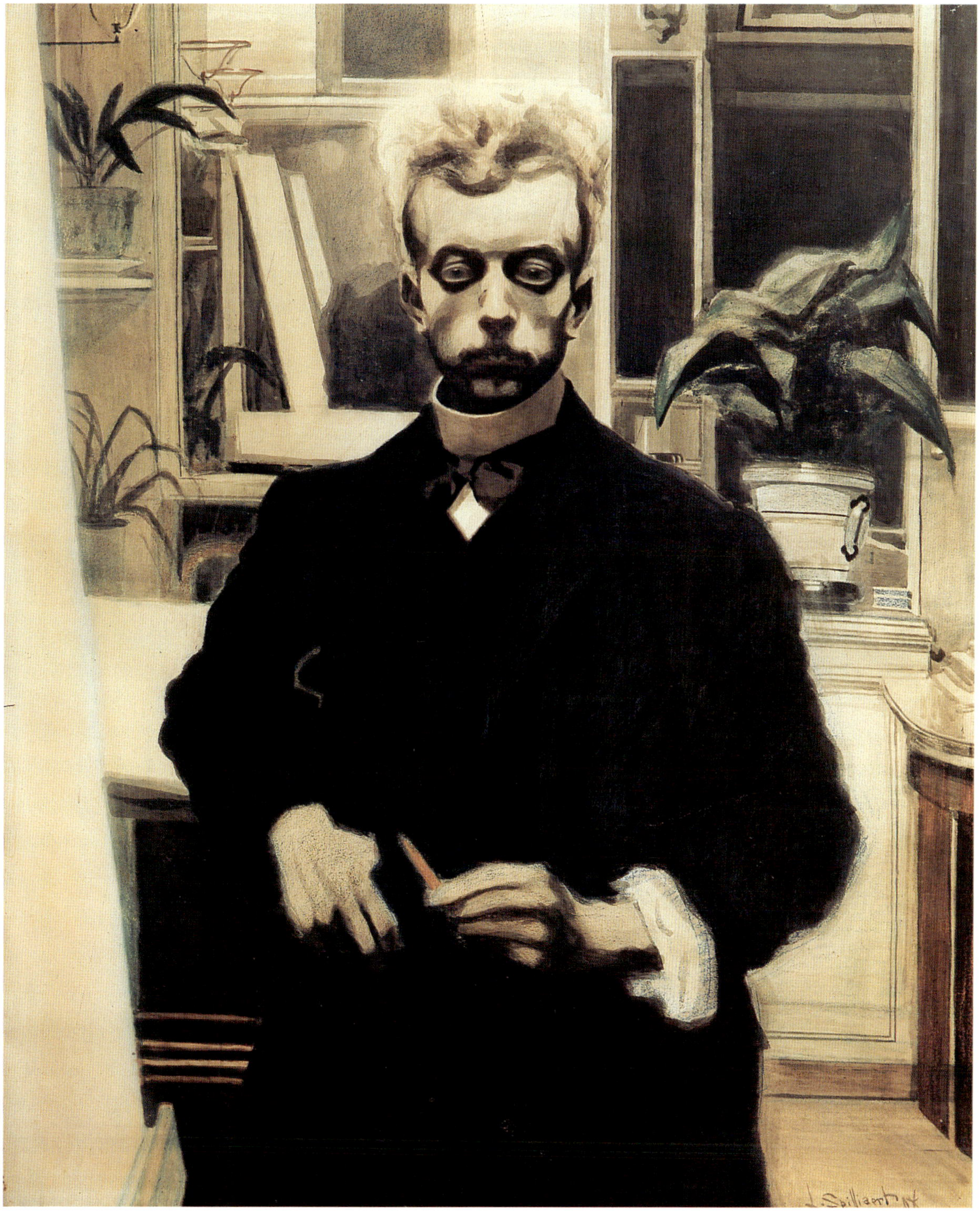

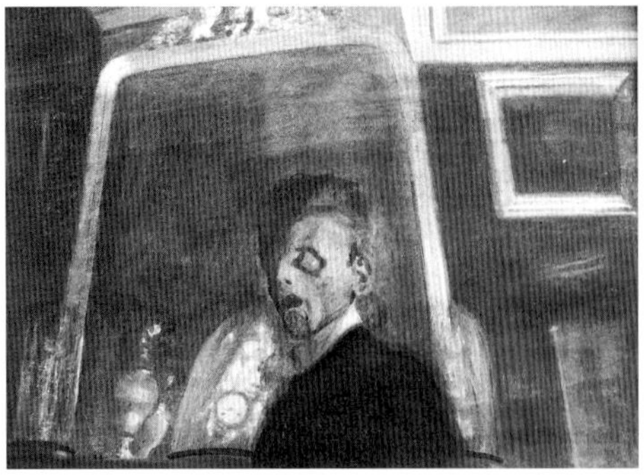

fig. a LÉON SPILLIAERT
Self-portrait with Mirror, 1908,
Museum voor Schone Kunsten, Ostend

Spilliaert's early work was dominated by a spiritual symbolism in which the sense of mystery is the most profound component, and literature the most intriguing source of inspiration. Later, the visionary Spilliaert turned his attention to the everyday world around him. His themes included the autonomous existence of objects, conveyed by means of complex perspectives (*Boxes in front of Mirror*, 1904, Musées royaux des Beaux-Arts de Belgique, Brussels), the human figure as manifested in the context of profound distress (*Vertigo*, 1908, Museum voor Schone Kunsten, Ostend) and the vastness of a natural element, treated in a manner that tends towards abstract composition (*Woman on the Sea Front*, 1908, Musées royaux des Beaux-Arts de Belgique, Brussels).

From 1907 Spilliaert regularly depicted his own image. He scrutinized and studied himself, making rapid drawings in his sketchbooks. A series of dark self-portraits done in Indian ink and reworked in coloured pastel was executed in the years up to 1909. Spilliaert depicts himself standing or sitting, in the daytime or at night, reading or working at his easel. Often his figure is reflected in a large mirror, and the view of the image disappearing into the distance evokes the flight of time into eternity (*Self-portrait with Easel and Mirror*, Koninklijk Museum voor Schone Kunsten, Antwerp).

The image Spilliaert has left us is of a singular-looking individual: in 1909 F. Jollivet Castelot talked of Spilliaert's 'amazing rumpled, quasi-fantastical, Hoffmanesque blond hair' (Jollivet Castelot 1912, 328). Spilliaert attached equal importance to the expressive representation of the figure as to the depiction of the interior in which he was working. In the present picture, he only simplifies the architecture a little and focuses on conveying the phantom-like presence of the still lifes that surround him, the green plants and the furniture, the only elements highlighted in light pastel. Positioned face to face with himself, the painter presents us with a figure full of self-confidence. He depicts the artist as an accomplished master. A simple gesture of the hand focuses attention on the instrument of his creativity – his stick of red pastel. The underlying attitude, however, borders on the nonchalant. This sharply contrasts with the insecurity which actually racked Spilliaert, and with the struggles he underwent for his art. Some years earlier he had confided to the daughter of the publisher Deman: 'Symbolism, mysticism, and so on – all that is a kind of breakdown, a disease. Everything I have done up to now, I should like to tear it all up, destroy it all. If only I could free myself of my anxious, feverish character; if only life did not have me in its grip'.[1] Spilliaert conveyed his inner turmoil in another self-portrait of the same year: '*Self-portrait with Mirror* [fig. a] is the most advanced development of this study of self, a probe in the questioning of the self and of the manifest nature of death as perceived through life' (Legrand 1988, 36). The power of the mute cry links Spilliaert spiritually with the symbolic expressionism of the Norwegian painter Edvard Munch. The depth of his inner gaze and his questioning of death establishes an affinity with the terrifying visions of James Ensor: 'M. Léon Spilliaert's art bears an unmistakable stamp. It is the stamp of an intellectual who is at the same time a highly emotional visionary. In this last aspect he resembles Ensor; but whereas Ensor moves us with colour, M. Spilliaert finds his emotive resources chiefly in line. He is, moreover, a realist, a ruthless observer. But his artistic realism is entirely internal, resorbed as it were' (Hellens 1919, 149). | APA

PROVENANCE Acquired from Mrs Léon Spilliaert, Brussels, 1953.
EXHIBITIONS Delft 1965 (no catalogue); Helsinki 1975, no. 20; Villeneuve-d'Ascq 1988, no. 18.
BIBLIOGRAPHY Hostyn 1990, 62–63.

1 Letter to Paule Deman, Ostend, 21 December 1904, Archives de l'Art contemporain belge, Brussels, Fonds Louvegné 2, inv. no. 558.

64 Night

La Nuit, 1908
Indian ink, wash, blue pastel on paper, 48 x 63 cm
Signed and dated upper left corner: L. Spilliaert 08
Musée d'Ixelles, Brussels, Collection de l'Etat Belge, inv. no. 7594

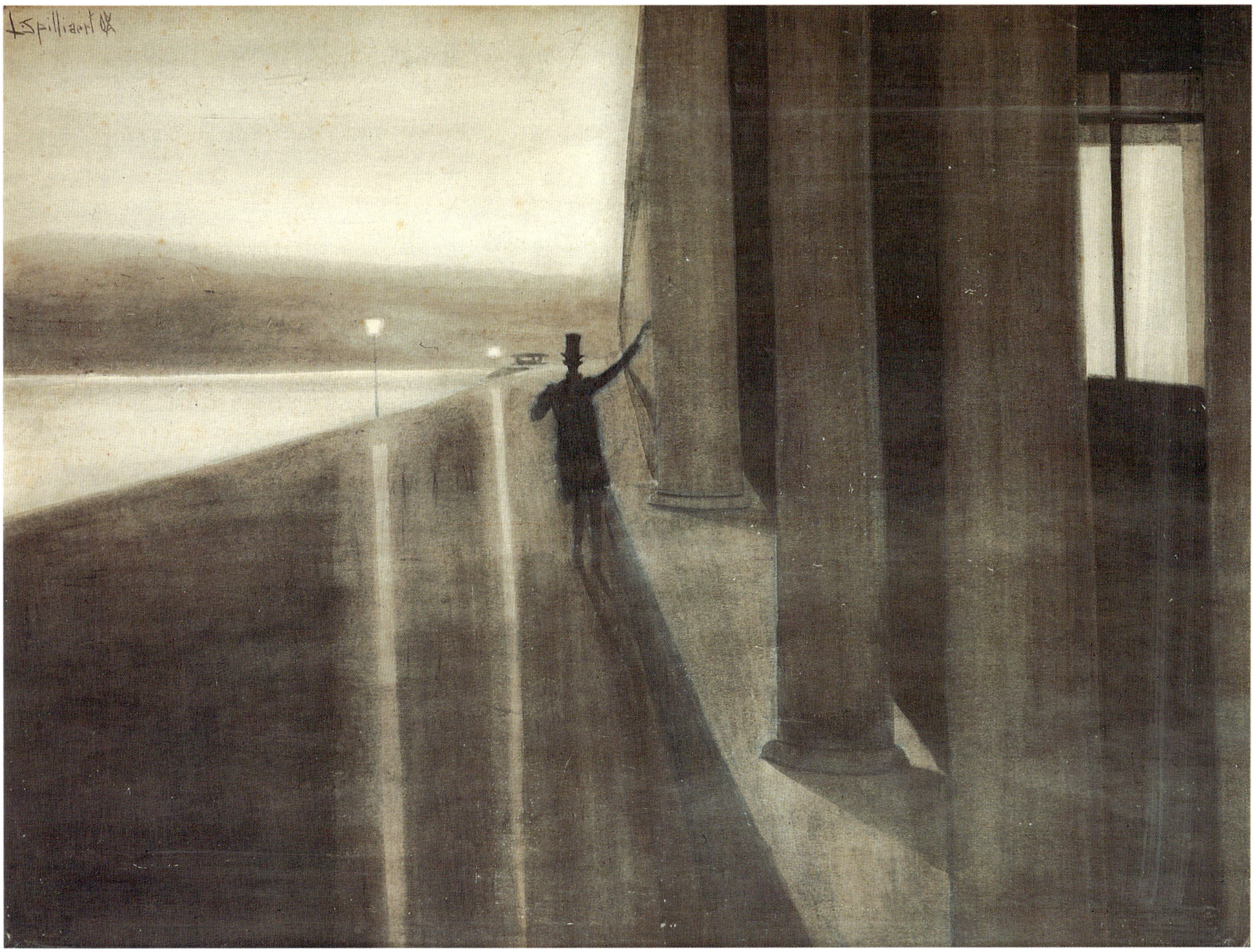

After a brief stay in Paris from 1904, during which he met members of the literary and artistic avant-garde through introductions provided by Emile Verhaeren, Spilliaert returned to the tranquillity and solitude of Ostend. In the words of Jean Clair: 'There is no doubt that in Spilliaert's eyes Ostend was not just a physical reality, but a mental space, an abstract configuration in which the two chasms of order and disorder were feverishly juxtaposed, as the straight line is opposed to the curve, and night is opposed to day – better still, as the illusion of surface is opposed to the reality of the abyss' (Paris, Brussels, Otterlo 1981–1982, 37). Being an insomniac, Spilliaert often took solitary walks along the beach at Ostend and paced the promenade in front of Ostend's classical arcades. The painting *Night* is pierced through with pallid moonlight that casts elongated shadows. The incandescent glow of the street-lamps is reflected on the damp pavement. Oblique lines come together to form triangle-like forms. The cinematographic framing, described by Francine Claire Legrand as 'wide-angle', accentuates the modernity of Spilliaert's compositions (Legrand 1981–1982, 93). The various natural elements are depicted motionless, in striking contrast to the vortex of wind and pallid light that Spilliaert breathed into *Beach in Moonlight* of the same year (Private Collection). Areas of light and shadow echo one another. A single rectangle of light pierces the rhythmic series of columns and restores the balance of black and grey surfaces. The vast horizon is sectioned off symmetrically. At the centre, a strange-looking human figure commands attention. The deserted expanse throws the tiny, unstable figure off balance. The columns of the arcade, with their rigid vertical disposition, provide a point of support for the anecdotal top-hatted figure. His arm raised, the man appears to be tracing out some incantatory movement. But the only reply he elicits is the rhythmic surge of the sea, stirred by the wind. The man advances slowly through the night, the enigmatic bearer of his torment and his freakish preoccupations. A single ring of blue pastel envelops the prophetic apparition.

The creative symbolism of this apparition emerging from the night, the favoured time for contemplation, highlights Spilliaert's novel contribution to art, which Franz Hellens so aptly described as 'fantastical reality': 'Imagination acquires the power to convey reality.'[1] In Spilliaert's work, this discreet form of the fantastical is often suffused with humour, even where he is translating spiritual concerns into visual form. In the reversed composition of *The Royal Galleries in Ostend* [fig. a], the nostalgic memory of the location and the notion of endless expectation give the work a universal resonance. This sense of expectation, devoid of any notion of time, displays affinities with Giorgio de Chirico's exercises in similarly silent, unpopulated urban spaces, such as *Place d'Italie*, painted some years later. | APA

PROVENANCE Acquired from Mrs Léon Spilliaert, 1955.
EXHIBITIONS Ixelles, Hasselt, Tournai 1961 (ex-catalogue); Vielsalm 1967 (no catalogue); Charleroi, Lobbes, Chimay *et al.* 1971–1972 (no catalogue); Savonlinna 1989, no. 77; Dixmude 1990 (no catalogue).
BIBLIOGRAPHY Legrand 1981–1982, 93.

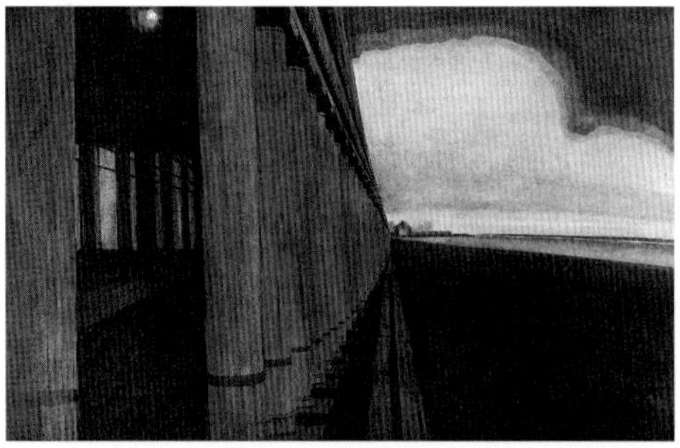

fig. a LÉON SPILLIAERT
The Royal Galleries in Ostend, 1908, Musées royaux des Beaux-Arts de Belgique, Brussels

1 F. Hellens, *Le Fantastique Réel*, Brussels 1946, 58.

Henry van de Velde

ANTWERP 1863 – OBERÄGERI (ZURICH) 1957

Henry van de Velde was born in Antwerp in 1863. Although his family wished him to pursue a career in law, Van de Velde remained resolutely committed to the visual arts. After secretly enrolling in the Antwerp Academy of Fine Arts in 1877–1879, he eventually won family approval and began his formal training there in the following year. He won a silver medal in his first year and in 1883 he entered the private studio of Charles Verlat (1824–1890). Through Verlat's patronage, Van de Velde became a member of Als Ik Kan, a group of artists who were associated with the Academy. He exhibited with Als Ik Kan in 1884, showing landscapes and portraits painted with a dark palette in the realist style approved by the Academy. Inspired by the art of Manet and Millet, Van de Velde left the Academy and joined the art colony at Wechelderzande. Due to his contact there with Adrien-Joseph Heymans (1839–1921) and other Northern 'Impressionist' painters, Van de Velde's palette lightened. He began painting scenes of farm life in a technique of interlocking diagonal brushstrokes to produce a rhythmic surface pattern. In 1887 Van de Velde saw Georges Seurat's *A Sunday Afternoon on the Island of the Grande Jatte* (1884–1887; Art Institute of Chicago) at Les XX. That same year, he and his high school friend, the poet Max Elskamp, created the exhibition society, L'Art Indépendant in Antwerp. After some initial hesitation, Van de Velde adopted the Neo-Impressionist palette and technique in 1888. His involvement with avant-garde art and ideas earned Van de Velde election to Les XX in November of 1888 and he showed paintings as a member in the 1889 Salon. The following year he was invited to show at the Salon des Indépendants in Paris. Although Van de Velde continued painting in a Neo-Impressionist technique until 1891, his contacts with the Symbolist poets Elskamp, Charles van Lerberghe, Stéphane Mallarmé and Paul Verlaine encouraged him to distance himself from the objective depiction of the external world and to pursue a more decorative, less descriptive style. In 1890, Van de Velde saw Van Gogh's paintings and drawings at Les XX, and a second viewing in 1891 led to a stylistic change in his painting in which he fused Seurat's colour theory with a pulsating, undulating line inspired by Van Gogh's late work. It was during this time that Van de Velde published his first critical essays in *L'Art moderne* and *La Wallonie*.

Van de Velde encountered the ideas and work of the Arts and Crafts Movement and the writings of John Ruskin through the *vingtistes* Finch (q.v.) and Lemmen (q.v.), and in 1891 began to explore the decorative arts, including tapestry. In the spring of 1892 he commenced his collaboration with Auguste Vermeylen on the Flemish literary journal *Van Nu en Straks*. Together with Elskamp and other Antwerp-based artists, including Georges Morren (q.v.), Van de Velde also formed L'Association pour l'Art, which held its first salon in May 1892. That same year, with Jan Toorop (1858–1928), and Van Rysselberghe (q.v.), he also put together an exhibition for the Panorama Group in The Hague. In 1893 Van de Velde met his future wife Maria Sèthe who helped him organize courses on industrial art at the Antwerp Academy of Fine Arts and the Université Nouvelle in Brussels. His readings of anarchist and socialist theory led him to question his painting career and in 1894 he gave up painting to pursue an influential career in architecture and design. Henry van de Velde died in Oberägeri near Zurich in 1957. | SC

SUMMARY BIBLIOGRAPHY

H. van de Velde, *Déblaiement d'Art* (Brussels 1895), Brussels 1979; H. van de Velde, *Geschichte meines Lebens*, Munich 1962 – Récit de ma vie, ed. A. van Loo and F. van de Kerckhove, Brussels 1992; *Henry van de Velde, 1863–1957*, Palais des Beaux-Arts, Brussels 1963 (Catalogue by R. L. Delevoy); *Henry van de Velde, 1863–1957*, Rijksmuseum Kröller-Müller, Otterlo 1964 (Catalogue by A. M. Hammacher, R. L. Delevoy *et al.*); A. M Hammacher, *Le Monde de Henry van de Velde*, Antwerp, Paris 1967; *Henry van de Velde: Paintings and Drawings*, Koninklijk Museum voor Schone Kunsten, Antwerp 1987 / Rijksmuseum Kröller-Müller, Otterlo 1988 (Catalogue by S. M. Canning); K.-J. Sembach, *Henry van de Velde*, Stuttgart 1989; *Henry van de Velde*, Bibliothèque Royale, Brussels 1993 (Catalogue by F. van de Kerckhove *et al.*).

65 The Beach at Blankenberghe with Beach Huts

Blankenberghe (La Plage à Blankenberghe avec cabines), 1888
Oil on canvas, 77.5 x 100 cm
Kunsthaus, Zurich, inv. no. 1964/30

In 1888, Van de Velde went to stay at his brother Laurent's villa on the boardwalk in the summer seaside resort of Blankenberghe. Profoundly depressed over his mother's death from cancer in July of that year, he sought desolation in the sand and dunes of the North Sea. The artist's emotional desolation is stated in the composition of this work. Taking up a viewpoint from inside a small beach hut, the artist/observer gazes out across the vast, empty expanse of beach to the distant spectacle of people playing or walking in the sand.

This painting is one of the first in which Van de Velde consistently applied both the Neo-Impressionist 'dot' or pointillist brushstroke and a colour scheme based upon divisionist theory. The palette is typical of his work at this time, for example, *Blankenberghe Beach* (Kunsthalle, Bremen), in which warm colour harmonies impart a sense of location and atmosphere. In *The Beach at Blankenberghe with Beach Huts*, Van de Velde creates space by contrasting the cool purple of the foreground shadow and green of the cabin door and wall to the yellow-orange of the beach and boardwalk hotels and villas. When combined with small strokes of white paint and applied in a precise and rhythmic manner across the surface, these oppositions of colour effectively recreate the bright luminosity of a sunlit beach.

Yet even as he evokes the humid air of a warm sunny day, Van de Velde's fascination with abstract compositional arrangements is already evident. The apparent simplicity of the scene belies a complex design which simultaneously asserts the painting's flat, decorative character. The broad horizontal of the beach, which takes up two-thirds of the painting's surface, is countered by the verticals of the cabin door in the foreground and the beach on the right. The underlying rectilinearity of these elements is then challenged by the diagonal of the foreground shadow which implies spatial depth while remaining a flat pattern. The result of this complex interplay of composition, colour and form is a scene which draws the observer inward toward the beach only to be left visually suspended between the empty foreground and the figures in the distance. In this fashion, Van de Velde visualizes the 'architecture of the idea' in which an Impressionist view of leisure is transformed into a private world expressive of solitary contemplation and emotional despair. Like Seurat, whose *La Grande Jatte* had so inspired him at the 1887 Les XX Salon, Van de Velde creates in *The Beach at Blankenberghe with Beach Huts* a synthesized arrangement of pictorial form which states the artist's expressive idea within a decorative arrangement of pictorial form. For his first exhibition as a member of Les XX (1892), Van de Velde exhibited this painting with three of his earlier experiments in Neo-Impressionism (*Soleil d'avril; Soleil* [*Matin*] *août 1888; Soleil* [*Midi*] *août 1888*) and a portrait of his brother Laurent (now lost). He later showed the painting at the first Salon of the Association pour l'Art held in Antwerp in 1892. | SC

PROVENANCE Collection of the artist; Thyl van de Velde, Brussels.
EXHIBITIONS *Les XX* 1889, no. 1; Antwerp 1892a; Hagen 1959, no. 23, ill.; Brussels, Otterlo 1962, no. 155; Vienna 1962, no. 125; New York 1968, no. 140, ill.; The Hague 1976–1977, no. 92; Munich 1977–1978; Düsseldorf 1977, no. 133; London 1979–1980, no. 423, ill.; Washington 1980, no. 423, ill.; Tokyo 1985, no. 53; Antwerp, Otterlo 1987–1988, no. 22.
BIBLIOGRAPHY E. Demolder, in *La Société Nouvelle* (March 1892); Van de Velde 1962, ill.; Hammacher 1967, no. 18; Sutter 1970, 209; S. Canning, in Antwerp, Otterlo 1987–1988, 144–146; Goyens de Heusch 1988, 174–175.

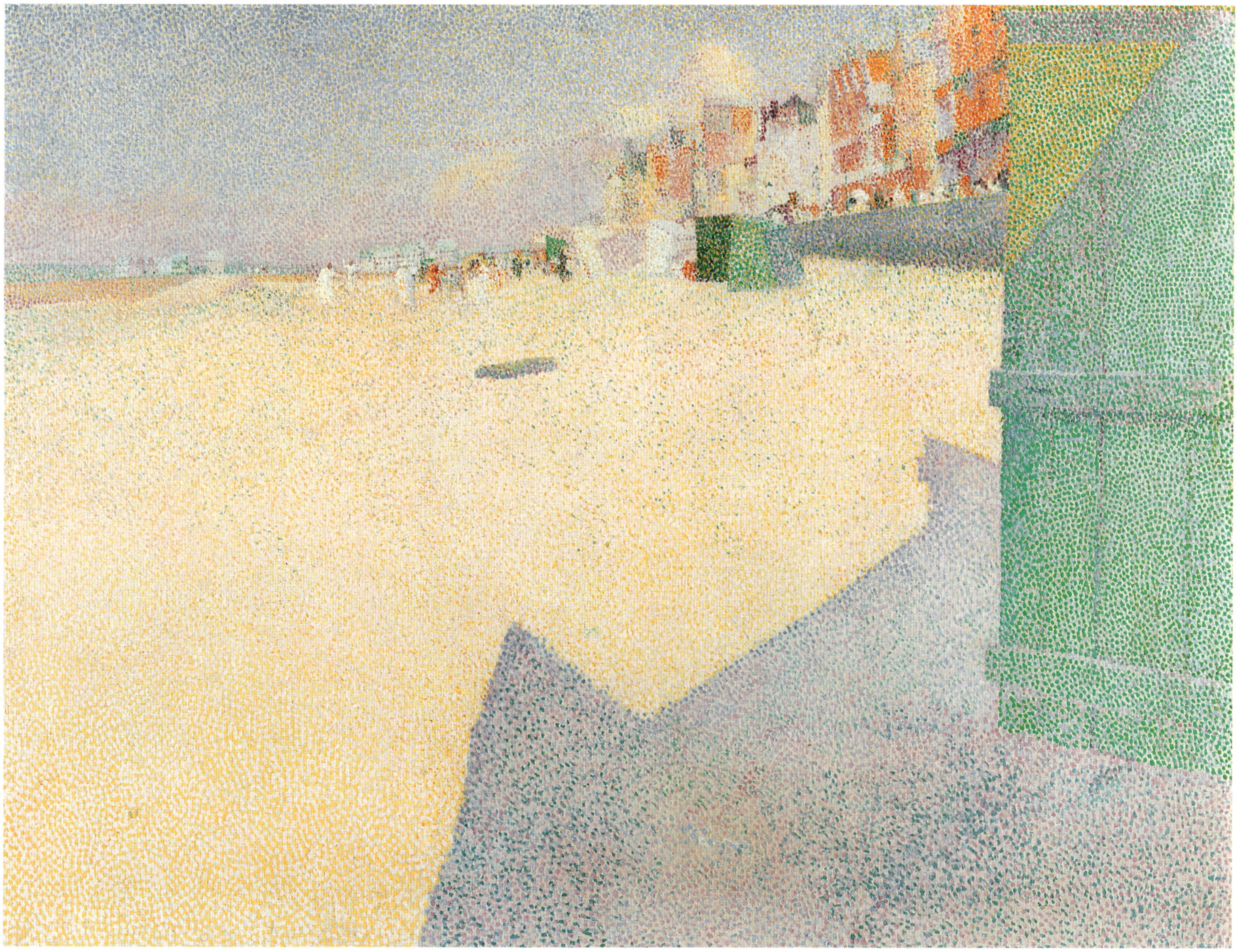

66 Père Biart reading in the Garden

Père Biart lisant dans le jardin, c. 1890–1891
Oil on brown paper mounted on canvas, 62.1 x 51.9 cm
Signed and dated with floral emblem
Indianapolis Museum of Art, The Holliday Collection, Indianapolis, inv. no. 79.320

By the time Van de Velde painted this portrait of his sister's father-in-law, he had become increasingly preoccupied with the evocative potential underlying the decorative arrangement of pictorial form. Although he uses divisionist technique, unlike *The Beach at Blankenberghe with Beach Huts* [cat. 65], there is little interest here in reproducing atmospheric effects. Indeed, the large, rounded, evenly applied dabs of paint on brown paper, a colour scheme dominated by a mixed palette of lavender, white, rose, pale green and blue, and an obtuse perspective which distorts the image of the seated Mr Biart, all collaborate to emphasize the scene's artificiality.

Van de Velde portrays a scene of middle-class leisure, here taking place in the garden of his sister Jeanne's summer home, Vogelenzang, near Antwerp. At once in control and unconcerned with his environment, Mr Biart, absorbed in his reading, evokes a proprietorial authority which is reinforced by his size and dominant placement within the space defined upon the canvas. While Van de Velde successfully conceals his awkward rendering of foreshortened form (with only two legs, the chair could hardly support Mr Biart and it casts no shadow), his focus moves beyond mere portraiture. The broad expanse of lavender and white brushstrokes, a rendering perhaps of a path or patio formed of white pebbles, envelops Mr Biart, setting him apart from the tree and lawn in the background. Unlike the numerous pastel drawings that Van de Velde executed in Wechelderzande in 1890 and 1891 and exhibited at Les XX in 1891 as 'attitudes' reflective of the peasant at work or at rest in harmony with nature, in this painting the artist emphasizes the sitter over the setting. When combined with the distancing effect of the path, the high perspective and the cool colour scheme of a background unrelieved by warm tints of sunshine, Van de Velde's scene of bourgeois leisure subtly takes on an aspect of estrangement from nature. In contrast to this painting, numerous pastel drawings of his sister and her children made during the same summer utilize warm colours, rhythmic line and intimate settings to evoke the harmony of family life and the comfort of the hearth. The emotional coolness and distancing of Mr Biart's portrait possibly points to the artist's own ambivalence toward his middle-class background and to his struggle to invest his art practice with personal and moral meaning. | SC

PROVENANCE Collection Léon Biart, Antwerp and Kalmthout; Edgar Biart, Lausanne; Mme Ionesco, Paris; Hammer Galleries, New York.
EXHIBITIONS Antwerp 1891, no. 262; Tokyo 1985, no. 54; Amsterdam 1988, no. 53.
BIBLIOGRAPHY Hammacher 1967, 43, ill., no. 22; R. Herbert, in New York 1968, 187; Sutter 1970, 211, ill.; Lee 1983, 74–75, ill.; S. Canning, in Antwerp, Otterlo 1987–1988, 160, ill.; Amsterdam 1988, 121–123, ill.; Goyens de Heusch 1988, 180.

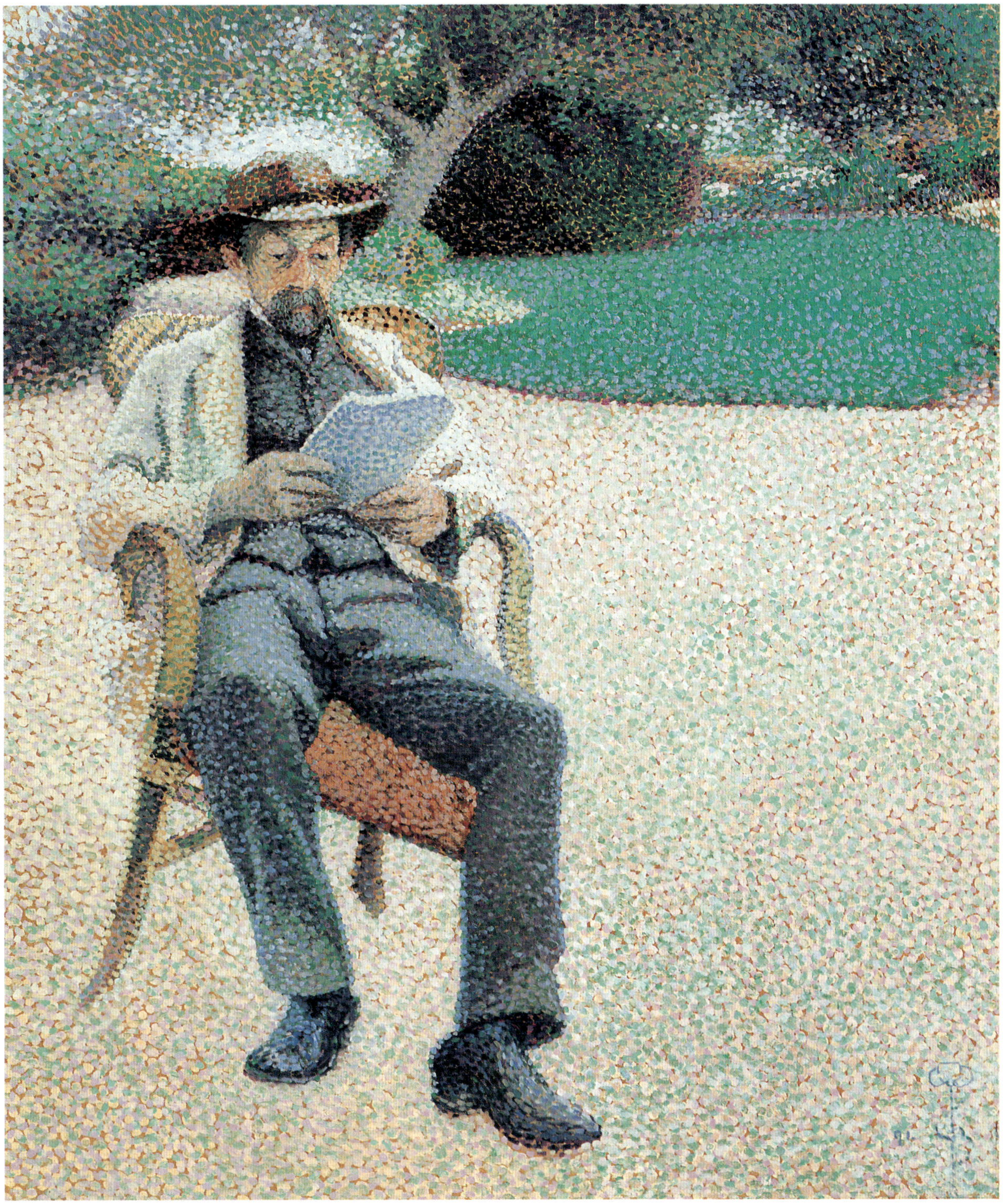

67 Garden in Summer (Kalmthout)

Le Jardin en été, 1892
Oil on canvas, 172 x 67.5 cm
Signed bottom right: H.v.d. Velde
Karl Ernst Osthaus-Museum, Hagen, inv. no. K 2449

Even though Van de Velde was a great admirer and follower of Georges Seurat, by 1891 he found the discipline of the Neo-Impressionist technique ill-suited to his nervous and high-strung temperament. As his own interest in Symbolism developed through conversations with Max Elskamp, Stéphane Mallarmé and Charles van Lerberghe, Van de Velde increasingly adopted a non-naturalist rather than Impressionist palette for his painting and simplified his compositions in order to distance his images from direct naturalistic description. Searching for a manner that would encompass both his personality and his emotions, Van de Velde turned to the expressive line of Vincent van Gogh. Van Gogh had exhibited at Les XX in 1890 and, as Van de Velde later wrote in his memoirs, at that time he was torn between Seurat's technique 'hopelessly peaceful and slow' and Van Gogh's 'impetuous technique fixing forever a moment of expressive emotion'.

In *Garden in Summer (Kalmthout)*, Van de Velde employs a tall, narrow format reminiscent of a Japanese print to represent a sunny day at his sister's estate in Kalmthout. Unlike his *Garden in Kalmthout* (1891, Staatsgemäldesammlungen, Neue Pinakothek, Munich), a view of the same garden which employs a pink-purple colour scheme to underscore the painting's decorative and artificial nature, here Van de Velde returns to an Impressionist palette first seen in his paintings of 1886–1887. Now the scene is imbued with warm sunlight and the humid atmosphere of a mid-summer day. The divisional brushstroke of earlier canvases [see cats. 65, 66] has given way to a curving, rhythmic line. Infusing every form with a sense of energy and movement, this emphatic arabesque combines with the extended vertical of the format and a high, bird's-eye perspective, to reinforce the decorative arrangement of the surface. Like the Japanese prints that he came to know through both the writer and critic Max Elskamp and the exhibition of Japanese art organized in 1889 in Brussels by Samuel Bing, collector, dealer and ultimately one of the leading supporters of Art Nouveau, Van de Velde creates an overall pictorial harmony in which composition, line, colour and form represent both the sensation of a summer's day and the energy of nature as viewed through a corner of his sister's garden. The identification with nature in this scene and others painted and drawn by Van de Velde between 1891 and 1892 indicate the solace and inspiration he found both in the countryside outside Antwerp and by the sea and on the dunes of Blankenberghe. As he arranged his expressive response to nature into the organic, energized line that became the symbol of his design aesthetic, he realized that painting no longer provided him with a broad enough arena for his ideas and social beliefs. Van de Velde's underlying interest in design is already evident in this painting, one of his last. The unusual dimensions of *Garden in Summer* suggest that it may have been part of a tripartite panel or multipaneled screen, perhaps originally painted as a wall decoration for the villa Vogelenzang. | SC

PROVENANCE Collection Wagemans, Berchem.
EXHIBITIONS Darmstadt 1976; Antwerp, Otterlo 1987–1988, no. 35 (ill.).
BIBLIOGRAPHY *Weltkunst* 36:2 (1966), 56; Hammacher 1967, no. 30 (ill.); S. Canning, in Antwerp, Otterlo 1987–1988, 172.

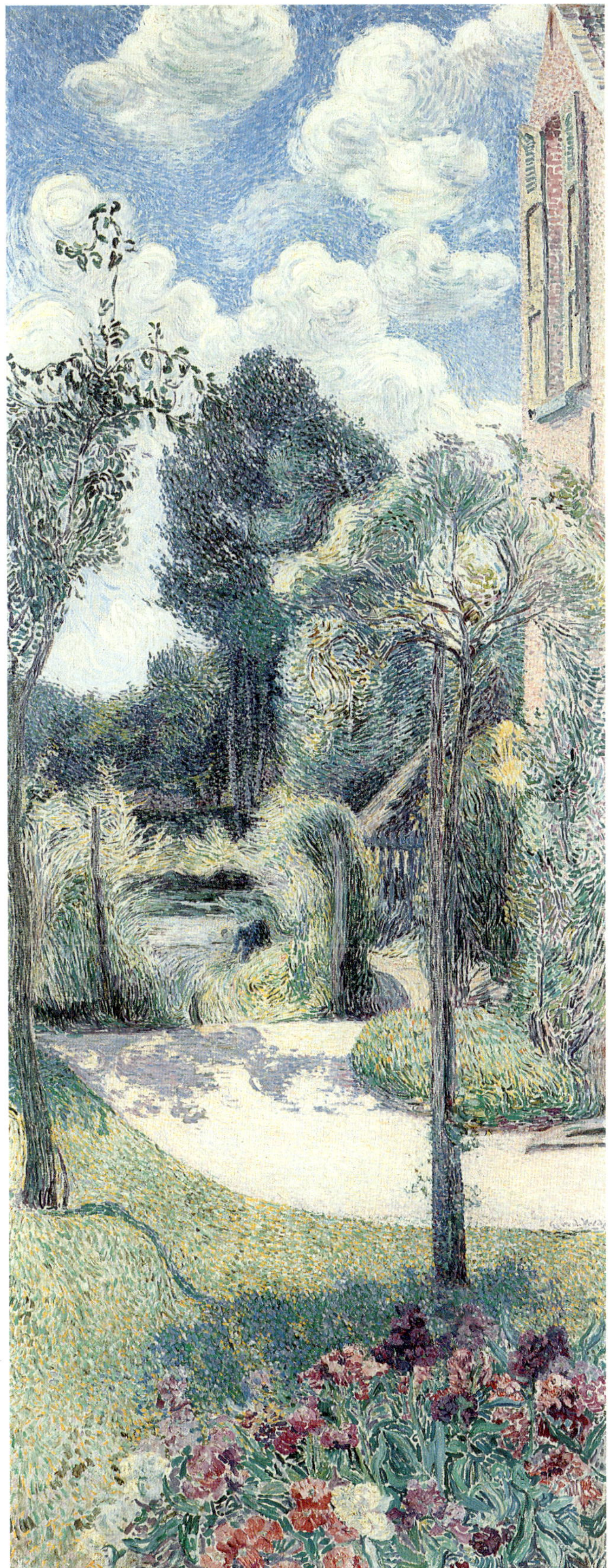

Frans van Leemputten

WERCHTER NEAR LOUVAIN 1850 – ANTWERP 1914

Frans van Leemputten came from a family of farmers that produced a surprising number of artists. Between 1865 and 1873, he followed evening classes at the Brussels Academy of Fine Arts where his teacher was the landscape painter Paul Lauters (1806–1876). He also knew and was advised by artists such as Constantin Meunier (q.v.) and the Dutchman (and member of The Hague School) P. J. C. Gabriel (1828–1903), who was then living in Brussels. He was influenced by the Realist Louis Dubois (1830–1880), and belonged to the free drawing club La Patte de Dindon, together with Meunier and Franz Courtens (1854–1943). He made his début at the 1873 Antwerp Salon with a work entitled *Orchard*.

Van Leemputten joined La Chrysalide, a society for progressive artists, shortly after its foundation in Brussels in 1875. He exhibited at three of the society's salons, in 1876, 1878 and 1881. He was also a member of L'Essor, a group set up in Brussels in 1876 chiefly to promote Realism. He settled in Brussels in 1876, and remained there until 1891, when he returned to Antwerp to take up a teaching post at the Hoger Instituut.

Van Leemputten was a landscape painter, but above all a narrator of country life. His paintings are generally set in the Antwerp Kempen region or in Brabant, and capture the piety of country folk, their dress, local manners and customs in a realistic style. These are not raw, naturalistic views of peasant life, nor do they display any social engagement. His approach is that of a neutral observer and is exemplified by the triptych *Candlelight Procession at Scherpenheuvel* (1903–1905; Koninklijk Museum voor Schone Kunsten, Antwerp). His palette was initially dominated by browns and dark tones, but became most closely allied to the brighter tones of the Luminists after 1900. | NH

SUMMARY BIBLIOGRAPHY

E. de Taeye, *Les artistes Belges contemporains. Leur vie, leur œuvre, leur place dans l'art*, Brussels 1894; *Kunst in Vlaanderen*, Brussels 1979, 212–213; *Schilders van het landelijke leven in België. Van realisme tot post-expressionisme*, Koninklijk Museum voor Schone Kunsten, Antwerp 1990; *In dienst van de kunst. Antwerps mecenaat rond Kunst van Heden 1905–1959*, Koninklijk Museum voor Schone Kunsten, Antwerp 1991; N. Hostyn, 'Frans Van Leemputten', *Nationaal Biografisch Woordenboek* 14 (1992).

68 Distribution of the Bread in the Village

Brooduitdeling op het dorp – Distribution du pain au village, 1892
Oil on canvas, 64 x 78 cm
Signed and dated bottom right: Frans Van Leemputten 1892
Koninklijk Museum voor Schone Kunsten, Antwerp, inv. no. 1293

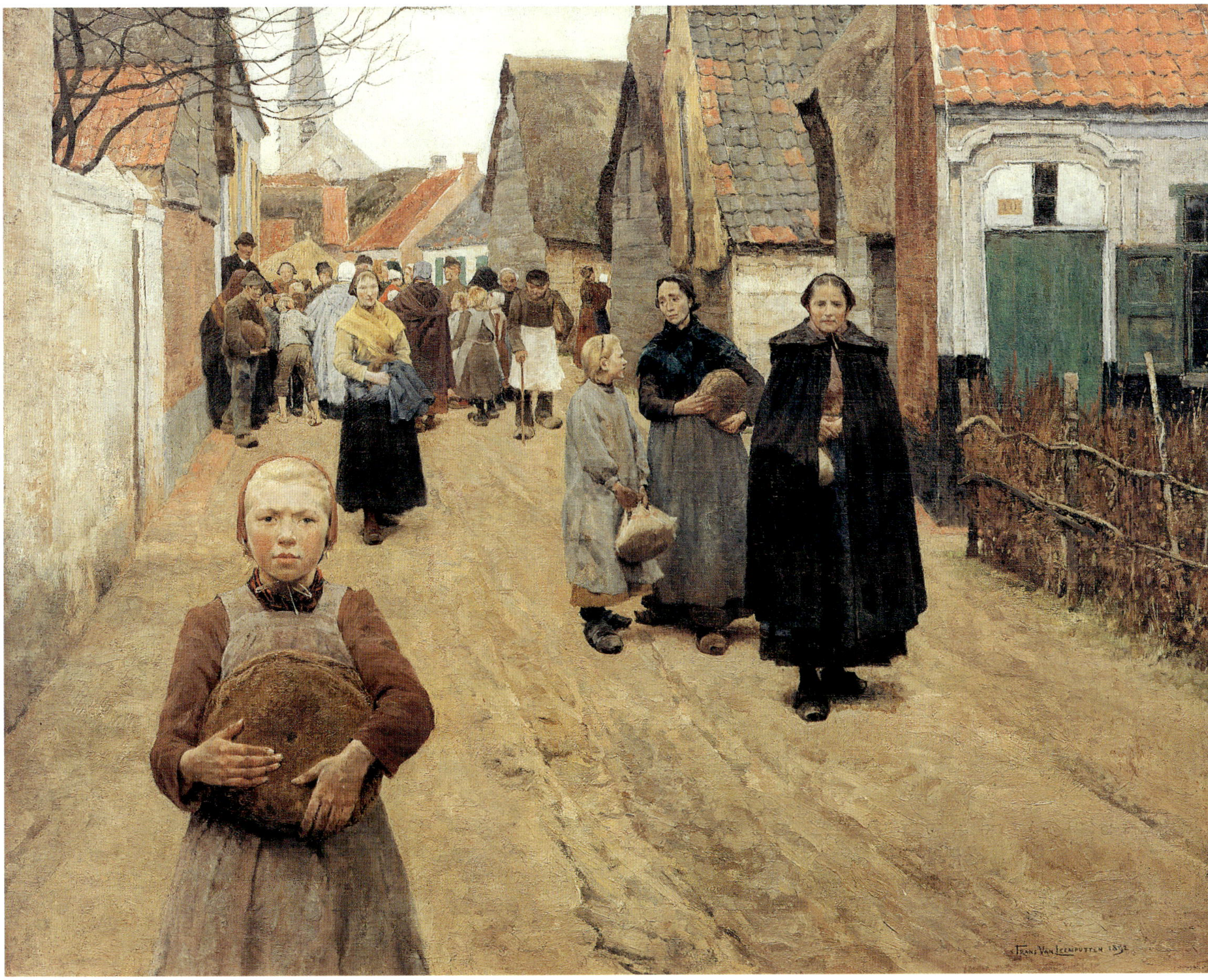

Van Leemputten was best known as a painter of the Kempen (La Campine). His love for the region, which remained relatively backward and unspoilt at that time, was fired by the stories of Hendrik Conscience. He was interested in the Brabant countryside, too, although it was the people there rather than the landscape that attracted him. In keeping with many of his contemporaries, from Jozef Israëls in Holland to J. F. Millet, Jules Bastien-Lepage and Léon Lhermitte in France, he became profoundly attached to the simple country folk, their customs and traditions. He recorded all facets of their rural existence, celebrating the mundane activities of walking down a village street or a country lane, going to market, or at work in the fields as well as the more particular moments in their lives when deep-seated faith found expression in pilgrimages, feasts on holy days and the burying of the dead.

Bread was widely distributed in Flanders until well into the twentieth century. It was intended first and foremost as a form of poor relief during the barren winter months, but it also often accompanied the funerals of prominent individuals within a local community. Like the *Candlelight Procession at Scherpenheuvel* (1903–1905; Koninklijk Museum voor Schone Kunsten, Antwerp), the *Distribution of the Bread,* which was painted ten years earlier, is already a synthesis of Van Leemputten's artistic concerns. He handles his subject with great objectivity and truthfulness, such that the elements of poverty, ignorance or social deprivation are not exaggerated but merely noted and recorded within the composition. Although less politically engaged than some of his more overtly committed socialist contemporaries such as Constantin Meunier (q.v.) and Léon Fréderic (q.v.), Van Leemputten saw his art as valuable documents of a culture which, like that in other more remote rural areas of Europe, such as Brittany, would soon be overwhelmed by social and economic change.

The sober reserve of Van Leemputten's pictorial approach has more in common with the directness of observation found in Léon Fréderic's *Funeral Wake* [cat. 26] than with the near contemporary representation of an important event in the life cycle of the rural peasant, *First Communion* (1893), executed by Emile Claus [cat. 4]. Rather than insisting upon the sombre, and often precarious, nature of rural life, Claus, in his *First Communion,* decked out the momentous religious event in the overtly innovative technique of Impressionism to create a scene where the sundrenched atmosphere becomes the dominant subject of the work. | NH

PROVENANCE Bought at the Antwerp Triennial Salon, 1894.
EXHIBITIONS / BIBLIOGRAPHY Antwerp 1894; Gaasbeek 1989; Antwerp 1990.

Théo van Rysselberghe

GHENT 1862 – SAINT CLAIR, LE LAVANDOU (FRANCE) 1926

Théo van Rysselberghe first studied at the Academy of Fine Arts in Ghent before following his brother, Octave, to Brussels, where he enrolled at the Academy of Fine Arts, studying with Jean Portaels (1818–1895) and the portraitist Léon Herbo (1850–1907). In 1882 he won a travelling fellowship from Ghent that allowed him, like Portaels before him, to visit Spain and Morocco, accompanied by the artists Meunier (q.v.), Dario de Regoyos (1857–1913) and Frantz Charlet (1862–1928). Captivated by the exoticism of these countries, he returned to Morocco twice more: in the autumn of 1883, when he rented a studio in Tangiers with Charlet for nearly a year, and late in 1887/early 1888 with the lawyer and co-founder of the periodical, *L'Art moderne*, Edmond Picard. This latter visit provided material for a joint publication, *El Moghreb-Al-Aksa*; published in Brussels in 1889, it set Van Rysselberghe's sketches from this trip beside Picard's text and opened with a frontispiece by Redon. Van Rysselberghe showed the products of his first Moroccan excursion at the 1883 exhibition of the Brussels society L'Essor. Shortly after his return, he met the writer and critic Emile Verhaeren, who was to become his life-long friend and collaborator. Van Rysselberghe was one of the founding members of Les XX in the autumn of 1883 where he was a loyal exhibitor showing in nine of the ten annual exhibitions. Van Rysselberghe regularly assisted the group's secretary, Octave Maus, by identifying prospective *invités* for subsequent exhibitions.

Georges Seurat's monumental *La Grande Jatte* (1884–1887; Art Institute of Chicago) formed the critical centre of the 8th and final Impressionist exhibition held in Paris in 1886. Van Rysselberghe visited the show with Verhaeren, and was so impressed by Seurat's work that he discarded the somewhat Whistlerian mode which currently dominated his work in favour of Neo-Impressionism, and advocated inviting Seurat to exhibit with Les XX in 1887. Van Rysselberghe greatly expanded the range of the style by applying pointillist theory to portraiture [see cats. 71, 72]. Around 1896 he began to adopt a larger, squarer brushstroke, abandoning some of the rigours of Neo-Impressionist theory. He ultimately discarded the technique after 1904. Apart from a prolific output of paintings, Van Rysselberghe also undertook several mural decorations (e.g. *Reading in the Garden*, 1902, Hôtel Solvay, Brussels), and later in his career, turned to sculpture.

In 1889 Van Rysselberghe's marriage to Maria Monnom, daughter of Sylvie Descamps Monnom, the publisher of *l'Art moderne* and Les XX's catalogues, encouraged his growing interest in book design, prints and posters. His pointillist design for the poster for the 1889 Salon des XX first revealed his success as a poster designer, which continued in his masterful posters for Les XX's successor, La Libre Esthétique. Van Rysselberghe was also active in the revival of book design, collaborating on the design and decoration for more than a dozen books by Verhaeren. He also created a significant body of prints.

In 1898 he moved to Paris and lived in France for the remainder of his life. He died in 1926, at his home at Saint Clair, Le Lavandou, which his brother, Octave, had designed for him in 1910. He exhibited with the Paris Indépendants from 1890 to 1895 and from 1901 until 1906. His important one-man shows were held in Paris in 1895 at the Galerie Laffitte, in 1905 at the Galerie Druet and at the Galerie Bernheim-Jeune in 1908, and in Brussels in 1922 and 1927 at the Galerie Giroux. | JB

SUMMARY BIBLIOGRAPHY

P. Fierens, *Théo Van Rysselberghe*, Brussels 1937; François Maret, *Théo Van Rysselberghe* (Monographies de l'art belge), Antwerp 1948; M.-J. Chartrain-Hebbelinck, 'Théo Van Rysselberghe, Le groupe des XX et La Libre Esthétique', *Revue Belge d'Archéologie et d'Histoire de l'Art* 34 (1965), 99–134; M.-J. Chartrain-Hebbelinck, 'Les lettres de Théo Van Rysselberghe à Octave Maus', *Bulletin des Musées Royaux des Beaux-Arts de Belgique* 15 (1966) no. 1/2, 55–130; *Rétrospective Théo Van Rysselberghe*, Museum voor Schone Kunsten, Ghent 1962; *Théo Van Rysselberghe, néo-impressionniste*, Museum voor Schone Kunsten, Ghent 1993.

69 Pool in the Kempen

Poel in de Kempen, 1882
Oil on canvas, 34 x 43 cm
Signed bottom left: Théo Van Rysselberghe Campine Août 82;
monogrammed and dated top right: Campine Août 84 TVR
Museum voor Schone Kunsten, Ghent, inv. no. 1914–HQ

Groups of landscape artists adopting a *plein-air* approach to the motif developed in several places in Belgium in the second half of the nineteenth century. The influence of certain pioneering figures was sometimes so great that actual 'schools' formed around them. The locations in question played a similar role in the development of Belgian landscape art as did those of Barbizon and Fontainebleau in France. Such 'schools' arose in Tervuren near Brussels, Anseremme in the Meuse region, Knokke on the North Sea coast, the island of Walcheren and the Scheldt region around Dendermonde and Antwerp. The Kempen (La Campine), an extensive and still undeveloped area in northern Belgium to the east of Antwerp, was another favourite location for these artists. In this flat, barren land, with its wide heaths, fens, swamps, pine forests and sand dunes, they found motifs that confounded the conventional aesthetics of the picturesque landscape.

Théo van Rysselberghe was an early *plein-airiste* who often painted on the Belgian coast and from time to time in the Kempen. This early landscape is still dominated by dark colours, with a tendency towards greys, a characteristic feature of Van Rysselberghe and other modernist Belgian masters in around 1880. The uncomplicated structure of the composition in four evenly-sized horizontal bands, alternating between light and dark, and the careful rendering of atmospheric effects, the scale of the work and the boldness with which the paint has been laid onto the canvas suggest that this is a study painted in the open air.

The work bears two dates – 1882 and 1884. If we are correct in assuming that the painting was made in front of the motif, then the earlier date must record the year in which it was made since Van Rysselberghe spent the period November 1883 to November 1884 in Spain and Morocco. The significance of the date '1884' is thus unclear. | NH

PROVENANCE Fernand Scribe Bequest, 1913.
EXHIBITIONS Ghent 1962, no. 15; Ghent 1980, no. 221; Ghent 1993, no. 4.

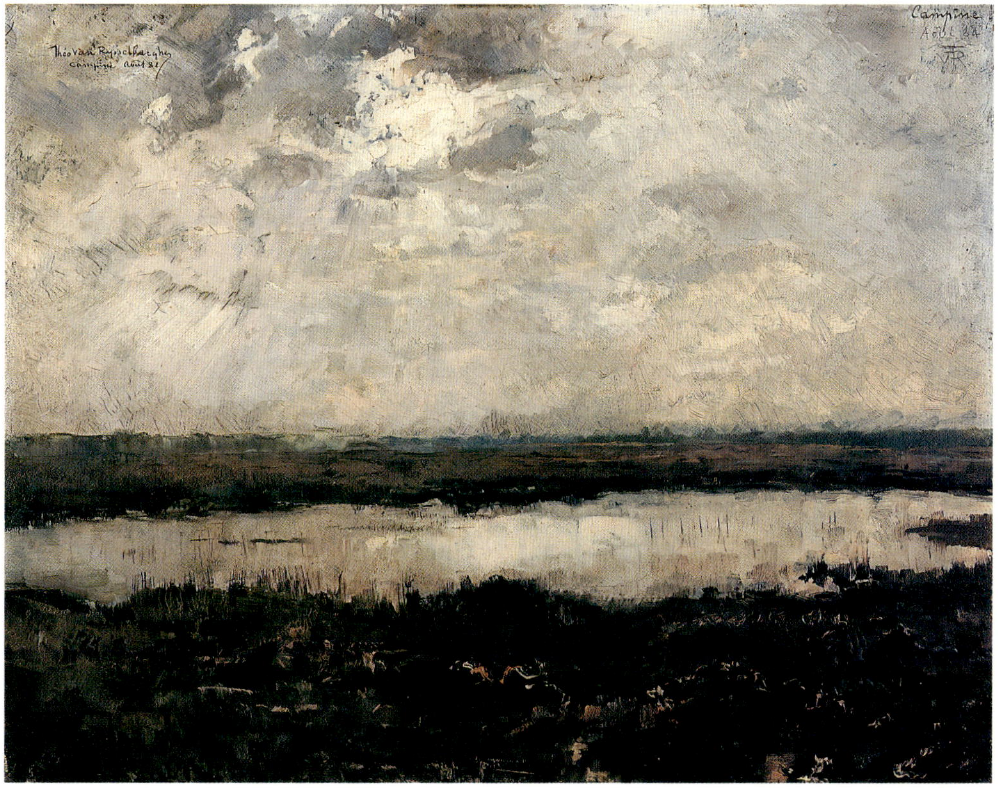
Campine

70 Portrait of Octave Maus

1885
Oil on canvas, 90 x 75.5 cm
Signed and dated bottom right: à mon ami O. Maus / Déc. 85 / TVR
Musées royaux des Beaux-Arts de Belgique / Koninklijke Musea voor Schone Kunsten van België, Brussels, inv. no. 6383

At the 1886 Salon des XX, Van Rysselberghe's entries for the first time emphasized portraiture over landscape: ten of the eleven submitted works were portraits. Prominent among them was this portrait of the artist's close friend, Octave Maus. The twenty-nine-year-old Maus – lawyer, co-founder of the radical review, *L'Art moderne* in 1881, creator of the Groupe des XX two years later and animator of the Les XX and La Libre Esthétique exhibitions, art patron, amateur musician and ardent devotee of Richard Wagner – stands beside his black laquer piano, confident and relaxed, if reflective. The Japanese-inspired lamp, delicately reflected in the mirror behind him, contributes to establish an elegant, artistic milieu.

With its self-consciously balanced blocks of colour and its elimination of sharp focus, the portrait reveals an obvious debt to Whistler, who was invited to exhibit at the very first Les XX show in 1884.[1] Indeed, this debt was noted by more than one critic. The *Journal des Beaux-Arts et de la Littérature* of 15 February 1886 declared: 'There M. Van Rysselberghe ... sets up some ten portraits which demonstrate a real decline and an infatuation with Whistler ...', while Georges Verdavainne, in *La Fédération Artistique* ('L'exposition des XX–II') stated that the first exhibition of Whistler at Les XX in 1884 'had left its marks. Some of the young, like M. Van Rysselberghe, to cite him alone, admirers of his symphonies, have adopted the principal aspects of his techniques in their own canvases.[2] The influence of Whistler upon the younger Belgian artists, while being regarded on the whole as detrimental by the critics, was indeed so pronounced among the members of Les XX that several of them supported the proposal of the anglophile *vingtiste*, Willy Finch, to accord him membership (Whistler was then living in London). Van Rysselberghe voted in favour of Whistler's admission, but it was decided to reserve the vacancy for a younger Belgian artist.

Many of the conservative critics were alarmed at Van Rysselberghe's change of style and longed for his earlier romantic landscapes from Morocco, such as *Fantasia* (1884, Musées royaux des Beaux-Arts de Belgique, Brussels) shown at the Salon des XX of 1885. They believed that the 'real decline and an infatuation with Whistler' which they recognized in Van Rysselberghe's 1886 portraits was to 'lead to the downfall of this young and so gifted artist'.[3] | JB

PROVENANCE Mme Octave Maus; acquired by the Museum in 1944.
EXHIBITIONS / BIBLIOGRAPHY *Les XX* 1886, no. 5; Brussels 1927, no. 9; Knokke 1955, no. 40; Brussels 1962, no. 119; Ghent 1962, no. 34; London 1965, no. 64; Brussels 1969a, no. 59; Brussels 1979, no. 82; New York 1980, no. 86; Brussels 1990, no. 37; Brussels 1993–1994, no. 73.

1 Whistler exhibited at Les XX in 1884 *Arrangement in Black no. v, Portrait of Miss C.; Arrangement in Grey and Green, Portrait of Miss Alexander, no I; Symphony in White no. III* and three etchings from his *Venice* series.
2 '... a laissé des traces. Des jeunes, comme M. Van Rysselberghe, pour ne citer que celui-là, admirateurs de ses symphonies, ont adopté dans plusieurs de leur toiles les principales lignes de son procédé.'
3 '... réel déclin et une infatuation de Whistler devant mener à sa perte ce jeune artiste si bien doué' (X., *Journal des Beaux-Arts et de la Littérature*, 15 February 1886, 20).

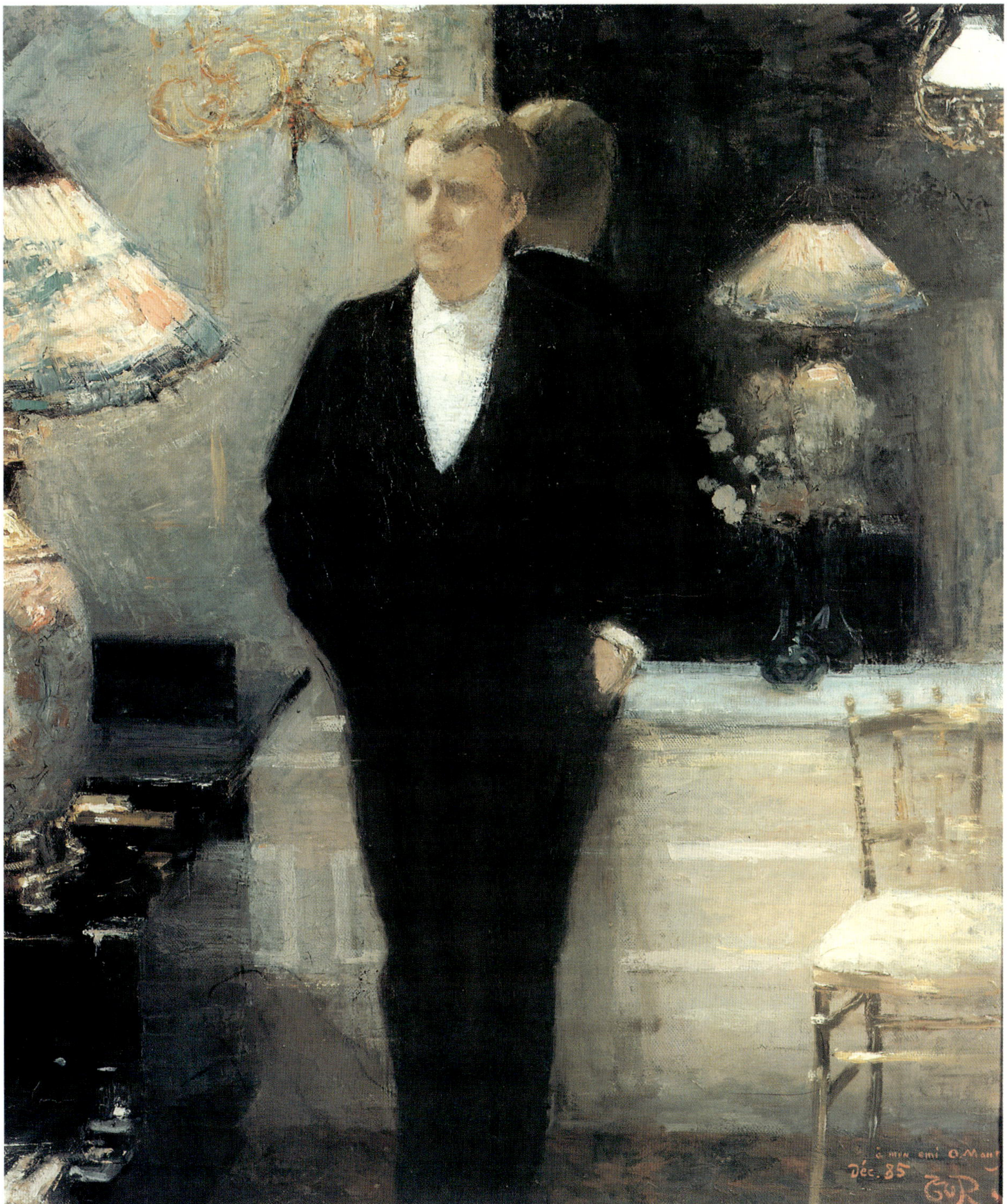
Déc. 85

71 Portrait of Anna Boch

1892
Oil on canvas, 95.2 x 64.8 cm
Monogrammed bottom right
Museum of Fine Arts, Springfield, Massachusetts, The James Philip Gray Collection, inv. no. 70.04

By the time Van Rysselberghe depicted the painter and *vingtiste*, Anna Boch (1848–1936), in her atelier with palette and brush in hand, he had already created some half-a-dozen Neo-Impressionist portraits. After seeing Seurat's *La Grande Jatte* (1884–1887; Art Institute of Chicago) in Paris in 1886, Van Rysselberghe adopted the pointillist technique, applying it to his land- and seascapes, but most notably to portraiture. He and Lemmen (q.v.) were the two Belgian pointillists who excelled and delighted at capturing the human form on canvas [see cats. 41, 42]. Van Rysselberghe's portraits are classically conceived, often monumental, but imbued with an essentially modern character through the application of the novel technique. Unlike the portraits of Lemmen, however, those of Van Rysselberghe tend to focus more on palpable physicality than on psychological portrayal.

Boch met Van Rysselberghe through her cousin, Octave Maus [see cat. 70], the lawyer, co-founder of *L'Art moderne*, patron of the arts and guiding force behind Les XX, and the two artists formed a strong friendship. Thus, the painting is very much a personal homage from one artist to another. Standing with palette and paintbrush as if caught in the process of creating a painting, Boch stands in front of a Japanese print, the neck and scroll of a violin immediately beneath. Not only is the latter a reference to her musical accomplishments,[1] but the print conveys the enthusiasm which both Anna and her brother, the artist Eugène Boch,[2] shared with so many Belgians in the 1880s for Japanese prints. Indeed, her pose and overall simplification of form echo the figure in the Japanese print. Van Rysselberghe's portrait of her held significant meaning for her, since she parted with it only in death, when it was sold at her estate sale in 1936.

Anna and Eugène Boch were the children of the wealthy porcelain manufacturer, Frédéric-Victor Boch, and his cousin Anne-Marie-Lucie Boch. Anna Boch, who became a student of Isidore Verheyden (q.v.) in 1876, was elected to membership of Les XX in 1885 together with her master. She remained the sole 'femme vingtiste', exhibiting annually at Les XX from 1886 to 1893 and subsequently virtually every year with La Libre Esthétique. Swept along by her friendship with Van Rysselberghe and the impact of Seurat's works shown at Les XX in 1887 and 1889, Anna Boch painted briefly in a pointillist style. Seurat himself identified her as one of the *vingtistes* 'favourably disposed to optical painting', and she was among the Belgian contingent who received a work by Seurat from the master's family after his untimely death.[3] She subsequently adopted a more generalized 'Impressionist' technique which she applied primarily to landscape and still-life subjects.

Boch is also remembered today for her important art collection, including works by Van Gogh, Ensor, Seurat, Signac and Gauguin, many of which she donated to the Musées royaux des Beaux-Arts de Belgique, Brussels. | JB

PROVENANCE Anna Boch; Jean Metthey; Galerie de l'Elysée, Paris; Walter P. Chrysler, Jr.; Coe Kerr Gallery, New York.

EXHIBITIONS Paris 1892, no. 1199; Brussels 1927, no. 23; Brussels 1936, no. 131; Venice 1952, no. 20; New York 1953, no. 98; Dayton 1960, no. 74; New York 1980, no. 88; Brussels 1990a, no. 57; Ghent 1993, no. 32; Pontoise 1994.

BIBLIOGRAPHY Faider-Thomas 1968, 402–410; Sutter 1970, 201; Robinson 1971; Faider-Thomas 1979, 9; *Handbook of the American and European Collections*, Museum of Fine Arts, Springfield, Mass., 1979, 164; J. Block, in Ghent 1993, 17.

1 Anna, an accomplished violinist, organist, and pianist, held weekly musical soirées at her home which many of her painter-friends attended.
2 For example, in 1887 Van Rysselberghe asked Eugène to mail a packet of Japanese woodblock prints from Paris (Van Rysselberghe to Eugène Boch, 11 October 1887; Archives de l'Art contemporain, Brussels, inv. no. 3862).
3 'Vingtistes favorables à la peinture optique'. Letter from Seurat to Félix Fénéon cited in C. M. de Hauke, *Seurat et son œuvre*, Paris 1961, 1: xx.

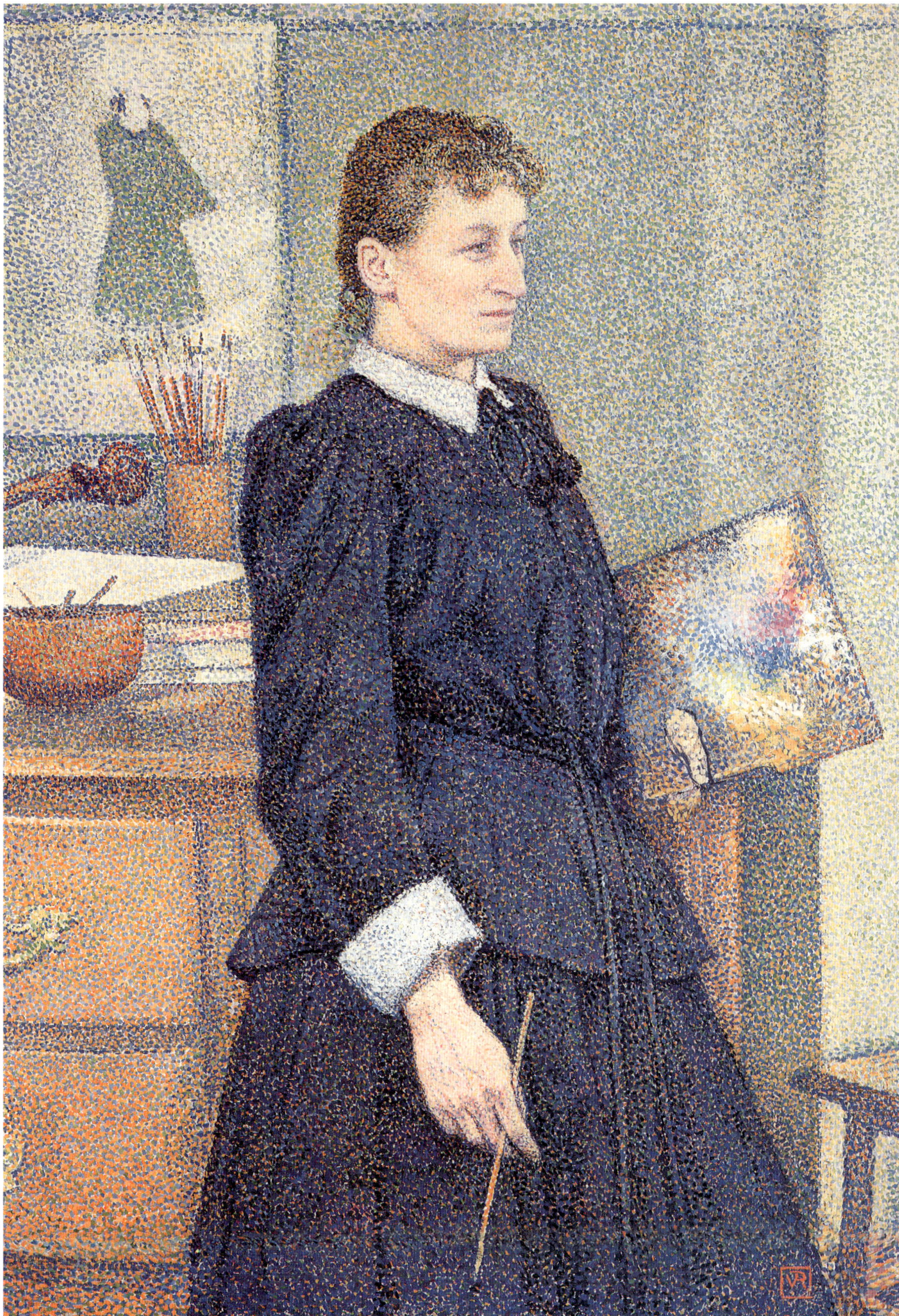

72 Portrait of the Violinist Irma Sèthe

Portrait de la violoniste Irma Sèthe, 1894
Oil on canvas, 197.5 x 114.5 cm
Monogrammed and dated bottom right: 18VR94
Musée du Petit Palais, Geneva, inv. no. 12277

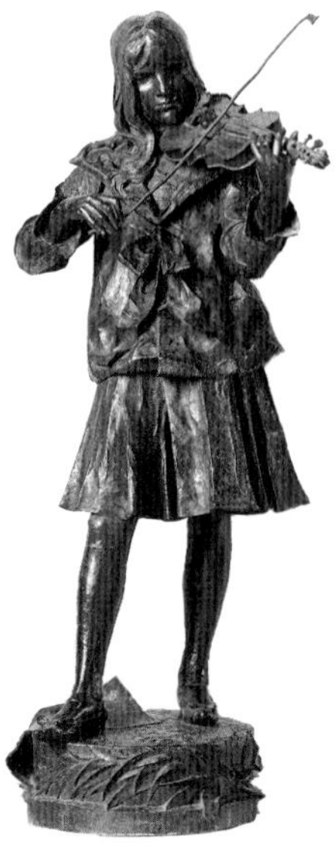

fig. a PAUL DU BOIS
Irma Sèthe playing the Violin, 1889, bronze, Conservatoire Royal, Brussels

Irma Sèthe (b. 1876) and her two older sisters, Maria (b. 1867) and Alice (b. 1869), were raised in a musical and artistic environment. The home of Gérard and Louise Sèthe was the centre of cultural soirées at which the girls were urged to play an active role. By the time he began Irma's portrait, Van Rysselberghe had already painted Alice in 1888 (now in the Musée du Prieuré, Saint-Germain-en-Laye) and Maria in 1891 (now in the Koninklijk Museum voor Schone Kunsten, Antwerp). This affinity with the arts led two of the sisters to marry *vingtistes*: Maria wed Henry van de Velde and Alice married the sculptor Du Bois. Irma, herself, was an irresistible subject, leading Du Bois to capture her at the tender age of thirteen, playing her violin [fig. a]. Van Rysselberghe showed her likewise, as she performed a duet at the Brussels Conservatory[1] with her renowned mentor Eugène Ysaÿe, the founder of the celebrated Ysaÿe Quartet which gave many of the first Belgian performances of compositions by Debussy, Ravel and César Franck.

In this full-length portrait, Irma Sèthe plays the violin while through the open door a female figure in the adjoining room listens to the music. While being unified by the power of music, the painting is built upon complementary elements. The standing, active Irma is counteracted by the seated, passive listener. This dichotomy is strengthened pictorially through divisionist colour oppositions: the pinks and greens that define Irma's world contrast with the lavenders and oranges of the auditor's space. The two framed prints on the wall are a subtle foil for the ephemeral nature of the musical performance. Irma's plastic form makes a sharp comparison with the geometrically conceived background. The extravagance of her puffed sleeves, bowed sash at her waist and wisps of her blond hair contrast with the rectilinear partitions behind her. The violinist's stunning pink dress is accented with greens and blues.

Van Rysselberghe reported his great pleasure with his portrait to his friend Paul Signac. Signac apparently concurred, for he noted in his diary: 'From Van Rysselberghe, a delicious portrait of Mlle Sèthe.'[2] | JB

PROVENANCE Mrs Irma Saenger-Sèthe; Mrs Elis Chapiro; sale London, Sotheby's, 3 April 1974 (no. 76); Hugo Perls, New York.
EXHIBITIONS Paris 1895, no. 1527; *La Libre Esthétique* 1898, no. 375; Vienna 1899, no. 46; New York 1971, no. 128; Ghent 1993, no. 37.
BIBLIOGRAPHY E. Verhaeren, 'Théo Van Rysselberghe', in *Ver Sacrum* (1899), 12; Maus 1926, 228, note 1; Fierens *s.d.*, 20; Mauclair 1903, 86; Rewald 1949, 118; J. Block, in Ghent 1993, 18.

1 In September 1890 Irma entered the Conservatoire de Musique in Brussels in the class of the violin virtuoso Eugène Ysaÿe. She had an international career as a concert violinist, making her London début in 1894. After marrying Dr Samuel Saenger (1864–1944), a Doctor of Philosophy in Berlin on 31 July 1897, she taught at the Berlin Hochschule. The couple remained in Germany until 1940, when they moved to Los Angeles to rejoin one of their daughters.
2 J. Rewald, 'Extraits du journal inédit de Paul Signac, Part I, 1894–1895', *Gazette des Beaux-Arts* 36:118 (July–September 1949).

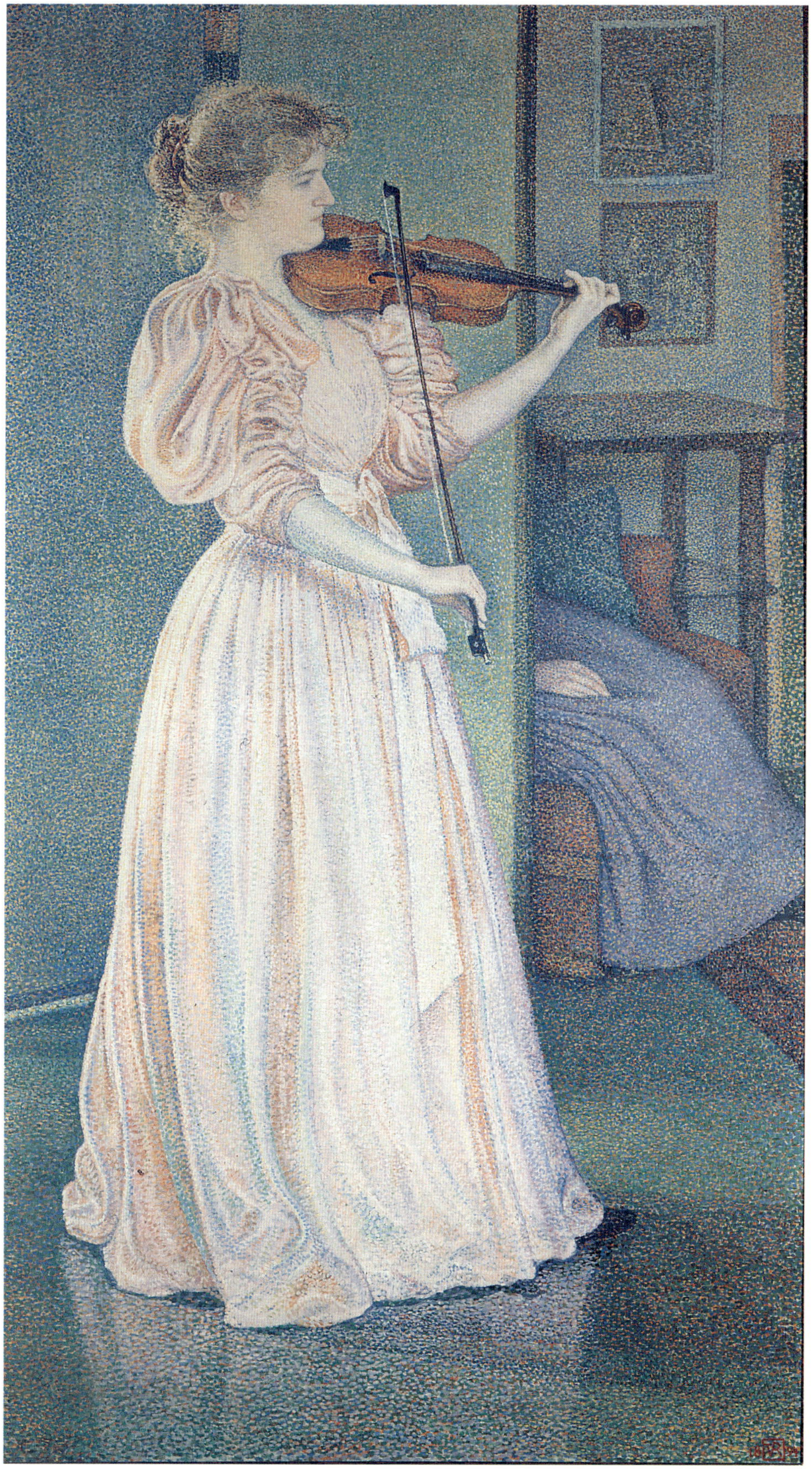

73 View of the Scheldt

Scheldegezicht – L'Escaut occidental vu des dunes de Cadzand, 1893
Oil on canvas, 55 x 75 cm
Signed and dated bottom right: 18 TVR 93
Lent by the Haags Gemeentemuseum, The Hague

Images of the River Scheldt, painted or engraved and often enlivened with sailing boats, feature regularly in Van Rysselberghe's work. This *View of the Scheldt* is one of his most straightforward and simple marine compositions. It consists of a view of the horizon from a dune, which fills up the foreground, inverting the traditional repoussoir or framing devices at each side of a landscape composition. The arrangement of the three horizontal strips of dune, water and sky creates balance and stability, and removes all hint of tension from the painting. Matching dimensions are also used: the maximum height of the water is the same as that of the sky, while the maximum height of the foreground is repeated in the sky at the edges. The parallel contours of the riverbank and clouds extend the horizontal structure of the composition beyond the confines of the edges of the canvas, thus investing the painting with a pronounced sense of space. Unlike the French Neo-Impressionists or their Belgian confrères such as Finch (q.v.) and Van de Velde (q.v.), Van Rysselberghe has presented a characteristic link with reality which prevents the picture plane from being organized in too complex or abstract a manner.

The observation of visual reality also dominates the technique. *View of the Scheldt* displays the characteristic interpretation of Seurat by his followers – a feature less evident in *Canal in Flanders* [cat. 74]. The pointillist technique is applied with caution and moderation. Adopting a palette far closer to that characteristic of Seurat than is found in *Canal in Flanders*, the clear northern light has been translated through primary and complementary colours, an even tonality being achieved by the application across the entire canvas of small white dots. The use of white as a highlight rather than as a foundation causes the light to fall on the scene from outside. The size and density of the dots also comply with the illusionistic laws governing the chosen subject: they are strongest around the edges, which the eye tends to skip over, and in the 'docile' strokes in the water or grass where they best serve the illusion of reality. They are least pronounced in the strips of sand and the pink clouds. This faithfulness to the strict laws of pointillism differs, for instance, from Van de Velde's far less naturalistic, more abstractly patterned application in *The Beach at Blankenberghe with Beach Huts* [cat. 65]. Seen against the earlier manifestations of realist landscape and the Belgian variant of Impressionism, the bright clarity of the optical mix in *View of the Scheldt* must have seemed innovative. Moreover, with its uncomplicated directness, the peace and stillness of the composition recall the contemplative and harmonious character of Seurat's marine paintings, a quality which is only rarely found elsewhere in such examples of Belgian Neo-Impressionism as Finch's *Cliffs at South Foreland* [cat. 24]. The dotted border painted around the scene is a device borrowed directly from Seurat. It is entirely faithful to divisionist theory in that its colours harmonize with the adjacent hues in the composition. In accordance with the same law the orange hue which is complementary to the darker part of the border is also used for the monogram. | ML

PROVENANCE H. Cleyndert, The Hague, who donated it to the Museum in 1958.
EXHIBITIONS Vienna 1899 (ex-catalogue); Rotterdam 1936–1937, no. 38a; Düsseldorf 1977, no. 97 (as 'View of The Scheldt'); Ghent 1980, no. 224 (idem); Ghent 1993, no. 46 (idem).
BIBLIOGRAPHY Hevesi 1906, 106.

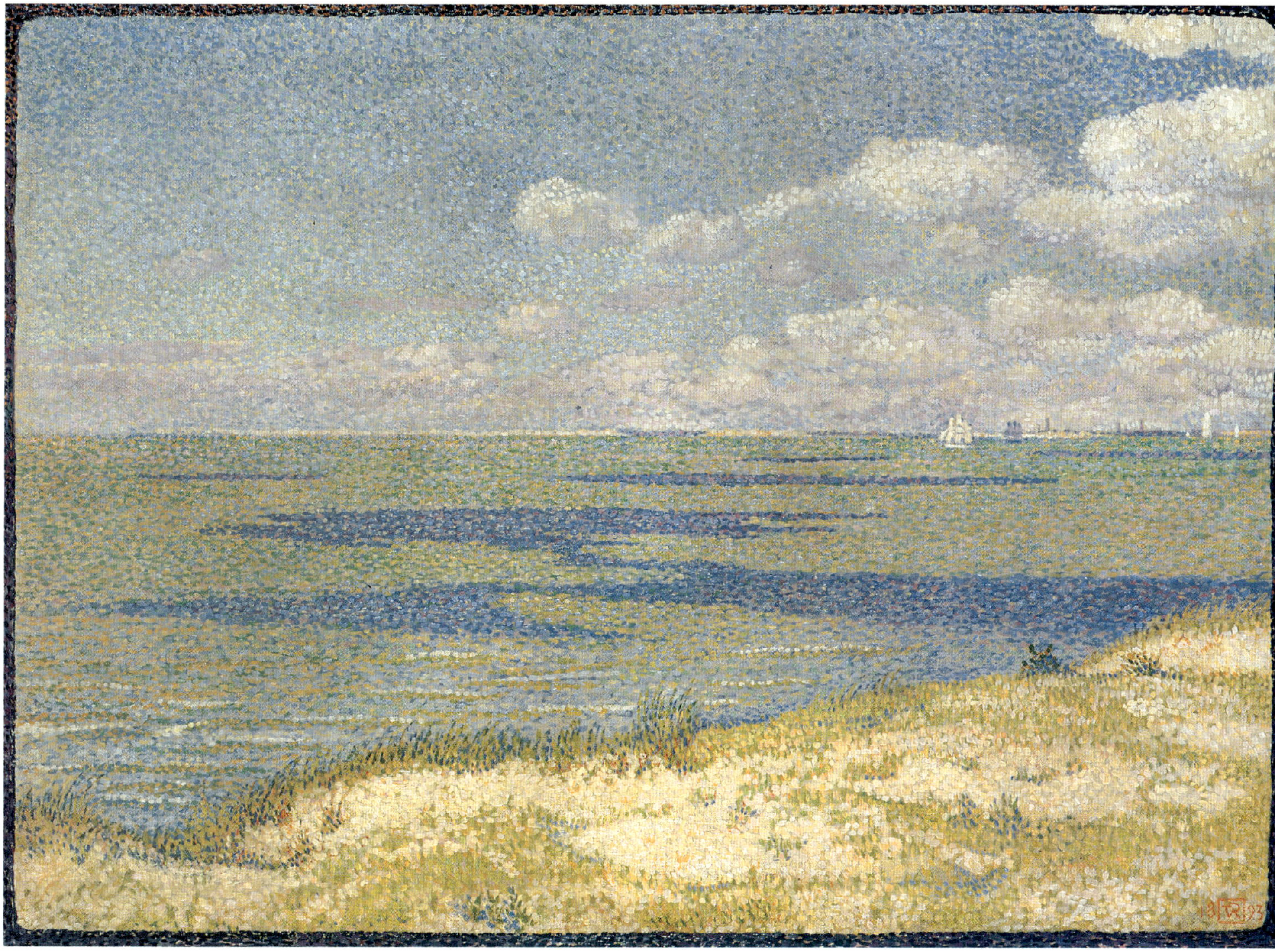

74 Canal in Flanders

Kanaal in Vlaanderen, 1894
Oil on canvas, 60 x 80 cm
Signed and dated bottom left: 18 TVR 94
Private Collection

Canal in Flanders has a more direct impact than the rich nuances of the *Portrait of Irma Sèthe* [cat. 72], painted in the same year. It belongs to a later stage of Van Rysselberghe's evolution towards a looser, less systematic use of Neo-Impressionist technique. The brushstrokes are broader and more varied, and their shape and direction are adapted to the forms they define in different parts of the painting. Even more so than in his earlier works, the artist renounces the use of the pointillist technique in certain key areas, including the water in the foreground and the row of trees. His use of colour suggests a desire for synthesis: unlike the swirling, divergent tones of the portrait, the colours in this painting come together in separate strips, where they are brought to life by the careful addition of chromatic components like orange dots on blue. The colour scheme thus appears limited to a pair of dominants, which alternate in segments and are attuned to one another: green with purplish or greyish blue. Together, they form a diffuse tone corresponding with the soft, simple rhythm of the lines. This allows the canvas to convey a specific mood. A similar effect is achieved in *The Scheldt upriver from Antwerp after a Fog* (1892; Private Collection),[1] through the same simplification of colour and form. In addition to Neo-Impressionist theories regarding the emotional value of the line, Van Rysselberghe must have been familiar with contemporary theories regarding colour as a determinant of mood. The latter had already been developed in three paintings by Louis Anquetin in which a dominant tone in each work served both to describe a specific time of day and to evoke an appropriate mood – morning, noon and evening. These three works were exhibited at Van Rysselberghe's behest at the 1888 Salon des XX.

Verhaeren described the evocative power of *Canal in Flanders* in 1898: 'Nuances of greys and greens merge to evoke the sad impression of heavy sky and rainy weather reaching to infinity. No violent oppositions, the nuances of the two basic colours counterbalance each other. They stretch out in nearly identical scales. And these lines, forever fleeing, forever plunging towards the horizon ..., they add to the bleak, cold idea, to the feeling of dampness, to the elongated spleen of the painting ... A complete unity.'[2]

The striking diagonals of the perspective which Verhaeren linked to the emotional expression of the painting was interpreted fifteen years later in a more strongly stylized manner and with an even more powerful psychological charge by Léon Spilliaert (q.v.). Van Rysselberghe ought not, however, to be characterized purely as a painter of mood similar to artists of a Symbolist bent both in Belgium and elsewhere in Europe. There is too little evidence of personal emotional involvement in his work. The main ambition of this landscape, as in all his work, was to represent external reality through the eyes of the artist.

Such an ambition tended to isolate his work from the mainstream of non-naturalistic or expressionist records of the external world. However, it would appear that Van Rysselberghe's art did have an impact on younger artists. Faistauer, in 1923 for instance,[3] pointed to the influence of Van Rysselberghe's technique on Gustav Klimt's landscapes. To be sure, Van Rysselberghe enjoyed great success in Vienna after 1899, the year in which the first of his four shows at the Secession was organized and a long article about him was published in *Ver Sacrum*. The Viennese public was won over by the modernity and mastery of technique in his work,[4] while artists like Klimt must have been attracted to the potential for decorative stylization and the combination of discreet detachment and emotionality – characteristics which are clearly present in *Canal in Flanders*.

It is possible that the painting had a wooden frame decorated in a pointillist style by the artist. The entry in the 1962 Ghent exhibition catalogue refers – probably erroneously – to a frame by Van de Velde. | ML

PROVENANCE Auguste Weber, Luxembourg; Hugo Perls, New York; Acquavelle Galleries, New York; John T. Dorrance, Pennsylvania.

EXHIBITIONS Dresden 1897; *La Libre Esthétique* 1898, no. 384; Vienna 1899 (ex-catalogue); Brussels 1927, no. 27; Ghent 1962, no. 62; New York 1968, no. 138; London 1979–1980, no. 411; Ghent 1980, no. 225; Washington 1980, no. 245; Ghent 1993, no. 48.

BIBLIOGRAPHY Verhaeren 1898, 86; Verhaeren 1899, 9; R. L. Herbert, in New York 1968, 186; M.A. Stevens, in London 1979–1980, 271–272.

1 New York 1968, no. 136; Ghent 1993, no. 42.
2 *L'Art moderne* (1898), 86. The same Salon de La Libre Esthétique also included a *Canal en Flandre par temps triste* (no. 385; letter of Van Rysselberghe, see Chartrain-Hebbelinck 1966, 78). However, *L'Art moderne* only mentioned *Canal en Flandre*, calling it one of the most important works in the show. Maus (1926, 228), on the other hand, called *Le Canal par temps triste* 'one of the most beautiful landscapes of the period'. Another variant emerged at the 1993 Ghent exhibition (no. 47): an unfinished canvas of the same size showing the same motif but seen from a different angle.
3 A. Faistauer, 'Neue Malerei in Österreich', reprint in O. Breicha (ed.), *Gustav Klimt. Die goldene Pforte. Werk – Wesen – Wirkung*, Salzburg 1978, 186.
4 Hevesi 1906, 102–107.

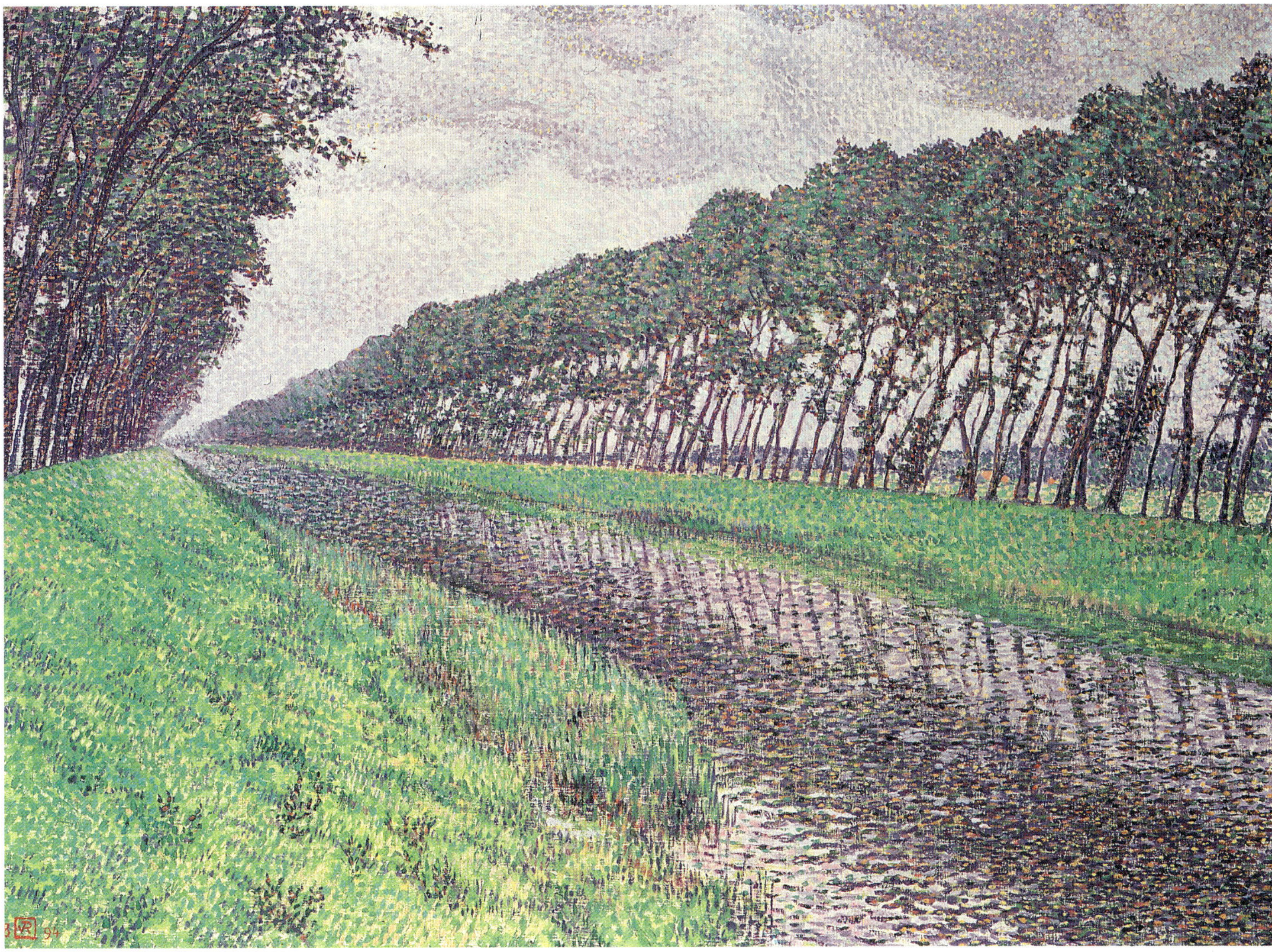

75 Tea in the Garden

Le Thé au jardin, c. 1904
Oil on canvas, 98 x 130 cm
Monogrammed bottom left: TVR
Musée d'Ixelles, Brussels, Octave Maus 184

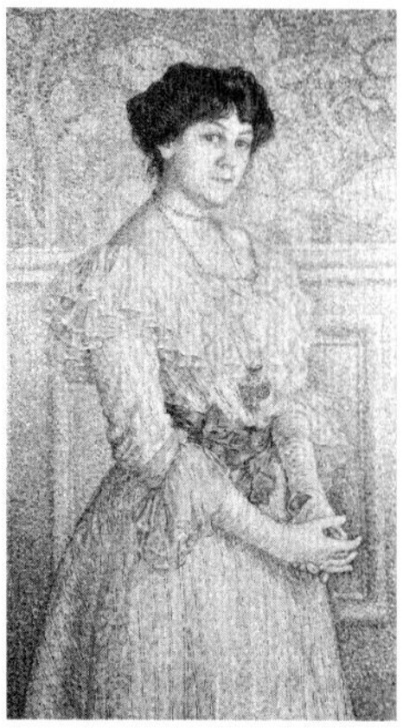

fig. a THÉO VAN RYSSELBERGHE
Portrait of Laure Flé, 1898,
Musée National d'Histoire et d'Art
du Grand-Duché de Luxembourg

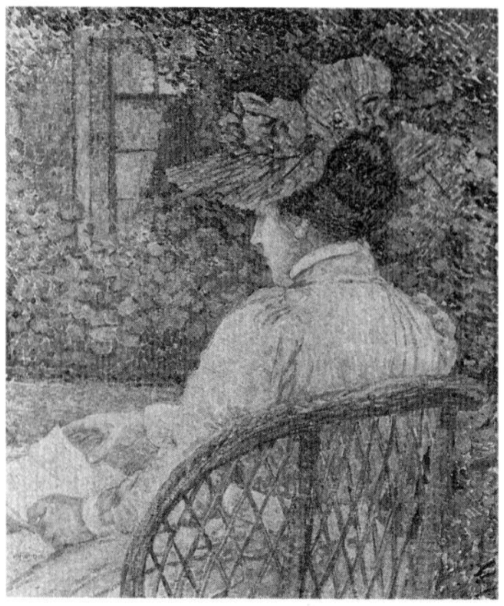

fig. b THÉO VAN RYSSELBERGHE
Woman wearing a Blue Hat, 1900,
Rijksmuseum Kröller-Müller, Otterlo

In *Tea in the Garden*, three women are seated in front of a country house, amusing themselves through such female pursuits as reading, sewing or simply taking tea. Each is self-absorbed, intently engaged in her particular activity. To capture the mid-morning, summer atmosphere, Van Rysselberghe employs a palette of cool greens, violets and blues. The woman at the right in the blue hat was the subject of an independent panel painting by Van Rysselberghe [fig. b].[1] The oil sketch shows the sitter in a similar wicker chair and in the same pose as the finished painting, but in the sketch she is seated closer to the house and her fringed shawl is absent. The rapidly applied, cross-hatched strokes of the study have disappeared in the final version, the overall touch of which is now more regularized and blended. Although the study is dated 1900, we know that in December 1901 Van Rysselberghe, still unsatisfied, had not completed the work.[2] That the finished oil both lacks a coherent treatment according to Van Rysselberghe's personal interpretation of Neo-Impressionist colour theory, and utilizes a squarer, longer brushstroke which gives the painting a more decorative rather than prismatic character, suggests that in its present state it must have been made after 1903, the year of Van Rysselberghe's last pointillist portrait group, *La Lecture* (*The Reading*, Museum voor Schone Kunsten, Ghent). In these two respects, while similar in subject matter to *A Family in an Orchard* (1890; Rijksmuseum Kröller-Müller, Otterlo), it marks a significant evolution in style and application of Neo-Impressionism.

Although technically not a group portrait, but a genre scene in a landscape, the three sitters in *Tea in the Garden* are individualized by their activities and their wonderfully flamboyant hats. Van Rysselberghe was careful to record their particular facial features. Thus, identification reveals something of the artist's choice of subject. No documents have come to light that might help us to identify the figures here or in *A Family in an Orchard*, and Van Rysselberghe himself did not provide any clues. Nevertheless identifications have been attempted. In the painting of 1890, although the emphasis also is on genre activity, two of the figures can be identified as part of the intimist circle of the painter: Marie van Rysselberghe and Maria van de Velde. In this later work, the woman in the blue hat has also been named as Maria Van de Velde, but this is clearly erroneous. She is more likely to have been the painter's wife, Marie.[3] The woman in the centre strongly resembles a close family friend, Laure Flé, whose portrait Van Rysselberghe had painted in 1898 [fig. a]. | JB

PROVENANCE Collection of Octave Maus.
EXHIBITIONS Charleroi 1960, no. 60; London 1965, no. 65; Tokyo 1981, no. 44; Kanagawa 1984, no. 22; Brussels 1990, no. 59; Ghent 1993, no. 61.
BIBLIOGRAPHY Mauclair 1903, 85, 87.

1 In addition, the 1993 Ghent exhibition (Ghent 1993, no. 60) identified an oil study for *Tea in the Garden*.
2 Letter from Van Rysselberghe to Van de Velde, 12 December 1901 (Bibliothèque Royale, Brussels, Musée de la Littérature, FSX 800/11).
3 Firstly, Mme Van de Velde was blonde. In addition, the sharp bridge of the nose and overall facial features correspond more closely with an identification of Marie van Rysselberghe than Maria van de Velde. In the *Paintings of the Rijksmuseum Kröller-Müller* (1969, 229), the figure in the painting *Woman wearing a Blue Hat* is identified as Mrs Van de Velde.

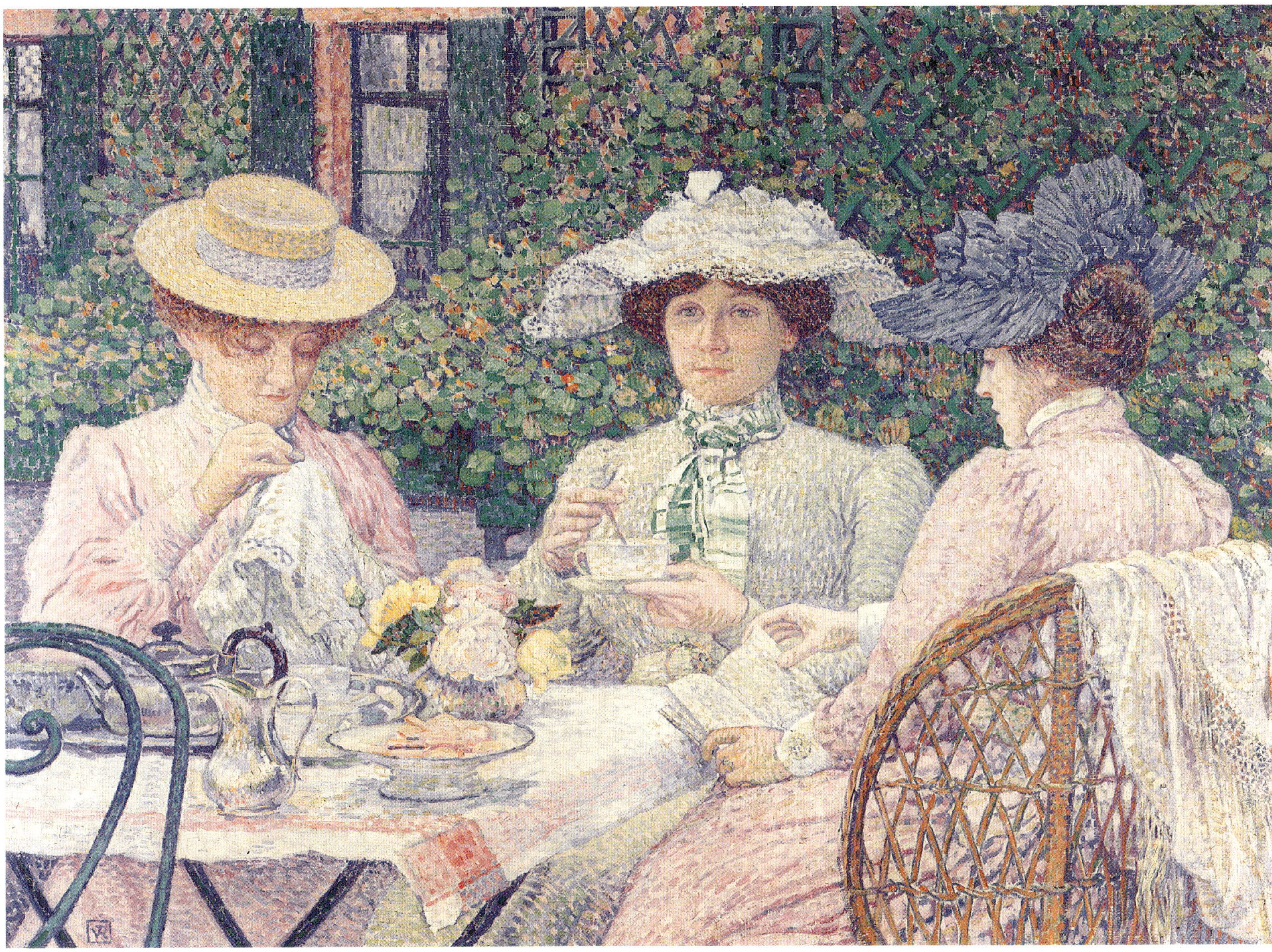

Guillaume-Séraphin van Strydonck

NAMSOS (NORWAY) 1861 – SAINT-GILLES (BRUSSELS) 1937

Guillaume-Séraphin van Strydonck was the son of Flemish parents then resident in the Norwegian city of Namsos. He received his first drawing lessons at the age of twelve in the Brussels studio of the figure painter Edouard Agneessens (1842–1885), a fine draughtsman and a friend of the family. He entered the Academy of Fine Arts in Brussels in 1876. In the early 1880s, he is reported to have attended Jean-Léon Gérôme's classes at the Ecole des Beaux-Arts in Paris. Although he failed to receive the Prix de Rome from the Brussels Academy in 1883, the following year he was awarded the Prix Godecharle for the painting *The History of Tobias*. In a notice, published in the periodical *L'Art moderne* in November 1883, Van Strydonck is listed as one of the founding members of the Brussels avant-garde circle Les XX. He made his public début by showing six paintings at the Salon of L'Essor in January of that year and presented four works at the first Salon des XX in February 1884. In May 1884, he shows three works at the annual Salon des Artistes Français in Paris. His contributions to the ten Salons des XX from 1884 until 1893 illustrate a young painter's development from Realism, through a moderate form of Impressionism to a cautious adoption of divisionist procedures. His initial work was strongly influenced by James Ensor (q.v.) and James McNeil Whistler, the latter being invited as a special guest for the first exhibition of Les XX. In 1888, Van Strydonck was invited by the Parisian Société des 33 to contribute to their Salon at the Galeries Georges Petit in Paris. Though he had been an active member of Les XX, he only exhibited in a few salons of its successor group, La Libre Esthétique.

Van Strydonck was an intrepid and extensive traveller. He went to Mandarin, a puritan community in northeastern Florida, USA, in 1886 [see cat. 76], and to India in 1891, where he stayed for five years. Upon his return from his many travels at the turn of the century, he settled in the countryside near Antwerp. Until his death in 1937 in Saint-Gilles (Brussels), he divided his time primarily between landscape painting and the drawing classes which he delivered at the Brussels Academy.

The special light and atmosphere of Mandarin near Jacksonville, Florida, may have encouraged Van Strydonck to adopt a form of Impressionism. During his stay, his palette lightened and he replaced the largely linear construction of volumes in space with forms created in terms of light and masses. | FL

SUMMARY BIBLIOGRAPHY

M. Haloche, *G. S. Van Strydonck*, Brussels 1922; *Exposition rétrospective de Julien Dillens Sculpteur (1849–1904) et de Guillaume S. Van Strydonck Peintre*, Cercle Artistique et Littéraire, Brussels 1933; B. de Clercq, 'Van Strydonck, Guillaume', in *Académie Royale des Beaux-Arts de Bruxelles. 275 ans d'enseignement*, Musées royaux des Beaux-Arts de Belgique, Brussels 1987, 248–249.

76 A Sunday at the Cracker's (Florida)

Les Quakers, 1886
Oil on canvas, 69 x 105 cm
Signed and dated bottom right: G.S. Van StrydoncK / A Sunday amongst / the CracKers Mandarin. Florida / 1–2–86
Musée des Beaux-Arts, Tournai

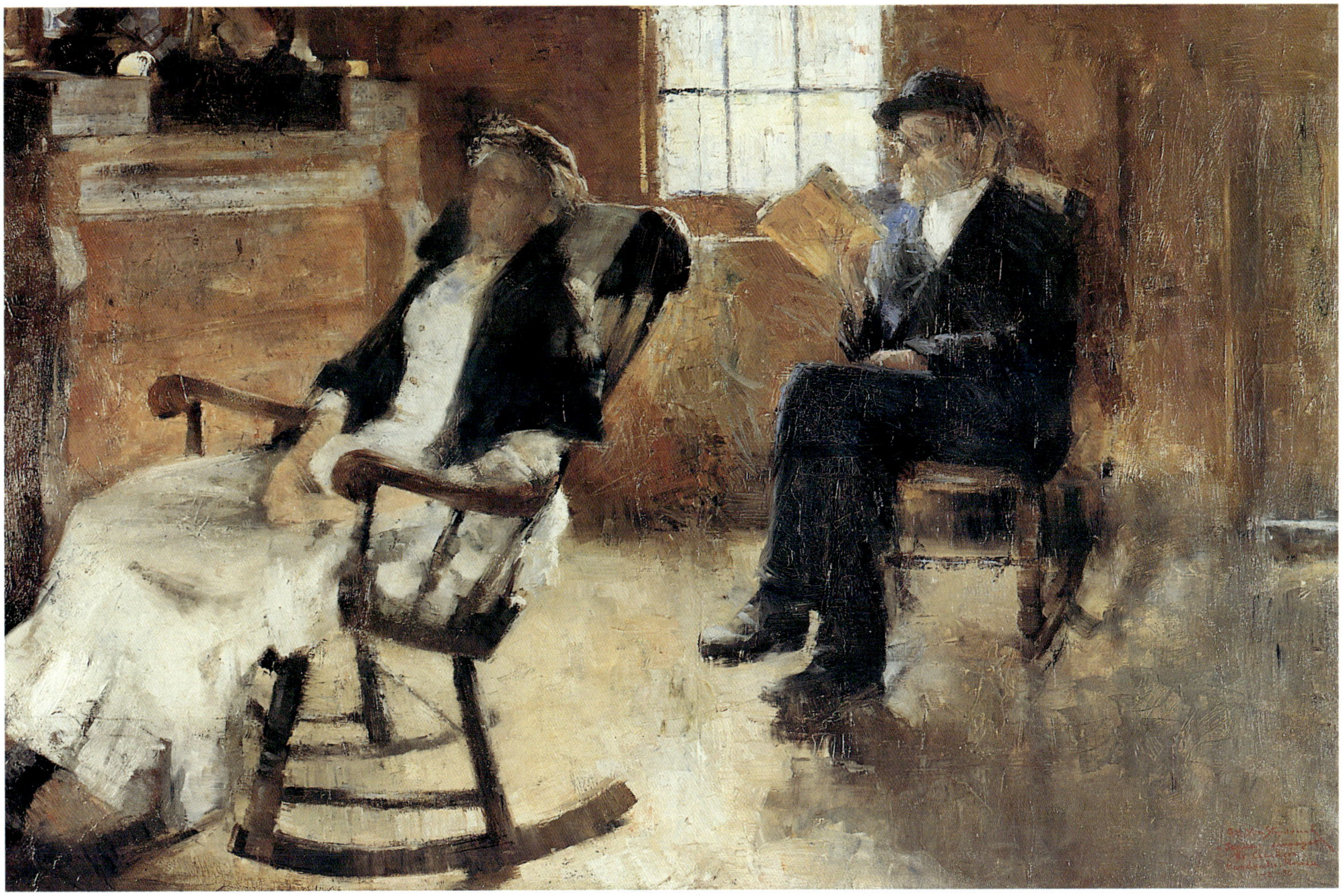

This peaceful impression of a Sunday afternoon in the home of a Cracker family in Florida belongs to a series of paintings that Van Strydonck finished during a journey to the United States in early 1886. The scene represents a sketchy interior and two people, rendered with little detail. Silence is captured by an older man, reading, and a younger woman in a rocking chair, leaning backwards in pensive mood. The clock on the mantelpiece registers the sound of time.

In keeping with many of Van Strydonck's paintings from this period, the light source is situated at the back of the pictorial space. The special conditions of lighting, provoked by the resulting *contre-jour*, dissolves the sharp edges of the forms. Van Strydonck clearly uses the opportunity presented by the unfamiliar setting and harsh southern light to explore the latter's translation onto canvas. This appears to have led him to adopt a more impressionistic palette and technique. The sombre, grey palette of his realist work (strongly influenced by French naturalist painters, notably Bastien-Lepage) gives way to brighter tonalities. Pictorial space is made more dependent upon explicit contrasts between light and dark. Although the need to retain a figurative coherence within the painting is resolutely persued, the lightening of the palette permits Van Strydonck to apply with even greater freedom the principles of painterly handling that he had already adopted from Ensor (q.v.). Thus, the forms within the composition have been built up in great slabs of impasto, frequently laid in with a palette knife. The effect is even more radical in its constructive approach to paint than many contemporaneous works by his mentor [see cats. 12–15]. On his return from Florida, Van Strydonck contributed four works to the Salon des XX of 1887, including the work shown here and its 'pendant' *News from Europe (Florida)* (no. 2; Hôtel Charlier, Brussels). Although he joined such artists as Ensor and Van Rysselberghe (q.v.) in their withdrawal from L'Essor in 1883 (shortly after Van Strydonck had exhibited with the group), he cannot be seen as one of the latter group's more innovative members. As *Sunday at the Cracker's (Florida)* demonstrates, Van Strydonck was essentially a realist painter who recognized and integrated some of the most significant technical innovations of his more audacious contemporaries. | FL

PROVENANCE Henri van Cutsem, Brussels, 1888; bequeathed to the Museum, 1904.
EXHIBITIONS *Les XX* 1887, no. 1; Paris 1888, no. 348; Brussels 1933, no. 126; Brussels, Otterlo 1962, no. 144; Brussels 1979, no. 88.
BIBLIOGRAPHY Haloche 1922, 20, 25 (ill.); Pierron 1926, 33, No. 118; Pion 1931, 61, No. 340; Pion, Pion-Leblanc 1971, 89, no. 596; Fondation Godecharle, 119, ill.

77 Portrait of Friends

Portrait d'amis, 1890
Oil on canvas, 120 x 146 cm
Signed and dated bottom right: G.S. VanStrydoncK / Blankenberghe.90
Musée des Beaux-Arts, Tournai

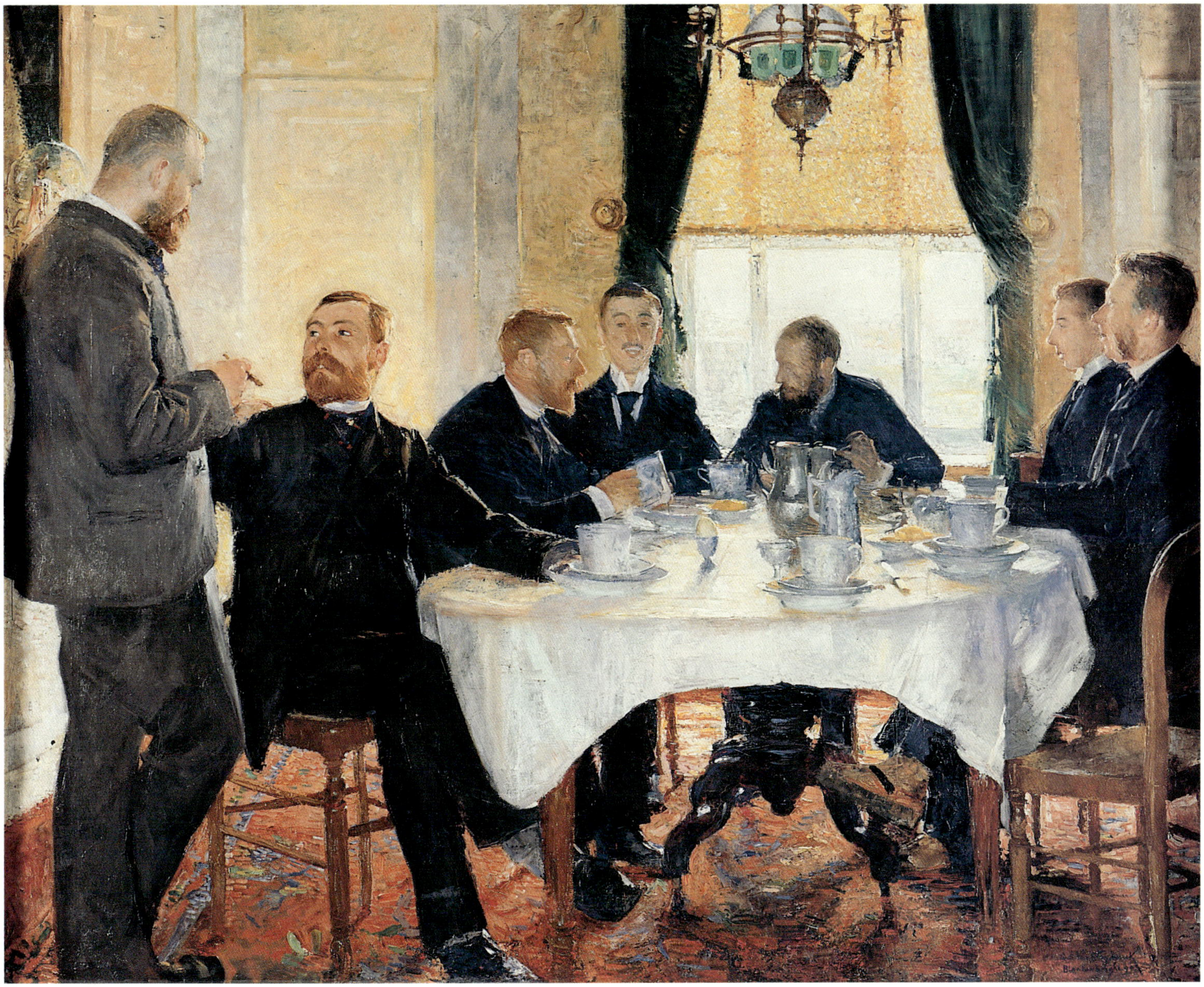

In this group portrait, Van Strydonck shows his friends in lively conversation. Breakfast is served. The setting is a spacious room in a villa in Blankenberghe on the Belgian coast, generously lit in *contre-jour* by a single window, positioned slightly off-centre.

It had been three years since Van Strydonck had seen Seurat's *Grande Jatte* at the Salon des XX in 1887. Unlike most of his fellow members of Les XX, he was reluctant wholeheartedly to embrace Neo-Impressionism. Although he has exchanged the bold blocking in of impasto, frequently with the use of a palette knife, for a more separated, dabbed brushstroke, there is only a discreet reference to divisionism in the handling of the sunlight filtered through the yellow blind. Here dabs of complementary colour (purple and green) have been placed upon the base of yellow. This overlay of related tones is somewhat comparable to the variant of divisionism created by the English artist, Philip Wilson Steer (1860–1942). Steer had also exhibited at the Salon des XX in 1887, showing amongst five works, *The Bridge* (no. 2). He exhibited again in 1892, showing nine works including *The Tidal Pool* (no. 2) and *Knucklebones* (no. 4). Van Strydonck shared with Steer a more synthetic pictorial approach to the record of figures set within a specific atmosphere. However, as an inheritance of his earlier, more constructive technique, he retained a concern for a rich and diversified painterly handling of surface which stands independently from its descriptive function.

The painting is an interesting historical document which represents some of the central figures in the famous Van Cutsem circle. Henri van Cutsem, a man of property and major Brussels collector of contemporary art, is seated first from the right next to Henri Damiens, a lawyer, archaeologist and collector. Van Cutsem used to invite his friends to his villa in Blankenberghe, a popular Belgian seaside resort. Professor François Henrijean, standing to the left, is listening to the sculptor Guillaume Charlier (1854–1925). The painter André Collin is seated to Charlier's left while the future notary Lucien Damiens stares full-faced out of the picture frame. In picturing himself *contre-jour* in the centre in front of the light source, Van Strydonck can create the most sketchy of the portraits, thus allowing himself a more discrete presence in this amiable company of friends.

In 1904, sensing his untimely death, Van Cutsem bequeathed his collection to the sculptor Charlier, who was primarily charged with arranging its donation to the Musée des Beaux-Arts in Tournai and supervising the construction of a new museum which was to be designed by Victor Horta and opened in 1928.

Portrait of Friends was bought by Van Cutsem, shortly after it was finished. It appears at first sight to be primarily a painting which celebrates Van Strydonck's fascination with light. However, it also documents the artist's equivocal attitude to the novel techniques of Impressionism and divisionism and his attachment to solid craftsmanship. In so far as this creates a tension between representational function and exploration of technique for its own sake, it bears certain affinities with such paintings of figures set in bourgeois interiors created by Ensor in the first half of the 1880s [see cat. 12] and by Mertens later in the decade [see cat. 46]. It also presages the similar tension between narrative representation, pictorial composition and the autonomy of artistic means so clearly illustrated in Van Rysselberghe's monumental group portrait of 1903, *La Lecture* (*The Reading*; Museum voor Schone Kunsten, Ghent) representing the artist's friend, Emile Verhaeren, reading to a group of literary and artistic friends in a domestic interior. | FL

PROVENANCE Henri van Cutsem, Brussels, 1890; bequeathed to the Museum, 1904.

EXHIBITIONS Brussels 1933, no. 131; Brussels 1979, no. 89; Brussels 1990a, no. 43.

BIBLIOGRAPHY Haloche 1922, 21 (ill.), 22; Pierron 1926, 34, no. 123; Pion 1931, 61, no. 334; Pion, Pion-Leblanc 1971, 90, no. 603; Goyens de Heusch 1988, 114; Le Bailly de Tilleghem 1989, 82, 103 (ill.).

Isidore Verheyden

ANTWERP 1846 – IXELLES (BRUSSELS) 1905

Throughout his artistic career, Isidore Verheyden tackled with equal competence such different genres as portraiture, figure subjects, landscapes and marine paintings. The son of the Belgian genre painter Jean François Verheyden (1806–1889), he enrolled as a student in the drawing classes at the Brussels Academy of Fine Arts in 1857 when only eleven years old. Contrary to earlier claims, his teacher there was not Joseph Quinaux since the latter was only appointed a professor at the Academy in 1876. Verheyden temporarily left the Academy in 1865, having won the first prize for drawing; he entered the free studio of Jean Portaels (1818–1895), but, in 1867 he returned for a further year of study at the Academy. His early works display a subdued tonal approach to realism, but his palette lightened and his technique became more broken as he came under the influence of Impressionism.

From 1870, Verheyden exhibited at the annual salon of the avant-garde society of Realist painters, the Société Libre des Beaux-Arts. In 1874 he settled in Hoeilaart, near Brussels. In this year he also briefly re-established his earlier relationship with Hippolyte Boulenger (1837–1874), the leader of the group of landscape painters known as the School of Tervuren, who, unfortunately, died that same year. Over the next ten years, Verheyden participated in most of the major official exhibitions in Brussels.

After an exhibition in 1883, reuniting the former students of the Portaels studio, Verheyden moved back to Brussels. On 22 November 1884, he was unanimously elected a member of Les XX. He exhibited with Les XX from 1885 to 1887, during which period he presented portraits of Anna Boch (1884; *Les XX* 1886, no. 3) and Constantin Meunier (1885; *Les XX* 1885, no. 1), but resigned on 23 May 1887 for 'purely personal reasons' (Letter to Octave Maus, Schaerbeek, 23 May 1887, Archives de l'Art contemporain belge, inv. no. 5071).

Verheyden belonged to the second generation of Belgian painters. He was reluctant fully to adopt the innovative technique of divisionism which was to dominate Les XX after 1887. However, his fascination with the role of light in the definition of form made him receptive to certain aspects of mature Impressionism, notably as practised by Camille Pissarro after 1890. Thus his own work created during the last decade of his life not only presents a looser painting technique, but also an even more heightened, brighter palette. From 1900 onwards, Verheyden taught at the Brussels Academy of Fine Arts and was appointed its director in 1904, one year before his death. | FL

SUMMARY BIBLIOGRAPHY

Isidore Verheyden 1848–1905, Palais des Beaux-Arts, Brussels 1942; M. France, 'Isidore Verheyden (1846–1905)', *Revue des archéologistes et historiens d'art* 17 (1984), 320; N. Hostyn, 'Verheyden, Isidore, landschaps- en portretschilder', *Nationaal biografisch woordenboek* 14 (1992), col. 709–713; G. Vanzype, *Notice sur Isidore Verheyden*, Brussels 1928.

78 The Gleaners

Les Glaneuses – De arenleessters, 1885–1886
Oil on canvas, 92 x 69 cm
Signed bottom right: Is. Verheyden
Collection Crédit Communal de Belgique / Collectie Gemeentekrediet van België, Brussels

Two peasant women, described with scant attention to detail are set within a geometrical composition on a flat surface against a flat sky. Such a description might well apply to the work of an adventurous modernist painter of the late nineteenth century but it might ring too radical a note in the context of Isidore Verheyden's oeuvre. Indeed, it would be difficult to consider, on pictorial evidence, Verheyden to have been either an innovator of pictorial space or a follower of Ockham's principle of the parsimony of means. Rather, Verheyden may have been expressing his adherence to the more traditional approaches to the painting of everyday life when he took the decision in May 1887 to resign from Les XX. Although he declared this to have been 'for purely personal reasons' in a letter to Octave Maus, his distancing from the avant-garde group may have been instigated by his suspicion of the more progressive Neo-Impressionism fast becoming the dominant style – albeit temporarily – of the more innovative members.

However, nor was Verheyden a conservative artist. He had been one of the first painters to celebrate the new Realism at the annual exhibition of the Société Libre des Beaux-Arts in Brussels in 1874. As such he declared his disregard for the grandiloquent or exotic themes of history painting, then regarded as the subject matter of the highest form of art. Instead, Verheyden was a painter's painter, captivated by his métier. His subjects were drawn from such mundane themes as landscape, portrait and still life. Modest subjects allowed an explicit demonstration of the application of technical and artistic skills to the objective recording of a specific motif. His numerous *plein-air* studies demonstrate a diversity of technique and unpretentious modes of composition, a freedom of handling and virtuosity which Verheyden could have applied to formal Salon works.

The subject of this picture – peasant women engaged in gleaning a field in the wake of the harvest – had been extensively treated in nineteenth-century art. Unlike such French prototypes as those by J.-F. Millet and Pierre Puvis de Chavannes, where religious or biblical references lie behind the initial description of the scene, Verheyden's composition appears to focus upon the timeless inevitability of the act of gleaning. As one year succeeds another, so too the act of gleaning is repeated. Such a sense of inevitability is reinforced by the reduction of detail to a bare minimum. In addition, in placing the figures in *contre-jour* against a sky suffused with evening light, the figures take on a monumental scale which celebrates the worthiness of the labour on the land.

The existence of paintings with similar treatment of surface and colour, and of a similar subject (e.g. *Glaneuses*; *Les XX* 1886, no. 12) suggests a date of c. 1885–1886 for this painting. | FL

PROVENANCE Eugène Flagey, 1971.
EXHIBITIONS Brussels 1942, no. 16, Tokyo 1981, no. 14; Albi 1985, no. 56; Paris 1990.
BIBLIOGRAPHY Goyens de Heusch 1988, 80, ill.

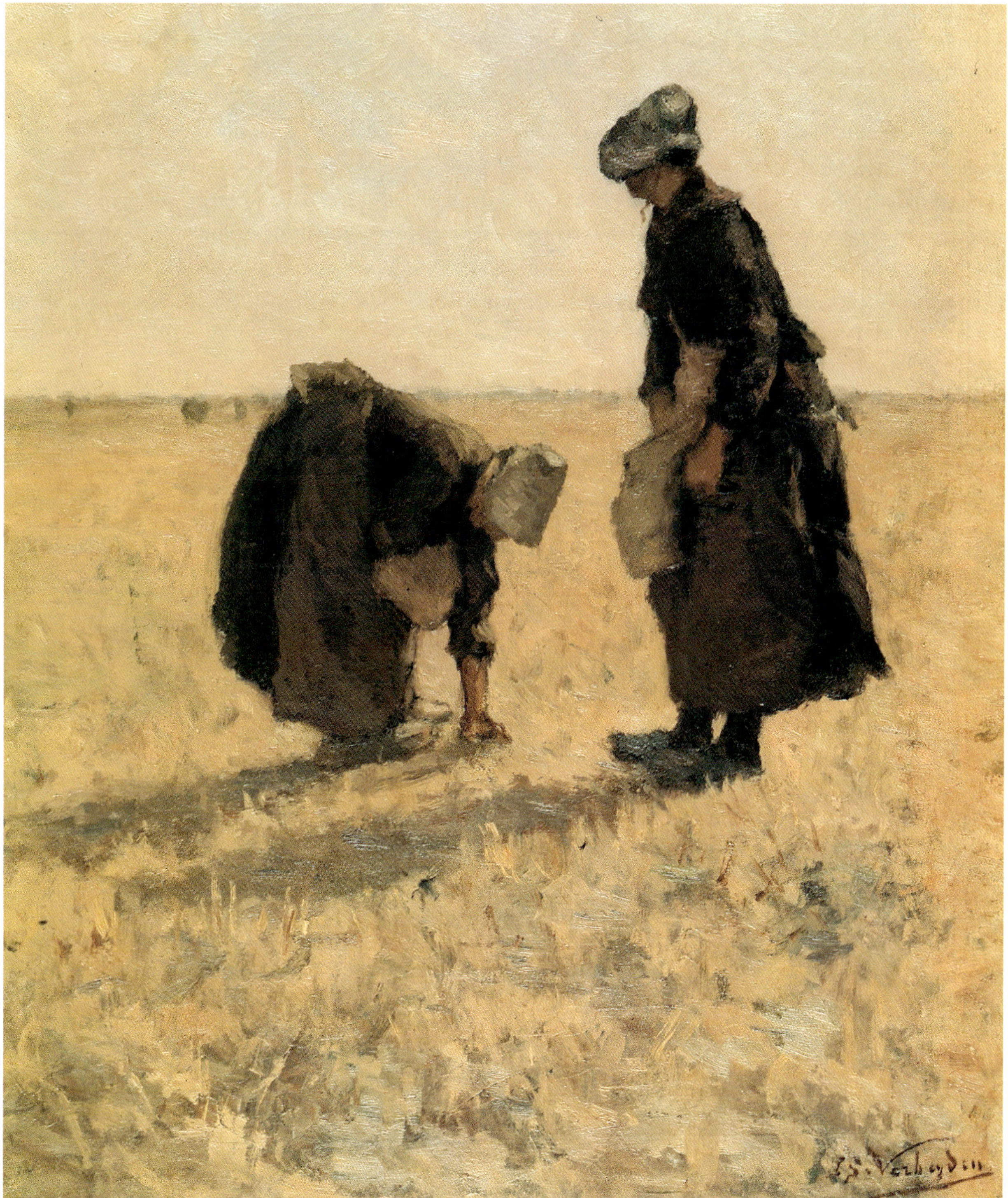

Theodoor Verstraete

GHENT 1850 – ANTWERP 1907

Theodoor Verstraete, the son of an actress and a musician, moved to Antwerp with his family in 1864. He enrolled at the Academy of Fine Arts in 1866, studying first in the engraving class run by J. Bal, and later in the studio of the landscape artist Jacob Jacobs (1812–1879). Verstraete continued to study at the Academy until 1877, but began to exhibit at the Antwerp Salon in 1873, and afterwards took part regularly in exhibitions in Belgium and abroad. He married in 1876, and looked for a house in or around Antwerp before finally settling in Brasschaat in 1880. His painting *On the Heath* (present location unknown) received special attention at the annual Paris exhibition in 1882. According to *L'Art moderne* (1882, 172), 'The painting is a success. Verstraete is an artist of delicacy, fondly in love with nature.' It comes as little surprise, then, to find him amongst the founders of Les XX in 1883. However, like the other Antwerp artists Isidore Verheyden (q.v.), Piet Verhaert (1852–1908), Frans Simons (1855–1919) and Jef Lambeaux (1852–1908), he belonged to the most conservative strand within the group. Before long, he and a number of others became the target of public criticism. While he reaped financial benefits from exhibiting with Les XX in 1884 (six works) and in 1885 (five works), he resigned from Les XX in 1885 after a public dispute in the press in which Emile Verhaeren, Georges Eekhoud and Edmond Picard attacked him for his conservatism. His involvement in organized artistic life continued in 1891 when he became a co-founder of the XIII, the Antwerp group set up to promote the work of local realists. Verstraete suffered a brain haemorrhage in 1893, which interrupted his career. He survived, in part through the support of his patron, the property owner Henri van Cutsem (1839–1904), who, after 1904, provided him with a monthly allowance, and in part through a retrospective exhibition held at Antwerp's Zaal Verlat in 1895, and through a tribute exhibition mounted by Kunst van Heden in 1906, shortly before his death.

Like many other artists (for example, Van Leemputten q.v., Van de Velde q.v.), Verstraete was inspired by the barren, unspoilt heathland around Kalmthout, and the unassuming life of its peasant farmers. He also shared his contemporaries' fascination for the landscape and picturesque local inhabitants of Zealand (see Baertsoen, Mellery, Mertens, q.v.). Towards the end of his life he also worked at Blankenberghe on the Channel coast, where Van Cutsem owned a villa. | LDJ

SUMMARY BIBLIOGRAPHY

F. L. de Taeye, *Les artistes belges contemporains*, Brussels 1894, 649–658; L. Solvay, *Le paysage et les paysagistes. Théodore Verstraete*, Brussels 1897; J. Dujardin, *L'Art flamand*, 6, Brussels 1900, 168–171; P. de Mont, *Vlaamsche Meesters der negentiende eeuw*, Antwerp, Ghent 1902, 274–278; S. Gilliams, *Marten Van der Loo - Theodoor Verstraete 1850–1907, Virtuoos van het doorleefde landschap*, Brasschaat 1980, 37–81; L. Pil, '"Brutale lelijkheid" of "onopgesmukte waarachtigheid". Controversen rond de voorstelling van landelijk leven in het kunstkritisch discours van het 19de-eeuwse België', in *Schilders van het landelijk leven in België. Van realisme tot post-expressionisme*, Koninklijk Museum voor Schone Kunsten, Antwerp 1990, 40–42, 172.

79 Barge Haulier

Le Haleur – De boottrekker, 1890
Oil on canvas, 108 x 218 cm
Signed bottom left: Verstraete
Musée des Beaux-Arts, Tournai

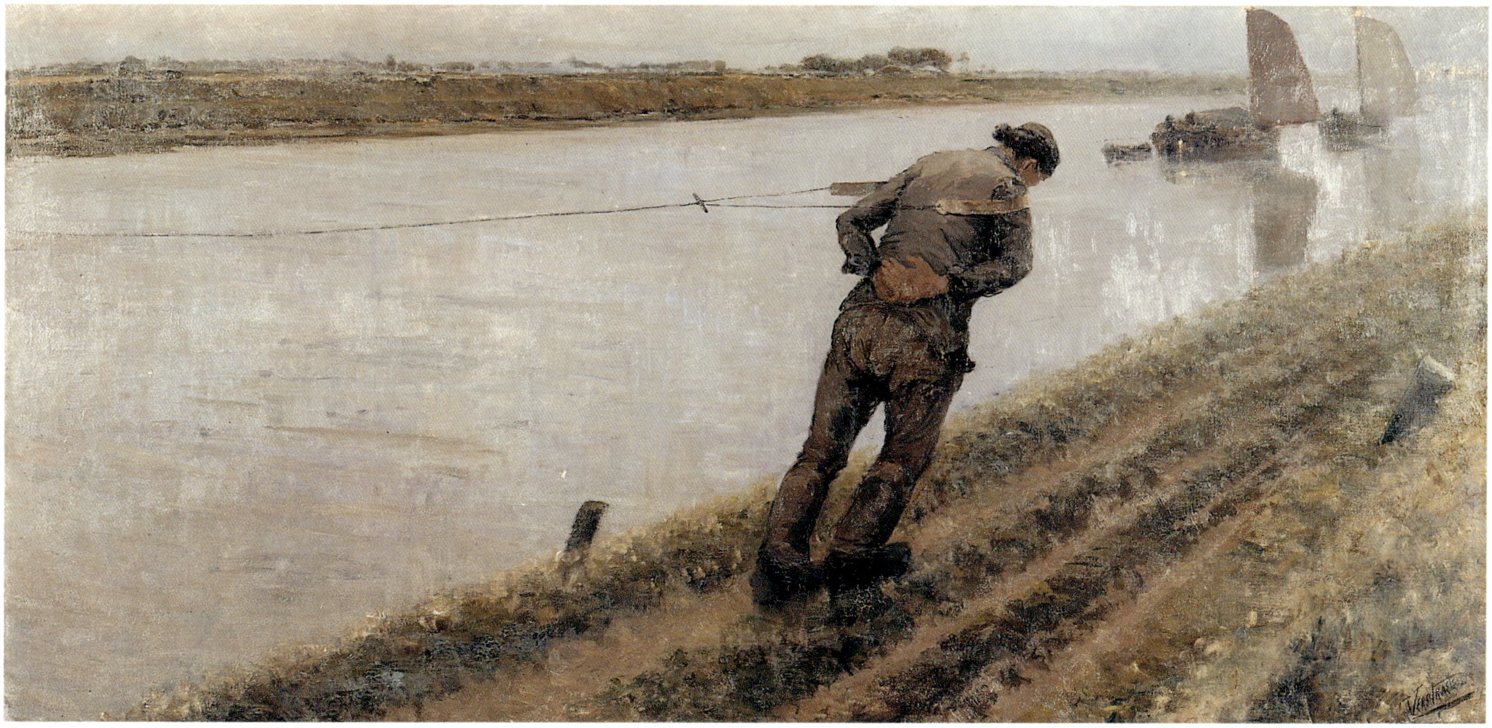

A man walks along the tow-path of a canalized river which runs through a desolate landscape. He is hauling a boat which lies beyond the left edge of the canvas. The high horizon line eliminates most of the sky, but the water, which takes up the larger part of the picture plane, reflects the blueness of the evening sky, punctuated by small lights and the glimmer of a few faint stars. The dramatic diagonal plunge of the river from lower left to upper right of the composition is reinforced by the low, parallel dikes and the bent posture of the boatman: 'The melancholy of things blended with that of living creatures' was how Lucien Solvay (1897, 68–70) described the *Barge Haulier* in his book on Verstraete, and he added elsewhere that it was in this painting that the artist achieved the most perfect harmony between nature and man. The realization of this harmony was the ideal pursued by Realists from Courbet, Millet, Bastien-Lepage and Breton to Mauve, Liebermann and Uhde – with all of whom Verstraete has strong affinities. Farmers, fishermen and labourers symbolize perfectly the unity between man and his environment.

The *Barge Haulier* is a dramatic, monumental work – broad and clear in composition and tonality. The man is seen from behind, and shares the compact outlines of the figures in *The Wake* (1889–1891; Koninklijk Museum voor Schone Kunsten, Antwerp) and *After the Funeral* (c. 1894; Musées royaux des Beaux-Arts de Belgique, Brussels), as well as those of Eugène Laermans and the later Belgian Expressionists. Whereas Verstraete's canvases are often narrative in approach – lovely and charming in his early works, melancholy and even sombre in his later works – in the *Barge Haulier* he has found a balance between narrative genre scene and landscape.

Verstraete was not a pure landscape painter, nor a pure Social Realist, but belonged instead to the best tradition of international Naturalism. Boatmen were, in fact, a favourite theme of the Naturalists (such as Ilya Repin, whose famous Volga boatmen [1870–1873] successfully toured Europe), and was a *leitmotiv* of the Hague School, used by Anton Mauve, Jacob Maris, J. H. Weissenbruch and Jozef Israëls.

Verstraete's cautious *pleinairisme* and social concern won the allegiance of the Brussels collector and patron of the arts, Henri van Cutsem (1839–1904) [see also cat. 76], who owned more than fifteen of Verstraete's paintings, including the *Barge Haulier*, and a hundred drawings (now deposited at the Musée des Beaux-Arts, Tournai, in a building commissioned by Van Cutsem from the Art Nouveau architect, Victor Horta). | LDJ

PROVENANCE Purchased by Henri van Cutsem, 1894; temporarily with Van Cutsem's universal heir, G. Charlier, 1904; acquired by the Museum in 1928.

EXHIBITIONS Brussels 1890, no. 818; Antwerp 1920, no. 219; Charleroi 1980, no. 158; Antwerp 1985–1986, no. 58.

BIBLIOGRAPHY Pion 1971; S. Le Bailly de Tilleghem, in Brussels 1988, 70–99.

Guillaume Vogels

BRUSSELS 1836 – IXELLES (BRUSSELS) 1896

Vogels belonged to a working-class family. He attended elementary school, and then became a house-painter. He studied at the Brussels Academy of Fine Arts between 1850 and 1853, but followed an unorthodox and very limited curriculum. In 1855, he became a master decorator and ultimately set up his own decorating firm in Brussels. While more or less abandoning his training in fine art after completion of his course in 1853, Vogels applied some of its principles to the provision of decorative panels with flowers and garlands and of ceiling paintings.

Shortly before or during 1873, Pericles Pantazis (1849–1884), a Greek artist who had recently arrived in Brussels, already imbued with the principles of French *pleinairisme*, joined Vogels's decorating firm. The two became friends, and Pantazis's influence led to the relaunching of Vogels's artistic career. They both exhibited at the Salons of Ghent and Namur in 1873. The works painted by Vogels between 1873 and 1878 owe a great deal both stylistically and thematically to those of Pantazis, although there are also similarities in subject matter and especially handling to the work of Hippolyte Boulenger (1837–1874) and Artan de Saint-Martin (q.v.). With Pantazis he joined the Brussels group La Chrysalide in 1878, and exhibited at three of its four Salons, in 1877, 1878 and 1881. James Ensor (q.v.) and Willy Finch (q.v.) showed there, as well as at the Brussels Cercle Artistique in 1884.

Vogels began to paint in a more radical, Impressionist style from 1880, evolving towards a daring 'tachisme', in which shapes are rendered by patches of boldly laid in paint to create an interplay of colour, light and shade. In this respect he not only influenced the palette and technique of James Ensor, a close friend although twenty years his junior, as well as of Willy Finch and Jan Toorop. His favoured themes were landscapes, seascapes, still lifes and city views.

He was one of the thirteen co-founders of Les XX in October 1883, and took part in eight of the group's ten annual exhibitions. He also exhibited at the 1894 and 1895 Salons of La Libre Esthétique. He was highly appreciated by both groups, most of whose members were significantly younger than him. Vogels also took part in a three-man exhibition – together with James Ensor and Louis Storm van 's Gravesande – at the Brussels Cercle Artistique et Littéraire in 1884.

Vogels must have been a singular character: not an intellectual, he was uncomplicated, jovial and happy. He sold few of his works, nor did he wish to part with them, except to close friends and genuine admirers. As an artist his was a truly natural talent which did not blossom until late in life. He died poverty-stricken and alcoholic, and remains poorly known and even mysterious to this day. At the behest of his friends, the 1896 Salon de La Libre Esthétique included a posthumous tribute to him. | NH

SUMMARY BIBLIOGRAPHY
Rétrospective Guillaume Vogels Palais des Beaux-Arts, Brussels 1936; *Vogels*, Musée d'Ixelles, Brussels 1968; *Post-Impressionism. Cross-Currents in European Painting*, Royal Academy of Arts, London 1979; *Het landschap in de Belgische kunst 1830–1914*, Museum voor Schone Kunsten, Ghent 1980; S. Goyens de Heusch, *L'Impressionnisme et le Fauvisme en Belgique*, Antwerp 1988; *L'Impressionnisme et le Fauvisme en Belgique*, Musée d'Ixelles, Brussels 1990.

80 The Storm

Het onweer – L'Orage, undated
Oil on canvas, 55 x 84 cm
Signed bottom right: G. Vogels
Musée de l'Art Wallon, Liège, Donation Jaumain-Jobert, inv. no. AW 2123

A landscape seen shortly before or after a storm could present an ideal subject for the landscape artist working out of doors in front of the motif. In many cases, the view is bathed in sunlight while the sky is a menacing lead-grey. This highly dramatic lighting can often be intensified further by a bolt of lightning or by reflections of the sky in puddles (as in Vogels's painting *L'Eclair* [*Lightning*], c. 1882–1883, Musées royaux des Beaux-Arts de Belgique, Brussels). Storm-torn landscapes were particularly popular subjects among romantic landscape painters of an earlier generation, but were also frequently realized by Vogels's contemporaries, including Hippolyte Boulenger (1837–1874), Joseph Coosemans (1828–1904) and Alphonse Asselbergs (1839–1916).

The Storm is stylistically linked to 'tachisme', the alternative to French Impressionism favoured by many progressive artists in Belgium. It was a loose style of painting – daring for its time – which evolved from the realism of the 1860s and 1870s. The fluent, sketchy technique which Vogels uses here enhances his depiction of this stormy landscape, as if he were seeking to 'experience' the storm as intensely as possible during its fleeting existence, and to capture it on canvas equally quickly. It was this translation of sensation in front of nature into a radically personal style which was remarked upon by Octave Maus in his oration delivered at Vogels's funeral on 9 January 1896 and subsequently published in *L'Art moderne* (12 January 1891): '[Vogels knew how to express] with a singularly expert hand [and] in a number of strokes with the brush, violent as sabre cuts, the summation of the impression felt and experienced.' In the same article, Maus also pointed to Vogels's role as 'a precursor and initiator', no doubt having in mind the influence that the artist had had upon both the approach to landscape and the painterly technique applied to its translation onto canvas which marks the works of James Ensor (q.v.) during the 1880s and the early paintings of Théo van Rysselberghe (q.v.) and Willy Finch (q.v.). | NH

PROVENANCE Désiré Jaumain-Ada Jobert Donation.
EXHIBITIONS Munich 1989; Brussels 1990a, no. 26, ill.
BIBLIOGRAPHY Goyens de Heusch 1988.

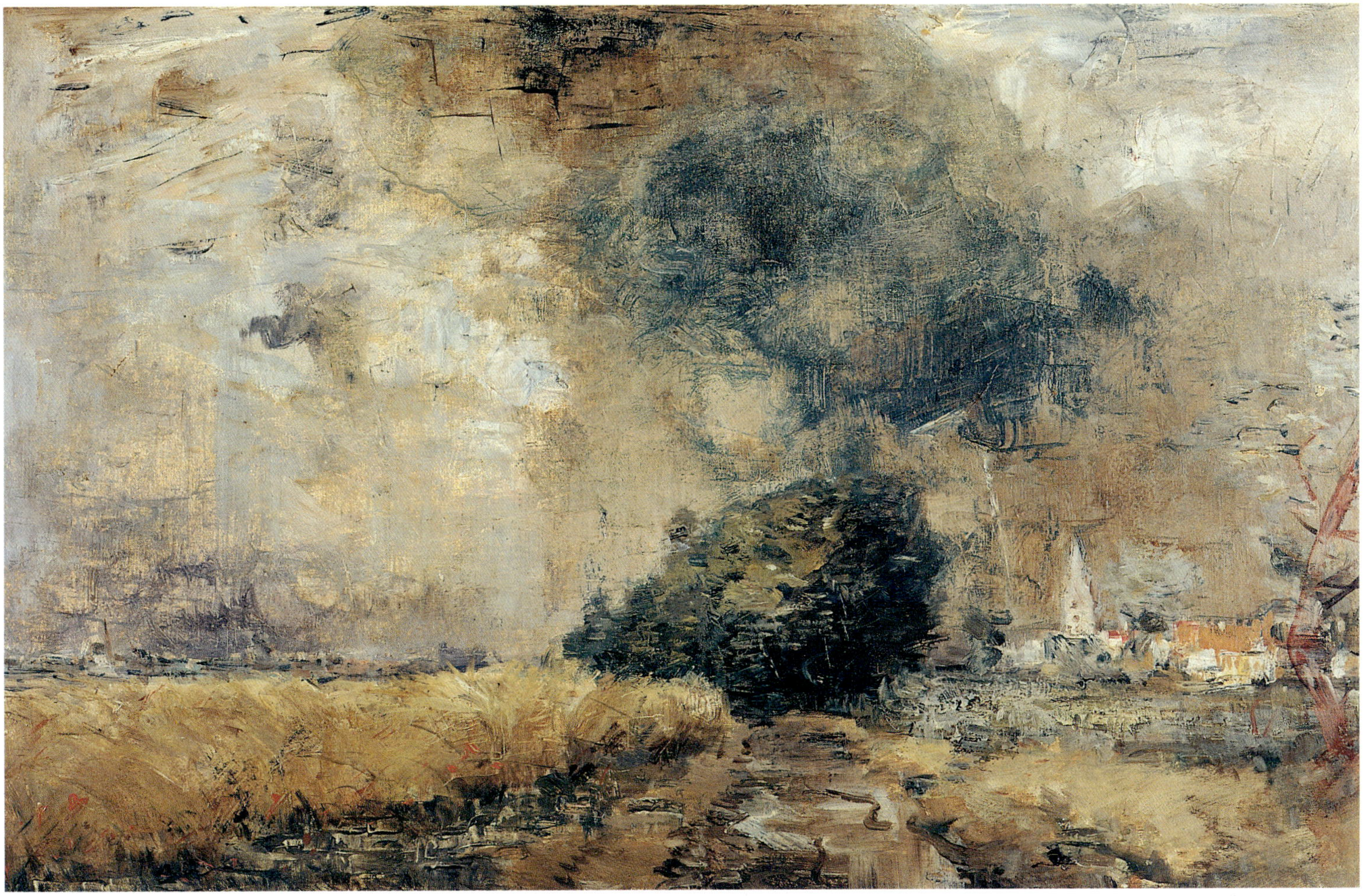

CHRONOLOGY

1868 | The army shoots down twenty demonstrators during a miners' strike in the Borinage. In response to this, dozens of sections of the International are established in the Charleroi region. The Brussels section of the International had been established in 1865 and sections are also active in Antwerp, Ghent, Liège and Verviers.

› The Third International Workers Congress, organized by the International Workers League, is held in Brussels.

› The new Liberal Rogier cabinet guarantees press freedom. This particularly benefits the Socialist press, which begins to organize itself throughout the country.

SOCIÉTÉ LIBRE DES BEAUX-ARTS

A number of young, already reasonably established artists found the Société Libre des Beaux-Arts (1868–1875) [fig. 1]. They are mainly landscape painters, influenced by the Barbizon School and the social-realists: Louis Artan, Alphonse Asselberghs, Théodore Baron, Hyppolyte de la Charlerie, Marie Collart, Joseph Coosemans, Louis Dubois, Constantin Meunier, Charles de Groux, Edouard Huberti, Edmond Lambrichs, Jules Raeymaekers, Félicien Rops, Eugène Smits, Camille van Camp, Henri van der Hecht and Alfred Verwee. The group opposes academicism and, although in principle open to all styles, it mainly promotes adherents of Realism. The Société Libre uses its influence to enable younger artists to participate in the annual official salons which are held in turn in Brussels, Ghent and Antwerp. The society organizes or participates in four exhibitions, one in 1868 and three in 1872. Their first exhibition is held in the offices of the newspaper, *La Chronique,* in the Galerie Royale in Brussels. Besides paintings they exhibit studies and sketches.

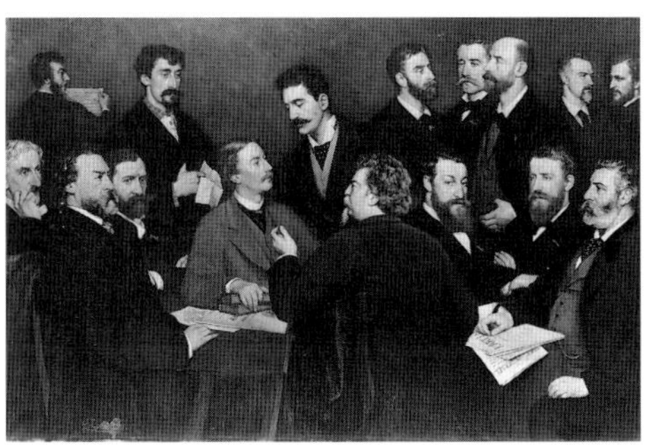

fig. 1 EDMOND LAMBRICHS, The Members of the Société Libre des Beaux-Arts, c. 1875, Musées royaux des Beaux-Arts de Belgique, Brussels

1869 | At the Brussels Salon, work by Eugène Boudin, Camille Corot, Gustave Courbet and Edouard Manet. The 'Impressionist' technique of Manet's Le Balcon causes a great stir.

› Establishment of the Société Internationale des Aquafortistes in Brussels under the chairmanship of Félicien Rops.

1870 | The Franco-Prussian War is in part fought out along the Franco-Belgian border. Belgium remains neutral.

› Première of the French-language version of Wagner's *Lohengrin* at the Théâtre de la Monnaie, Brussels.

1871 | After the failure of the Paris Commune, some 1500 communards, who were sentenced in France in their absence, flee to Belgium and, more particularly, to Brussels. Some will play an important part in the development of Socialism in Belgium.

L'ART LIBRE

Establishment of the bi-monthly journal *L'Art libre* (1871–1872) as the mouthpiece of the Société Libre des Beaux-Arts. The editors are Félicien Rops, Camille van Camp, Louis Artan and Louis Dubois. The contributors include Camille Lemonnier, Léon Dommartin and the French critic Champfleury. The journal's articles of association can be read as the group's manifesto: '… elle ne connaît d'autre point de départ pour les recherches de l'artiste que celui d'où procède le renouvellement de l'Art à toutes les époques, c'est-à-dire l'interprétation libre et individuelle de la nature'. The use of a journal to propagate the programme of a group of artists will later be continued by La Chrysalide and Les XX.

1872 | The Société Libre cooperates in the organization of a charitable exhibition in Brussels; it also organizes exhibitions in the Cercle artistique in Brussels at and the seaside resort of Blankenberghe. Realism gradually conquers official art circles, and the majority of its practitioners are admitted to the Brussels Salon.

› Première of the French-language version of Richard Wagner's *Der Fliegende Holländer (The Flying Dutchman)* at the Théâtre de la Monnaie, Brussels.

1873 | L'ART UNIVERSEL

After the closure of L'Art libre, Camille Lemonnier founds the bi-monthly journal L'Art universel (1873–1876) with the motto 'Liberté, sincérité'. Like L'Art libre, it is a defender of naturalism. Besides the visual arts it devotes attention to literature and music. Editions of etchings and musical compositions are included in the subscription. In 1875 the paper opens an office in Paris, which stimulates contacts between French and Belgian writers.

1874 | The first Impressionist Exhibition is held in the studio of the photographer Nadar in Paris. Birth of the term 'Impressionism'.

1875 | LA CHRYSALIDE

Establishment of La Chrysalide (1875–1881) on the initiative of Félicien Rops, a rejuvenated continuation of the Société Libre des Beaux-Arts. The members include Louis Artan, Louis Dubois, Théodore Baron, Constantin Meunier, Alfred Verwee, Guillaume Vogels, Pericles Pantazis, Jean-Baptiste Degreef and Théo Hannon. Besides artists, the group also includes musicians and singers.

1876 | Establishment of the association Le Cercle d'Elèves et Anciens Elèves des Académies des Beaux-Arts as a reaction against academicism and its associated salons, with all their restrictions, rules and regulations. The founders, who include Julien Dillens, Henri Permeke, Leon Herbo, Louis Cambier, Emile Hoeterickx, were initially concerned to defend Realism.

› La Chrysalide holds its first exhibition in Le Ballon, a cabaret theatre on the Cantersteen in Brussels. The invitations are designed by Félicien Rops [fig. 2].

L'ACTUALITÉ

After the failure of *L'Art universel*, Camille Lemonnier establishes a new journal, *L'Actualité* (1876–1877). Although the journal is mainly literary, it also includes photographic reproductions of the work of Belgian artists. It publishes work by the most important naturalist writers such as Joris-Karl Huysmans, Emile Zola and Théo Hannon.

› The Belgian publisher Deman starts the publication of de luxe editions which would later include the work of Stéphane Mallarmé, with frontispieces by Edouard Manet, James McNeil Whistler, Auguste Renoir and Odilon Redon.

1877 | In Ghent, Edmond van Beveren and Edward Anseele found the Flemish Socialist Party; the Brabant Socialist Party is established in Brussels under the leadership of Cesar de Paepe. The two merge to form the Belgian Socialist Party.

L'ARTISTE

The poet and art critic, Théo Hannon, gathers together the former staff of *L'Actualité* and establishes the new journal *L'Artiste* (1877–1880) with the motto 'Naturalisme, Modernité'. The paper takes up the defence of the Chrysalide group: 'Bonsoir aux Vieux, Salut aux Jeunes, Nargue au cocon des Vieux, Les Jeunes ont fait leur Chrysalide, Les roses en émoi hâtent leur floraison' (Hannon).

1879 | L'ESSOR

The Cercle d'Elèves et Anciens Elèves des Académies des Beaux-Arts (1876) changes its name into L'ESSOR (1879–1891) in order to distance itself from the Academy. L'Essor organizes one or more exhibitions each year. The artists may exhibit there without having taken part in the official salons. Nevertheless, L'Essor will never be more than an eclectic grouping of moderate modernists. The members include Albert Baertsoen, Frantz Charlet, Jean Degreef, Jean Delville, James Ensor, Charles van den Eycken, Léon Fréderic, Henri de Groux, Fernand Khnopff, Jacques de Lalaing, Frans van Leemputten, Alexandre Marcette, Guillaume van Strydonck, Jan Toorop, Rodolphe Wytsman.

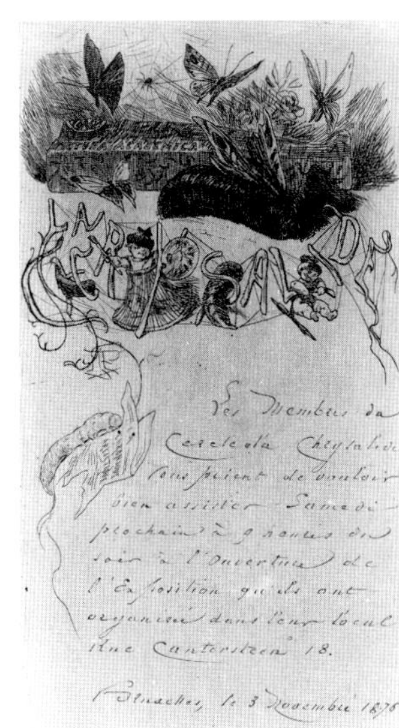

fig. 2 FÉLICIEN ROPS La Chrysalide, 1876, invitation to the first exhibition, etching and drypoint, Stedelijk Prentenkabinet, Antwerp

1880 | In Ghent and Antwerp the Socialists establish cooperative bakeries. Their example will be followed throughout the country during the next few years and signifies an important factor in the development of the Socialist movement.

› Women are admitted to the university for the first time; three succeed in registering.
› Belgium celebrates 50 years of independence with two major exhibitions. Two exhibition buildings are erected on the old parade ground of the Belgian army, laid out afresh as the Parc du Centenaire – the present Musées royaux d'Art et d'Histoire and the Musée de l'Armée – designed by Gidéon Bordiau, where an international exhibition of science and industry is held. The new Palais des Beaux-Arts (now the Musées royaux des Beaux-Arts de Belgique) designed by Alphonse Balat, opens on the Rue de la Régence in Brussels with a major retrospective exhibition of Belgian Art from 1830 to 1880.

› Auguste Rodin and Edouard Manet participate in the Ghent Salon, Willy Finch makes his début there.
› The writer Camille Lemonnier travels through the Walloon industrial region with Xavier Mellery and Constantin Meunier gathering material for his book, *La Belgique* (1884). Meunier shows his first scenes of factory life in Walllonia at the Ghent and Paris Salons.

› French publication of Engels's *Socialisme utopique et socialisme scientifique*. Jules Guesde founds the Parti Ouvrier in France.

› Fifth Impressionist Exhibition in Paris, this time under the title 'Exposition de Peintres indépendants'. The newcomers are Paul Gauguin and Jean-François Raffaëlli; important absentees are Auguste Renoir and Claude Monet, who prefer to exhibit at the official Salon.
› Thematic exhibition on Metal at the Union Centrale des Beaux-Arts appliqués à l'Industrie in Paris. Establishment of the Musée des Arts Décoratifs in Paris; commissioning of the portal *(Porte de l'Enfer)* from Auguste Rodin; first volume of the *Revue des Arts Décoratifs* (1880–1902).

› Henrik Ibsen, *The Dolls House*; Dostoyevski, *The Brothers Karamazov*.

† Louis Dubois, Albrecht Rodenbach, Gustave Flaubert

1881 | The radical group within the Liberal Party, including Victor Arnould and Eugène Robert, joint founders of the journal L'Art moderne, argues in the Chamber of Deputies for the introduction of universal suffrage.

› Henry Morton Stanley, on an expedition in the Congo on behalf of King Leopold II, founds Leopoldville.

LA JEUNE BELGIQUE

Founding of the literary journal, *La Jeune Belgique* (1881–1896), by alumni of the Catholic University of Louvain and the Université Libre de Bruxelles. The paper is edited by Max Waller (until his death in 1889). It becomes a forum for young writers, who are opposed to the academicism of the 'official' writers. As a younger sister of *La Jeune France* (established 1878), the journal gives form to the literary renewal which is emerging in Belgium. *La Jeune Belgique* largely defends the elitist principle of 'l'art pour l'art' and contests the idea that all art is social. Emile Verhaeren, Albert Giraud and Emile van Arenbergh are members of the editorial board. The Jeune Belgique movement in the early years includes: Georges Eekhoud, Iwan Gilkin, Henri Maubel, Georges Rodenbach, André Fontainas, Fernand Séverin, Valère Gille, Jules Destrée, Eugène Demolder, Louis Delattre, Maurice des Ombiaux, Charles van Lerberghe, Grégoire Le Roy and Maurice Maeterlinck. The paper prints unpublished work by Stéphane Mallarmé, Joséphin Péladan, Joris-Karl Huysmans, Dante-Gabriel Rossetti, Paul Verlaine and others. It at once becomes an major mouthpiece for Symbolism.

L'ART MODERNE

Establishment of the weekly journal *L'Art moderne: Revue critique des arts et de la littérature (1881–1914)*, by the progressive Liberal Brussels lawyers Edmond Picard, Octave Maus, and two radical members of the Liberal Party, Victor Arnould and Eugène Robert. The subscribers of the former paper *L'Artiste* (1877–1880) are transferred to the new journal. It emphasizes the social role of art and becomes, until the outbreak of the First World War, the principal mouthpiece of the avant-garde in Belgium and, more particularly, of the art associations, Les XX (1883–1893) and La Libre Esthétique (1894–1914). The articles are seldom signed, which underlines the paper's anarchist standpoint.

› Last exhibition of La Chrysalide (1875–1881). It includes work by Félicien Rops, Fernand Dubois, Pericles Pantazis, Willy Finch, Louis Artan, Jean-Baptiste Degreef, Constantin Meunier, Théo Hannon, Amedée Lynen, Maurice Hagemans, Guillaume Vogels, Eugène Maus, Jef Lambeaux, Gustave Vanaise and by the 21-year-old James Ensor, who exhibits for the first time.
› First one-man show by Fernand Khnopff at L'Essor in Brussels.
› Constantin Meunier exhibits his paintings, drawings, studies and sketches of the mining district of Le Borinage in the Cercle Artistique et Littéraire in Brussels.
› Jules Bastien-Lepage and Henri Fantin-Latour participate in the Brussels Salon.

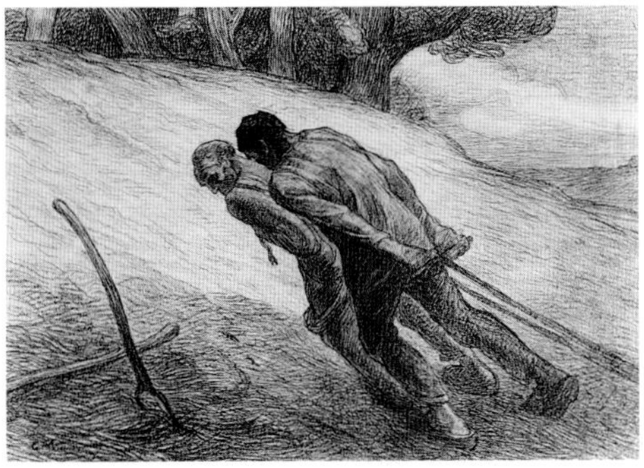

fig. 3 CONSTANTIN MEUNIER, Peasants in the Field, 1881, Illustration for Camille Lemonnier's *Le Mort*, charcoal, Musées royaux des Beaux-Arts de Belgique, Brussels

- The art bookshop Dietrich & Cie opens in Brussels. It is the first bookshop in Belgium which also serves as a gallery where permanent exhibitions of the work of living artists are held: they will include Louis Artan, Franz Courtens, Louis Dubois, Constantin Meunier, Isidore Verheyden, Guillaume Vogels. The bookshop will play an important role over the next few years in the spread of the contemporary English art and literature in Belgium.

- Publication of Camille Lemonnier's naturalistic novel *Un Mâle* in serial form in *L'Europe*; causes a scandal in Belgium and is a great success in France.
- Camille Lemonnier, *Le Mort* [fig. 3].
- Première of Jules Massenet's opera *Hérodiade* at the Théâtre de la Monnaie, Brussels.

- In Paris, reform of the official Salon, which now comes solely under the control of the artists. It is renamed the Société des Artistes Français.
- Edgar Degas causes a sensation at the sixth Impressionist Exhibition in Paris with *La Petite Danseuse*, a small clothed sculpture in painted wax.
- Excluded from the Paris Salon, Odilon Redon holds his first one-man show in the offices of the journal *La Vie moderne*.
- *Théorie scientifique des couleurs et leurs applications à l'art et à l'industrie,* French translation of *Modern Chromatics* by the American painter and physicist Ogden Rood, an important theoretical work for the development of Neo-Impressionism.
- Paul Verlaine, *Sagesse*.

1882 | L'Essor is permitted to exhibit in the Palais des Beaux-Arts for the first time; the show includes Impressionist works by younger painters: James Ensor, Albert Baertsoen, Frantz Charlet, Willy Finch, Fernand Khnopff, Alexandre Marcette, Théo van Rysselberghe, Guillaume van Strydonck, Willy Schlobach, Dario de Regoyos, Rodolphe Wytsman and Jan Toorop. These had been admitted to the society in 1881, creating potential conflict with their older confrères who are committed to a more traditional form of Realism. L'Essor organizes its first 'Noir et Blanc' exhibition (drawings).
- *The Oyster Eater* by the 22-year-old Ensor is refused at the Antwerp Salon.
- Félicien Rops illustrates title pages for the publishers Gay et Doucé and makes *Les Sataniques*, a series of etchings. He has become one of the best-known and highest paid illustrators in Paris.
- Théo van Rysselberghe, Dario De Regoyos, Frantz Charlet and Constantin Meunier spend the winter of 1882–1883 in Spain and Morocco.
- Auguste Rodin and Edouard Manet participate in the Antwerp Salon.

- Georges Rodenbach, *Gudrun*; Pol de Mont, *Loreley*.

- In France, the collapse of the Union Générale bank temporarily ruins the Paris dealer and principal promoter of the Impressionists, Paul Durand-Ruel.
- Opening of the luxurious Galerie Georges Petit on the rue Laffitte in Paris; holds first Exposition internationale.
- Courbet retrospective in the Ecole des Beaux-Arts, Paris.
- Thematic exhibition on wood, paper and textiles of the Union Centrale des Beaux-Arts appliqués à l'Industrie in Paris.
- In London, Durand-Ruel organizes a small exhibition of French Impressionists with works by Degas, Monet, Renoir and Sisley.

- Walter Crane, *Art and the Formation of Taste*; William Morris, *Hopes and Fears for Art*.
- First performance of Wagner's *Parsifal* in Bayreuth.

† Dante-Gabriel Rossetti

1883 | Salon de L'Essor with James Ensor, Léon Fréderic, Fernand Khnopff, Théo van Rysselberghe, Dario de Regoyos, Guillaume van Strydonck, Willy Finch and others. L'Essor organizes concerts for the first time in the rooms where the salon is held. This will be copied immediately in other exhibition circles.

LES XX

Disagreements within L'Essor lead to the establishment on 23 October of Les XX (1883–1893), a group of independent artists without a programme or manifesto. The founder members are the painters Frantz Charlet, Jean Delvin, Dario de Regoyos, James Ensor, Willy Finch, Charles Goethals, Fernand Khnopff, Pericles Pantazis, Willy Schlobach, Frans Simons, Gustave Vanaise, Théo van Rysselberghe, Guillaume van Strydonck, Piet Verhaert, Theodoor Verstraete, Guillaume Vogels, Rodolphe Wytsman, and the three sculptors Achille Chainaye, Paul Du Bois and Jef Lambeaux. The group refuses to have any binding aesthetic criteria, chairman or administrative committee, only a secretary. For the latter post they choose the lawyer, art critic and collector, Octave Maus. Each member may make suggestions about the invitation of artists to the salons and may vote on the admittance of new members. Some of the founder members soon resign and are replaced by figures who are more in sympathy with the avant-garde character of the group. *L'Art moderne*, the journal of which Maus is the joint founder, becomes the mouthpiece of the group. During the salons, Les XX also organize regular lectures and concerts which embody the aesthetic theory of the group. Over the next few years the salons of Les XX form the focus par excellence of the confrontations of the European avant-garde, a place of revelations and scandals, a meeting place of the visual arts, applied art, literature and music.

ALS IK KAN

Some young Antwerp artists, including Henry van de Velde, found the Als Ik Kan association (1883–1954). It is a group of like-minded young people rather than a group with a programme of aesthetic renewal. They oppose the Antwerp Cercle Artistique which admits to its exhibitions only artists who have participated at least twice in the official Triennial Salons. Members include Evert Larock and Charles Mertens.

› Fernand Khnopff paints his first Symbolist canvas, *D'après Flaubert*.
› The first masks appear in James Ensor's work.
› First exhibition of the Cercle des Aquarellistes et des Aquafortistes in Brussels.
› Théo van Rysselberghe meets the poet Emile Verhaeren. He travels again with Frantz Charlet to Morocco, where he stays about a year.
› Jan Toorop shares his studio with William Degouve de Nuncques in Mechelen. They become friendly with Emile Verhaeren and make contact with most of the writers of *La Jeune Belgique*.

› In protest against the fact that Camille Lemonnier has not won the quinquennial state prize for literature, Max Waller and *La Jeune Belgique* organize a huge banquet in his honour, which is attended by 200 artists, writers and left-wing politicians. Speeches by Georges Rodenbach, Edmond Picard and Emile Verhaeren.
› Encouraged by Lemonnier, Verhaeren publishes his first collection of poems: *Les Flamandes*.
› The writer Georges Rodenbach settles in Paris, where he is admitted to the literary circles. He forms a close friendship with Stéphane Mallarmé.

› Completion of the monumental Palais de Justice in Brussels (arch. Joseph Poelaert)
› The Bayreuth company produces Wagner's *Ring Cycle* at the Théâtre de la Monnaie, Brussels.

› In Paris, 'Exposition des portraits du Siècle', a celebration of official art, at the Palais de l'Ecole des Beaux-Arts.
› In Paris, Louis Gonse publishes two richly illustrated albums on Japanese art, containing works by Hokusai, Utamaro, Hiroshige...
› In London, Exhibition of French Impressionists with Mary Cassatt, Degas, Manet, Monet, Camille Pissarro, Renoir, Sisley.
› The 19-year-old Edvard Munch causes a scandal at the Salon for Applied Arts in Christiania.

› Joris-Karl Huysmans, *L'Art moderne*; Robert Louis Stevenson, *Treasure Island*; Emile Zola, *Au bonheur des dames*; Villiers de l'Isle-Adam, *Contes cruels*; Friedrich Nietzsche, *Also sprach Zarathoustra*.

† Gustave Doré, Edouard Manet, Karl Marx, Richard Wagner

1884 | The Liberals suffer heavy losses in the parliamentary elections. During the next thirty years Belgium is governed by Catholic right-wing cabinets.
› In Ghent the flourishing Socialist cooperative, Vooruit, transforms its weekly paper of the same name into a daily newspaper, the first Socialist daily paper in Belgium.
› In Great Britain, Hyndman establishes the Social Democratic Federation .

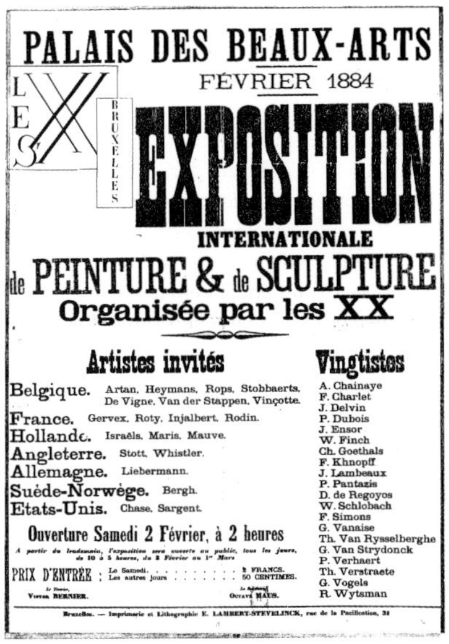

fig. 4 Poster for the First Salon des XX, 1884, Archives de l'Art contemporain, Brussels

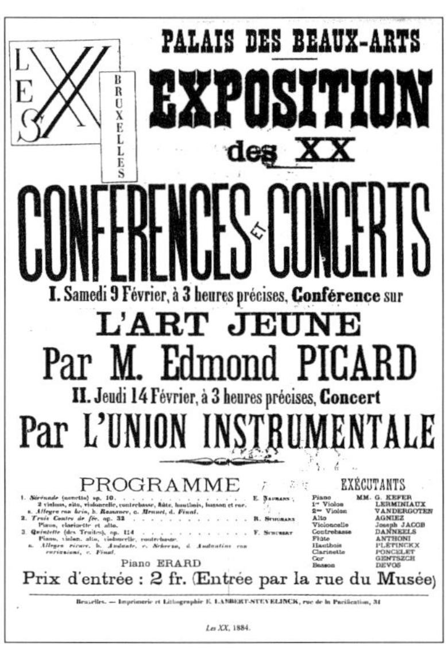

fig. 5 Poster announcing Edmond Picard's lecture at Les XX, 1884

LES XX: FIRST SALON

VINGTISTES Chainaye, Charlet, Delvin, Dubois, Ensor, Finch, Goethals, Khnopff, Lambeaux, Pantazis, Regoyos, Schlobach, Simons, Vanaise, Van Rysselberghe, Van Strydonck, Verhaert, Verstraete, Vogels and Wytsman.
INVITÉS *Belgium*: L. Artan, P. de Vigne, A.-J. Heymans, F. Rops, J. Stobbaerts, C. van der Stappen, T. Vinçotte; *England*: W. Stott; *France*: F. Gervex, J.-A. Injalbert, A. Rodin, O. Roty; *Germany*: M. Liebermann; *Holland*: J. Israëls, M. Maris, A. Mauve; *Sweden–Norway*: S. R. Bergh; *United States*: M. Chase, J. Singer Sargent, J. M. Whistler [fig. 4].
› Ensor causes a scandal with *Les Masques* and Rops with *La Tentation de Saint Antoine*. Whistler is invited at the suggestion of Khnopff and Finch. Les XX are allowed to exhibit in the Palais des Beaux-Arts, as are the official Triennials and the L'Essor Salons.
› The sculptor Jef Lambeaux leaves Les XX one week after the exhibition. Isidore Verheyden, the Dutchman Jan Toorop and the sculptor Guillaume Charlier join. Verheyden is one of the oldest of the group and is regarded as an establishment counterweight to the younger, avant-garde members. He resigns in 1887.
LECTURES Edmond Picard, 'L'Art jeune' [fig. 5]; Georges Rodenbach, 'Les Jeunes Belgique'; Albert Giraud, 'La Petite Presse en Belgique'; Catulle Mendès, 'Richard Wagner'.
CONCERTS Works by Naumann, Mendelssohn, Schubert, Grieg, Reyer, Wagner, Godard and Moszkowski.

› All the works of James Ensor, Guillaume Vogels, Achille Chainaye and Willy Finch are refused at the Brussels Salon. Anna Boch, Isidore Verheyden and Fernand Khnopff are given poor positions. According to Maus, Ensor and Finch swear not to invite Alfred Verwee, a member of the organizing committee, to the next Salon des XX.
› The photographer Alexandre gives a slide show at L'Essor with the title 'La Lanterne Magique'. Khnopff will later collaborate closely with him.
› Théo van Rysselberghe and Frantz Charlet spend the winter in Tangiers.
› James Ensor publishes in *L'Art moderne* the satire, *Trois semaines à l'Académie*.

LA BASOCHE

Establishment in Brussels of the Symbolist journal *La Basoche* (1884–1886) by Charles-Henry de Tombeur and André Fontainas, alumni of the Université Libre de Bruxelles. The journal introduces the Symbolist poets Stéphane Mallarmé, Stuart Merrill and René Ghil to Belgium.

› Emile Verhaeren, *Contes de minuit*; Théo van Rysselberghe makes his début as an illustrator, with designs for Georges Eekhoud, *Les Kermesses*.
› Camille Lemonnier publishes *La Belgique*, an accurate account of contemporary life in Belgium, with illustrations by Constantin Meunier, Xavier Mellery, Emile Claus, Theodoor Verstraete and others.
› Gustave Serrurier-Bovy discovers the School of Handicrafts and the Liberty shops in England. He opens a shop for interior design in Liège analogous with Liberty in London, whose products he in fact distributes. He abandons architecture and starts making furniture. He is soon employing about 100 furniture makers and has sales outlets in Paris, Nice, Brussels and The Hague.

› As a reaction to the many refusals of the Paris Salon jury, the *refusés* Auguste Dubois-Pillet, Odilon Redon, Georges Seurat, Paul Signac, Charles Angrand and Henri-Edmond Cross establish the Société des Artistes Indépendants. The artists wish to be able to present their works freely to the general public irrespective of style or taste. The first exhibition, which is held in temporary sheds, shows over one thousand works by four hundred artists.
› Manet retrospective in the Ecole des Beaux-Arts, Paris.
› Puvis de Chavannes paints *Le Bois sacré* for the staircase of the Musée des Beaux-Arts in Lyons.
› Establishment of the Union Centrale des Arts Décoratifs in Paris, as a merger of the Union Centrale des Beaux-Arts appliqués à l'Industrie and the Société du Musée des Arts Décoratifs.
› Thematic exhibition of the Union Centrale des Arts Décoratifs in Paris including stone, wood, ceramics, glass.

› First volume of *The Hobby Horse* (1884–1892), organ of The Century Guild of Artists, by Arthur H. Mackmurdo and Selwyn Image.

› Joris-Karl Huysmans, *A Rebours*; Joséphin Péladan, *Le Vice suprême*, with a frontispiece by Félicien Rops; August Strindberg, *Mariés*.

† Jules Bastien-Lepage, Pericles Pantazis

1885 | The Congress of Berlin on Africa recognizes Leopold II, King of the Belgians, as sovereign of the Independent Congo state.

- Because of very high unemployment, strikes break out in the Borinage. Large quantities of bread are sent to the strikers by the Ghent cooperative bakeries (established by the Socialists in 1880).
- Establishment of the Belgian Labour Party (Parti Ouvrier Belge/Belgische Werklieden Partij). There are great differences of opinion over the choice of the name. Many Belgian workers' associations have an anarchist tradition or tend towards the Progressive Liberals. In order to recruit members more easily from among the Christian workers, the appellation 'socialist' is dropped and the name is taken from the French Parti Ouvrier. The new Party starts up the newspaper, *Le Peuple*. Emile Zola's *Germinal* is featured as a serial on the front page. Many progressive young intellectuals, including Edmond Picard, Jules Destrée, Emile Vandervelde, Léon Furnemont and Max Hallet, leave the Liberal camp to join the new Party, in which they quickly occupy leading positions.
- Colonial exhibition in Antwerp with pavilions from twenty countries.

- Under the leadership of William Morris, the Socialist League splits from the Social Democratic Federation. Morris publishes the manifesto of the Socialist League in his weekly *The Commonwealth*.
- Kropotkin's anarchist journal, *Le Révolté* (editor Jules Grave), is transferred from Geneva to Paris.

LES XX: SECOND SALON

VINGTISTES Chainaye, Charlet, Delvin, Du Bois, Ensor, Finch, Goethals, Khnopff, Regoyos, Schlobach, Simons, Vanaise, Van Rysselberghe, Van Strydonck, Verstraete, Vogels, Wytsman, and the new members Guillaume Charlier, Jan Toorop and Isidore Verheyden. Frans Simons and Theodoor Verstraete leave Les XX; Anna Boch and Félicien Rops take their places.

INVITÉS *Belgium*: L.-H. Devillez, L. Le Nain, X. Mellery, C. Meunier, F. Ter Linden; *Denmark*: P. S. Kröyer; *England*: M. Fisher, J. Swan; *France*: F. Bracquemond, M. Cazin, H. Fantin-Latour, A. Lanson, J.-F. Raffaëlli; *Germany*: F. von Uhde; *Holland*: H. W. Mesdag; *Italy*: A. Mancini, F. P. Michetti; *Switzerland*: L. Breslau; *United States*: C. F. Ulrich.

- Constantin Meunier exhibits sculpture for the first time, including two little waxes of workers: *Puddler* [cat. 48] and *The Stevedore*; Fantin-Latour shows *Parsifal* and *La Prise de Troie*.

LECTURES Emile Sigogne, 'La Tentation de Saint Antoine d'après Flaubert'; Jean-François Raffaëlli, 'Le Laid, l'Intimité, la Sensation et le Caractère dans l'art'.

- An exhibition of drawings by Frantz Charlet, Fernand Khnopff, Constantin Meunier, Théo van Rysselberghe and Guillaume van Strydonck as illustrations to Joséphin Péladan's *Le Vice Suprême*, is held in parallel with the Salon des XX.
- After Emile Verhaeren joins the editorial board of *L'Art moderne*, the paper becomes more oriented towards Symbolism. Emile Verhaeren, Jules Destrée and Jan Toorop travel to England, where they make contact with James Whistler and the William Morris circle. Through his journeys to London, Verhaeren plays a role in transmitting the ideas of Morris and Crane to Les XX. Frantz Charlet and Théo van Rysselberghe meet Whistler when he travels to the Netherlands.
- The 'Grande Zwans' (Big Joke) exhibition opens in the Musée du Nord, Passage du Nord, in Brussels, as a joke of the L'Essor circle aimed at Les XX.
- Exhibition of French Impressionists organized by Durand-Ruel in a Brussels hotel.
- Jean Delville makes his début with L'Essor.
- James Ensor draws *Les Auréoles du Christ (The Halos of Christ)*.
- Georges Rodenbach gives a lecture on Schopenhauer in Brussels.
- The Théâtre de la Monnaie, Brussels, presents Wagner's *Meistersinger von Nürnberg (Mastersingers of Nuremberg)* in French.

- Bastien-Lepage retrospective at the Ecole des Beaux-Arts, Paris.
- An exhibition of works by Paul Gauguin organized by the Danish Academy in Copenhagen is closed after five days.
- The French mathematician Charles Henry publishes *Introduction à une esthétique scientifique*.
- First volume of *Kunstgewerbeblatt* in Leipzig (1885–1917).
- First issue of *La Revue wagnérienne* (founded by Houston Chamberlain, Edouard Dujardin, Téodor de Wyzéwa, in Munich, 1884). Contributors include Villiers de l'Isle-Adam, Huysmans, Mallarmé ('Richard Wagner, Rêverie d'un poète français', 1885), Redon and Fantin-Latour.

- Guy de Maupassant, *Bel ami*; Emile Zola, *Germinal*; Kropotkin, *Paroles d'un révolté* (selected essays, 1879–1882).

† Charles Goethals, Victor Hugo

1886 | The economic depression which began around 1874 reaches its absolute trough. Companies shift the general fall in the prices of manufactures onto their employees. In the coal industry, for example, wages fall to the pre-1865 level. In addition, the depression period is marked by major technical innovations in the steel, coal and glass industries. New machines replace human labour. Besides the wage cuts there are large-scale redundancies and forced unemployment in the majority of industries, as well as in agriculture. The depression will drag on until around 1895.

› The lawyer Alfred Defuisseaux publishes his *Catéchisme du peuple* – 'A People's Catechism', of which 200,000 copies are printed. He calls for a general strike as a means of obtaining universal suffrage. In Brussels some 30,000 workers demonstrate for universal suffrage.

› Disorders break out after a commemoration of the 15th anniversary of the Paris Commune by an anarchist group at Liège. The disorder spreads across Hainaut and from there to the other industrial centres. Rioters plunder and lay waste factories and houses of factory owners in the coal basins of Hainaut. The army is deployed on a large scale and shoots down 24 agitators; hundreds of workers are arrested and given heavy sentences. Alarmed by the spontaneous and massive labour unrest, however, the government appoints a commission to examine working conditions. This marks the first step towards social legislation, which will be voted on during the next few years. Various artists, including Constantin Meunier, James Ensor, Eugène Laermans and Félicien Rops, portray the strike movement [fig. 6].

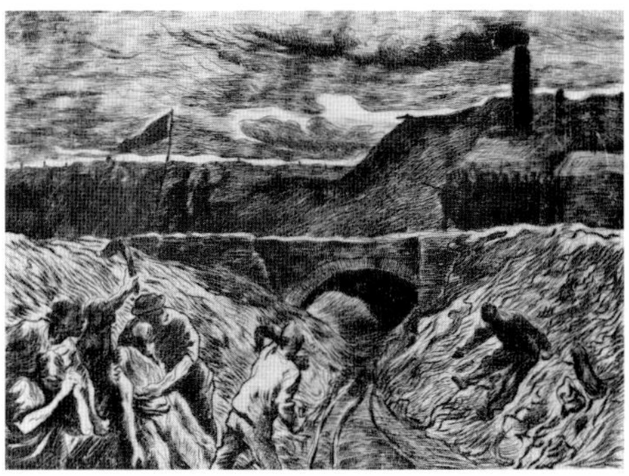

fig. 6 KARL MEUNIER after CONSTANTIN MEUNIER, The Strike, before 1889, etching on parchment

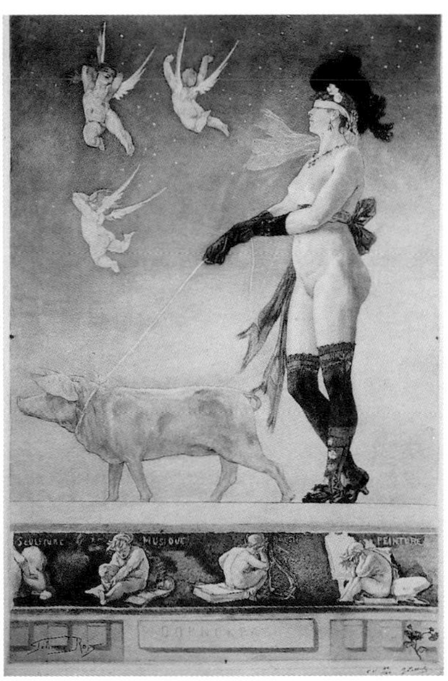

fig. 7 FÉLICIEN ROPS, Pornocrates, after 1878, etching

LES XX: THIRD SALON

VINGTISTES Chainaye, Charlet, Charlier, Du Bois, Ensor, Finch, Khnopff, Regoyos, Rops, Schlobach, Toorop, Van Rysselberghe, Van Strydonck, Verheyden, Vogels, Wytsman, and the new members: Anna Boch and Félicien Rops.

INVITÉS *Belgium*: A. Danse, C. Hermans, L. Speekaert; *England* C. Montalba; *France*: A. Besnard, J. Carriès, F. Gaillard, H. Guérard, C. Monet, O. Redon, A. Renoir, O. Roty, F. Zandomeneghi; *Holland*: I. Israëls, G. H. Breitner; *Italy*: A. Monticelli; *Norway*: F. Kolstö, C. Krohg; *United States*: J. M. Whistler.

› The opening takes place in the presence of Claude Monet, Odilon Redon, Auguste Renoir and James Whistler. An innovation in installation is the stylistic grouping of artists.

› Important submissions by Claude Monet (10 works) and Auguste Renoir (7). It is the first time that Belgium is confronted with Impressionism on this scale. The watercolour *Pornocrates* by Félicien Rops [fig. 7] causes considerable commotion among the visitors. A separate exhibition by Constantin Meunier: paintings, sketches and sculptures, largely inspired by living and working conditions in the Borinage.

› Jean Delvin leaves Les XX because one of his works is refused. Gustave Vanaise leaves Les XX because he no longer identifies with the spirit of the group. Henri de Groux replaces the deceased Charles Goethals. Auguste Rodin and James McNeil Whistler express a wish to become members of Les XX, but are refused after a ballot. James Ensor is one of Whistler's fiercest opponents.

LECTURES Edmond Haraucourt, 'Les Reines de Village' (attack on decadent poetry); Georges Rodenbach, 'Camille Lemonnier'.

CONCERT Works by Schumann, Tartini and Wagner.

LA WALLONIE

Albert Mockel, Hector Chainaye and Charles de Tombeur found the journal *La Wallonie* (1886–1892) in Liège. The editorial staff include Gustave Rahlenbeck, Maurice Siville, Ernest Mahaim, Pierre-M. Olin and Henri de Régnier. The journal develops into the most important medium for the Belgian and French Symbolists. It publishes, for example, work by Emile Verhaeren, Georges Rodenbach, Maurice Maeterlinck, Francis Viélé-Griffin, Stéphane Mallarmé and André Gide.

› James Ensor makes his first etchings.

› At the invitation of James McNeil Whistler, Willy Finch exhibits at the Royal Society of British Artists. Finch pays frequent visits to England and makes contact with the Arts and Crafts Movement.

› First exhibition of Fernand Khnopff in England, at the Art Club in Liverpool.

› George Minne makes his first sculptures. First contacts between Minne and Maurice Maeterlinck.

› The French art critic Félix Fénéon introduces the term Neo-Impressionism in a review of the Paris Salon des Indépendants (see below) in *L'Art moderne*.

› Camille Lemonnier, *Happe-Chair* (novel set round a coal mine); Max Elskamp has his collection of poems *L'Eventail japonais* printed on Japanese woodcuts; Odilon Redon illustrates *Le Juré* by Edmond Picard and makes his first illustrations for Belgian authors: Jules Destrée, Iwan Gilkin and Emile Verhaeren.

› Première of Emmanuel Chabrier's *Gwendoline*, with a 'Wagnerian' libretto by Catulle Mendès, at the Théâtre de la Monnaie, Brussels.

› In Paris, Eighth and last Impressionist Exhibition. There is disagreement about whether they should continue to exhibit as a revolutionary group separately from the other stylistic tendencies or mingle with other artists. It becomes clear that the 'Impressionists' have less and less in common with each other. 'Impressionism' was even deleted from the title of the exhibition. Artists such as Renoir, Monet, Sisley, Cézanne are absent. Georges Seurat exhibits *La Grande Jatte*.

› Salon des Indépendants in Paris. After the exhibition of the Impressionists, Georges Seurat exhibits *La Grande Jatte* in the midst of works by his friends Camille Pissarro, Paul Signac, Henri-Edmond Cross, Charles Angrand as a manifesto of a new style in painting. Le Douanier Rousseau makes his first appearance there. Emile Verhaeren and Théo van Rysselberghe propose inviting Seurat to the next Salon des XX in Brussels.

› Vincent van Gogh settles in Paris, where he meets Louis Anquetin, André Guillaumin and Camille Pissarro.

› Paul Gauguin settles in Pont-Aven and meets Emile Bernard and Charles Laval. He makes his first ceramic sculptures there.

› Jean Moréas and Gustave Kahn publish manifestos for Symbolism in *Le Figaro* and *L'Evénement* respectively. The Belgian journals *L'Art moderne* and *La Jeune Belgique* publish excerpts from Moréas's text.

› Whistler retrospective at Galerie Georges Petit, Paris. Whistler becomes chairman of the Society of British Artists.

› First exhibition of the New English Art Club at the Marlborough Gallery, London.
› In New York, Paul Durand-Ruel organizes an exhibition of over 300 Impressionist canvases, which arouses great interest.

› Robert Louis Stevenson, *Dr Jekyll and Mr Hyde*; Tolstoy, *The Death of Ivan Illitch*; Friedrich Nietzsche, *Jenseits von Gut und Böse*.

1887 | Establishment of the newspaper, *Le Soir*, which is distributed free in Brussels.

› Alfred Defuisseaux, who is regarded by the government as the person mainly responsible for the bloody strikes of 1886, flees to Paris, where he is sentenced to four years imprisonment in his absence. He is expelled from the Belgian Labour Party (POB) and founds the Parti Républicain Socialiste. A third of the POB associations, mainly from Hainaut, follow him. Further violent strikes break out, with universal suffrage as the principal demand.
› The radical Liberals split from the Liberal Party and establish a Progressive Party under the leadership of Paul Janson. As strong supporters of universal suffrage, they maintain close contacts with the Socialists. Many progressives will in fact transfer their allegiance after the breakthrough of the POB in 1894.

LES XX: FOURTH SALON

VINGTISTES Boch, Chainaye, Charlet, Charlier, De Groux, Du Bois, Ensor, Finch, Khnopff, Regoyos, Rops, Schlobach, Toorop, Van Rysselberghe, Van Strydonck, Verheyden, Vogels, Wytsman.

INVITÉS *Belgium*: L. Artan, H. de Braekeleer, C. Meunier, E. Smits, A. Verhaeren; *England*: W. Sickert; *France*: M. Cazin, A. Lebourg, B. Morisot, C. Pissarro, J. F. Raffaëlli, A. Renan, A. Rodin, G. Seurat; *Holland*: W. and M. Maris, M. van der Maarel, P. Zilcken; *Norway*: F. Thaulow.

› After Paris, Georges Seurat – who is present at the opening – now confronts the Brussels art scene with *La Grande Jatte* and six other works painted in the pointillist style. He makes his first sales there. During the next few years various *vingtistes* will go over to Neo-Impressionism. It is also the first time that works by Camille Pissarro are on view in Belgium. Auguste Rodin exhibits *L'Eve* and *L'Homme au nez cassé*. Other eye-catchers include a series of drawings by James Ensor: *Les Auréoles du Christ ou les sensibilités de la lumière (The Halos of Christ or the Sensibilities of Light)* including *The Entry of Christ into Jerusalem*.
› Edmond Picard reads from his work, *Le Juré*. The illustrations by Odilon Redon are exhibited at the Salon.

L'ASSOCIATION POUR L'ART INDÉPENDANT

The group L'Association pour l'Art Indépendant (1887–1892) is established in Antwerp through the actions of Henry van de Velde. The aim is to make the innovative force of Les XX felt in Antwerp too. Only one Salon is held (1887) because of the opposition of the city council. The members are: Léon Abry, Florent Crabeels, Maurice Hagemans, Alexandre Marcette, Isidore Meyers, George Morren, Jacques Rosseels, Henry van de Velde, and the secretary is the writer Max Elskamp. Work by the *vingtistes* Ensor, Khnopff, Rops, Van Rysselberghe and Vogels is shown at the exhibition alongside that of the association's own members.

› Théo van Rysselberghe visits the studio of Georges Seurat in Paris, where he meets Henri de Toulouse-Lautrec, whom he recommends for exhibition with Les XX.
› After staying in The Hague for a year, Jan Toorop returns to Brussels, where he remains until 1889.
› The Palais des Beaux-Arts in Brussels is converted into the Musée d'Art Ancien. 'The living artists have made way for the dead!' *(L'Art moderne)*.
› Victor Horta joins the Brussels freemasons' lodge, Les Amis Philantropes, who play an important role in the development of Belgian Liberalism. There he meets the engineer Tassel, for whom he will build one of his first houses. The majority of Horta's clients will in fact be progressive Liberals: Autrique, Winssinger, Solvay, Furnemont, Hallet, Dubois, Sander Pierron and Feron.
› Gustave Serrurier-Bovy imports Oriental objects.

› Emile Verhaeren, *Quelques notes sur l'œuvre de Fernand Khnopff, 1881–1887*, Editions Monnom, Brussels (collected articles published in *L'Art moderne*); Emile Verhaeren, *L'Idole*, with a frontispiece by Odilon Redon.
› Première of Richard Wagner's *Valkyrie* (in French) at the Théâtre de la Monnaie, Brussels.

› On the initiative of the French artists Louis Roll, Albert Besnard and the Belgian Guillaume van Strydonck, the Société des XXXIII is established in Paris, following the example of Les XX. Belgian members include Fernand Khnopff, Theodoor Verstraete, Félicien Rops, Guillaume Charlier and Théo van Rysselberghe. The first exhibition is held at the Galerie Georges Petit.
› Exhibition of Japanese art at the Union Centrale des Arts Décoratifs, Paris.
› Vincent van Gogh paints in Paris and frequents the circles of the Impressionists and the Neo-Impressionists. He exhibits with Bernard, Anquetin and Toulouse-Lautrec.
› Puvis de Chavannes exhibition at the Galerie Durand-Ruel; J.-F. Millet exhibition at the Ecole Nationale des Beaux-Arts, Paris.
› Paul Gauguin travels around Martinique.
› Thousands demonstrate against the performance of Wagner's *Lohengrin* at the Eden-Concert in Paris.

› Emile Zola, *La Terre*.
› Gabriel Fauré, *Réquiem*.

› Max Klinger's *The Judgement of Paris*, a monumental work combining painting, sculpture and architecture, is shown in Berlin.

1888 | Belgian banknotes become bilingual and part of the Belgian State Gazette is published in Dutch.
› Julius Hoste founds the freethinking Liberal popular newspaper, *Het Laatste Nieuws*.

LES XX: FIFTH SALON
VINGTISTES Boch, Chainaye, Charlet, Charlier, De Groux, Du Bois, Ensor, Finch, Khnopff, Regoyos, Rops, Schlobach, Toorop, Van Rysselberghe, Van Strydonck, Vogels. Achille Chainaye, Isidore Verheyden and Rodolphe Wytsman withdraw from Les XX and are replaced by Henry van de Velde, Auguste Rodin and Georges Lemmen.
INVITÉS *Belgium*: X. Mellery, C. van der Stappen; *France*: L. Anquetin, C. Besnard, J.-E. Blanche, G. Caillebotte, J. C. Chaplain, H. Cros, H. de Toulouse-Lautrec, A. Dubois-Pillet, J.-L. Forain, J. Gonzales, A. Guillaumin, P. Helleu, P. Signac; *United States*: J. M. Whistler.
› Through Théo Van Rysselberghe, Louis Anquetin, Henri de Toulouse-Lautrec, Paul Helleu, Armand Guillaumin, Jean-Louis Forain, Gustave Caillebotte, Paul Signac (13 works) and Auguste Dubois-Pillet exhibit for the first time with Les XX. It is Toulouse-Lautrec's first participation in an important exhibition. The exhibition is largely given over to Neo-Impressionism, with works by Dubois-Pillet, Signac and Willy Finch, the first Belgian artist to exhibit Neo-Impressionist work.
› Each participant designs his own page for the catalogue – a handwritten list of the submitted works sometimes embellished with a drawing – which is reproduced and printed using photomechanical plates.
› As soon as he is admitted, Henry van de Velde begins to work for the inclusion of applied art in the Salons.
LECTURES Octave Maus: 'La Recherche de la lumière dans la peinture' (introductory speech); Villiers de l'Isle-Adam reads three *Histoires insolites*.
CONCERTS French contemporary music with works by d'Indy, Franck, Fauré, de Castillon, with the young Belgian violinist Eugène Ysaÿe, and Vincent d'Indy and Gabriel Fauré themselves as performers; contemporary Spanish music with works by Sarasate, Cinna, Arbos and Guelbenzu (programme illustrated by Regoyos); works by Schumann, Scarlatti and Bach.

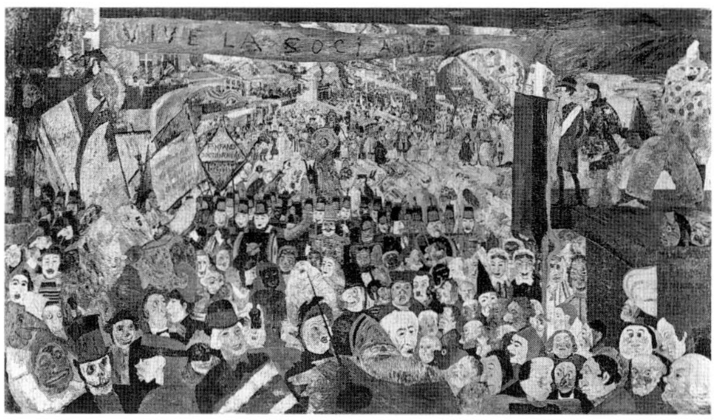
fig. 8 JAMES ENSOR, The Entry of Christ into Brussels, 1888–1889, J. P. Getty Museum, Malibu

› James Ensor starts work on his most important work: *The Entry of Christ into Brussels* (completed 1889) [fig. 8].
› Théo van Rysselberghe and Henry van de Velde paint their first Neo-Impressionist works.
› Fernand Khnopff increasingly frequents literary circles. Josephin Péladan asks him to make the frontispieces for *Istar* and *Femmes honnêtes*.
› The painter Jean Delville publishes his first sonnets in the Symbolist journal *La Wallonie*.
› Establishment of the Union des Arts Décoratifs, Brussels.

› Octave Maus, *Souvenirs d'un wagnériste. Le Théâtre de Bayreuth*; Emile Verhaeren, *Les Soirs* and *Les Débâcles*, dedicated to his friends, the painters Théo van Rysselberghe, Willy Schlobach and Dario de Regoyos, frontispieces by Odilon Redon.

› Van Gogh settles in Arles, where Gauguin joins him later in the year.
› Gauguin and Bernard work in Pont-Aven.
› Paul Sérusier founds the group Les Nabis ; members are Pierre Bonnard, Henri Gabriel Ibels, Paul Ranson, Maurice Denis, René Piot, Ker-Xavier Roussel and Edouard Vuillard, and later, Aristide Maillol and Félix Vallotton.
› First one-man show by Maximilien Luce in the offices of *La Revue indépendante*, the review founded by Edouard Dujardin and Félix Fénéon.
› Samuel Bing opens a gallery in Paris which specializes in Japanese prints and founds the journal *Le Japon artistique* (1888–1891).

› Charles R. Ashbee establishes the Guild of Handicraft (1888–1891) in London.
› George Eastman produces the first box camera: Kodak.

› Maurice Barrès, *Sous l'œil des barbares*; Stéphane Mallarmé translates Whistler's *Ten o'clock Lecture*; Friedrich Nietzsche, *Der Antichrist*.

1889 | Acquittal of the workers arrested during the strikes of 1887 and sentencing of the moles of the state security service. Defuisseaux's revolutionaries rejoin the reformist Belgian Labour Party (POB). The POB becomes a member of the Second International, established in Paris with the collaboration of the Belgian Socialists César de Paepe, Edward Anseele and Emile Vandervelde.
› Parliament passes the first laws to regulate female and child labour.
› Thousands of Belgians emigrate to the United States, Canada and Argentina.

LES XX: SIXTH SALON
VINGTISTES Boch, Charlet, Charlier, De Groux, Du Bois, Ensor, Finch, Khnopff, Regoyos, Rops, Schlobach, Toorop, Van Rysselberghe, Van Strydonck, Vogels, and the new members: Georges Lemmen, Auguste Rodin and Henry van de Velde.
INVITÉS *Belgium*: P. de Vigne, C. Meunier; *England*: P. Wilson Steer, W. Stott; *France*: A. Besnard, F. Bracquemond, H.-E. Cross, M. Desboutin, E. Frémiet, P. Gauguin, M. Luce, C. Monet, E. Moreau-Nélaton, C. Pissarro, G. Seurat; *Germany*: M. Klinger; *Holland*: W. B. van Tholen.
› Triumph of Neo-Impressionism with works by the Seurat, Pissarro, Luce and Cross, and by Van Rysselberghe, Anna Boch, Toorop and Van de Velde, who present Neo-Impressionist work for the first time. Gauguin causes a scandal with his Breton, Provençal and Martinique paintings.
LECTURE Téodor de Wyzéwa, 'Les Origines de la Littérature décadente: Verlaine, Laforgue, Mallarmé'.
CONCERTS Contemporary French music with works by Franck, d'Indy, Tiersot, Chausson, De Bréville, Fauré, Duparc and Bordes performed by the Ysaÿe Quartet, d'Indy and Fauré.

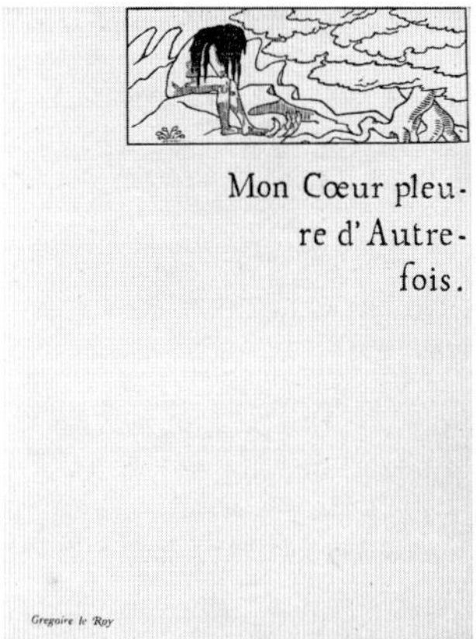

fig. 9 GEORGE MINNE, Cover for Grégoire Le Roy's *Mon cœur pleure d'autrefois* (1889), Private Collection

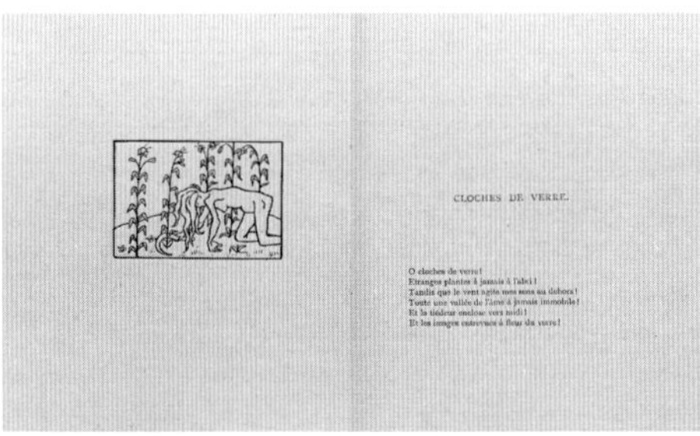

fig. 10 GEORGE MINNE, Illustration for Maurice Maeterlinck's *Serres chaudes* (1889), Private Collection, Brasschaat

- Through the intervention of Henry van de Velde an exhibition of Les XX is organized in Zaal Verlat, Antwerp. Jan Toorop organizes an exhibition of works by twelve *vingtistes* in Kunstzaal Panorama, Amsterdam: Boch, De Groux, Regoyos, Du Bois, Finch, Lemmen, Rops, Schlobach, Toorop, Van Rysselberghe, Van Strydonck and Vogels. The exhibition causes violent arguments in the Netherlands.
- Fernand Khnopff becomes increasingly interested in photography; he buys photographic apparatus and technical manuals. Photographs are enhanced with coloured pencils and pastels. Close collaboration with the photographer Alexandre.
- Emile Claus who exhibits regularly at the Paris Salon, rents a studio in Paris and works there during three successive winters.
- Exhibition of Japanese art at the Cercle Artistique et Littéraire, Brussels.

- Maurice Maeterlinck, *La Princesse Maleine* (his début as a playwright); Maurice Maeterlinck, *Serres chaudes* (collection of poems published in Paris), with illustrations by George Minne [fig. 10]; Grégoire Le Roy, *Mon cœur pleure d'autrefois* with illustrations by George Minne [fig. 9] and Fernand Khnopff; Jules Destrée, *Les Chimères*, with a frontispiece by Odilon Redon.
- Performances of Wagner's *Lohengrin* at the Théâtre de la Monnaie, Brussels.

- Exposition Universelle, Paris: the triumph of industry and technology (Eiffel Tower, Halle des Machines) alongside the celebration of colonialism (exotic pavilions). The official exhibition of a century of French painting includes works by Monet, Manet, Pissarro and Cézanne.
- 'Exposition du Groupe impressionniste et synthétiste' in Volpini's Café des Arts immediately adjoining the Champ-de-Mars: Gauguin, Anquetin, Bernard, Laval, Fouché, Daniel, Roy and Schuffenecker.
- Double retrospective of Auguste Rodin and Claude Monet in the Galerie Georges Petit, Paris.
- First exhibition of posters by Jules Chéret in Paris.
- First one-man show of Edvard Munch in Oslo.
- Exhibition of London Impressionists at the Goupil Gallery, London, organized by Walter Richard Sickert and Frederick Brown.

- The mathematician Charles Henry, a friend of Georges Seurat and Paul Signac, publishes his *Cercle chromatique*, a scientific study of colours.
- First volume of the French Symbolist journal *Le Moderniste* under the direction of Albert Aurier.
- Emile Pouget founds the anarchist journal *Père Peinard* in Paris; Camille Pissarro, Maximilien Luce and Adolphe Willette provide the illustrations.
- Paul Verlaine, *Parallèlement*; Paul Bourget, *Le Disciple*; Francis Viélé-Griffin, *Joies*; Joris-Karl Huysmans, *Certains*; Louis Couperus, *Eline Vere*; Herman Gorter, *Mei*; Yeats, *Wanderings of Oisin*.
- Walter Crane illustrates *Flora's Feast*.
- Richard Strauss, *Don Juan*.

† Max Waller, Villiers de l'Isle-Adam

1890

fig. 11 'Le Salon des XX', *Le Patriote Illustré* (2 February 1890)

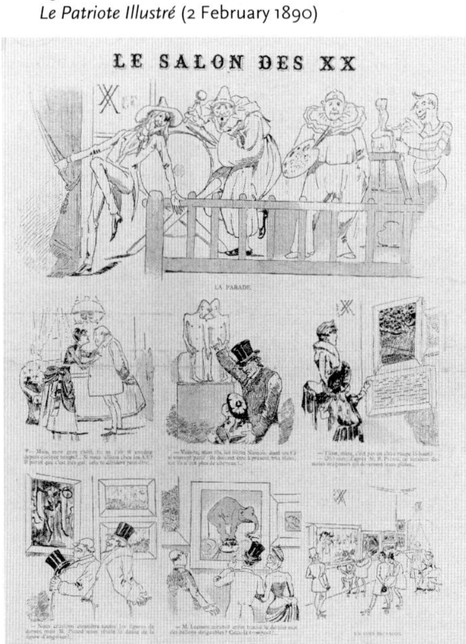

Eighty thousand demonstrate in Brussels for the introduction of universal suffrage. A compromise between the revolutionaries and the reform movement results in a strategy of preparing for a general strike in the whole country. This compromise is confirmed by an oath sworn after the demonstration in the park at Saint-Gilles (Brussels).
- King Leopold II receives a credit from the Belgian state running into millions – to be paid after his death – in return for handing over sovereignty of the Congo.

LES XX: SEVENTH SALON

VINGTISTES Boch, Charlet, Charlier, De Groux, Du Bois, Ensor, Finch, Khnopff, Lemmen, Regoyos, Rodin, Rops, Schlobach, Toorop, Van de Velde, Van Rysselberghe, Van Strydonck, Vogels, and the new member: Robert Picard.

INVITÉS *Belgium*: E. Boch, X. Mellery, G. Minne; *England*: G.W. Thornley; *France*: P. Cézanne, A. Charpentier, A. Dubois-Pillet, L. Hayet, L. Pissarro, O. Redon, A. Renoir, O. Roty, P. Signac, A. Sisley, H. de Toulouse-Lautrec; *Holland*: C. Storm van 's Gravesande, V. van Gogh; *Italy*: G. Segantini [fig. 11].

- Cézanne makes an exception to not exhibiting by sending three works to Brussels. Van Gogh apologizes in a letter to Octave Maus for exceeding the four metres, and sends seven works. This is where he sells his first painting. First exhibits by Alfred Sisley and Giovanni Segantini. Van Gogh is the cause of great argument within the Society; Henri de Groux withdraws his entry because he does not want to exhibit in the same gallery as Van Gogh. After a vote De Groux is expelled from the society.
- For the first time a significant presence of Symbolist works: Odilon Redon, Willy Schlobach, Jan Toorop, Fernand Khnopff and George Minne. Paul Signac and Henri de Toulouse-Lautrec attend the opening.
- George Minne and Paul Signac become members of Les XX.

LECTURES Edmond Picard, 'Trois poètes belges d'exception: Emile Verhaeren, Maurice Maeterlinck, Charles van Lerberghe' [fig. 12]; Stéphane Mallarmé, 'Villiers de l'Isle-Adam'.

CONCERTS Contemporary Belgian music: Dupont, Franck, Soubre, Huberti, Gilson, Kéfer, Jouret, Jacob, Mathieu; contemporary French music: De Castillon, Fauré, d'Indy; including some first performances.

- Fernand Khnopff acquires a growing reputation in England. Walter Shaw-Sparrow publishes a long article about him in the *Magazine of Art*. His first one-man show is held in the Hanover Gallery, London, and his work is also shown in two group exhibitions.
- Willy Finch works as a 'decorative painter on faience' for the Boch-Keramis ceramics studio in La Louvière (–1892).
- First Symbolist works by Léon Fréderic.
- Debut of William Degouve de Nuncques in the Paris Salon, where he meets Auguste Rodin, Puvis de Chavannes and Maurice Denis.
- Anna Boch, Robert Picard and the Belgian Neo-Impressionists Henry van de Velde, Georges Lemmen, Willy Finch and Théo van Rysselberghe exhibit in the Salon des Indépendants in Paris.

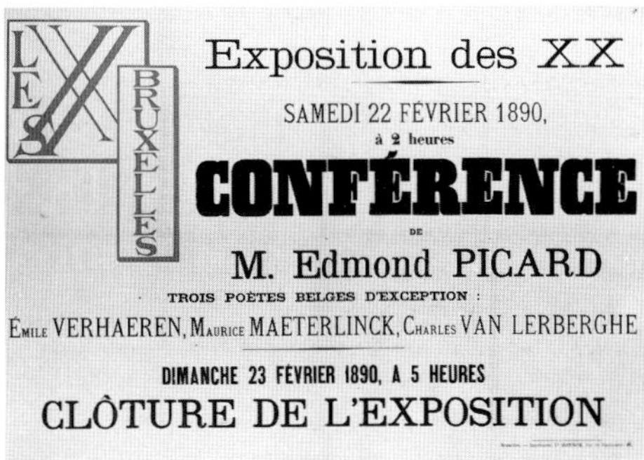

fig. 12 Poster announcing Edmond Picard's lecture at Les XX, 1890

L'ERMITAGE
Establishment of the monthly journal, *L'Ermitage* (1890–1906), on French-language literature and art in Belgium. Contributors include Emile Verhaeren, Camille Lemonnier, Albert Mockel, Georges Rodenbach, Charles van Lerberghe. Théo van Rysselberghe is in charge of cover and design.

› Maurice Maeterlinck, *Les Aveugles* and *L'Intruse*; Iwan Gilkin, *La Damnation de l'artiste*, with a frontispiece by Odilon Redon.
› Stéphane Mallarmé lectures in five Belgian cities, including Antwerp.

› First Salon of the Société Nationale des Beaux-Arts (Salon du Champ-de-Mars) in Paris, an alternative annual salon to the Salon des Artistes Français (Salon des Champs-Elysées).

› Exhibition of Japanese prints at the Ecole des Beaux-Arts, Paris.
› Toulouse-Lautrec produces his first posters.
› Gauguin is again working in Pont-Aven together with Paul Sérusier, Charles Filiger and the Dutchman Meyer de Haan.
› Maurice Denis publishes his 'Définition du néo-traditionalisme' – the Nabis manifesto – in the journal *Art et Critique*.

› First volume of the Symbolist journal *Mercure de France*.
› Emile Zola, *La Bête humaine*; Paul Claudel, *Tête d'or*.

› First exhibition of the Arts and Crafts Exhibition Society, London (founded 1888).
› First volume of *Das Kunstgewerbe* (1890–1895), Dresden.

† Louis Artan de Saint-Martin, Auguste Dubois-Pillet, Vincent van Gogh, César Franck

1891

The Belgian Catholics – Christian Democrats – who defend the workers' interest, feel encouraged by the encyclical 'Rerum Novarum' in which Pope Leo XIII associates himself with more liberal doctrines.
› After the annual May-Day demonstration there are massive strikes in the mining industry in support of universal suffrage, higher pay and an eight-hour working day. After twenty days of strikes, the House of Representatives, fearing a general strike, declare themselves in agreement with the progressive Liberals' proposals of 1889 for the revision of the constitution in respect of suffrage, as had been proposed the previous year by the progressive liberals. The Belgian Labour Party calls off a general strike.

LES XX: EIGHTH SALON
VINGTISTES Boch, Charlet, Charlier, Du Bois, Ensor, Finch, Khnopff, Lemmen, Picard, Regoyos, Rodin, Rops, Schlobach, Toorop, Van de Velde, Van Rysselberghe, Van Strydonck, Vogels, and the new members: George Minne and Paul Signac.
INVITÉS *Belgium*: E. Smits, C. van der Stappen; *England*: W. Crane, P. Wilson Steer; *France*: C. Angrand, J. Baffier, J. Chéret, C. Filiger, P. Gauguin, A. Guillaumin, C. Pissarro, Seurat, Sisley; *Germany*: A. Oberländer; *Holland*: M. Bauer, F. Verster; *Sweden*: C. Larsson. As a tribute to Vincent van Gogh, who had died the previous year, fifteen of his works are exhibited, chosen by Theo van Gogh's wife [fig. 13].
› Fernand Khnopff designs the poster and Georges Lemmen the cover of the catalogue. Octave Maus refuses to hang Ensor's *The Righteous Judges* (an indictment of the Belgian legal system). Paul Gauguin's works again cause great stir among the general public. Filiger is invited at Gauguin's request. A significant amount of applied arts: illustrated books by Walter Crane, decorative panels by Willy Finch, ceramics and bas-reliefs in polychromed wood by Gauguin and posters by Jules Chéret. Decorative art objects are for the first time given equal prominence with the paintings and sculptures.
LECTURES Henry van de Velde, 'Le Paysan en peinture'; Georges Lecomte, 'Les Néo-Impressionnistes'; Gustave Kahn, 'Le Vers libre'; Edmond Picard: 'Jules Laforgue et la femme'.

fig. 13 FERNAND KHNOPFF
Poster for the Eighth Salon des XX, 1891

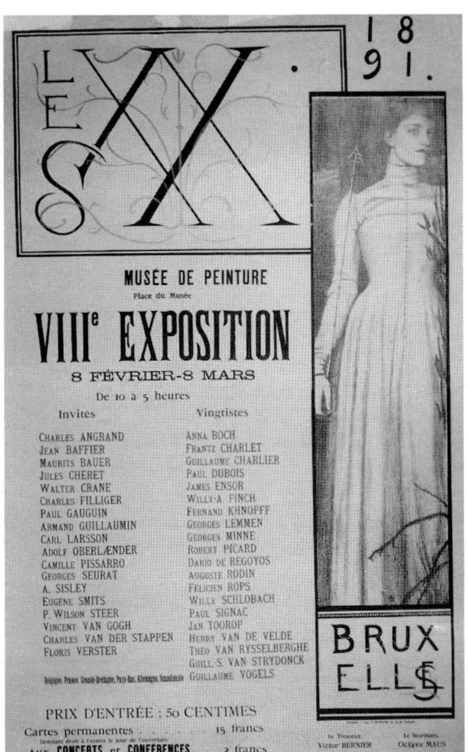

CONCERTS Unpublished works by Franck – who had died the previous year – performed by the Ysaÿe Quartet, Vincent d'Indy and the newly formed choir of Les XX; contemporary French music by Fauré, Duparc, Chausson *et al.*; and Russian music, in which works by Tchaikovsky, Borodin, Cherbatchov, Kopylov and Rimsky-Korsakov are performed for the first time in Brussels.

THE XIII
Emile Claus, Edgard Farasyn and Edward de Jans form the XIII in Antwerp. Their aim is to bring about a revival of Antwerp's artistic life following the example of Les XX. Members are Léon Abry, Leo van Aken, Emile Claus, Louis van Engelen, Edgard Farasyn, Frans Hens, Edward de Jans, Romain Looymans, Hendrik Luyten, Charles Mertens, Henri de Smeth, Piet Verhaert, Theodoor Verstraete.

SECTION FOR ART AND PUBLIC EDUCATION
Establishment of the Section d'Art et d'Enseignement populaire (1891–1911) in the Maison du Peuple in Brussels. This cultural department of the Belgian Labour Party organizes lectures (by, among others, Henry van de Velde, Max Elskamp, Emile Vandervelde, Jules Destrée, Fernand Khnopff, Octave Maus, Edmond Picard, Emile Verhaeren), practical courses, concerts and exhibitions for the workers of Brussels and encourages artists to put their work and skills at the service of the social struggle. Every year visits are organized to exhibitions and to the Salons of Les XX and later of La Libre Esthétique. Membership of the Party is not a condition of taking part. Among those showing at the exhibitions were: Constantin Meunier, Willy Finch, Guillaume van Strydonck, Anna Boch, Paul Signac, Georges Lemmen, Eugène Laermans, Henry van de Velde. Octave Maus organizes a whole series of concerts, including, in 1891, a lecture by Kufferath on Wagner, followed by a Wagner concert.
› Fernand Khnopff begins to spend a few months in England each year at the time of the main salons. He makes his first sculpture in polychromed plaster: a mask of a young English woman.
› Anna Boch, Willy Finch, George Lemmen and Théo van Rysselberghe exhibit in the Salon des Indépendants, Paris.

- Maurice Maeterlinck, *Les Sept Princesses*; Emile Verhaeren, *Les Flambeaux noirs*.
- World première of the French-language version of Wagner's *Siegfried* at the Théâtre de la Monnaie, Brussels.
- The Brussels art bookseller, Dietrich, exhibits a series of large-size photographic reproductions of works by Burne-Jones and Rossetti, and of albums and books illustrated by Walter Crane.
- Brussels is the first city on the Continent where the English store, Liberty's, offers its textile designs for sale: linen and decorative articles can be bought there.
- In Paris (–1897), first Exhibition of Impressionnist and Symbolist painters by Le Barc de Boutteville .
- For the first time the Nabis exhibit as a group in the First Exhibition for Fine Arts at the Château at Saint-Germain-en-Laye.
- Applied arts are included in the Salon du Champ-de-Mars in Paris.
- Paul Gauguin shows ceramics and woodcarving in the Salon des Indépendants, Paris.

LA REVUE BLANCHE

Establishment in Paris of the Symbolist journal, *La Revue Blanche*, by the Nathanson brothers. After a few issues published in Liège and Brussels, publication moves permanently to Paris. The editor is Lucien Muhlfeld and from 1894 Félix Fénéon. The journal becomes the mouthpiece of the avant-garde, the anarchists and the supporters of Dreyfus. The paper can call on a long list of contributors: Jules Renard, Stéphane Mallarmé, André Gide, Tristan Bernard, Guillaume Apollinaire, Georges Clemenceau, Léon Blum; Jules Chéret, Henri de Toulouse-Lautrec and all members of the Nabis work on the illustrations. Edouard Vuillard's first one-man exhibition is held on the premises of *La Revue Blanche*.

- The anarchist journal, *En Dehors*, is founded by Zo D'Axa in Paris. Contributors include Félix Fénéon, Emile Verhaeren, Octave Mirbeau, Emile Henry and Georges Lecomte.
- Théâtre d'Art: first performance in Paris of a work *(L'Intruse)* by Maurice Maeterlinck.
- Théâtre du Vaudeville in Paris benefit performance for Paul Gauguin – on his departure for Tahiti – and Paul Verlaine. The programme includes work by Stéphane Mallarmé, Paul Verlaine, Catulle Mendès and Maurice Maeterlinck *(L'Intruse)*.

- Jean Moréas, *Pélerin passionné*; Selma Lagerlöf, *Gösta Berling*; Stéphane Mallarmé, *Pages*, with an etching by Renoir (published in Brussels).
- William Morris sets up the Kelmscott Press.

† Arthur Rimbaud, Georges Seurat

1892

Various anarchist outrages in Paris, Ravachol is executed.

LES XX: NINTH SALON

VINGTISTES Boch, Charlet, Charlier, Du Bois, Ensor, Finch, Khnopff, Lemmen, Minne, Picard, Regoyos, Rodin, Rops, Schlobach, Signac, Toorop, Van de Velde, Van Rysselberghe, Van Strydonck, Vogels.
INVITÉS *Belgium*: X. Mellery, C. Meunier; *England*: H. Horne, S. Image; *France*: A. Bartholomé, A. Besnard, M. Cassatt, A. Delaherche, M. Denis, L. Gausson, M. Luce, L. Pissarro, C. Serret, H. de Toulouse-Lautrec.

- Georges Lemmen designs the Les XX catalogue cover. Retrospective homage to the late Georges Seurat with forty of his works. First exhibits by Maurice Denis; substantial contribution of French and English applied art not previously seen in Brussels; Selwyn Image and Horne are invited on the suggestion of Fernand Khnopff and Georges Lemmen. Embroidery by Henry van de Velde: his first step in the direction of applied art. The alliance of Socialism, Symbolism and the decorative arts, which has grown steadily stronger over the previous few exhibitions, for the first time confronts the public with the new aesthetic which is soon to be known as 'Art Nouveau'.

LECTURES Georges Lecomte, 'Des Tendances de la Peinture moderne'; M. Roland, 'Lecture de quelques contes de Camille Lemonnier'.
CONCERTS Contemporary music, with works by Rimsky-Korsakov, Lekeu, Gilson, Glazunov, Servais, De Castillon, Bordes, Franck, Chabrier, De Serres and d'Indy. Lekeu conducts his own work.

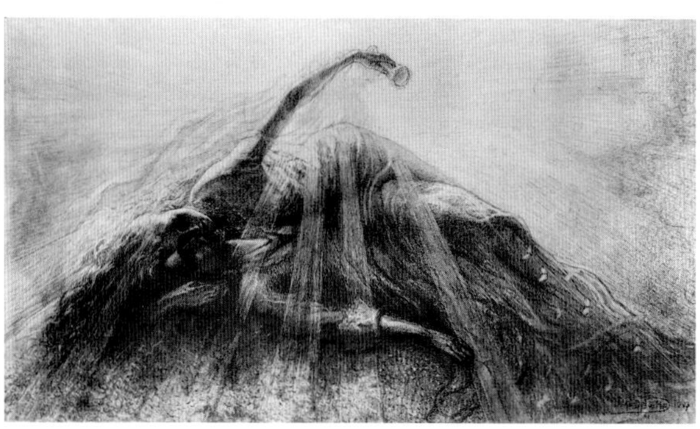

fig. 14 JEAN DELVILLE, Tristan and Isolde, 1887, Pencil, black chalk and charcoal, Musées royaux des Beaux-Arts de Belgique, Brussels

POUR L'ART

After the collapse of L'Essor, Jean Delville [fig. 14] sets up the society, Pour L'Art, in Brussels (1892–1941). Founded as a society of Symbolists, with Xavier Mellery, George Minne, Albert Ciamberlani, Emile Fabry, Félicien Rops, the Swiss Carlos Schwabe and the Dutchman Jan Verkade as members, the society evolves after a few years into an eclectic group whose primary emphasis lay in a belief in the independence of the artist.

L'ASSOCIATION POUR L'ART

Establishment in Antwerp of L'Association pour L'Art (1892–1893) as a successor to L'Art Indépendant. The society's object is, in the spirit of Les XX, to provide a forum for contemporary artistic expression. The founding committee consists of Charles Dumercy, Max Elskamp, George Morren, Gustave Serigiers and Henry van de Velde. Following the example of Les XX, they organize exhibitions, lectures and concerts. Their first Salon consists largely of works by those who took part the Salons des XX in 1891 and 1892, including Finch, Lemmen, Boch, Van de Velde, Signac, Van Rysselberghe, Minne and Toorop. During the Salon there is a Hiroshige retrospective from the Lemmen and Van Rysselberghe collections.

- Through the agency of Jan Toorop, works by Van Rysselberghe and Van de Velde are exhibited in the Kunstkring, The Hague. Lectures by Van de Velde ('Du Paysan en peinture') and Emile Verhaeren. Van de Velde meets Jan Thorn-Prikker there.
- Khnopff gives a lecture in the Cercle des Arts et de la Presse, Brussels, on the occasion of an exhibition of Hollyer's photographs after G F. Watts, Ford Madox Brown, Rossetti and Burne-Jones.
- Degouve de Nuncques' first Symbolist canvases.
- Henri Evenepoel is in Paris, attending classes at the Ecole Nationale des Beaux-Arts.

LE RÉVEIL AND FLORÉAL

Théo van Rysselberghe designs the cover and decoration for the Ghent Symbolist journal *Le Réveil*. The trendsetting Liège journal *La Wallonie* is succeeded by *Floréal*, with which *Le Réveil* merges in 1894 (until 1896). Apart from Van Rysselberghe, George Minne, Georges Lemmen, Charles Doudelet and to a lesser degree Henry van de Velde also provide illustrations. Other contributors include: Max Elskamp, André Fontainas, Emile Verhaeren, Maurice Maeterlinck, Charles van Lerberghe, Grégoire Le Roy, Stéphane Mallarmé, Henri de Régnier, Viélé-Griffin.

› The Art and Education Section of the Brussels Maison du Peuple organizes a series of lectures on a variety of subjects. The lecturers include: Jules Destrée, Georges Eekhoud, Fernand Khnopff (art in England), Maurice Maeterlinck, Edmond Picard, Eugène Robert.
› Joséphin Péladan lectures in the Cercle Pour l'Art in Brussels on the aesthetic theories of the Rosicrucians, and in the Cercle Artistique on 'Mystery, Love and Art'. Fernand Khopff lectures on Hamlet.

› Georges Rodenbach publishes *Bruges-la-Morte* in Paris (Flammarion). This best-selling novel is later serialized in ten instalments in *Le Figaro*.
› Maurice Maeterlinck, *Pelléas et Mélisande*; Max Elskamp, *Dominical* (first book design by Henry van de Velde, who abandons painting for the decorative arts and design); Emile Verhaeren, *Les Flambeaux noirs*, with a frontispiece by Odilon Redon; Friedrich Nietzsche, *Le Cas Wagner*, first French translation appears in *La Société Nouvelle*, a cosmopolitan Brussels review.
› First Salon of the Symbolist Ordre de la Rose+Croix, du Temple et du Graal (–1897) founded by Merodack (Sâr) Péladan in Paris in 1890. George Minne, Fernand Khnopff and Jean Delville are invited to exhibit at this first exhibition in the Galerie Durand-Ruel. Works by Ciamberlani, Filiger, Schwabe, Vallotton, Séon, Hodler, Toorop, Grasset and Bernard are also shown.
› First exhibition of 'Neo-Impressionist Painters' in Paris with work by Alexandre Charpentier, Henri-Edmond Cross, Léo Gausson, Maximilien Luce, Hippolyte Petitjean, Lucien Pissarro, Paul Signac, Georges Seurat (d. 1891) and Théo van Rysselberghe (the only non-Frenchman). The catalogue is printed in Belgium by Veuve Monnom, who also publish the journals *L'Art moderne*, *La Jeune Belgique* and the catalogues of Les XX.
› Georges Seurat retrospective in the Salon des Indépendants, Paris.
› An exhibition of the work of Edvard Munch, organized by the Verein Bildender Künstler in Berlin, arouses so much scandal that it is closed the day after the vernissage. In reaction Max Liebermann, Walter Leistikow, Franz Skarbina, Max Klinger, Ludwig von Hofmann and others set up the Berlin Secession on the model of Les XX. Fritz von Uhde, Franz von Stuck and Wilhelm Trübner found the Munich Secession in parallel.
› Louis Comfort Tiffany establishes the Tiffany Glass and Decorating Co. in New York.

› Walter Crane, *The Claims of Decorative Art* (1893).

1893 | After months of discussion the Parliament rejects the introduction of universal suffrage. As a result the Socialists call a general strike, which is well observed, particularly in key industries. There are disturbances, with several deaths. Finally the radical Liberals in Parliament and the labour leaders, to the great dissatisfaction of the rank and file, submit to a compromise proposal: the universal plural vote. All males over the age of 25 are given one vote, and if they are heads of families or have educational or property qualifications, may have two or three.
› In Alost the priest, Adolf Daens, founds a new political party, the Christene Volkspartij (Christian People's Party), in addition to the Catholic Party.
› Keir Hardie founds the Independent Labour Party in Great Britain.

LES XX: TENTH SALON

VINGTISTES Boch, Charlet, Charlier, Du Bois, Ensor, Finch, Khnopff, Lemmen, Minne, Picard, Regoyos, Rodin, Rops, Schlobach, Signac, Toorop, Van de Velde, Van Rysselberghe, Van Strydonck, Vogels.
INVITÉS *Belgium*: W. Degouve de Nuncques, C. Doudelet, L. Fréderic, J. Gaspar, M. Holeman; *England*: Ford Madox Brown, E.A. Hornel, P. Wilson Steer; *France*: E. Bernard, A. Besnard, A. Charpentier, H. Cros, H.-E. Cross, J. Jacquemin, H. Petitjean, H. de Toulouse-Lautrec; *Holland*: F. Thorn Prikker.
› First submissions by Thorn Prikker, Degouve de Nuncques and the former Pre-Raphaelite Ford Madox Brown. Two complete rooms are devoted to applied art.
LECTURES Paul Verlaine, 'La Poésie contemporaine'; Edmond Picard, 'L'Evolution de la poésie française contemporaine (Henry de Régnier)'. At Verlaine's request Octave Maus organizes a series of lectures in a number of Belgian towns, including Verviers, Charleroi, Liège, Antwerp, Ghent.
CONCERTS Contemporary Belgian and French music, with works by Franck, d'Indy, De Bréville, Chabrier, Fauré, De Castillon, Smulders, Van Reysschoot, Lekeu, Gilson and Chausson (first performance), performed by the Ysaÿe Quartet.
› Group exhibition by Les XX at the Cercle Artistique et Littéraire, Ghent.

› Fernand Khnopff exhibits in the New Gallery and the Grafton Galleries, London.

LA LIBRE ESTHÉTIQUE

L'Art moderne announces the foundation of the art society La Libre Esthétique. Les XX is dissolved. The question is submitted to the vote. In favour: Paul Du Bois, Fernand Khnopff, Robert Picard, Van de Velde, Van Rysselberghe, Dario de Regoyos, Anna Boch, Jan Toorop, Paul Signac and Félicien Rops. James Ensor votes against. George Lemmen, Guillaume Charlier and Willy Finch abstain. The object of La Libre Esthétique is to offer a forum to 'independent' Belgian and foreign artists, in which they can present their work in the best possible conditions. Unlike past practice, the choice of artists lies with one man, Octave Maus, former secretary and animator of Les XX, who asks Théo van Rysselberghe to assist him. Eugène Ysaÿe is in charge of concerts and Léon de Lantsheere of lectures. The greatest virtue of the society, particularly in its early years, lies in its presentation of the latest international developments in applied art and in confronting them with each other. In the visual arts the innovatory role of La Libre Esthétique is, however, relatively small. Their Salons become social events and are much less controversial than those of Les XX. An annual visit by King Leopold II, accompanied by his ministers is symptomatic of the development.

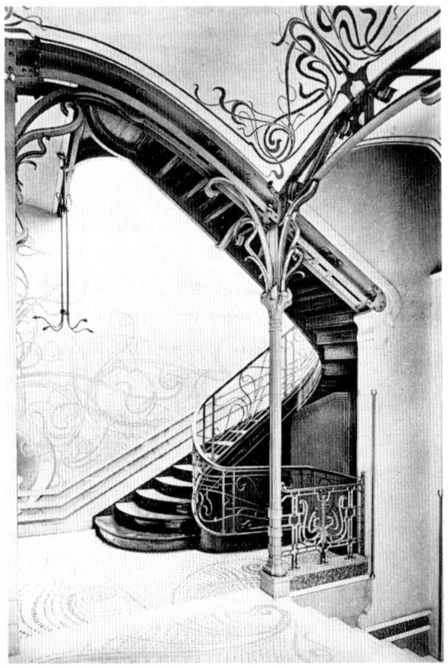

fig. 15 VICTOR HORTA, Tassel House, Brussels, 1893–1895

› Second exhibition of L'Association pour L'Art in Antwerp. Mainly by members of Les XX and supplemented with works of the Nabis: Pierre Bonnard, Maurice Denis, Henri Gabriel Ibels, Paul Ranson, Edouard Vuillard.

LE SILLON

Jef Lambeaux, Frans Smeers and Alfred Bastien found Le Sillon, a society of non-progressive, mainly realist painters and sculptors, alumni of the Brussels Academy. First Le Sillon exhibition in Brussels.

› Henri Evenepoel enrols at Gustave Moreau's art studio in the Ecole Nationale des Beaux-Arts, Paris.
› Henry van de Velde publishes his *Première prédication d'art* on the unity of the arts in *L'Art moderne*.

VAN NU EN STRAKS

Founding of the Flemish literary journal *Van Nu en Straks* (Present and Future) in Antwerp, 'devoted to the art of the Present, curious about the art-still-being-created – that of the Future – here and abroad', modelled on journals such as *The Hobby Horse* (first series 1893–1894). Editors are Cyriel Buysse, Emmanuel de Bom, August Vermeylen and Prosper van Langendonck. Henry van de Velde is responsible for the design. In the first series up to 1894 complete issues are devoted to the visual arts, i.e. to Van Gogh, or to the Symbolist drawings of George Minne. Théo van Rysselberghe designs the cover. Illustrations and full-page plates by Xavier Mellery, Marguerite Holeman, George Minne, James Ensor, Théo van Rysselberghe, Georges Lemmen, Richard Baseleer, George Morren, Victor Hageman and Willy Finch; from the Netherlands: Jan Toorop, Jan Veth, Johan Thorn Prikker, Richard Roland Hols and Gerrit Deysselhof; from Britain: Charles Ricketts; from France: Lucien Pissarro (living in England). The innovative typography and illustrations, however, prevent the magazine being economically viable, so that it ceases to appear after about a year. The articles are mainly devoted to theoretical discussions about the avant-garde and anarchism.
› Victor Horta builds a house for E. Tassel [fig. 15], the engineer who is a close colleague of the industrialist Ernest Solvay, and starts building the Autrique and Frison houses. Between 1893 and 1903 he builds more than thirty important architectural Art-Nouveau buildings, also designing the interiors and furniture.
› Henri Balat finishes the Royal Green Houses (1879–1893) at the Royal Palace, Laeken, including the so-called 'Iron Church'.
› Première of the French-language version of Wagner's *Tristan und Isolde* at the Théâtre de la Monnaie, Brussels.
› Lugné-Poë's Théâtre d'Art (Symbolist theatre established in Paris, 1890) performs Maurice Maeterlinck's *Pelléas et Mélisande* in Brussels.

› Exhibitions of prints by Utamaro and Hiroshige, by Gauguin (Polynesia) and by Degas at the Galerie Durand-Ruel, Paris.
› Second Exhibition of Neo-Impressionist Painters in Paris, at the Galerie Laffitte. Van Rysselberghe is again the only non-French exhibitor. He designs the fleurons of the catalogue, which is printed in Belgium.
› Lugné-Poë's new Théâtre de l'Œuvre opens in Paris with Maurice Maeterlinck's *Pelléas et Mélisande*. Drawings in the programme are by Maurice Denis.
› First edition of *L'Estampe originale* in Paris.
› Opening of the Galerie Vollard, Paris.

› Stéphane Mallarmé, *Vers et prose*.

† Guy de Maupassant, Piotr Tchaikovsky

1894 | First elections held under the universal plural vote system. The Socialists win 28 seats, more than they and their opponents expected. They have a majority in the large Walloon industrial centres such as Liège, Mons and Charleroi. This victory is celebrated in Socialist circles not only in Belgium, but also internationally. Among the Socialists elected are Edmond Picard, co-founder of *L'Art moderne*, Jules Destrée, Emile Vandervelde and Max Hallet, who have close contacts with the avant-garde artists.
The Socialists establish the Université Nouvelle and the Institut des Hautes Etudes in Brussels, inspired by Emile Vandervelde, Jules Destrée, Edmond Picard and others. Henry van der Velde gives lectures there.

› At the World Exhibition in Antwerp fourteen Belgian sculptors, including Philippe Wolfers, Julien Dillens and Thomas Vinçotte, show chryselephantine sculptures.

LA LIBRE ESTHÉTIQUE: FIRST SALON

EXHIBITORS Ashbee, Baffier, Bartholomé, Beardsley, Besnard, Boch, Cameron, Carabin, Carrière, Charlier, Charpentier, Chéret, Claudel, Claus, Craco, Cros, Dalpayrat et Lesbros, Danse, Degouve de Nuncques, Delaherche, Denis, Devillez, Donnay, Doudelet, Paul du Bois, Fernand Dubois, Ensor, Frampton, Gaspar, Gauguin, Gilsoul, Grasset, Welden Hawkins, Heymans, Ibels, Image, Khnopff, Lane, Laermans, Lemmen, Lerolle, Levêque, Lunois, Maillol, Mathews, Mellery, C. Meunier, K. Meunier, Michel, De Montesquiou-Fézensac, Morisot, Morris, Motte, Murray, Niederkorn, Paul, C. Pissarro, G. Pissarro, L. Pissarro, Puvis de Chavannes, Ranson, Redon, Renoir, Rivière, Samuel, Sauter, Serrurier-Bovy, Signac, Sisley, Storm van 's Gravesande, Stremel, Summer, Thaulow, Thesmar, Toorop, Toulouse-Lautrec, Tourteau, Van der Stappen, Van Rysselberghe, Vinçotte, Vogels, Wallaert, Watts, Whall, Guild School of Handicraft, The Fitzroy Society.
› Théo van Rysselberghe designs the cover of the catalogue which is used until 1914.
› Important exhibits by Puvis de Chavannes, Carrière, Watts, Renoir, Gauguin, Redon, Ibels, Sisley, C. Pissarro, Morisot, Signac and Denis. Belgian painters who had never exhibited at Les XX are: Claus, Baertsoen and Laermans. There is a large section for the applied arts, completely devoted to Art Nouveau: for example, a whole room of furniture ('cabinet de travail') by Serrurier-Bovy, books and wallpaper by Morris, jewellery designed by Ashbee and made by the Guild and School of Handicraft, decorative panels by Ranson, carpets and embroidery by Maillol, Gauguin, Redon, Lemmen, Signac and Denis ..., books produced by William Morris, book illustrations by Ricketts, Housman and Beardsley (Oscar Wilde's *Salome*). Many foreign artists, among them Gauguin, Carrière, Charpentier, Signac, Toulouse-Lautrec, Carabin, De Régnier, Vallotton, Toorop, are present at the opening of the exhibition.

LECTURES Henri de Régnier, 'Le Bosquet de Psyché'; Henri Carton de Wiart, 'Léon Bloy'; Henry van de Velde, 'L'Art futur'; Edmond Picard, 'Dialégomènes artistiques'.
CONCERTS Works by Schubert, d'Indy, Beethoven, Franck, Bach, Chausson, De Bréville, and a concert with a first performance of works by Debussy.

- Fernand Khnopff's first submission to the Munich Secession. Stefan George publishes a work by Khnopff in *Blätter für die Kunst*. He contributes to the third Salon de la Rose+Croix, Paris. Joséphin Péladan personally selects works.
- Walter Crane exhibits in the Cercle Artistique, Brussels. Khnopff lectures about the artist.
- Henri Evenepoel makes his début at the Salon des Artistes Français, Paris.
- Henry van de Velde publishes and illustrates *Déblaiement d'art*.

- Maurice Maeterlinck, *Alladine et Pallomides*, illustrations by George Minne.

- Anti-anarchist laws are approved in France; Camille Pissarro escapes to Belgium; Emile Henry is executed; Félix Fénéon arrested; start of the Dreyfus affair.
- Gustave Caillebotte leaves his most important Impressionist works to the French State. After three years of argument only half of them are accepted.
- Odilon Redon exhibition at the Galerie Durand-Ruel, Paris, and at the Kunstkring, The Hague, with works from Belgian and Dutch collections.
- Alfred Jarry, Rémy de Gourmont, Charles Filiger and Joséphin Péladan found the monthly journal *L'Ymagier*.
- Lalique exhibits jewellery at the Salon of the Société des Artistes Français in Paris for the first time.

- The publisher John Lane and the artist Aubrey Beardsley start *The Yellow Book* (1894–1895), an illustrated art journal, in London.
- Establishment of the American Symbolist journal *The Chap Book*.

- Oscar Wilde, *Salome*, with illustrations by Aubrey Beardsley; Rudyard Kipling, *Jungle Book*; Marcel Prévost, *Les Demi-Vierges*; Jules Renard, *Poil de carotte*.
- Claude Debussy, *La Demoiselle élue* after D.G. Rossetti, and *Prélude à l'après-midi d'un faune* after Stéphane Mallarmé.

† Gustave Caillebotte

1895 | After a crisis, which had dragged on for some twenty years, the Belgian economy gradually recovers. The driving forces behind the new prosperity are still metal-working and mechanical engineering. Sales of consumer goods, which had suffered a severe decline during the crisis years, again experience a satisfying growth curve. As well as traditional industries new ones appear, often based on traditional crafts, making bicycles, motors, cars, cameras, fashion accessories, ornamental metalwork and all the articles typical of the *Belle Epoque*. By the turn of the century Belgium is enjoying unprecedented prosperity.

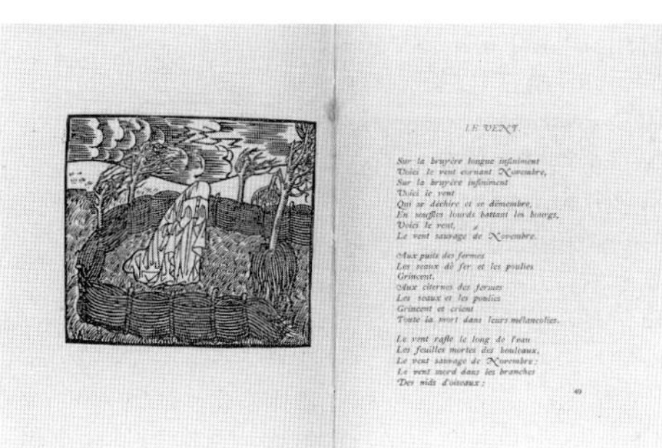

fig.16 GEORGE MINNE, Illustration for Emile Verhaeren's *Les Villages illusoires* (1895)

LA LIBRE ESTHETIQUE: SECOND SALON
EXHIBITORS Allen, Ashbee, Aubert, Baertsoen, Beardsley, Berchmans, Besnard, Bigot, Boch, Bradley, Breslau, Carabin, Carter, Charlier, Charpentier, Chéret, Claus, Cobden Sanderson, Coppens, Craco, Crane, Cros, Cross, Dalpayrat et Lesbros, Dammouse, Dampt, Debienne, Regoyos, Daum frères et Cie, Degouve de Nuncques, De Groux, Delaherche, Denis, Dent, De Swart, Deysselhof, Doudelet, Du Bois, Dubois, Ensor, Ford, Frampton, Fréderic, Gaskin, Gaspar, Grasset, Guillaumin, Hageman, Heyman, Heymans, Hobé, Holman Hunt, Housman, Ibels, Jeanniot, Jossot, Kay, Khnopff, Klinger, Lepère, Lerolle, Luce, Lunois, Maris, Martin, Mellery, Morren, Morris, Moulijn, Paul, Picard, C. Pissarro, F. Pissarro, G. Pissarro, L. Pissarro, Polignac, Powell, Prouvé, Ranson, Redon, Reid-Murray, Reynolds-Stephens, Rippl-Ronaï, Roche, Rousseau, Serrurier-Bovy, Servat, Signac, E. Smits, Stremel, Summer, Swan, Thaulow, Thesmar, Toulouse-Lautrec, Thys, Vallgren, Vallotton, Van den Eekhoudt, Van der Stappen, Van Hoytema, Vogels, Von Hoffmann, Voysey, Watts, White, Wiener, L'Epreuve, L'Estampe originale, the Fitzroy Picture Society.
- The Salon differs little from the previous one. There is great interest in English applied arts, the first of the Daum brothers' glassware; *La Chambre d'artisan* by Gustave Serrurier-Bovy, the furniture designer, gets a special section in the catalogue; furniture by the architect Georges Hobé; important exhibits by Maurice Denis, Henry-Edmond Cross and Maximilien Luce.

LECTURES Camille Mauclair, 'L'Aristocratie intellectuelle'; Henry Maubel, 'Psychologie musicale'; Lugné-Poë (director of the Théâtre de l'Œuvre, Paris), 'Pour être un acteur d'aujourd'hui'; Edmond Picard, 'La Socialisation de l'Art'.
CONCERTS Works by Saint-Saëns, Lalo, Fauré, d'Indy, Duparc, Huberti, Chabrier, Gilson, Franck; first performances of works by Glazunov, Lazzari, Sokolov, Jacob, Chabrier, Chausson, Fauré, Ysaÿe, Magnard, Marchot.

- Fernand Khnopff illustrates a sonnet by Stéphane Mallarmé, *A la nue accablante tu*, which appears in the recently founded Berlin journal *Pan* and publishes an illustrated poem in the same journal. He becomes correspondent for the English journal *The Studio*, contributing to the column, 'Studio Talk Brussels'.
- James Ensor's first one-man exhibition is held in the Brussels carpet store of the writer Eugène Demolder's father.

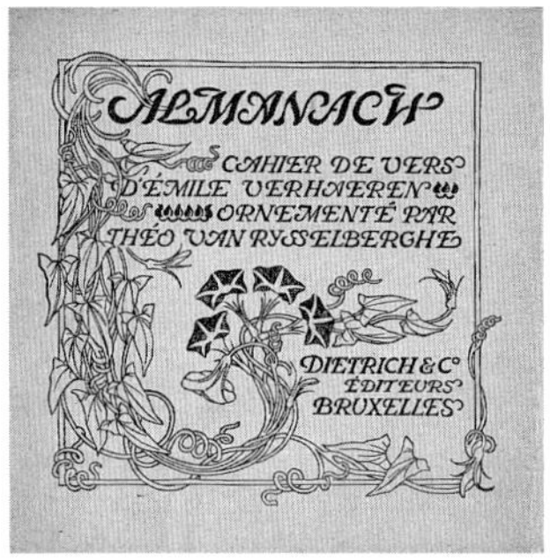

fig.17 THÉO VAN RYSSELBERGHE
Cover for Emile Verhaeren's *Almanach* (1895)

› Théo van Rysselberghe retrospective in the Galerie Laffitte, Paris; Van Rysselberghe also exhibits in the Salon des Indépendants, Paris.

› Victor Horta starts building the new Maison du Peuple in Brussels: a complex scheme including a co-operative department store, offices, canteen, meeting rooms and a theatre. The fact that the Maison du Peuple is executed in the same style as the houses built by Horta for his progressive Liberal clients acts as visual evidence in the Brussels street scene of the alliance between the Socialists and the progressive Liberals.
› Henry van de Velde draws up plans for his own house, 'Bloemenwerf', and its interior decoration in Uccle (outside Brussels). This marks his definitive shift from painting and graphic art to architecture and applied art.
› H. Van de Velde, *Aperçus en vue d'une synthèse d'art.*
› Gustave Serrurier-Bovy shows furniture by Charles Rennie Mackintosh in L'Œuvre Artistique, Liège.
› First showing of the 'cinematograph' by the Lumière brothers in the Palais du Midi, Brussels.

› Emile Verhaeren, *Les Villages illusoires* [fig.16], with illustrations by George Minne, and *Almanach* [fig.17], with illustrations by Théo van Rysselberghe.
› Establishment of the Société des Concerts Ysaÿe in Brussels.

› Paul Gauguin returns to Tahiti, taking final leave of France.
› First Cézanne one-man exhibition at Galerie Ambroise Vollard, Paris.
› Samuel Bing opens Galerie L'Art Nouveau, Paris. The front is decorated with designs by Frank Brangwyn and Victor Horta, the poster and invitation are by Georges Lemmen. The first exhibition includes interiors by Henry van de Velde, and decorative work by Maurice Denis, Edouard Vuillard, Albert Besnard, Charles Conder and Fernand Khnopff.
› First Venice Biennale.
› Establishment of the quarterly journal *Pan* by the art critic Julius Meier-Graefe in Berlin.
› Establishment of the Birmingham Guild of Handicraft.

› H. P. Berlage, *Over architectuur*; Otto Wagner, *Moderne Architektur.*

› First public cinema showing by the Lumière brothers in Paris.

› Thomas Hardy, *Jude the Obscure*; H. G. Wells, *The Time Machine.*

† Berthe Morisot

1896 | LA LIBRE ESTHÉTIQUE: THIRD SALON

EXHIBITORS Baffier, Bauer, Berchmans, Besnard, Bigot, Boch, Bradley, Carabin, Carrière, Chaplet, Charpentier, Claessens, Claus, Colenbrander, Cornette, Cottet, Degouve de Nuncques, De Groux, Delaunois, Denis, Destrée-Danse, Doudelet, Donnay, Du Bois, Ensor, Fehr, Finch, Frampton, Gallé, Guillaumin, Hall, Hart-Nibbrig, Welden Hawkins, Hestaux, Heymans, Jourdain, Khnopff, Lebourg, Lemmen, Lunois, Martin, Maufra, Maurin, Melchers, Meunier, Monet, Moret, Morren, Muller, Paillard, L. Pissarro, Rassenfosse, Renoir, Roche, Rops, Saverny, Serrurier-Bovy, Signac, Mowbray-Taubman, Thesmar, Thorn Prikker, Tiffany, Toulouse-Lautrec, Van den Eeckhoudt, Van der Stappen, Van de Velde, Vogels, Zandomeneghi.
› Important submission by Eugène Carrière; first inclusion of the Belgians Auguste Donnay, Alfred Delaunois and Armand Rassenfosse; 'favrile glass' by Louis C. Tiffany; 'Salle de five o'clock' by Henry van de Velde, in which he assembled a whole range of applied art: furniture, textiles, carpets and lighting.
LECTURES Camille Mauclair, 'La Tradition et la Mode en Art; Paul Gérardy, 'L'Ame allemande aujourd'hui' (more particularly about *Blätter für die Kunst* and Stefan George); Roland de Marès, 'La Révolte dans l'Art'; L'Abbé Charbonnel, 'Art religieux, Art ecclésiastique'.
CONCERTS Works by Bordes, d'Indy, Brahms, Grieg, Fauré and first performances of works by Glazunov, Wallner, Franck, Eibenschutz, Ropartz, Duparc, Lekeu, Chausson, Crickboom.

L'ART IDÉALISTE
As a reaction against Realism and Impressionism the society L'Art Idéaliste (1896–1898) is established in Brussels, on the example of Joséphin Péladan's Ordre du Temple de la Rose+Croix (1892–1897) in Paris. The leader is Jean Delville and members are Emile Fabry, Victor Hageman, Léon Fréderic, Auguste Levêque and Isidore de Rudder. The society arranges an annual Salon.

› Fernand Khnopff produces some of his most important work, such as *L'Art* (or *Les Caresses, Le Sphinx*). He creates costumes for the opera singer Jeanne Maubourg, a member of the opera company of the Théâtre de la Monnaie, Brussels. In Le Sillon (1893) he lectures on William Morris, who had just died, and appeals for a renaissance of applied art on the English model.
› Retrospective exhibition of work by Constantin Meunier in Samuel Bing's Galerie L'Art Nouveau in Paris marks the start of international recognition for Meunier. Maximilien Luce makes a series of drawings of the figures, which are published by Emile Pouget in the anarchist weekly *La Sociale.*
› Retrospective exhibition of Félicien Rops, organized by the journal *La Plume* in the Hôtel Drouot, Paris.

VAN NU EN STRAKS
August Vermeylen starts a new series of the Flemish social and literary journal *Van Nu en Straks* (–1901). In contrast with the earlier issues few contributions by artists are included and the design is very restrained. With its radical outlook the journal contributes to the politicizing of the Flemish Movement.

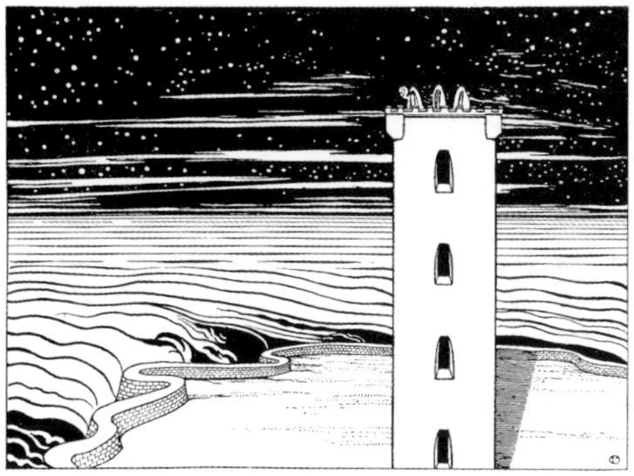

fig. 18 CHARLES DOUDELET, Illustration for Maurice Maeterlinck's *Douze chansons* (1896), woodcut, Museum A. Vander Haeghen, Ghent

› Maurice Maeterlinck, *Douze Chansons*, with illustrations by Charles Doudelet [fig. 18].

› Opening of the first cinema in the Galerie Royale in Brussels with electrically operated photographs by the Lumière brothers. Cinematographic experiments in the theatre.

› First Salon of the Peintres de l'Ame in the Galerie de la Bodinière, Paris.
› Ambroise Vollard publishes the first volume of *Album des Peintres Graveurs* in Paris.
› Publication of *L'Estampe nouvelle* in France.

› Georg Hirth starts publication in Munich of the popular journal *Jugend* (1896–1933), from which 'Jugendstil', the German variant of Art Nouveau, derived its name.
› Paul Cassirer publishes the satirical illustrated journal *Simplicissimus* in Munich (1896–1914).
› First volume of *The Pageant*, London (1896–1897).

› Walter Crane, *The Decorative Illustration of Books Old and New*.

† Guillaume Vogels, Paul Verlaine, William Morris

1897 | Colonial Exhibition in Tervuren (Brussels) [fig. 19]. The secretary of the Congo Free State, Edmond van Eetvelde, arranges for the young Art Nouveau architects Paul Hankar, Georges Hobé, Gustave Serrurier-Bovy and Henry van de Velde each to design a hall in the colonial pavilion. It is the first time that the general public is confronted with Art Nouveau on this scale. In the Salle d'Honneur there is an exhibition of chryselephantine sculpture – for which the ivory had been donated to the artists by King Leopold II – by, among others, Philippe Wolfers, Charles van der Stappen, Fernand Dubois, Arthur Craco, Constantin Meunier, Fernand Khnopff (a mask [fig. 20]), Josué Dupon, Charles Samuel.

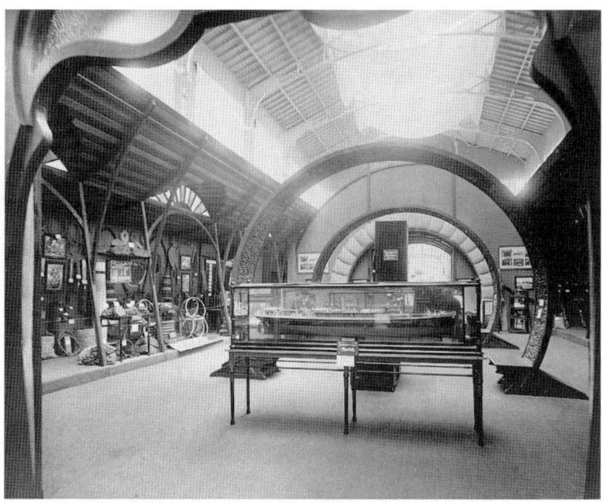

fig. 19 Colonial Exhibition in Tervuren

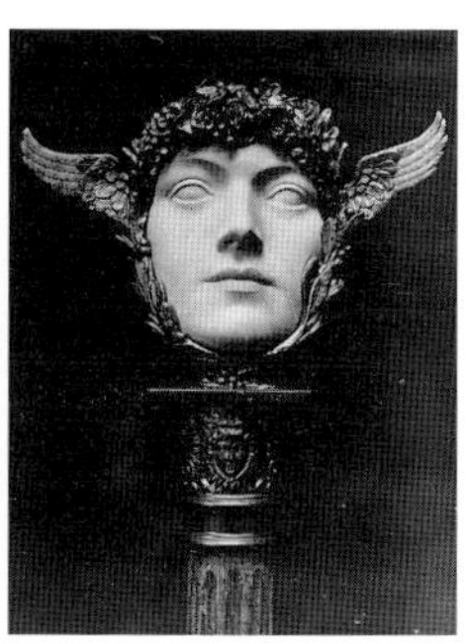

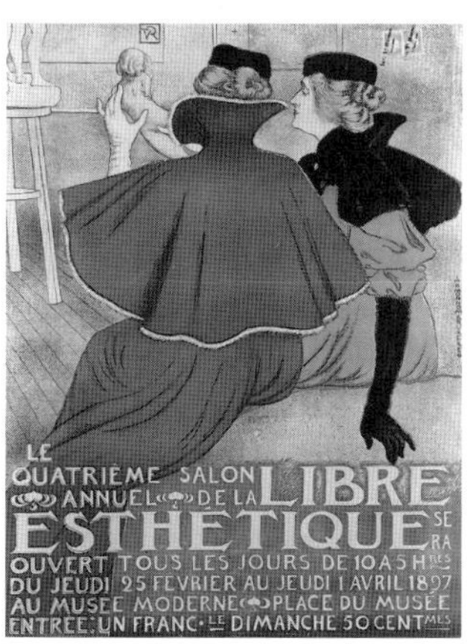

fig. 21 THÉO VAN RYSSELBERGHE Poster for the Fourth Salon de La Libre Esthétique, 1897

fig. 20 FERNAND KHNOPFF, *Mask*, retouched photograph, Bibliothèque Royale Albert Ier, Cabinet des Estampes, Brussels

LA LIBRE ESTHÉTIQUE: FOURTH SALON

EXHIBITORS Barbotin, Besnard, Bird, Blanche, Boch, Bonnard, Bussy, Carabin, Chaplet, Charlet, Charpentier, Claus, Cobden-Sanderson, Combaz, Cottet, Craco, Crespin, Cros, Cross, Degouve de Nuncques, De Groux, Delvin, De Moor, De Morgan, Doudelet, Du Bois, Dubois, Duhem, Ensor, Fauché, Finch, Fisher, Gauguin, Grasset, Hazenplug, Helleu, Heymans, Horta, Jack, Jeanniot, Khnopff, Kaelher, Koepping, Legrand, Lemmen, Luce, Lunois, Maurin, Melchers, Ménard, Meunier, Monet, Munch, Nocq, Penfield, Plumet, Rassenfosse, Rathbone, Rhead, Roche, Romberg, Rops, Rousseau, Samuel, Saverny, E. Smits, Thesmar, Thoma, Toorop, Toulouse-Lautrec, Van der Stappen, Van Strydonck, Voysey, Wytsman, Les Peintres Graveurs, Birmingham School of Handicraft, the Fitzroy Picture Society [fig. 21].
› First showing by Edvard Munch with seven works; Claude Monet shows three canvases from his Rouen Cathedral series; six canvases by Paul Gauguin, painted in Tahiti; Victor Horta presents the complete interior for a dining room.
› A memorial gathering for Verlaine is held during the Salon of La Libre Esthétique, with an address by Emile Verhaeren and others.

CONCERTS Seventeenth- and eighteenth-century French and German music.

› Henry van de Velde and Constantin Meunier are successful at the Internationale Kunstausstellung, Dresden. Van de Velde founds the firm of Van de Velde S.A. in Ixelles, with Finch, Lemmen, Thorn Prikker and others. Their activities include the establishment of the Keller und Reiner gallery in Berlin.
› Henri Evenepoel travels through Algeria. His first one-man exhibition is held at the Cercle Artistique et Littéraire, Brussels.
› Théo van Rysselberghe designs the cover of the journal, *Dekorative Kunst*, founded in Munich by the German critic Julius Meier-Graefe.
› Willy Finch becomes manager of the ceramic studio of the Iris company in Borgå (Finland) and settles in Finland.
› First exhibition of Monumental, Decorative and Applied Art organized by De Scalden (founded 1889) in Antwerp: a confrontation between traditional style and Art Nouveau.
› First volume of *L'Art appliqué* (1897–1898), Brussels.
› Establishment of the Société Belge des Affichophiles, Antwerp.
› Establishment of the Union des Arts Décoratifs et Industriels de Belgique, Brussels.

› World première of *Fervaal* by Vincent d'Indy at the Théâtre de la Monnaie, Brussels.

› Eighteen artists, including the architects Josef Maria Olbrich and Josef Hoffmann, and the painters Carl Moll and Koloman Moser, led by Gustav Klimt, form the Vienna Secession.
› Establishment of the Vereinigte Werkstätte für Art im Handwerk in Munich.
› Pierre Bonnard exhibition at the Galerie Ambroise Vollard, Paris.

› Publication of *La Lithographie* and *L'Estampe et l'Affiche* in France.
› First volumes of *Art et Décoration* in Paris (–1913), *Dekorative Kunst* (–1929) in Munich, *Deutsche Kunst und Dekoration* in Darmstadt (–1934) and *The Dome* in London (–1900).
› H. G. Wells, *War of the Worlds*; Léon Bloy, *La Femme pauvre*; Anatole France, *L'Orme du mail*; André Gide, *Les Nourritures terrestres*; first performance of Edmond Rostand's *Cyrano de Bergerac*.

† Johannes Brahms

1898 | LA LIBRE ESTHÉTIQUE: FIFTH SALON

EXHIBITORS Alexander, Baertsoen, Bartlett, Bing and Groendahl, Brangwyn, I. and C. Brinckmann, Cazin, Charpentier, Claus, Combaz, Hermann, Denis, Desbois, De Uranga, Deysselhof, Durrio de Madron, Eeckmann, Ensor, Evaldre, Fréderic, Fromuth, Gross, Hassam, Hawkins, Hazledine, Heymans, Hitz, Huez, Humphreys-Johnston, Illies, Jungmann, Kayser, Koster, Leistikow, Le Sidaner, Liebermann, Maillol, Mertens, Meunier, Minne, Morren, O'Connor, Picard, Plumet, Ranson, Rentsch, Selmersheim, Simon, Thaulow, Thorn Prikker, Tiffany, Vallgren, Van Hoytema, Van Mattemburgh, Van Rysselberghe, A. Verhaeren, Von Ehren, Willumsen, Royal Porcelain Works Copenhagen, Société Nationale du Livre, Librairie d'Art.

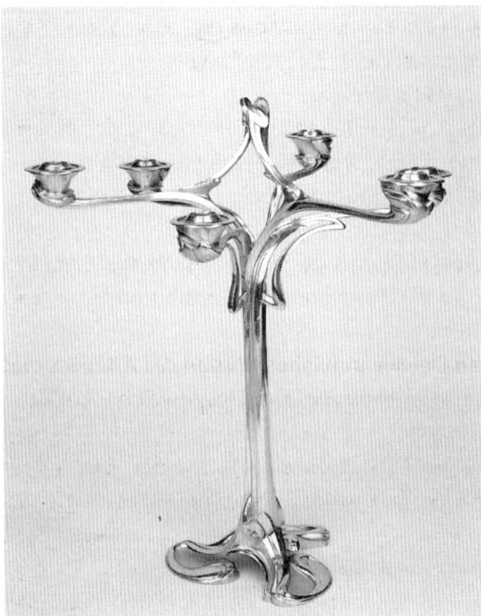

fig. 22 HENRY VAN DE VELDE, Six-light candelabrum, 1898, silver-plated bronze, Musées royaux d'Art et d'Histoire, Brussels

› Series of figures by George Minne, including *Kneeling Youth*, and Aristide Maillol; a large number of German decorative artists accepted on the advice of Henry van de Velde; ceramics by various Danish artists; Jan Thorn Prikker's first batiks. Painting is completely crowded out. The leading Impressionists and their successors are all under contract to dealers and can hardly submit any work, while applied art has become extremely popular. The significance and influence of La Libre Esthétique as an international forum for innovation in painting and sculpture is steadily declining; the Salon is in this respect clearly past its peak.

LECTURES Camille Mauclair, 'L'Homme moderne, moral et social, devant l'avenir'; Charles Morice, 'Au temps de Van Eyck', Gabriel Mourey, 'Dante-Gabriel Rossetti'; Jules Destrée, 'Benozzo Gozzoli'.

› Constantin Meunier exhibition at Galerie Keller und Reiner, Berlin.
› James Ensor one-man exhibition in the Paris gallery, Salon des Cent. A special issue of the journal *La Plume* is devoted entirely to Ensor.
› Théo van Rysselberghe travels in the Netherlands and Britain with Paul Signac and settles in Paris. Van Rysselberghe designs the cover for Stéphane Mallarmé's *Poésies*, and illustrates *Poésies mises en musique*, a collection of songs by his friend, the composer Georges Flé, set to words by Banville, Gautier, Hugo, Lecomte de Lisle, Villiers de l'Isle-Adam and Verlaine.

› Fernand Khnopff scores a success at the first Vienna Secession exhibition. A whole room is reserved for him, where he is represented by 21 works. A complete issue of *Ver Sacrum* (see below) is devoted to Khnopff and Maurice Maeterlinck.
The first issue of *L'Art Décoratif* (Paris) is entirely devoted to Henry van de Velde [fig. 22].

› Maurice Maeterlinck leaves Ghent and settles in Paris.
› Production of Wagner's *Rheingold* (in French) at the Théâtre de la Monnaie, Brussels.
› Toulouse-Lautrec exhibition at the Goupil Gallery, London.

VER SACRUM

The artists of the Vienna Secession found their own journal *Ver Sacrum* (1898–1921) on the model of *Pan* and *Jugend* in Germany. Contributors to the journal include the writers Rilke, Hofmannsthal, the art critic Hermann Bahr; illustrators include Loos, Hoffmann, Olbrich, Klimt, Kolo Moser, Wilhelm List. Josef Maria Olbrich builds the Vienna Secession pavilion.

› First volume of *L'Art Décoratif* in Paris (1898–1913), and of *Kunst und Handwerk* (1898–1914) in Munich.

› Establishment of the International Society of Sculptors, Painters and Engravers in London with James McNeil Whistler in the chair.
› Charles Rennie Mackintosh builds the Glasgow School of Art.
› Establishment of the Dresdner Werstätte für Handwerkskunst.

› Gabriël Fauré, *Pelléas et Mélisande*, after Maurice Maeterlinck.

› André Messager, *Véronique*; Joseph Conrad, *The Nigger of the Narcissus*.

† Aubrey Beardsley, Edward Burne-Jones (Fernand Khnopff writes his obituary in *The Magazine of Art*), Stéphane Mallarmé, Gustave Moreau, Pierre Puvis de Chavannes, Georges Rodenbach, Félicien Rops

1899 | After a year of violent demonstrations, the principle of simple majority voting in elections is abolished, and universal plural franchise with proportional representation introduced.

› Opening of the Socialist Party's Maison du Peuple in Brussels (arch. Victor Horta) [fig. 23].

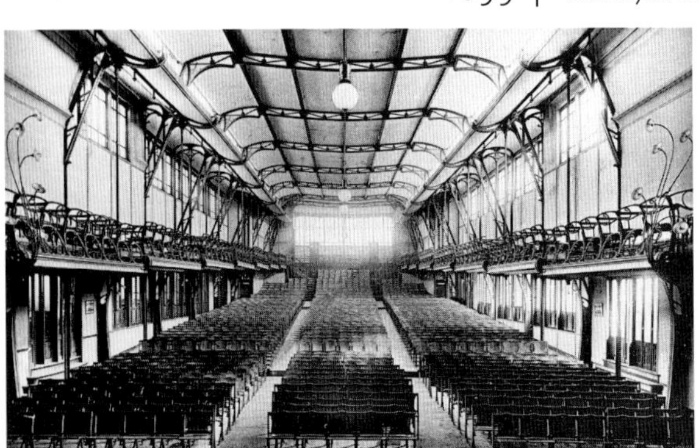

fig. 23 VICTOR HORTA, Theatre of the Maison du Peuple, Brussels, 1896–1899

LA LIBRE ESTHÉTIQUE: SIXTH SALON

EXHIBITORS Anquetin, Artot, Berchmans, Bernard, Boch, Brangwyn, Carrière, Charpentier, Colonna, Combaz, Cottet, De Brouckère, Degouve de Nuncques, Delaunois, De Samblanx and Weckesser, De Cressonnières, d'Espagnat, Donnay, Du Bois, Dubois, Finch, Greiffenhagen, Gubicy de Dragon, Heaton, Hens, Holbach and A. Huez, Inness Jr., Isaacson, Jo, Jourdain, Koopman, Läuger, Lemmen, Levêque, Mellery, Meunier, Minne, Moreau-Nélaton, Motte, Raffaëlli, Rassenfosse, Roche, Rousseau, J. Smits, Speekaert, Van Assendelft, Verheyden, Von Brocken, Von Hoffmann, Von Zumbusch, Zitzmann, L'Atelier de Glatigny, Vereinigte Werkstätte für Art im Handwerk.

› Retrospective exhibition in tribute to Félicien Rops (d. 1898). First entry by Jacob Smits; George Minne shows his *Fountain of Kneeling Youths*; important submission by Jean-François Raffaëlli; ceramics by Willy Finch, sent from Finland; a very large representation of German applied artists, through the agency of Henry van de Velde.

LECTURES Charles Morice, 'Le Christ de Carrière'; Henri Carton de Wiart, 'Vieux poètes belges'; Edouard Schuré, 'Le Théâtre de Rêve'; F. André: 'Lettres belges d'aujourd'hui'.

› Eugène Laermans's first one-man exhibition at the Galerie La Toison d'Or, Brussels.
› Henri Evenepoel's second one-man exhibition at the Cercle Artistique et Littéraire, Brussels.
› Théo van Rysselberghe joins the Vienna Secession.
› Fernand Khnopff makes his first prints.

› The architects Emile van Averbeke and Jan van Asperen design the Liberal Party's headquarters in Antwerp in Art Nouveau style.

› Villiers de l'Isle-Adam, *Histoires Souveraines*, layout by Théo van Rysselberghe.

› First exhibition of the Pastel Society, London.
› First volume of *Die Kunst* (1899–1945), Munich.

› Paul Signac, *D'Eugène Delacroix au néo-impressionnisme*.

† Henri Evenepoel, Alfred Sisley

1900 | Belgian industry rated fifth in world foreign trade, and if calculated per head of population, heads the list. The Socialists submit a proposal to extend the suffrage to women for regional and local elections.
› In the first parliamentary elections held under the system of proportional representation the Catholics lose more than 20% of their seats to the advantage of the Socialists, and particularly of the Liberals. They still, however, hold an absolute majority.

LA LIBRE ESTHÉTIQUE: SEVENTH SALON
EXHIBITORS André, Aubert, Bourdelle, Bussy, Buysse, Charpentier, Claus, Cornette, De Beys, De Brouckère, De Decker, Dejean, Delville, Delvin, Destrée-Danse, Du Bois, Dufrène, Ensor, Fréderic, Geyger, Hart Nibbrig, Hazledine, Heymans, Holbach, Huklenbrok, Israëls, Jo, Jourdain, Onnes, Kersten, Laermans, Le Brun, Lhommel, Luce, McAdam, Melchers, Meunier, Melcendeau, Morren, Morrice, Nieuwenkamp, Picard, Pirenne, Pirie, Powell, Rhead, Rivière, Roussel, Schmidt-Pecht, Schuster-Woldan, Serrurier-Bovy, Signac, Thooft et Labouchère, Toorop, Valtat, Van de Velde, Van Hoytema, A. Verhaeren, E. Verwee, Zuloaga, Rörstand Porcelain Works.
› Retrospective section of paintings by Henri Evenepoel (d. 1899); important submission by the Spaniard Ignacio Zuloaga; pastels by Ker-Xavier Roussel; sculptures by Antoine Bourdelle; paintings and watercolours by Paul Signac; views of the Mons region by Maximilien Luce; Symbolist works by Jean Delville.
LECTURES Thomas Bran, 'Des Poètes simples'; Tristan Klingsor, 'Les Poètes mis en musique'; Francis Jammes, 'Les Poètes contre la Littérature'; André Gide, 'De l'Influence en littérature'.

› George Minne scores a success in the Vienna Secession.
› Fernand Khnopff one-man exhibition at the Galerie Keller, Berlin.
› Jean Delville publishes *Mission de l'Art*, becomes a teacher and later director of the Glasgow School of Art.

› Richard Strauss conducts his works, *Ein Heldenleben* and *Don Quixote*, at the Théâtre de la Monnaie, Brussels.

› The French Impressionists triumph in the Decennial Exhibition of Fine Art in the Paris Exposition Universelle. The works of Paul Cézanne are given a place of honour and there is a separate exhibition of works by Auguste Rodin.
› Claude Monet exhibits his first series of *Waterlilies* at the Galerie Durand-Ruel, Paris.
› Walter Crane, *Line and Form*.

† Friedrich Nietzsche, William Ruskin, Oscar Wilde

EPILOGUE

1904 | VIE ET LUMIÈRE
Emile Claus and Georges Buysse found the Vie et Lumière society in Brussels to promote 'Luminism'. Among the members are Anna Boch, Georges Buysse, Emile Claus, William Degouve de Nuncques, Anna de Weert, Aloïs de Laet, Rodolphe de Saegher, James Ensor, Alfred Hazledine, Adrien-Joseph Heymans, Georges Lemmen, Jenny Montigny, George Morren, Edmond Verstraeten.

LA LIBRE ESTHÉTIQUE
The annual Salon of La Libre Esthétique is entirely devoted to Impressionism. All the great French Impressionists are represented there. Simultaneously, Octave Maus conducts an enquiry in the journal, *L'Art moderne*, about the influence of Impressionism on contemporary painting.

First Salon of the Cercle d'Art, Les Indépendants in the Musée Moderne in Brussels. Les Indépendants want to create exhibition opportunities for young artists who do not belong to a traditional society.

1905 | KUNST VAN HEDEN
François Franck and his brothers Louis and Charles found Kunst van Heden in Antwerp. The society's object is to encourage and promote modern Belgian art by bringing together artists and patrons, and by lectures, publications and exhibitions at home and abroad. The original artist members are: Albert Baertsoen, Richard Baseleer, Emile Claus, Jean Delvin, James Ensor, Victor Hageman, Eugène Laermans, Hendrik Luyten, Charles Mertens, George Minne, Georges Morren, Ernest Rombaux, Jacob Smits and Walter Vaes.

LA LIBRE ESTHÉTIQUE
The Salon de La Libre Esthétique is dominated by 'internatioal' Impressionism, in which a significant number of Belgian Impressionists are included, e.g. Anna Boch, Georges Buysse, Emile Claus, Jenny Montigny, George Morren.

† Constantin Meunier

Bibliography

Adams 1980 B. Adams, 'Symbolism in the Flesh: the Fernand Khnopff Retrospective', *Arts Magazine* (Feb. 1980)
Alexandre 1897 A. Alexandre, *Félicien Rops et son œuvre*, Brussels
Alhadeff 1966 A. Alhadeff, 'George Minne, Maeterlinck's Fin de Siècle Illustrator', *Annales de la Fondation Maurice Maeterlinck* 12
Alhadeff 1973 —, 'Narcissism and Symbolist Sculpture', in: *Studies in Western Art, Acts of the XXIInd International Congres of the History of Art, Hungarian Academy of Sciences*
[Antell] 1975 *Antellin kokoelmat [The Antell Collection]*, Helsinki
Arwas 1972 V. Arwas, *Félicien Rops*, London 1972
Babut du Mares 1971 J.P. Babut du Mares, *Félicien Rops*, Ostend
Baudson 1979 P. Baudson, *Les trois Vies de Constantin Meunier*, Brussels
Baudson 1985–1988 —, 'La Collection du Musée Constantin Meunier. Approche de trois modes d'expression d'un artiste', *Miscellanea Philippe Roberts-Jones, Bulletin Musées royaux des Beaux-Arts de Belgique* 1–3
Baudson 1990 —, 'La Représentation du travail dans la sculpture – Autour de Constantin Meunier', in: *La Sculpture belge au 19ème siècle*, Brussels
Baudson 1991 —, 'Un artista del lavoro: Constantin Meunier', in: *Il lavoro dell' Uomo nella pittura da Goya a Kandinskij*, Città del Vaticano, Rome
Behets 1942 A. Behets, *Constantin Meunier, l'homme, l'artiste et l'œuvre*, Brussels
Benedetti 1981 M.T. Benedetti, 'Khnopff e Burne-Jones', *Storia dell'Arte* 43
Bénédite 1910 L. Bénédite, *De Schilderkunst der 19de eeuw*, Amsterdam
Biermé 1911 M. Biermé, *Les Artistes de la pensée et du sentiment*, Brussels
Biermé 1924 —, 'Nos Peintres: Emile Claus', *La Revue belge* III/1 (July 1924)
Blei 1907 F. Blei, *Félicien Rops*, Berlin
Block 1984 J. Block, *Les XX and Belgian Avant-Gardism*, Ann Arbor
Boenders 1979–1980 F. Boenders, 'Mascarade à propos de Fernand Khnopff', in: *Fernand Khnopff*, Paris–Brussels
Boenders 1980 —, 'Maskerada zu Fernand Khnopff', in: *Fernand Khnopff*, Hamburg
Bonneure *et al.* 1992 F. Bonneure, M. van Houtryve, K. Puype, *Het Stille Brugge. 100 jaar Bruges-la-Morte*, Bruges
Bosmant 1930 J. Bosmant, *La Peinture et la sculpture au pays de Liège de 1793 à nos jours*, Liège
Bosmant 1967 —, *Auguste Donnay* (Monographies de l'Art belge), Brussels
Boyens 1992 P. Boyens, *Sint-Martens-Latem, Kunstenaarsdorp in Vlaanderen*, Tielt
Buyck 1977 J.F. Buyck (ed.), *Catalogus Schilderijen 19de en 20ste eeuw*, Koninklijk Museum voor Schone Kunsten, Antwerp
Brison 1969 C. Brison, *Pornocrates, an Introduction to the Life and Work of Félicien Rops (1833–1898)*, London
Carluccio 1974 L. Carluccio, *La Grande Histoire de la peinture. XV. Du Symbolisme à l'Expressionnisme. XIXe et XXe siècles*, Geneva
Chartrain-Hebbelinck 1966 M.J. Chartrain-Hebbelinck, 'Les Lettres de Théo van Rysselberghe à Octave Maus', *Bulletin Musées royaux des Beaux-Arts de Belgique* 1–2
Chartrain-Hebbelinck 1976 M.J. Chartrain-Hebbelinck, 'Henri Evenepoel', *Biographie Nationale* XXXIX/1
Colin 1930a P. Colin, *La Peinture belge depuis 1830*, Brussels
Colin 1930b —, *La Première Exposition centennale de la peinture belge*, Brussels
Cuvelier 1987 G. Cuvelier, *Félicien Rops au Musée de Namur* (Musées vivants de Wallonie et de Bruxelles) Brussels-Liège
D'Agen, De Roig 1924 B. d'Agen and J. de Roig, *Rops...iana*, Paris
Dalemans 1986 R. Dalemans, *100 Ans d'arts plastiques en Belgique*, Brussels
Dasnoy 1965–1966 A. Dasnoy, 'Henri Evenepoel. La dame au chapeau vert', *Peinture vivante*
D.D.C. [D. Derrey-Capon] 1987 D. Derrey-Capon, 'A.W. Finch', in: *Académie Royale des Beaux-Arts de Bruxelles. 275 ans d'enseignement*, Brussels
De Clercq 1987 B. de Clercq, 'Van Strydonck, Guillaume', in: *Académie Royale des Beaux-Arts de Bruxelles. 275 ans d'enseignement*, Brussels
De Croës 1990 C. de Croës, 'Blanc, noir et or', in: *Fernand Khnopff 1858–1921*, Tokyo, Himeji, Nagoya, Yamanashi
Delevoy 1977 R.L. Delevoy, *Journal du Symbolisme*, Geneva
Delevoy 1981 —, *James Ensor*, Antwerp
Delevoy 1985 —, G. Lascault, J.-P. Verheggen and Guy Cuvelier, *Félicien Rops*, Brussels
Delevoy, De Croës, Ollinger-Zinque 1979 R.L. Delevoy, C. de Croës and G. Ollinger-Zinque, *Fernand Khnopff*, Brussels
Delevoy, De Croës, Ollinger-Zinque 1987 —, *Fernand Khnopff*, Brussels
Delville 1925 J. Delville, 'Notice sur Fernand Khnopff', *Annuaire de l'Académie Royale des Sciences, des Lettres et des Beaux-Arts de Belgique* 91
Demolder 1889 —, 'Constantin Meunier', *La Société Nouvelle* 49 (31 Jan. 1889)
Demolder 1892 E. Demolder, *La Société nouvelle*, s.l.
Demolder 1894 —, *Félicien Rops – Etude patronymique avec quelques reproductions brutales de devises inédites de Rops*, Paris
Demolder 1901 —, *Constantin Meunier*, Brussels
De Mont 1891 P. de Mont, 'Fernand Khnopff', *De Nederlandsche Spectator* 34 (22 Aug. 1891)
De Mont 1901 —, *Fernand Khnopff (Het Schildersboek)*, Amsterdam
De Mont 1921 —, *De Schilderkunst in België*, The Hague
De Ridder 1947 A. de Ridder, *George Minne* (Monographies de l'Art belge), Antwerp
De Ridder 1957 —, *William Degouve de Nuncques*, Brussels
Derrey-Capon 1991–1992 D. Derrey-Capon, in: *Alfred William Finch 1854–1930*, Helsinki–Brussels
Derrey-Capon 1994 —, Ph. Roberts-Jones, G. Ollinger-Zinque *et al.*, *Henri Evenepoel*, Brussels
De Taeye 1894 E.L. de Taeye, *Les Artistes belges contemporains. Leur vie – Leurs œuvres – Leur place dans l'art*, Brussels
Detouche 1906 H. Detouche, *Les Peintres de la femme intégrale: Félicien Rops et A. Willette*, Paris
Devigne 1919 M. Devigne, *Constantin Meunier*, Turnhout
Dorival 1969 B. Dorival, *Histoire de l'Art*, IV, Paris
Draguet [1991] M. Draguet, 'Le Paysage fin de siècle entre Impressionnisme et Symbolisme. Monet, Redon, Seurat et Khnopff', in: *Irréalisme et Art moderne. Les voies de l'imaginaire dans l'art des XVIIIe, XIXe et XXe siècles* (Mélanges Philippe Roberts-Jones), Brussels
Draguet 1992 —, 'Khnopff et la Philosophie du visage: les mascarades du regard interdit', *Académie Royale de Belgique. Bulletin de la Classe des Beaux-Arts* 10–12
Dubray 1928 Jean Dubray (Jean-Dubray), *Félicien Rops. Essai critique*, Paris
Dufey 1985 F. Dufey, 'L'Art baroque de la représentation', in: *La Musique source d'inspiration dans l'art belge, XIIIe–XXe siècle*, Brussels
Duvosquel 1988 J.M. Duvosquel (ed.), *La Collection. Crédit Communal*, Brussels
Du Jardin 1900 J. Du Jardin, *L'Art flamand. II. Les Artistes contemporains*, Brussels
Dumont-Wilden 1907 L. Dumont-Wilden, *Fernand Khnopff*, Brussels
Edebau 1950 Fr. Edebau, *Léon Spilliaert* (Monographies de l'Art belge), Antwerp
Eemans 1950 N. Eemans, *Fernand Khnopff*, Antwerp
Evenepoel 1994 H. Evenepoel, *Lettres à mon père*, Brussels, 2 vols.
Faistauer [1923] 1978 A. Faistauer, 'Neue Malerei aus Österreich', Zürich–Leipzig–Vienna 1923, reprint in O. Breicha (ed.), *Gustav Klimt. Die goldene Pforte. Werk – Wesen – Wirkung. Bilder und Schriften zu Leben und Werk*, Salzburg 1978
Fierens 1922 P. Fierens, 'Trois Disparus: Xavier Mellery, Fernand Khnopff, Auguste Donnay', *La Renaissance de l'Art Français* 2 (Feb. 1922)
Fierens 1939 —, *L'Art en Belgique, du Moyen-Age à nos jours*, Brussels
Fierens 1943 —, *James Ensor*, Paris
Fierens 1947–1948 —, 'Evenepoel et l'Algérie', *Etudes d'Art* III
Fierens-Gevaert 1904 H. Fierens-Gevaert, 'Albert Baertsoen', *L'Art moderne* 4 (Sept. 1904)
Fierens-Gevaert 1910 —, *Albert Baertsoen*, Brussels
Fierens-Gevaert 1928 —, A. Laes, *Musées royaux des Beaux-Arts de Belgique. Catalogue de la peinture moderne*, Brussels
Fontainas 1925 A. Fontainas, *Rops*, Paris
Fontaine 1923 A. Fontaine, *Constantin Meunier*, Paris
France 1984 M. France, 'Isidore Verheyden (1846–1905)', *Revue des Archéologistes et Historiens d'art* 17
Friedman 1984 D.F. Friedman, 'Fernand Khnopff', *Arts Magazine* (April 1984)
Frosterus 1907 S. Frosterus, 'A.W. Finch's atelierexposition', *Nya Pressen* (8 Dec. 1907)
Gensel 1907 W. Gensel, *Constantin Meunier*, Bielefeld–Leipzig
Gibson 1984 M. Gibson, *Les Symbolistes*, Paris
Goldwater 1979 R. Goldwater, *Symbolism*, London
Gorceix 1982 P. Gorceix, *Le Symbolisme en Belgique. Etude de textes*, Heidelberg
Goyens de Heusch 1985 S. Goyens de Heusch, 'Musique et art belge contemporain', in: *La Musique source d'inspiration dans l'art belge XIIIe–XXe siècle*, Brussels
Goyens de Heusch 1988 —, *L'Impressionnisme et le Fauvisme en Belgique*, Antwerp–Paris
GOZ 1987 [G. Ollinger-Zinque], 'James Ensor', in: *Académie Royale des Beaux-Arts de Bruxelles. 275 ans d'enseignement*, Brussels
Guenther 1968 P.W. Guenther, *Stefan Georg und Die Bildenden Künste*, Austin
Haas 1967 W. Haas, *Die Belle Epoque*, Munich
Haesaerts 1931 L. and P. Haesaerts, *Flandre*, Paris
Haesaerts 1932 —, *Henri Evenepoel*, Brussels
Haesaerts 1935 —, *William Degouve de Nuncques*, Brussels
Haesaerts (1939)a P. Haesaerts, *Beeldhouwwerken en tekeningen van George Minne*, Amsterdam
Haesaerts (1939)b —, *George Minne ou le repliement sur soi-même*, Amsterdam
Haesaerts 1942 L. Haesaerts, *Histoire du Portrait de Navez à Ensor*, Brussels
Haesaerts 1960 P. Haesaerts, *Histoire de la Peinture moderne en Flandre*, Brussels
Haesaerts 1965 —, *Sint-Martens-Latem, gezegend oord van de Vlaamse kunst*, Brussels
Haesaerts 1973 —, *James Ensor*, Brussels
Haloche 1922 M. Haloche, *G. S. Van Strydonck*, Brussels
Hellens 1919 F. Hellens, 'Les Lithographies de Léon Spilliaert', *Le Thyrse* 16 (1 Sept. 1919)
Hellens 1932 F. Hellens, *Xavier Mellery*, Brussels
Herbert 1968 R.L. Herbert, *Neo-Impressionism*, New York
Hevesi [1906] 1984 L. Hevesi, *Acht Jahre Sezession. Kritik – Polemik – Chronik*, Vienna 1906; reprint Klagenfurt 1984
Hintze 1966 B. Hintze, 'A.W. Finch, som nyimpressionistisk malare. A.W. Finch, peintre néo-impressionniste', *Ateneumin Taidemuseo, Museojulkaisu* 1–2
Hostyn 1990 N. Hostyn, *Catalogus van de verzameling. Museum voor Schone Kunsten – Oostende*, Ostend
Hostyn 1992 —, 'Verheyden, Isidore, landschaps- en portretschilder', in: *Nationaal Biografisch woordenboek* 14
Houbart-Wilkin 1964a S. Houbart-Wilkin, 'Baertsoen (Albert)', *Biographie Nationale* XXXII/1
Houbart-Wilkin 1964b —, 'La maison du peintre Xavier Mellery', *Bulletin Musées royaux des Beaux-Arts de Belgique* 1–2
Houbart-Wilkin 1970 S. Houbart-Wilkin, 'Introduction', in: *Le Clair et l'obscur. Dessins belges*, Brussels
Howe 1980 J.W. Howe, 'Fernand Khnopff's Depictions of Bruges: Medievalism, Mysticism and Socialism', *Arts Magazine* 4 (Dec. 1980)
Howe 1982 —, *The Symbolist Art of Fernand Khnopff*, Ann Arbor
Hymans 1906 H. Hymans, 'Belgische Kunst des 19. Jahrhunderts', Leipzig

Hyslop 1975 F. E. Hyslop, *Henri Evenepoel, Belgian Painter in Paris 1892–1899*, s.l.
Jollivet-Castelot 1912 Fr. Jollivet-Castelot, 'Léon Spilliaert', *Croquis scientifiques et philosophiques, (Publication de psychisme experimental)* (article dated Ostend, 3 Sept. 1909)
Joly 1896 E. Joly, 'Le Salon de La Libre Esthétique', *La Libre Critique* (15 March 1896)
Joly 1924 —, 'Un Peintre symboliste belge. Fernand Khnopff', *Le Figaro artistique* (3 April 1924)
Jones 1953 Ph. Jones, 'Evenepoel ou La Vie mesurée', *Les Arts plastiques* 4 (July–Sept. 1953)
Juin 1980 H. Juin, *Fernand Khnopff et la littérature de son temps*, Brussels
Jullian 1969 Ph. Jullian, *Esthètes et magiciens*, Paris
Kahn (1909?) G. Kahn, *Félicien Rops*, Paris
Kelder 1986 D. Kelder, *L'Héritage de l'Impressionnisme*, Paris–New York
Klein (1909?) R. Klein, *Félicien Rops*, Paris, s.d.
Kluncker 1974 K. Kluncker, *Blätter für die Kunst*, Frankfurt
Koninckx 1931 W. Koninckx, *Eloge de Rops*, Antwerp
Koyanagi 1990 R. Koyanagi, *Fernand Khnopff*, Tokyo
Kultermann 1977 U. Kultermann, 'Fountain of Youth: the Folkwang Fountain by George Minne', *Konsthistorisk Tidskrift*, 46/3 (Dec. 1977)
Kunel 1923 M. Kunel, *Aug. Donnay. Peintre de Wallonie*, Liège
Laclotte 1976 M. Laclotte, *Le Larousse des grands peintres*, Paris
Lambotte 1908 P. Lambotte, *Henri Evenepoel*, Brussels
Lambotte 1913 —, *Les Peintres de portraits*, Brussels–Paris
Langui 1961 E. Langui, *Les Sources du xxe siècle*, Brussels
Legrand 1971a F.C. Legrand, *Ensor, cet inconnu*, Brussels
Legrand 1971b —, *Le Symbolisme en Belgique*, Brussels
Legrand 1979 — *et al.*, *Le Symbolisme dans le dessin belge*, Brussels
Legrand 1981 —, *Léon Spilliaert et son époque*, Antwerp
Legrand, Ollinger-Zinque 1966 —, G. Ollinger-Zinque, 'Lettres de James Ensor à Octave Maus', *Bulletin Musées royaux des Beaux-Arts de Belgique* 1–2
Lemonnier 1887 C. Lemonnier, *Histoire des Beaux-Arts en Belgique*, Brussels
Lemonnier 1904 —, *Constantin Meunier, sculpteur et peintre*, Paris
Lemonnier 1906 —, *L'Ecole belge de peinture – 1830–1905*, Brussels
Lemonnier 1908a —, *Emile Claus*, Brussels
Lemonnier 1908b —, *Félicien Rops, l'homme et l'artiste*, Paris
Leppert 1993 R. Leppert, *The Sight of Sound. Music, Representation and the History of the Body*, Berkeley–Los Angeles–London
Les XX 1981 *Les XX. Catalogue des dix expositions annuelles*, Brussels (reprint)
Lindström 1966 A. Lindström, *Ateneumin Taidemuseo* [Catalogue of the collections], Helsinki
Louis 1901 E. Louis, 'Au Salon des aquarellistes', *La Fédération artistique* (22 Dec. 1901)
Mascha 1910 O. Mascha, *Félicien Rops und sein werk*, Munich
Maeterlinck *et al.* 1923 M. Maeterlinck, G. Chabot, P. Fierens, P. Desmedt, 'George Minne', *La Nervie* 8
Marcel 1910 H. Marcel, 'Peintres contemporains. Emile Claus', *Gazette des Beaux-Arts* 1910 (1st semester)
Marchal 1966–1967 A. Marchal, *Fernand Khnopff. Portrait d'enfant (Peinture vivante)*, Brussels
Marechal 1992 D. Marechal, 'Bruges Painting from Mannerism to Symbolism', in: *Bruges and Europe*, Antwerp
Maret 1949 F. Maret, *Emile Claus*, Antwerp
Marmori 1979 G. Marmori, 'Mia sorella, mia sposa, mia modella', *Espresso* (28 Oct. 1979)
Mathieu 1990 P.L. Mathieu, *La Génération symboliste, 1870–1910*, Zurich
Mauclair 1906 C. Mauclair, *Trois Crises de l'art actuel. Un chercheur, Félicien Rops*, Paris 1906
Maus 1901 O. Maus, 'Le Salon des aquarellistes', *L'Art moderne* (15 Dec. 1901)
Maus 1905 —, 'Exposition Albert Baertsoen', *L'Art moderne* 3 (Dec. 1905)
Maus 1926 M.O. Maus, *Trente Années de lutte pour l'art (1884–1914)*, Brussels
Meier-Graefe 1900 J. Meier-Graefe, 'George Minne', *Ver Sacrum*
Mertens 1984 Ph. Mertens (ed.), *Musées royaux des Beaux-Arts de Belgique. Département d'Art Moderne. Catalogue inventaire de la peinture moderne*, Brussels
Metken 1979–1980 G. Metken, 'Fernand Khnopff et la modernité', in: *Fernand Khnopff*, Paris–Brussels 1979–1980
Metken 1983 —, *Lokaltermin*, Munich
Micha 1980 R. Micha, 'Fernand Khnopff figure centrale du Symbolisme', *Vie des Arts* xxv/100
Milner 1971 J. Milner, *Symbolists and Decadents*, London
Mirbeau 1893 O. Mirbeau, 'Nos Artistes jugés à l'étranger, Constantin Meunier', *L'Art moderne* (18 June 1893)
Mockel 1922 A. Mockel, *Auguste Donnay, souvenirs et réflexions*, Liège
Mourey 1901 G. Mourey, 'Albert Baertsoen', *L'Art moderne* 20 (Oct. 1901)
Mourey 1902 —, 'Some Paintings and Sculpture at the Paris Salons', *The Studio* (Aug. 1902)
M.W. 1885 M.W. [Max Waller], 'L'Exposition des xx', *La Réforme* (5 Feb. 1885)
Neter 1914 R. Neter, 'Fernand Khnopff', *Die Kunst für Alle* xxix/15
Norman 1990 A. Norman, 'Le Temps de la peinture symboliste', *De Facto* (Dec. 1990)
Ollinger-Zinque 1969 G. Ollinger-Zinque, *Blanc, noir et or (Huit Siècles de Peinture)*, Brussels
Ollinger-Zinque 1990 G. Ollinger-Zinque, 'En écoutant du Schumann', in: *Fernand Khnopff*, Tokyo
Parisse 1991 J. Parisse, *Auguste Donnay, un visage de la terre wallonne*, Brussels
Pica 1902 V. Pica, 'Artisti Contemporanei: Fernand Khnopff', *Emporium* xvi/93
Pica 1909 —, *La Galleria d'Arte Moderna di Venezia*, Bergamo
Pica 1927 —, *Fernand Khnopff (Allgemeines Lexikon der Bildenden Künstler)*, Leipzig
Piérard 1937 L. Piérard, *Constantin Meunier*, Brussels
Piérard 1952 —, *Félicien Rops*, Antwerp
Pierron 1926 S. Pierron, *Collection Henri Van Cutsem. Catalogue descriptif des peintures et sculptures*, Paris
Pion 1931 L. Pion, *Musée des Beaux-Arts de Tournai. Catalogue général des œuvres exposées*, Tournai
Pion, Pion-Leblanc 1971 L. Pion, I. Pion-Leblanc, *Musée des Beaux-Arts Tournai. Catalogue des peintures et des sculptures*, Tournai
Poirier 1953 P. Poirier, *La Peinture belge d'autrefois 1830–1930*, Brussels
Ramiro 1905 E. Ramiro, *Félicien Rops*, Paris
Rebell 1901 H. Rebell, *Trois Artistes étrangers: Robert Sherard, Sattler, Félicien Rops*, Paris
Rewald 1956 J. Rewald, *Post-Impressionism*, New York
Roberts-Jones 1978 Ph. Roberts-Jones, *La Peinture irréaliste au xixe siècle*, Freiburg
Roberts-Jones 1980 —, 'Khnopff revisited', *Bulletin de l'Académie Royale de Belgique (Classe des Beaux-Arts)* 72/3
Roberts-Jones 1981 —, *L'Alphabet des circonstances*, Brussels
Roelandts 1928 O. Roelandts, *Albert Baertsoen*, Koninklijke Academie van Schone Kunsten van Gent, Ghent
Saarikivi 1949 S. Saarikivi, 'Le Groupe Septem et l'Impressionnisme finlandais', *Revue Taïde* 1
Sabatini 1988 L. Sabatini, *Le Musée de l'Art wallon* (Musea Nostra), Brussels
Sarfatti 1906 M.G. Saarfatti, 'Profili d'Artisti. Fernand Khnopff', *Il Rinascimento* (April 1906)
Sauton 1946 A. Sauton, *Un Prince du Luminisme, Emile Claus (1849–1924)*, Brussels
Schmutzler 1962 R. Schmutzler, *Art Nouveau. Jugendstil*, Stuttgart
Schultze-Naumburg 1900 P. Schultze-Naumburg, 'Fernand Khnopff', *Die Kunst für Alle* xv/19
Shaw-Sparrow 1897 W. Shaw-Sparrow, 'Constantin Meunier: the Artist of the Flemish Collieries', *The Studio* ix/52 (15 July 1897)
Stevens 1979 M.A. Stevens, A.W. Finch, in: *Post-Impressionism*, London
Sulzberger 1937 M. Sulzberger, *Profils perdus*, Brussels
Sutter 1970 J. Sutter *et al.*, *Les Néo-impressionnistes*, Lausanne
Thiery, Van Drievoet [1909] A. Thiery, E. van Drievoet, *Catalogue complet des œuvres dessinées peintes et sculptées de Constantin Meunier*, Louvain
Treu 1898 G. Treu, *Constantin Meunier*, Dresden
Tschudi Madsen 1967 S. Tschudi Madsen, *L'Art Nouveau*, Paris
[Turku] 1984 *Turun Taideyhdistyksen kokoelmat. Luettelo* [Catalogue of the collection, Museum of Fine Arts, Turku], Turku
Van Hassel 1927 V. van Hassel, *Sur les Sentiers infinis de la souffrance humaine*, Brussels
Vanbeselaere 1961 W. Vanbeselaere, *De Vlaamse Schilderkunst van 1850 tot 1950*, Brussels
Van de Velde 1962 H. van de Velde, *Geschichte meines Lebens*, Munich
Van de Woestijne 1911 K. van de Woestijne, *Kunst en geest in Vlaanderen*, Bussum
Van de Woestijne 1928 —, *De Schroeflijn*, I, *Opstellen over plastische kunst*, Brussels
Van Kerckhoven 1980 M. van Kerckhoven, 'Muziek en plastische kunsten', *Vlaanderen* (Aug. 1980)
Van Kerckhoven 1981 M. van Kerckhoven, 'Fernand Khnopff en de Muziek', *Bulletin Musées royaux des Beaux-Arts de Belgique* 1–3
Van Maris 1982 L. van Maris, 'Félicien Rops, over kunst, melancholie & perversiteit', *Synopsis*
Van Puyvelde 1930 L. van Puyvelde, *George Minne*, Brussels
Vanzype 1903 G. Vanzype, *Nos Peintres*, I, Brussels
Vanzype 1923 —, *L'Art belge au xixe siècle*, Brussels–Paris
Vanzype 1926 —, 'Notice sur Albert Baertsoen', *Annuaire de l'Académie royale des Sciences, des Lettres et des Beaux-Arts de Belgique*
Vanzype 1928 —, *Notice sur Isidore Verheyden*, Brussels
Vanzype 1930 —, *Les Peintres de genre et d'intérieur. Les Idéalistes (Histoire de la peinture et de la sculpture en Belgique. 1830–1930)*, Brussels–Paris
Verhaeren 1886 E. Verhaeren, 'Silhouettes d'artistes. Fernand Khnopff', *L'Art moderne* (10 Oct. 1886)
Verhaeren 1891 —, 'Constantin Meunier', *La Nation* (5 Dec. 1891)
[Verhaeren] 1893 —, 'Le Salon des XX. Les invités', *L'Art moderne* (5 March 1893)
[Verhaeren] 1896 —, 'Le Salon de La Libre Esthétique', *L'Art moderne* (8 March 1896)
Verhaeren 1899 —, 'Théo van Rysselberghe', *Ver Sacrum* II/11
Verhaeren 1908 —, *James Ensor*, Brussels
Vermeylen 1903 A. Vermeylen, 'Constantin Meunier', *Onze Kunst* (Feb. 1903)
Wangermée 1985 R. Wangermée, 'Musique et peinture au xixe siècle', in: *La Musique source d'inspiration dans l'art belge xiiie–xxe siècle*, Brussels
X., 'Nacht te Venetië', *Stedelijke Musea Brugge. Informatiebulletin* 1 (Jan. 1985)
X.,'Petite Chronique', *L'Art moderne* (12 Jan. 1902)
Y., 'La Libre Esthétique', *L'Art moderne* (7 April 1895)
Zeno 1985 Th. Zeno, *Les Muses sataniques. Félicien Rops. Œuvre graphique et lettres choisies*, Brussels

Exhibitions

Albi 1985 — *Du Réalisme au Surréalisme en Belgique. Collection du Crédit Communal de Belgique*, Musée Toulouse-Lautrec
Amsterdam 1988 — *Neo-Impressionisten*, Rijksmuseum Vincent van Gogh
Amsterdam–Bern–Paris 1945–1946 — *Sept Peintres belges*, Stedelijk Museum Amsterdam, 1945–1946; Kunsthalle, Berne 1946; Musée de l'Orangerie, Paris 1946
Antwerp 1887 — *L'Art Indépendant. 1er Salon annuel*, Palais de l'Industrie des Arts et du Commerce
Antwerp 1892 — *Association pour l'Art, 1ère exposition annuelle*, Ancien Musée de Peinture
Antwerp 1922 — *Kunst van Heden*
Antwerp 1936 — *William Degouve de Nuncques*, Cercle Royal Artistique. L'Art Contemporain
Antwerp 1953 — *Evenepoel*, Koninklijk Museum voor Schone Kunsten
Antwerp 1985 — *Aspecten van het Symbolisme. Tekeningen en pastels*, Koninklijk Museum voor Schone Kunsten
Antwerp 1985–1986 — *Antwerpen 1900: Schilderijen en tekeningen 1880–1914*, Koninklijk Museum voor Schone Kunsten
Antwerp 1990 — *Schilders van het landelijke leven in België. Van realisme tot post-expressionisme*, Koninklijk Museum voor Schone Kunsten
Antwerp 1991 — *In dienst van de kunst. Antwerps mecenaat rond 'Kunst van Heden' (1905–1959)*, Koninklijk Museum voor Schone Kunsten
Atlanta 1962 — *Landscape into Art*, Art Association
Baden-Baden 1976 — *Symbolismus in Europa*, Staatliche Kunsthalle
Beijing 1988 — *Constantin Meunier*, Museum of Fine Arts
Belgrade 1953 — *Izlozba. Rada I Folklora U Belgijskoj Umetnosti xix i xx Veka*
Berlin 1908 — *Ausstellung Belgischer Kunst*, Lokal der Sezession
Berlin 1914 — *Grosse Berliner Kunstausstellung 1914*
Berlin 1933 — *Hundert Jahre Belgischer Kunst*, Preussische Akademie der Künste
Berlin 1971 — *Constantin Meunier*, Orangerie, Charlottenburg
Berlin 1979 — *Arbeit und Alltag. Soziale Wirklichkeit in der belgischen Kunst, 1830–1914*, Staatliche Kunsthalle
Bochum 1970–1971 — *Constantin Meunier*, Bergbau-Museum
Brussels 1883 — *xie Exposition d'œuvres d'art*, Cercle Artistique et Littéraire
Brussels 1886 — [L'Essor]
Brussels 1889 — *Société royale belge des aquarellistes. Vingt-neuvième exposition annuelle*,
Brussels 1890 — *Exposition générale des Beaux-Arts*
Brussels 1891 — *Jan Verhas, Den Duyts, Coosemans, Fernand Khnopff, Maurice Vauthier*, Cercle Artistique et Littéraire
Brussels 1893 — *Exposition générale des Beaux-Arts*, Musée Moderne
Brussels 1897–1898 — *Exposition d'œuvres de Henri Evenepoel*, Cercle Artistique et Littéraire
Brussels 1901–1902 — *Société Royale belge des Aquarellistes. 42e Exposition*, Musées royaux de Peinture
Brussels 1904 — *Société Royale belge des Aquarellistes. 45e Exposition*, Musées royaux de Peinture
Brussels 1905 — *Exposition rétrospective de l'art belge*, Palais du Cinquantenaire
Brussels 1912a — *Société royale belge des aquarellistes. 53e exposition*
Brussels 1912b — *ive Salon de printemps (Société Royale des Beaux-Arts)*, Palais du Cinquantenaire
Brussels 1912c — *Quelques peintres de la figure*, Waux-Hall
Brussels 1913 — *H. Evenepoel*, Galerie Georges Giroux
Brussels 1915 — *Salon d'automne*, Musée Moderne
Brussels 1922 — *Exposition jubilaire*
Brussels 1923–1924 — *Exposition d'œuvres de Henri Evenepoel*, Cercle Artistique et Littéraire
Brussels 1926 — *Rétrospective William Degouve de Nuncques*, Galerie Georges Giroux
Brussels 1927 — *Théo van Rysselberghe. Exposition d'ensemble*, Galerie Giroux
Brussels 1928 — *Exposition Constantin Meunier. Peintures – Dessins – Sculptures*, Galerie Georges Giroux
Brussels 1930 — *Exposition centennale de l'art belge, 1830–1930. Un siècle d'art*, Palais des Beaux-Arts
Brussels 1931 — *Exposition rétrospective du portrait de la femme 1830–1930*, Cercle Artistique et Littéraire
Brussels 1932a — *Henri Evenepoel*, Galerie Georges Giroux
Brussels 1932b — *La Musique dans l'art*, Palais des Beaux-Arts
Brussels 1932c — *Les Maîtres de la Société libre des Beaux-Arts*, Palais des Beaux-Arts
Brussels 1933 — *Exposition rétrospective de Julien Dillens Sculpteur (1849–1904) et de Guillaume – S. Van Strydonck Peintre, catalogue*, Cercle Artistique et Littéraire
Brussels 1935 — *L'Art contemporain*, Palais des Beaux-Arts
Brussels 1937 — *Xavier Mellery*, Palais des Beaux-Arts
Brussels 1942a — *Trente Chefs-d'Œuvre de la peinture belge*, 234 avenue de Longchamp
Brussels 1942b — *Isidore Verheyden 1848–1905*, Palais des Beaux-Arts
Brussels 1942–1943 — *Henri Evenepoel*, Musées royaux des Beaux-Arts de Belgique
Brussels 1947 — *Centenaire du Cercle Artistique*, Cercle Royal Artistique et Littéraire et Royal Gaulois
Brussels 1948 — *Rétrospective Léon Fréderic*, Palais des Beaux-Arts
Brussels 1949 — *De schilders van de zee*, Palais des Beaux-Arts
Brussels 1957 — *Le Mouvement Symboliste*, Palais des Beaux-Arts
Brussels 1961 — *Les Loisirs et les jeux*, Musées royaux des Beaux-Arts de Belgique
Brussels 1962 — *Le Groupe des XX et son temps*, Musées royaux des Beaux-Arts de Belgique
Brussels 1963 — *Henry van de Velde*, Palais des Beaux-Arts
Brussels 1964 — *Aquarelles, gouaches et pastels du xixe siècle à nos jours*, Musées royaux des Beaux-Arts de Belgique
Brussels 1966 — *Evocation des XX et de La Libre Esthétique*, Musées royaux des Beaux-Arts de Belgique
Brussels 1967 — *Rétrospective A.W. Finch*, Palais des Beaux-Arts
Brussels 1967–1968 — *Regards et attitudes d'un siècle*, Musées royaux des Beaux-Arts de Belgique
Brussels 1968 — *De l'Allégorie au symbole*, Musées royaux des Beaux-Arts de Belgique
Brussels 1969 — *Constantin Meunier – George Minne. Dessins et sculptures*, Musées royaux des Beaux-Arts de Belgique
Brussels 1970a — *Le Clair et l'obscur. Dessins belges*, Musées royaux des Beaux-Arts de Belgique
Brussels 1970b — *Œuvres des xixe et xxe siècles*, Musées royaux des Beaux-Arts de Belgique
Brussels 1971 — *Fernand Khnopff*, Galerie L'Ecuyer
Brussels 1976 — *Le Symbolisme en Europe*, Musées royaux des Beaux-Arts de Belgique
Brussels 1977 — *W. Degouve de Nuncques*, Hôtel de ville
Brussels 1978 — *L'Art en Belgique, 1880–1950. Hommage à Luc et Paul Haesaerts*, Palais des Beaux-Arts
Brussels 1979 — *Jean Portaels et ses élèves*, Musées royaux des Beaux-Arts de Belgique
Brussels 1980–1981 — *150 Ans d'art belge*, Musées royaux des Beaux-Arts de Belgique
Brussels 1981 — *Les XX au Musée de Bruxelles*, Musées royaux des Beaux-Arts de Belgique
Brussels 1983–1984 — *L'enfant dans l'art belge de 1800 à nos jours*, Galerie CGER
Brussels 1985 — *La Musique source d'inspiration dans l'art belge. xiiie–xxe siècle*, Galerie CGER
Brussels–Paris–Nice 1985 — *Félicien Rops 1833–1898*, Musées royaux des Beaux-Arts de Belgique and Le Botanique, Brussels; Musée des Arts Décoratifs, Paris; Musée des Beaux-Arts Jules Chéret, Nice
Brussels 1987a — *Académie Royale des Beaux-Arts de Bruxelles. 275 ans d'enseignement*, Musées royaux des Beaux-Arts de Belgique
Brussels 1987b — *Fernand Khnopff et ses rapports avec la Sécession viennoise*, Musées royaux des Beaux-Arts de Belgique
Brussels 1989 — *La Collection du Crédit Communal. Art belge xixe–xxe* siècle, Palais des Beaux-Arts
Brussels 1990 — *L'Impressionnisme et le Fauvisme en Belgique*, Musée d'Ixelles
Brussels 1991 — *Fin de siècle. Dessins, pastels et estampes en Belgique de 1885 à 1905*, Galerie CGER
Brussels 1993–1994 — *Les XX & La Libre Esthétique. Cent ans après*, Musées royaux des Beaux-Arts de Belgique
Brussels 1994 — *Henri Evenepoel*, Musées royaux des Beaux-Arts de Belgique
Budapest 1902 — *Tavaszi Nemzetközi Kiallitas*, Mücsarnok
Cairo 1947 — *Exposition Internationale d'art contemporain*, s.l.
Charleroi 1952 — *Auguste Oleffe*, Cercle Artistique et Littéraire
Charleroi 1960 — *xxxive Salon du Cercle Artistique et Littéraire. Trente ans de peinture belge*, Palais des Beaux-Arts
Charleroi 1980 — *Art et Société en Belgique, 1848–1914*, Palais des Beaux-Arts
Chicago–New York–Wilmington 1984 — *Fernand Khnopff and the Belgian Avant-Garde*, David and Alfred Smart Gallery, Chicago; Barry Friedman Ltd, New York; Delaware Art Museum, Wilmington
Cologne 1981 — *Georges Le Brun, 1873–1914*, Belgisches Haus
Colonster 1968 — *Rétrospective Auguste Donnay*, Université de Liège, Château de Colonster
Copenhagen 1931 — *Belgisk Kunst fra xv–xx Aarhundrede*, Carlsberg Glyptotek
Dresden 1897 — *Internationale Kunstausstellung*
Düsseldorf 1977 — *Vom Licht zur Farbe. Nachtimpressionistische Malerei zwischen 1886 und 1912*, Städtische Kunsthalle
Finland 1973 — *1800 – Luvun Taidetta Nils Dahlström Kokoelmasta*, travelling exhibition
Florence 1896–1897 — *Festa dell'Arte e dei Fiori. Esposizione di Belle Arti*
Florence 1973 — *Aspetti del Simbolismo*, Galleria Menghelli
Frankfurt 1988 — *Pastelle und Zeichnungen des Belgischen Symbolismus*, Kunstverein
Ghent 1883 — *xxxiie Exposition triennale de Gand. Salon de 1883*, Casino
Ghent 1886 — *33e Salon triennal*
Ghent 1924 — *L'Œuvre de Constantin Meunier*, Palais des Fêtes
Ghent 1962 — *Retrospectieve Théo van Rysselberghe*, Museum voor Schone Kunsten
Ghent 1972–1973 — *Retrospectieve tentoonstelling Albert Baertsoen, 1866–1922*, Museum voor Schone Kunsten
Ghent 1974 — *Rétrospective Emile Claus, 1849–1924*, Museum voor Schone Kunsten
Ghent 1975 — *Gent. Duizend jaar kunst en cultuur*, Museum voor Schone Kunsten
Ghent 1979 — *Veertig kunstenaars rond Karel van de Woestyne*, Museum voor Schone Kunsten
Ghent 1980 — *Het landschap in de Belgische kunst, 1830–1914*, Museum voor Schone Kunsten
Ghent 1982 — *George Minne en de kunst rond 1900*, Museum voor Schone Kunsten
Ghent 1985 — *Tekeningen, pastels en aquarellen uit eigen collectie*, Museum voor Schone Kunsten
Ghent 1993 — *Théo van Rysselberghe, neo-impressionist*, Museum voor Schone Kunsten
Ghent–Lawrence–Williamstown–Cleveland 1992–1993 — *Les XX and The Belgian Avant-Garde. Prints, Drawings and Books ca. 1890*, Museum voor Schone Kunsten, Ghent; Spencer Museum of Art, University of Kansas, Lawrence; Sterling and Francine Clark Art Institute, Williamstown; Cleveland Museum of Art, Cleveland
Hagen 1959 — *Der Junge van de Velde und sein Kreis*, Osthaus Museum
Hamburg 1980 — *'Im Lebenstraum gefangen'. Fernand Khnopff. 1858–1921*, Kunsthalle
Helsinki 1901 — *Finska Konstnärernas xi utställning*, Ateneum
Helsinki 1910 — *A.W. Finch*, University of Helsinki
Helsinki 1928 — *Avajaisnäyttely*, Taidehalli
Helsinki 1929 — *Retrospektiivinen näyttely A.W. Finch*, Taidehalli
Helsinki 1930 — *Suomalaista taidetta Ateneumin kokoelmasta*, Taidehalli
Helsinki 1943 — *Vanhaa ja uutta suomalaista maalaustaidetta*, Galerie Hörhammer
Helsinki 1946 — *A.W. Finch Muistonäyttely*, Galerie Hörhammer
Helsinki 1948 — *Edelfeltistä midän päiviimme*, Galerie Hörhammer
Helsinki 1948b — *Belgisk Konstutställning Hundra Mästerverk Fran Ett Århundrade*, Konstakademi
Helsinki 1955 — *A.W. Finch Satavuotisnäyttely*, Galerie Hörhammer
Helsinki 1975 — *Léon Spilliaert 1881–1946*, Kluuvin galleria
Helsinki–Brussels 1991–1992 — *Alfred William Finch 1854–1930*, The Art Museum of Ateneum, Helsinki 1991;

Musées royaux des Beaux-Arts de Belgique, Brussels 1992
Hokkaido–Tokyo–Fukuoka–Itami 1988 — *Les Feux de L'Art Nouveau*, Hakodate Museum of Art, Hokkaido; Tokyo Art Gallery, Shibuya, Tokyo; The Seibu Art Museum, Tokyo; Fukuoka Art Museum, Fukuoka; Itami City Museum of Art, Itami
Ixelles–Hasselt–Ostend–Tournai 1961 — *Spilliaert*, Musée d'Ixelles, Ixelles; Begijnhof, Hasselt; Stedelijk Museum voor Schone Kunsten, Ostend; Musée des Beaux-Arts, Tournai
Ixelles 1969 — *Félicien Rops*, Musée d'Ixelles
Ixelles 1975 — *Georges Le Brun*, Musée d'Ixelles
Ixelles 1991 — *Rops et la modernité (Œuvres de la Communauté française de Belgique)*, Musée d'Ixelles
Knokke 1949 — *La Flandre maritime dans la peinture moderne*, La Réserve
Knokke 1974 — *Het Symbolisme in België. Le Symbolisme en Belgique*, Casino
Lausanne 1988–1989 — *Chefs-d'œuvre des musées de Liège*, Fondation de l'Hermitage
Louvain 1894 — *Exposition des Beaux-Arts*, La Table Ronde
Louvain 1909 — *Constantin Meunier*, KUL, Institute of Chemistry
La Libre Esthétique 1894 — *La Libre Esthétique*, Musée Moderne, Brussels
La Libre Esthétique 1895 — *La Libre Esthétique, Deuxième Exposition*, Musée Moderne, Brussels
La Libre Esthétique 1896 — *La Libre Esthétique. Troisième Exposition*, Musée Moderne, Brussels
La Libre Esthétique 1898 — *La Libre Esthétique. Cinquième exposition*, Musée Moderne, Brussels
La Libre Esthétique 1901 — *La Libre Esthétique. Huitième Exposition*, Musée Moderne, Brussels
La Libre Esthétique 1908 — *La Libre Esthétique. Salon jubilaire*, Musée Moderne, Brussels
Les XX 1885, Palais des Beaux-Arts
Les XX 1886, *IIIe exposition annuelle des XX*
Les XX 1886, *IVe exposition annuelle des XX*, Musée de Peinture
Les XX 1889, *VIe exposition annuelle des XX*
Les XX 1891, *VIIIe exposition annuelle des XX*, Musée Moderne
Les XX 1892, *IXe exposition annuelle des XX*, Musée Moderne
Les XX 1893, *Xe exposition annuelle des XX*, Musée Moderne
Liège 1905 — *Exposition Internationale de Liège. Beaux-Arts*, Palais des Beaux-Arts
Liège 1912 — *Fernand Khnopff*, Salles des fêtes
Liège 1920 — *Salon de 1920*, Palais des Beaux-Arts
Liège 1922 — *Rétrospective des œuvres d'Auguste Donnay*, Musée des Beaux-Arts
Liège 1978 — *La Donation Désiré Jaumain Ada Jobart au Musée de l'Art wallon*, Musée de l'Art wallon
Liège 1981 — *Du réalisme à l'expressionnisme dans l'art belge. Collection du Crédit Communal*, Musée Saint-Georges En Feronstrée
Liège 1991 — *Auguste Donnay, un visage de la terre wallonne*, Musée de l'Art wallon
London 1890 — *Fernand Khnopff*, Hannover Gallery
London 1892 — *Society of Portrait Painters. Second Exhibition*, Royal Institute
London 1897 — Continental Gallery (no catalogue)
Londen 1897b — *Ninth Summer Exhibition*, The New Gallery
London 1927 — *Flemish and Belgian Art*, The Royal Academy of Arts
London 1965 — *Autour de 1900. L'art belge (1884–1901)*, The Arts Council
London 1968 — *Les Salons de La Rose+Croix. 1892–1897*, The Piccadilly Gallery
London 1979–1980 — *Post-Impressionism. Cross-Currents in European Painting*, Royal Academy of Arts
London 1983 — *Summer Exhibition*, Whitford & Hughes
Los Angeles 1983 — *German Expressionist Sculpture*, Los Angeles County Museum of Art
Luxemburg 1993 — *Hunderd Years of Belgian Art. The Crédit Communal Collection*, Musée National d'Histoire et d'Art à Luxembourg
Mannheim 1916–1917 — *Ausstellung aus Mannheimer Privatbesitz*, Kunsthalle
Marbach 1968 — *Stefan Georg*, Schiller-Nationalmuseum
Marcq-en-Baroeul 1986 — *Le Symbolisme et la femme*, Fondation Septentrion
Milan 1970 — *Fernand Khnopff*, Galleria del Levante
Milan–Rome–Caserta 1985–1986 — *Aspetti del Simbolismo in Belgio. Disegni e Pastelli*, Accademia di Brera, Palazzo Clerici, Milan; Palazzo Braschi, Rome; Palazzo reale, Caserta
Moscow 1985 — *L'Art et la société dans les musées de Wallonie et Bruxelles fin 19e–début 20e siècle*, Pouchkine Museum
Munich 1894 — *Internationale Kunst-Ausstellung des Vereins Bildender Künstler Münchens. Secession*
Munich 1898 — *Internationale Kunst-Ausstellung des Vereins Bildender Künstler Münchens. Secession*, Königliches Kunstausstellungsgebäude
Munich 1901 — *VIII. Internationale Kunstausstellung 'Münchener Sezession'*, Königliches Glaspalast
Munich 1913 — *XI. Internationale Kunstausstellung*, Königliches Glaspalast
Munich 1964 — *Secession. Europaïsche Kunst um die Jahrhundertwende*, Haus der Kunst
Munich 1973 — *Symbolismus*, Galerie Michael Hasenclever
Munich 1989 — *James Ensor et ses contemporains*, Kunsthalle
Namur 1889 — *VIIe Expositio n internationale et triennale des beaux-arts*, Cercle Artistique et Littéraire
New York 1968 — *Neo-Impressionism*, Solomon R. Guggenheim Museum
New York 1980 — *Belgian Art, 1880–1914*, Brooklyn Museum
New York–Houston 1974 — *Painters of the Mind's Eye. Belgian Symbolists and Surrealists*, New York Cultural Center, New York; Museum of Fine Arts, Houston
Oslo 1948–1949 — *Belgisk kunst Gjennom hundre ar hundre mesterverk*, Kunstnernes Hus
Ostend 1951 — *La Peinture sous le signe de la mer*, Museum voor Schone Kunsten
Ostend 1952 — *La Femme dans l'art*, Kursaal
Ostend 1967 — *Europa 1900*, Kursaal and Museum voor Schone Kunsten
Otterlo 1962 — *De Twintig en hun tijdgenoten*, Rijksmuseum Kröller-Müller
Ouderghem 1972 — *Rétrospective Auguste Oleffe*, Centre Culturel d'Ouderghem
Ouderghem 1979 — *Rétrospective Auguste Oleffe*, Cultureel Centrum van het Rood Klooster
Oviedo 1985 — *Arte y Sociedad en Belgica 1848–1914*, Museo de Bellas Artes de Asturias
Paris 1888 — Salon des XXXIII, Galérie Georges Petit
Paris 1890 — *Salon de la Société nationale des Beaux-Arts*, Palais du Champ-de-Mars
Paris 1893 — *Salon de la Société nationale des Beaux-Arts*, Palais du Champ-de-Mars
Paris 1895–1896 — *Salon de L'Art Nouveau*, Salon Bing
Paris 1896 — *Exposition Constantin Meunier*, Salon de l'Art Nouveau
Paris 1897 — *Société nationale des Beaux-Arts. Exposition de 1897*, Palais du Champ-de-Mars
Paris 1902 — *Salon de 1902*, Grand Palais des Champs-Elysées
Paris 1906 — *Première Exposition de la Société internationale de la Peinture à l'Eau*, Galerie des Artistes Modernes
Paris 1907 — *Société du Salon d'Automne. 5ème Exposition. Exposition belge*, Grand Palais des Champs-Elysées
Paris 1923 — *L'Art belge ancien et moderne*, Musée du Jeu de Paume
Paris 1972 — *Peintres de l'imaginaire*, Galeries nationales du Grand Palais
Paris 1976 — *Le Symbolisme en Europe*, Galeries nationales du Grand Palais
Paris–Brussels 1979–1980 — *Fernand Khnopff. 1858–1921*, Musée des Arts Décoratifs, Paris; Musées royaux des Beaux-Arts de Belgique, Brussels
Paris–Brussels–Otterlo 1981–1982 — *Léon Spilliaert 1881–1946*, Galeries Nationales, Paris 1981; Musées royaux des Beaux-Arts, Brussels 1982; Rijksmuseum Kröller-Müller, Otterlo 1982
Paris 1988 — *Le Symbolisme – Le Réalisme*, Centre Wallonie–Bruxelles
Paris 1990 — *Cent Ans d'art belge. La collection du Crédit Communal de Belgique*, Grande Arche de la Défense
Pontoise–Charleroi 1990 — *Néo-impressionnistes belges dans les collections privées de Belgique*, Musées Tavet et Pissarro, Pontoise; Musée des Beaux-Arts, Charleroi
Prague 1949 — *Sto let Belgického Umeni*, S.V.U. Manes (Rooms of the Manes Artists' Society)
Rome 1955 — *Arte nordica contemporanea*, Palazzo delle Esposizioni
Rome 1991–1992 — *Il Lavoro dell' Uomo nella pittura da Goya a Kandinskij*, Città del Vaticano, Braccio di Carlo Magno
Rotterdam 1936–1937 — *De Divisionisten, van Georges Seurat tot Jan Toorop*, Museum Boymans
Rotterdam 1975–1976 — *Het Symbolisme in Europa*, Museum Boymans-van Beuningen
Saint-Josse-ten-Noode 1973 — *Rétrospective Léon Fréderic*, Hôtel Charlier
Savonlinna (Finland) 1989 — *Valon Juhlaa – Fête de la Lumière*, Taidekeskus Pyrri
Schaerbeek 1954 — *Rétrospective W. Degouve de Nuncques*, Musée Communal
Stavelot 1963 — *William Degouve de Nuncques*, Musée de l'Ancienne Abbaye
Stavelot 1990 — *William Degouves de Nuncques et les intimistes verviétois*, Musée d'art religieux régional et de l'ancienne Abbaye
St. Louis 1914 — *Constantin Meunier*, The City Art Museum
Stockholm 1981 — *A.W. Finch*, Prins Eugens Waldemarsudde
The Hague 1892 — *Tentoonstelling van Schilderijen en Teekeningen van eenigen uit de «XX» en uit de «Association pour l'Art»*, Haagschen Kunstkring
Tokyo 1981 — *Vingtistes*, Tobu department store
Tokyo 1983 — *Symbolism in Belgium*, National Museum of Modern Art
Tokyo–Kyoto 1985 — *Exposition du Pointillisme*, National Museum of Occidental Art, Tokyo; City Museum, Kyoto
Tokyo et al. 1988 — *Chefs-d'œuvre des musées de Liège*, Takamatsu City Museum of Art, *et al.*, 1988.
Tokyo–Himeji–Nagoya–Yamanashi 1990 — *Fernand Khnopff 1858–1921*, Bunkamura Museum, Tokyo; Himeji, City Art Museum, 1990; City Art Museum, Nagoya; Art Museum, Yamanashi
Tokyo–Hyogo–Hokkaido 1992–1993 — *Symbolisme en Belgique*, National Museum of Modern Art, Tokyo 1992–1993; Museum of Modern Art, Hyogo 1993; Museum of Modern Art, Hokkaido 1993
Turku 1973 — *Turun Taideyhdistyksen 81. Vuosinäyttely, Kokoelma Nils Dahlström*, Turun Taidemuseo
Venice 1899 — *Biennale. Terza Esposizione internazionale d'Arte della Città du Venezia*
Venice 1905 — *VI. Esposizione Internazionale d'Arte della citta di Venezia*, Palazzo dell'Esposizione
Venice 1912 — *X. Esposizione internazionale d'Arte della Città di Venezia*
Verviers 1904 — *Berthe Centner, Georges Le Brun, Maurice Pirenne*, Salle des Beaux-Arts
Verviers 1936 — *Georges Le Brun*, Société royale des Beaux-Arts
Verviers 1973 — *Georges Le Brun*, Musée communal des Beaux-Arts
Verviers 1975 — *Philippe Derchain, Georges Le Brun, Maurice Pirenne*, Cercle des Beaux-Arts
Vienna 1888 — *[International art-exhibition on the occasion of the 40th anniversary of the accession to the throne by the emperor Franz-Joseph]*
Vienna 1898 — *Sezession (II). Kunstausstellung der Vereinigung Bildender Künstler Oesterreichs*, Neues Haus
Vienna 1899 — *Sezession (III)*
Vienna 1907 — *XXIX. Ausstellung der Vereinigung bildender Künstler Osterreichs Sezession Wien*, s.l.
Vienna 1962 — *Belgische Malerei seit 1900*, Museum des 20. Jahrhunderts
Villeneuve d'Ascq 1988 — *Expressions flamandes, 1900–1930*, Musée d'art moderne
Waregem 1985 — *Retrospektieve Emile Claus*, Kultuurcentrum 'De Schakel'
Washington 1980 — *Post-Impressionism. Cross-Currents in European and American Painting, 1880–1906*, National Gallery of Art
Zurich 1952 — *Um 1900, Art Nouveau und Jugendstil. Kunst und Kunstgewerbe aus Europa und Amerika zur Zeit der Stilwende*, Kunstgewerbemuseum

Index

Page numbers in italics refer to illustrations

Photographic credits

Antwerp, Felix Tirry, p. 26 fig. 10
Antwerp, Pelegrie, cat. 1, 3, 14, 16, 27, 38, 68, 44, 46, 47
Antwerp, Stedelijk Prentenkabinet, p. 267 fig. 2, p. 273 fig. 7
Bibliotheca Regia, p. 36 fig. 18
Brussels, ACL, p. 16 fig. 1, p. 17 fig. 2, p. 17 fig. 3, p. 18 fig. 5, p. 19 fig. 6, p. 25 fig. 9, p. 27 fig. 11, p. 37 fig. 20, p. 38 fig. 23, p. 41 fig. 26, p. 41 fig. 27, p. 42 fig. 28, p. 43 fig. 30, p. 47 fig. 32, p. 53 fig. 37, p. 53 fig. 38, p. 60 fig. 40, p. 61 fig. 41, p. 64 fig. 42, p. 66 fig. 45, p. 67 fig. 46, p. 80 fig. a, p. 120 fig. a, p. 120 fig. b, p. 174 fig. a, p. 186 fig. a, p. 188 fig. a, p. 190 fig. a, p. 194, fig. a, p. 196 fig. a, p. 196 fig. b, p. 226 fig. a, p. 244 fig. a, p. 267 fig. 1, p. 269 fig. 3, p. 275 fig. 8
Brussels, Cabinet des Estampes, Bibliothèque royale Albert Ier, p. 277 fig. 13, p. 48 fig. 33
Brussels, Hervé Goffin, Art Promotion s.c., cat. 59
Brussels, Musées royaux des Beaux-Arts de Belgique, Archives de l'Art contemporain, p. 43 fig. 29, p. 44 fig. 31, p. 146 fig. a, p. 152 fig. a, p. 276 fig. 11, p. 277 fig. 12, p. 278, fig. 14
Brussels, Speltdoorn et fils, cat. 2, 6, 12, 28, 32, 35, 48, 49, 50, 51, 52, 53, 55, 57, 70, p. 155 fig. a, p. 283 fig. 18
Brussels, Vincent Everaerts, cat. 34
Cathy Carver, cat. 40
Douglas Sivén, cat. 22, 25
Friedrich Rosenstiel, cat. 67
Ghent, Ditmar Bollaert & Karel Moortgat, cat. 26, 69
Ghent, Foto-archief AMSAB v.z.w., p. 280 fig. 15, p. 285 fig. 23
Ghent, Piet Ysabie, p. 21 fig. 7, p. 202 fig. a, p. 206 fig. a
The Hague, Rob Koclaard ILL, cat. 73
Helsinki, Central Art Archives, Hannu Aaltonen, cat. 23, 24
London, Christie's Colour Library, cat. 29
Michel Bockian, cat. 11, 20, 80
Michael Bodycomb, cat. 17
New York, Ali Elai, Comerarts, cat. 31
Otterlo, Rijksmuseum Kröller-Müller, p. 88 fig. a, p. 250 fig. b,
Photo RMN, p. 92 fig. a

Friends of the Royal Academy

SPONSORS

Mrs Denise Adeane
Mr Brian Bailey
Air Marshal Sir Erik Bennett
Mr P.F.J. Bennett
Mrs J. Brice
Mr Jeremy Brown
Mrs L. Cantor
Mr and Mrs Christopher Cates
Mrs Elizabeth Corob
Mr and Mrs S. Fein
Mr and Mrs R. Gapper
Mr and Mrs Michael Godbee
Lady Gosling
Mr Peter G. Goulandris
Lady Grant
Mr J.P. Jacobs
Mr Harold Joels
Mr J. Kirkman
Dr Abraham Marcus
The Oakmoor Trust
Ocean Group p.l.c. (P.H. Holt Trust)
Mr J.P. Onions
Mr and Mrs R. Roberts
The Worshipful Company of Saddlers
Lady Samuel
Mrs M.C. Slawson
Dr and Mrs M.L. Slotover
The Stanley Foundation
Mr Robin Symes
Sir Brian Wolfson

ASSOCIATE SPONSORS

Mr Richard B. Allan
Mr Richard Alston
Mr Ian F.C. Anstruther
Mrs Ann Appelbe
Mr John R. Asprey
Mr Edgar Astaire
Lady Attenborough
Mr J.M. Bartos
Mrs Olive Bell
Mr N.S. Bergel
Mr David Berman
Mrs Susan Besser
Mrs Linda Blackstone
Mrs C.W.T. Blackwell
Mr Peter Boizot
C.T. Bowring (Charities Trust) Ltd
Mrs J.M. Bracegirdle
Mr Cornelius Broere
Lady Brown
Mr P.J. Brown Jr
Mrs Susan Burns
Mrs A. Cadbury
Mr and Mrs P.H.G. Cadbury
Mr and Mrs R. Cadbury
Mrs C.A. Cain
Carroll Foundation
Mr E.V. Cass
Miss E.M. Cassin
Mr R.A. Cernis
Mr W.J. Chapman
Mrs J.V. Clarke
Mr John Cleese
Mrs D. Cohen
Mrs R. Cohen
Mrs N.S. Conrad
Mr C. Cotton
Mrs Saeda H. Dalloul
Mr and Mrs D. de Laszlo
Mr John Denham
Mr Richard Dobson
The Marquess of Douro
Mr D.P. Duncan
Mr J. Edwards
Mr Kenneth Edwards
Falle Fine Art Ltd
Mrs K.W. Feesey MSc
Mrs B.D. Fenton
Mr J.G. Fogel
Mr Graham Gauld
Mr Robert Gavron
Mr Stephen A. Geiger
Mrs E.J. Gillespie
Mrs R.H.I. Goddard
Mrs P. Goldsmith
Mr Gavin Graham
Mr R.W. Gregson-Brown
Mrs O. Grogan
Mr J.A. Hadjipateras
Mr and Mrs D. Hallam-Peel
Mr and Mrs Richard Harris
Miss Julia Hazandras
Mr M.Z. Hepker
Mr Malcolm Herring
Mrs K.S. Hill
Mr R.J. Hoare
Mr Reginald Hoe
Mr Charles Howard
Mrs A. Howitt
Mr Christopher Hull
Mr Norman J. Hyams
Mr David Hyman
Mrs Manya Igel
Mr C.J. Ingram
Mr S. Isern-Feliu
The Rt. Hon. The Countess of Iveagh
Mrs I. Jackson
Lady Jacobs
Mrs G. Jungels-Winkler
Mr and Mrs S.D. Kahan
Mr Simon Karmel
Mr D.H. Killick
Mr P.W. Kininmonth
Mrs L. Kosta
Mrs. E. Landau
Mrs J.H. Lavender
Mr Ronald A. Lee
Mr Morris Leigh
Mr and Mrs J.R.A. Leighton
Mr and Mrs R. Leiman
Mr David Levinson
Mr Owen Luder
Mrs G.M.S. McIntosh
Mr Peter I. McMean
The Hon. Simon Marks
Mr and Mrs V.J. Marmion
Mr B.P. Marsh
Mr and Mrs J.B.H. Martin
Mr and Mrs G. Mathieson
Mr. R. Matthews
Mr J. Menasakanian
Mr J. Moores
Mrs A. Morgan
Mrs A. Morrison
Mr A.H.J. Muir
Mr David H. Nelson
Mrs E.M. Oppenheim-Sandelson
Mr Brian R. Oury
Mrs J. Palmer
Mr J.H. Pattisson
Mrs M.C.S. Philip
Mrs Anne Phillips
Mr Ralph Picken
Mr G.B. Pincus
Mr W. Plapinger
Mrs J. Rich
Mr Clive and Mrs Sylvia Richards
Robinson Charitable Trust
Mr F.P. Robinson
Mr D. Rocklin
Mrs A. Rodman
Lady Rootes
Mr and Mrs O. Roux
The Hon. Sir Stephen Runciman CH
Sir Robert Sainsbury
Mr G. Salmanowitz
Mrs Bernice Sandelson
Mrs Bernard L. Schwartz
Mr and Mrs D.M. Shalit
Shell UK Ltd
Mr Mark Shelmerdine
P. Sheridan Charitable Trust
Mr Mohamed Shourbaji
Mr R.J. Simmons
Mr John H.M. Sims
Mr and Mrs R. Slotover
The Spencer Wills Trust
Mrs B. Stubbs
Mr J.A. Tackaberry
Mr and Mrs L. Tanner
Mr G.C.A. Thom
Ms Britt Tidelius
Mr H.R. Towning
Mrs Andrew Trollope
Mr E. Victor
Mr A.J. Vines
Mrs C.H. Walton
Mr D.R. Walton Masters
Mr Neil Warren
Miss J. Waterous
Mrs J.M. Weingarten
Mrs E.S. Weiss
Mrs C. Weldon
Mr Frank S. Wenstrom
Mr R.A.M. Whitaker
Mr J. Wickham
Mr Colin C. Williams
Mrs I. Wolstenholme
Mr W.M. Wood
Mr R.M. Woodhouse
Mr F.S. Worms

Royal Academy Trust

BENEFACTORS

H.M. The Queen
Mr and Mrs Russell B. Aitken
The Annie Laurie Aitkin Charitable Trust
American Associates of the Royal Academy Trust
American Express Company
Mrs John W. Anderson II
The Hon. Walter H. and Mrs Annenberg
Mr Walter Archibald
Marilyn B. Arison
The Hon. Anne and Mr Tobin Armstrong
Asprey
AT & T
AT & T (UK) Ltd
Miss Nancy Balfour
The Bank of England
Barclays Bank plc
The Baring Foundation
B.A.T. Industries plc
Mr Tom Bendhem
Benihana Group
Mr and Mrs James Benson
In Memoriam: Ida Rose Biggs
Dame Elizabeth Blackadder RA
Charlotte Bonham-Carter Charitable Trust
Bowne of New York City
Mr Peter Bowring
British Airways, North America
British Gas plc
The British Petroleum Company plc

BP America
British Steel plc
Mr Keith Bromley
The Brown Foundation Inc.
BT
Bunzl plc
Iris and B. Gerald Cantor
The Rt. Hon. the Lord Carrington
The Trustees of the Clore Foundation
The John S. Cohen Foundation
The Cohen Family Charitable Trust
The Colby Trust
Commercial Union Assurance Company PLC
The Ernest Cook Trust
Mrs Jan Cowles
Credit Suisse First Boston
Sir Roger de Grey PRA
Sir Harry and Lady Djanogly
In Memoriam: Miss W.A. Donner
Alfred Dunhill Limited
Miss Jayne Edwardes
The John Ellerman Foundation
English Heritage
Mrs Roberta Entwistle
Esso UK PLC
The Esmée Fairbairn Charitable Trust
Kenneth Fang
Lord and Lady Faringdon
Mr and Mrs Eugene V. Fife
Mr and Mrs Donald R. Findlay
The Hon. Leonard K. and Mrs Firestone
Mr Walter Fitch III
Mrs Henry Ford II
The Henry Ford II Fund
The Late John Frye Bourne
The Garfield Weston Foundation
The Gatsby Foundation
The Getty Grant Program
The J. Paul Getty Jr Trust
The Lady Gibson
Glaxo
Mrs Mary Graves
The Jack Goldhill Charitable Trust
The Horace W. Goldsmith Foundation
The Worshipful Company of Goldsmiths
Mr and Mrs John Gore
The Gosling Foundation Ltd
The Greentree Foundation
Mr Lewis Grinnan Jr
The Worshipful Company of Grocers
The Worshipful Company of Haberdashers
The Paul Hamlyn Foundation
The Late Dr and Mrs Armand Hammer
Mrs Sue Hammerson
Philip and Pauline Harris Charitable Trust
The Hayward Foundation
Mr and Mrs Randolph A. Hearst
Klaus and Belinda Hebben
The Hedley Foundation
Mrs Henry J. Heinz
The Henry J. and Drue Heinz Foundation
The Heritage of London Trust
IBM United Kingdom Limited
The Idlewild Trust
The Inchcape Charitable Trust
The Worshipful Company of Ironmongers
Mr and Mrs Ralph Isham
The J.P. Jacobs Charitable Trust
Mr and Mrs Donald P. Kahn
Mrs D. King
Irene and Hyman Kreitman
The Kresge Foundation
The Kress Foundation
Mr and Mrs Sol Kroll
Ladbroke Group Plc
Mr D.E. Laing
The Maurice Laing Foundation
The Landmark Trust
The Lankelly Foundation
Mr John S. Latsis
The Leche Trust
Mr and Mrs Panagiotis Lemos
Mr Leon Levy and Ms Shelby White
Mr J.H. Lewis
Lex Services PLC
The Linbury Trust
The Ruth and Stuart Lipton Charitable Trust
Sir Sydney and Lady Lipworth
Lloyds Bank PLC
Mrs T.S. Mallinson
The Manifold Trust
The Stella and Alexander Margulies Charitable Trust
Mr and Mrs John L. Marion
Mrs W. Marks
Marks & Spencer
Mrs Jack C. Massey
Paul Mellon KBE
The Anthony and Elizabeth Mellows Charitable Trust
The Mercers Company
Museums and Galleries Improvement Fund
National Westminster Bank PLC
Mr Stavros S. Niarchos
Ms Diane A. Nixon
Orrin Charitable Trust
Otemae College
The Peacock Charitable Trust
Mr and Mrs Frank Pearl
The Pennycress Trust
In Memoriam: Mrs Olive Petit
Mr and Mrs Milton Petrie
The P.F. Charitable Trust
The Pilgrim Trust
Mr A.N. Polhill
The Hon. and Mrs Leon B. Polsky
The Hon. Charles H. Price II and Mrs Price
Prudential Assurance Company Ltd
Mr and Mrs John Raisman
The Rayne Foundation
The Regent Hotel
Mr and Mrs Laurance S. Rockefeller
The Ronson Charitable Foundation
The J. Rothschild Group Charitable Trust
Rothschilds Inc
The RTZ Corporation Plc
The Late Dr Arthur M. Sackler
Mrs Arthur M. Sackler
The Sainsbury Family Charitable Trusts
Mrs Jean Sainsbury
Mrs Basil Samuel
The Peter Samuel Charitable Trust
Mrs Louisa Sarofim
Save & Prosper Educational Trust
Sea Containers Limited
The Rt Hon. the Lord Sharp
Shell UK Ltd
Mr and Mrs James C. Slaughter
The Late Mr Robert Slaughter
Mr and Mrs Kenneth Snowman
The Spencer Charitable Trust
Miss K. Stalnaker
Mr and Mrs Stephen Stamas
The Starr Foundation
Bernard Sunley Charitable Foundation
John Swire and Son
Mr and Mrs A. Alfred Taubman
Mr and Mrs Vernon Taylor Jr.
Texaco Inc
G. Ware and Edythe Travelstead
The TSB Foundation for England and Wales
Seiji Tsutsumi
The Douglas Turner Charitable Trust
The 20th May 1961 Charitable Trust
Unilever PLC
Mr Alexander Von Auersperg
The Henry Vyner Charitable Trust
S.G. Warburg Limited
Dorothy, Viscountess Weir
The Weldon UK Charitable Trust
Mr and Mrs Keith S. Wellin
The Welton Foundation
Westminster City Council
Mr and Mrs Garry H. Weston
Mr Anthony Whishaw RA
Mr Frederick B. Whittemore
The Hon. John and Mrs Whitehead
Mrs John Hay Whitney
Mr and Mrs Wallace S. Wilson
Mr A. Witkin
The Wolfson Foundation
The Late Mr Charles Wollaston
The Late Mr Ian Woodner
Mr and Mrs William Wood Prince

CORPORATE MEMBERS

Amdahl UK Limited
Arthur Andersen and Andersen Consulting
Atlantic Plastics Limited
A.T. Kearney Limited
Barclays de Zoete Wedd
Bankers Trust Company
BAT Industries plc
BP Chemicals Limited
British Petroleum
British Alcan Aluminium plc
British Gas plc
BT
Bunzl plc
Chubb Insurance Company
Courage Limited
C.S. First Boston Group
The Daily Telegraph plc
The Diamond Trading Company (Pty) Limited
Gartmore plc
Goldman Sachs International Limited
Glaxo Holdings p.l.c.
Grand Metropolitan plc
Hay Management Consultants
Hill Samuel Bank Limited
Hillier Parker May & Rowden
IMS A6 UK Branch
Industrial Bank of Japan Limited
Jaguar Cars Ltd
John Laing plc
Lehman Brothers International
Lloyds Bank Plc
Lloyds Private Banking Limited
London & Edinburgh Trust plc
E.D.& F. Man Limited Charitable Trust
Marks & Spencer
Midland Group
MoMart PLC
J.P. Morgan
Morgan Stanley International
The Peninsular and Oriental Steam Navigation Co
The Reader's Digest Association
Reed Elsevier (UK) Limited
Republic National Bank of New York
Reuters
Rothmans International p.l.c.
Rothmans International Tobacco (UK) Ltd
The RTZ Corporation PLC
Salomon Brothers
Santa Fe Exploration (UK) Limited
Smith & Williamson
Southern Water plc
St James's Place Capital plc
TI Group Plc
Trafalgar House Construction Holdings Ltd
Unilever Plc

CORPORATE ASSOCIATES

3i PLC
Allen & Overy
American Express Europe Ltd
Barclays Bank plc
BDO Binder Hamlyn
Belron International BV
BMP DDB Needham
BMW (GB) Ltd
The BOC Group
Booker plc
Bovis Construction Ltd
Burmah Castrol PLC

Cable and Wireless plc
Charterhouse plc
Christie's
CJA (Management Recruitment Consultants) Limited
Clifford Chance
Coopers & Lybrand
Courage Charitable Trust
Coutts & Co
Credit Lyonnais Laing
The Dai-Ichi Kangyo Bank Limited
Dalgleish & Co
De La Rue plc
Denton Hall
Durrington Corporation Limited
Enterprise Oil plc
Fina plc
Foreign & Colonial Management Ltd
Forte Plc
General Accident plc
The General Electric Company plc
Granada Group
Guardian Royal Exchange plc
Hamilton Oil Company Ltd
Heidrick & Struggles Int.
H.J. Heinz Company Limited
IBM UK Ltd
Inchcape plc
S.C. Johnson
Kleinwort Benson Limited
Kodak Limited
Lex Service PLC
Linklaters and Pains
John Lewis Partnership plc
London Weekend Television
Macfarlanes
Mars GB Limited
Nat West Investment Management
Nabarro Nathanson
NEC (UK) Ltd
The Nestlé Charitable Trust
Nihon Keizai Shimbun Europe Ltd
Northern Telecom Europe Ltd
Occidental International Oil Inc
Olivetti UK Limited
Ove Arup Partnership
Pearson plc
Pentland Group plc
The Post Office
The Rank Organisation Plc
Reliance National Insurance Company (UK) Ltd
Robert Fleming & Co Limited
The Royal Bank of Scotland
Royal Insurance Holdings plc
Sainsbury's PLC
Save & Prosper Educational Trust
Schroder Investment Management Ltd
J. Henry Schroder Wagg & Co Limited
Sears plc
Sedgwick Group plc
Slough Estates plc
Smith Kline Beecham
Smith Systems Engineering
Sony United Kingdom Limited
Sotheby's
Stanhope Properties plc
Sun Life Assurance Society plc
Tate & Lyle Plc
Tomkins PLC
Toyota Motor Corporation
United Biscuits (UK) Ltd
Vistech International
S.G. Warburg Group plc
The Wellcome Foundation Ltd

Sponsors of past exhibitions

The Council of the Royal Academy thanks sponsors of past exhibitions for their support. Sponsors of major exhibitions during the last ten years have included the following:

ALITALIA
Italian Art in the 20th Century 1989

AMERICAN EXPRESS FOUNDATION
Masters of 17th-Century Dutch Genre Painting 1984
Je suis le cahier: The Sketchbooks of Picasso 1986

ARTS COUNCIL OF GREAT BRITAIN
Peter Greenham 1985

THE BANQUE INDOSUEZ GROUP
Pissarro: The Impressionist and the City 1993

BANQUE INDOSUEZ AND W.I. CARR
Gauguin and The School of Pont-Aven: Prints and Paintings 1989

BAT INDUSTRIES PLC
Paintings from the Royal Academy US Tour 1982/84
RA 1984

BBC RADIO ONE
The Pop Art Show 1991

BECK'S BIER
German Art in the 20th Century 1985

BMW 8 SERIES
Georges Rouault: The Early Years, 1903–1920 1993

ROBERT BOSCH LIMITED
German Art in the 20th Century 1985

BOVIS CONSTRUCTION LTD
New Architecture 1986

BRITISH ALCAN ALUMINIUM
Sir Alfred Gilbert 1986

BRITISH PETROLEUM PLC
British Art in the 20th Century 1987

BT
Hokusai 1991

CANARY WHARF DEVELOPMENT
New Architecture 1986

THE CAPITAL GROUP COMPANIES
Drawings from the J. Paul Getty Museum 1993

THE CHASE MANHATTAN BANK
Cézanne: the Early Years 1988

CLASSIC FM
Goya: Truch and Fantasy, The Small Paintings 1994

THE DAI ICHI KANGYO BANK LIMITED
222nd Summer Exhibition 1990

THE DAILY TELEGRAPH
American Art in the 20th Century 1993

DEUTSCHE BANK AG
German Art in the 20th Century 1985

DIGITAL EQUIPMENT CORPORATION
Monet in the '90s: The Series Paintings 1990

THE DUPONT COMPANY
American Art in the 20th Century 1993

THE ECONOMIST
Inigo Jones Architect 1989

EDWARDIAN HOTELS
The Edwardians and After: Paintings and Sculpture from the Royal Academy's Collection, 1900–1950 1990

ELECTRICITY COUNCIL
New Architecture 1986

ELF
Alfred Sisley 1992

ESSO PETROLEUM COMPANY LTD
220th Summer Exhibition 1988

FIAT
Italian Art in the 20th Century 1989

FINANCIAL TIMES
Inigo Jones Architect 1989

FIRST NATIONAL BANK OF CHICAGO
Chagall 1985

FONDATION ELF
Alfred Sisley 1992

FORD MOTOR COMPANY LIMITED
The Fauve Landscape: Matisse, Derain, Braque and their Circle 1991

FRIENDS OF THE ROYAL ACADEMY
Peter Greenham 1985
Sir Alfred Gilbert 1986

GAMLESTADEN
Royal Treasures of Sweden, 1550–1700 1989

JOSEPH GARTNER
New Architecture 1986

J. PAUL GETTY JR CHARITABLE TRUST
The Age of Chivalry 1987

GLAXO HOLDINGS PLC
From Byzantium to El Greco 1987
Great Impressionist and other Master Paintings from the Emil G. Bührle Collection, Zurich 1991
The Unknown Modigliani 1994

THE GUARDIAN
The Unknown Modigliani 1994

GUINNESS PLC
Twentieth-Century Modern Masters: The Jacques and Natasha Gelman Collection 1990
223rd Summer Exhibition 1991
224th Summer Exhibition 1992
225th Summer Exhibition 1993
226th Summer Exhibition 1994

GUINNESS PEAT AVIATION
Alexander Calder 1992

HARPERS & QUEEN
Georges Rouault: The Early Years, 1903–1920 1993
Sandra Blow 1994

THE HENRY MOORE FOUNDATION
Henry Moore 1988
Alexander Calder 1992

HOECHST (UK) LTD
German Art in the 20th Century 1985

THE INDEPENDENT
The Art of Photography 1839–1989 1989
The Pop Art Show 1991

THE INDUSTRIAL BANK OF JAPAN
Hokusai 1991

INTERCRAFT DESIGNS LIMITED
Inigo Jones Architect 1989

JOANNOU & PARASKE-VAIDES (OVERSEAS) LTD
From Byzantium to El Greco 1987

THE KLEINWORT BENSON GROUP
Inigo Jones Architect 1989

LLOYDS BANK
The Age of Chivalry 1987

LOGICA
The Art of Photography, 1839–1989 1989

LUFTHANSA
German Art in the 20th Century 1985

THE MAIL ON SUNDAY
Royal Academy Summer Season 1992
Royal Academy Summer Season 1993

MARTINI & ROSSI LTD
The Great Age of British Watercolours, 1750–1880 1993

MARKS & SPENCER PLC
Royal Academy Schools Premiums 1994
Royal Academy Schools Final Year Show 1994

MELITTA
German Art in the 20th Century 1985

PAUL MELLON KBE
The Great Age of British Watercolours, 1750–1880 1993

MERCEDES-BENZ
German Art in the 20th Century 1985

MERCURY COMMUNICATIONS
The Pop Art Show 1991

MERRILL LYNCH
American Art in the 20th Century 1993

MIDLAND BANK PLC
The Art of Photography 1839–1989 1989
Lessons in Life 1994

MITSUBISHI ESTATE COMPANY UK LIMITED
Sir Christopher Wren and the Making of St Paul's 1991

MOBIL
Modern Masters from the Thyssen-Bornemisza Collection 1984
From Byzantium to El Greco 1987

NATIONAL WESTMINSTER BANK
Reynolds 1986

OLIVETTI
Andrea Mantegna 1992

OTIS ELEVATORS
New Architecture 1986

PARK TOWER REALTY CORPORATION
Sir Christopher Wren and the Making of St Paul's 1991

PEARSON PLC
Eduardo Paolozzi Underground 1986

PILKINGTON GLASS
New Architecture 1986

REDAB (UK) LTD
Wisdom and Compassion: The Sacred Art of Tibet 1992

REED INTERNATIONAL PLC
Toulouse-Lautrec: The Graphic Works 1988
Sir Christopher Wren and the Making of St Paul's 1991

REPUBLIC NATIONAL BANK OF NEW YORK
Sickert: Paintings 1992

ARTHUR M. SACKLER FOUNDATION
Jewels of the Ancients 1987

SALOMON BROTHERS
Henry Moore 1988

SIEMENS
German Art in the 20th Century 1985

SILHOUETTE EYEWEAR
Egon Schiele and His Contemporaries: From the Leopold Collection, Vienna 1990
Wisdom and Compassion: The Sacred Art of Tibet 1992
Sandra Blow 1994

SPERO COMMUNICATIONS
The Schools Final Year Show 1992

SWAN HELLENIC
Edward Lear 1985

TEXACO
Selections from the Royal Academy's Private Collection 1991

THE TIMES
Old Master Paintings from the Thyssen-Bornemisza Collection 1988
Wisdom and Compassion: The Sacred Art of Tibet 1992
Drawings from the J. Paul Getty Museum 1993
Goya: Truth and Fantasy, The Small Paintings 1994

TRACTEBEL
Impressionism to Symbolism: The Belgian Avant-Garde 1880–1900 1994

TRAFALGAR HOUSE
Elisabeth Frink 1985

TRUSTHOUSE FORTE
Edward Lear 1985

UNILEVER
Frans Hals 1990

VISTECH INTERNATIONAL LTD
Wisdom and Compassion: The Sacred Art of Tibet 1992

WALKER BOOKS LIMITED
Edward Lear 1985

Other Sponsors

Sponsors of events, publications and other items in the past two years:

Academy Group Limited
Air Namibia
Air Seychelles
Air UK
American Airlines
Arthur Andersen
Austrian Airlines
Berggruen & Zevi Limited
British Airways
Bulgari Jewellery
Cable & Wireless
Christies International plc
Citibank N.A.
Columbus Communications
Condé Nast Publications
Brenda Evans
Fina Plc
Forte Plc
The Four Seasons Hotels
Häagen-Dazs
Tim Harvey Design
Hyundai Car (UK) Ltd
IBM United Kingdom Limited
Inter-Continental Hotels
Intercraft Designs Limited
Jaguar Cars Limited
A.T. Kearney Limited
KLM
The Leading Hotels of the World
Martini & Rossi Ltd
May Fair Inter-Continental Hotels
Mercury Communications Ltd
Merrill Lynch
Midland Bank Plc
Anton Mosimann
NK
Novell U.K. Ltd
Patagonia
Penshurst Press Ltd
Percy Fox and Co
Polaroid (UK) Ltd
The Regent Hotel
The Robina Group
Royal Mail International
Sears Plc
Swan Hellenic Ltd
Mr and Ms Daniel Unger
Kurt Unger
Venice Simplon-Orient Express
Vista Bay Club Seychelles
Vorwerk Carpets Limited
Louis Vuitton Ltd
White Dove Press
Winsor & Newton
Mrs George Zakhem